MICROECONOMICS

A Free Market Approach

Revised Edition

Edited by Thomas Rustici, Carrie Milton, and Nathanael Snow

George Mason University

First published in the United States of America in 2010 by Cognella, a division of University Readers, Inc.

Trademark Notice: Product or corporate names may be trademarks or registered trademarks, and are used only for identification and explanation without intent to infringe.

14 13 12 11 10   1 2 3 4 5

Printed in the United States of America

ISBN: 978-1-935551-11-9

cognella
academic publishing
www.cognella.com   800-200-3908

Contents

SECTION ONE:

Introduction / Spontaneous Order

Introduction

By Thomas Rustici

ECONOMIC LITERACY

ECONOMICS IS OFTEN thought of as the application of mathematics to social science. While economists make heavy use of mathematical tools, for the sake of logical rigor, economics as a science has a rich literary heritage. Consider the wealth of insight shared by the classical economists such as Adam Smith and David Ricardo, classical liberals similar to Frédéric Bastiat, leaders of the marginal revolution like the Austrian, Carl Menger, articulators of essential economic truths such as Leonard Reed, Nobel Laureates such as Milton Friedman, Friedrich von Hayek and George Stigler, and finally, today's writers like Walter Williams, Terry Anderson, Hugh Rockoff, Thomas DiLorenzo, and Daniel Klein. Far too often this literature is overlooked, many students come to despise the graphs and equations of textbooks, and the rich insights to be gained from the economic way of thinking are never absorbed. This anthology consists of selections from this literature highlighting the fundamental principles of microeconomics.

The editors of this volume are unapologetically free market economists. Our attitude reflects a belief in emerging systems, such as prices, which efficiently communicate relevant bits of information throughout the economy and all of society. We have discovered these essays to be some of the best literature available for grasping the subtleties of the market process. They range from very simple to very technical and everything in between. Even the most complicated of these, however, may be grasped by novice students with the guidance of an instructor reinforcing fundamental principles. The readings have been broken down into 13 sections: 12 of basic principles, and a final section on applied economics.

SPONTANEOUS ORDER

Economics may be described as the science of spontaneous unplanned order emerging from seeming chaos. Leonard Read demonstrates how even the humble pencil is a product of these emerging systems in the classic *I, Pencil.* Economics has no designed plan yet activities are co-ordinated in a logically coherent fashion such that life is made possible. This is the window into the science of microeconomics. It is the art of seeing what you don't see, the life behind things. Economics is about hidden order, or what Adam Smith in *An Inquiry Into the Nature and Causes of the Wealth of Nations* calls "the Invisible Hand." These essays illustrate the spontaneous nature of market emergence.

HISTORY OF IDEAS

How do we get things in life that we need? What are the moral ground rules by which people engage with each other? What are the economic consequences of relationships based on different institutions? The *normative* aspect of the history of ideas and social cooperation is explained through the essays in this section. *Mercantilistic*, or pre-economic ways of looking at life, understood human relations as a zero-sum game, where if anyone were to gain, necessarily someone else must lose. But markets can only exist where there are mutual gains and creation of new wealth unconstrained by the zero-sum perspective. To cooperate well with others may be the most relevant demonstration of morality regularly practiced. Every peaceful exchange contributes to the moral institutional infrastructure of the marketplace that makes civilization appreciable.

PRICE FORMATION

The crown jewel of economics, the positive contribution to scientific inquiry, is *price theory*. The formation, function, and interaction of relative prices direct the choices of individuals. The relevance of the basic theory is illustrated in practice. Even in the most unlikely of places markets and prices emerge as R. A. Radford shows in *The Economic Organization of a POW Camp*.

Nobel Laureate Friedrich von Hayek's *The Use of Knowledge in Society* is possibly the richest essay in this book. Hayek shows that the price system is a grand information system. Prices communicate information about human values in a world with scarce resources for storing information and making calculations. They tell us what we don't know. Prices allow us to give knowledge in ways we could never access through reason alone. The price system is spontaneous, unplanned, undefined. It is, "the result of human *action* but *not* of human *design*." This essay deserves multiple readings.

PRICE CONTROLS

Often government will try to manipulate the human values expressed in the price system and use coercion to dictate terms of trade that do not reflect the underlying reality of values of buyers and sellers. There are consequences of course. Economics is about revealing the law of unintended consequences. Whether well-intentioned or not, price controls force institutionalized chaos on a dynamically emergent market process, creating surpluses and shortages of vital goods and services, and hurting people in the process. Specifically, where prices are held too high relative to the market, surpluses are created; where held below market equilibrium, shortages are created.

The essay *The Energy Crisis is Over!* by Charles Maurice and Charles Smithson clearly outlines the process by which price controls created the energy crisis of the 1970's, and the proliferating array of excuses and desperate policy measures created to deal with the consequences of price controls. The student will learn the crisis did not end until price controls were repealed in the early 1980's.

Prices tell us about the trade-offs, opportunities, and values of other people when not controlled by coercive threat. When prices are controlled misinformation creates disharmony and disorder. The price system is like the thermometer attached to the thermostat in your home. The temperature in the room is gauged by the mercury in the thermometer. But the mercury in the thermometer does not directly affect the temperature in the room.

If the room is on fire and the mercury reads 120°F, we don't cool the room by artificially sticking a needle in the thermometer and taking out mercury until it reads 30° F. Causation does not run from the mercury to the room, but from the room to the mercury. Misinformation gets forced into the system by such a control. If there is a fire in the room we should call the fire department to change the underlying variables—put the fire out. However, there are unintended consequences of policy adjustments, one of which is unintended feedback. The thermostat reads 30° F when it is really 120° F in the room. Exactly when we want the room cooler, it gets hotter, the heater comes on when thermostat is tricked into believing the temperature is only 30° F, exactly the opposite of what we would want to have happen.

Conversely, if there is a hole in the roof in the winter, which allowed snow and ice to accumulate in the room, so that the temperature is only 10° F in the room, we would have a maintenance company come fix the hole, changing the underlying variables. If the mercury reads 10° F we don't make it warmer by putting a lit match under the mercury. The thermometer would then be communicating false information. Exactly when we want it warmer the thermostat starts the air conditioning. Now we not only have ice and snow, but it is even colder, the exact opposite of what we wanted.

OPPORTUNITY COST AND COMPARATIVE ADVANTAGE.

Economics has always sought to be practical. The economic way of thinking has helped shift public opinion on many issues, leading to better efficiency, and higher standards of living. Among the oldest of insights, David Ricardo in *On Foreign Trade,* and Frédéric Bastiat in *The Candlemaker's Petition, and The Balance of Trade* used opportunity cost and comparative advantage to play key roles in destroying mercantilist myths.

Many resources are scarce. Using a quart of milk to make ice cream requires that we forego the use of that milk in making cheese. Every choice therefore must consider the trade-offs of multiple options. The final course of action always involves sacrificed opportunities. To get some goods or services, we always have to give up others. The next best option; what you would have done if your first preferred course of action were made impossible: this is the opportunity cost of that decision.

Comparative advantage is applied opportunity cost. Why do people engage in the activities they do? What is the economic logic of the division of labor? Specialization in production

 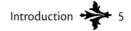

increases the benefits of exchange. This has implications for social cooperation locally, nationally, and internationally. Were you and a friend to paint a room together you might first have a little competition to see who was better at cutting in the edges and who was better at rolling. By so discovering your comparative advantages you can work together to finish the job more quickly. Such trade is mutually beneficial regardless of where one lives and works.

Many times politicians and journalists will spread the idea that trade deficits are harmful. Such thinking reflects a zero-sum game mentality. Once nations began working to improve standards of living, and stopped focusing on national cash reserves, trade relations improved and all parties were better off. Unfortunately, these lessons are often forgotten or misunderstood.

THE FIRM

Why do firms exist and what is their functional role in the marketplace? Why can't we rely on the price system alone to allocate all scarce resources? Why do we find, in every market economy, entrepreneurs running businesses instead of everyone operating as sole proprietors?

Firms exist to make money, a profit. Firms not in the market for profit go bankrupt and leave the market. Ronald Coase received his Nobel Prize for showing in *The Nature of the Firm* how transaction costs lead to the creation of the firm. Entrepreneurs internalize market externalities and replace the price system when they are efficient. When they are not, the market replaces them through bankruptcy. Factors of production revert to other entrepreneurs in the open market.

The essay by Nobel Laureate Milton Friedman, *The Social Responsibility of Business to Increase its Profits,* illustrates this process and why it is good they do so.

The prisoner's dilemma is an idea we owe to John Nash, about whom the book and movie *A Beautiful Mind* were written. His insights into *game theory* explain strategic behavior in group settings. Among the applications of this theory is Alchian and Demsetz's *Production, Information Costs, and Economic Organization.* While rather technical for the principles student, this paper is profound, and worth working through. Alchian and Demsetz argue there is an alternative explanation for the formation of the firm. They do not deny Coase's transactions costs explanation, but they address the prisoner's dilemma and shirking costs problems. Students should get an appreciation for entrepreneurs and how they help each of us actualize our full productive potential by pulling us out of dilemmas.

COMPETITION AND MONOPOLY

There are many myths surrounding the issue of market structure in a free market economy. Among these is a fear of monopoly, or competitive behavior which forces all of one firm's competitors out of its industry, and gives it the power to restrict output and raise prices indeterminately. Fear of monopolists has spawned much anti-monopoly policy by government, but these policies may have horrible unintended consequences.

Monopoly, rightly understood, is actually a creation of privilege on the market by the state, and yet many people believe that the competitive marketplace never existed based on historical myths. These essays, including an early work of Alan Greenspan's, former Chairman of the Board of Governors of the United States Federal Reserve, and a rousing history of *J. D. Rockefeller and the Oil Industry* by Burton Folsom, deal with the theory of antitrust, the policy of antitrust, as well as the history of the origin of the Sherman Act.

Competition comes from greed in a world of scarcity. Other capitalists greedy to earn abnormally high returns on the capital market guarantee the process of competition will discipline the behavior of firms unless government prohibits it. Historically, those whom trust-busters accuse of being monopolies have actually been those who have lowered prices, and expanded output. In fact, the Thomas DiLorenzo article *Competition (Except Where Prohibited by Law)* points out that the main reason the Sherman Act passed was because outputs were expanding and prices were falling! Other firms which were not able to match the productivity of the dominant firm pushed for government favor to keep them, inefficiently, in business.

Finally, the essay *Occupational Licensure* by Milton Friedman illustrates the many ways the government creation of monopoly is guised under the public interest to serve consumer quality, when really it is an expense to consumers.

INFORMATION, MIDDLEMEN, AND SPECULATORS

If we assume information is a free economic good it can be difficult to justify the presence of middlemen and speculators. However, as Nobel Laureate George Stigler showed, information is a scarce economic good that must be economized. People only search for information until the marginal benefit of searching is equal to its marginal cost. Middlemen specialize in searching for relevant information, bringing it to consumers at less cost than they would incur from searching for it themselves.

Speculators are messengers of the future that forewarn what is to come based on best guesses. They take on the risk of getting the guesses right, and relieve the rest of us of much of that risk. They help bring future information to bear on current prices, which then transmit this information to the rest of the market. Speculators are the shock absorbers for any economic system. They further coordinate trade through time and thus expand the gains from trade.

Other market institutions provide information as well. Israel Kirzner in *Advertising* illustrates how advertising is beneficial not only to producers, but also to consumers who are not necessarily knowledgeable of all their choices. No one can make use of an opportunity they don't know about. Advertising bridges this gap, and can no longer be viewed as social waste but as a necessary component for an efficient large economy.

Finally, public policy in information acquisition for drug licensing by the Food and Drug Administration (FDA) is examined in two of these readings. The FDA claims to help people by keeping bad drugs off the market. They want to avoid the *Type I* error of allowing a drug to go to market even though it may have harmful effects. They spend a great deal of time testing and observing the side effects of medicines to avoid this mistake.

But as a result, they fall into the *Type II* error of excessive skepticism. They often keep a good drug off the market far too long. All of the people who could have benefited from the use of

the medicine will then never have the opportunity. Many of them will have already died while waiting.

It is easier to see and measure the consequences of a Type I error. You see the patient suffering from the side effects. It is harder to notice the person who suffers due to a Type II error. Government agencies therefore receive more pressure to avoid Type I errors than Type II. We want public health to be protected by regulation, yet regulation hurts public health because information about potentially useful drugs is held back from consumers, and is not free.

INCOME DETERMINATION

Who gets what? What are the economic forces involved? What determines the division of income? Businesses derive profits, workers receive real wages, and savers receive interest. These three are not each hermetically sealed, people usually draw from multiple sources. Economics can explain the basic determinates in each.

Entrepreneurs earn profits by serving society, but also may take losses to capital if they do not it do well. With respect to real wages, an important concept emerges: what are the determinate variables that make workers real standard of living rise? In economics it is called marginal productivity of labor. Based on that, the worker receives the value of their contribution to the revenues of the firm. If for any reason workers receive less than their marginal productivity their greed leads them to say, as the old Johnny Paycheck song says, "Take this job and shove it." Who has ever quit a job because they were being paid too much? Yet, many quit jobs in search of higher wages every year. The underpaid worker's greed leads them to quit. On the other hand, if workers are overpaid by entrepreneurs the firm moves toward bankruptcy. Wages tend toward marginal productivity over the long run.

Wage is a composite variable. What a worker receives for his work is not just the money, but also non-monetary in-kind benefits, working conditions, and amenities. The total of these describes the *real* wage. What makes marginal productivity increase is the message of *The Wealth of Nations*: division of labor, human capital, education, and improvements in tools.

These essays also deal with certain fallacies on labor markets that politicians and journalists often make about why workers are paid what they are. Much of this is shrouded in the mythology of unions. The essay by Isaac DiIanni *Three Myths About Labor Unions* shows that unions are labor cartels which hurt most non-union members.

Finally, savers receive interest. *Gumballs Now or Ice Cream Later?* by Nathanael Snow illustrates how goods though time are not the same, even if identical, because people dislike waiting. If time is scarce it has a price; the interest rate. The present value of goods, services, and financial instruments forms markets to better satisfy our inter-temporal desires.

ENVIRONMENTAL ECONOMICS

What can an economist say about the environment? Students are regularly turned toward biology or ecology to answer questions about the environment, however economics can bring its unique way of thinking to illuminate often overlooked truths about the environment. We are dealing with humans, their values, and scarce resources. We can look at unintended consequences which result from interactions among these variables.

Why are some species endangered? How might laws to protect them accelerate their rates of extinction? The essay *The Endangered Species Act* by Richard Stroup illustrates this point very clearly. *Communal resources* have no real owners. Unlike private property whose owner protects its value, communal resources are free for the taking, thus end up on a race to the bottom through the first extraction rule: Individuals line up to extract the maximum out of communal resources and minimize any future reinvestment.

Incentives matter. Ownership matters. People take care of what they own because they are greedy. Future residual claimants, because they are greedy, will not trash what they own. Property rights channel investment into the future quality and quantity of land, water, air, and other environmental resources. The commons quickly dive to the bottom.

Other issues on environmental economics become very clear here. Public policy which tries to manage an endangered species habitat often overrides private property rights and leads to the "Three S's Rule": Shoot, Shovel, and Shut up. These essays illustrate that under current environmental regulations the presence of an endangered species on one's property is a liability and not an asset. The essay *Enclosing the Environmental Commons* by Fred Smith deals with these broad issues from several angles.

In politics we have the phrase "politics makes strange bedfellows." Many times public policy for environmental protection looks well-intentioned on the surface and yet certain alliances are created with diametrically opposite values. Why might a coal company support an environmental group that is ostensibly anti-coal? This phenomenon is described by Bruce Yandle in *Bootleggers and Baptists*. Regulation imposes costs and benefits. Just as the environmentalists may believe targeting certain types of coal use is a good thing, so does the competitor who has an advanced technology. If the government will restrict his competitor's use of coal, he will have an advantage in the marketplace. One desires clean environment the other desires to monopolize.

PUBLIC CHOICE AND GOVERNMENT

Why does government exist? Why not allow private anarchy to allocate all scarce resources? Why do we allow a coercive agent called "the state" to take our money? The economic defense for government is usually the need to supply *public goods.* The essays in this section will deal with the role and limits of governments constitutionally, economically, and morally. From the *Federalist Papers 10 and 51,* by James Madison to the "Schools Brief" from *The Economist* magazine these limits are explored.

The essay by Robert Rush explores the economics of regulation. Students wishing to pursue regulatory economics or public policy courses should examine this essay and those cited in it, especially Nobel Laureate George Stigler's *The Theory of Economic Regulation,* to understand how producers will lobby the government for entry restrictions against competitors. This creates a monopoly at the expense of consumers. This is exactly opposite of any "Civics Course" notion of government regulation for the public good. Rather it is about private greed, using

government, under guise of serving the public, through taxes, fees, permits, licenses, and barriers, limiting the entry of competitors.

MARKETS AND LIBERTY

We must address certain myths about markets, capitalism, and economic growth on positive and normative grounds. The two essays from *The Economist* magazine, "Ungenerous Endowments," and "Economic Freedom, of Liberty, and Prosperity" deal with some of the positive fallacies, such as natural resources as the cause of wealth of nations, or government central planning as an improvement on markets for prosperity. The essay by Dwight Lee, *Political Economics and US Constitution,* ties together public choice insights with the founders' original intent in the U.S. Constitution. The last essay, *What is Capitalism?,* by philosopher Ayn Rand ties together positive and normative elements about market capitalism, what it is dependent on, and what it is not. It explains that the wisdom of the founding fathers was to limit government power and what the economic and moral implications of these limits are.

APPLIED ECONOMICS

Technical in nature yet understandable to students with guidance from a professor, these essays take the lessons learned in previous sections and demonstrate how all the tools of the economic science can be brought to bear in harmony on particular issues. First, *A Public Choice View of the Minimum Wage* by Thomas Rustici, ties together income determination, price theory, price controls, government in politics, public choice in government, and markets in liberty.

Jennifer Roback's *Exploitation in the Jim Crow South: The Market or the Law* is an applied historical case study of labor markets in the time of segregation. Again, many of the same broad themes are tied together in this essay with relevant empirical data. Our view of segregation and economics under segregation starts to change when we read Roback. The culprit was certainly the state and not the market.

Carrie Milton applies microeconomic concepts to the current financial crisis (2008-9) in markets in *The Emergence of Nonperforming Loans: From the Commons of Risk.* Concepts such as moral hazard, the financial commons, regulatory economics, and many different microeconomic tools are employed here to explain larger macroeconomic movements. This essay illustrates how government policies laid the foundation for our current crises.

In the final essay *Public Goods and Public Choice* by Thomas Rustici all the tools of microeconomics: price theory, history of ideas, competition, environment, and public choice are woven together and applied within the broad economy. This chapter is a good introduction to international economics. Students taking future classes in economics will find this analysis helpful in dissecting new material.

CONCLUSION

We know these readings will provide the reader a strong literacy in economics. The economic way of thinking is useless if it is not put into practice. Essays like these should prompt the reader to observe economics in action in their daily lives, applying the lessons to personal decisions, and directing their analysis of public policy. With a strong foundation in economic literacy the economic intuition is formed, and the mysteries of complex theory are revealed. We are confident this anthology provides such a foundation, and does so while maintaining the interest and curiosity of the reader.

 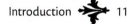

I, Pencil

By Leonard E. Read

I AM A LEAD pencil—the ordinary wooden pencil familiar to all boys and girls and adults who can read and write.

Writing is both my vocation and my avocation; that's all I do.

You may wonder why I should write a genealogy. Well, to begin with, my story is interesting. And, next, I am a mystery—more so than a tree or a sunset or even a flash of lightning. But, sadly, I am taken for granted by those who use me, as if I were a mere incident and without background. This supercilious attitude relegates me to the level of the commonplace. This is a species of the grievous error in which mankind cannot too long persist without peril. For, the wise G. K. Chesterton observed, "We are perishing for want of wonder, not for want of wonders."

I, Pencil, simple though I appear to be, merit your wonder and awe, a claim I shall attempt to prove. In fact, if you can understand me—no, that's too much to ask of anyone—if you can become aware of the miraculousness which I symbolize, you can help save the freedom mankind is so unhappily losing. I have a profound lesson to teach. And I can teach this lesson better than can an automobile or an airplane or a mechanical dishwasher because—well, because I am seemingly so simple.

Simple? Yet, *not a single person on the face of this earth knows how to make me.* This sounds fantastic, doesn't it? Especially when it is realized that there are about one and one-half billion of my kind produced in the U.S.A. each year.

Pick me up and look me over. What do you see? Not much meets the eye—there's some wood, lacquer, the printed labeling, graphite lead, a bit of metal, and an eraser.

Innumerable Antecedents

Just as you cannot trace your family tree back very far, so is it impossible for me to name and explain all my antecedents. But I would like to suggest enough of them to impress upon you the richness and complexity of my background.

My family tree begins with what in fact is a tree, a cedar of straight grain that grows in Northern California and Oregon. Now contemplate all the saws and trucks and rope and the countless other gear used in harvesting and carting the cedar logs to the railroad siding. Think of all the persons and the numberless skills that went into their fabrication: the mining of ore, the making of steel and its refinement into saws, axes, motors; the growing of hemp and bringing it through all the stages to heavy and strong rope; the logging camps with their beds and mess halls, the cookery and the raising of all the foods. Why, untold thousands of persons had a hand in every cup of coffee the loggers drink!

The logs are shipped to a mill in San Leandro, California. Can you imagine the individuals who make flat cars and rails and railroad engines and who construct and install the communication systems incidental thereto? These legions are among my antecedents.

Consider the millwork in San Leandro. The cedar logs are cut into small, pencil-length slats less than one-fourth of an inch in thickness. These are kiln dried and then tinted for the same reason women put rouge on their faces. People prefer that I look pretty, not a pallid white. The slats are waxed and kiln dried again. How many skills went into the making of the tint and the kilns, into supplying the heat, the light and power, the belts, motors, and all the other things a mill requires? Sweepers in the mill among my ancestors? Yes, and included are the men who poured the concrete for the dam of a Pacific Gas & Electric Company hydroplant which supplies the mill's power!

Don't overlook the ancestors present and distant who have a hand in transporting sixty carloads of slats across the nation.

Once in the pencil factory—$4,000,000 in machinery and building, all capital accumulated by thrifty and saving parents of mine—each slat is given eight grooves by a complex machine, after which another machine lays leads in every other slat, applies glue, and places another slat atop—a lead sandwich, so to speak. Seven brothers and I are mechanically carved from this "wood-clinched" sandwich.

My "lead" itself—it contains no lead at all—is complex. The graphite is mined in Ceylon [Sri Lanka]. Consider these miners and those who make their many tools and the makers of the paper sacks in which the graphite is shipped and those who make the string that ties the sacks and those who put them aboard ships and those who make the ships. Even the lighthouse keepers along the way assisted in my birth—and the harbor pilots.

The graphite is mixed with clay from Mississippi in which ammonium hydroxide is used in the refining process. Then wetting agents are added such as sulfonated tallow—animal fats chemically reacted with sulfuric acid. After passing through numerous machines, the mixture finally appears as endless extrusions—as from a sausage grinder—cut to size, dried, and baked for several hours at 1,850 degrees Fahrenheit. To increase their strength and smoothness the leads are then treated with a hot mixture which includes candelilla wax from Mexico, paraffin wax, and hydrogenated natural fats.

My cedar receives six coats of lacquer. Do you know all the ingredients of lacquer? Who would think that the growers of castor beans and the refiners of castor oil are a part of it? They are. Why, even the processes by which the lacquer is made a beautiful yellow involve the skills of more persons than one can enumerate!

Observe the labeling. That's a film formed by applying heat to carbon black mixed with resins. How do you make resins and what, pray, is carbon black?

My bit of metal—the ferrule—is brass. Think of all the persons who mine zinc and copper and those who have the skills to make shiny sheet brass from these products of nature. Those black rings on my ferrule are black nickel. What is black nickel and how is it applied? The complete story of why the center of my ferrule has no black nickel on it would take pages to explain.

Then there's my crowning glory, inelegantly referred to in the trade as "the plug," the part man uses to erase the errors he makes with me. An ingredient called "factice" is what does the erasing. It is a rubberlike product made by reacting rape-seed oil from the Dutch East Indies [Indonesia] with sulfur chloride. Rubber, contrary to the common notion, is only for binding purposes. Then, too, there are numerous vulcanizing and accelerating agents. The pumice comes from Italy; and the pigment which gives "the plug" its color is cadmium sulfide.

No One Knows

Does anyone wish to challenge my earlier assertion that no single person on the face of this earth knows how to make me?

Actually, millions of human beings have had a hand in my creation, no one of whom even knows more than a very few of the others. Now, you may say that I go too far in relating the picker of a coffee berry in far-off Brazil and food growers elsewhere to my creation; that this is an extreme position. I shall stand by my claim. There isn't a single person in all these millions, including the president of the pencil company, who contributes more than a tiny, infinitesimal bit of know-how. From the standpoint of know-how the only difference between the miner of graphite in Ceylon and the logger in Oregon is in the *type* of know-how. Neither the miner nor the logger can be dispensed with, any more than can the chemist at the factory or the worker in the oil field—paraffin being a by-product of petroleum.

Here is an astounding fact: Neither the worker in the oil field nor the chemist nor the digger of graphite or clay nor any who mans or makes the ships or trains or trucks nor the one who runs the machine that does the knurling on my bit of metal nor the president of the company performs his singular task because he wants me. Each one wants me less, perhaps, than does a child in the first grade. Indeed, there are some among this vast multitude who never saw a pencil nor would they know how to use one. Their motivation is other than me. Perhaps it is something like this: Each of these millions sees that he can thus exchange his tiny know-how for the goods and services he needs or wants. I may or may not be among these items.

No Master Mind

There is a fact still more astounding: The absence of a master mind, of anyone dictating or forcibly directing these countless actions which bring me into being. No trace of such a person can be found. Instead, we find the Invisible Hand at work. This is the mystery to which I earlier referred.

It has been said that "only God can make a tree." Why do we agree with this? Isn't it because we realize that we ourselves could not make one? Indeed, can we even describe a tree? We cannot, except in superficial terms. We can say, for instance, that a certain molecular configuration manifests itself as a tree. But what mind is there among men that could even record, let alone direct, the constant changes in molecules that transpire in the life span of a tree? Such a feat is utterly unthinkable!

I, Pencil, am a complex combination of miracles: a tree, zinc, copper, graphite, and so on. But to these miracles which manifest themselves in Nature an even more extraordinary miracle has been added: the configuration of creative human energies—millions of tiny know-hows configurating naturally and spontaneously in response to human necessity and desire and *in the absence of any human masterminding!* Since only God can make a tree, I insist that only God could make me. Man can no more direct these millions of know-hows to bring me into being than he can put molecules together to create a tree.

The above is what I meant when writing, "If you can become aware of the miraculousness which I symbolize, you can help save the freedom mankind is so unhappily losing." For, if one is aware that these know-hows will naturally, yes, automatically, arrange themselves into creative and productive patterns in response to human necessity and demand—that is, in the absence of governmental or any other coercive masterminding—then one will possess an absolutely essential ingredient for freedom: *a faith in free people.* Freedom is impossible without this faith.

Once government has had a monopoly of a creative activity such, for instance, as the delivery of the mails, most individuals will believe that the mails could not be efficiently delivered by men acting freely. And here is the reason: Each one acknowledges that he himself doesn't know how to do all the things incident to mail delivery. He also recognizes that no other individual could do it. These assumptions are correct. No individual possesses enough know-how to perform a nation's mail delivery any more than any individual possesses enough know-how to make a pencil. Now, in the absence of faith in free people—in the unawareness that millions of tiny know-hows would naturally and miraculously form and cooperate to satisfy this necessity—the individual cannot help but reach the erroneous conclusion that mail can be delivered only by governmental "masterminding."

Testimony Galore

If I, Pencil, were the only item that could offer testimony on what men and women can accomplish when free to try, then those with little faith would have a fair case. However, there is testimony galore; it's all about us and on every hand. Mail delivery is exceedingly simple when compared, for instance, to the making of an automobile or a calculating machine or a grain combine or a milling machine or to tens of thousands of other things. Delivery? Why, in this area where men have been left free to try, they deliver the human voice around the world in less than one second; they deliver an event visually and in motion to any person's home when it is happening; they deliver 150 passengers from Seattle to Baltimore in less than four hours; they deliver gas from Texas to one's range or furnace in New York at unbelievably low rates and without subsidy; they deliver each four pounds of oil from the Persian Gulf to our Eastern

Seaboard—halfway around the world—for less money than the government charges for delivering a one-ounce letter across the street!

The lesson I have to teach is this: *Leave all creative energies uninhibited.* Merely organize society to act in harmony with this lesson. Let society's legal apparatus remove all obstacles the best it can. Permit these creative know-hows freely to flow. Have faith that free men and women will respond to the Invisible Hand. This faith will be confirmed. I, Pencil, seemingly simple though I am, offer the miracle of my creation as testimony that this is a practical faith, as practical as the sun, the rain, a cedar tree, the good earth.

Rinkonomics: A Window on Spontaneous Order

By Daniel B. Klein

"An important quality of collision is mutuality. If I collide with you, then you collide with me. And if I don't collide with you, you don't collide with me. In promoting my interest in avoiding collision with you, I also promote your interest in avoiding collision with me." At a roller rink you can see something that holds insights into great questions of politics and society.

At a roller rink you see 100 people skating—but wait!—

Rather than imagine what you know happens at a roller rink, imagine that you have never seen or heard of a roller rink. Nor an ice-skating rink. Long ago people didn't know anything of skating. Imagine yourself one of them. Imagine that a friend walks up to you and tells you with great enthusiasm about his new idea for a business:

> "I'll build a huge arena with a smooth hard wooden floor and around the perimeter a naked iron hand-rail. I'll invite people to come down to the arena and strap wheels onto their feet and skate round n' round the arena floor. They won't be equipped with helmets, shoulder-pads, or knee-pads. I won't test their skating competence, nor separate skaters into lanes. Speedsters will intermingle with toddlers and grandparents, all together they will just skate just as they please. They'll have great fun. And they'll pay me richly for it!"

Knowing nothing of skating, you would probably expect catastrophe. You exclaim:

> "How are 100 people supposed to skate around the arena without guidance or direction? Each skater traces out a pattern, and the patterns must mesh so skaters avoid injury. That's a complex problem. It would require smart leadership. But it won't get solved! The arena will be a scene of collision, injury, and stagnation. Who will pay for that?!"

If you knew nothing of skating, you would expect catastrophe. Before they knew of skating, people knew of dance performance such as ballet, and to achieve a complex coordination requires a choreographer. Everyone knows that.

Intuition leads us to think that complex problems require complex, deliberate solutions. In a roller rink, the social good depends on getting the patterns to mesh. But no one is minding that good. As your friend describes the business idea, not even the owner intends to look after it. How can the social good be achieved if no one is looking after it?

Yet, we have all witnessed roller skating, and we know that somehow it does work out. There are occasional accidents, but mostly people stay whole and have fun, so much so that they pay good money to participate. The spectacle is counter-intuitive. How does it happen?

Suppose you and I step into roller-skates and join the other skaters on the floor of the rink. In skating, I do not aim to solve the big problem of coordinating all the skaters. I do not try to get all 100 patterns to mesh. I show common courtesy, but basically I am out for myself. I want to have fun, and so certainly don't want to get hurt. Looking out for myself, I promote my interest in avoiding collision with you.

An important quality of collision is *mutuality*. If I collide with you, then you collide with me. And if I don't collide with you, you don't collide with me. In promoting my interest in avoiding collision with you, *I also promote your interest in avoiding collision with me.*

The key to social order at the roller rink is this *coincidence of interest*. I do not intend to promote your interest. I am not necessarily even aware of it. Still, by looking out for myself I am to that extent also looking out for you. My actions promote your interest.

Skating on the floor of the roller rink is an example of what Friedrich Hayek called *spontaneous order*. The process is beneficial and orderly, but also spontaneous. No one plans or directs the overall order. Decision making is left to the individual skater. It is decentralized.

The contrast is centralized decision making. Again, intuition tells us that the only way the complex social good can be achieved is by central planning. Yet Hayek tells us that sometimes another way it can work is "decentral" planning. He tells us, in fact, that, often, decentral planning is the *only* way it can work.

Suppose the social good on the floor of the roller rink were entrusted to central planning. The rink owner appoints a really smart, really nice guy to look out for the social good. He hires a man with the reputation of a saint, and with two PhDs from Yale, one in Civil Engineering and one in Ethics. This smart saint stands in the organ booth, holds a bullhorn up to his mouth, and calls out directions: "You in the blue jacket, speed up and veer to the left." "You in the black overalls, I want you to slow down and move toward the inside." And so on.

The results would be terrible. The smart saint could not come close to achieve the brisk dynamic order that spontaneous skating achieves. The main reason he could not is that he lacks knowledge of individual conditions. Using his Yale learning, he looks closely and does his best. But he has 100 skaters to watch, and the conditions of each are changing moment by moment. The planner's college knowledge is useless in informing him of the particular conditions of your situation. The planner tries to apply engineering principles, but each skater has principles of motion all his own: Do I feel like going faster? Am I losing my balance? Can I handle this turn? Do I have to go to the bathroom? Am I content to follow the planner's directions?

Your local conditions—your opportunities, constraints, and aspirations—are best known by you. No one else comes close. College knowledge is no substitute for what Hayek called *local knowledge.*

Moreover, even if somehow the smart saint from Yale has all the local knowledge of the individual skaters, what would he do with it? How would he interpret it? How would he integrate it? And if he came up with orders for how to direct our skating, how would he communicate those orders to 100 people simultaneously?

Being smart and saintly, the planner would recognize his limitations and just slow things down. To prevent collisions, he would have to impose regimentation. Skating would be slow and simple. Skaters would be bored. Moreover, they would not find the joy and dignity that come from making one's own course.

On the floor of the roller rink, the social good can *only* be achieved by spontaneous order. As Hayek explained, the case for leaving action spontaneous is stronger *the more complex social affairs are*, because greater complexity only exacerbates the planner's knowledge problems. When the situation is simple, central planning can succeed. If there were just four skaters on the floor of the rink, central planning might not be so bad. But with 100 skaters, it is preposterous.

If, besides being smart and saintly, the planner were also *wise*, he would beseech the rink owner to relieve him of his assigned task. He would renounce central planning. He would recommend spontaneous order.

The principles find direct application in economics. Just as we want to discourage collisions, we want to encourage voluntary exchange. In both cases, the key is mutuality. Gains from trade are mutual, giving rise to coincidence of interest: In promoting my interest in gaining in a voluntary exchange with you, *I also promote your interest in gaining in a voluntary exchange with me.* You would not enter into the exchange if you did not stand to gain.

Once again, actors buzz about spontaneously to advance their own interest, but in the process advancing the social good. As merchants, we garner the honest dollar by serving our customers—that is, by serving society. As consumers, we obtain stuff by rewarding suppliers for services rendered.

Again, individuals act on their knowledge of local conditions, which change moment by moment. A chief component of your local conditions is the array of prices you face. If you produce comic books, you mind the prices of the ink, the paper, the labor that go into your comic books, and you mind the prices you can command for your product. The array of prices, for inputs and outputs, is how the business owner adjusts his activities to the activities of the vast number of players. Myriad players work to satisfy the comic reader, who, after all, provides the funding for all the activities flowing into comic book production. If you don't adjust properly, the reader will buy from another comic-book provider, who offers better quality or lower prices.

Again, if someone were to presume to plan the economy, the result would be disaster. The social patterns in an economy are fabulously complex, making decentral planning all the more necessary.

In economics, the substance of "spontaneous" is liberty. Liberty means freedom from others messing with your stuff, including yourself, your person. When the government tells you that you can't enter certain contracts, can't use your property in certain ways, and can't keep 35 percent of your earnings, it treads on your liberty. It is making affairs less spontaneous and more centrally directed or controlled.

It sounds self-centered—freedom from others messing with your stuff. But the principle would go for everyone, so it also requires you not to mess with others' stuff. Liberty implies not only security and freedom in ownership, but duties to respect ownership by others.

But more importantly, we live in a world of mutualities. I want others not to mess with my stuff so that I can use my stuff to best participate in mutual relationships. The point is not self-centeredness; it is to center control over stuff in the owner, so that action draws on local conditions and advances mutual betterment. The bonds of mutual relationships form the vast network of society, and when its members are individually empowered and motivated to advance those bonds, we have a society that is well cared for.

Spontaneous-order principles argue against full-fledged central planning, but do they condemn all incursions on liberty? The key is coincidence of interest. In some activities, such as polluting the air, maybe there isn't coincidence of interest. Maybe there is conflict of interest. In cases like that there is less of a case for spontaneous arrangements.

Likewise, in the roller rink, there are occasions for simple rules, such as signaling to skaters when the direction for skating is to be reversed, or when the floor is open only to ladies, or only to couples. These rules are largely self-enforcing.

But in the great roller rink of human society, many government restrictions are more like the central planner imposing foolish restrictions on ordinary skating. Spontaneous-order principles ought to have more purchase than they do.

Consider restrictions on the freedom to sell your services in certain occupations. Occupational licensing restrictions are justified by the idea of protecting consumers from quacks and charlatans. Supposedly, there is a conflict of interest, not a beneficent coincidence of interest.

What the regulators neglect is that the very hazard or problem posited would generate awareness and opportunity for new practices and institutions, which reassert the primacy of coincidence of interest. Just as skaters will spontaneously adjust to an aberration on the floor of the rink, such as an obstruction, people in the market creatively adjust to aberrations from coincidence of interest. The aberrations create new opportunities for mutual gains, opportunities that summon our entrepreneurial propensities to resolve or avoid the initial aberration. We witness myriad private institutions and practices to certify practitioners and assure the quality of their services. Economists who study occupational licensing agree that, rather than protect consumers, the requirements hurt consumers by restricting the range and competition of spontaneous developments.

The principle of spontaneity, of liberty, is not an all-or-nothing proposition. But the principles of local knowledge, coincidence of interest, and spontaneous adaptation have much more power than is generally recognized. People have a hard time understanding how spontaneous order works, or even that it exists. At a roller rink, spontaneous order happens before our very eyes. But in the great rink of society, each of us is immersed deep within the spontaneous order, focused on our own particular situation. Each has no window on the whole, not even a glimpse. Although economics cannot make the whole actually visible to us, it can help us see the principles at work.

Jonathan Swift's quote is from Thoughts on Various Subjects; from Miscellanies, 1726, Bartlett's Familiar Quotations, (1980) p. 322.

Jonathan Swift said that vision is the art of seeing things invisible. In that sense, economics gives us vision.

The skating rink is an analogy for human society. In the following quotation from *Theory of Moral Sentiments*, par. VI.II.42 Adam Smith used the metaphor of a chessboard:

> The man of system … is apt to be very wise in his own conceit; and is often so enamoured with the supposed beauty of his own ideal plan of government, that he cannot suffer the smallest deviation from any part of it. He goes on to establish it completely and in all its parts, without any regard either to the great interests, or to the strong prejudices which may oppose it. He seems to imagine that he can arrange the different members of a great society with as much ease as the hand arranges the different pieces upon a chess-board. He does not consider that the pieces upon the chess-board have no other principle of motion besides that which the hand impresses upon them; but that, in the great chess-board of human society, every single piece has a principle of motion of its own, altogether different from that which the legislature might chuse to impress upon it. If those two principles coincide and act in the same direction, the game of human society will go on easily and harmoniously, and is very likely to be happy and successful. If they are opposite or different, the game will go on miserably, and the society must be at all times in the highest degree of disorder.

[*The Theory of Moral Sentiments*, p. 233–234.]

REFERENCES

Barry, Norman. 1982. "The Tradition of Spontaneous Order." *Literature of Liberty* 5(2), Summer: 7–58.

Cannan, Edwin. 1926. "Adam Smith as Economist: The Gospel of Mutual Service." *Economica*, June: 123–134.

Hayek, Friedrich A. 1948. "The Use of Knowledge in Society." *Individualism and Economic Order*. Chicago: University of Chicago Press.

Hayek, Friedrich A. 1973. *Law, Legislation and Liberty, Vol. 1, Rules and Order*. Chicago: University of Chicago Press.

Smith, Adam. 1776. *An Inquiry into the Nature and Causes of the Wealth of Nations*. R. H. Campbell and A. S. Skinner, ed. Indianapolis: Liberty Fund, 1981. Oxford U. Press edition. Online: *An Inquiry into the Nature and Causes of the Wealth of Nations*. Edwin Cannan edition, full text, notes, and editorial notes free, fully searchable.

Smith, Adam. 1790. *The Theory of Moral Sentiments*. D. D. Raphael and A. L. Macfie, ed. Indianapolis: Liberty Fund, 1982. Online: *The Theory of Moral Sentiments*. Full text and notes free, fully searchable.

Order from Chaos

By Thomas Rustici

We can see the greatest miracles are before our very eyes if we just take the time to notice them.

Frédéric Bastiat[1]

THE AMAZING ECONOMIC SYMPHONY

THE GLOBAL MARKETPLACE is a fantastic symphony of economic production. Think about the task carried out by the conductor in an orchestra. The conductor harmonizes a vast array of musical instruments and produces a synchronized rhythm of sounds. Instead of random noise, we experience the pleasures of Beethoven, Mozart, or Tchaikovsky. Patrons of the philharmonic marvel at the conductor creating order from seeming chaos.

The economy is like the symphony, only much more spectacular. In the international economy, the *price system* acts as the grand conductor harmonizing our economic life. Inseparable from the people who comprise it, the price system reflects human values in a world of scarcity. Even more astounding, you, I and billions of anonymous individuals perform simultaneously as the instruments, composers and, through the price system, the conductor in the worldwide symphony of production and exchange. *We are the economy.* Imagine, 6 ½ billion different instruments playing their own song, yet anarchy does not reign. As the conductor harmonizes the cacophony of sound, the price system coordinates our values and actions. The economic symphony of the international marketplace creates social order out of apparent chaos.

---

1   Frédéric Bastiat, *Economic Harmonies*, (Irvington-on-the-Hudson, NY: Foundation for Economic Education, 1957)

Thomas Rustici, "Order from Chaos." Permission to reprint granted by the professor.

SEEING THE UNSEEN

> *[E]very individual necessarily labours to render the annual revenue of the society as great as he can. He ... neither intends to promote the public interest, nor knows how much he is promoting it ... he intends only his own gain, and he is in this, as in many other cases, <u>led by an invisible hand to promote an end which was no part of his intention</u>. Nor is it always the worse for the society that it was no part of it. By pursuing his own interest he frequently promotes that of the society more effectually than when he really intends to promote it.*
>
> *Adam Smith*[2] (emphasis added)

International economics explores the logical structure of unplanned social order—global harmony—from seeming chaos. Adam Smith's "invisible hand,"[3] points the way in the study of economic theory.

Many of our daily experiences are seen or visible. However, the central lesson of economic theory involves the unseen or unintended consequences of human interaction.[4] Economists investigate the immediate effects of human choices, as well as the long-term consequences of human interaction.

The long understood concept of the division of labor provides an example. When looking at the production within the firm, it becomes immediately apparent that different individuals perform different tasks. Inside an auto assembly plant, a complex organization involving hundreds of people harmonizes its collective knowledge and labor toward the goal of producing a car. Thousands of parts from hundreds of suppliers must arrive daily at the plant. The engine-fitters, the body part hangers, the windshield installers, the final assemblers, the painters, the detailers, the accountants, the senior VPs, the financiers, and everyone else from the janitor to the CEO aspire to provide you with a car. Assembling a car from thousands of parts involves substantial division of labor and knowledge. The coordination of these efforts appears monumental. Most car-buyers never see the production process of or its sophisticated level of coordination. Consumers only see the finished product on the showroom floor. The interesting events remain unseen. Yet, the really dazzling story comes from the larger market processes that make even the assembly of an automobile seem trivial.

THE WORLD-CLASS PENCIL

For the moment, reflect upon the remarkable amount of social cooperation occurring without our conscious awareness. Every day, we only interact with a few individuals. Yet, we depend on

---

2   Adam Smith, *An Inquiry into the Nature and Causes of the Wealth of Nations*, The Modern Library: New York (1937). P. 423.

3   Nobel Laureate Friedrich von Hayek calls Smith's invisible hand a "spontaneous order," which is the product of human action, but not of human design.

4   Frédéric Bastiat, *Selected Essays on Political Economy*, (Irvington-on-the-Hudson, NY: Foundation for Economic Education, 1964), pp.1-50.

millions of people for our survival. Economics explores this paradox: the unplanned processes that permit human survival in a world where no one possesses the knowledge needed to create all but the simplest of goods and services.

Making a pencil illustrates this point.[5] To those untrained in economics, an object like a pencil appears simple to make. Still, the production of a trivial pencil exemplifies the economic complexity resulting from a highly interdependent division of labor and division of knowledge within a global economy.

While some only see a pencil, economists see a wonder. *No one person on Earth knows how to make a pencil.* Read on and judge for yourself whether economists exaggerate.

Let's start with the pencil lead. How many know that the graphite comes from Sri Lanka? Most people could not find Sri Lanka on a map, but they can find a pencil. Sri Lanka is in the Indian Ocean. Who knows the location of Sri Lankan graphite mines, or how to mine and process graphite? How many speak the Sri Lankan's native languages of Sinhala or Tamil? Sri Lanka has starkly different religious and cultural norms from most Americans. However, our ignorance of each other's customs does not prevent us from coordinating our values through trade. After obtaining the graphite, adding Mississippi clay hardens the pencil lead. Where is the clay located in Mississippi? What grade of clay goes into making a Number 2 pencil, since a different pencil hardness requires different clay?

The wood that usually encases the pencil lead comes from huge trees grown in the Pacific northwest. How many people can fell a ten-foot diameter tree without killing themselves or others? Manufacturing a chainsaw involves mechanical engineering. How many pencil users have engineering degrees? Once harvested, the lumber mill cuts the huge trunk into tapered and grooved strips which are eventually glued together around the lead. How many individuals have designed or organized a lumber mill and built or operated its complicated and dangerous machinery?

---

5   The author is indebted to Leonard Read's "I Pencil," *The Freeman* (Dec. 1958), from which this vignette is based. Adam Smith uses a similar example:

> The woolen coat, for example ... is the produce of the joint labour of a great multitude of workmen. The shepherd, the sorter of the wool, the wool-comber or carder, the dyer, the scribbler, the spinner, the weaver, the fuller, the dresser, with many others, must all join their different arts in order to complete even this homely production. How many merchants and carriers, besides, must have been employed in transporting the materials from some of those workmen to others who often live in a very distant part of the country! how much commerce and navigation in particular, how many ship-builders, sailors, sail-makers, rope-makers, must have been employed in order to bring together the different drugs made use of by the dyer, which often come from the remotest corners of the world! What a variety of labour too is necessary in order to produce the tools of the meanest of those workmen! ... The miner, the builder of the furnace for smelting the ore, the feller of the timber, the burner of the charcoal to be made use of in the smelting-house, the brick-maker, the brick-layer, the workmen who attend the furnace, the mill-wright, the forger, the smith, must all of them join their different arts in order to produce them.

Smith at pp. 11-12

Consider the eraser. How many consumers know it's made from rape seed oil, or could even identify a rape seed? Who knows Indonesia is the primary exporter of rape seeds? How do you extract the oil? Rape seed oil crosses the Pacific Ocean in tankers. How many people possess the ability to construct a tanker and navigate it across the ocean? Once the rape seed oil safely arrives, it must be chemically converted into an eraser. How many pencil users understand the advanced knowledge in chemistry required to transform the rape seed oil into a solid eraser?

Take the tin band holding the eraser to the wood. How many people know that the tin comes from Bolivia, Rwanda or Malaysia? Do they know how to remove the tin ore, or possess the knowledge of metallurgy needed for smelting and rolling tin into paper-thin strips?

What about the paint derived from petroleum? Who knows how to conduct geological surveys to find and drill for oil? How many pencil users have the knowledge of chemistry demanded for refining crude oil into a nice, shiny yellow paint?

Alone, no one could make a pencil in his lifetime. The tasks involved in producing this extremely uncomplicated item require the coordinated knowledge and effort of millions of people from around the world. Millions of people directly and indirectly labor to make a pencil available. Amazingly, no individual understands the entire set of economic relationships. Furthermore, the overwhelming majority of people in this nexus of exchange remain unaware of each other's existence.

Still, we have pencils that no one knows how to make. Billions and billions of pencils! So many pencils that people take pencils for granted. Consumers believe pencils will always be there when they want them. Only when the market's seamless interconnected web of exchange breaks down do we notice its importance in supplying goods like the miraculous pencil. And, look how people treat these little wonders. They bite a pencil when bored, bang it on the desk when impatient, break it in half when angry, and worst of all, heartlessly throw it away before it's half used.

The story of the pencil reveals the fundamental nature of the modem market economy. Billions of individuals from around the world voluntarily cooperate to produce economic goods and services. People trade their labor and knowledge with unnamed multitudes to create the goods and services for their survival. The result is order from chaos.

WE NEED EACH OTHER

Some readers probably wonder about the connection between a pencil and their survival. Ask yourself this question: if no one knows how to make a pencil, who knows how to feed New York City or your hometown? Every day, 8 ½ million people in New York City depend on others to grow, harvest, transport, process, warehouse and sell food. Who feeds New York City? While a fascinating place, Manhattan is not famous for its farms. New Yorkers depend on nearly everyone in the world to feed them, except fellow New Yorkers. The same is true for your hometown. You depend on people in the Caribbean or Latin America for bananas, people in the Midwest and South America for beef and people in faraway factories to manufacture your eating utensils. What appears on your breakfast table on any given day would take a lifetime to acquire without trade or exchange. Yet, no one loses sleep at night worrying what might happen if the farmers in Kansas or Mexico quit growing food or other events that prevent the general migration of food from around the world to your plate.

Who feeds you? Who furnished your clothes, car, house, or electricity? It was primarily someone else in the world, not you. Other people sustain our daily existence. In the international marketplace, we trust other people with our life. We cooperate and trade with farmers in Australia, food processors in Italy, warehouses in Canada, and the grocery store down the street. A typical grocer stocks over 20,000 items on the shelves—twenty thousand intricate stories, each involving an unplanned global effort, and waiting to satisfy your every whim. This leads to an ironclad law of economics: *we need each other, because economic isolation leads to death.* Our life depends on the talents and knowledge of people we will never know.

By specializing in our productive activities, we produce a few economic goods or services and trade for thousands of others. We do not have to know how to make the things we want to get them. We are involved in one large worldwide network of indirect production and indirect exchange. In an infinite number of small ways, others from around the world affect our life. Understanding the complex social order arising from human interaction necessitates seeing the unseen. International economics explores the logic that underpins the structure of civilization, something too often taken for granted.

SECTION TWO:

History of Ideas

Greed Versus Compassion

By Walter Williams

WHAT'S THE NOBLEST of human motivations? Some might be tempted to answer: charity, love of one's neighbor, or, in modern, politically correct language, giving something back or feeling another's pain. In my book, these are indeed noble motivations, but they pale in comparison to a much more potent motivation for human action. For me the noblest of human motivations is greed. I don't mean theft, fraud, tricks, or misrepresentation. By greed I mean being only or mostly concerned with getting the most one can for oneself and not necessarily concerned about the welfare of others. Social consternation might cause one to cringe at the suggestion that greed might possibly be seen as a noble motivation. "Enlightened self-interest" might be a preferable term. I prefer greed since it is far more descriptive and less likely to be confused with other human motives.

That greed is the greatest of human motivations should be obvious to all; however, a few examples will make it more concrete. Texas cattle ranchers make enormous sacrifices to husband and insure the safety and well-being of their herds: running down stray cattle in the snow to care for and feed them, hiring veterinarians to safeguard their health, taking them to feed yards in time to fatten them up prior to selling them to slaughterhouses. The result of these sacrifices is that New Yorkers can enjoy having beef on their supermarket shelves. Idaho potato farmers arise early in the morning. They do backbreaking work in potato fields, with the sun beating down on them and the bugs maybe eating them. Similarly, the result of their sacrifices is that New Yorkers can also enjoy having potatoes on their supermarket shelves.

Why do Texas cattle ranchers and Idaho potato farmers make these sacrifices? Is it because they love New Yorkers? Only the most naïve would chalk their motivation up to one of concern for their fellow man in New York. The reason Texas cattle ranchers and Idaho potato farmers make those sacrifice is that they love themselves. They want more for themselves. In a word, they are greedy!

But that is the miracle of the market. Through serving the wants of one's fellow man, one acquires more for oneself. That is precisely what Adam Smith meant when he said, "It is not from the benevolence of the butcher, the brewer, or the baker, that we expect our dinner, but from their regard to their own interest. We address ourselves, not to their humanity but to their

Walter Williams, "Greed Versus Compassion," from *The Freeman*, *50, 10*, October 2000, pp. 1–2. Copyright © 2000 The Foundation for Economic Education. Permission to reprint granted by the publisher.

self-love, and never talk to them of our own necessities but of their advantages." He added, "By pursuing his own interest he frequently promotes that of the society more effectually than when he really intends to promote it. I have never known much good done by those who affected to trade for the public good." One might pause here for a moment and ask: How much beef and potatoes would New Yorkers enjoy if it all depended on human love, charity, and kindness? I'd be worried about New Yorkers.

Greed promotes other wonderful outcomes. It's nice that present generations conserve on scarce resources in order to make those resources available to future generations. Owners of buildings make sacrifices of current consumption and spend resources on maintenance that extends the useful life of the building—long past their own lives. For example, the original owners of the Empire State Building are now dead; however, the sacrifices they made to maintain the building mean that today's generations can enjoy it. When timber companies harvest trees on their land, they spend the resources necessary to plant seedlings and insure that the forest will continue to produce trees long after the owners are dead.

Can one realistically produce an argument that present generations make sacrifices of current consumption to insure that goods such as buildings and lumber will be available for future generations because they actually care about future generations? After all there's no quid pro quo, no way for future generations to compensate them for the sacrifices made on their behalf. So why? Again, it's greed but with its facilitator, private property rights (rights residing in the owner to acquire, keep, use, and dispose of property as deemed fit so long as that use does not violate similar rights held by another).

The present value, or selling price, of say 10,000 acres of forest depends not only on how much lumber the forest will yield in the year 2000, but also in the years 2005, 2010, 2030, and so on. The forest's capacity to produce lumber in these out years is summarized in its present selling price. The longer the forest will produce trees, the greater will be its price. Therefore, the current owner of the forest has a vested financial interest in doing those things that protect the forest's productivity whether or not he will be alive in 2010 or 2030. In other words, his wealth is held hostage to his doing the socially responsible thing—conserving society's scarce resources. Thus one easily predicts that goods privately held will receive better care than goods communally held no matter what the good: cars, houses, land, and so forth. Owners tend to take better care of cars, houses, and land than renters or other non-owners.

We should hasten to add that for private property to have these beneficial effects it requires more than simply holding its title. The owner must have options. One could hold title to land but be restricted by government in its use. An example is when a person holds title to a 1,000-acre plot of forest land but the U.S. Fish and Wildlife Service decrees that some or all of it cannot be used, for fear of threatening an endangered species. Such a decree reduces the private use-value of the land and hence weakens incentives to care for it. Similarly, if there were high transfer taxes for land sales, it too would weaken incentives to care for the land. In fact, anything that weakens the owner's private property rights in the land weakens his incentives to do the socially responsible thing—conserve society's scarce resources.

While human motivations such as charity, love, or concern for others are important and salutary, they are nowhere nearly as important as people's desire to have more for themselves.

We all know that, but we pretend it is not so. That unwillingness to acknowledge personal greed as vital to human welfare, and instead view it with disapproval, makes us easy prey to charlatans and quacks who'd take away our liberties in the name of combating greed.

 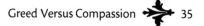

Morality as
Cooperation

By Peter J. Boettke

L IVING A "MORAL" life is often contrasted with living a "prosperous" life. Major philosophers, ancient and modern, have tended to praise the virtuous life of personal sacrifice for the public good, while discounting the moral worth of the individual's pursuit of individual happiness. When an individual's pursuit of his own interests generates socially desirable outcomes it is understood as a mere accident, and when attempts by political leaders to achieve a defined social virtue result in degradation (economic and moral) of the people, it is explained as an accident of history or the corruption of an ideal by unscrupulous individuals.

If in the aftermath of a natural disaster that knocks out electricity, the local hardware dealer increases the price of battery-run electric generators, complaints abound that this individual is taking unfair advantage of the situation to personally profit. The fact that in raising the price of generators, he inadvertently rations the scarce supply of generators so as to eliminate the possibility of current and future shortages is missed by many because it is *not* the hardware dealers purpose. Despite the social function served, our moral imagination has been outraged and we feel justified in condemnation.

On the other hand, had the dealer acted "morally" he would have lowered the price of generators under the desire to increase their availability and inadvertently reinforced the crisis situation, and he would be hailed as a moral man. Something is wrong with our moral imagination when morality and consequentialism are in such conflict.

There are many examples that can be offered which reflect this tension. Many still believe—including most of our influential intellectual, political, and moral leaders—that socialism did not collapse due to internal weaknesses in the idea itself, but due to the weaknesses of the flesh attributed to the populations that happen to live under socialist rules (including the rulers).

But socialism did not fail because of the sinful weaknesses of people; humanity did not fail to live up to a worthy doctrine of social cooperation. Socialism was an impractical and unworthy ideal. Socialism failed because the idea was inconsistent with the demands of humanity. I would like to suggest that in being inconsistent with these demands socialism was not only impractical, but fundamentally immoral.

This does not mean that the market economy is therefore necessarily moral, if by a market all we mean is that monetary bids and offers are what guide resource allocation. On the contrary, markets exist everywhere and always wherever there are gaps and opportunities for individuals to gain from exchange. Illicit markets existed even during the most enthusiastic periods of socialism in the former Soviet Union. Not all markets, however, are equally beneficial for social cooperation. The relationship of markets to the ideal of social cooperation is dependent on the rules and institutions within which markets are embedded. But if we specify the rules under which markets operate, then perhaps we can assess the moral worthiness of the arrangement. In order to make such an assessment, however, we require a standard of judgement.

SOCIAL COOPERATION AS A STANDARD

Can economics answer the question of whether a social arrangement is moral or not? Perhaps not. But if we admit the limits of economic science to address question of moral worth we must insist on what questions economics *can* answer. For example, economics might not be able to answer directly whether profits are deserved or not, but it can inform on the consequences of different answers to that question.

Moral reasoning that discounts the information that economics can provide risks advocating moral actions that generate deprivation and increased suffering. In other words, while economics cannot provide all the answers to our questions about how we should organize our affairs, to ignore its teachings would mean that we risk adopting social arrangements which entrap us in poverty and enslave us in tyranny. And there is nothing virtuous about either poverty or slavery.

"Rights" talk independent of attention to consequences is hollow. Distinctions between negative and positive liberties, while conceptually useful, do not perform the necessary task. Who cares if we can conceptually distinguish between negative and positive liberties when if sticking to negative liberties we entrap individuals in poverty? The fact that in many modern libertarian writings, the institutionalization of negative liberties leads to favorable consequences appears as a happy coincidence. But this type of reasoning simply reinforces the artificial split between morality and consequentialism that must be rejected.

Instead, we would do better to explain the coincidence between "right" and "good" as a systematic outcome of particular institutional arrangements. We desire the institutional arrangements associated with negative liberties for it is these arrangements which channel individual activity in a direction which increases social cooperation and improves the lot of the population. If this means that absolute economics becomes absolute ethics, then so be it. Notice, however, that I am leaving moral assessment at the level of social rules and not addressing questions of individual behavior—I'll come back to that later.

Social cooperation is desirable because it ensures that individuals who can mutually gain from voluntarily interacting will do so, and that through doing so, a division of labor in society will result that increases "wealth" and, thus, the range of opportunities that individuals face to pursue their own idea of the "good life." Social philosophers such as David Hume, Ludwig von Mises, Henry Hazlitt and F.A. Hayek have made extended arguments on why social cooperation should be elevated to a norm in assessing social arrangements. It is through voluntary exchange and the recognition of the benefits of the division of labor, that humanity both learns to cooperate with fellow men and generate wealth.

Mises' student, Murray Rothbard, has argued that if the division of labor was not productive, then it would be easy to see how life would devolve into a world marked by violence and perpetual war as each individual could gain from others only at their expense. Life would become a bitter struggle for survival. In the world as we know it, however, the voluntary contractual behavior of individuals is mutually beneficial and the division of labor increases productivity, and as such affords individuals the opportunity to develop friendships and a sense of social sympathy with others.

MORAL LEARNING & THE MORAL SENSE

Economics as science informs us both of the consequences of the division of labor for our material well-being, and of the institutional preconditions for the contractual society which gives rise to extended specialization and exchange. The rejoining of economics with its sister discipline of moral philosophy has been a project pursued vigorously by Nobel Laureate James Buchanan. His work signals a return of political economy. "The great scientific discovery of the eighteenth century, out of which political economy (economics) emerged as an independent academic discipline," Buchanan has written, "embodies the recognition that the complementary values of liberty, prosperity, and peace can be attained. It is not surprising that my eighteenth- and early nineteenth-century counterparts were so enthusiastic in their advocacy of market organization. So long as the state provides and maintains the appropriate structural constraints (the 'laws and institutions,' the rules of the game), individuals, as economic actors, can be left alone to pursue their own privately determined purposes, and in so doing enjoy the values of liberty, prosperity and peace in reciprocal and mutual respect, one for another." Unfortunately, the classical political economist's ideal was never fully realized and the vision failed to capture the imagination of intellectual leaders for more than a few generations. Buchanan conjectures that this failure was due to the omission of concerns with justice in the classical political economy vision. This omission, however, was only an apparent one and not real.

The experiments in the twentieth century in egalitarian justice have failed miserably. Socialism's only success was in making the masses of people equally deprived. The social democratic vision of welfare state justice that was embraced in Western Europe and then in the United States has eroded the wealth of these countries and created a culture of dependence. Egalitarian notions of justice deplete a country's material and spiritual reserves.

Justice was not omitted in the classical political economy vision, but rather embodied in the values of liberty, prosperity and peace. Liberty here was defined in terms of the freedom of individuals to pursue their projects in living, provided they didn't interfere with the projects of others. Justice was a procedural concept, not a distributional one. Justice was served by establishing a social arrangement which promoted the complementary values of liberty, prosperity and peace. Within such a social arrangement, individuals did not need either the moral preacher or the legislator to inform them on how to behave. Individuals, free to behave as they see fit and reap the reward or suffer the consequences of those choices, would learn how to behave "morally."

In a contractual society, with clearly defined and strictly enforced property rules, all are required to honor contracts, abstain from using force, be truthful in deals, etc. Being "good" does not necessarily translate into doing "well" more often than not, but in a truly contractual society one cannot do well unless by doing good. In other words, individuals can only acquire material wealth by satisfying the demands of others. Profit from theft, for example, is eliminated from consideration in this equation by definition since theft would violate the norms of the contractual society.

That is why Walter Williams is correct in stating in an interview published in *Religion & Liberty* [Nov./Dec. 1994] that: "The market talks about moral relationships among individuals. The free market asks us to serve our fellow man in order to have a claim on what he produces." These claims (often summarized in monetary terms) are "certificates of performance." The morality of the market is that individuals can only prosper by satisfying the demands of others in the market. Neither their birth nor race nor religion are the primary cause of economic success in life (as was [is] the case in a non-contractual society). Success is a result of many factors (including dumb luck), but that success is only possible if others are made "better off."

Where does that leave individual morality? Well, at the level of the individual. By establishing social rules which give individuals the freedom to act and pursue their experiments in living, these individuals learn how to behave and develop a moral sense. The liberal (in the classical sense) does not seek freedom for the individual so as to promote lewd and irresponsible behavior, but rather in order to create the conditions necessary for individuals to learn and acquire a moral sense by reaping the rewards and bearing the consequences of their actions. That some may use this freedom to act in self-destructive ways is unfortunate. The moral policemen of the "Nanny State" certainly does not provide the answer to solving our personal moral conundrums—just consider consequences for the social order of the "war on drugs" or the attempts at censorship.

Furthermore, if we sought to entrust our moral learning to others and their attempts at the micromanagment of our lives, what moral sense would we ourselves ever possess? How do we know that we will learn what the "right thing" to do is, unless we are left free to choose our path? In this regard, we can see the consequentialist foundations not only of the social rules implied in negative liberty, but also the individual behavioral norms associated with a contractual society.

THE CRUCIAL MORAL QUESTION

In the introduction to their recently published collection of articles, *Profits and Morality*, Robin Cowan and Mario Rizzo begin with a moral puzzle. The day before Iraq invaded Kuwait, the price of crude oil was $21, five days later the price was $28, and the quarterly reports of the big oil companies showed a strong rise in profits. Sorting out whether moral outrage over this is justified, Cowan and Rizzo point out, is difficult on both theoretical and empirical grounds. It may well be that reaping profits from the invasion does not break a moral code though we don't particular consider such behavior as morally superior. The crucial distinction for political economy, however, is not between acts that are morally permissible (but disliked) and actions which are morally superior. The key distinction which must be addressed is whether an act is morally permissible or not independent of whether the act disturbs our moral intuitions.

Michael Jordan, for example, has recently returned to professional basketball after "retiring" and trying his hand at professional baseball. His return has been hailed by sportswriters as the major sporting event of this year (even overshadowing to some degree the baseball strike itself). And Jordan's return has been special. Just the other night, he scored 55 points in Madison Square Garden while leading the Chicago Bulls to a victory over the New York Knicks—the best offensive performance by any player in the NBA this season. But Jordan has also returned with a flood of commercials designed in the wake of his comeback. A commercial for Wheaties cereal, a few for McDonald's restaurants, and of course a new one from Nike shoes cannot be far off. In addition, his return was also marked by the unveiling of a new Michael Jordan number—45 as opposed to his old number 23—and with that the marketing of a new basketball jersey to adoring fans. Jordan explained the change of number in a very sincere and touching way: his father (who was murdered just prior to Jordan's original decision to retire) had last seen him play as number 23 and that is how Jordan wanted it to stay, for his second basketball career he would be number 45, his junior high number and baseball number for his brief career as a Chicago White Sox minor league player. But cynics abound—just another marketing ploy to maximize his value some assert. Why should we care? Whether we buy the cynical conspiracy theory or the sincere bereavement story should be irrelevant. The crucial question is whether it is moral for Jordan to financially benefit from his return to basketball. If we answer no, then would we still be able to enjoy watching Michael Jordan do the things that only he appears to be able to do on the basketball court? If we stave off his ability to capitalize on the rare talents he has been given in whatever manner he sees fit, then are we "better off"?

The crucial moral question which economics is well-equipped to answer is not one concerning the motives of any individual, but rather the examination of the consequences of the rules of the game in which the individual finds himself. The foundation of morality, as Hazlitt so cogently argued, can be found in an examination of the consequences of different social rules. The rules which enhance social cooperation and as such allow the simultaneous achievement of liberty, prosperity, and peace are *moral* rules. Moral rules which promise justice, but deliver reduced liberty, lower levels of prosperity, and the breakdown of peaceful harmony do not deserve to be described by terms such as "just" and "moral."

If people object by stating that the utilitarian rule truncates moral discourse with concepts of efficiency and wealth, the doctrine is being misunderstood. Moral discourse must return to a central place in political economy. But moral discourse that is ignorant of the teachings of economics is bound to be found wanting on theoretical and practical grounds—if not also downright dangerous when applied in the social world to assess the daily behavior of human actors.

WHERE MARKET MORALITY LIES

The morality of the market lies not in the idea of monetary calculation and the tug and pull of bids and offers. As I said above, markets have existed under every conceivable moral system; markets are like weeds, they emerge whenever there are gains to be had from exchange, the attempt to stamp markets out here, means they grow over there. Markets themselves are neither moral or immoral. But the rules within which markets are embedded should be held up to critical scrutiny.

Not all markets are equal. The "market" for hitmen as recently examined in the film "Pulp Fiction" is different from the market for shrimping in "Forest Gump." The underbelly of society reflected in "Pulp" contrasts greatly with the windfall profit realized by Gump because his was the only shrimp-boat to survive the hurricane that fateful season. Gump in accidentally reaping rewards, improves the lives of his customers. In "Pulp" the success of the hitmen is at the expense of their target. Both examples speak to the universal existence of markets, but the contrast is vitally important for moral discourse.

Outside the framework of liberalism, the market mechanism can be relied on to allocate resources, but not with any degree of confidence in terms of promoting social cooperation and the prosperity of the society in question. When markets are embedded in a private property order governed by a rule of law, then they can be reasonably relied on to allocate resources effectively and to channel behavior in a manner consistent with the values of individual liberty, personal responsibility, honesty in dealing, respect for the property of others, etc. Such moral learning takes place not because individuals are striving to create heaven on earth, but because the rules of private property and contract reward such behavior and punish deviations.

In other words, an individual ends up living a "moral life" as the unintended, though desirable, consequence of following social rules of the game which promote social cooperation and the harmony of rightly-understood interest on the market. The market economy can teach its participants many lessons, the lesson learned however is dependent on the political/legal/social infrastructure within which the market is embedded. The contractual society of the liberal order transforms markets into vehicles for growth and prosperity and cooperation. In doing so, the great eighteenth century discovery by political economists of the complementary values of liberty, prosperity and peace is affirmed once again.

Peter J. Boettke is Assistant Professor of Economics at New York University. He is the author of The Political Economy of Soviet Socialism (Kluwer, 1990) and Why Perestroika Failed (Routledge, 1993).

Capitalist Ethics—Tough or Soft?

By Jack Hershleifer

I have never known much good done by those who affected to trade for the public good. It is an affectation, indeed, not very common among merchants, and very few words need be employed in dissuading them from it.

Sometimes it is said that man cannot be trusted with the government of himself. Can he, then, be trusted with the government of others?

FEW WORLD OUTLOOKS have been responsible for greater social mischief than the ideology or social philosophy which might be called "sentimental socialism"—the cluster of ideas centering upon a contrast between the evil capitalist ethic and its supposedly superior socialist counterpart. Sentimental socialists maintain, for one thing, that, since the system of private enterprise for profit rewards pursuit of self-interest, it cannot serve the general interest. Consequently, a system banning selfish private enterprise for profit is bound to encourage economic activity in the public interest in the place of the proscribed private interest.

What is sentimental here is the belief that a change in social organization is all that is required to abolish human selfishness. As Mr. Dooley said, "A man that'd expect to train lobsters to fly in a year is called a lunatic; but a man that thinks men can be turned into angels by an election is called a reformer and remains at large." Among sentimental socialists are such disparate modern thinkers as Albert Einstein, Jawaharlal Nehru, and R. H. Tawney. Sentimental or "soft" socialism has an extraordinary appeal to gentle physicists, non-materialistic statesmen, Unitarian ministers, and social workers—to mention just a few vulnerable categories. The appalling experience of this century with an actual socialist system in Russia has shaken this set of beliefs, to the limited extent by which mere evidence can sway opinion, but even so the world-wide influence of the ideology of soft socialism is an incalculable asset to the system of organized terror now ruling most of the Eurasian continent.

By way of contrast, it is worth mentioning that Karl Marx was primarily a realistic or "tough" socialist. He despised the Utopians with their proposed ethical reconstitutions of society. Basically, Marx understood both capitalism and socialism as systems of power relations developing out of an ineluctable historical process. Marx did not deny that the system of bourgeois capitalism had made enormous productive contributions to social advancement. Rather, his view was that, having served this purpose and also having performed its historical function of crushing feudal remnants and developing an aroused proletariat, capitalism had evolved within itself the seeds of its successor—socialism. It is true that Marx's thought was infected by certain ethical considerations; his dictatorship of the proletariat was not utopia, but it was supposed to lead to a utopia in which the state would wither away with the disappearance of the economic disparities responsible for human conflict. For this reason, the true exemplar of socialist reality is not the inconsistent theoretician Marx but the practitioners Lenin, Stalin, and Mao, a group more consistently free of the taint of softness.

This, however, is an aside. Our concern here is with sentimental socialism in the realm of ideology, not with experienced socialism in the world of affairs. Now soft socialism as an ideology has two outlooks—one upon the capitalist system as seen or imagined, and one upon the socialist system. Proponents of capitalism have often, on varying grounds, attacked the beautiful image of beneficent socialism as a false picture. Alternatively, there have been attempts to construct an ideology of capitalism which will be less vulnerable to socialist criticism.

Such an attempt appears in a recent article by James C. Worthy, a vice-president of a leading American corporation, entitled "Religion and Its Role in the World of Business."[1] "Soft socialism" regards the business system as convicted of encouraging selfishness and, consequently, of failing to serve humanity. Speaking before a religious conference, an audience which he may (perhaps wrongly) have suspected of being especially likely to hold a soft view of human nature, Worthy propounded an ideology which might be called "sentimental capitalism" as the answer to sentimental socialism. Admitting that selfishness is socially harmful, Worthy declares that businessmen, despite appearances, are really unselfish. Modern management is faithfully responsive to the interests of employees and of the public. But, strangely, businessmen perform their good acts while avowing only that they pursue self-interest. The businessman's bark is worse than his bite; his harsh talk only masks his generous motives. He is like a doting father whose gruffness hides genuine affection for his son.

In Worthy's view, the reason for the businessman's odd behavior is the outmoded theory of laissez-faire economics, which justifies and condones "rational" conduct based exclusively on self-interest. Businessmen, influenced by this ideology, feel constrained to explain their behavior in these terms. But this explanation constitutes a grave liability for the business system: in the first place, society is unlikely to turn for leadership to a group which avows its merely selfish interest, and in the second place the actions of businessmen are less generous than they would be because they themselves cannot help but be influenced somewhat by their ethically barren ideology. In short, businessmen need to see themselves

---

1   31 J. Business 293 (1958).

 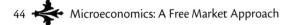

not as selfish agents, which they really are not, but as stewards for the welfare of others, which is their true role and one which they have essentially played in the past, though no doubt with lapses and imperfections.

There are several interesting things about this defense of capitalism—that capitalists are really not selfish after all. The first is that, as a defense, it is a hopeless failure. There are many reasons why this argument must fail, but perhaps the most conspicuous reason is that it is untrue. Instances of "generous" practice whether or not masked by "selfish" talk may exist, but they are not the characteristic examples that come immediately to mind as representative of business behavior. One doubts, for example, that the cigarette companies are giving serious consideration these days to stopping sales of their product merely because there is a strong suspicion that cigarette smoking causes lung cancer. Industries often ask to be relieved of tax burdens and only rarely that their taxes be increased. It is no revelation to note that "unselfish" talk or rationalization more typically accompanies "selfish" practices than the reverse. When firms raise prices, they rarely declare that they wish to increase their profits but rather that they must unavoidably meet an increase in costs. Firms seeking tariffs declare not that their objective is greater profits but rather that it is necessary to protect the jobs and living standard of American labor from foreign competition.

Of course, selfishness is not limited to capitalists, in our society or in any other. A gentle physicist may rise to wrath when someone steals his ideas or perhaps only disagrees with them; a non-materialistic statesman may call on the troops when the populace of a province prefers another government. Even socialist writers are rarely unconcerned with their royalties—unless, indeed, as is likely in a socialist society, this concern becomes trivial because of the more pressing need to keep head and neck firmly attached. The coalminer does not engage in his unpleasant job because he feels his responsibility to prevent people from freezing in the winter. The Chicago city councilman, whatever he may say, is rarely credited with a single-minded urge to serve the community, and so it goes.

What does all this prove? Simply that all the world is largely governed by self-interest, and all the world knows it. Consequently, the assertion that capitalists are exempt from this failing is unlikely to win many converts to capitalism.

The second interesting—even amazing—thing about Mr. Worthy's argument is that he, as defender of the capitalist system, completely misunderstands the fundamental nature of that system as viewed by the laissez-faire ideology he attacks. Worthy's basic ideas are expressed in the following sentences:

> The ideas of fair play and self-restraint are essentially religious. They help keep dog-eat-dog practices in check and enable the economy to operate without strict governmental supervision and control: self-restraint rather than legal restraint is the rule …
>
> The great weakness of laissez-faire economics (both the earlier and the later variety) is not so much the reliance on individual freedom and the distrust of government controls but rather the absence—indeed, the explicit denial in official business theory—of any responsibility of the businessman to anyone but himself …

The principle that self-interest is a sufficient guide for personal and public policy (that private vices make for public good) makes the demand for greater public control inevitable…

In other words, the alternatives Worthy recognizes are self-restraint or legal restraint. But the essence of the laissez-faire idea is that there is a third form of "restraint" against antisocial practices—not so frail a reed as the hope of self-restraint, nor such a threat to individual freedom as legal restraint. I refer, of course, to the *market* restraint of competition. Under laissez-faire, if a business charges high prices, either because of inefficiency or because it is attempting to exploit its position, competitors rush in to serve the public in the place of the firm which is failing to do so. It is competition, not self-interest or the lack of it, which forces businessmen (if they wish to succeed) to give the public what it wants at the lowest attainable price.

The third interesting point in Mr. Worthy's presentation is his implicit acceptance of the ideas of the "new managerialism"—that the corporate manager (the typical "capitalist" of today) should serve the interest of all affected groups (owners, employees, customers, suppliers, and the community) rather than seek profits (i.e., serve stockholders) alone. Now, a corporate manager pursuing profits exclusively would at least be loyal to one master—the stockholder—and not be attempting to represent conflicting interests. No one can represent conflicting interests; he can at best mediate among them. Where there are conflicting masters, the servant is responsible to none. In this case the temptation is for the managers to serve neither their employers (the stockholders), other employees, customers, *nor* the public—but rather the interest of the managerial group itself. In this interpretation "unselfishness" of managers who deal with corporate funds (other people's money) may not be much of a virtue.

On all these grounds, a sentimental defense of capitalism cannot be accepted. Is it possible to give a tough-minded defense of capitalism—that is, to show that, taking people as they really are, capitalism can convert their energies to useful social results more effectively than other systems? The answer to this question, I believe, is "Yes." It is not capitalism which makes people selfish—people other than saints simply are more interested in their own health, comfort, and safety than in other people's and will continue to be until the establishment of the Kingdom of God on earth. All *actual* social systems, though not all social philosophies, must recognize and cope with this fact.

Under the system of private enterprise for profit, men enjoy the opportunity to receive high returns if they provide people with goods and services that people are willing to pay for. The disciplining rod is competition; if some producers do not fill an existing public need or do not fill it well, others can begin to do so. In this system everyone can be selfish— consumers buy what they like, businessmen produce what they can sell, laborers work for whoever pays most—but the market forces them to serve one another's interests, the laborer by working, the employer by paying labor and organizing production, and the consumer by paying for the final product. (Of course, it is not true that everyone *must* be selfish under this system—all who choose to serve others without reward may do so, but the choice is their own.) In the laissez-faire ideology, the major role for government is to insure the preservation of competition, as well as to provide for certain communal needs like national defense. To be sure, the system has more or less serious failings: among those usually cited are the arbitrariness of the distribution of inherited wealth, and possible divergences between what the public wants and what it ought to have. These and other real objections to the capitalist system can be raised, but it remains to be shown how alternative systems will perform better. Capitalism has the decisive merit, at least, of being based on human motives as they actually are.

If we ask how an actual socialist system would have to cope with the same motives, we see that the consumers, managers, workers, and government officials of a socialist system can on no reasonable ground be assumed to be less selfish than their equivalents in a capitalist society. The distinctive characteristic of the socialist system is that it encourages and gratifies a rather different aspect of human self-interest. The main rewards in capitalism go to those who serve others through providing services and products for which others are willing to pay. In a socialist system, the monopolization of the economic (together with the political) sphere by government eliminates the check of competition. The great rewards will then go not to those who serve the public but to those who control government and thereby *rule* the public. If a system of democratic socialism were really possible, rewards under it would be shared between a hypertrophied government bureaucracy and political parties. In dictatorial socialism, the rewards go, as they have gone in Russia, to "the fittest" in seizing power. In either variant, the unsentimental case for socialism is a much harder one to defend than that for the system of private enterprise.

Corresponding to the alternative "soft" and "tough" defenses which have been given for the private enterprise system in the economic sphere, it is of interest to note that there are both sentimental and realistic defenses for democracy in the political realm. The sentimental argument runs that the people are "good" (unselfish) and so deserve to rule. The unsentimental argument, in contrast, says that all are humanly selfish—rulers and ruled alike. Democracy is a good system because it sets up a regularized procedure whereby those in the seats of power are held in check by the necessity for election by the people they govern. As in the economic sphere, the test of a desirable social system is not whether the group to whom it grants power constitutes an unselfish class but whether the holders of power are effectively checked in their exercise of it.

In the economic sphere, the crucial check on private enterprise is market competition. In the political sphere, the crucial check on democratic rulers is the requirement that they be chosen over alternative groups who also seek to become the leaders—we might say that competition here also is the check—the competition for political leadership.

Men are selfish, so who can trust self-restraint? Since rulers are selfish and terrifyingly powerful as well, to put all trust in their guardianship is folly twice over. The true principle is to associate self-interest with public interest—by offering rewards for service to the public, and by insuring that all may compete for these rewards. Competition for reward is thus the key feature of those twin liberating social inventions—capitalism in the economic sphere and democracy in the political realm.

SECTION THREE

Price Formation

The Formation and
Function of Prices

By Hans Sennholz

FOR ALMOST TWO thousand years economic investigation was handicapped by the common notion that economic exchange is fair only as long as each party gets exactly as much as he gives the other. This notion of equality in exchange even permeated the writings of the classical economists.

Back in the 1870's the Englishman Jevons, the Swiss Walras, and the Austrian Menger irrefutably exploded this philosophical foundation. The Austrian School, especially, built a new foundation on the cognition that economic exchange results from a *difference in individual valuations*, not from an equality of costs. According to Menger, "the principle that leads men to exchange is the same principle that guides them in their economic activity as a whole; it is the endeavor to insure the greatest possible satisfaction of their wants." Exchange comes to an end as soon as one party to the exchange should judge both goods of equal value.

In the terminology of the economists, the value of a good is determined by its marginal utility. This means that the value of a good is determined by the importance of the least important want that can be satisfied by the available supply of goods. A simple example first used by Böhm-Bawerk, the eminent Austrian economist, may illustrate this principle.

A pioneer farmer in the jungle of Brazil has just harvested five sacks of grain. They are his only means of subsistence until the next harvest. One sack is absolutely essential as the food supply which is to keep him alive. A second sack is to assure his full strength and complete health until the next harvest. The third sack is to be used for the raising of poultry which provides nutriment in the form of meat. The fourth sack is devoted to the distilling of brandy. And finally, after his modest personal wants are thus provided for, he can think of no better use for his fifth sack than to feed it to a number of parrots whose antics give him some entertainment.

It is obvious that the various uses to which the grain is put do not rank equally in importance to him. His life and health depend on the first two sacks, while the fifth and last sack "at the margin" has the least importance or "utility." If he were to lose this last sack, our frontier farmer would suffer a loss of well-being no greater than the

Hans Sennholz, "The Formation and Function of Prices," from *The Freeman*, *15*, *2*, February 1965, pp. 3–9. Copyright © 1965 The Foundation for Economic Education. Permission to reprint granted by the publisher.

pleasure of parrot entertainment. Or, if he should have an opportunity to trade with another frontiersman who happens to pass his solitary log cabin, he will be willing to exchange one sack for any other good that in his judgment exceeds the pleasure of parrot entertainment.

But now let us assume that our frontier farmer has a total supply of only three sacks. His valuation of any one sack will be the utility provided by the third and last sack, which affords him the meat. Loss of any one of three sacks would be much more serious, its value and price therefore much higher. Our farmer could be induced to exchange this sack only if the usefulness of the good he is offered would exceed the utility derived from the consumption of meat.

And finally, let us assume that he possesses only a single sack of grain. It is obvious that any exchange is out of the question as his life depends on it. He would rather fight than risk loss of this sack.

THE LAW OF SUPPLY AND DEMAND

This discussion of the principles of valuation is not merely academic. In a highly developed exchange economy these principles explain the familiar observation that the value and price of goods vary inversely to their quantity. The larger the supply of goods the lower will be the value of the individual good, and vice versa. This elementary principle is the basis of the price doctrine known as the *law of supply and demand*. Stated in a more detailed manner, the following factors determine market prices: the value of the desired good according to the subjective judgment of the buyer and his subjective value of the medium of exchange; the subjective value of the good for the seller and his subjective value of the medium of exchange.

In a given market there can be only *one* price. Whenever businessmen discover discrepancies in prices of goods at different locations, they will endeavor to buy in the lower-price markets and sell in the higher-price markets. But these operations tend to equalize all prices. Or, if they discover discrepancies between producers' goods prices and the anticipated prices of consumers' goods, they may embark upon production in order to take advantage of the price differences.

Value and price constitute the very foundation of the economics of the market society, for it is through value and price that the people give purpose and aim to the production process. No matter what their ultimate motivation may be, whether material or ideal, noble or base, the people judge goods and services according to their suitability for the attainment of their desired objectives. They ascribe value to consumers' goods and determine their prices. And according to Böhm-Bawerk's irrefutable "imputation theory," they even determine indirectly the prices of all factors of production and the income of every member of the market economy.

The prices of the consumers' goods condition and determine the prices of the factors of production: land, labor, and capital. Businessmen appraise the production factors in accordance with the anticipated prices of the products. On the market, the price and remuneration of each factor then emerges from the bids of the competing highest bidders. The businessmen, in order to acquire the necessary production factors, outbid each other by bidding higher prices than their competitors. Their bids are limited by their anticipation of the prices of the products.

The pricing process thus reveals itself as a social process in which all members of society participate. Through buying or abstaining from buying, through cooperation and competition, the millions of consumers ultimately determine the price structure of the market and the allocation of the income of each individual.

PRICES ARE PRODUCTION SIGNALS

Market prices direct economic production. They determine the selection of the factors of production, particularly the land and resources that are employed—or left unused. Market prices are the essential signals that provide meaning and direction to the market economy. The entrepreneurs and capitalists are merely the consumers' agents, and must cater to their wishes and preferences. Through their judgments of value and expressions of price, the consumers decide what is to be produced and in what quantity and quality; where it is to be produced and by whom; what method of production is to be employed; what material is to be used; and they make numerous other decisions. Indeed, the baton of price makes every member of the market economy a conductor of the production process.

Prices also direct investments. True, it may appear that the businessman determines the investment of savings and the direction of production. But he does not exercise this control arbitrarily, as his own desires dictate. On the contrary, he is guided by the prices of products. Where lively demand assures or promises profitable prices, he expands his production. Where prices decline, he restricts production. Expansion and contraction of production tend to alternate until an equilibrium has been established between supply and demand. In final analysis, then, it is the consumer—not the businessman—who determines the direction of production through his buying or abstention from buying.

If, for instance, every individual member of the market society were to consume all his income, then the demand for consumers' goods would determine prices in such a way that businessmen would be induced to produce consumers' goods only. The stock of capital goods will stay the same, provided people do not consume more than their income. If they consume more, the stock of capital goods is necessarily diminished.

If, on the other hand, people save part of their incomes and reduce consumption expenditures, the prices of consumption goods decline. Businessmen thus are forced to adjust their production to the changes demanded. Let us assume that people, on the average, save 25 percent of their incomes. Then, businessmen, through the agency of prices, would assign only 75 percent of production to immediate consumption and the rest to increasing capital.

Our knowledge of prices also discloses the most crucial shortcoming of socialism and the immense superiority of the market order. Without the yardstick of prices, economic calculation is impossible. Without prices, how is the economic planner to calculate the results of production ? He cannot compare the vast number of different materials, kinds of labor, capital goods, land, and methods of production with the yields of production. Without the price yardstick, he cannot ascertain whether certain procedures actually increase the productivity and output of his system. It is true, he may calculate in kind. But such a calculation permits no value comparison between the costs of production and its yield. Other socialist substitutes for the price denominator, such as the calculation of labor time, are equally spurious.

GOVERNMENT INTERFERENCE WITH PRICES

Economic theory reveals irrefutably that government intervention causes effects that tend to be undesirable, even from the point of view of those who design that intervention. To interfere with prices, wages, and the rates of interest through government orders and prohibitions is to deprive the people of their central position as sovereigns of the market process. It compels entrepreneurs to obey government orders rather than the value judgments and price signals of consumers. In short, government intervention curtails the economic freedom of the people and enhances the power of politicians and government officials.

The price theory also explains the various other economic problems of socialism and the interventionist state. It explains, for instance, the unemployment suffered in the industrial areas, the agricultural surpluses accumulated in government bins and warehouses; it even explains the gold and dollar shortages suffered by many central banks all over the world.

The market price equates the demand for and the supply of goods and services. It is the very function of price to establish this equilibrium. At the free market price, anyone willing to sell can sell, and anyone willing to buy can buy. Surpluses or shortages are inconceivable where market prices continuously adjust supply and production to the demand exerted by the consumers.

But whenever government by law or decree endeavors to raise a price, a surplus inevitably results. The motivation for such a policy may indeed be laudable: to raise the farmers' income and improve their living conditions. But the artificially high price causes the supply to increase and the demand to decline. A surplus is thus created, which finds some producers unable to sell their goods at the official price. This very effect explains the $8 billion agricultural surplus now held by the U.S. Government.

It also explains the chronic unemployment of some 5 million people in the United States. For political and social reasons and in attempted defiance of the law of supply and demand, the U.S. Government has enacted minimum wage legislation that is pricing millions of workers right out of the market. The minimum wage is set at $1.25 per hour—to which must be added approximately 30¢ in fringe costs such as social security, vacations and paid holidays, health, and other benefits—so that the minimum employment costs of an American worker exceed $1.55 an hour. But in the world of economic reality, there are millions of unskilled workers, teenagers, and elderly workers whose productivity rates are lower than this minimum. Consequently, no businessman will employ them unless he is able to sustain continuous losses on their employment. In fact, these unfortunate people are unemployable as long as the official minimum wage exceeds their individual productivity in the market. This kind of labor legislation, even when conceived in good intentions, has bred a great variety of problems which give rise and impetus to more radical government intervention.

The price theory also explains most money problems in the world. For several years after World War II, many underdeveloped countries suffered a chronic gold and dollar shortage. And in recent years, the United States itself has had serious balance-of-payments problems, which are reflected in European countries as a dollar flood.

No matter what the official explanations may be, our knowledge of prices provides us with an understanding of these international money problems. Price theory reveals the operation of "Gresham's Law," according to which an inflated depreciated currency causes gold to leave the country. Gresham's Law merely constitutes the monetary case of the general price theory, which teaches that a shortage inevitably results whenever the government fixes an official price that is below the market price. When the official exchange ratio between gold and paper money understates the value of gold, or overstates the paper, a shortage of gold must inevitably emerge.

And finally, our knowledge of the nature of prices and of the consequences of government interference with prices also explains the "shortages" of goods and services suffered in many countries. Whether the interference is in the form of emergency or wartime controls, international commodity agreements, price stops, wage stops, rent stops, or "usury laws" that artificially limit the yield of capital—and whether they are imposed on the people of America, Africa, Asia, or Europe—government controls over prices control and impoverish the people. And yet, omnipotent governments all over the world are bent on substituting threats and coercion for the laws of the market.

The Economic Organization
of a POW Camp

By R. A. Radford

AFTER ALLOWANCE HAS been made for abnormal circumstances, the social institutions, ideas and habits of groups in the outside world are to be found reflected in a Prisoner of War Camp. It is an unusual but a vital society. Camp organization and politics are matters of real concern to the inmates, as affecting their present and perhaps their future existences. Nor does this indicate any loss of proportion. No one pretends that camp matters are of any but local importance or of more than transient interest, but their importance there is great. They bulk large in a world of narrow horizons and it is suggested that any distortion of values lies rather in the minimisation than in the exaggeration of their importance. Human affairs are essentially practical matters and the measure of immediate effect on the lives of those directly concerned in them is to a large extent the criterion of their importance at that time and place. A prisoner can hold strong views on such subjects as whether or not all tinned meats shall be issued to individuals cold or be centrally cooked, without losing sight of the significance of the Atlantic Charter.

One aspect of social organization is to be found in economic activity, and this, along with other manifestations of a group existence, is to be found in any P.O.W. camp. True, a prisoner is not dependent on his exertions for the provision of the necessaries or even the luxuries of life, but through his economic activity, the exchange of goods and services, his standard of material comfort is considerably enhanced. And this is a serious matter to the prisoner: he is not "playing at shops" even though the small scale of the transactions and the simple expression of comfort and wants in terms of cigarettes and jam, razor blades and writing paper, make the urgency of those needs difficult to appreciate, even by an ex-prisoner of some three months' standing.

Nevertheless, it cannot be too strongly emphasized that economic activities do not bulk so large in prison society as they do in the larger world. There can be little production; as has been said, the prisoner is independent of his exertions for the provision of the necessities and luxuries of life ; the emphasis lies in exchange and the media of exchange. A prison camp is not to be compared with the seething crowd of hagglers in a street market, any more than it is to be compared with the economic inertia of a family dinner table.

Naturally then, entertainment, academic and literary interests, games and discussions of the "other world" bulk larger in everyday life than they do in the life of more normal societies. But it would be wrong to underestimate the importance of economic activity. Everyone receives a roughly equal share of essentials ; it is by trade that individual preferences are given expression and comfort increased All at some time, and most people regularly, make exchanges of one sort or another.

Although a P.O.W. camp provides a living example of a simple economy which might be used as an alternative to the Robinson Crusoe economy beloved by the text-books, and its simplicity renders the demonstration of certain economic hypotheses both amusing and instructive, it is suggested that the principal significance is sociological. True, there is interest in observing the growth of economic institutions and customs in a brand new society, small and simple enough to prevent detail from obscuring the basic pattern and disequilibrium from obscuring the working of the system. But the essential interest lies in the universality and the spontaneity of this economic life; it came into existence not by conscious imitation but as a response to the immediate needs and circumstances. Any similarity between prison organization and outside organization arises from similar stimuli evoking similar responses.

The following is as brief an account of the essential data as may render the narrative intelligible. The camps of which the writer had experience were Oflags and consequently the economy was not complicated by payments for work by the detaining power. They consisted normally of between 1,200 and 2,500 people, housed in a number of separate but intercommunicating bungalows, one company of 200 or so to a building. Each company formed a group within the main organization and inside the company the room and the messing syndicate, a voluntary and spontaneous group who fed together, formed the constituent units.

Between individuals there was active trading in all consumer goods and in some services. Most trading was for food against cigarettes or other foodstuffs, but cigarettes rose from the status of a normal commodity to that of currency. RMk.s existed but had no circulation save for gambling debts, as few articles could be purchased with them from the canteen.

Our supplies consisted of rations provided by the detaining power and (principally) the contents of Red Cross food parcels-tinned milk, jam, butter, biscuits, bully, chocolate, sugar, etc., and cigarettes. So far the supplies to each person were equal and regular. Private parcels of clothing, toilet requisites and cigarettes were also received, and here equality ceased owing to the different numbers despatched and the vagaries of the post. All these articles were the subject of trade and exchange.

THE DEVELOPMENT AND ORGANIZATION OF THE OF MARKET

Very soon after capture people realized that it was both undesirable and unnecessary, in view of the limited size and the equality of supplies, to give away or to accept gifts of cigarettes or food. "Goodwill" developed into trading as a more equitable means of maximizing individual satisfaction.

We reached a transit camp in Italy about a fortnight after capture and received 1/4 of a Red Cross food parcel each a week later. At once exchanges, already established, multiplied in volume. Starting with simple direct barter, such as a non-smoker giving a smoker friend his cigarette issue in exchange for a chocolate ration, more complex exchanges soon became an accepted custom. Stories circulated of a padre who started off round the camp with a tin of cheese and five cigarettes and returned to his bed with a complete parcel in addition to his original cheese and cigarettes; the market was not yet perfect. Within a week or two, as the volume of trade grew, rough scales of exchange values came into existence. Sikhs, who had at first exchanged tinned beef for practically any other foodstuff, began to insist on jam and margarine. It was realized that a tin of jam was worth 4 lb. of margarine plus something else; that a cigarette issue was worth several chocolate issues: and a tin of diced carrots was worth practically nothing.

In this camp we did not visit other bungalows very much and prices varied from place to place; hence the germ of truth in the story of the itinerant priest. By the end of a month, when we reached our permanent camp, there was a lively trade in all commodities and their relative values were well known, and expressed not in terms of one another-one didn't quote bully in terms of sugar-but in terms of cigarettes. The cigarette became the standard of value. In the permanent camp people started by wandering through the bungalows calling their offers—"cheese for seven" (cigarettes)—and the hours after parcel issue were Bedlam. The inconveniences of this system soon led to its replacement by an Exchange and Mart notice board in every bungalow, where under the headings "name," "room number," "wanted" and "offered" sales and wants were advertised. When a deal went through, it was crossed off the board. The public and semi-permanent records of transactions led to cigarette prices being well known and thus tending to equality throughout the camp, although there were always opportunities for an astute trader to make a profit from arbitrage. With this development everyone, including nonsmokers, was willing to sell for cigarettes, using them to buy at another time and place. Cigarettes became the normal currency, though, of course, barter was never extinguished.

The unity of the market and the prevalence of a single price varied directly with the general level of organization and comfort in the camp. A transit camp was always chaotic and uncomfortable: people were overcrowded, no one knew where anyone else was living, and few took the trouble to find out. Organization was too slender to include an Exchange and Mart board, and private advertisements were the most that appeared. Consequently a transit camp was not one market but many. The price of a tin of salmon is known to have varied by two cigarettes in 20 between one end of a hut and the other. Despite a high level of organization in Italy, the market was morcellated in this manner at the first transit camp we reached after our removal to Germany in the autumn of 1943. In this camp—Stalag VIIA at Moosburg in Bavaria—there were up to 50,000 prisoners of all nationalities. French, Russians, Italians and Jugo-Slavs were free to move about within the camp : British and Americans were confined to their compounds, although a few cigarettes given to a sentry would always procure permission for one or two men to visit other compounds. The people who first visited the highly organized French trading centre, with its stalls and known prices, found coffee extract-relatively cheap among the tea-drinking English-commanding a fancy price in biscuits or cigarettes, and some enterprising people made small fortunes that way. (Incidentally we found out later that much of the coffee went "over the wire" and sold for phenomenal prices at black market cafes in Munich: some of the French prisoners were said to have made substantial sums in RMk.s. This has one of the few occasions on which our normally closed economy came into contact with other economic worlds.)

Eventually public opinion grew hostile to these monopoly profits- not everyone could make contact with the French-and trading with them was put on a regulated basis. Each group of beds was given a quota of articles to offer and the transaction was carried out by accredited representatives from the British compound, with monopoly rights. The same method was used for trading with sentries elsewhere, as in this trade secrecy and reasonable prices had a peculiar importance, but as is ever the case with regulated companies, the interloper proved too strong.

The permanent camps in Germany saw the highest level of commercial organization. In addition to the Exchange and Mart notice boards, a shop was organized as a public utility, controlled by representatives of the Senior British Officer on a no profit basis. People left their surplus clothing, toilet requisites and food there until they were sold at a fixed price in cigarettes. Only sales in cigarettes were accepted-there was no barter-and there was no haggling. For food at least there were standard prices: clothing is less homogeneous and the price was decided around a norm by the seller and the shop manager-in agreement; shirts would average, say 80, ranging from 60 to 120 according to quality and age. Of food, the shop carried small stocks for convenience ; the capital was provided by a loan from the bulk store of Red Cross cigarettes and repaid by a small commission taken on the first transactions. Thus the cigarette attained its fullest currency status, and the market was almost completely unified.

It is thus to be seen that a market came into existence without labour or production. The B.R.C.S. map be considered as "Nature" of the text-book, and the articles of trade—food, clothing and cigarettes—as free gifts-land or manna. Despite this, and despite a roughly equal distribution of resources, a market came into spontaneous operation, and prices were fixed by the operation of supply and demand. It is difficult to reconcile this fact with the labour theory of value.

Actually there was an embryo labour market. Even when cigarettes were not scarce, there was usually some unlucky person willing to perform services for them. Laundrymen advertised at two cigarettes a garment. Battle-dress was scrubbed and pressed and a pair of trousers lent for the interim period for twelve. A good pastel portrait cost thirty or a tin of "Kam." Odd tailoring and other jobs similarly had their prices.

There were also entrepreneurial services. There was a coffee stall owner who sold tea, coffee or cocoa at two cigarettes a cup, buying his raw materials at market prices and hiring labour to gather fuel and to stoke; he actually enjoyed the services of a chartered accountant at one stage. After a period of great prosperity he overreached himself and failed disastrously for several hundred cigarettes. Such large-scale private enterprise was rare but several middlemen or professional traders existed. The padre in Italy, or the men at Moosburg who opened trading relations with the French, are examples: the more subdivided the market, the less perfect the advertisement of prices, and the less stable the prices, the greater was the scope for these operators. One man capitalized his knowledge of Urdu by buying meat from the Sikhs and selling butter and jam in return: as his operations became better known more and more people entered this trade, prices in the Indian Wing approximated more nearly to those elsewhere, though to the end a "contact" among the Indians was valuable, as linguistic difficulties prevented the trade from being quite free. Some were specialists in the Indian trade, the food, clothing or even the watch trade. Middlemen traded on their own account or on commission. Price rings and agreements were suspected and the traders certainly cooperated. Nor did they welcome newcomers. Unfortunately the writer knows little of the workings of these people: public opinion was hostile and the professionals were usually of a retiring disposition.

One trader in food and cigarettes, operating in a period of dearth, enjoyed a high reputation. His capital, carefully saved, was originally about 50 cigarettes, with which he bought rations on issue days and held them until the price rose just before the next issue. He also picked up a little by arbitrage; several times a day he visited every Exchange or Mart notice board and took advantage of every discrepancy between prices of goods offered and wanted. His knowledge of prices, markets and names of those who had received cigarette parcels was phenomenal. By these means he kept himself smoking steadily—his profits—while his capital remained intact.

Sugar was issued on Saturday. About Tuesday two of us used to visit Sam and make a deal: as old customers he would advance as much of the price as he could spare then, and entered the transaction in a book. On Saturday morning he left cocoa tins on our beds for the ration, and picked them up on Saturday afternoon. We were hoping for a calendar at Christmas, but Sam failed too. He was left holding a big black treacle issue when the price fell, and in this weakened state was unable to withstand an unexpected arrival of parcels and the consequent price fluctuations. He paid in full, but from his capital. The next Tuesday, when I paid my usual visit he was out of business.

Credit entered into many, perhaps into most, transactions, in one form or another. Sam paid in advance as a rule for his purchases of future deliveries of sugar, but many buyers asked for credit, whether the commodity was sold spot or future. Naturally prices varied according to the terms of sale. A treacle ration might be advertised for four cigarettes now or five next week. And in the future market "bread now" was a vastly different thing from "bread Thursday." Bread was issued on Thursday and Monday, four and three days' rations respectively, and by Wednesday and Sunday night it had risen at least one cigarette per ration, from seven to eight, by supper time. One man always saved a ration to sell then at the peak price: his offer of "bread now" stood out on the board among a number of "bread Monday's" fetching one or two less, or not selling at all—and he always smoked on Sunday night.

THE CIGARETTE CURRENCY

Although cigarettes as currency exhibited certain peculiarities, they performed all the functions of a metallic currency as a unit of account, as a measure of value and as a store of value, and shared most of its characteristics. They were homogeneous, reasonably durable, and of convenient size for the smallest or, in packets, for the largest transactions. Incidentally, they could be clipped or sweated by rolling them between the fingers so that tobacco fell out.

Cigarettes were also subject to the working of Gresham's Law. Certain brands were more popular than others as smokes, but for currency purposes a cigarette was a cigarette. Consequently buyers used the poorer qualities and the Shop rarely saw the more popular brands: cigarettes such as Churchman's No. 1 were rarely used for trading. At one time cigarettes hand-rolled from pipe tobacco began to circulate. Pipe tobacco was issued in lieu of cigarettes by the Red Cross at a rate of 25 cigarettes to the ounce and this rate was standard in exchanges, but an ounce would produce 30 home-made cigarettes. Naturally, people with machine-made cigarettes broke them down and re-rolled the tobacco, and the real cigarette virtually disappeared from the market. Hand-rolled cigarettes were not homogeneous and prices could no longer be quoted in them with safety: each cigarette was examined before it was accepted and thin ones were rejected, or extra demanded as a make-weight. For a time we suffered all the inconveniences of a debased currency.

Machine-made cigarettes were always universally acceptable, both for what they would buy and for themselves. It was this intrinsic value which gave rise to their principal disadvantage as currency, a disadvantage which exists, but to a far smaller extent, in the case of metallic currency; that is, a strong demand for non-monetary purposes. Consequently our economy was repeatedly subject to deflation and to periods of monetary stringency. While the Red Cross issue of 50 or 25 cigarettes per man per week came in regularly, and while there were fair stocks held, the cigarette currency suited its purpose admirably. But when the issue was interrupted, stocks soon ran out, prices fell, trading declined in volume and became increasingly a matter of barter. This deflationary tendency was periodically offset by the sudden injection of new currency. Private cigarette parcels arrived in a trickle throughout the year, but the big numbers came in quarterly when the Red Cross received its allocation of transport. Several hundred thousand cigarettes might arrive in the space of a fortnight. Prices soared, and then began to fall, slowly at first but with increasing rapidity as stocks ran out, until the next big delivery. Most of our economic troubles could be attributed to this fundamental instability.

PRICE MOVEMENTS

Many factors affected prices, the strongest and most noticeable being the periodical currency inflation and deflation described in the last paragraphs. The periodicity of this price cycle depended on cigarette and, to a far lesser extent, on food deliveries. At one time in the early days, before any private parcels had arrived and when there were no individual stocks, the weekly issue of cigarettes and food parcels occurred on a Monday. The non-monetary demand for cigarettes was great and less elastic than the demand for food: consequently prices fluctuated weekly, falling towards Sunday night and rising sharply on Monday morning. Later, when many people held reserves, the weekly issue had no such effect, being too small a proportion of the total available. Credit allowed people with no reserves to meet their non-monetary demand over the weekend.

The general price level was affected by other factors. An influx of new prisoners, proverbially hungry, raised it. Heavy air raids in the vicinity of the camp probably increased the non-monetary demand for cigarettes and accentuated deflation. Good and bad war news certainly had its effect, and the general waves of optimism and pessimism which swept the camp were reflected in prices. Before breakfast one morning in March of this year, a rumor of the arrival of parcels and cigarettes was circulated. Within ten minutes I sold a treacle ration, for four cigarettes (hitherto offered in vain for three), and many similar deals went through. By 10 o'clock the rumor was denied, and treacle that day found no more buyers even at two cigarettes.

More interesting than changes in the general price level were changes in the price structure. Changes in the supply of a commodity, in the German ration scale or in the make-up of Red Cross parcels, would raise the price of one commodity relative to others. Tins of oatmeal, once a rare and much sought after luxury in the parcels, became a commonplace in 1943, and the price fell. In hot weather the demand for cocoa fell, and that for soap rose. A new recipe would be reflected in the price level: the discovery that raisins and sugar could be turned into an alcoholic liquor of remarkable potency reacted permanently on the dried fruit market. The invention of electric immersion heaters run off the power points made tea, a drug on the market in Italy, a certain seller in Germany.

In August, 1944, the supplies of parcels and cigarettes were both halved. Since both sides of the equation were changed in the same degree, changes in prices were not anticipated. But this was not the case: the non-monetary demand for cigarettes was less elastic than the demand for food, and food prices fell a little. More important however were the changes in the price structure. German margarine and jam, hitherto valueless owing to adequate supplies of Canadian butter and marmalade, acquired a new value. Chocolate, popular and a certain seller, and sugar, fell. Bread rose; several standing contracts of bread for cigarettes were broken, especially when the bread ration was reduced a few weeks later.

In February, 1945, the German soldier who drove the ration waggon was found to be willing to exchange loaves of bread at the rate of one loaf for a bar of chocolate. Those in the know began selling bread and buying chocolate, by then almost unsalable in a period of serious deflation. Bread, at about 40, fell slightly; chocolate rose from 15; the supply of bread was not enough for the two commodities to reach parity, but the tendency was unmistakable.

The substitution of German margarine for Canadian butter when parcels were halved naturally affected their relative values, margarine appreciating at the expense of butter. Similarly, two brands of dried milk, hitherto differing in quality and therefore in price by five cigarettes a tin, came together in price as the wider substitution of the cheaper raised its relative value.

Enough has been cited to show that any change in conditions affected both the general price level and the price structure. It was this latter phenomenon which wrecked our planned economy.

PAPER CURRENCY—BULLY MARKS

Around D-Day, food and cigarettes were plentiful, business was brisk and the camp in an optimistic mood. Consequently the Entertainments Committee felt the moment opportune to launch a restaurant where food and hot drinks were sold while a band and variety turns performed. Earlier experiments, both public and private, had pointed the way, and the scheme was a great success. Food was bought at market prices to provide the meals and the small profits were devoted to a reserve fund and used to bribe Germans to provide grease-paints and other necessities for the camp theatre. Originally meals were sold for cigarettes but this meant that the whole scheme was vulnerable to the deflationary waves, and furthermore heavy smokers were unlikely to attend much. The whole success of the scheme depended on an adequate amount of food being offered for sale in the normal manner.

To increase and facilitate trade, and to stimulate supplies and customers therefore. and secondarily to avoid the worst effects of deflation when it should come, a paper currency was organized by the Restaurant and the Shop. The Shop bought food on behalf of the Restaurant with paper notes and the paper was accepted equally with the cigarettes in the Restaurant or Shop, and passed back to the Shop to purchase more food. The Shop acted as a bank of issue. The paper money was backed 100 percent. by food ; hence its name, the Bully Mark. The BMk. was backed 100 percent by food: there could be no over-issues, as is permissible with a normal bank of issue, since the eventual dispersal of the camp and consequent redemption of all BMk.s was anticipated in the near future.

Originally one BMk. was worth one cigarette and for a short time both circulated freely inside and outside the Restaurant. Prices were quoted in BMk.s and cigarettes with equal freedom-and for a short time the BMk. showed signs of replacing the cigarette as currency. The BMk. was tied to food, but not to cigarettes: as it was issued against food, say 45 for a tin of milk and so on, any reduction in the BMk. prices of food would have meant that there were unbacked BMk.s in circulation. But the price of both food and BMk.s could and did fluctuate with the supply of cigarettes.

While the Restaurant flourished, the scheme was a success: the Restaurant bought heavily, all foods were saleable and prices were stable.

In August parcels and cigarettes were halved and the Camp was bombed. The Restaurant closed for a short while and sales of food became difficult. Even when the Restaurant reopened, the food and cigarette shortage became increasingly acute and people were unwilling to convert such valuable goods into paper and to hold them for luxuries like snacks and tea. Less of the right kinds of food for the Restaurant were sold, and the Shop became glutted with dried fruit, chocolate, sugar, etc., which the Restaurant could not buy. The price level and the price structure changed. The BMk. fell to four-fifths of a cigarette and eventually farther still, and it became unacceptable save in the Restaurant. There was a flight from the BMk., no longer convertible into cigarettes or popular foods. The cigarette re-established itself.

But the BMk. was sound! The Restaurant closed in the New Year with a progressive food shortage and the long evenings without lights due to intensified Allied air raids, and BMk.s could only be spent in the Coffee Bar—relict of the Restaurant—or on the few unpopular foods in the Shop, the owners of which were prepared to accept them. In the end all holders of BMk.s were paid in full, in cups of coffee or in prunes. People who had bought BMk.s for cigarettes or valuable jam or biscuits in their heyday were aggrieved that they should have stood the loss involved by their restricted choice, but they suffered no actual loss of market value.

PRICE FIXING

Along with this scheme came a determined attempt at a planned economy, at price fixing. The Medical Officer had long been anxious to control food sales, for fear of some people selling too much, to the detriment of their health. The deflationary waves and their effects on prices were inconvenient to all and would be dangerous to the Restaurant which had to carry stocks. Furthermore, unless the BMk. was convertible into cigarettes at about par it had little chance of gaining confidence and of succeeding as a currency. As has been explained, the BMk, was tied to food but could not be tied to cigarettes, which fluctuated in value. Hence, while BMk, prices of food were fixed for all time, cigarette prices of food and BMk.s varied.

The Shop, backed by the Senior British Officer, was now in a position to enforce price control both inside and outside its walls. Hitherto a standard price had been fixed for food left for sale in the shop, and prices outside were roughly in conformity with this scale, which was recommended as a "guide" to sellers, but fluctuated a good deal around it. Sales in the Shop at recommended prices were apt to be slow though a good price might be obtained: sales outside could be made more quickly at lower prices. (If sales outside were to be at higher prices, goods were withdrawn from the Shop until the recommended price rose: but the recommended price was sluggish and could not follow the market closely by reason of its very purpose, which was stability.) The Exchange and Mart notice boards came under the control of the Shop: advertisements which exceeded a 5 percent departure from the recommended scale were liable to be crossed out by authority: unauthorized sales were discouraged by authority and also by public opinion, strongly in favour of a just and stable price. (Recommended prices were fixed partly from market data, partly on the advice of the M.O.)

At first the recommended scale was a success: the Restaurant, a big buyer, kept prices stable around this level: opinion and the 5 percent tolerance helped. But when the price level fell with the August cuts and the price structure changed, the recommended scale was too rigid. Unchanged at first, as no deflation was expected, the scale was tardily lowered, but the prices of goods on the new scale remained in the same relation to one another owing to the BMk., while on the market the price structure had changed. And the modifying influence of the Restaurant had gone. The scale was moved up and down several times, slowly following the inflationary and deflationary waves, but it was rarely adjusted to changes in the price structure. More and more advertisements were crossed off the board, and black market sales at unauthorized prices increased : eventually public opinion turned against the recommended scale and authority gave up the struggle. In the last few weeks, with unparalleled deflation, prices fell with alarming rapidity, no scales existed, and supply and demand, alone and unmellowed, determined prices.

PUBLIC OPINION

Public opinion on the subject of trading was vocal if confused and changeable, and generalizations as to its direction are difficult and dangerous. A tiny minority held that all trading was undesirable as it engendered an unsavory atmosphere; occasional frauds and sharp practices were cited as proof. Certain forms of trading were more generally condemned; trade with the Germans was criticized by many, Red Cross toilet articles, which were in short supply and only issued in cases of actual need, were excluded from trade by law and opinion working in unshakable harmony. At one time, when there had been several cases of malnutrition reported among the more devoted smokers, no trade in German rations was permitted, as the victims became an additional burden on the depleted food reserves of the Hospital. But while certain activities were condemned as anti-social, trade itself was practiced, and its utility appreciated, by almost everyone in the camp.

More interesting was opinion on middlemen and prices. Taken as a whole, opinion was hostile to the middleman. His function, and his hard work in bringing buyer and seller together, were ignored; profits were not regarded as a reward for labour, but as the result of sharp practices. Despite the fact that his very existence was proof to the contrary, the middleman was held to be redundant in view of the existence of an official Shop and the Exchange and Mart. Appreciation only came his way when he was willing to advance the price of a sugar ration, or to buy goods spot and carry them against a future sale. In these cases the element of risk was obvious to all, and the convenience of the service was felt to merit some reward. Particularly unpopular was the middleman with an element of monopoly, the man who contacted the ration wagon driver, or the man who utilized his knowledge of Urdu. And middlemen as a group were blamed for reducing prices. Opinion notwithstanding, most people dealt with a middleman, whether consciously or unconsciously, at some time or another.

There was a strong feeling that everything had its "just price" in cigarettes. While the assessment of the just price, which incidentally varied between camps, was impossible of explanation, this price was nevertheless pretty closely known. It can best be defined as the price usually fetched by an article in good times when cigarettes were plentiful. The "just price" changed slowly; it was unaffected by short-term variations in supply, and while opinion might be resigned to departures from the "just price," a strong feeling of resentment persisted. A more satisfactory definition of the "just price" is impossible. Everyone knew what it was, though no one could explain why it should be so.

As soon as prices began to fall with a cigarette shortage, a clamor arose, particularly against those who held reserves and who bought at reduced prices. Sellers at cut prices were criticized and their activities referred to as the black market. In every period of dearth the explosive question of "should non-smokers receive a cigarette ration?" was discussed to profitless length. Unfortunately, it was the non-smoker, or the light smoker with his reserves, along with the hated middleman, who weathered the storm most easily.

The popularity of the price-fixing scheme, and such success as it enjoyed, were undoubtedly the result of this body of opinion. On several occasions the fall of prices was delayed by the general support given to the recommended scale. The onset of deflation was marked by a period of sluggish trade; prices stayed up but no one bought. Then prices fell on the black market, and the volume of trade revived in that quarter. Even when the recommended scale was revised, the volume of trade in the Shop would remain low. Opinion was always overruled by the hard facts of the market.

Curious arguments were advanced to justify price fixing. The recommended prices were in some way related to the calorific values of the foods offered: hence some were overvalued and never sold at these prices. One argument ran as follows: not everyone has private cigarette parcels, thus, when prices were high and trade good in the summer of 1944, only the lucky rich could buy. This was unfair to the man with few cigarettes. When prices fell in the following winter, prices should be pegged high so that the rich, who had enjoyed life in the summer, should put many cigarettes into circulation. The fact that those who sold to the rich in the summer had also enjoyed life then, and the fact that in the winter there was always someone willing to sell at low prices were ignored. Such arguments were hotly debated each night after the approach of Allied aircraft extinguished all lights at 8 p.m. But prices moved with the supply of cigarettes, and refused to stay fixed in accordance with a theory of ethics.

CONCLUSION

The economic organization described was both elaborate and smooth-working in the summer of 1944. Then came the August cuts and deflation. Prices fell, rallied with deliveries of cigarette parcels in September and December, and fell again. In January, 1945, supplies of Red Cross cigarettes ran out: and prices slumped still further: in February the supplies of food parcels were exhausted and the depression became a blizzard. Food, itself scarce, was almost given away in order to meet the non-monetary demand for cigarettes. Laundries ceased to operate, or worked for £s or RMk.s: food and cigarettes sold for fancy prices in £s, hitherto unheard of. The Restaurant was a memory ad the BMk. a joke. The Shop was empty and the Exchange and Mart notices were full of unaccepted offers for cigarettes. Barter increased in volume, becoming a larger proportion of a smaller volume of trade. This, the first serious and prolonged food shortage in the writer's experience, caused the price structure to change again, partly because German rations were not easily divisible. A margarine ration gradually sank in value until it exchanged directly for a treacle ration. Sugar slumped sadly. Only bread retained its value. Several thousand cigarettes, the capital of the Shop, were distributed without any noticeable effect. A few fractional parcel and cigarette issues, such as one-sixth of a parcel and twelve cigarettes each, led to momentary price recoveries and feverish trade, especially when they coincided with good news from the Western Front, but the general position remained unaltered.

By April, 1945, chaos had replaced order in the economic sphere : sales were difficult, prices lacked stability. Economics has been defined as the science of distributing limited means among unlimited and competing ends. On 12th April, with the arrival of elements of the 30th U.S. Infantry Division, the ushering in of an age of plenty demonstrated the hypothesis that with infinite means economic organization and activity would be redundant, as every want could be satisfied without effort.

The Use of Knowledge
in Society

By F. A. Hayek

I.

WHAT IS THE problem we wish to solve when we try to construct a rational economic order? On certain familiar assumptions the answer is simple enough. *If* we possess all the relevant information, *if* we can start out from a given system of preferences, and *if* we command complete knowledge of available means, the problem which remains is purely one of logic. That is, the answer to the question of what is the best use of the available means is implicit in our assumptions. The conditions which the solution of this optimum problem must satisfy have been fully worked out and can be stated best in mathematical form: put at their briefest, they are that the marginal rates of substitution between any two commodities or factors must be the same in all their different uses.

This, however, is emphatically *not* the economic problem which society faces. And the economic calculus which we have developed to solve this logical problem, though an important step toward the solution of the economic problem of society, does not yet provide an answer to it. The reason for this is that the "data" from which the economic calculus starts are never for the whole society "given" to a single mind which could work out the implications and can never be so given.

The peculiar character of the problem of a rational economic order is determined precisely by the fact that the knowledge of the circumstances of which we must make use never exists in concentrated or integrated form but solely as the dispersed bits of incomplete and frequently contradictory knowledge which all the separate individuals possess. The economic problem of society is thus not merely a problem of how to allocate "given" resources—if "given" is taken to mean given to a single mind which deliberately solves the problem set by these "data." It is rather a problem of how to secure the best use of resources known to any of the members of society, for ends whose relative importance only these individuals know. Or, to put it briefly, it is a problem of the utilization of knowledge which is not given to anyone in its totality.

This character of the fundamental problem has, I am afraid, been obscured rather than illuminated by many of the recent refinements of economic theory, particularly by many of the uses made of mathematics. Though the problem with which I want primarily to deal in this paper is the problem of a rational economic organization, I shall in its course be led again and again to point to its close connections with certain methodological questions. Many of the points I wish to make are indeed conclusions toward which diverse paths of reasoning have unexpectedly converged. But, as I now see these problems, this is no accident. It seems to me that many of the current disputes with regard to both economic theory and economic policy have their common origin in a misconception about the nature of the economic problem of society. This misconception in turn is due to an erroneous transfer to social phenomena of the habits of thought we have developed in dealing with the phenomena of nature.

II.

In ordinary language we describe by the word "planning" the complex of interrelated decisions about the allocation of our available resources. All economic activity is in this sense planning; and in any society in which many people collaborate, this planning, whoever does it, will in some measure have to be based on knowledge which, in the first instance, is not given to the planner but to somebody else, which somehow will have to be conveyed to the planner. The various ways in which the knowledge on which people base their plans is communicated to them is the crucial problem for any theory explaining the economic process, and the problem of what is the best way of utilizing knowledge initially dispersed among all the people is at least one of the main problems of economic policy—or of designing an efficient economic system.

The answer to this question is closely connected with that other question which arises here, that of *who* is to do the planning. It is about this question that all the dispute about "economic planning" centers. This is not a dispute about whether planning is to be done or not. It is a dispute as to whether planning is to be done centrally, by one authority for the whole economic system, or is to be divided among many individuals. Planning in the specific sense in which the term is used in contemporary controversy necessarily means central planning—direction of the whole economic system according to one unified plan. Competition, on the other hand, means decentralized planning by many separate persons. The halfway house between the two, about which many people talk but which few like when they see it, is the delegation of planning to organized industries, or, in other words, monopoly.

Which of these systems is likely to be more efficient depends mainly on the question under which of them we can expect that fuller use will be made of the existing knowledge. And this, in turn, depends on whether we are more likely to succeed in putting at the disposal of a single central authority all the knowledge which ought to be used but which is initially dispersed among many different individuals, or in conveying to the individuals such additional knowledge as they need in order to enable them to fit their plans with those of others.

III.

It will at once be evident that on this point the position will be different with respect to different kinds of knowledge; and the answer to our question will therefore largely turn on the relative importance of the different kinds of knowledge; those more likely to be at the disposal of particular individuals and those which we should with greater confidence expect to find in the possession of an authority made up of suitably chosen experts. If it is today so widely assumed that the latter will be in a better position, this is because one kind of knowledge, namely, scientific knowledge, occupies now so prominent a place in public imagination that we tend to forget that it is not the only kind that is relevant. It may be admitted that, as far as scientific knowledge is concerned, a body of suitably chosen experts may be in the best position to command all the best knowledge available—though this is of course merely shifting the difficulty to the problem of selecting the experts. What I wish to point out is that, even assuming that this problem can be readily solved, it is only a small part of the wider problem.

Today it is almost heresy to suggest that scientific knowledge is not the sum of all knowledge. But a little reflection will show that there is beyond question a body of very important but unorganized knowledge which cannot possibly be called scientific in the sense of knowledge of general rules: the knowledge of the particular circumstances of time and place. It is with respect to this that practically every individual has some advantage over all others because he possesses unique information of which beneficial use might be made, but of which use can be made only if the decisions depending on it are left to him or are made with his active cooperation. We need to remember only how much we have to learn in any occupation after we have completed our theoretical training, how big a part of our working life we spend learning particular jobs, and how valuable an asset in all walks of life is knowledge of people, of local conditions, and of special circumstances. To know of and put to use a machine not fully employed, or somebody's skill which could be better utilized, or to be aware of a surplus stock which can be drawn upon during an interruption of supplies, is socially quite as useful as the knowledge of better alternative techniques. And the shipper who earns his living from using otherwise empty or half-filled journeys of tramp-steamers, or the estate agent whose whole knowledge is almost exclusively one of temporary opportunities, or the *arbitrageur* who gains from local differences of commodity prices, are all performing eminently useful functions based on special knowledge of circumstances of the fleeting moment not known to others.

It is a curious fact that this sort of knowledge should today be generally regarded with a kind of contempt and that anyone who by such knowledge gains an advantage over somebody better equipped with theoretical or technical knowledge is thought to have acted almost disreputably. To gain an advantage from better knowledge of facilities of communication or transport is sometimes regarded as almost dishonest, although it is quite as important that society make use of the best opportunities in this respect as in using the latest scientific discoveries. This prejudice has in a considerable measure affected the attitude toward commerce in general compared with that toward production. Even economists who regard themselves as definitely immune to the crude materialist fallacies of the past constantly commit the same mistake where activities directed toward the acquisition of such practical knowledge are concerned—apparently because in their scheme of things all such knowledge is supposed to be "given." The common idea now seems to be that all such knowledge should as a matter of course be readily at the command of everybody, and the reproach of irrationality leveled against the existing economic order is frequently based on the fact that it is not so available. This view disregards the fact that the method by which such knowledge can be made as widely available as possible is precisely the problem to which we have to find an answer.

IV.

If it is fashionable today to minimize the importance of the knowledge of the particular circumstances of time and place, this is closely connected with the smaller importance which is now attached to change as such. Indeed, there are few points on which the assumptions made (usually only implicitly) by the "planners" differ from those of their opponents as much as with regard to the significance and frequency of changes which will make substantial alterations of production plans necessary. Of course, if detailed economic plans could be laid down for fairly long periods in advance and then closely adhered to, so that no further economic decisions of importance would be required, the task of drawing up a comprehensive plan governing all economic activity would be much less formidable.

It is, perhaps, worth stressing that economic problems arise always and only in consequence of change. So long as things continue as before, or at least as they were expected to, there arise no new problems requiring a decision, no need to form a new plan. The belief that changes, or at least day-to-day adjustments, have become less important in modern times implies the contention that economic problems also have become less important. This belief in the decreasing importance of change is, for that reason, usually held by the same people who argue that the importance of economic considerations has been driven into the background by the growing importance of technological knowledge.

Is it true that, with the elaborate apparatus of modern production, economic decisions are required only at long intervals, as when a new factory is to be erected or a new process to be introduced? Is it true that, once a plant has been built, the rest is all more or less mechanical, determined by the character of the plant, and leaving little to be changed in adapting to the ever-changing circumstances of the moment?

The fairly widespread belief in the affirmative is not, as far as I can ascertain, borne out by the practical experience of the businessman. In a competitive industry at any rate—and such an industry alone can serve as a test—the task of keeping cost from rising requires constant struggle, absorbing a great part of the energy of the manager. How easy it is for an inefficient manager to dissipate the differentials on which profitability rests, and that it is possible, with the same technical facilities, to produce with a great variety of costs, are among the commonplaces of business experience which do not seem to be equally familiar in the study of the economist. The very strength of the desire, constantly voiced by producers and engineers, to be allowed to proceed untrammeled by considerations of money costs, is eloquent testimony to the extent to which these factors enter into their daily work.

One reason why economists are increasingly apt to forget about the constant small changes which make up the whole economic picture is probably their growing preoccupation with statistical aggregates, which show a very much greater stability than the movements of the detail. The comparative stability of the aggregates cannot, however, be accounted for—as the statisticians occasionally seem to be inclined to do—by the "law of large numbers" or the mutual compensation of random changes. The number of elements with which we have to deal is not large enough for such accidental forces to produce stability. The continuous flow of goods and services is maintained by constant deliberate adjustments, by new dispositions made every day in the light of circumstances not known the day before, by *B* stepping in at once when *A* fails to deliver. Even the large and highly mechanized plant keeps going largely because of an environment upon which it can draw for all sorts of unexpected needs; tiles for its roof, stationery for its forms, and all the thousand and one kinds of equipment in which it cannot be self-contained and which the plans for the operation of the plant require to be readily available in the market.

This is, perhaps, also the point where I should briefly mention the fact that the sort of knowledge with which I have been concerned is knowledge of the kind which by its nature cannot enter into statistics and therefore cannot be conveyed to any central authority in statistical form. The statistics which such a central authority would have to use would have to be arrived at precisely by abstracting from minor differences between the things, by lumping together, as resources of one kind, items which differ as regards location, quality, and other particulars, in a way which may be very significant for the specific decision. It follows from this that central planning based on statistical information by its nature cannot take direct account of these circumstances of time and place and that the central planner will have to find some way or other in which the decisions depending on them can be left to the "man on the spot."

V.

If we can agree that the economic problem of society is mainly one of rapid adaptation to changes in the particular circumstances of time and place, it would seem to follow that the ultimate decisions must be left to the people who are familiar with these circumstances, who know directly of the relevant changes and of the resources immediately available to meet them. We cannot expect that this problem will be solved by first communicating all this knowledge to a central board which, after integrating *all* knowledge, issues its orders. We must solve it by some form of decentralization. But this answers only part of our problem. We need decentralization because only thus can we insure that the knowledge of the particular circumstances of time and place will be promptly used. But the "man on the spot" cannot decide solely on the basis of his limited but intimate knowledge of the facts of his immediate surroundings. There still remains the problem of communicating to him such further information as he needs to fit his decisions into the whole pattern of changes of the larger economic system.

How much knowledge does he need to do so successfully? Which of the events which happen beyond the horizon of his immediate knowledge are of relevance to his immediate decision, and how much of them need he know?

There is hardly anything that happens anywhere in the world that *might* not have an effect on the decision he ought to make. But he need not know of these events as such, nor of *all* their effects. It does not matter for him *why* at the particular moment more screws of one size than of another are wanted, *why* paper bags are more readily available than canvas bags, or *why* skilled labor, or particular machine tools, have for the moment become more difficult to obtain. All that is significant for him is *how much more or less* difficult to procure they have become compared with other things with which he is also concerned, or how much more or less urgently wanted are the alternative things he produces or uses. It is always a question of the relative importance of the particular things with which he is concerned, and the causes which alter their relative importance are of no interest to him beyond the effect on those concrete things of his own environment.

It is in this connection that what I have called the "economic calculus" proper helps us, at least by analogy, to see how this problem can be solved, and in fact is being solved, by the price system. Even the single controlling mind, in possession of all the data for some small, self-contained economic system, would not—every time some small adjustment in the allocation of resources had to be made—go explicitly through all the relations between ends and means which might possibly be affected. It is indeed the great contribution of the pure logic of choice that it has demonstrated conclusively that even such a single mind could solve this kind of problem only by constructing and constantly using rates of equivalence (or "values," or "marginal rates of substitution"), *i.e.,* by attaching to each kind of scarce resource a numerical index which cannot be derived from any property possessed by that particular thing, but which reflects, or in which is condensed, its significance in view of the whole means-end structure. In any small change he will have to consider only these quantitative indices (or "values") in which all the relevant information is concentrated; and, by adjusting the quantities one by one, he can appropriately rearrange his dispositions without having to solve the whole puzzle *ab initio* or without needing at any stage to survey it at once in all its ramifications.

Fundamentally, in a system in which the knowledge of the relevant facts is dispersed among many people, prices can act to coordinate the separate actions of different people in the same way as subjective values help the individual to coordinate the parts of his plan. It is worth contemplating for a moment a very simple and commonplace instance of the action of the price system to see what precisely it accomplishes. Assume that somewhere in the world a new opportunity for the use of some raw material, say, tin, has arisen, or that one of the sources of supply of tin has been eliminated. It does not matter for our purpose—and it is very significant that it does not matter—which of these two causes has made tin more scarce. All that the users of tin need to know is that some of the tin they used to consume is now more profitably employed elsewhere and that, in consequence, they must economize tin. There is no need for the great majority of them even to know where the more urgent need has arisen, or in favor of what other needs they ought to husband the supply. If only some of them know directly of the new demand, and switch resources over to it, and if the people who are aware of the new gap thus created in turn fill it from still other sources, the effect will rapidly spread throughout the whole economic system and influence not only all the uses of tin but also those of its substitutes and the substitutes of these substitutes, the supply of all the things made of tin, and their substitutes, and so on; and all his without the great majority of those instrumental in bringing about these substitutions knowing anything at all about the original cause of these changes. The whole acts as one market, not because any of its members survey the whole field, but because their limited individual fields of vision sufficiently overlap so that through many intermediaries the relevant information is communicated to all. The mere fact that there is one price for any commodity—or rather that local prices are connected in a manner determined by the cost of transport, etc.—brings about the solution which (it is just conceptually possible) might have been arrived at by one single mind possessing all the information which is in fact dispersed among all the people involved in the process.

VI.

We must look at the price system as such a mechanism for communicating information if we want to understand its real function—a function which, of course, it fulfils less perfectly as prices grow more rigid. (Even when quoted prices have become quite rigid, however, the forces which would operate through changes in price still operate to a considerable extent through changes in the other terms of the contract.) The most significant fact about this system is the economy of knowledge with which it operates, or how little the individual participants need to know in order to be able to take the right action. In abbreviated form, by a kind of symbol, only the most essential information is passed on and passed on only to those concerned. It is more than a metaphor to describe the price system as a kind of machinery for registering change, or a system of telecommunications which enables individual producers to watch merely the movement of a few pointers, as an engineer might watch the hands of a few dials, in order to adjust their activities to changes of which they may never know more than is reflected in the price movement.

Of course, these adjustments are probably never "perfect" in the sense in which the economist conceives of them in his equilibrium analysis. But I fear that our theoretical habits of approaching the problem with the assumption of more or less perfect knowledge on the part of almost everyone has made us somewhat blind to the true function of the price mechanism and led us to apply rather misleading standards in judging its efficiency. The marvel is that in a case like that of a scarcity of one raw material, without an order being issued, without more than perhaps a handful of people knowing the cause, tens of thousands of people whose identity could not be ascertained by months of investigation, are made to use the material or its products more sparingly; *i.e.*, they move in the right direction. This is enough of a marvel even if, in a constantly changing world, not all will hit it off so perfectly that their profit rates will always be maintained at the same constant or "normal" level.

I have deliberately used the word "marvel" to shock the reader out of the complacency with which we often take the working of this mechanism for granted. I am convinced that if it were the result of deliberate human design, and if the people guided by the price changes understood that their decisions have significance far beyond their immediate aim, this mechanism would have been acclaimed as one of the greatest triumphs of the human mind. Its misfortune is the double one that it is not the product of human design and that the people guided by it usually do not know why they are made to do what they do. But those who clamor for "conscious direction"—and who cannot believe that anything which has evolved without design (and even without our understanding it) should solve problems which we should not be able to solve consciously—should remember this: The problem is precisely how to extend the span of out utilization of resources beyond the span of the control of any one mind; and therefore, how to dispense with the need of conscious control, and how to provide inducements which will make the individuals do the desirable things without anyone having to tell them what to do.

The problem which we meet here is by no means peculiar to economics but arises in connection with nearly all truly social phenomena, with language and with most of our cultural inheritance, and constitutes really the central theoretical problem of all social science. As Alfred Whitehead has said in another connection, "It is a profoundly erroneous truism, repeated by all copy-books and by eminent people when they are making speeches, that we should cultivate the habit of thinking what we are doing. The precise opposite is the case. Civilization advances by extending the number of important operations which we can perform without thinking about them." This is of profound significance in the social field. We make constant use of formulas, symbols, and rules whose meaning we do not understand and through the use of which we avail ourselves of the assistance of knowledge which individually we do not possess. We have developed these practices and institutions by building upon habits and institutions which have proved successful in their own sphere and which have in turn become the foundation of the civilization we have built up.

The price system is just one of those formations which man has learned to use (though he is still very far from having learned to make the best use of it) after he had stumbled upon it without understanding it. Through it not only a division of labor but also a coördinated utilization of resources based on an equally divided knowledge has become possible. The people who like to deride any suggestion that this may be so usually distort the argument by insinuating that it asserts that by some miracle just that sort of system has spontaneously grown up which is best suited to modern civilization. It is the other way round: man has been able to develop that division of labor on which our civilization is based because he happened to stumble upon a method which made it possible. Had he not done so, he might still have developed some other, altogether different, type of civilization, something like the "state" of the termite ants, or some other altogether unimaginable type. All that we can say is that nobody has yet succeeded in designing an alternative system in which certain features of the existing one can be preserved which are dear even to those who most violently assail it—such as particularly the extent to which the individual can choose his pursuits and consequently freely use his own knowledge and skill.

VII.

It is in many ways fortunate that the dispute about the indispensability of the price system for any rational calculation in a complex society is now no longer conducted entirely between camps holding different political views. The thesis that without the price system we could not preserve a society based on such extensive division of labor as ours was greeted with a howl of derision when it was first advanced by von Mises twenty-five years ago. Today the difficulties which some still find in accepting it are no longer mainly political, and this makes for an atmosphere much more conducive to reasonable discussion. When we find Leon Trotsky arguing that "economic accounting is unthinkable without market relations"; when Professor Oscar Lange promises Professor von Mises a statue in the marble halls of the future Central Planning

Board; and when Professor Abba P. Lerner rediscovers Adam Smith and emphasizes that the essential utility of the price system consists in inducing the individual, while seeking his own interest, to do what is in the general interest, the differences can indeed no longer be ascribed to political prejudice. The remaining dissent seems clearly to be due to purely intellectual, and more particularly methodological, differences.

A recent statement by Professor Joseph Schumpeter in his *Capitalism, Socialism, and Democracy* provides a clear illustration of one of the methodological differences which I have in mind. Its author is pre-eminent among those economists who approach economic phenomena in the light of a certain branch of positivism. To him these phenomena accordingly appear as objectively given quantities of commodities impinging directly upon each other, almost, it would seem, without any intervention of human minds. Only against this background can I account for the following (to me startling) pronouncement. Professor Schumpeter argues that the possibility of a rational calculation in the absence of markets for the factors of production follows for the theorist "from the elementary proposition that consumers in evaluating ('demanding') consumers' goods *ipso facto* also evaluate the means of production which enter into the production of these goods."

Taken literally, this statement is simply untrue. The consumers do nothing of the kind. What Professor Schumpeter's *"ipso facto"* presumably means is that the valuation of the factors of production is implied in, or follows necessarily from, the valuation of consumers' goods. But this, too, is not correct. Implication is a logical relationship which can be meaningfully asserted only of propositions simultaneously present to one and the same mind. It is evident, however, that the values of the factors of production do not depend solely on the valuation of the consumers' goods but also on the conditions of supply of the various factors of production. Only to a mind to which all these facts were simultaneously known would the answer necessarily follow from the facts given to it. The practical problem, however, arises precisely because these facts are never so given to a single mind, and because, in consequence, it is necessary that in the solution of the problem knowledge should be used that is dispersed among many people.

The problem is thus in no way solved if we can show that all the facts, *if* they were known to a single mind (as we hypothetically assume them to be given to the observing economist), would uniquely determine the solution; instead we must show how a solution is produced by the interactions of people each of whom possesses only partial knowledge. To assume all the knowledge to be given to a single mind in the same manner in which we assume it to be given to us as the explaining economists is to assume the problem away and to disregard everything that is important and significant in the real world.

That an economist of Professor Schumpeter's standing should thus have fallen into a trap which the ambiguity of the term "datum" sets to the unwary can hardly be explained as a simple error. It suggests rather that there is something fundamentally wrong with an approach which habitually disregards an essential part of the phenomena with which we have to deal: the unavoidable imperfection of man's knowledge and the consequent need for a process by which knowledge is constantly communicated and acquired. Any approach, such as that of much of mathematical economics with its simultaneous equations, which in effect starts from the assumption that people's *knowledge* corresponds with the objective *facts* of the situation, systematically leaves out what is our main task to explain. I am far from denying that in our system equilibrium analysis has a useful function to perform. But when it comes to the point where it misleads some of our leading thinkers into believing that the situation which it describes has direct relevance to the solution of practical problems, it is high time that we remember that it does not deal with the social process at all and that it is no more than a useful preliminary to the study of the main problem.

NOTES FOR THIS CHAPTER

J. Schumpeter, *Capitalism, Socialism, and Democracy* (New York; Harper, 1942), p. 175. Professor Schumpeter is, I believe, also the original author of the myth that Pareto and Barone have "solved" the problem of socialist calculation. What they, and many others, did was merely to state the conditions which a rational allocation of resources would have to satisfy and to point out that these were essentially the same as the conditions of equilibrium of a competitive market. This is something altogether different from knowing how the allocation of resources satisfying these conditions can be found in practice. Pareto himself (from whom Barone has taken practically everything he has to say), far from claiming to have solved the practical problem, in fact explicitly denies that it can be solved without the help of the market. See his *Manuel d'économie pure* (2nd ed., 1927), pp. 233–34. The relevant passage is quoted in an English translation at the beginning of my article on "Socialist Calculation: The Competitive 'Solution,'" in *Economica,* New Series, Vol. VIII, No. 26 (May, 1940), p. 125.

SECTION FOUR

Price Control

Price Controls

By Hugh Rockoff

G OVERNMENTS HAVE BEEN trying to set maximum or minimum prices since ancient times. The Old Testament prohibited interest on loans to fellow Israelites; medieval governments fixed the maximum price of bread; and in recent years, governments in the United States have fixed the price of gasoline, the rent on apartments in New York City, and the wage of unskilled labor, to name a few. At times, governments go beyond fixing specific prices and try to control the general level of prices, as was done in the United States during both world wars and the Korean War, and by the Nixon administration from 1971 to 1973.

The appeal of price controls is understandable. Even though they fail to protect many consumers and hurt others, controls hold out the promise of protecting groups that are particularly hard-pressed to meet price increases. Thus, the prohibition against usury—charging high interest on loans—was intended to protect someone forced to borrow out of desperation; the maximum price for bread was supposed to protect the poor, who depended on bread to survive; and rent controls were supposed to protect those who were renting when the demand for apartments exceeded the supply, and landlords were preparing to "gouge" their tenants.

Despite the frequent use of price controls, however, and despite their appeal, economists are generally opposed to them, except perhaps for very brief periods during emergencies. In a survey published in 1992, 76.3 percent of the economists surveyed agreed with the statement: "A ceiling on rents reduces the quality and quantity of housing available." A further 16.6 percent agreed with qualifications, and only 6.5 percent disagreed. The results were similar when the economists were asked about general controls: only 8.4 percent agreed with the statement: "Wage-price controls are a useful policy option in the control of inflation." An additional 17.7 percent agreed with qualifications, but a sizable majority, 73.9 percent, disagreed (Alston et al. 1992, p. 204).

The reason most economists are skeptical about price controls is that they distort the allocation of resources. To paraphrase a remark by Milton Friedman, economists may not know much, but they do know how to produce a shortage or surplus. Price ceilings, which prevent prices from exceeding a certain maximum, cause shortages. Price floors, which prohibit prices below a certain minimum, cause surpluses, at least for a time. Suppose that the supply and demand for wheat flour are balanced at the current price, and that the government then fixes a lower maximum price. The supply of flour will decrease, but the demand for it will increase. The result will be excess demand and empty shelves. Although some consumers will be lucky enough to purchase flour at the lower price, others will be forced to do without.

Because controls prevent the price system from rationing the available supply, some other mechanism must take its place. A queue, once a familiar sight in the controlled economies of Eastern Europe, is one possibility. When the United States set maximum prices for gasoline in 1973 and 1979, dealers sold gas on a first-come-first-served basis, and drivers had to wait in long lines to buy gasoline, receiving in the process a taste of life in the Soviet Union. The true price of gasoline, which included both the cash paid and the time spent waiting in line, was often higher than it would have been if the price had not been controlled. In 1979, for example, the United States fixed the price of gasoline at about $1.00 per gallon. If the market price had been $1.20, a driver who bought ten gallons would apparently have saved $.20 per gallon, or $2.00. But if the driver had to wait in line for thirty minutes to buy gasoline, and if her time was worth $8.00 per hour, the real cost to her was $10.00 for the gas and $4.00 for the time, an overall cost of $1.40 per gallon. Some gasoline, of course, was held for friends, longtime customers, the politically well connected, and those who were willing to pay a little cash on the side.

The incentives to evade controls are ever present, and the forms that evasion can take are limitless. The precise form depends on the nature of the good or service, the organization of the industry, the degree of government enforcement, and so on. One of the simplest forms of evasion is quality deterioration. In the United States during World War II, fat was added to hamburger, candy bars were made smaller and of inferior ingredients, and landlords reduced their maintenance of rent-controlled apartments. The government can attack quality deterioration by issuing specific product standards (hamburger must contain so much lean meat, apartments must be painted once a year, and so on) and by government oversight and enforcement. But this means that the bureaucracy controlling prices tends to get bigger, more intrusive, and more expensive.

Sometimes more subtle forms of evasion arise. One is the tie-in sale. To buy wheat flour at the official price during World War I, consumers were often required to purchase unwanted quantities of rye or potato flour. "Forced up-trading" is another. Consider a manufacturer that produces a lower-quality, lower-priced line sold in large volumes at a small markup, and a higher-priced, higher-quality line sold in small quantities at a high markup. When the government introduces price ceilings and causes a shortage of both lines, the manufacturer may discontinue the lower-priced line, causing the consumer to "trade up" to the higher-priced line. During World War II, the U.S. government made numerous unsuccessful attempts to force clothing manufacturers to continue lower-priced lines.

Not only do producers have an incentive to raise prices, but some consumers also have an incentive to pay them. The result may be payments on the side to distributors (a bribe for the superintendent of a rent-controlled building, for example), or it may be a full-fledged black market in which goods are bought and sold clandestinely. Prices in black markets may be above not only the official price but even the price that would prevail in a free market, because the buyers are unusually desperate and because sellers face penalties if their transactions are detected, and this risk is reflected in the price.

The obvious costs of queuing, evasion, and black markets often lead governments to impose some form of rationing. The simplest is a coupon entitling a consumer to buy a fixed quantity of the controlled good. For example, each motorist might receive a coupon permitting the purchase of one set of new tires. Rationing solves some of the shortage problems created by controls. Producers no longer find it easy to divert supplies to the black market since they must have ration tickets to match their production; distributors no longer have as much incentive to accept bribes or demand tie-in purchases; and consumers have a smaller incentive to pay high prices because they are assured a minimum amount. Rationing, as Forrest Capie and Geoffrey Wood (2002) pointed out, increases the integrity and efficiency of a system of price controls.

Rationing, however, comes at a cost. The government must undertake the difficult job of adjusting rations to reflect fluctuating supplies and demands and the needs of individual consumers. While an equal ration for each consumer makes sense in a few cases—bread in a city under siege is the classic example—most rationing programs must face the problem that consumer needs vary widely. One solution is to tailor the ration to the needs of individuals: people with a long commute to work can be given a larger ration of gasoline. In World War II, community boards in the United States had the power to issue extra rations to particularly needy individuals. The danger of favoritism and corruption in such a scheme, particularly if continued after the spirit of patriotism has begun to erode, is obvious. One way of ameliorating some of the problems created by rationing is to permit a free market in ration tickets. The free exchange of ration tickets has the advantages of providing additional income for consumers who sell their extra tickets and improving the well-being of those who buy. A "white market" in ration tickets, however, does nothing to encourage additional production, an end that can be accomplished by removing price controls. Also, a white market in ration tickets will not necessarily cause the product sold to be moved to the same regions of the country where the tickets are sold. Thus, a white market will not necessarily eliminate regional shortages.

With all of the problems generated by controls, we can well ask why they are ever imposed and why they are sometimes maintained for so long. The answer, in part, is that the public does not always see the links between controls and the problems they create. The elimination of lower-priced lines of merchandise may be interpreted simply as callous disregard for the poor rather than a consequence of controls. But price controls almost always benefit a subset of consumers who may have a particular claim to public sympathy and who, in any case, have a strong interest in lobbying for controls. Minimum-wage laws may create unemployment among the unskilled or drive them into the black market, but minimum wages do raise the income of those poor workers who remain employed in regulated markets. Rent controls make it difficult for young people to find an apartment, but they do hold down the rent for those who already have an apartment when controls are instituted (see rent control).

General price controls—controls on prices of many goods—are often imposed when the public becomes alarmed that inflation is out of control. In the twentieth century, war has frequently been the occasion for general price controls. Here, the case can be made that controls have a positive psychological benefit that outweighs the costs, at least in the short run. Surging

inflation may lead to panic buying, strikes, animosity toward racial or ethnic minorities who are perceived as benefiting from inflation, and so on. Price controls may make a positive contribution by calming these fears, particularly if patriotism can be counted on to limit evasion. This was the limited case for controls made by Frank W. Taussig, a member of the Price Fixing Committee in World War I, in his famous essay "Price-Fixing as seen by a Price-Fixer." A somewhat similar case can be made for removing controls cautiously when suppressed inflation—that is, inflation that the government holds down forcibly by price controls—is significant. Toward the end of World War II, more than fifty leading economists, including friends of the free market such as Frank H. Knight and Henry Simons, wrote to the New York Times (April 9, 1946, p. 23) calling on Congress to continue controls for another year until supplies and demands were more nearly in equilibrium in order to prevent the inflationary spiral they feared would arise if controls were removed suddenly.

However, most inflation, even in wartime, is due to inflationary monetary and fiscal policies rather than to panic buying. To the extent that wartime controls suppress price increases produced by monetary and fiscal policies, controls only postpone the day of reckoning, converting what would have been a steady inflation into a period of slow inflation followed by more rapid inflation. Also, part of the apparent stability of the price indexes under wartime controls is an illusion. All of the problems with price controls—queuing, evasion, black markets, and rationing—raise the real price of goods to consumers, and these effects are only partly taken into account when the price indexes are computed. When controls are removed, the hidden inflation is unveiled.

Inflation is extremely difficult to contain through general controls, in part because the attempt to limit control to a manageable sector of the economy is usually hopeless. John Kenneth Galbraith, in A Theory of Price Control, which was based on his experience as deputy administrator of the Office of Price Administration in World War II, argued that the prices of goods produced by large industrial oligopolists were relatively easy to control. These firms had large numbers of administrators who could be pressed into service—administrators who were willing, moreover, to shift their allegiance from their employers to the government, at least during the war. Galbraith overstated the market power of large firms, most of which were in highly competitive industries. But even if he had been right about these firms' market power, the problem with limiting controls to a particular sector of the economy is that when demand is surging, it tends to shift from the controlled to the uncontrolled sector, forcing prices in the uncontrolled sector to rise even faster than before. Resources follow prices, and supplies tend to rise in the uncontrolled sector at the expense of supplies in the controlled sector. Thus, a government that begins by controlling prices on selected goods tends to end with across-the-board controls. This is what happened in the United States during World War II. The attempt to confine controls to a limited sector of highly concentrated industrial firms simply did not work.

A second problem with general controls is the trade-off between the need to have a simple program generally perceived as fair and the need for sufficient flexibility to maintain efficiency. Creating an appearance of fairness requires holding most prices constant, but efficiency requires making frequent changes. Adjustments of relative prices, however, subject the bureaucracy administering controls to a barrage of lobbying and complaints of unfairness. This conflict was brought out sharply by the American experience in World War II. At first, relative prices were changed frequently on the advice of economists who maintained that this was necessary to eliminate problems in specific markets. However, mounting complaints that the program was unfair and was not stopping inflation led to President Franklin D. Roosevelt's famous "hold-the-line" order, issued in April 1943, that froze most prices. Whatever its defects as economic policy, the hold-the-line order was easy to justify to the public.

The best case for imposing general controls in peacetime turns on the possibility that controls can ease the transition from high to low inflation. If a tight monetary policy is introduced after a long period of inflation, the long-run effect will be for prices and wages to rise more slowly. But in the short run, some prices may continue to rise at the older rate. Wages also may continue to rise because of long-term contracts or because workers fail to appreciate the extent of the change in policy and, therefore, hold out for higher wages than they otherwise would. Rising wages and prices may keep output and employment below their potential. Price and wage controls may limit these temporary costs of disinflation by prohibiting wage increases that are out of line with the new trends in demand and prices. From this viewpoint, restrictive monetary policy is the operation that cures inflation, and price and wage controls are the anesthesia that suppresses the pain.

But this best case for price controls is weak. The danger is that the painkiller may be mistaken for the cure. In the eyes of the public, price controls free the monetary authority from responsibility for inflation. As a result, the pressures on the monetary authority to avoid recession may lead to a continuation or even acceleration of excessive growth in the money supply. Something very like this happened in the United States under the controls imposed by President Richard M. Nixon in 1971. Although controls were justified on the grounds that they were being used to "buy time" while more fundamental cures for inflation were put in place, monetary policy continued to be expansionary, perhaps even more so than before.

The study of price controls teaches important lessons about free competitive markets. By examining cases in which controls have prevented the price mechanism from working, we gain a better appreciation of its usual elegance and efficiency. This does not mean that there are no circumstances in which temporary controls may be effective. But a fair reading of economic history shows just how rare those circumstances are.

ABOUT THE AUTHOR

Hugh Rockoff is a professor of economics at Rutgers University in New Brunswick, New Jersey, and a research associate of the National Bureau of Economic Research.

FURTHER READING

Alston, Richard M., J. R. Kearl, and Michael B. Vaughan. "Is There a Consensus Among Economists in the 1990's?" *American Economic Review* 82 (1992): 203–209.

Capie, Forrest, and Geoffrey Wood. "Price Controls in War and Peace: A Marshallian Conclusion." *Scottish Journal of Political Economy* 49 (2002): 39–60.

Clinard, Marshall Barron. *The Black Market: A Study of White Collar Crime.* New York: Rinehart, 1952.

Galbraith, John Kenneth. *A Theory of Price Control.* Cambridge: Harvard University Press, 1952.

Grayson, C. Jackson. *Confessions of a Price Controller.* Homewood, Ill.: Dow Jones–Irwin, 1974.

Jonung, Lars. *The Political Economy of Price Controls: The Swedish Experience 1970–1987.* Brookfield, Mass.: Avebury, 1990.

Rockoff, Hugh. *Drastic Measures: A History of Wage and Price Controls in the United States.* New York: Cambridge University Press, 1984.

Schultz, George P., and Robert Z. Aliber, eds. *Guidelines: Informal Controls and the Market Place.* Chicago: University of Chicago Press, 1966.

Taussig, Frank W. "Price-Fixing as Seen by a Price-Fixer." *Quarterly Journal of Economics* 33 (1919): 205–241.

Rent Control

By Walter Block

New York State legislators defend the War Emergency Tenant Protection Act—also known as rent control—as a way of protecting tenants from war-related housing shortages. The war referred to in the law is not the 2003 war in Iraq, however, or the Vietnam War; it is World War II. That is when rent control started in New York City. Of course, war has very little to do with apartment shortages. On the contrary, the shortage is created by rent control, the supposed solution. Gotham is far from the only city to have embraced rent control. Many others across the United States have succumbed to the blandishments of this legislative "fix."

Rent control, like all other government-mandated **price controls**, is a law placing a maximum price, or a "rent ceiling," on what landlords may charge tenants. If it is to have any effect, the rent level must be set at a rate below that which would otherwise have prevailed. (An enactment prohibiting apartment rents from exceeding, say, $100,000 per month would have no effect since no one would pay that amount in any case.) But if rents are established at less than their equilibrium levels, the quantity demanded will necessarily exceed the amount supplied, and rent control will lead to a shortage of dwelling spaces. In a competitive market and absent controls on prices, if the amount of a commodity or service demanded is larger than the amount supplied, prices rise to eliminate the shortage (by both bringing forth new **supply** and by reducing the amount demanded). But controls prevent rents from attaining market-clearing levels and shortages result.

With shortages in the controlled sector, this excess **demand** spills over onto the noncontrolled sector (typically, new upper-bracket rental units or condominiums). But this noncontrolled segment of the market is likely to be smaller than it would be without controls because property owners fear that controls may one day be placed on them. The high demand in the noncontrolled segment along with the small quantity supplied, both caused by rent control, boost prices in that segment. Paradoxically, then, even though rents may be lower in the controlled sector, they rise greatly for uncontrolled units and may be higher for rental housing as a whole.

As in the case of other price ceilings, rent control causes shortages, diminution in the quality of the product, and queues. But rent control differs from other such schemes. With price controls on gasoline, the waiting lines worked on a first-come-first-served basis. With rent control, because the law places sitting tenants first in the queue, many of them benefit.

THE EFFECTS OF RENT CONTROL

Economists are virtually unanimous in concluding that rent controls are destructive. In a 1990 poll of 464 economists published in the May 1992 issue of the *American Economic Review,* 93 percent of U.S. respondents agreed, either completely or with provisos, that "a ceiling on rents reduces the quantity and quality of housing available."[1] Similarly, another study reported that more than 95 percent of the Canadian economists polled agreed with the statement.[2] The agreement cuts across the usual political spectrum, ranging all the way from Nobel Prize winners **Milton Friedman** and **Friedrich Hayek** on the "right" to their fellow Nobel laureate **Gunnar Myrdal**, an important architect of the Swedish Labor Party's **welfare** state, on the "left." Myrdal stated, "Rent control has in certain Western countries constituted, maybe, the worst example of poor planning by governments lacking courage and vision."[3] His fellow Swedish economist (and socialist) Assar Lindbeck asserted, "In many cases rent control appears to be the most efficient technique presently known to destroy a city—except for bombing."[4] That cities like New York have clearly not been destroyed by rent control is due to the fact that rent control has been relaxed over the years.[5] Rent stabilization, for example, which took the place of rent control for newer buildings, is less restrictive than the old rent control. Also, the decades-long boom in the New York City housing market is not in rent-controlled or rent-stabilized units, but in condominiums and cooperative housing. But these two forms of housing ownership grew important as a way of getting around rent control.

Economists have shown that rent control diverts new **investment**, which would otherwise have gone to rental housing, toward greener pastures—greener in terms of consumer need. They have demonstrated that it leads to housing deterioration, fewer repairs, and less maintenance. For example, Paul Niebanck found that 29 percent of rent-controlled housing in the United States was deteriorated, but only 8 percent of the uncontrolled units were in such a state of disrepair. Joel Brenner and Herbert Franklin cited similar statistics for England and France.

The economic reasons are straightforward. One effect of government oversight is to retard investment in residential rental units. Imagine that you have five million dollars to invest and can place the funds in any industry you wish. In most businesses, governments will place only limited controls and taxes on your enterprise. But if you entrust your money to rental housing, you must pass one additional hurdle: the rent-control authority, with its hearings, red tape, and rent ceilings. Under these conditions is it any wonder that you are less likely to build or purchase rental housing?

This line of reasoning holds not just for you, but for everyone else as well. As a result, the quantity of apartments for rent will be far smaller than otherwise. And not so amazingly, the preceding analysis holds true not only for the case where rent controls are in place, but even where they are only threatened. The mere anticipation of controls is enough to have a chilling effect on such investment. Instead, everything else under the sun in the real estate market has been built: condominiums, office towers, hotels, warehouses, commercial space. Why? Because such investments have never been subject to rent controls, and no one fears that they ever will be. It is no accident that these facilities boast healthy vacancy rates and relatively slowly increasing rental rates, while residential space suffers from a virtual zero vacancy rate in the controlled sector and skyrocketing prices in the uncontrolled sector.

Although many rent-control ordinances specifically exempt new rental units from coverage, investors are too cautious (perhaps too smart) to put their faith in rental housing. In numerous cases housing units supposedly exempt forever from controls were nevertheless brought under the provisions of this law due to some "emergency" or other. New York City's government, for example, has three times broken its promise to exempt new or vacant units from control. So prevalent is this practice of rent-control authorities that a new term has been invented to describe it: "recapture."

Rent control has destroyed entire sections of sound housing in New York's South Bronx and has led to decay and abandonment throughout the entire five boroughs of the city. Although hard statistics on abandonments are not available, William Tucker estimates that about 30,000 New York apartments were abandoned annually from 1972 to 1982, a loss of almost a third of a million units in this eleven-year period. Thanks to rent control, and to potential investors' all-too-rational fear that rent control will become even more stringent, no sensible investor will build rental housing unsubsidized by government.

EFFECTS ON TENANTS

Existing rental units fare poorly under rent control. Even with the best will in the world, the landlord sometimes cannot afford to pay his escalating fuel, labor, and materials bills, to say nothing of refinancing his mortgage, out of the rent increase he can legally charge. And under rent controls he lacks the best will; the incentive he had under free-market conditions to supply tenant services is severely reduced.

The sitting tenant is "protected" by rent control but, in many cases, receives no real rental bargain because of improper maintenance, poor repairs and painting, and grudging provision of services. The enjoyment he can derive out of his dwelling space ultimately tends to be reduced to a level commensurate with his controlled rent. This may take decades, though, and meanwhile he benefits from rent control.

In fact, many tenants, usually rich or middle-class ones who are politically connected or who were lucky enough to be in the right place at the right time, can gain a lot from rent control. Tenants in some of the nicest neighborhoods in New York City pay a scandalously small fraction of the market price of their apartments. In the early 1980s, for example, former mayor Ed Koch paid $441.49 for an apartment then worth about $1,200.00 per month. Some people in this fortunate position use their apartments like hotel rooms, visiting only a few times per year.

Then there is the "old lady effect." Consider the case of a two-parent, four-child family that has occupied a ten-room rental dwelling. One by one the children grow up, marry, and move elsewhere. The husband dies. Now the lady is left with a gigantic apartment. She uses only two or three of the rooms and, to save on heating and cleaning, closes off the remainder. Without rent control she would move to a smaller accommodation. But rent control makes that option unattractive. Needless to say, these practices further exacerbate the housing crisis. Repeal of rent control would free up thousands of such rooms very quickly, dampening the impetus toward vastly higher rents.

What determines whether or not a tenant benefits from rent control? If the building in which he lives is in a good neighborhood where rents would rise appreciably if rent control were repealed, then the landlord has an incentive to maintain the building against the prospect of that happy day. This incentive is enhanced if there are many decontrolled units in the building (due to "vacancy decontrol" when tenants move out) or privately owned condominiums for which the landlord must provide adequate services. Then the tenant who pays the scandalously low rent may "free ride" on his neighbors. But in the more typical case the quality of housing services tends to reflect rental payments. This, at least, is the situation that will prevail at equilibrium.

If government really had the best interests of tenants at heart and was for some reason determined to employ controls, it would do the very *opposite* of imposing rent restrictions: it would instead control the price of every *other* good and service available, apart from residential suites, in an attempt to divert resources out of all those other opportunities and into this one field. But that, of course, would bring about full-scale socialism, the very system under which the Eastern Europeans suffered so grimly. If the government wanted to help the poor and was for some reason constrained to keep rent controls, it would do better to tightly control rents on luxury unit rentals and to eliminate rent controls on more modest dwellings—the very opposite of the present practice. Then, builders' incentives would be turned around. Instead of erecting luxury dwellings, which are now exempt, they would be led, "as if by an invisible hand," to create housing for the poor and middle classes.

SOLUTIONS

The negative consequences of rent legislation have become so massive and perverse that even many of its former supporters have spoken out against it. Instead of urging a quick termination of controls, however, some pundits would only allow landlords to buy tenants out of their controlled dwellings. That they propose such a solution is understandable. Because tenants outnumber landlords and are usually convinced that rent control is in their best interests, they are likely to invest considerable political energy (see rent seeking) in maintaining rent control. Having landlords "buy off" these opponents of reform, therefore, could be a politically effective way to end rent control.

But making property owners pay to escape a law that has victimized many of them for years is not an effective way to make them confident that rent controls will be absent in the future. The surest way to encourage private investment is to signal investors that housing will be safe from rent control. And the most effective way to do that is to eliminate the possibility of rent control with an amendment to the state constitution that forbids it. Paradoxically, one of the best ways to help tenants is to protect the **economic freedom** of landlords.

RENT CONTROL: IT'S WORSE THAN BOMBING

NEW DELHI—A "romantic conception of socialism" … destroyed Vietnam's economy in the years after the Vietnam war, Foreign Minister Nguyen Co Thach said Friday. Addressing a crowded news conference in the Indian capital, Mr. Thach admitted that controls …had artificially encouraged demand and discouraged supply … House rents had … been kept low … so all the houses in Hanoi had fallen into disrepair, said Mr. Thach.

"The Americans couldn't destroy Hanoi, but we have destroyed our city by very low rents. We realized it was stupid and that we must change policy," he said.

—From a news report in *Journal of Commerce*, quoted in Dan Seligman, "Keeping Up," *Fortune*, February 27, 1989

ABOUT THE AUTHOR

Walter Block (wbock@loyno.edu) holds the Harold E. Wirth Eminent Scholar Chair in Economics at Loyola University's Joseph A. Butt, S.J., College of Business Administration.

FURTHER READING

Arnott, Richard. "Time for Revisionism on Rent Control?" *Journal of Economic Perspectives* 9, no. 1 (1995): 99–120.

Baird, Charles. *Rent Control: The Perennial Folly.* Washington D.C.: Cato Institute, 1980.

Block, Walter. "A Critique of the Legal and Philosophical Case for Rent Control." *Journal of Business Ethics* 40 (2002): 75–90. Online at: http://www.mises.org/etexts/rentcontrol.pdf.

Block, Walter, and Edgar Olsen, eds. *Rent Control: Myths and Realities.* Vancouver: Fraser Institute, 1981.

Brenner, Joel F., and Herbert M. Franklin. *Rent Control in North America and Four European Countries.* Rockville, Md.: Council for International Urban Liaison, 1977.

Grampp, W. S. "Some Effects of Rent Control." *Southern Economic Journal* (April 1950): 425–426.

Johnson, M. Bruce, ed. *Resolving the Housing Crisis: Government Policy, Decontrol, and the Public Interest.* San Francisco: Pacific Institute, 1982.

Niebanck, Paul L. *Rent Control and the Rental Housing Market in New York City.* New York: Housing and Development Administration, Department of Rent and Housing Maintenance, 1968.

Salins, Peter D. *The Ecology of Housing Destruction: Economic Effects of Public Intervention in the Housing Market.* New York: New York University Press, 1980.

Tucker, William. *The Excluded Americans: Homelessness and Housing Policies.* Washington, D.C.: Regnery Gateway, 1990.

FOOTNOTES

1. Richard M. Alson, J. R. Kearl, and Michael B. Vaughan, "Is There a Consensus Among Economists in the 1990's?" *American Economic Review* 82, no. 2 (1992): 203–209.

2. Walter Block and Michael A. Walker, "Entropy in the Canadian Economics Profession: Sampling Consensus on the Major Issues," *Canadian Public Policy* 14, no. 2 (1988): 137–150, online at: http://141.164.133.3/faculty/Block/Blockarticles/Entropy.htm.

3. Gunnar Myrdal, "Opening Address to the Council of International Building Research in Copenhagen," *Dagens Nyheter* (Swedish newspaper), August 25, 1965, p. 12; cited in Sven Rydenfelt, "The Rise, Fall and Revival of Swedish Rent Control," in *Rent Control: Myths and Realities,* Walter Block and Edgar Olsen, eds. (Vancouver: The Fraser Institute, 1981), p. 224.

4. Assar Lindbeck, *The Political Economy of the New Left* (New York: Harper and Row, 1972); cited in Sven Rydenfelt, "The Rise, Fall and Revival of Swedish Rent Control," in *Rent Control: Myths and Realities,* Walter Block and Edgar Olsen, eds. (Vancouver: The Fraser Institute, 1981), pp. 213, 230.

5. States New York "public advocate" Mark Green: "the number of rent-controlled apartments fell 18.2% between 1991 and 1993 and the new data we have analyzed shows an even greater decline—30%—from 1993 to 1996. Indeed, the total number of rent-controlled apartments has fallen by 75% from its peak of 285,000 in 1981" (http://www.tenant.net/Alerts/Guide/papers/mgreen1.html). This is due to the fact that when rents reach a certain level ($2,000 per month under certain conditions), apartments leave the controlled sector altogether. Inflation plus a "hot" New York City housing market have pushed many units above this level. See on this http://www.housingnyc.com/html/resources/faq/decontrol.html. Ken Rosenblum, Mike Golden, and Deborah Poole provided the above cites.

The Energy Crisis Is Over!

By Charles Maurice and Charles Smithson

---

1   We take our title for this chapter and parts of the discussion from an excellent article by William Tucker that appeared in the November 1981 issue of *Harper's*.

WHO IN 1979 would have believed that by the early 1980s our concern with energy would have diminished to such an extent? How do you suppose a person waiting in one of those enormous gasoline lines would have reacted to the suggestion that by 1983 we would be talking about the collapse of OPEC and the "problems" of a rapidly falling petroleum price? Confronted with odd/even rationing and red flags signaling that service stations had no more gasoline to sell, how many people would have believed that in a span of only four years gasoline stations would once again be handing out glassware in order to attract customers?

Looking back over the period 1972–1983, we find the changes in public sentiment concerning energy to be nothing short of amazing. Permit us to review this cycle in public opinion as it was reflected in the headlines of some of the most widely read periodicals.

1972	"U.S. Energy Still Abundant ..." *New York Times*, January 9
1973	"Who Shut the Heat Off?" *Time*, February 12 "Summer 1973: The Economics of Scarcity," *Newsweek*, July 9
1974	"Energy: How High is Up?" *Newsweek* (cover story), January 7
1975	"Energy Conservation Is Becoming a Habit," *New York Times*, October 30
1976	"Autos: Thinking Not So Small," *Newsweek*, March 1 "Back on a Dangerous Binge," *Time*, August 30
1977	"Yes, There *IS* an Energy Crisis" *Time*, October 10
1978	"Energy: Where Did the Crisis Go?" *New York Times*, April 16
1979	"A Long Dry Summer," *Newsweek* (cover story), April 21 "Over a Barrel," *Newsweek* (cover story), July 9
1980	"Gasoline Gauges Rest on Full," *Time*, July 28

1981	"The Good News About Oil," *Newsweek*, April 27
1982	"Down, Down, Down: OPEC Finds That It Is a Crude, Crude World," *Time*, March 15
	"OPEC Tries Again to Sop Up the Glut," *Newsweek*, March 29
1983	"Oil Prices Hit the Skids," *Newsweek*, January 24

These headlines indicate that over the period 1972–1983 Americans' attitudes concerning energy ran full cycle—from optimism (or even indifference) to panic and then back to guarded optimism.

Perhaps even more than headlines, editorial cartoons may be viewed as a reflection of prevailing public opinion. Here again we see a massive change in public opinion from 1973 to 1983. For example, in 1973, an Arabian sheik holds up a U.S. consumer with a gasoline-nozzle pistol. But in 1983, the OPEC sheiks were depicted in a far less menacing manner.

How can such a radical shift in public opinion be explained? The explanation is found in the energy market itself. Something happened to negate the forecasts of gloom and doom that were being widely publicized in the mid-1970s. In this chapter, we will review the events of the last several decades in order to identify the factors that eliminated the crisis in the energy market. (Once we finish our history of the last decade, it might be useful to return to the headlines we have presented to see how they look in the light of the events that were occurring at the time.)

The Good Old Days

Before the 1970s, very few people were interested in energy except in finding more ways to use it—bigger cars, bigger houses, and so forth. It got very little attention in the press, with the possible exception of some stories about the behavior of Texas oil millionaires. Why? The answer is very simple. Before the decade of the 1970s—indeed, before 1973—the real price (price net of inflation) of oil was declining. (We definitely look back with fondness on the gas wars of the 1960s.) Let's look at the history of oil prices in the United States and in the world

Table 1: Crude Oil Prices, 1950–1970

	Average U.S. Wellhead Price (dollars per barrel)	World Price Estimated Actual Transaction Price (dollars per barrel)
1950	$2.51	$1.71
1955	2.77	1.63
1960	2.88	1.53
1965	2.86	1.33
1970	3.18	1.26

Source: James M. Griffin and Henry B. Steele, Energy Economics and Policy, p. 18.

market for the period 1950–1970. Table 1 lists the prices for a barrel of crude oil that prevailed during this period.

It's very easy to see two major features in this price series. First, oil prices in the United States rose very little from 1950 to 1970. Second, the world price of oil stayed much below the U.S. price through 1970 and was actually falling.

FIGURE 1: CRUDE OIL PRICES, 1950–1970 (IN CONSTANT 1982 DOLLARS)

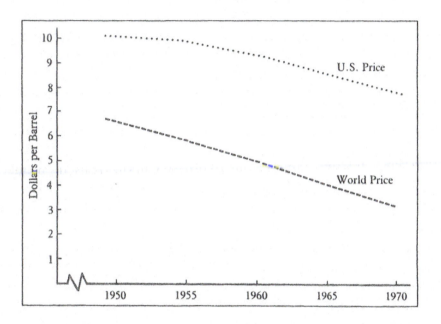

SOURCE: J.M. GRIFFIN AND H.B. STEELE, ENERGY ECONOMICS AND POLICY, P. 18.

These prices, however, do not take into account the effect of inflation during this period—the value of a dollar was certainly less in 1970 than it was in 1950. Hence we need to deflate these prices by a consumer price index in order to express all prices in constant dollars.

In order to compare these historical prices to the prices that we are currently experiencing, we will express all of them in 1982 dollars. For those not familiar with this technique, let us explain briefly how it is done. From the published consumer price index, we know that a good that sold for $1 in 1950 sold for $4 in 1982—a 1950 dollar was worth four times as much as a dollar in 1982. Thus, a barrel of crude oil that sold for $2.51 in 1950 would carry a price tag of $10.04 in 1982. Doing the same thing for each of the prices in Table 1, we obtain the real prices of crude oil in constant 1982 dollars. We have graphed these real prices in Figure 1.

It is evident from this figure that the real price of oil fell between 1950 and the early 1970s. Is it surprising then that the 1950s and 1960s were the era of the gas guzzler in America? Is it shocking that homes built during this period were poorly insulated and energy inefficient? Of course not. If any product becomes cheaper, don't people use more of it? Don't you? Gasoline and heating oil are not exceptions. As the price of oil—and thus gasoline—dropped, cars got bigger. It wasn't a plot by the big three car manufacturers. We wanted big cars because gasoline was cheap. Efficient home energy was a rarity. Why spend a lot of money for expensive home Insulation when heating oil was so cheap?

Americans weren't wasteful during this period, in spite of the editorial criticism we heard after prices rose in the 1970s. People used more of the cheap resource, oil, to save on the expensive resources—time, in the case of automobiles, and building materials, in the case of homes. This reaction is precisely what we would expect.

But during these happy days of the 1950s and 1960s, some of the seeds of the coming crisis were planted. As shown in Table 1, the world price of energy—the price of imported oil—was far below the U.S. price. So, during this period the United States began to actively follow a policy of restricting imports in order to protect domestic producers from cheap foreign crude. Ostensibly designed for national security, an oil import quota system was put in place in 1959 during the Eisenhower administration. The objective of the quota system was to limit imports to 12 percent of total U.S. consumption.

Faced with this quota system in the United States, the countries exporting that cheap crude reacted. On September 14, 1960, Iran, Iraq, Kuwait, Saudi Arabia, and Venezuela formed the Organization of Petroleum Exporting Countries (OPEC). In later years, the membership would rise to thirteen with the addition of Qatar, Indonesia, Libya, Abu Dhabi, Nigeria, Ecuador, and Gabon. However, in the 1960s, OPEC lacked the strength to become an effective cartel. The United States was producing too much oil.

Looking back at the 1960s, we can see that there was no real problem. Although OPEC existed, the demand for imported crude was insufficient for OPEC to exercise any real monopoly power. During the 1960s, there was even excess production capacity in the United States. Had OPEC attempted to reduce imports, the shortfall could easily have been covered by domestic production. What then swung the balance of power to the foreign suppliers?

Imports did not maintain a 12 percent share of U.S. consumption. The import restrictions did not work. Instead, in the 1960s, the share was closer to 20 percent. Foreign crudes were very attractive. One reason the foreign crudes were so attractive—other than the obvious reason that they were lower priced—is that many of them are low-sulfur crudes and are therefore cleaner burning. With the increasing environmental concerns of the 1960s, these clean-burning crudes became more and more desirable. And, with increasing use of these crudes, many people began to argue, quite convincingly, that elimination of import quotas would be a bonanza—it would apparently both clean up the environment and benefit consumers with lower prices. Thus, the demand for foreign crude oils increased substantially.

While this increase in the demand for foreign crude oils may have been troublesome by permitting OPEC more power, it would not have in itself led to a crisis. Instead, we would expect it to lead to higher world oil prices, although still below the U.S. price, resulting in U.S. crude becoming relatively more attractive. Rather, it was another factor that set the stage for the crisis. This factor was the price ceiling imposed on domestically produced petroleum.

FIGURE 2: COST OF IMPORTED OIL, 1970–1980 (IN CONSTANT 1982 DOLLARS)

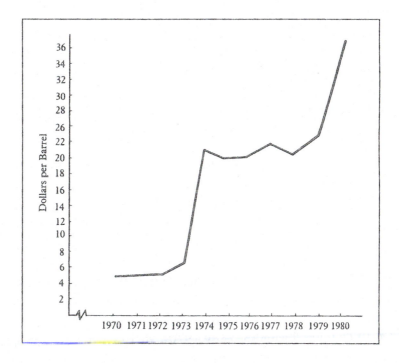

SOURCE: AMERICAN PETROLEUM INSTITUTE, BASIC PETROLEUM DATA BOOK, JANUARY 1983.

A DECADE OF PANIC

In contrast to the falling real oil prices that we had experienced in the past, the decade of the 1970s was one that will be remembered for the massive increases in oil prices—particularly the price of imported oil. It was a decade of panic. Before we begin our explanation of the events of this period, let's take a moment to look at the magnitude of this increase in price. In 1970, the average cost per barrel for imported crude oil was $2.16. In 1980, it was $30.60. In order to account for the inflation that we were also experiencing during this period, it is again necessary to express these prices in constant dollars. In 1982 dollars, these values are $5.35 and $35.69, respectively. Over the eleven years from 1970 to 1980, the price of imported oil rose by over 500 percent! Figure 2 graphs the path of real price over this period. Who was responsible? Unfortunately, it turns out that we ourselves were responsible. Let us explain why.

In August 1971, the Nixon administration imposed a wage and price freeze. Think for a moment how this price ceiling affected the market for crude oil. Look first at domestic supplies. In order to obtain more energy, producers were being forced to use more and more expensive techniques—deeper wells, fracturing, steam or water injection, and so on. However, these more expensive techniques required that the producers get a higher price for the crude. Put yourself in their shoes for a moment. How long would you go on spending more and more to extract oil for which you could not charge a higher price? It is therefore not at all surprising that the peak of U.S. oil production had occurred in 1970 before the imposition of controls (at 9.6 million barrels a day). With the imposition of price controls, domestic production began its decline—a decline that would haunt us in coming years.

Next, let's look at the impact of the price ceiling on the consumption of petroleum. With declining production, consumption would also have to decline in order to avoid a shortage. Instead, consumption continued to increase at the same rate as during the oil-rush decade of the 1960s. The price controls kept the price of gasoline and heating oil from rising, so Americans continued to use oil as if nothing had happened.

By this time, the storm clouds were looming. The United States was faced with rising consumption and declining production. (Indeed, it is precisely this realization that led many to predict a collapse of the developed economies, a point we will take up later.) How then did Americans react to this situation? They imported more crude oil. By 1973, imports were approaching 30 percent of U.S. consumption. In the summer of 1973, the price controls on other products were allowed to expire; but oil was an exception. With the existing trends in consumption and production, it was clear that decontrol would lead to an increase in price; so the controls were extended through 1975 (and later until 1981). In order to avoid the price increase dictated by the market, this decision set the stage for the winter of 1973.

What was OPEC doing during the early 1970s? In 1969, the rich but feeble Libyan monarchy had been overthrown by Arab radicals led by Col. Muammar Qaddafi. This political event marked the turning point in OPEC's position. Although Libya was the smallest member of OPEC in population and GNP, its leadership excelled in fanaticism. Led by Libya, OPEC forced through a 21 percent price increase in 1971 and agreed to a program that would have amounted to a 52 percent increase (over the 1970 level) by 1976. OPEC was beginning to flex its muscles.

It was, however, in the winter of 1973 that OPEC discovered the extent of its power. As a result of the Arab-Israeli War, OPEC imposed an embargo in October. At that time, the posted price of Persian Gulf crude oils was $3.01. By the end of the year, that price had risen to $11.65—an increase of almost 300 percent in only ten weeks! (So much for OPEC's 1971 goal of a 52 percent increase over five years.) Although the embargo ended in March 1974, the remainder of the decade was one of gas lines, heating oil shortages, and OPEC price increases.

Faced with this crisis situation, how then did we, or more correctly our government, react? The obvious solution was to increase domestic production and decrease consumption. In 1975, President Gerald Ford presented a program that would have accomplished this. He proposed abolishing price controls on crude oil and imposing a $2 per barrel tax on foreign oil. Decontrol would have stimulated domestic production, while the tax would have led to a reduction in the consumption of imported oil. Instead, in 1975, Congress voted to continue the price controls. Moreover, in 1976, the governmentally-determined price of domestic crude oil was actually lowered—further reducing the incentives for domestic production.

How did we, the consumers, respond? During the embargo and immediately following, there was a massive movement toward energy efficiency. Small, fuel efficient automobiles were being sold at a substantial premium, while the large gas guzzlers sat on the lots.

Homeowners began to insulate their homes and tried to reduce their use of oil and electricity. However, once the memory of the embargo faded, the conservation movement lost its momentum. With the government artificially holding down the prices the consumer had to pay, Americans returned to big cars, and it was then the small cars that were left on the used car lots. Gasoline consumption resumed its climb; indeed, consumption in 1978 was even higher than the pre-embargo record. Why did gasoline consumption remain so high in the period between 1975 and 1978? Due to price controls on petroleum, the real price of gasoline actually fell during this period. Figure 3 graphs the real prices of unleaded gasoline (in 1982 dollars) for 1970–1978. The embargo did raise the gasoline price in 1973–74; but, following this increase, the real price that consumers paid again began to decline. Price controls insulated the consumers; so what reason existed for them to conserve gasoline?

FIGURE 3: UNLEADED GASOLINE PRICE, 1970–1978 (IN CONSTANT 1982 DOLLARS)

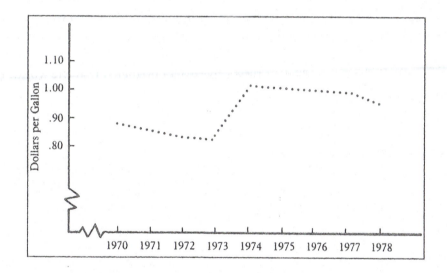

SOURCE: AMERICAN PETROLEUM INSTITUTE, BASIC PETROLEUM DATA BOOK, JANUARY 1983.

Why then were there no gasoline lines between 1975 and 1979? The answer is simple. We imported more and more foreign crude oil. With domestic production stagnating under price controls, imports rose to almost 50 percent of total U.S. consumption.

To give more perspective on the situation that existed in the late 1970s, we have graphed consumption and production of petroleum in the United States from 1950 to 1977 in Figure 4. The imposition of price controls in 1971 led to a decline in domestic production. But these same price controls insulated consumers from the higher world price. With the exception of the temporary decline in consumption that followed the 1973 embargo, consumption continued to increase. As we neared the end of the 1970s, the gap between domestic consumption and production was getting wider and wider. The price controls begun in 1971 had set us up for the events that were to come in 1979.

The turmoil in Iran in 1979 marked the beginning of the second period of severe gasoline shortage. However, all this really did was to indicate the level of our dependence on imports. With the cutbacks in foreign production and the resultant increases in the price of crude oil, Americans experienced once again the depths of a crisis. The worst of the energy crisis was upon us; a solution to the problem became essential.

THE DOOM MERCHANTS

In light of the events that occurred during the 1970s, it is not surprising that some people predicted the imminent collapse of the world as we know it due to shortages in energy and other natural resources. When faced with a period of scarcity, there are always those who will argue that the shortages will only get worse, leading finally to DOOM. Looking at figures like the one we presented above, the doom merchants predicted that we are going to run out of oil. Indeed, if we were to look only at such a figure, it is not hard to see how they came to such a conclusion. But the important thing is that such a figure does not tell the whole story.

While we will concentrate on the more recent prophecies of doom in the energy market, we should note that this was not the first time experts had predicted that the world would run out of petroleum. Let us give you a few examples:

1891	The U.S. Geological Survey predicted that there was little or no chance of finding oil in Texas.
1926	The Federal Oil Conservation Board predicted the United States had only a seven-year supply of petroleum remaining. Senator LaFollette predicted that the price of gasoline would soon rise to $1 per gallon.
1939	The Interior Department predicted that U.S. petroleum supplies would last for less than two decades.
1949	The Secretary of the Interior predicted that the end to U.S. supplies of oil was almost in sight.

FIGURE 4: U.S. PETROLEUM CONSUMPTION AND PRODUCTION, 1950–1977

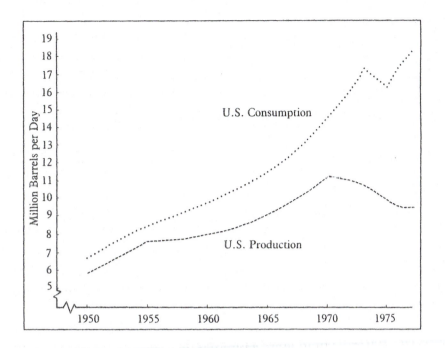

SOURCE: AMERICAN PETROLEUM INSTITUTE, BASIC PETROLEUM DATA BOOK, JANUARY 1983.

There were many doomsday theses advanced during the 1970s. Probably the best known is that in *The Limits to Growth* by Donella H. Meadows et al. Permit us to concentrate on the authors' argument as an illustration of the arguments proposed by the group we label the "doom merchants."

They argued that there were five prevailing trends in the world: (1) accelerating industrialization, (2) rapid population growth, (3) widespread malnutrition, (4) depletion of nonrenewable resources, and (5) deteriorating environment.

Furthermore, they asserted that in general these prevailing trends are characterized by exponential growth. Viewing these prevailing trends, the authors then made their crucial assumption: They assumed that the prevailing trends would continue in the future. Put another way, their forecasts for future levels of consumption and production were simply extrapolations from the existing trend lines. Although they argued that "extrapolation is a time-honored way of looking into the future," we will demonstrate that it certainly did not prove valid for energy. In Chapter 2, we will confront this questionable assumption more directly.

Given their assumption of prevailing trend. Meadows et al. proceeded to make some dismal forecasts for the future. They asserted that "industrial growth will certainly stop within the next century, at the latest." The limits to growth will, in their scenario, be reached within 100 years and the result will be a sudden and uncontrollable decline in both population and industrial capacity. In their view, "the basic behavior mode of the world system is exponential growth of population and capital, followed by collapse." The forecast was, then, that the future holds "a dismal, depleted existence" because of resource shortages.

What about technological progress? Can't we avert the collapse through technological advancement? Not according to these prophets of doom. They asserted that "the application of technology to apparent problems of resource depletion … has no impact on the *essential* problem, which is exponential growth." In essence, this statement again asserts that the prevailing trends in production and consumption will continue unchanged—technological progress cannot alter these trends.

What then was their solution? Only one solution was offered—"deliberate checks on growth." In this dismal view of the future, it was argued that we can only avert the inevitable collapse by learning to live with less. And advocates of this policy were not in short supply.

As will be demonstrated in the following sections, recent history does not bear out these dire predictions. Why not? The answer is very simple. The trends in consumption and production have changed. In the case of energy, the rate of growth in consumption declined while that for production increased. What caused these changes in trend? In their analysis, Meadows et al. neglected one crucial point—the impact of price in a marketplace. They understood that shortages lead to increases in price: "Given present resource consumption rates and the projected increase in these rates, the great majority of the currently important nonrenewable resources will be extremely costly 100 years from now." However, they failed to realize that price influences prevailing trends. For example, the trend they observed in consumption was due, to a large extent, to falling resource prices (especially energy) in the 1960s and early 1970s. However, how do consumers react if the price increases? Obviously, they consume less; so with rising prices, the rate of increase in consumption declines. With rising prices, the users of a resource begin to conserve it. Thus, our assertion is that these doom merchants failed to consider the impact of price on trends. In the following sections, we will demonstrate this point in the case of energy and we will return to a general consideration of this issue in Chapter 2.

THE SOLUTION TO THE ENERGY CRISIS

We left our discussion of the events of the last decade in 1979—the depth of the energy crisis. At the time, it appeared to many Americans that the problem might never be solved—that the doom merchants might have been correct. This pessimistic attitude is probably best reflected in the headline that appeared on the cover of *Newsweek* on November 19, 1973:

"ARE WE RUNNING OUT OF EVERYTHING?"

How gloomy can you get? But happily this was an instance in which it was indeed darkest before the dawn. The shortages of 1979 forced us to realize that price controls were a self-defeating strategy. There was no quick fix; no painless solution. The energy problem could not be wished away or legislated away; it had to be faced. In the midst of a storm of angry protest from consumer groups, President Jimmy Carter announced that, beginning in late 1979, oil price controls would be phased out with final decontrol occurring in the fall of 1981.

FIGURE 5: U.S. PETROLEUM CONSUMPTION AND PRODUCTION, 1970–1982

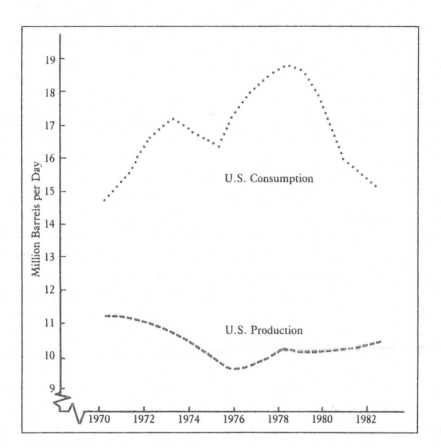

SOURCES: AMERICAN PETROLEUM INSTITUTE, **BASIC PETROLEUM DATA BOOK,** JANUARY 1983; U.S. DEPARTMENT OF ENERGY, **MONTHLY ENERGY REVIEW**, JANUARY 1983

By the end of 1980, imports had fallen by 25 percent. Both consumers and producers saw that, once again, the price of energy was to be controlled by supply and demand—not by government fiat. Consumers realized that the era of artificially cheap energy was over, so they began to conserve energy. The important point to realize here is that this was not just a panic reaction to short-term shortages and gasoline lines—like the winter of 1973—but rather was a reaction to the realization that more and more oil could be obtained only at higher and higher prices. Faced with this realization, Americans began to conserve gasoline and other petroleum products.

It is, however, on the production side that the impact of deregulation was most pronounced. As we have noted earlier, over time it has become more difficult and more expensive to find and extract new supplies of crude oil. In 1970, the average cost of drilling an onshore well was about $15 per foot. By 1980, this cost had risen to $60 per foot. Higher prices were needed to induce suppliers to find and extract new deposits of crude oil. And that is precisely what decontrol did. The rising price of crude oil made it feasible to drill deeper, use more expensive recovery techniques, and generally undertake more risky projects. Examples of the exotic new technologies include infrared photographs taken from satellites to find promising exploration sites and horizontal drilling that permits wheel spoke patterns from an original hole to drain the oil more completely from a given area.

Deregulation was completed by President Ronald Reagan in January 1981—nine months earlier than planned. What happened then? By the end of the year, consumption had dropped by 20 percent. On the other side of the coin, the drilling for new sources had increased by 50 percent. Indeed, in 1981, the number of oil rigs working in the United States was almost double that in 1979; and, not surprisingly, this number is approximately six times the number of rigs working in 1971. The result was that, for the first time in more than a decade, petroleum reserves in the United States rose. Within a month following decontrol, the price of gasoline had risen about 10 cents per gallon, with heating oil increasing by about the same amount. The price of domestic crude oil jumped from $29 to $36 per barrel, a rise that indicated a forthcoming increase in the price of gasoline of another 14 cents. However, by March the oil companies found themselves in a situation that was unusual given their experience of the past decade—a surplus of oil products at the existing prices. They reacted as any market reacts; the major oil companies cut the price of oil products. By the summer of 1981, consumers were faced with a happy situation, falling energy prices.

By the end of 1982, the ability of a functioning marketplace to eliminate a shortage had become even more evident. As shown in Figure 5, domestic consumption of petroleum had dropped radically while U.S. production continued to increase. The gap between domestic consumption and production had declined to its pre-control magnitude. Imports were at the lowest level in eleven years. As Figure 6 illustrates, imports as a percentage of total U.S. demand have dropped steadily since decontrol. The workings of a marketplace have broken the stranglehold OPEC held on America!

What about OPEC? With decontrol, America and other Western countries became less dependent on OPEC oil. In 1973, OPEC accounted for almost 60 percent of the oil supply of the West, but by 1982 this share had fallen below 45 percent. In 1981 and, most particularly, in 1982, OPEC was producing more high priced oil than the world wanted. In an effort to maintain its price, OPEC members—led by Saudi Arabia—tried to reduce production. But this move met with little success. Iran, for one, increased its production sixfold—from one half million to over three million barrels per day—in only the last six months of 1982. The world was virtually awash in oil. In 1982, we saw something we had not seen for a long time—a decline in the price of imported oil. According to the U.S. Department of Energy, the average acquisition cost of a barrel of imported crude oil fell from $37.05 in 1981 to $33.72 in 1982. Even more significantly, we began to read about "the end of OPEC." Permit us to show you two of the headlines appearing in early 1983.

"OPEC Output Pact Collapses"
Washington Post, January 28, 1983

"OPEC: From Cartel to Chaos"
Newsweek, March 7, 1983

While it may be a little too early for us to write the final obituary for OPEC, it is clear that the energy crisis we suffered through in the 1970s is over. OPEC will probably continue to exist, but it does not today and will not in the future have the power it had during the 1970s (unless we again hand it that power). By allowing the market to function 3 we survived the energy crisis.

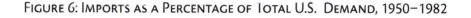

FIGURE 6: IMPORTS AS A PERCENTAGE OF TOTAL U.S. DEMAND, 1950–1982

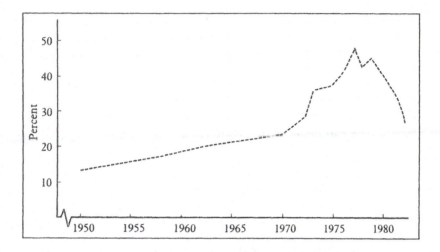

SOURCES: AMERICAN PETROLEUM INSTITUTE,
BASIC PETROLEUM DATA BOOK, JANUARY 1983; U.S. DEPARTMENT OF ENERGY,
MONTHLY ENERGY REVIEW, JANUARY 1983.

THE MORAL

In *Poor Richard's Almanac*, Benjamin Franklin said something about experience keeping a hard school. Since we have all had to suffer through the harsh experience of this recent energy crisis, we need to make sure we have learned the lessons it taught. Permit us to summarize what we feel are the most important of these lessons as the answers to three questions.

What caused the crisis? As Richard Hofstadter has pointed out, Americans have formed conspiracy theories before. At various times, the conspirators have been the Masons, Catholics, slaveholders, international bankers, munitions manufacturers, and the House of Hapsburg. During the decade of the 1970s, many persons again turned to a conspiracy theory in which OPEC and the oil companies were the villains. (Indeed, a reader of *Science Digest* noted to the editors the diabolical fact that OPEC had thirteen members; and we all know about the dark forces involved in the number thirteen.) However, although OPEC raised the price of oil and the oil companies charged us higher prices, the truth is that we ourselves, not some outside agent, caused the crisis. Instead of permitting the marketplace to function, we, through our agents the government, attempted to keep the price of oil artificially low. In doing so, we caused consumption to increase and domestic production to decline. With this growing gap between domestic consumption and production, we placed ourselves at the mercy of foreign suppliers.

What about the forecasts of doom for the developed economies? Those who predicted doom did so on the basis of trends prevailing at that time. They saw that the rate of growth in consumption exceeded the rate of growth for production. Obviously, if that trend continued, we would run out of oil. However, those trends changed. Once price was permitted to rise, the rate of growth in consumption declined while the rate of growth of production increased. Look at Figure 5. The upshot of this is that in the 1980s we find ourselves not faced by a shortage of oil but rather with the happy circumstance of falling prices. The doom merchants neglected a critical variable: price. In a market economy, a shortage leads to an increase in price, which always has and always will result in a decline in consumption and an increase in production.

What eliminated the crisis? Here the answer is very simple; our market economy eliminated the energy crisis of the 1970s. Once the price mechanism was permitted to function—after a delay of ten years—the gap between domestic consumption and production began to narrow rapidly. With increasing energy prices, consumption declined. Conservation was accomplished by the consumers substituting other commodities for the relatively expensive energy. We substituted newer, more fuel efficient autos for those of an earlier decade. In 1973, the average auto in the United States obtained 13.1 miles per gallon. By 1981 the average miles per gallon for autos in the United States was 15.5. The fuel efficiency of U.S. autos has increased by over 18 percent. In our homes, we substituted insulation (and sometimes sweaters) for energy. Firms also substituted capital for energy by switching from inefficient machines to more energy efficient machines. Hence, we argue that one of the primary factors is the price-induced substitution away from energy. Looking at the production of oil, we saw that rising oil prices led to a massive increase in domestic exploration and drilling. The resulting increase in production can, to a great extent, be said to involve price-induced technical change. As prices rose, the producers were induced to use newer and more expensive technology in order to drill deeper, drill in more difficult formations and locations, and extract more of the available deposit. With the new technology, oil fields that were previously not counted as reserves began pumping oil. Therefore, we feel that price-induced substitution and price-induced technical change are responsible for solving the energy crisis.

We might ask the question, "Was it a miracle?" Well, if one remembers those long gas lines back in 1979, the answer is "yes." How else could so serious a problem go away in such a short period of time? And we would probably have to agree. Sometimes the results of freely functioning markets seem like a miracle. No one person, no government, no regulatory body was needed to solve the crisis. The real miracle was that individual consumers and producers, acting independently in their own self-interest, eliminated the crisis by responding to price changes.

We might also ask, "Was it unprecedented?" To this question we answer, "no." As we shall show, this miracle had occurred many times before. Crises that were thought to be insurmountable were overcome in the same way that the energy crisis was solved. This then is the theme of our book: these miracles have happened in the past, and there is no reason to believe that they won't continue to happen in the future.

IS THE ENERGY CRISIS *REALLY* OVER?

At this time, imports have declined from almost 50 percent to less than 30 percent of domestic consumption. To that extent, we no longer have to fear upheavals caused by a curtailment of foreign oil, like those of 1973 or 1979. Hence, the energy crisis in the sense of massive shortages is over.

On a larger scale, an energy crisis still may exist. It is getting harder and more expensive to find and extract crude oil. In a free market, this means that the future might hold higher prices for energy products. While we are sure the world will never run out of oil, it is possible that sometime in the future oil may become so expensive that it is no longer feasible to use it as an energy source. What then? Permit us to hold the answer to this question for a later chapter. Once we have seen what has happened in the past, we will be in a much better position to answer that question.

SOURCES

CHAPTER 1

American Petroleum Institute. *Basic Petroleum Data Book*. January 1983.

Chapman, Stephen. "The Gas Lines of 79." *Public Interest*, Summer 1980.

Griffin, James M., and Steele, Henry B. *Energy Economics and Policy*. New York: Academic Press, 1980.

Howard, Frank A. *Buna Rubber: The Birth of an Industry*. New York: D. Van
Nostrand Co., 1947.

Meadows, Donella H.; Meadows, Dennis L.; Randers, Jørgen; and Behrens, William W., III. *The Limits to Growth*. New York: Universe Books, 1972.

Tucker, William. "The Energy Crisis Is Over!" *Harper's*, November 1981.

U.S. Department of Energy. *Monthly Energy Review*, January 1983.

SECTION FIVE

Opportunity Cost and Comparative Advantage

A PETITION From the Manufacturers of Candles, Tapers, Lanterns, Sticks, Street Lamps, Snuffers, and Extinguishers, and from Producers of Tallow, Oil, Resin, Alcohol, and Generally of Everything Connected with Lighting

By Frédéric Bastiat

TO THE HONOURABLE MEMBERS OF THE CHAMBER OF DEPUTIES.

GENTLEMEN:

You are on the right track. You reject abstract theories and have little regard for abundance and low prices. You concern yourselves mainly with the fate of the producer. You wish to free him from foreign competition, that is, to reserve the *domestic market* for *domestic industry*.

We come to offer you a wonderful opportunity for your—what shall we call it? Your theory? No, nothing is more deceptive than theory. Your doctrine? Your system? Your principle? But you dislike doctrines, you have a horror of systems, as for principles, you deny that there are any in political economy; therefore we shall call it your practice—your practice without theory and without principle.

We are suffering from the ruinous competition of a rival who apparently works under conditions so far superior to our own for the production of light that he is *flooding* the *domestic market* with it at an incredibly low price; for the moment he appears, our sales cease, all the consumers turn to him, and a branch of French industry whose ramifications are innumerable is all at once reduced to complete stagnation. This rival, which is none other than the sun, is waging war on us so mercilessly we suspect he is being stirred up against us by perfidious Albion (excellent diplomacy nowadays!), particularly because he has for that haughty island a respect that he does not show for us.

Frédéric Bastiat, "The Candlemakers' Petition," from <http://bastiat.org/en/petition.html>.

We ask you to be so good as to pass a law requiring the closing of all windows, dormers, skylights, inside and outside shutters, curtains, casements, bull's-eyes, deadlights, and blinds— in short, all openings, holes, chinks, and fissures through which the light of the sun is wont to enter houses, to the detriment of the fair industries with which, we are proud to say, we have endowed the country, a country that cannot, without betraying ingratitude, abandon us today to so unequal a combat.

Be good enough, honourable deputies, to take our request seriously, and do not reject it without at least hearing the reasons that we have to advance in its support.

First, if you shut off as much as possible all access to natural light, and thereby create a need for artificial light, what industry in France will not ultimately be encouraged?

If France consumes more tallow, there will have to be more cattle and sheep, and, consequently, we shall see an increase in cleared fields, meat, wool, leather, and especially manure, the basis of all agricultural wealth.

If France consumes more oil, we shall see an expansion in the cultivation of the poppy, the olive, and rapeseed. These rich yet soil-exhausting plants will come at just the right time to enable us to put to profitable use the increased fertility that the breeding of cattle will impart to the land.

Our moors will be covered with resinous trees. Numerous swarms of bees will gather from our mountains the perfumed treasures that today waste their fragrance, like the flowers from which they emanate. Thus, there is not one branch of agriculture that would not undergo a great expansion.

The same holds true of shipping. Thousands of vessels will engage in whaling, and in a short time we shall have a fleet capable of upholding the honour of France and of gratifying the patriotic aspirations of the undersigned petitioners, chandlers, etc.

But what shall we say of the *specialities* of *Parisian manufacture*? Henceforth you will behold gilding, bronze, and crystal in candlesticks, in lamps, in chandeliers, in candelabra sparkling in spacious emporia compared with which those of today are but stalls.

There is no needy resin-collector on the heights of his sand dunes, no poor miner in the depths of his black pit, who will not receive higher wages and enjoy increased prosperity.

It needs but a little reflection, gentlemen, to be convinced that there is perhaps not one Frenchman, from the wealthy stockholder of the Anzin Company to the humblest vendor of matches, whose condition would not be improved by the success of our petition.

We anticipate your objections, gentlemen; but there is not a single one of them that you have not picked up from the musty old books of the advocates of free trade. We defy you to utter a word against us that will not instantly rebound against yourselves and the principle behind all your policy.

Will you tell us that, though we may gain by this protection, France will not gain at all, because the consumer will bear the expense?

We have our answer ready:

You no longer have the right to invoke the interests of the consumer. You have sacrificed him whenever you have found his interests opposed to those of the producer. You have done so in order *to encourage industry and to increase employment*. For the same reason you ought to do so this time too.

Indeed, you yourselves have anticipated this objection. When told that the consumer has a stake in the free entry of iron, coal, sesame, wheat, and textiles, "Yes," you reply, "but the producer has a stake in their exclusion." Very well, surely if consumers have a stake in the admission of natural light, producers have a stake in its interdiction.

"But," you may still say, "the producer and the consumer are one and the same person. If the manufacturer profits by protection, he will make the farmer prosperous. Contrariwise, if agriculture is prosperous, it will open markets for manufactured goods." Very well, If you grant us a monopoly over the production of lighting during the day, first of all we shall buy large amounts of tallow, charcoal, oil, resin, wax, alcohol, silver, iron, bronze, and crystal, to supply our industry; and, moreover, we and our numerous suppliers, having become rich, will consume a great deal and spread prosperity into all areas of domestic industry.

Will you say that the light of the sun is a gratuitous gift of Nature, and that to reject such gifts would be to reject wealth itself under the pretext of encouraging the means of acquiring it?

But if you take this position, you strike a mortal blow at your own policy; remember that up to now you have always excluded foreign goods *because* and *in proportion* as they approximate gratuitous gifts. You have only *half* as good a reason for complying with the demands of other monopolists as you have for granting our petition, which is in *complete* accord with your established policy; and to reject our demands precisely because they are *better founded* than anyone else's would be tantamount to accepting the equation: + × + = -; in other words, it would be to heap *absurdity* upon *absurdity*.

Labour and Nature collaborate in varying proportions, depending upon the country and the climate, in the production of a commodity. The part that Nature contributes is always free of charge; it is the part contributed by human labour that constitutes value and is paid for.

If an orange from Lisbon sells for half the price of an orange from Paris, it is because the natural heat of the sun, which is, of course, free of charge, does for the former what the latter owes to artificial heating, which necessarily has to be paid for in the market.

Thus, when an orange reaches us from Portugal, one can say that it is given to us half free of charge, or, in other words, at *half price* as compared with those from Paris.

Now, it is precisely on the basis of its being *semigratuitous* (pardon the word) that you maintain it should be barred. You ask: "How can French labour withstand the competition of foreign labour when the former has to do all the work, whereas the latter has to do only half, the sun taking care of the rest?" But if the fact that a product is *half* free of charge leads you to exclude it from competition, how can its being *totally* free of charge induce you to admit it into competition? Either you are not consistent, or you should, after excluding what is half free of charge as harmful to our domestic industry, exclude what is totally gratuitous with all the more reason and with twice the zeal.

To take another example: When a product—coal, iron, wheat, or textiles—comes to us from abroad, and when we can acquire it for less labour than if we produced it ourselves, the difference is a *gratuitous gift* that is conferred up on us. The size of this gift is proportionate to the extent of this difference. It is a quarter, a half, or three-quarters of the value of the product if the foreigner asks of us only three-quarters, one-half, or one-quarter as high a price. It is as complete as it can be when the donor, like the sun in providing us with light, asks nothing from us. The question, and we pose it formally, is whether what you desire for France is the benefit of consumption free of charge or the alleged advantages of onerous production. Make your choice, but be logical; for as long as you ban, as you do, foreign coal, iron, wheat, and textiles, *in proportion* as their price approaches zero, how inconsistent it would be to admit the light of the sun, whose price is *zero* all day long!

Frédéric Bastiat (1801–1850), *Sophismes économiques, 1845.*

The Balance of Trade

By Frédéric Bastiat

THE BALANCE OF trade is an article of faith.

We know what it consists in: if a country imports more than it exports, it loses the difference. Conversely, if its exports exceed its imports, the excess is to its profit. This is held to be an axiom, and laws are passed in accordance with it.

On this hypothesis, M. Mauguin warned us the day before yesterday, citing statistics, that France carries on a foreign trade in which it has managed to lose, out of good will, without being required to do so, two hundred million francs a year.

"You have lost by your trade, in eleven years, two billion francs. Do you understand what that means?"

Then, applying his infallible rule to the facts, he told us: "In 1847 you sold 605 million francs' worth of manufactured products, and you bought only 152 millions' worth. Hence, you *gained* 450 million.

"You bought 804 millions' worth of raw materials, and you sold only 114 million; hence, you *lost* 690 million."

This is an example of the dauntless naïveté of following an absurd premise to its logical conclusion. M. Mauguin has discovered the secret of making even Messrs. Darblay and Lebeuf laugh at the expense of the balance of trade. It is a great achievement, of which I cannot help being jealous.

Allow me to assess the validity of the rule according to which M. Mauguin and all the protectionists calculate profits and losses. I shall do so by recounting two business transactions which I have had the occasion to engage in.

I was at Bordeaux. I had a cask of wine which was worth 50 francs; I sent it to Liverpool, and the customhouse noted on its records an *export* of 50 francs.

At Liverpool the wine was sold for 70 francs. My representative converted the 70 francs into coal, which was found to be worth 90 francs on the market at Bordeaux. The customhouse hastened to record an *import* of 90 francs.

Balance of trade, or the excess of imports over exports: 40 francs.

These 40 francs, I have always believed, putting my trust in my books, I had gained. But M. Mauguin tells me that I have lost them, and that France has lost them in my person.

And why does M. Mauguin see a loss here? Because he supposes that any excess of imports over exports necessarily implies a balance that must be paid in cash. But where is there in the transaction that I speak of, which follows the pattern of all profitable commercial transactions, any balance to pay? Is it, then, so difficult to understand that a merchant compares the prices current in different markets and decides to trade only when he has the certainty, or at least the probability, of seeing the exported value return to him increased? Hence, what M. Mauguin calls *loss* should be called *profit*.

A few days after my transaction I had the simplicity to experience regret; I was sorry I had not waited. In fact, the price of wine fell at Bordeaux and rose at Liverpool; so that if I had not been so hasty, I could have bought at 40 francs and sold at 100 francs. I truly believed that on such a basis my *profit* would have been greater. But I learn from M. Mauguin that it is the *loss* that would have been more ruinous.

My second transaction had a very different result.

I had had some truffles shipped from Périgord which cost me 100 francs; they were destined for two distinguished English cabinet ministers for a very high price, which I proposed to turn into pounds sterling. Alas, I would have done better to eat them myself (I mean the truffles, not the English pounds or the Tories). All would not have been lost, as they were, for the ship that carried them off sank on its departure. The customs officer, who had noted on this occasion an export of 100 francs, never had any re-import to enter in this case.

Hence, M. Mauguin would say, France gained 100 francs; for it was, in fact, by this sum that the export, thanks to the shipwreck, exceeded the import. If the affair had turned out otherwise, if I had received 200 or 300 francs worth of English pounds, then the balance of trade would have been unfavorable, and France would have been the loser.

From the point of view of science, it is sad to think that all the commercial transactions which end in loss according to the businessmen concerned show a profit according to that class of theorists who are always declaiming against theory.

But from the point of view of practical affairs, it is even sadder, for what is the result?

Suppose that M. Mauguin had the power (and to a certain extent he has, by his votes) to substitute his calculations and desires for the calculations and desires of businessmen and to give, in his words, "a good commercial and industrial organization to the country, a good impetus to domestic industry." What would he do?

M. Mauguin would suppress by law all transactions that consist in buying at a low domestic price in order to sell at a high price abroad and in converting the proceeds into commodities eagerly sought after at home; for it is precisely in these transactions that the imported value exceeds the exported value.

Conversely, he would tolerate, and, indeed, he would encourage, if necessary by subsidies (from taxes on the public), all enterprises based on the idea of buying dearly in France in order to sell cheaply abroad; in other words, exporting what is useful to us in order to import what is useless. Thus, he would leave us perfectly free, for example, to send off cheeses from Paris to Amsterdam, in order to bring back the latest fashions from Amsterdam to Paris; for in this traffic the balance of trade would always be in our favor.

Yet, it is sad and, I dare add, degrading that the legislator will not let the interested parties decide and act for themselves in these matters, at their peril and risk. At least then everyone bears the responsibility for his own acts; he who makes a mistake is punished and is set right. But when the legislator imposes and prohibits, should he make a monstrous error in judgment, that error must become the rule of conduct for the whole of a great nation. In France we love freedom very much, but we hardly understand it. Oh, let us try to understand it better! We shall not love it any the less.

M. Mauguin has stated with imperturbable aplomb that there is not a statesman in England who does not accept the doctrine of the balance of trade. After having calculated the loss which, according to him, results from the excess of our imports, he cried out: "If a similar picture were to be presented to the English, they would shudder, and there is not a member in the House of Commons who would not feel that his seat was threatened."

For my part, I affirm that if someone were to say to the House of Commons: "The total value of what is exported from the country exceeds the total value of what is imported," it is then that they would feel threatened; and I doubt that a single speaker could be found who would dare to add: "The difference represents a profit."

In England they are convinced that it is important for the nation to receive more than it gives. Moreover, they have observed that this is the attitude of all businessmen; and that is why they have taken the side of *laissez faire* and are committed to restoring free trade.

 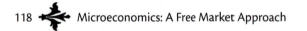

On Foreign Trade[1]

By David Ricardo

1   Excerpted from Chapter VII of *Principles of Political Economy and Taxation* (1817). Ricardo, an economist of the "Classical School," deserves credit for having been among the first to point out the advantages of specialization and trade, even if one party to the transaction could produce everything better and cheaper than the other.

UNDER A SYSTEM of perfectly free commerce, each country naturally devotes its capital and labour to such employments as are most beneficial to each. This pursuit of individual advantage is admirably connected with the universal good of the whole. By stimulating industry, by rewarding ingenuity, and by using most efficaciously the peculiar powers bestowed by nature, it distributes labour most effectively and most economically: while, by increasing the general mass of productions, it diffuses general benefit, and binds together, by one common tie of interest and intercourse, the universal society of nations throughout the civilised world. It is this principle which determines that wine shall be made in France and Portugal, that corn shall be grown in America and Poland, and that hardware and other goods shall be manufactured in England.

In one and the same country, profits are, generally speaking, always on the same level; or differ only as the employment of capital may be more or less secure and agreeable. It is not so between different countries. If the profits of capital employed in Yorkshire should exceed those of capital employed in London, capital would speedily move from London to Yorkshire, and an equality of profits would be effected; but if in consequence of the diminished rate of production in the lands of England, from the increase of capital and population, wages should rise and profits fall, it would not follow that capital and population would necessarily move from England to Holland, or Spain, or Russia, where profits might be higher.

If Portugal had no commercial connection with other countries, instead of employing a great part of her capital and industry in the production of wines, with which she purchases for her own use the cloth and hardware of other countries, she would be obliged to devote a part of that capital to the manufacture of those commodities, which she would thus obtain probably inferior in quality as well as quantity.

The quantity of wine which she shall give in exchange for the cloth of England is not determined by the respective quantities of labour devoted to the production of each, as it would be if both commodities were manufactured in England, or both in Portugal.

England may be so circumstanced that to produce the cloth may require the labour of 100 men for one year; and if she attempted to make the wine, it might require the labour of 120 men for the same time. England would therefore find it her interest to import wine, and to purchase it by the exportation of cloth.

To produce the wine in Portugal might require only the labour of 80 men for one year, and to produce the cloth in the same country might require the labour of 90 men for the same time. It would therefore be advantageous for her to export wine in exchange for cloth. This exchange might even take place notwithstanding that the commodity imported by Portugal could be produced there with less labour than in England. Though she could make the cloth with the labour of 90 men, she would import it from a country where it required the labour of 100 men to produce it, because it would be advantageous to her rather to employ her capital in the production of wine, for which she would obtain more cloth from England, than she could produce by diverting a portion of her capital from the cultivation of vines to the manufacture of cloth.

Thus England would give the produce of the labour of 100 men for the produce of the labour of 80. Such an exchange could not take place between the individuals of the same country. The labour of 100 Englishmen cannot be given for that of 80 Englishmen, but the produce of the labour of 100 Englishmen may be given for the produce of the labour of 80 Portuguese, 60 Russians, or 120 East Indians. The difference in this respect, between a single country and many, is easily accounted for, by considering the difficulty with which capital moves from one country to another, to seek a more profitable employment, and the activity with which it invariably passes from one province to another in the same country.[1]

It would undoubtedly be advantageous to the capitalists of England, and to the consumers in both countries, that under such circumstances the wine and the cloth should both be made in Portugal, and therefore that the capital and labour of England employed in making cloth should be removed to Portugal for that purpose. In that case, the relative value of these commodities would be regulated by the same principle as if one were the produce of Yorkshire and the other of London: and in every other case, if capital freely flowed towards those countries where it could be most profitably employed, there could be no difference in the rate of

---

NOTE

1   It will appear, then, that a country possessing very considerable advantages in machinery and skill, and which may therefore be enabled to manufacture commodities with much less labour than her neighbours, may, in return for such commodities, import a portion of the corn required for its consumption, even if its land were more fertile and corn could be grown with less labour than in the country from which it was imported. Two men can both make shoes and hats, and one is superior to the other in both employments; but in making hats he can only exceed his competitor by one-fifth or 20 percent, and in making shoes he can excel him by one-third or 33 percent—will it not be for the interest of both that the superior man should employ himself exclusively in making shoes, and the inferior man in making hats?

profit, and no other difference in the real or labour price of commodities than the additional quantity of labour required to convey them to the various markets where they were to be sold.

Experience, however, shows that the fancied or real insecurity of capital, when not under the immediate control of its owner, together with the natural disinclination which every man has to quit the country of his birth and connections, and intrust himself, with all his habits fixed, to a strange government and new laws, check the emigration of capital …

SECTION SIX

The Firm

The Social Responsibility of Business is to Increase its Profits

By Milton Friedman

WHEN I HEAR businessmen speak eloquently about the "social responsibilities of business in a free-enterprise system," I am reminded of the wonderful line about the Frenchman who discovered at the age of 70 that he had been speaking prose all his life. The businessmen believe that they are defending free enterprise when they declaim that business is not concerned "merely" with profit but also with promoting desirable "social" ends; that business has a "social conscience" and takes seriously its responsibilities for providing employment, eliminating discrimination, avoiding pollution and whatever else may be the catchwords of the contemporary crop of reformers. In fact they are—or would be if they or anyone else took them seriously—preaching pure and unadulterated socialism. Businessmen who talk this way are unwitting puppets of the intellectual forces that have been undermining the basis of a free society these past decades.

The discussions of the "social responsibilities of business" are notable for their analytical looseness and lack of rigor. What does it mean to say that "business" has responsibilities? Only people can have responsibilities. A corporation is an artificial person and in this sense may have artificial responsibilities, but "business" as a whole cannot be said to have responsibilities, even in this vague sense. The first step toward clarity in examining the doctrine of the social responsibility of business is to ask precisely what it implies for whom.

Presumably, the individuals who are to be responsible are businessmen, which means individual proprietors or corporate executives. Most of the discussion of social responsibility is directed at corporations, so in what follows I shall mostly neglect the individual proprietors and speak of corporate executives.

In a free-enterprise, private-property system, a corporate executive is an employee of the owners of the business. He has direct responsibility to his employers. That responsibility is to conduct the business in accordance with their desires, which generally will be to make as much money as possible while conforming to the basic rules of the society, both those embodied in law and those embodied in ethical custom. Of course, in some cases his employers may have a different objective. A group of persons might establish a corporation for an eleemosynary purpose—for example, a hospital or a school. The manager of such a corporation will not have money profit as his objective but the rendering of certain services.

In either case, the key point is that, in his capacity as a corporate executive, the manager is the agent of the individuals who own the corporation or establish the eleemosynary institution, and his primary responsibility is to them.

Needless to say, this does not mean that it is easy to judge how well he is performing his task. But at least the criterion of performance is straightforward, and the persons among whom a voluntary contractual arrangement exists are clearly defined.

Of course, the corporate executive is also a person in his own right. As a person, he may have many other responsibilities that he recognizes or assumes voluntarily—to his family, his conscience, his feelings of charity, his church, his clubs, his city, his country. He may feel impelled by these responsibilities to devote part of his income to causes he regards as worthy, to refuse to work for particular corporations, even to leave his job, for example, to join his country's armed forces. If we wish, we may refer to some of these responsibilities as "social responsibilities." But in these respects he is acting as a principal, not an agent; he is spending his own money or time or energy, not the money of his employers or the time or energy he has contracted to devote to their purposes. If these are "social responsibilities," they are the social responsibilities of individuals, not of business.

What does it mean to say that the corporate executive has a "social responsibility" in his capacity as businessman? If this statement is not pure rhetoric, it must mean that he is to act in some way that is not in the interest of his employers. For example, that he is to refrain from increasing the price of the product in order to contribute to the social objective of preventing inflation, even though a price increase would be in the best interests of the corporation. Or that he is to make expenditures on reducing pollution beyond the amount that is in the best interests of the corporation or that is required by law in order to contribute to the social objective of improving the environment. Or that, at the expense of corporate profits, he is to hire "hardcore" unemployed instead of better qualified available workmen to contribute to the social objective of reducing poverty.

In each of these cases, the corporate executive would be spending someone else's money for a general social interest. Insofar as his actions in accord with his "social responsibility" reduce returns to stockholders, he is spending their money. Insofar as his actions raise the price to customers, he is spending the customers' money. Insofar as his actions lower the wages of some employees, he is spending their money.

The stockholders or the customers or the employees could separately spend their own money on the particular action if they wished to do so. The executive is exercising a distinct "social responsibility," rather than serving as an agent of the stockholders or the customers or the employees, only if he spends the money in a different way than they would have spent it.

But if he does this, he is in effect imposing taxes, on the one hand, and deciding how the tax proceeds shall be spent, on the other.

This process raises political questions on two levels: principle and consequences. On the level of political principle, the imposition of taxes and the expenditure of tax proceeds are governmental functions. We have established elaborate constitutional, parliamentary and judicial provisions to control these functions, to assure that taxes are imposed so far as possible in accordance with the preferences and desires of the public—after all, "taxation without representation" was one of the battle cries of the American Revolution. We have a system of checks and balances to separate the legislative function of imposing taxes and enacting expenditures from the executive function of collecting taxes and administering expenditure programs and from the judicial function of mediating disputes and interpreting the law.

Here the businessman—self-selected or appointed directly or indirectly by stockholders—is to be simultaneously legislator, executive and, jurist. He is to decide whom to tax by how much and for what purpose, and he is to spend the proceeds—all this guided only by general exhortations from on high to restrain inflation, improve the environment, fight poverty and so on and on.

The whole justification for permitting the corporate executive to be selected by the stockholders is that the executive is an agent serving the interests of his principal. This justification disappears when the corporate executive imposes taxes and spends the proceeds for "social" purposes. He becomes in effect a public employee, a civil servant, even though he remains in name an employee of a private enterprise. On grounds of political principle, it is intolerable that such civil servants—insofar as their actions in the name of social responsibility are real and not just window-dressing—should be selected as they are now. If they are to be civil servants, then they must be elected through a political process. If they are to impose taxes and make expenditures to foster "social" objectives, then political machinery must be set up to make the assessment of taxes and to determine through a political process the objectives to be served.

This is the basic reason why the doctrine of "social responsibility" involves the acceptance of the socialist view that political mechanisms, not market mechanisms, are the appropriate way to determine the allocation of scarce resources to alternative uses.

On the grounds of consequences, can the corporate executive in fact discharge his alleged "social responsibilities?" On the other hand, suppose he could get away with spending the stockholders' or customers' or employees' money. How is he to know how to spend it? He is told that he must contribute to fighting inflation. How is he to know what action of his will contribute to that end? He is presumably an expert in running his company—in producing a product or selling it or financing it. But nothing about his selection makes him an expert on inflation. Will his holding down the price of his product reduce inflationary pressure? Or, by leaving more spending power in the hands of his customers, simply divert it elsewhere? Or, by forcing him to produce less because of the lower price, will it simply contribute to shortages? Even if he could answer these questions, how much cost is he justified in imposing on his stockholders, customers and employees for this social purpose? What is his appropriate share and what is the appropriate share of others?

And, whether he wants to or not, can he get away with spending his stockholders', customers' or employees' money? Will not the stockholders fire him? (Either the present ones or those who take over when his actions in the name of social responsibility have reduced the corporation's profits and the price of its stock.) His customers and his employees can desert him for other producers and employers less scrupulous in exercising their social responsibilities.

This facet of "social responsibility" doctrine is brought into sharp relief when the doctrine is used to justify wage restraint by trade unions. The conflict of interest is naked and clear when union officials are asked to subordinate the interest of their members to some more general purpose. If the union officials try to enforce wage restraint, the consequence is likely to be wildcat strikes, rank-and-file revolts and the emergence of strong competitors for their jobs. We thus have the ironic phenomenon that union leaders—at least in the U.S.—have objected to Government interference with the market far more consistently and courageously than have business leaders.

The difficulty of exercising "social responsibility" illustrates, of course, the great virtue of private competitive enterprise—it forces people to be responsible for their own actions and makes it difficult for them to "exploit" other people for either selfish or unselfish purposes. They can do good—but only at their own expense.

Many a reader who has followed the argument this far may be tempted to remonstrate that it is all well and good to speak of Government's having the responsibility to impose taxes and determine expenditures for such "social" purposes as controlling pollution or training the hard-core unemployed, but that the problems are too urgent to wait on the slow course of political processes, that the exercise of social responsibility by businessmen is a quicker and surer way to solve pressing current problems.

Aside from the question of fact—I share Adam Smith's skepticism about the benefits that can be expected from "those who affected to trade for the public good"—this argument must be rejected on grounds of principle. What it amounts to is an assertion that those who favor the taxes and expenditures in question have failed to persuade a majority of their fellow citizens to be of like mind and that they are seeking to attain by undemocratic procedures what they cannot attain by democratic procedures. In a free society, it is hard for "evil" people to do "evil," especially since one man's good is another's evil.

I have, for simplicity, concentrated on the special case of the corporate executive, except only for the brief digression on trade unions. But precisely the same argument applies to the newer phenomenon of calling upon stockholders to require corporations to exercise social responsibility (the recent G.M. crusade for example). In most of these cases, what is in effect involved is some stockholders trying to get other stockholders (or customers or employees) to contribute against their will to "social" causes favored by the activists. Insofar as they succeed, they are again imposing taxes and spending the proceeds.

The situation of the individual proprietor is somewhat different. If he acts to reduce the returns of his enterprise in order to exercise his "social responsibility," he is spending his own money, not someone else's. If he wishes to spend his money on such purposes, that is his right, and I cannot see that there is any objection to his doing so. In the process, he, too, may impose costs on employees and customers. However, because he is far less likely than a large corporation or union to have monopolistic power, any such side effects will tend to be minor.

Of course, in practice the doctrine of social responsibility is frequently a cloak for actions that are justified on other grounds rather than a reason for those actions.

To illustrate, it may well be in the long run interest of a corporation that is a major employer in a small community to devote resources to providing amenities to that community or to improving its government. That may make it easier to attract desirable employees, it may reduce the wage bill or lessen losses from pilferage and sabotage or have other worthwhile effects. Or it may be that, given the laws about the deductibility of corporate charitable contributions, the stockholders can contribute more to charities they favor by having the corporation make the gift than by doing it themselves, since they can in that way contribute an amount that would otherwise have been paid as corporate taxes.

In each of these—and many similar—cases, there is a strong temptation to rationalize these actions as an exercise of "social responsibility." In the present climate of opinion, with its wide spread aversion to "capitalism," "profits," the "soulless corporation" and so on, this is one way for a corporation to generate goodwill as a by-product of expenditures that are entirely justified in its own self-interest.

It would be inconsistent of me to call on corporate executives to refrain from this hypocritical window-dressing because it harms the foundations of a free society. That would be to call on them to exercise a "social responsibility"! If our institutions, and the attitudes of the public make it in their self-interest to cloak their actions in this way, I cannot summon much indignation to denounce them. At the same time, I can express admiration for those individual proprietors or owners of closely held corporations or stockholders of more broadly held corporations who disdain such tactics as approaching fraud.

Whether blameworthy or not, the use of the cloak of social responsibility, and the nonsense spoken in its name by influential and prestigious businessmen, does clearly harm the foundations of a free society. I have been impressed time and again by the schizophrenic character of many businessmen. They are capable of being extremely farsighted and clearheaded in matters that are internal to their businesses. They are incredibly shortsighted and muddleheaded in matters that are outside their businesses but affect the possible survival of business in general. This shortsightedness is strikingly exemplified in the calls from many businessmen for wage and price guidelines or controls or income policies. There is nothing that could do more in a brief period to destroy a market system and replace it by a centrally controlled system than effective governmental control of prices and wages.

The shortsightedness is also exemplified in speeches by businessmen on social responsibility. This may gain them kudos in the short run. But it helps to strengthen the already too prevalent view that the pursuit of profits is wicked and immoral and must be curbed and controlled by external forces. Once this view is adopted, the external forces that curb the market will not be the social consciences, however highly developed, of the pontificating executives; it will be the iron fist of Government bureaucrats. Here, as with price and wage controls, businessmen seem to me to reveal a suicidal impulse.

The political principle that underlies the market mechanism is unanimity. In an ideal free market resting on private property, no individual can coerce any other, all cooperation is voluntary, all parties to such cooperation benefit or they need not participate. There are no values, no "social" responsibilities in any sense other than the shared values and responsibilities of individuals. Society is a collection of individuals and of the various groups they voluntarily form.

The political principle that underlies the political mechanism is conformity. The individual must serve a more general social interest—whether that be determined by a church or a dictator or a majority. The individual may have a vote and say in what is to be done, but if he is over-ruled, he must conform. It is appropriate for some to require others to contribute to a general social purpose whether they wish to or not.

Unfortunately, unanimity is not always feasible. There are some respects in which conformity appears unavoidable, so I do not see how one can avoid the use of the political mechanism altogether.

But the doctrine of "social responsibility" taken seriously would extend the scope of the political mechanism to every human activity. It does not differ in philosophy from the most explicitly collectivist doctrine. It differs only by professing to believe that collectivist ends can be attained without collectivist means. That is why, in my book *Capitalism and Freedom*, I have called it a "fundamentally subversive doctrine" in a free society, and have said that in such a society, "there is one and only one social responsibility of business—to use it resources and engage in activities designed to increase its profits so long as it stays within the rules of the game, which is to say, engages in open and free competition without deception or fraud."

The Nature of the Firm

By Ronald Coase

Economic theory has suffered in the past from a failure to state clearly its assumption. Economists in building up a theory have often omitted to examine the foundations on which it was erected. This examination is, however, essential not only to prevent the misunderstanding and needless controversy which arise from a lack of knowledge of the assumptions on which a theory is based, but also because of the extreme importance for economics of good judgment in choosing between rival sets of assumptions. For instance, it is suggested that the use of the word "firm" in economics may be different from the use of the term by the "plain man."[1] Since there is apparently a trend in economic theory towards starting analysis with the individual firm and not with the industry,[2] it is all the more necessary not only that a clear definition of the word *"firm"* should be given but that its difference from a firm in the "real world," if it lists, should be made clear. Mrs. Robinson has said that "the two questions to be asked of a set of assumptions in economics are: Are they tractable? and: Do they correspond with the real world?"[3] Though, as Mrs. Robinson points out, "More often one set will be manageable and the other realistic," yet there may well be branches of theory where assumptions may be both manageable and realistic. It is hoped to show in the following paper that a definition of a firm may be obtained which is not only realistic in that it corresponds to what is meant by a firm in the real world, but is tractable by two of the most powerful instruments of economic analysis developed by Marshall, the idea of the margin and that of substitution, together giving the idea of substitution at the margin.[4] Our definition must, of course, "relate to formal relations which are capable of being *conceived* exactly."[5]

I.

It is convenient if, in searching for a definition of a firm, we first consider the economic system as it is normally treated by the economist. Let us consider the description of the economic system given by Sir Arthur Salter.[6] "The normal economic system works itself. For its current operation it is under no central control, it needs no central survey. Over the whole range of human activity and human need, supply is adjusted to demand, and production to consumption, by a process that is automatic, elastic and responsive." An economist thinks of the economic system as being co-ordinated by the price mechanism and society becomes not an organization but an organism.[7] The economic system "works itself." This does not mean that there is no planning by individuals. These exercise foresight and choose between alternatives. This is necessarily so if there is to be order in the system. But this theory assumes that the direction of resources is dependent directly on the price mechanism. Indeed, it is often considered to be an objection to economic planning that it merely tries to do what is already done by the price mechanism.[8] Sir Arthur Salter's description, however, gives a very incomplete picture of our economic system. Within a firm, the description does not fit at all. For instance, in economic theory we find that the allocation of factors of production between different uses is determined by the price mechanism. The price of factor A becomes higher in X than in Y. As a result, A moves from Y to X until the difference between the prices in X and Y, except if so far as it compensates for other differential advantages, disappears. Yet in the real world, we find that there are many areas where this does not apply. If a workman moves from department Y to department X, he does not go because of a change in relative prices, but because he is ordered to do so. Those who object to economic planning on the grounds that the problem is solved by price movements can be answered by pointing out that there is planning within our economic system which is quite different from the individual planning mentioned above and which is akin to what is normally called economic planning. The example given above is typical of a large sphere in our modern economic system. Of course, this fact has not been ignored by economists. Marshall introduces organization as a fourth factor of production; J.B. Clark gives the coordinating function to the entrepreneur; Professor Knight introduces managers who coordinate. As D. H. Robertson points out, we find "islands of conscious power in this ocean of unconscious cooperation like lumps of butter coagulating in a pail of buttermilk."[9] But in view of the fact that it is usually argued that coordination will be done by the price mechanism, why is such organization necessary? Why are there these "islands of conscious power?" Outside the firm, price movements direct production, which is coordinated through a series of exchange transactions on the market. Within a firm, these markets transactions are eliminated and in place of the complicated market structure with exchange transactions is substituted the entrepreneur-coordinator, who directs production.[10] It is clear that these are alternative methods of coordinating production. Yet, having regard to the fact that if production is regulated by price movements, production could be carried on without any organization at all, well might we ask, why is there any organization?

Of course, the degree to which the price mechanism is superseded varies greatly. In a department store, the allocation of the different sections to the various locations in the building may be done by the controlling authority or it may be the result of competitive price bidding for space. In the Lancashire cotton industry, a weaver can rent power and shop-room and can obtain looms and yarn on credit. [11]

This coordination of the various factors of production is, however, normally carried out without the intervention of the price mechanism. As is evident, the amount of "vertical" integration, involving as it does the supersession of the price mechanism, varies greatly from industry to industry and from firm to firm.

It can, I think, be assumed that the distinguishing mark of the firm is the supersession of the price mechanism. It is, of course, as Professor Robbins points out, "related to an outside network of relative prices and costs,"[12] but it is important to discover the exact nature of this relationship. This distinction between the allocation of resources in a firm and the allocation in the economic system has been very vividly described by Mr. Maurice Dobb when discussing Adam Smith's conception of the capitalist: "It began to be seen that there was something more important than the relations inside each factory or unit captained by an undertaker; there were the relations of the undertaker with the rest of the economic world outside his immediate sphere … the undertaker busies himself with the division of labour inside each firm and he plans and organizes consciously," but "he is related to the much larger economic specialization, of which he himself is merely one specialised unit. Here, he plays his part as a single cell in a larger organism, mainly unconscious of the wider role he fills."[13]

In view of the fact that while economists treat the price mechanism as a coordinating instrument, they also admit the coordinating function of the "entrepreneur," it is surely important to enquire why coordination is the work of the price mechanism in one case and of the entrepreneur in another. The purpose of this paper is to bridge what appears to be a gap in economic theory between the assumption (made for some purposes) that resources are allocated by means of the price mechanism and the assumption (made for other purposes) that this allocation is dependent on the entrepreneur-coordinator. We have to explain the basis on which, in practice, this choice between alternatives is effected.[14]

II.

Our task is to attempt to discover why a firm emerges at all in a specialized exchange economy. The price mechanism (considered purely from the side of the direction of resources) might be superseded if the relationship which replaced it was desired for its own sake. This would be the case, for example, if some people preferred to work under the direction of some other person. Such individuals would accept less in order to work under someone, and firms would arise naturally from this. But it would appear that this cannot be a very important reason, for it would rather seem that the opposite tendency is operating if one judges from the stress normally laid on the advantage of "being one's own master."[15] Of course, if the desire was not to be controlled but to control, to exercise power over others, then people might be willing to give up something in order to direct others; that is, they would be willing to pay others more than they could get under the price mechanism in order to be able to direct them. But this implies that those who direct pay in order to be able to do this and are not paid to direct, which is clearly not true in the majority of cases.[16] Firms might also exist if purchasers preferred commodities which are produced by firms to those not so produced; but even in spheres where one would expect such preferences (if they exist) to be of negligible importance, firms are to be found in the real world.[17] Therefore there must be other elements involved.

The main reason why it is profitable to establish a firm would seem to be that there is a cost of using the price mechanism. The most obvious cost of "organizing" production through the price mechanism is that of discovering what the relevant prices are.[18] This cost may be reduced but it will not be eliminated by the emergence of specialists who will sell this information. The costs of negotiating and concluding a separate contract for each exchange transaction which takes place on a market must also be taken into account.[19] Again, in certain markets, e.g., produce ex-changes, a technique is devised for minimizing these contract costs; but they are not eliminated. It is true that contracts are not eliminated when there is a firm but they are greatly reduced. A factor of production (or the owner thereof) does not have to make a series of contracts with the factors with whom he is cooperating within the firm, as would be necessary, of course, if this cooperation were as a direct result of the working of the price mechanism. For this series of contracts is substituted one. At this stage, it is important to note the character of the contract into which a factor enters that is employed within a firm. The contract is one whereby the factor, for a certain remuneration (which may be fixed or fluctuating), agrees to obey the directions of an entrepreneur *within certain limits*.[20] The essence of the contract is that it should only state the limits to the powers of the entrepreneur; Within these limits, he can therefore direct the other factors of production.

There are, however, other disadvantages—or costs—of using the price mechanism. It may be desired to make a long-term contract for the supply of some article or service. This may be due to the fact that if one contract is made for a longer period, instead of several shorter ones, then certain costs of making each contract will be avoided. Or, owing to the risk attitude of the people concerned, they may prefer to make a long rather than a short-term contract. Now, owing to the difficulty of forecasting, the longer the period of the contract is for the supply of the commodity or service, the less possible, and indeed, the less desirable it is for the person purchasing to specify what the other contracting party is expected to do. It may well be a matter of indifference to the person supplying the service or commodity which of several courses of action is taken, but not to the purchaser of that service or commodity. But the purchaser will not know which of these several courses he will want the supplier to take. Therefore, the service which is being provided is expressed in general terms, the exact details being left until a later date. All that is stated in the contract is the limits to what the persons supplying the commodity or service is expected to do. The details of what the supplier is expected to do is not stated in the contract but is decided later by the purchaser. When the direction of resources (within the limits of the contract) becomes dependent on the buyer in this way, that relationship which I term a "firm" may be obtained.[21] A firm is likely therefore to emerge in those cases where a very short-term contract would be unsatisfactory. It is obviously of more importance in the case of services—labor—than it is in the case of the buying of commodities. In the case of commodities, the main items can be stated in advance and the details which will be decided later will be of minor significance.

We may sum up this section of the argument by saying that the operation of a market costs something and by forming an organization and allowing some authority (an "entrepreneur") to direct the resources, certain marketing costs are saved. The entrepreneur has to carry out his function at less cost, taking into account the fact that he may get factors of production at a lower price than the market transactions which he supersedes, because it is always possible to revert to the open market if he fails to do this. The question of uncertainty is one which is often considered to be very relevant to the study of the equilibrium of the firm. It seems improbable that a firm would emerge without the existence of uncertainty. But those, for instance, Professor Knight, who make the *mode of payment* the distinguishing mark of the firm—fixed incomes being guaranteed to some of those engaged in production by a person who takes the residual, and fluctuating, income—would appear to be introducing a point which is irrelevant to the problem we are considering. One entrepreneur may sell his services to another for a certain sum of money, while the payment to his employees may be mainly or wholly a share in profits.[22] The significant question would appear to be why the allocation of resources is not done directly by the price mechanism.

Another factor that should be noted is that exchange transactions on a market and the same transactions organized within a firm are often treated differently by Governments or other bodies with regulatory powers. If we consider the operation of a sales tax, it is clear that it is a tax on market transactions and not on the same transactions organized within the firm. Now since these are alternative methods of organization"—by the price mechanism or by the entrepreneur—such a regulation would bring into existence firms which otherwise would have no *raison d'être*. It would furnish a reason for the emergence of a firm in a specialized exchange economy. Of course, to the extent that firms already exist, such a measure as a sales tax would merely tend to make them larger than they would otherwise be. Similarly, quota schemes, and methods of price control which imply that there is rationing, and which do not apply to firms producing such products for themselves, by allowing advantages to those who organize within the firm and not through the market, necessarily encourage the growth of firms. But it is difficult to believe that it is measures such as have been mentioned in this paragraph which have brought firms into existence. Such measures would, however, tend to have this result if they did not exist for other reasons.

These, then, are the reasons why organizations such as firms exist in a specialized exchange economy in which it is generally assumed that the distribution of resources is "organized" by the price mechanism. A firm, therefore, consists of the system of relationships which comes into existence when the direction of resources is dependent on an entrepreneur; The approach which has just been sketched would appear to offer an advantage in that it is possible to give a scientific meaning to what is meant by saying that a firm gets larger or smaller. A firm becomes larger as additional transactions (which could be exchange transactions coordinated through the price mechanism) are organized by the entrepreneur and becomes smaller as he abandons the organization of such transactions. The question which arises is whether it is possible to study the forces which determine the size of the firm. Why does the entrepreneur not organize one less transaction or one more? It is interesting to note that Professor Knight considers that:

> The relation between efficiency and size is one of the most serious problems of theory, being, in contrast with the relation for a plant, largely a matter of personality and historical accident rather than of intelligible general principles.
> But the question is peculiarly vital because the possibility of monopoly gain offers a powerful incentive to *continuous and unlimited* expansion of the firm, which force must be offset by some decreased efficiency (in the production of money income) with growth in size, if even boundary competition is to exist.[23]

Professor Knight would appear to consider that it is impossible to treat scientifically the determinants of the size of the firm. On the basis of the concept of the firm developed above, this task will now be attempted.

It was suggested that the introduction of the firm was due primarily to the existence of marketing costs. A pertinent question to ask would appear to be (quite apart from the monopoly considerations raised by Professor Knight), why, if by organizing one can eliminate certain costs and in fact reduce the cost of production, are there any market transactions at all?[24] Why is not all production carried on by one big firm? There would appear to be certain possible explanations.

First, as a firm gets larger, there may be decreasing returns to the entrepreneur function, that is, the costs of organizing additional transactions within the firm may rise.[25] Naturally, a point must be reached where the costs of organizing an extra transaction within the firm are equal to the costs involved in carrying out the transaction in the open market, or; to the costs of organizing by another entrepreneur. Secondly, it may be that as the transactions which are organized increase, the entrepreneur fails to place the factors of production in the uses where their value is greatest, that is, fails to make the best use of the factors of production. Again, a point must be reached where the loss through the waste of resources is equal to the marketing costs of the exchange transaction in the open market or to the loss if the transaction was organized by another entrepreneur. Finally, the supply price of one or more of the factors of production may rise, because the "other advantages" of a small firm are greater than those of a large firm.[26] Of course, the actual point where the expansion of the firm ceases might be determined by a combination of the factors mentioned above. The first two reasons given most probably correspond to the economists' phrase of "diminishing returns to management."[27]

The point has been made in the previous paragraph that a firm will tend to expand until the costs of organizing an extra transaction within the firm become equal to the costs of carrying out the same transaction by means of an exchange on the open market or the costs of organizing in another firm. But if the firm stops its expansion at a point below the costs of marketing in the open market and at a point equal to the costs of organizing in another firm, in most cases (excluding the case of "combination"[28]), this will imply that there is a market transaction between these two procedures, each of whom could organize it at less than the actual marketing costs. How is the paradox to be resolved? If we consider an example the reason for this will become clear. Suppose *A* is buying a product from *B* and that both *A* and *B* could organize this marketing transaction at less than its present cost. *B,* we can assume, is not organizing one process or stage of production, but several. If *A* therefore wishes to avoid a market transaction, he will have to take over all the processes of production controlled by *B*. Unless *A* takes over all the processes of production, a market transaction will still remain, although it is a different product that is bought. But we have previously assumed that as each producer expands he becomes less efficient; the additional costs of organizing extra transactions increase. It is probable that *A's* cost of organizing the transactions previously organized by *B* will be greater than *B's* costs of doing the same thing. *A* therefore will take over the whole of *B's* organization only if his cost of organizing *B's* work is not greater than *B's* cost by an amount equal to the costs of carrying out an exchange transaction on the open market. But once it becomes economical to have a market transaction, it also pays to divide production in such a way that the cost of organizing an extra transaction in each firm is the same.

Up to now it has been assumed that the exchange transactions which take place through the price mechanism are homogeneous. In fact, nothing could be more diverse than the actual transactions which take place in our modern world. This would seem to imply that the costs of carrying out exchange transactions through the price mechanism will vary considerably as will also the costs of organizing these transactions within the firm. It seems therefore possible that quite apart from the question of diminishing returns the costs of organizing certain transactions within the firm may be greater than the costs of carrying out the exchange transactions in the open market. This would necessarily imply that there were exchange transactions carried out through the price mechanism, but would it mean that there would have to be more than one firm? Clearly not, for all those areas in the economic system where the direction of resources was not dependent directly on the price mechanism could be organized within one firm. The factors which were discussed earlier would seem to be the important ones, though it is difficult to say whether "diminishing returns to management" or the rising supply price of factors is likely to be the more important. Other things being equal, therefore, a firm will tend to be larger:

a. The less the costs of organizing and the slower these costs rise with an increase in the transactions organized.
b. The less likely the entrepreneur is to make mistakes and the smaller the increase in mistakes with an increase in the transactions organized.
c. The greater the lowering (or the less the rise) in the supply price of factors of production to firms of larger size.

Apart from variations in the supply price of factors of production to firms of different sizes, it would appear that the costs of organizing and the losses through mistakes will increase with an increase in the spatial distribution of the transactions organized, in the dissimilarity of the transactions, and in the probability of changes in the relevant prices.[29] As more transactions are organized by an entrepreneur, it would appear that the transactions would tend to be either different in kind or in different places. This furnishes an additional reason why efficiency will tend to decrease as the firm gets larger. Inventions which tend to bring factors of production nearer together, by lessening spatial distribution, tend to increase the size of the firm.[30] Changes like the telephone and the telegraph which tend to reduce the cost of organizing spatially will tend to increase the size of the firm. All changes which improve managerial technique will tend to increase the size of the firm. [31/32] It should be noted that the definition of a firm which was given above can be used to give more precise meanings to the terms "combination" and "integration."[33] There is a combination when transactions which were previously organized by two or more entrepreneurs become organized by one. This becomes integration when it involves the organization of transactions which were previously carried out between the entrepreneurs on a market. A firm can expand in either or both of these two ways. The whole of the "structure of competitive industry" becomes tractable by the ordinary technique of economic analysis.

The problem which has been investigated in the previous section has not been entirely neglected by economists and it is now necessary to consider why the reasons given above for the emergence of a firm in a specialized exchange economy are to be preferred to the other explanations which have been offered.

It is sometimes said that the reason for the existence of a firm is to be found in the division of labor. This is the view of Professor Usher, a view which has been adopted and expanded by Mr. Maurice Dobb. The firm becomes "the result of an increasing complexity of the division of labour ... The growth of this economic differentiation creates the need for some integrating force without which differentiation would collapse into chaos; and it is as the integrating force in a differentiated economy that industrial forms are chiefly significant.[34] The answer to this argument is an obvious one. The "integrating force in a differentiated economy" already exists in the form of the price mechanism. It is perhaps the main achievement of economic science that it has shown that there is no reason to suppose that specialization must lead to chaos.[35] The reason given by Mr. Maurice Dobb is therefore inadmissible. What has to be explained is why one integrating force (the entrepreneur) should be substituted for another integrating force (the price mechanism). The most interesting reasons (and probably the most widely accepted) which have been given to explain this fact are those to be found in Professor Knight's *Risk, Uncertainty and Profit*. His views will be examined in some detail.

Professor Knight starts with a system in which there is no uncertainty:

> Acting as individuals under absolute freedom but without collusion men are supposed to have organized economic life with the primary and secondary division of labour, the use of capital, etc., developed to the point familiar in present-day America. The principal fact which calls for the exercise of the imagination is the internal organization of the productive groups or establishments. With uncertainty entirely absent, every individual being in possession of perfect knowledge of the situation, there would be no occasion for anything of the nature of responsible management or control of productive activity. Even marketing transactions in any realistic sense would not be found. The flow of raw materials and productive services to the consumer would be entirely automatic.[36]

Professor Knight says that we can imagine this adjustment as being "the result of a long process of experimentation worked out by trial-and-error methods alone," while it is not necessary "to imagine every worker doing exactly the right thing at the right time in a sort of 'pre-established harmony' with the work of others. There might be managers, superintendents, etc., for the purpose of coordinating the activities of individuals," though these managers would be performing a purely routine function, "without responsibility of any sort."[37]

Professor Knight then continues:

> With the introduction of uncertainty—the fact of ignorance and the necessity of acting upon opinion rather than knowledge—into this Eden-like situation, its character

is entirely changed ... With uncertainty present doing things, the actual execution of activity, becomes in a real sense a secondary part of life; the primary problem or function is deciding what to do and how to do.

This fact of uncertainty brings about the two most important characteristics of social organization.

> In the first place, goods are produced for a market, on the basis of entirely impersonal prediction of wants, not for the satisfaction of the wants of the producers themselves. The producer takes the responsibility of forecasting the consumers' wants. In the second place, the work of forecasting and at the same time a large part of the technological direction and control of production are still further concentrated upon a very narrow class of the producers, and we meet with a new economic functionary, the entrepreneur ... When uncertainty is present and the task of deciding what to do and how to do it takes the ascendancy over that of execution the internal organization of the productive groups is no longer a matter of indifference or a mechanical detail. Centralisation of this deciding and controlling function is imperative, a process of "cephalisation" is inevitable.[39]

The most fundamental change is:

> the system under which the confident and venturesome assume the risk or insure the doubtful and timid by guaranteeing to the latter a specified income in return for an assignment of the actual results ... With human nature as we know it it would be impracticable or very unusual for one man to guarantee to another a definite result of the latter's actions without being given power to direct his work. And on the other hand the second party would not place himself under the direction of the first without such a guarantee ... The result of this manifold specialization of function is the enterprise and wage system of industry. Its existence in the world is the direct result of the fact of uncertainty.[40]

These quotations give the essence of Professor Knight's theory. The fact of uncertainty means that people have to forecast future wants. Therefore, you get a special class springing up who direct the activities of others to whom they give guaranteed wages. It acts because good judgment is generally associated with confidence in one's judgment.[41] Professor Knight would appear to leave himself open to criticism on several grounds. First of all, as he himself points out, the fact that certain people have better judgment or better knowledge does not mean that they can only get an income from it by themselves actively taking part in production. They can sell advice or knowledge. Every business buys the services of a host of advisers. We can imagine a system where advice or knowledge was bought as required. Again, it is possible to get a reward from better knowledge or judgment not by actively taking part in production but by making contracts with people who are producing. A merchant buying for future delivery represents an example of this. But this merely illustrates the point that it is quite possible to give a guaranteed reward providing that certain acts are performed without directing the performance of those acts. Professor Knight says that "with human nature as we know it, it would be impracticable or very unusual for one man to guarantee to another a definite result of the latter's actions without being given power to direct his work." This is surely incorrect. A large proportion of jobs are done to contract, that is, the contractor is guaranteed a certain sum providing he performs certain acts. But this does not involve any direction. It does mean, however, that the system of relative prices has been changed and that there will be a new arrangement of the factors of production.[42] The fact that Professor Knight mentions that the "second party would not place himself under the direction of the first without such a guarantee" is irrelevant to the problem we are considering. Finally, it seems important to notice that even in the case of an economic system where there is no uncertainty Professor Knight considers that there would be coordinators, though they would perform only a routine function. He immediately adds that they would be "without responsibility of any sort," which raises the question by whom are they paid and why? It seems that nowhere does Professor Knight give a reason why the price mechanism should be superseded.

IV.

It would seem important to examine one further point and that is to consider the relevance of this discussion to the general question of the "cost-curve of the firm."

It has sometimes been assumed that a firm is limited in size under perfect competition if its cost curve slopes upward,[43] while under imperfect competition, it is limited in size because it will not pay to produce more than the output at which marginal cost is equal to marginal revenue. But it is clear that a firm may produce more than one product and, therefore, there appears to be no prima facie reason why this upward slope of the cost curve in the case of perfect competition or the fact that marginal cost will not always be below marginal revenue in the case of imperfect competition should limit the size of the firm.[45] Mrs. Robinson[46] makes the simplifying assumption that only one product is being produced. But it is clearly important to investigate how the number of products produced by a firm is determined, while no theory which assumes that only one product is in fact produced can have very great practical significance.

It might be replied that under perfect competition, since everything that is produced can be sold at the prevailing price, then there is no need for any other product to be produced. But this argument ignores the fact that there may be a point where it is less costly to organize the exchange transactions of a new product than to organize further exchange transactions of the old product. This point can be illustrated in the following way. Imagine, following von Thunen, that there is a town, the consuming center, and that industries are located around this central point in rings. These conditions are illustrated in the following diagram in which *A, B,* and *C* represent different industries.

Imagine an entrepreneur who starts controlling exchange transactions from x. Now as he extends his activities in the same product *(B),* the cost of organizing increases until at some point it becomes equal to that of a dissimilar product which is nearer. As the firm expands, it will therefore from this point include more than one product *(A and C)*. This treatment of the problem is obviously incomplete,[47] but it is necessary to show that merely proving that the cost curve turns upwards does not give a limitation to the size of the firm. So far we have only considered the case of perfect competition; the case of imperfect competition would appear to be obvious.

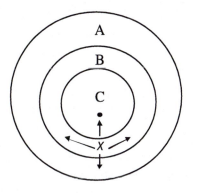

To determine the size of the firm, we have to consider the marketing costs (that is, the costs of using the price mechanism), and the costs of organizing the different entrepreneurs and then we can determine how many products will be produced by each firm and how much of each it will produce. It would, therefore, appear that Mr. Shove[48] in his article on "Imperfect Competition" was asking questions which Mrs. Robinson's cost curve apparatus cannot answer; The factors mentioned above would seem to be the relevant ones.

V.

Only one task now remains; and that is, to see whether the concept of a firm which has been developed fits in with that existing in the real world. We can best approach the question of what constitutes a firm in practice by considering the legal relationship normally called that of "master and servant" or "employer and employee."[49] The essentials of this relationship have been given as follows:

(1) The servant must be under the duty of rendering personal services to the master or to others on behalf of the master, otherwise the contract is a con-tract for sale of goods or the like.

(2) The master must have the right to control the servant's work, either personally or by another servant or agent. It is this right of control or interference, of being entitled to tell the servant when to work (within the hours of service) and when not to work, and what work to do and how to do it (within the terms of such service) which is the dominant characteristic in this relation and marks off the servant from

an independent contractor, or from one employed merely to give to his employer the fruits of his labour. In the latter case, the contractor or performer is not under the employer's control in doing the work or effecting the service; he has to shape and manage his work so as to give the result he has contracted to effect.[50]

We thus see that it is the fact of direction which is the essence of the legal concept of "employer and employee," just as it was in the economic concept which was developed above. It is interesting to note that Professor Batt says further:

> That which distinguishes an agent from a servant is not the absence or presence of a fixed wage or the payment only of commission on business done, but rather the freedom with which an agent may carry out his employment.[51]

We can therefore conclude that the definition we have given is one which approximates closely to the firm as it is considered in the real world.

Our definition is, therefore, realistic. Is it manageable? This ought to be clear; When we are considering how large a firm will be the principle of marginalism works smoothly. The question always is, will it pay to bring an extra exchange transaction under the organizing authority? At the margin, the costs of organizing within the firm will be equal either to the costs of organizing in another firm or to the costs involved in leaving the transaction to be "organized" by the price mechanism. Business men will be constantly experimenting, controlling more or less, and in this way, equilibrium will be maintained. This gives the position of equilibrium for static analysis. But it is clear that the dynamic factors are also of considerable importance, and an investigation of the effect changes have on the cost of organizing within the firm and on marketing costs generally will enable one to explain why firms get larger and smaller; We thus have a theory of moving equilibrium. The above analysis would also appear to have clarified the relationship between initiative or enterprise and management. Initiative means forecasting and operates through the price mechanism by the making of new contracts. Management proper merely reacts to price changes, rearranging the factors of production under its control. That the business man normally combines both functions is an obvious result of the marketing costs which were discussed above. Finally, this analysis enables us to state more exactly what is meant by the "marginal product" of the entrepreneur. But an elaboration of this point would take us far from our comparatively simple task of definition and clarification.

NOTES

1. Joan Robinson, *Economics Is a Serious Subject* (1932), 12.
2. See N. Kaldor, "The Equilibrium of the Firm," 44 The Economic Journal (1934), 60–76.
3. Op. cit., 6.
4. J M. Keynes, *Essays in Biography* (1933), 223–24.
5. L. Robbins, *Nature and Significance of Economic Science* (1935), 63.

6. This description is quoted with approval by D. H. Robenson, *Control Of Industry* (1923), *85,* and by Professor Arnold Plant, "Trends in Business Administration," 12 *Economica* (1932) *45–62. It* appears in *Allied Shipping Control,* pp. 16–17.

7. See F. A. Hayek, "The Trend of Economic Thinking," 13 *Economica* (1933)121–37.

8. See *R* A. Hayek, op. cit.

9. Op. cit., *85.*

10. In the rest of this paper I shall use the term entrepreneur to refer to the person or persons who, in a competitive system, take the place of the price mechanism in the direction of resources.

11. *Survey of Textile Industries,* 26.

12. *Op. cit.,* 71.

13. *Capitalist Enterprise and Social Progress (1925),* 20. *Cf,* also, Henderson, *Supply and Demand* (1932), 3–5.

14. It is easy to see when the State takes over the direction of an industry that, in planning it, it is doing something which was previously done by the price mechanism. What is usually not realized is that any business man in organizing the relations between his departments is also doing something which could be organized through the price mechanism. There is therefore point in Mr. Durbin's answer to those who emphasize the problems involved in economic planning that the same problems have to be solved by business men in the competitive system. (Sec "Economic Calculus in a Planned Economy," 46 *The Economic Journal* [1936] 676–90.) The important difference between these two cases is that economic planning is imposed on industry while firms arise voluntarily because they represent a more efficient method of organizing production. In a competitive system, there is an "optimum" amount of planning!

15. Cf. Harry Dawes, "Labour Mobility in the Steel Industry," 44 *The Economic Journal* (1934) 84–94, who instances "the trek to retail shopkeeping and insurance work by the better paid of skilled men due to the desire (often the main aim in life of a worker) to be independent" (86).

16. Nonetheless, this is not altogether fanciful. Some small shopkeepers are said to earn less than their assistants.

17. G. F. Shove, "The Imperfection of the Market: a Further Note," 44 *The Economic Journal* (1933)113–24, n. 1, points out that such preferences may exist, although the example he gives is almost the reverse of the instance given in the text.

18. According to N. Kaldor, "A Classificatory Note of the Determinanteness of Equilibrium," I *The Review Of Economic Studies* (1934)122–36, his one of the assumptions of static theory that "Ail the relevant prices are known to ail individuals." But this is clearly not true of the real world.

19. This influence was noted by Professor Usher when discussing the development of capitalism. He says: "The successive buying and selling of partly finished products were sheer waste of energy." *(Introduction to the Industrial History Of England* (1920), 13.) But he does not develop the idea nor consider why it is that buying and selling operations still exist.

20. It would be possible for no limits to the powers of the entrepreneur to be fixed. This would be voluntary slavery. According to Professor Batt, *The Law o! Master and Servant* (1933), 18, such a contract would be void and unenforceable.

21. Of course, it is not possible to draw a hard and fast line which determines whether there is a firm or not. There may be more or less direction. It is similar to the legal question of whether there is the relationship of master and servant or principal and agent. Sec the discussion of this problem below.

22. The views of Professor Knight are examined below in more detail.

23. *Risk, Uncertainty and Profit,* Preface to the Re-issue, London School of Economics Series of Reprints, No. 16 (1933).

24. There are certain marketing costs which could only be eliminated by the abolition of "consumers' choice" and these arc the costs of retailing. It is conceivable that these costs might be so high that people would be willing to accept rations because the extra product obtained was worth the loss of their choice.

25. This argument assumes that exchange transactions on a market can be considered as homogeneous; which is clearly untrue in fact. This complication is taken into account below.

26. For a discussion of the variation of the supply price of factors and production to firms of varying size, see E. A. G. Robinson, *The Structure of Competitive Industry* (1932). It is sometimes said that the supply price of organizing ability increases as the size of the firm increases because men prefer to be the heads of small independent businesses rather than the heads of departments in a large business. Sec Jones, *The Trust Problem* (1921), 531, and Macgregor, *Industrial Combination* (1935), 63. This is a common argument of those who advocate Rationalization. It is said that larger units would be more efficient, but owing to the individualistic spirit of the smaller entrepreneurs, they prefer to remain independent, apparently in spite of the higher income which their increased efficiency under Rationalization makes possible.

27. This discussion is, of course, brief and incomplete. For a more thorough discussion of this particular problem, see N. Kaldor, "The Equilibrium of the Firm," 44 *The Economic Journal* (1934) 60–76, and E. A. G. Robinson, "The Problem of Management and the Size of the Firm," 44 *The Economic Journal* (1934) 242–57.

28. A definition of this term is given below.

29. This aspect of the problem is emphasized by N. Kaldor, op. cit. Its importance in this connection had been previously noted by E. A. G. Robinson, *The Structure Of Competitive Industry* (1932), 83–106. This assumes that an increase in the probability of price movements increases the costs of organizing within a firm more than it increases the cost of carrying out an exchange transaction on the market—which is probable.

30. This would appear to be the importance of the treatment of the technical unit by E. A. G. Robinson, op. cit., 27–33. The larger the technical unit, the greater the concentration of factors and therefore the firm is likely to be larger.

31. It should be noted that most inventions will change both the costs of organizing and the costs of using the price mechanism. In such cases, whether the invention tends to make firms larger or smaller will depend on the relative effect on these two sets of costs. For instance, if the telephone reduces the costs of using the price mechanism more than it reduces the costs of organizing, then it will have the effect of reducing the size of the firm.

32. An illustration of these dynamic forces is furnished by Maurice Dobb, *Russian Economic Development* (1928), 68. "With the passing of bonded labour the factory, as an establishment where work was organized under the whip of the overseer, lost its raison d'être until this was restored to it with the introduction of power machinery after 1846." It seems important to realize that the passage from the domestic system to the factory system is not a mere historical accident, but is conditioned by economic forces. This is shown by the fact that it is possible to move from the factory system to the domestic system, as in the Russian example, as well as vice versa. It is the essence of serfdom that the price mechanism is not allowed to operate. Therefore, there has to be direction from some organizer. When, however, serfdom passed, the price mechanism was allowed to operate. It was not until machinery drew workers into one locality that it paid to supersede the price mechanism and the firm again emerged.

33. This is often called "vertical integration," combination being termed "lateral integration."

34. Op. cit., 10. Professor Usher's views are to be found in his *Introduction to the Industrial History of England* (1920), 1–18.

35. Cf. J.B. Clark, *Distribution of Wealth* (1899), 19, who speaks of the theory of exchange as being the "theory of the organisation of industrial society."

36. *Risk, Uncertainty and Profit,* 267.

37. Op. cit., 267–68.

38. Op. cit., 268.

39. Op. cit., 268–95.

40. Op. cit., 269–70.

41. Op. cit., 270.

42. This shows that it is possible to have a private enterprise system without the existence of firms. Though, in practice, the two functions of enterprise, which actually influences the system of relative prices by forecasting wants and acting in accordance with such forecasts, and management, which accepts the system of relative prices as being given, are normally carried out by the same persons, yet it seems important to keep them separate in theory. This point is further discussed below.

43. See Kaidor, op. cit., and Robinson, *The Problem of Management and the Size of the Firm.*

44. Mr. Robinson calls this the Imperfect Competition solution for the survival of the small firm.

45. Mr. Robinson's conclusion, op. cit., 249, n. 1, would appear to be definitely wrong. He is followed by Horace J. White, Jr, "Monopolistic and Perfect Competition," 26 *The American Economic Review* (1936) 645, n. 27. Mr. White states "It is obvious that the size of the firm is limited in conditions of monopolistic competition."

46. *Economics Imperfect Competition* (1934).

47. As has been shown above, location is only one of the factors influencing the cost of organizing.

48. G. F. Shove, "The Imperfection of the Market," 43 *The Economic Journal* (1933). 115. In connection with an increase in demand in the suburbs and the effect on the price charged by suppliers, Mr. Shove asks "… why do not the old firms open branches in the suburbs?" If the argument in the text is correct, this is a question which Mrs. Robinson's apparatus cannot answer.

49. The legal concept of "employer and employee" and the economic concept of a firm are not identical, in that the firm may imply control over another person's property as well as over their labor. But the identity of these two concepts is sufficiently close for an examination of the legal concept to be of value in appraising the worth of the economic concept.

50. Batt, *The Law of Master and Servant,* 6.

51. Op. cit., 7.

Production, Information Costs, and Economic Organization

By Armen A. Alchian and Harold Demsetz

T HE MARK OF a capitalistic society is that resources are owned and allocated by such nongovernmental organizations as firms, households, and markets. Resource owners increase productivity through cooperative specialization and this leads to the demand for economic organizations which facilitate cooperation. When a lumber mill employs a cabinetmaker, cooperation between specialists is achieved within a firm, and when a cabinetmaker purchases wood from a lumberman, the cooperation takes place across markets (or between firms). Two important problems face a theory of economic organization-to explain the conditions that determine whether the gains from specialization and cooperative production can better be obtained within an organization like the firm, or across markets, and to explain the structure of the organization.

It is common to see the firm characterized by the power to settle issues by fiat, by authority, or by disciplinary action superior to that available in the conventional market. This is delusion. The firm does not own all its inputs. It has no power of fiat, no authority, no disciplinary action any different in the slightest degree from ordinary market contracting between any two people. I can "punish" you only by withholding future business or by seeking redress in the courts for any failure to honor our exchange agreement. That is exactly all that any employer can do. He can fire or sue, just as I can fire my grocer by stopping purchases from him or sue him for delivering faulty products. What then is the content of the presumed power to manage and assign workers to various tasks? Exactly the same as one little consumer's power to manage and assign his grocer to various tasks. The single consumer can assign his grocer to the task of obtaining whatever the customer can induce the grocer to provide at a price acceptable to both parties. That is precisely all that an employer can do to an employee. To speak of managing, directing, or assigning workers to various tasks is a deceptive way of noting that the employer continually is involved in renegotiation of contracts on terms that must be acceptable to both parties. Telling an employee to type this letter rather than to file that document is like my telling a grocer to sell me this brand of tuna rather than that brand of bread. I have no contract to continue to purchase from the grocer and neither the employer nor the employee is bound

Armen A. Alchian and Harold Demsetz, "Production, Information Costs, and Economic Organization," from *Engineering Management Review, IEEE*, 1975, pp. 21–41. Copyright © 1975 Institute of Electrical and Electronics Engineers. Permission to reprint granted by the publisher.

by any contractual obligations to continue their relationship. Long-term contracts between employer and employee are not the essence of the organization we call a firm. My grocer can count on my returning day after day and purchasing his services and goods even with the prices not always marked on the goods—because I know what they are—and he adapts his activity to conform to my directions to him as to what I want each day ... he is not my employee.

Wherein then is the relationship between a grocer and his employee different from that between a grocer and his customers? It is in a *team* use of inputs and a centralized position of some party in the contractual arrangements of all other inputs. It is the *centralized contractual agent in a team productive process*—not some superior authoritarian directive or disciplinary power. Exactly what is a team process and why does it induce the contractual form, called the firm? These problems motivate the inquiry of this paper.

I. THE METERING PROBLEM

The economic organization through which input owners cooperate will make better use of their comparative advantages to the extent that it facilitates the payment of rewards in accord with productivity. If rewards were random, and without regard to productive effort, no incentive to productive effort would be provided by the organization; and if rewards were negatively correlated with productivity the organization would be subject to sabotage. Two key demands are placed on an economic organization—metering input productivity and metering rewards.[1]

Metering problems sometimes can be resolved well through the exchange of products across competitive markets, because in many situations markets yield a high correlation between rewards and productivity. If a farmer increases his output of wheat by 10 percent at the prevailing market price, his receipts also increase by 10 percent. This method of organizing economic activity meters the *output directly*, reveals the marginal product and apportions the *rewards* to resource owners in accord with that direct measurement of their outputs. The success of this decentralized, market exchange in promoting productive specialization requires that changes in market rewards fall on those responsible for changes in *output*.[2]

---

1   Meter means to measure and also to apportion. One can meter (measure) output and one can also meter (control) the output. We use the word to denote both; the context should indicate which.

2   A producer's wealth would be reduced by the present capitalized value of the future income lost by loss of reputation. Reputation, i.e., credibility, is an asset, which is another way of saying that reliable information about expected performance is both a costly and a valuable good. For acts of God that interfere with contract performance, both parties have incentives to reach a settlement akin to that which would have been reached if such events had been covered by specific contingency clauses. The reason, again, is that a reputation for "honest" dealings—i.e., for actions similar to those that would probably have been reached had the contract provided this contingency—is wealth.

Almost every contract is open-ended in that many contingencies are uncovered. For example, if a fire delays production of a promised product by A to B, and if B contends that A has not fulfilled the contract, how is the dispute settled and what recompense, if any, does A grant to B? A person uninitiated in such questions may be surprised by the extent to which contracts permit either party to escape performance or to nullify the contract. In fact, it is hard to imagine any contract, which, when taken solely in terms of its stipulations, could not be evaded

The classic relationship in economics that runs from marginal productivity to the distribution of income implicitly assumes the existence of an organization, be it the market or the firm, that allocates rewards to resources in accord with their productivity. The problem of economic organization, the economical means of metering productivity and rewards, is not confronted directly in the classical analysis of production and distribution. Instead, that analysis tends to assume sufficiently economic or zero cost means, as if productivity automatically created its reward. We conjecture the direction of causation is the reverse the specific system of rewarding which is relied upon stimulates a particular productivity response. If the economic organization meters poorly, with rewards and productivity only loosely correlated, then productivity will be smaller; but if the economic organization meters well productivity will be greater. What makes metering difficult and hence induces means of economizing on metering costs?

II. TEAM PRODUCTION

Two men jointly lift heavy cargo into trucks. Solely by observing the total weight loaded per day, it is impossible to determine each person's marginal productivity. With team production it is difficult, solely by observing total output, to either define or determine each individual's contribution to this output of the cooperating inputs. The output is yielded by a team, by definition, and it is not a *sum* of separable outputs of each of its members. Team production of Z involves at least two inputs, X_i and X_j, with $\partial^2 Z/\partial X_i \partial X_j \neq 0$.[3] The production function is not separable into two functions each involving only inputs X_i or only inputs X_j. Consequently there is no *sum* of Z of two separable functions to treat as the Z of the team production function. (An example of a *separable* case is $Z = aX_i^2 + bX_j^2$, which is separable into $Z_i = aX^2$ and $Z_j = bX_j^2$, and $Z = Z_i + Z_j$. This is not team production.) There exist production techniques in which the Z obtained is greater than if X_i and X_j had produced separable Z. Team production will be used if it yields an output enough larger than the sum of separable production of Z to cover the costs of organizing and disciplining team members-the topics of this paper.[4]

Usual explanations of the gains from cooperative behavior rely on exchange and production in accord with the comparative advantage specialization principle with separable additive production. However, as suggested above there is a source of gain from cooperative activity

---

by one of the parties. Yet that is the ruling, viable type of contract. Why? Undoubtedly the best discussion that we have seen on this question is by Stewart Macaulay.

There are means not only of detecting or preventing cheating, but also for deciding how to allocate the losses or gains of unpredictable events or quality of items exchanged. Sales contracts contain warranties, guarantees, collateral, return privileges and penalty clauses for specific nonperformance. These are means of assignment of *risks* of losses of cheating. A lower price without warranty—an "as is" purchase—places more of the risk on the buyer while the seller buys insurance against losses of his "cheating." On the other hand, a warranty or return privilege or service contract places more risk on the seller with insurance being bought by the buyer.

3   The function is separable into additive functions if the cross partial derivative is zero, i.e., if $\partial^2 Z/\partial X_i \partial X_j = 0$.

4   With sufficient generality of notation and conception this team production function could be formulated as a case of the generalized production function interpretation given by our colleague, E. A. Thompson.

involving working as a *team*, wherein individual cooperating inputs do not yield identifiable, separate products which can be *summed* to measure the total output. For this cooperative productive activity, here called "team" production, measuring *marginal* productivity and making payments in accord therewith is more expensive by an order of magnitude than for separable production functions.

Team production, to repeat, is production in which 1) several types of resources are used and 2) the product is not a sum of separable outputs of each cooperating resource. An additional factor creates a team organization problem—3) not all resources used in team production belong to one person.

We do not inquire into why all the jointly used resources are not owned by one person, but instead into the types of organization, contracts, and informational and payment procedures used among owners of teamed inputs. With respect to the one-owner case, perhaps it is sufficient merely to note that (a) slavery is prohibited, (b) one might assume risk aversion as a reason for one person's not borrowing enough to purchase all the assets or sources of services rather than renting them, and (c) the purchase-resale spread may be so large that costs of short-term ownership exceed rental costs. Our problem is viewed basically as one of organization among different people, not of the physical goods or services, however much there must be selection and choice of combination of the latter.

How can the members of a team be rewarded and induced to work efficiently? In team production, marginal products of cooperative team members are not so directly and separably (i.e., cheaply) observable. What a team offers to the market can be taken as the marginal product of the team but not of the team members. The costs of metering or ascertaining the marginal products of the team's members is what calls forth new organizations and procedures. Clues to each input's productivity can be secured by observing behavior of individual inputs. When lifting cargo into the truck, how rapidly does a man move to the next piece to be loaded, how many cigarette breaks does he take, does the item being lifted tilt downward toward his side?

If detecting such behavior were costless, neither party would have an incentive to shirk, because neither could impose the cost of his shirking on the other (if their cooperation was agreed to voluntarily). But since costs must be incurred to monitor each other, each input owner will have more incentive to shirk when he works as part of a team, than if his performance could be monitored easily or if he did not work as a team. If there is a net increase in productivity available by team production, net of the metering cost associated with disciplining the team, then team production will be relied upon rather than a multitude of bilateral exchange of separable individual outputs.

Both leisure and higher income enter a person's utility function.[5] Hence, each person should adjust his work and realized reward so as to equate the marginal rate of substitution between leisure and production of real output to his marginal rate of substitution in consumption. That is, he would adjust his rate of work to bring his demand prices of leisure and output to equality

---

5   More precisely: "if anything other than pecuniary income enters his utility function." Leisure stands for all nonpecuniary income for simplicity of exposition.

with their true costs. However, with detection, policing, monitoring, measuring or metering costs, each person will be induced to take more leisure, because the effect of relaxing on *his realized* (reward) rate of substitution between output and leisure will be less than the effect on the true rate of substitution. His realized cost of leisure will fall more than the *true* cost of leisure, so he "buys" more leisure (i.e., more nonpecuniary reward).

If his relaxation cannot be detected perfectly at zero cost, part of its effects will be borne by others in the team, thus making his realized cost of relaxation less than the true total cost to the team. The difficulty of detecting such actions permits the private costs of his actions to be less than their full costs. Since each person responds to his private realizable rate of substitution (in production) rather than the true total (i.e., social) rate, and so long as there are costs for other people to detect his shift toward relaxation, it will not pay (them) to force him to readjust completely by making him realize the true cost. Only enough efforts will be made to equate the marginal gains of detection activity with the marginal costs of detection; and that implies a lower rate of productive effort and more shirking than in a costless monitoring, or measuring, world. In a university, the faculty use office telephones, paper, and mail for personal uses beyond strict university productivity.

The university administrators could stop such practices by identifying the responsible person in each case, but they can do so only at higher costs than administrators are willing to incur. The extra costs of identifying each party (rather than merely identifying the presence of such activity) would exceed the savings from diminished faculty "turpitudinal peccadilloes." So the faculty is allowed some degree of "privileges, perquisites, or fringe benefits." And the total of the pecuniary wages paid is lower because of this irreducible (at acceptable costs) degree of amenity-seizing activity. Pay is lower in pecuniary terms and higher in leisure, conveniences, and ease of work. But still every person would prefer to see detection made more effective (if it were somehow possible to monitor costlessly) so that he, as part of the now more effectively producing team, could thereby realize a higher pecuniary pay and less leisure. If everyone could, at zero cost, have his reward-realized rate brought to the true production possibility real rate, all could achieve a more preferred position. But detection of the responsible parties is costly; that cost acts like a tax on work rewards.[6] Viable shirking is the result.

What forms of organizing team production will lower the cost of detecting "performance" (i.e., marginal productivity) and bring personally realized rates of substitution closer to true rates of substitution? Market competition, in principle, could monitor some team production. (It already organizes teams.) Input owners who are not team members can offer, in return for a smaller share of the team's rewards, to replace excessively (i.e., overpaid) shirking members. Market competition among potential team members would determine team membership and

---

6   Do not assume that the sole result of the cost of detecting shirking is one form of payment (more leisure and less take home money). With several members of the team, each has an incentive to cheat against each other by engaging in more than the average amount of such leisure if the employer can not tell at zero cost which employee is taking more than average. As a result the total productivity of the team is lowered. Shirking detection costs thus change the form of payment and also result in lower total rewards. Because the cross partial derivatives are positive, shirking reduces other people's marginal products.

individual rewards. There would be no team leader, manager, organizer, owner, or employer. For such decentralized organizational control to work, outsiders, possibly after observing each team's total output, can speculate about their capabilities as team members and, by a market competitive process, revised teams with greater productive ability will be formed and sustained. Incumbent members will be constrained by threats of replacement by outsiders offering services for lower reward shares or offering greater rewards to the other members of the team. Any team member who shirked in the expectation that the reduced output effect would not be attributed to him will be displaced if his activity is detected. Teams of productive inputs, like business units, would evolve in apparent spontaneity in the market-without any central organizing agent, team manager, or boss.

But completely effective control cannot be expected from individualized market competition for two reasons. First, for this competition to be completely effective, new challengers for team membership must know where, and to what extent, shirking is a serious problem, i.e., know they can increase net output as compared with the inputs they replace. To the extent that this is true it is probably possible for existing fellow team members to recognize the shirking. But, by definition, the detection of shirking by observing team output is costly for team production. Secondly, assume the presence of detection costs, and assume that in order to secure a place on the team a new input owner must accept a smaller share of rewards (or a promise to produce more). Then his incentive to shirk would still be at least as great as the incentives of the inputs replaced, because he still bears less than the entire reduction in team output for which he is responsible.

III. THE CLASSICAL FIRM

One method of reducing shirking is for someone to specialize as a monitor to check the input performance of team members.[7] But who will monitor the monitor? One constraint on the monitor is the aforesaid market competition offered by other monitors, but for reasons already given, that is not perfectly effective. Another constraint can be imposed on the monitor: give him title to the net earnings of the team, net of payments to other inputs. If owners of cooperating inputs agree with the monitor that he is to receive any residual product above prescribed amounts (hopefully, the marginal value products of the other inputs), the monitor will have an added incentive not to shirk as a monitor. Specialization in monitoring plus reliance on a residual claimant status will reduce shirking; but additional links are needed to forge the firm of classical economic theory. How will the residual claimant monitor the other inputs?

---

7   What is meant by performance? Input energy, initiative, work attitude, perspiration, rate of exhaustion? Or output? It is the latter that is sought-the effect or output. But performance is nicely ambiguous because it suggests both input and output. It is nicely ambiguous because as we shall see, sometimes by inspecting a team member's input activity we can better judge his output effect, perhaps not with complete accuracy but better than by watching the output of the team. It is not always the case that watching input activity is the only or best means of detecting, measuring or monitoring output effects of each team member, but in some cases it is a useful way. For the moment the word performance glosses over these aspects and facilitates concentration on other issues.

We use the term monitor to connote several activities in addition to its disciplinary connotation. It connotes measuring output performance, apportioning rewards, observing the input behavior of inputs as means of detecting or estimating their marginal productivity and giving assignments or instructions in what to do and how to do it. (It also includes, as we shall show later, authority to terminate or revise contracts.) Perhaps the contrast between a football coach and team captain is helpful. The coach selects strategies and tactics and sends in instructions about what plays to utilize. The captain is essentially an observer and reporter of the performance at close hand of the members. The latter is an inspector-steward and the former a supervisor manager. For the present all these activities are included in the rubric "monitoring." All these tasks are, in principle, negotiable across markets, but we are presuming that such market measurement of marginal productivities and job reassignments are not so cheaply performed for team production. And in particular our analysis suggests that it is not so much the costs of spontaneously negotiating contracts in the markets among groups for team production as it is the detection of the performance of individual members of the team that calls for the organization noted here.

The specialist who *receives the residual rewards* will be the monitor of the members of the team (i.e., will manage the use of cooperative inputs). The monitor earns his residual through the reduction in shirking that he brings about, not only by the prices that he agrees to pay the owners of the inputs, but also by observing and directing the actions or uses of these inputs. *Managing or examining the ways to which inputs are used in team production is a method of metering the marginal productivity of individual inputs to the team's output.*

To discipline team members and reduce shirking, the residual claimant must have power to revise the contract terms and incentives of *individual* members without having to terminate or alter every other input's contract. Hence, team members who seek to increase their productivity will assign to the monitor not only the residual claimant right but also the right to alter individual membership and performance on the team. Each team member, of course, can terminate his own membership (i.e., quit the team), but only the monitor may unilaterally terminate the membership of any of the other members without necessarily terminating the team itself or his association with the team; and he alone can expand or reduce membership, alter the mix of membership, or sell the right to be the residual claimant-monitor of the team. It is this entire bundle of rights: 1) to be a residual claimant; 2) to observe input behavior; 3) to be the central party common to all contracts with inputs; 4) to alter the membership of the team; and 5) to sell these rights, that defines the *ownership* (or the employer) of the *classical* (capitalist, free-enterprise) firm. The coalescing of these rights has arisen, our analysis asserts, because it resolves the shirking-information problem of team production better than does the noncentralized contractual arrangement.

The relationship of each team member to the owner of the firm (i.e., the party common to all input contracts and the residual claimant) is simply a "quid pro quo" contract. Each makes a purchase and sale. The employee "orders" the owner of the team to pay him money in the same sense that the employer directs the team member to perform certain acts. The employee can terminate the contract as readily as can the employer, and longterm contracts, therefore, are not an essential attribute of the firm. Nor are "authoritarian," "dictational," or "fiat" attributes relevant to the conception of the firm or its efficiency.

In summary, two necessary conditions exist for the emergence of the firm on the prior assumption that more than pecuniary wealth enter utility functions: 1) It is possible to increase productivity through team-oriented production, a production technique for which it is costly to directly measure the marginal outputs of the cooperating inputs. This makes it more difficult to restrict shirking through simple market exchange between cooperating inputs. 2) It is economical to estimate marginal productivity by observing or specifying input behavior. The simultaneous occurrence of both these preconditions leads to the contractual organization of inputs, known as the *classical capitalist firms* with (a) joint input production, (b) several input owners, (c) one party who is common to all the contracts of the joint inputs, (d) who has rights to renegotiate any input's contract independently of contracts with other input owners, (e) who holds the residual claim, and (f) who has the right to sell his central contractual residual status.[8]

Other Theories of the Firm

At this juncture, as an aside, we briefly place this theory of the firm in the contexts of those offered by Ronald Coase and Frank Knight.[9] Our view of the firm is not necessarily inconsistent with Coase's; we attempt to go further and identify refutable implications. Coase's penetrating insight is to make more of the fact that markets do not operate costlessly, and he relies on the cost of using markets to form contracts as his basic explanation for the existence of firms. We do not disagree with the proposition that, *ceteris paribus*, the higher is the cost of transacting across markets the greater will be the comparative advantage of organizing resources within the firm; it is a difficult proposition to disagree with or to refute. We could with equal ease subscribe to a theory of the firm based on the cost of managing, for surely it is true that, *ceteris paribus*, the lower is the cost of managing the greater will be the comparative advantage of organizing resources within the firm. To move the theory forward, it is necessary to know what is meant by a firm and to explain the circumstances under which the cost of "managing" resources is low relative to the cost of allocating resources through market transaction. The conception of and rationale for the classical firm that we propose takes a step down the path pointed out by Coase toward that goal. Consideration of team production, team organization, difficulty in metering outputs, and the problem of shirking are important to our explanation but, so far as we can ascertain, not in Coase's. Coase's analysis insofar as it had heretofore been developed would suggest open-ended contracts but does not appear to imply anything more-neither the residual claimant status nor the distinction between employee and subcontractor status (nor any of the implications indicated below). And it is not true that employees are generally employed on the basis of long-term contractual arrangements any more than on a series of short-term or indefinite length contracts.

---

8   Removal of (b) converts a capitalist proprietary firm to a socialist firm

9   Recognition must also be made to the seminal inquiries by Morris Silver anid Richard Auster, and by H. B. Malmgren.

The importance of our proposed additional elements is revealed, for example, by the explanation of why the person to whom the control monitor is responsible receives the residual, and also by our later discussion of the implications about the corporation, partnerships, and profit sharing. These alternative forms for organization of the firm are difficult to resolve on the basis of market transaction costs only. Our exposition also suggests a definition of the classical firm-something crucial that was heretofore absent.

In addition, sometimes a technological development will lower the cost of market transactions while, at the same time, it expands the role of the firm. When the "putting out" system was used for weaving, inputs were organized largely through market negotiations. With the development of efficient central sources of power, it became economical to perform weaving in proximity to the power source and to engage in team production. The bringing in of weavers surely must have resulted in a reduction in the cost of negotiating (forming) contracts. Yet, what we observe is the beginning of the factory system in which inputs are organized within a firm. Why? The weavers did not simply move to a common source of power that they could tap like an electric line, purchasing power while they used their own equipment. Now team production in the joint use of equipment became more important. The measurement of marginal productivity, which now involved interactions between workers, especially through their joint use of machines, became more difficult though contract negotiating cost was reduced, while managing the *behavior* of inputs became easier because of the increased centralization of activity. The firm as an organization expanded even though the cost of transactions was reduced by the advent of centralized power. The same could be said for modern assembly lines. Hence the emergence of central power sources expanded the scope of productive activity in which the firm enjoyed a comparative advantage as an organizational form.

Some economists, following Knight, have identified the bearing of risks of wealth changes with the director or central employer without explaining why that is a viable arrangement. Presumably, the more risk-averse inputs become employees rather than owners of the classical firm. Risk averseness and uncertainty *with regard to the firm's fortunes* have little, if anything, to do with our explanation although it helps to explain why all resources in a team are not owned by one person. That is, the role of risk taken in the sense of absorbing the windfalls that buffet the firm because of unforeseen competition, technological change, or fluctuations in demand are not central to our theory, although it is true that imperfect knowledge and, therefore, risk, in *this* sense of risk, underlie the problem of monitoring team behavior. We deduce the system of paying the manager with a residual claim (the equity) from the desire to have efficient means to reduce shirking so as to make team production economical and not from the smaller aversion to the risks of enterprise in a dynamic economy. We conjecture that "distribution-of-risk" is not a valid rationale for the *existence* and organization of the *classical* firm.

Although we have emphasized team production as creating a costly metering task and have treated team production as an essential (necessary?) condition for the firm, would not other obstacles to cheap metering also call forth the same kind of contractual arrangement here denoted as a firm? For example, suppose a farmer produces wheat in an easily ascertained quantity but with subtle and difficult to detect quality variations determined by how the farmer grew the wheat. A vertical integration could allow a purchaser to control the farmer's behavior in order to more economically estimate productivity. But this is not a case of joint or team production, unless "information" can be considered part of the product. (While a good case could be made for that broader conception of production, we shall ignore it here.) Instead of forming a firm, a buyer can contract to have his inspector on the site of production, just as home builders contract with architects to supervise building contracts; that arrangement is not a firm. Still, a firm might be organized in the production of many products wherein no team production or jointness of use of separately owned resources is involved.

This possibility rather clearly indicates a broader, or complementary, approach to that which we have chosen. 1) As we do in this paper, it can be argued that the firm is the particular policing device utilized when joint team production is present. If other sources of high policing costs arise, as in the wheat case just indicated, some other form of contractual arrangement will be used. Thus to each source of informational cost there may be a different type of policing and contractual arrangement. 2) On the other hand, one can say that where policing is difficult across markets, various forms of contractual arrangements are devised, but there is no reason for that known as the firm to be uniquely related or even highly correlated with team production, as defined here. It might be used equally probably and viably for other sources of high policing cost. We have not intensively analyzed other sources, and we can only note that our current and readily revisable conjecture is that 1) is valid, and has motivated us in our current endeavor. In any event, the test of the theory advanced here is to see whether the conditions we have identified are necessary for firms to have long-run viability rather than merely births with high infant mortality. Conglomerate firms or collections of separate production agencies into one owning organization can be interpreted as an investment trust or investment diversification device—probably along the lines that motivated Knight's interpretation. A holding company can be called a firm, because of the common association of the word firm with any ownership unit that owns income sources. The term firm as commonly used is so turgid of meaning that we can not hope to explain every entity to which the name is attached in common or even technical literature. Instead, we seek to identify and explain a particular contractual arrangement induced by the cost of information factors analyzed in this paper.

IV. TYPES OF FIRMS

A. Profit-Sharing Firms

Explicit in our explanation of the capitalist firm is the assumption that the cost of *managing* the team's inputs by a central monitor, who disciplines himself because he is a residual claimant, is low relative to the cost of metering the marginal outputs of team members.

If we look within a firm to see who monitors-hires, fires, changes, promotes, and renegotiates-we should find him being a residual claimant or, at least, one whose pay or reward is more than any others correlated with fluctuations in the residual value of the firm. They more likely will have options or rights or bonuses than will inputs with other tasks.

An implicit "auxiliary" assumption of our explanation of the firm is that the cost of team production is increased if the residual claim is not held entirely by the central monitor. That is, we assume that if profit sharing had to be relied upon for *all* team members, losses from the resulting increase in central monitor shirking would exceed the output gains from the increased incentives of other team members not to shirk. If the optimal team size is only two owners of inputs, then an equal division of profits and losses between them will leave each with stronger incentives to reduce shirking than if the optimal team size is large, for in the latter case only a smaller percentage of the losses occasioned by the shirker will be borne by him. Incentives to shirk are positively related to the optimal size of the team under an equal profit-sharing scheme.[10]

The preceding does not imply that profit sharing is never viable. Profit sharing to encourage self-policing is more appropriate for small teams. And, indeed, where input owners are free to make whatever contractual arrangements suit them, as generally is true in capitalist economies, profit sharing seems largely limited to partnerships with a relatively small number of *active* partners.[11] Another advantage of such arrangements for smaller teams is that it permits more effective reciprocal monitoring among inputs. Monitoring need not be entirely specialized.

Profit sharing is more viable if small team size is associated with situations where the cost of specialized management of inputs is large relative to the increased productivity potential in team effort. We conjecture that the cost of managing team inputs increases if the productivity of a team member is difficult to correlate with his behavior. In "artistic" or "professional" work, watching a man's activities is not a good clue to what he is actually thinking or doing with his mind. While it is relatively easy to manage or direct the loading of trucks by a team of dock workers where input activity is so highly related in an obvious way to output, it is more difficult to manage and direct a lawyer in the preparation and presentation of a case. Dock workers can be directed in detail without the monitor himself loading the truck, and assembly line workers can be monitored by varying the speed of the assembly line, but detailed direction in the preparation of a law case would require in much greater degree that the monitor prepare the case himself. As a result, artistic or professional inputs, such as lawyers, advertising specialists, and doctors, will be given relatively freer reign with regard to individual behavior. If the management of inputs is relatively costly, or ineffective, as it would seem to be in these cases, but, nonetheless if team effort is more productive than separable production with exchange across markets, then there will develop a tendency to use profit-sharing schemes to provide incentives to avoid shirking.[12]

---

10 While the degree to which residual claims are centralized will affect the size of the team, this will be only one of many factors that determine team size, so as an approximation, we can treat team size as exogenously determined. Under certain assumptions about the shape of the "typical" utility function, the incentive to avoid shirking with unequal profit-sharing can be measured by the Herfindahl index.

11 The use of the word active will be clarified in our discussion of the corporation, which follows below.

12 Some sharing contracts, like crop sharing, or rental payments based on gross sales in retail stores, come close to profit sharing. However, it is gross output sharing rather than profit sharing. We are unable to specify the implications of the difference. We refer the reader to S. N. Cheung.

B. Socialist Firms

We have analyzed the classical proprietorship and the profit-sharing firms in the context of free association and choice of economic organization. Such organizations need not be the most viable when political constraints limit the forms of organization that can be chosen. It is one thing to have profit sharing when professional or artistic talents are used by small teams. But if political or tax or subsidy considerations induce profit-sharing techniques when these are not otherwise economically justified, then additional management techniques will be developed to help reduce the degree of shirking.

For example, most, if not all, firms in Jugoslavia are owned by the employees in the restricted sense that all share in the residual. This is true for large firms and for firms which employ nonartistic, or nonprofessional, workers as well. With a decay of political constraints, most of these firms could be expected to rely on paid wages rather than shares in the residual. This rests on our auxiliary assumption that general sharing in the residual results in losses from enhanced shirking by the monitor that exceed the gains from reduced shirking by residual-sharing employees. If this were not so, profit sharing with employees should have occurred more frequently in Western societies where such organizations are neither banned nor preferred politically. Where residual sharing by employees is politically imposed, as in Jugoslavia, we are led to expect that some management technique will arise to reduce the shirking by the central monitor, a technique that will not be found frequently in Western societies since the monitor retains all (or much) of the residual in the West and profit sharing is largely confined to small, professional-artistic team production situations. We do find in the larger scale residual-sharing firms in Jugoslavia that there are employee committees that can recommend (to the state) the termination of a manager's contract (veto his continuance) with the enterprise. We conjecture that the workers' committee is given the right to recommend the termination of the manager's contract precisely because the general sharing of the residual increases "excessively" the manager's incentive to shirk.[13]

C. The Corporation

All firms must initially acquire command over some resources. The corporation does so primarily by selling promises of future returns to those who (as creditors or owners) provide financial capital. In some situations resources can be acquired in advance from consumers by promises of future delivery (for example, advance sale of a proposed book). Or where the firm is a few artistic or professional persons, each can "chip in" with time and talent until the sale of services brings in revenues. For the most part, capital can be acquired more cheaply if many (risk-averse)

---

13   Incidentally, investment activity will be changed. The inability to capitalize the investment value as "take-home" proviate property *wealth* of the members of the firm means that the benefits of the investment must be taken as annual income by those who are employed at the time of the income. Investment will be confined more to those with shorter life and with higher rates or pay-offs if the alternative of investing is paying out the firm's income to its employees to take home and use as private property. For a development of this proposition, see the papeis by Eirik Furobotn and Svetozar Pejovich, and by Pejovich.

investors contribute small portions to a large investment. The economies of raising large sums of equity capital in this way suggest that modifications in the relationship among corporate inputs are required to cope with the shirking problem that arises with profit sharing among large numbers of corporate stockholders. One modification is limited liability, especially for firms that are large relative to a stockholder's wealth. It serves to protect stockholders from large losses no matter how they are caused.

If every stock owner participated in each decision in a corporation, not only would large bureaucratic costs be incurred, but many would shirk the task of becoming well informed on the issue to be decided, since the losses associated with unexpectedly bad decisions will be borne in large part by the many other corporate shareholders. More effective control of corporate activity is achieved for most purposes by transferring decision authority to a smaller group, whose main function is to negotiate with and manage (renegotiate with) the other inputs of the team. The corporate stockholders retain the authority to revise the membership of the management group and over major decisions that affect the structure of the corporation or its dissolution.

As a result a new modification of partnerships is induced-the right to sale of corporate shares without approval of any other stockholders. Any shareholder can remove his wealth from control by those with whom he has differences of opinion. Rather than try to control the decisions of the management, which is harder to do with many stockholders than with only a few, unrestricted salability provides a more acceptable escape to each stockholder from continued policies with which he disagrees.

Indeed, the policing of managerial shirking relies on across-market competition from new groups of would-be managers as well as competition from members within the firm who seek to displace existing management. In addition to competition from outside and inside managers, control is facilitated by the temporary congealing of share votes into voting blocs owned by one or a few contenders. Proxy battles or stock-purchases concentrate the votes required to displace the existing management or modify managerial policies. But it is more than a change in policy that is sought by the newly formed financial interests, whether of new stockholders or not. It is the capitalization of expected future benefits into stock prices that concentrates on the innovators the wealth gains of their actions if they own large numbers of shares. Without capitalization of future benefits, there would be less incentive to incur the costs required to exert informed decisive influence on the corporation's policies and managing personnel. Temporarily, the structure of ownership is reformed, moving away from diffused ownership into decisive power blocs, and this is a transient resurgence of the classical firm with power again concentrated in those who have title to the residual.

In assessing the significance of stockholders' power it is not the usual diffusion of voting power that is significant but instead the frequency with which voting congeals into decisive changes. Even a one-man owned company may have a long term with just one manager—continuously being approved by the owner. Similarly a dispersed voting power corporation may be also characterized by a long-lived management. The question is the probability of replacement of the management if it behaves in ways not acceptable to a majority of the stockholders. The unrestricted salability of stock and the transfer of proxies enhances the probability of decisive action in the event current stockholders or any outsider believes that management is not doing a good job with the corporation. We are not comparing the corporate responsiveness to that of a single proprietorship; instead, we are indicating features of the corporate structure that are induced by the problem of delegated authority to manager-monitors.[14]

---

14 Instead of thinking of shareholders as joint *owners*, we can think of them as investors, like bondholders, except that the stockholders are more optimistic than bondholders about the enterprise prospects. Instead of buying bonds in the corporation, thus enjoying smaller risks, shareholders prefer to invest funds with a greater realizable return if the firm prospers as expected, but with smaller (possibly negative) returns if the firm performs in a manner closer to that expected by the more pessimistic investors. The pessimistic investors, in turn, regard only the bonds as likely to pay off.

If the entrepreneur-organizer is to raise capital on the best terms to him, it is to his advantage, as well as that of prospective investors, to recognize these differences in expectations. The residual claim on earnings enjoyed by shareholders does not serve the function of enhancing their efficiency as monitors in the general situation. The stockholders are "merely" the less risk-averse or the more optimistic member of the group that finances the firm. Being more optimistic than the average and seeing a higher mean value future return, they are willing to pay more for a certificate that allows them to realize gain on their expectations. One method of doing so is to buy claims to the distribution of returns that "they see" while bondholders, who are more pessimistic, purchase a claim to the distribution that they see as more likely to emerge. Stockholders are then comparable to warrant holders. They care not about the voting rights (usually not attached to warrants); they are in the same position in so far as voting rights are concerned as are bondholders. The only difference is in the probability distribution of rewards and the terms on which they can place their bets.

If we treat bondholders, preferred and convertible preferred stockholders, and common stockholders and warrant holders as simply different classes of investors—differing not only in their risk averseness but in their beliefs about the probability distribution of the firm's future earnings, why should stockholders be regarded as "owners" in any sense distinct from the other financial investors? The entrepreneur-organizer, who let us assume is the chief operating officer and sole repository of control of the corporation, does not find his authority residing in common stockholders (except in the case of a take over). Does this type of control make any difference in the way the firm is conducted? Would it make any difference in the kinds of behavior that would be tolerated by competing managers and investors (and we here deliberately refrain from thinking of them as owner-stockholders in the traditional sense)?

Investment old timers recall a significant incidence of nonvoting common stock, now prohibited in corporations whose stock is traded on listed exchanges. (Why prohibited?) The entrepreneur in those days could hold voting shares while investors held nonvoting shares, which in every other respect were identical. Nonvoting share holders were simply investors devoid of ownership connotations. The control and behavior of inside owners in such corporations has never, so far as we have ascertained, been carefully studied. For example, at the simplest level of interest, does the evidence indicate that nonvoting shareholders fared any worse because of not having voting rights? Did owners permit the nonvoting holders the normal return available to voting shareholders? Though evidence is prohibitively expensive to obtain, it is remarkable that voting and nonvoting shares sold for essentially identical prices, even during some proxy battles. However, our casual evidence deserves no more than interest-initiating weight.

One more point. The facade is deceptive. Instead of nonvoting shares, today we have warrants, convertible preferred stocks all of which are solely or partly "equity" claims without voting rights, though they could be converted into voting shares.

In sum, is it the case that the stockholder-investor relationship is one emanating from the *division* of *ownership* among several people, or is it that the collection of investment funds from people of varying anticipations is the underlying factor? If the latter, why should any of them be thought of as the owners in whom voting rights, whatever they may signify or however exercisable, should reside in order to enhance efficiency? Why voting rights in any of the outside, participating investors?

D. Mutual and Nonprofit Firms

The benefits obtained by the new management are greater if the stock can be purchased and sold, because this enables capitalization of anticipated future improvements into present *wealth* of new managers who bought stock and created a larger capital by their management changes. But in nonprofit corporations, colleges, churches, country clubs, mutual savings banks, mutual insurance companies, and "coops," the future consequences of improved management are not capitalized into present wealth of stockholders. (As if to make more difficult that competition by new would-be monitors, multiple shares of ownership in those enterprises cannot be bought by one person.) One should, therefore, find greater shirking in nonprofit, mutually owned enterprises. (This suggests that nonprofit enterprises are especially appropriate in realms of endeavor where more shirking is desired and where redirected uses of the enterprise in response to market-revealed values is less desired.)

E. Partnerships

Team production in artistic or professional intellectual skills will more likely be by partnerships than other types of team production. This amounts to market-organized team activity and to a nonemployer status. Self-monitoring partnerships, therefore, will be used rather than employer-employee contracts, and these organizations will be small to prevent an excessive dilution of efforts through shirking. Also, partnerships are more likely to occur among relatives or long-standing acquaintances, not necessarily because they share a common utility function, but also because each knows better the other's work characteristics and tendencies to shirk.

F. Employee Unions

Employee unions, whatever else they do, perform as monitors for employees. Employers monitor employees and similarly employees monitor an employer's performance. Are correct wages paid on time and in good currency? Usually, this is extremely easy to check. But some forms of employer performance are less easy to meter and are more subject to employer shirking. Fringe benefits often are in nonpecuniary, contingent form; medical, hospital, and accident insurance, and retirement pensions are contingent payments or performances partly in *kind* by employers to employees. Each employee cannot judge the character of such payments as easily as money wages. Insurance is a contingent payment-what the employee will get upon the contingent event may come as a disappointment. If he could easily determine what other employees had gotten

---

Our initial perception of this possibly significant difference in interpretation was precipitated by Henry Manne. A reading of his paper makes it clear that it is hard to understand why an investor who wishes to back and "share" in the consequences of some new business should necessarily have to acquire voting power (i.e., power to change the manager-operator) in order to invest in the venture. In fact, we invest in some ventures in the hope that no other stockholders will be so "foolish" as to try to toss out the incumbent management. We want him to have the power to stay in office, and for the prospect of sharing in his fortunes we buy nonvoting common stock. Our willingness to invest is enhanced by the knowledge that we can act legally via fraud, embezzlement and other laws to help assure that we outside investors will not be "milked" beyond our initial discounted anticipations

upon such contingent events he could judge more accurately the performance by the employer. He could "trust" the employer not to shirk in such fringe contingent payments, but he would prefer an effective and economic monitor of those payments. We see a specialist monitor-the union employees' agent-hired by them and monitoring those aspects of employer payment most difficult for the employees to monitor. Employees should be willing to employ a specialist monitor to administer such hard-to-detect employer performance, even though their monitor has incentives to use pension and retirement funds not entirely for the benefit of employees.

V. TEAM SPIRIT AND LOYALTY

Every team member would prefer a team in which no one, not even himself, shirked. Then the true marginal costs and values could be equated to achieve more preferred positions. If one could enhance a common interest in nonshirking in the guise of a team loyalty or team spirit, the team would be more efficient. In those sports where team activity is most clearly exemplified, the sense of loyalty and team spirit is most strongly urged. Obviously the team is better, with team spirit and loyalty, because of the reduced shirking—not because of some other feature inherent in loyalty or spirit as such.[15]

Corporations and business firms try to instill a spirit of loyalty. This should not be viewed simply as a device to increase profits by over-working or misleading the employees, nor as an

---

15 *Sports Leagues*: Professional sports contests among teams is typically conducted by a league of teams. We assume that sports consumers are interested not only in absolute sporting skill but also in skills relative to other teams. Being slightly better than opposing teams enables one to claim a major portion of the receipts; the inferior team does not release resources and reduce costs, since they were expected in the play of contest. Hence, absolute skill is developed beyond the equality of marginal investment in sporting skill with its true social marginal value product. It follows there will be a tendency to overinvest in training athletes and developing teams. "Reverse shirking" arises, as budding players are induced to overpractice hyperactively relative to the social marginal value of their enhanced skills. To prevent overinvestment, the teams seek an agreement with each other to restrict practice, size of teams, and even pay of the team members (which reduces incentives of young people to overinvest in developing skills). Ideally, if all the contestant teams were owned by one owner, overinvestment in sports would be avoided, much as ownership of common fisheries or underground oil or water reserve would prevent overinvestment. This hyperactivity (to suggest the opposite of shirking) is controlled by the league of teams, wherein the league adopts a common set of constraints on each team's behavior. In effect, the teams are no longer really owned by the team owners but are supervised by them, much as the franchisers of some product. They are not full-fledged owners of their business, including the brand name, and can not "do what they wish" as franchises. Comparable to the franchiser, is the league commissioner or conference president, who seeks to restrain hyperactivity, as individual team supervisors compete with each other and cause external diseconomies. Such restraints are usually regarded as anticompetitive, anti-social, collusive-cartel devices to restrain free open competition, and reduce players' salaries. However, the interpretation presented here is premised on an attempt to avoid hyperinvestment in team sports production. Of course, the team operators have an incentive, once the league is formed and restraints are placed on hyperinvestment activity, to go further and obtain the private benefits of monopoly restriction. To what extent overinvestment is replaced by monopoly restriction is not yet determinable; nor have we seen an empirical test of these two competing, but mutually consistent interpretations. (This interpretation of league-sports activity was proposed by Earl Thompson and formulated by Michael Canes.) Again, athletic teams clearly exemplify the specialization of monitoring with captains and coaches; a captain detects shirkers while the coach trains and selects strategies and tactics. Both functions may be centralized in one person.

adolescent urge for belonging. It promotes a closer approximation to the employees' potentially available true rates of substitution between production and leisure and enables each team member to achieve a more preferred situation. The difficulty, of course, is to create economically that team spirit and loyalty. It can be preached with an aura of moral code of conduct a morality with literally the same basis as the ten commandments to restrict our conduct toward what we would choose if we bore our full costs.

VI. KINDS OF INPUTS OWNED BY THE FIRM

To this point the discussion has examined why firms, as we have defined them, exist? That is, why is there an owner-employer who is the common party to contracts with other owners of inputs in team activity? The answer to that question should also indicate the kind of the jointly used resources likely to be owned by the central-owner-monitor and the kind likely to be hired from people who are not team-owners. Can we identify characteristics or features of various inputs that lead to their being hired or to their being owned by the firm?

How can residual-claimant, central-employer-owner demonstrate ability to pay the other hired inputs the promised amount in the event of a loss? He can pay in advance or he can commit wealth sufficient to cover negative residuals. The latter will take the form of machines, land, buildings, or raw materials committed to the firm. Commitments of labor wealth (i.e., human wealth) given the property rights in people, is less feasible. These considerations suggest that residual claimants owners of the firm will be investors of resalable capital equipment in the firm. The goods or inputs more likely to be invested, than rented, by the owners of the enterprise, will have higher resale values relative to the initial cost and will have longer expected use in a firm relative to the economic life of the good.

But beyond these factors are those developed above to explain the existence of the institution known as the firm the costs of detecting output performance. When a durable resource is used it will have a marginal product and a depreciation. Its use requires payment to cover at least use-induced depreciation; unless that user cost is specifically detectable, payment for it will be demanded in accord with *expected* depreciation. And we can ascertain circumstances for each. An indestructible hammer with a readily detectable marginal product has zero user cost. But suppose the hammer were destructible and that careless (which is easier than careful) use is more abusive and causes greater depreciation of the hammer. Suppose in addition the abuse is easier to detect by observing the way it is used than by observing only the hammer after its use, or by measuring the output scored from a hammer by a laborer. If the hammer were rented and used in the absence of the owner, the depreciation would be greater than if the use were observed by the owner and the user charged in accord with the imposed depreciation. (Careless use is more likely than careful use-if one does not pay for the greater depreciation.) An absentee owner would therefore ask for a higher rental price because of the higher *expected* user cost than if the item were used by the owner. The expectation is higher because of the greater difficulty of observing specific user cost, by inspection of the hammer after use. Renting is therefore in this case more costly than owner use. This is the valid content of the misleading expressions about ownership being more economical than renting ignoring all other factors that may work in the opposite direction, like tax provision, short-term occupancy and capital risk avoidance.

Better examples are tools of the trade. Watch repairers, engineers, and carpenters tend to own their own tools especially if they are portable. Trucks are more likely to be employee owned rather than other equally expensive team inputs because it is relatively cheap for the driver to police the care taken in using a truck. Policing the use of trucks by a nondriver owner is more likely to occur for trucks that are not specialized to one driver, like public transit busses.

The factor with which we are concerned here is one related to the costs of monitoring not only the gross product performance of an input but also the abuse or depreciation inflicted on the input in the course of its use. If depreciation or user cost is more cheaply detected when the owner can see its use than by only seeing the input before and after, there is a force toward owner use rather than renting. Resources whose user cost is harder to detect when used by someone else, tend on this count to be owner-used. Absentee ownership, in the lay language, will be less likely. Assume momentarily that labor service cannot be performed in the absence of its owner. The labor owner can more cheaply monitor any abuse of himself than if somehow labor-services could be provided without the labor owner observing its mode of use or knowing what was happening. Also his incentive to abuse himself is increased if he does not own himself.[16]

The similarity between the preceding analysis and the question of absentee landlordism and of sharecropping arrangements is no accident. The same factors which explain the contractual arrangements known as a firm help to explain the incidence of tenancy, labor hiring or sharecropping.[17]

---

16 Professional athletes in baseball, football, and basketball, where athletes having sold their source of service to the team owners upon entering into sports activity, are owned by team owners. Here the team owners must monitor the athletes' physical condition and behavior to protect the team owners' wealth. The athlete has less (not, no) incentive to protect or enhance his athletic prowess since capital value changes have less impact on his own wealth and more on the team owners. Thus, some athletes sign up for big initial bonuses (representing present capital value of future services). Future salaries are lower by the annuity value of the prepaid "bonus" and hence the athlete has less to lose by subsequent abuse of his athletic prowess. Any decline in his subsequent service value would in part be borne by the team owner who owns the players' future service. This does not say these losses of future salaries have no effect on preservation of athletic talent (we are not making a "sunk cost" error). Instead, we assert that the preservation is reduced, not eliminated, because the amount of loss of wealth suffered is smaller. The athlete will spend less to maintain or enhance his prowess thereafter. The effect of this revised incentive system is evidenced in comparisons of the kinds of attention and care imposed on the athletes at the "expense of the team owner" in the case where athletes' future services are owned by the team owner with that where future labor service values are owned by the athlete himself. Why athletes' future athletic services are owned by the team owners rather than being hired is a question we should be able to answer. One presumption is cartelization and monopsony gains to team owners. Another is exactly the theory being expounded in this paper-costs of monitoring production of athletes; we know not on which to rely.

17 The analysis used by Cheung in explaining the prevalence of sharecropping and land tenancy arrangements is built squarely on the same factors-the costs of detecting output performance of jointly used inputs in team production and the costs of detecting user costs imposed on the various inputs if owner used or if rented.

VII. FIRMS AS A SPECIALIZED MARKET INSTITUTION FOR COLLECTING, COLLATING, AND SELLING INPUT INFORMATION

The firm serves as a highly specialized surrogate market. Any person contemplating a joint-input activity must search and detect the qualities of available joint inputs. He could contact an employment agency, but that agency in a small town would have little advantage over a large firm with many inputs. The employer, by virtue of monitoring many inputs, acquires special superior information about their productive talents. This aids his *directive* (i.e., market hiring) efficiency. He "sells" his information to employee-inputs as he aids them in ascertaining good input combinations for team activity. Those who work as employees or who rent services to him are using him to discern superior combinations of inputs. Not only does the director-employer "decide" what each input will produce, he also estimates which heterogeneous inputs will work together jointly more efficiently, and he does this in the context of a privately owned market for forming teams. The department store is a firm and is a superior private market. People who shop and work in one town can as well shop and work in a privately owned firm.

This marketing function is obscured in the theoretical literature by the assumption of homogeneous factors. Or it is tacitly left for individuals to do themselves via personal market search, much as if a person had to search without benefit of specialist retailers. Whether or not the firm arose because of this efficient information service, it gives the director-employer more knowledge about the productive talents of the team's inputs, and a basis for superior decisions about efficient or profitable combinations of those heterogeneous resources.

In other words, opportunities for profitable team production by inputs already within the firm may be ascertained more economically and accurately than for resources outside the firm. Superior combinations of inputs can be more economically identified and formed from resources already used in the organization than by obtaining new resources (and knowledge of them) from the outside. Promotion and revision of employee assignments (contracts) will be preferred by a firm to the hiring of new inputs. To the extent that this occurs there is reason to expect the firm to be able to operate as a conglomerate rather than persist in producing a single product. Efficient production with heterogeneous resources is a result not of having *better* resources but in *knowing more accurately* the relative productive performances of those resources. Poorer resources can be paid less in accord with their inferiority; greater accuracy of knowledge of the potential and actual productive actions of inputs rather than having high productivity resources makes a firm (or an assignment of inputs) profitable.[18]

---

18   According to our interpretation, the firm is a specialized surrogate for a market for team use of inputs; it provides superior (i.e., cheaper) collection and collation of knowledge about heterogeneous resources. The greater the set of inputs about which knowledge of performance is being collated within a firm the greater are the present costs of the collation activity. Then, the larger the firm (market) the greater the attenuation of monitor control. To counter this force, the firm will be divisionalized in ways that economize on those costs—just as will the market be specialized. So far as we can ascertain, other theories of the reasons for firms have no such implications.

In Japan, employees by custom work nearly their entire lives with one firm, and the firm agrees to that expectation. Firms will tend to be large and conglomerate to enable a broader scope of input revision. Each firm is, in effect, a small economy engaging in "intranational and international" trade. Analogously, Americans expect to spend their whole lives in the United States, and the bigger the country, in terms of variety of resources, the easier it is to adjust

VIII. SUMMARY

While ordinary contracts facilitate efficient specialization according to comparative advantage, a special class of contracts among a group of joint inputs to a team production process is commonly used for team production. Instead of multilateral contracts among all the joint inputs' owners, a central common party to a set of bilateral contracts facilitates efficient organization of the joint inguts in team production. The terms of the contracts form the basis of the entity called the firm—especially appropriate for organizing team production processes.

Team productive activity is that in which a union, or joint use, of inputs yields a larger output than the sum of the products of the separately used inputs. This team production requires—like all other production processes—an assessment of marginal productivities if efficient production is to be achieved. Nonseparability of the products of several differently owned joint inputs raises the cost of assessing the marginal productivities of those resources or services of each input owner. Monitoring or metering the productivities to match marginal productivities to costs of inputs and thereby to reduce shirking can be achieved more economically (than by across market bilateral negotiations among inputs) in a firm.

The essence of the classical firm is identified here as a contractual structure with: 1) joint input production; 2) several input owners; 3) one party who is common to all the contracts of the joint inputs; 4) who has rights to renegotiate any input's contract independently of contracts with other input owners; 5) who holds the residual claim; and 6) who has the right to sell his central contractual residual status. The central agent is called the firm's owner and the employer. No authoritarian control is involved; the arrangement is simply a contractual structure subject to continuous renegotiation with the central agent. The contractual structure arises as a means of enhancing efficient organization of team production. In particular, the ability to detect shirking among owners of jointly used inputs in team production is enhanced (detection costs are reduced) by this arrangement and the discipline (by revision of contracts) of input owners is made more economic.

Testable implications are suggested by the analysis of different types of organizations -nonprofit, proprietary for profit, unions, cooperatives, partnerships, and by the kinds of inputs that tend to be owned by the firm in contrast to those employed by the firm.

We conclude with a highly conjectural but possibly significant interpretation. As a consequence of the flow of information to the central party (employer), the firm takes on the characteristic of an efficient market in that information about the productive characteristics of a large set of specific inputs is now more cheaply available. Better recombinations or new uses of resources can be more efficiently ascertained than by the conventional search through the general market. In this sense inputs compete with each other within and via a firm rather than solely across markets as conventionally conceived. Emphasis on interfirm competition obscures intrafirm competition among inputs. Conceiving competition as the *revelation and exchange* of knowledge or information about qualities, potential uses of different inputs in different

---

to changing tastes and circumstances. Japan, with its lifetime employees, should be characterized more by large, conglomerate firms. Presumably, at some size of the firm, specialized knowledge about inputs becomes as expensive to transmit across divisions of the firms as it does across markets to other firms.

potential applications indicates that the firm is a device for enchancing competition among sets of input resources as well as a device for more efficiently rewarding the inputs. In contrast to markets and cities which can be viewed as publicly or nonowned market places, the firm can be considered a privately owned market; if so, we could consider the firm and the ordinary market as competing types of markets, competition between private proprietary markets and public or communal markets. Could it be that the market suffers from the defects of communal property rights in organizing and influencing uses of valuable resources?

REFERENCES

M. Canes, "A Model of a Sports League," unpublished doctoral dissertation, UCLA 1970.

S. N. Cheung, *The Theory of Share Tenancy*, Chicago 1969.

R. H. Coase, "The Nature of the Firm," *Economica*, Nov. 1937, 4, 386–405; reprinted in G. J. Stigler and K. Boulding, eds., *Readings in Price Theory*, Homewood 1952, 331–51.

E. Furobotn and S. Pejovich, "Property Rights and the Behavior of the Firm in a Socialist State," *Zeitschrift für Nationalokonomie*, 1970, 30, 431–454.

F. H. Knight, *Risk, Uncertainty and Profit*, New York 1965.

S. Macaulay, "Non-Contractual Relations in Business: A Preliminary Study," *Amer. Sociological Rev.*, 1968, 28, 55–69.

H. B. Malmgren, "Information, Expectations and the Theory of the Firm," *Quart J. Econ.*, Aug. 1961, 75, 399–421.

H. Manne, "Our Two Corporation Systems: Law and Economics," *Virginia Law Rev.*, Mar. 1967, 53, No. 2, 259–84.

S. Pejovich, "The Firm, Monetary Policy and Property Rights in a Planned Economy," *Western Econ. J.*, Sept. 1969, 7, 193–200.

M. Silver and R. Auster, "Entrepreneurship, Profit, and the Limits on Firm Size," *J. Bus. Univ. Chicago*, Apr. 1969, 42, 277–81.

E. A. Thompson, "Nonpecuniary Rewards and the Aggregate Production Function," *Rev. Econ. Statist.*, Nov. 1970, 52, 395–404.

SECTION SEVEN

Competition and Monopoly

Antitrust

By Alan Greenspan

Memo To: SSU Students on summer break
From: Jude Wanniski
Re: Guest Lecture

(Based on a paper given at the Antitrust Seminar of the National Association of Business Economists, Cleveland, September 25, 1961. Published by Nathaniel Branden Institute, New York, 1962.)

T HE WORLD OF antitrust is reminiscent of Alice's Wonderland: everything seemingly is, yet apparently isn't, simultaneously. It is a world in which competition is lauded as the basic axiom and guiding principle, yet "too much" competition is condemned as "cutthroat." It is a world in which actions designed to limit competition are branded as criminal when taken by businessmen, yet praised as "enlightened" when initiated by the government. It is a world in which the law is so vague that businessmen have no way of knowing whether specific actions will be declared illegal until they hear the judge's verdict—after the fact.

In view of the confusion, contradictions, and legalistic hairsplitting which characterize the realm of antitrust, I submit that the entire antitrust system must be opened for review. It is necessary to ascertain and to estimate: (a) the historical roots of the antitrust laws, and (b) the economic theories upon which these laws were based.

Americans have always feared the concentration of arbitrary power in the hands of politicians. Prior to the Civil War, few attributed such power to businessmen. It was recognized that government officials had the legal power to compel obedience by the use of physical force—and that businessmen had no such power. A businessman needed customers. He had to appeal to their self-interest.

This appraisal of the issue changed rapidly in the immediate aftermath of the Civil War, particularly with the coming of the railroad age. Outwardly, the railroads did not have the backing of legal force. But to the farmers of the West, the railroads seemed to hold the arbitrary power previously ascribed solely to the government. The railroads appeared unhampered by the laws of competition. They seemed able *to* charge rates calculated *to* keep the fanners in seed grain—no higher, no lower. The farmer's protest took the form of the National Grange movement, the organization responsible for the passage of the Interstate Commerce Act of 1887.

The industrial giants, such as Rockefeller's Standard Oil Trust, which were rising during this period, were also alleged to be immune from competition, from the law of supply and demand. The public reaction against the trusts culminated in the Sherman Act of 1890.

It was claimed then—as it is still claimed today—that business, if left free, would necessarily develop into an institution vested with arbitrary power. Is this assertion valid? Did the post-Civil War period give birth to a new form of arbitrary power? Or did the government remain the source of such power, with business merely providing a new avenue through which it could be exercised? This is the crucial historical question.

The railroads developed in the East, prior to the Civil War, in stiff competition with one another as well as with the older forms of transportation—barges, riverboats, and wagons. By the 1860's there arose a political clamor demanding that the railroads move west and tie California to the nation: national prestige was held to be at stake. But the traffic volume outside of the populous East was insufficient to draw commercial transportation westward. The potential profit did not warrant the heavy cost of investment in transportation facilities. In the name of "Public policy" it was, therefore, decided to subsidize the railroads in their move to the West.

Between 1863 and 1867, close to one hundred million acres of public lands were granted to the railroads. Since these grants were made to individual roads, no competing railroads could vie for traffic in the same area in the West. Meanwhile, the alternative forms of competition (wagons, riverboats, etc.) could not afford to challenge the railroads in the West. Thus, with the aid of the federal government, a segment of the railroad industry was able to "break free" from the competitive bounds which had prevailed in the East.

As might be expected, the subsidies attracted the kind of promoters who always exist on the fringe of the business community and who are constantly seeking an "easy deal." Many of the new western railroads were shabbily built: they were not constructed to carry traffic, but to acquire land grants. The western railroads were true monopolies in the textbook sense of the word. They could, and did, behave with an aura of arbitrary power. But that power was not derived from a free market. It stemmed from governmental subsidies and governmental restrictions.

When, ultimately, western traffic increased to levels which could support other profit-making transportation carriers, the railroads' monopolistic power was soon undercut. In spite of their initial privileges, they were unable to withstand the pressure of free competition. In the meantime, however, an ominous turning point had taken place in our economic history: the Interstate Commerce Act of 1887. That Act was not necessitated by the "evils" of the free market. Like subsequent legislation controlling business, the Act was an attempt to remedy the economic distortions which prior government interventions had created, but which were blamed on the free market. The Interstate Commerce Act, in turn, produced new distortions in the structure and finances of the railroads. Today, it is proposed that these distortions be corrected by means of further subsidies. The railroads are on the verge of final collapse, yet no one challenges the original misdiagnosis to discover—and correct—the actual cause of their illness.

To interpret the railroad history of the nineteenth century as "proof" of the failure of a free market, is a disastrous error. The same error—which persists to this day—was the nineteenth century's fear of the "trusts." The most formidable of the "trusts" was Standard Oil. Nevertheless, at the time of the passage of the Sherman Act, a pre-automotive period, the entire petroleum industry amounted to less than one percent of the Gross National Product and was barely one-third as large as the shoe industry. It was not the absolute size of the trusts, but their dominance within their own industries that gave rise to apprehension. What the observers failed to grasp, however, was the fact that the control by Standard Oil, at the turn of the century, of more than eighty percent of refining capacity made economic sense and accelerated the growth of the American economy.

Such control yielded obvious gains in efficiency, through the integration of divergent refining, marketing, and pipeline operations; it also made the raising of capital easier and cheaper. Trusts came into existence because they were the most efficient units in those industries which, being relatively new, were too small to support more than one large company.

Historically, the general development of industry has taken the following course: an industry begins with a few small firms; in time, many of them merge; this increases efficiency and augments profits. As the market expands, new firms enter the field, thus cutting down the share of the market held by the dominant firm. This has been the pattern in steel, oil, aluminum, containers, and numerous other major industries. The observable tendency of an industry's dominant companies eventually to lose part of their share of the market, is not caused by antitrust legislation, but by the fact that it is difficult to prevent new firms from entering the field when the demand for a certain product increases. Texaco and Gulf, for example, would have grown into large firms even if the original Standard Oil Trust had not been dissolved. Similarly, the United States Steel Corporation's dominance of the steel industry half a century ago would have been eroded with or without the Sherman Act.

It takes extraordinary skill to hold more than fifty percent of a large industry's market in a free economy. It requires unusual productive ability, unfailing business judgment, unrelenting effort at the continuous improvement of one's product and technique. The rare company which is able to retain its share of the market year after year and decade after decade does so by means of productive efficiency—and deserves praise, not condemnation.

The Sherman Act may be understandable when viewed as a projection of the nineteenth century's fear and economic ignorance. But it is utter nonsense in the context of today's economic knowledge. The seventy additional years of observing industrial development should have taught us something. If the attempts to justify our antitrust statutes on historical grounds are erroneous and rest on a misinterpretation of history, the attempts to justify them on theoretical grounds come from a still more fundamental misconception.

In the early days of the United States, Americans enjoyed a large measure of economic freedom. Each individual was free to produce what he chose, and sell to whomever he chose, at a price mutually agreed upon. If two competitors concluded that it was to their mutual self-interest to set joint price policies, they were free to do so. If a customer requested a rebate in exchange for his business, a firm (usually a railroad) could comply or deny as it saw fit.

According to classical economics, which had a profound influence on the nineteenth century, competition would keep the economy in balance.

But while many theories of the classical economists—such as their description of the working of a free economy—were valid, their concept of competition was ambiguous and led to confusion in the minds of their followers. It was understood to mean that competition consists merely of producing and selling the maximum possible, like a robot, passively accepting the market price as a law of nature, never making any attempt to influence the conditions of the market.

The businessmen of the latter half of the nineteenth century, however, aggressively attempted to affect the conditions of their markets by advertising, varying production rates, and bargaining on price with suppliers and customers. Many observers assumed that these activities were incompatible with the classical theory. They concluded that competition was no longer working effectively. In the sense in which they understood competition, it had never worked or existed, except possibly in some isolated agricultural markets. But in a meaningful sense of the word, competition did, and does, exist-in the nineteenth century as well as today.

"Competition" is an active, not a passive, noun. It applies to the entire sphere of economic activity, not merely to production, but also to trade; it implies the necessity of taking action to affect the conditions of the market in one's own favor. The error of the nineteenth-century observers was that they restricted a wide abstraction—competition—to a narrow set of particulars, to the "passive" competition projected by their own interpretation of classical economics. As a result, they concluded that the alleged "failure" of this fictitious "passive competition" negated the entire theoretical structure of classical economics, including the demonstration of the fact that laissez-faire is the most efficient and productive of all possible economic systems. They concluded that a free market, by its nature, leads to its own destruction—and they came to the grotesque contradiction of attempting to preserve the freedom of the market by government controls, i.e., to preserve the benefits of laissez-faire by abrogating it.

The crucial question which they failed to ask is whether "active" competition does inevitably lead to the establishment of coercive monopolies, as they supposed—or whether a laissez-faire economy of "active" competition has a built-in regulator that protects and preserves it. That is the question which we must now examine.

A "coercive monopoly" is a business concern that can set its prices and production policies independent of the market, with immunity from competition, from the law of supply and demand. An economy dominated by such monopolies would be rigid and stagnant. The necessary precondition of a coercive monopoly is closed entry—the barring of all competing producers from a given field. This can be accomplished only by an act of government intervention, in the form of special regulations, subsidies, or franchises. Without government assistance, it is impossible for a would-be monopolist to set and maintain his prices and production policies independent of the rest of the economy. For if he attempted to set his prices and production at a level that would yield profits to new entrants significantly above those available in other fields, competitors would be sure to invade his industry.

The ultimate regulator of competition in a free economy is the capital market. So long as capital is free to flow, it will tend to seek those areas which offer the maximum rate of return.

The potential investor of capital does not merely consider the actual rate of return earned by companies within a specific industry. His decision concerning where to invest depends on what he himself could earn in that particular line. The existing profit rates within an industry are calculated in terms of existing costs. He has to consider the fact that a new entrant might not be able to achieve at once as low a cost structure as that of experienced producers.

Therefore, the existence of a free capital market does not guarantee that a monopolist who enjoys high profits will necessarily and immediately find himself confronted by competition. What it does guarantee is that a monopolist whose high profits are caused by high prices, rather than low costs, will soon meet competition originated by the capital market.

The capital market acts as a regulator of prices, not necessarily of profits. It leaves an individual producer free to earn as much as he can by lowering his costs and by increasing his efficiency relative to others. Thus, it constitutes the mechanism that generates greater incentives to increased productivity and leads, as a consequence, to a rising standard of living.

The history of the Aluminum Company of America prior to World War II illustrates the process. Envisaging its self-interest and long-term profitability in terms of a growing market, ALCOA kept the price of primary aluminum at a level compatible with the maximum expansion of its Market. At such a price level, however, profits were forthcoming only by means of tremendous efforts to step up efficiency and productivity. ALCOA was a monopoly—the only producer of primary aluminum—but it was not a coercive monopoly, i.e., it could not set its price and production policies independent of the competitive world. In fact, only because the company stressed cost-cutting and efficiency, rather than raising prices, was it able to maintain its position as sole producer of primary aluminum for so long. Had ALCOA attempted to increase its profits by raising prices, it soon would have found itself competing with new entrants in the primary aluminum business.

In analyzing the competitive processes of a laissez-faire economy, one must recognize that capital outlays (investments in new plant and equipment either by existing producers or new entrants) are not determined solely by current profits. An investment is made or not made depending upon the estimated discounted present worth of expected future profits. Consequently, the issue of whether or not a new competitor will enter a hitherto monopolistic industry, is determined by his expected future returns. The present worth of the discounted expected future profits of a given industry is represented by the market price of the common stock of the companies in that industry. If the price of a particular company's stock (or an average for a particular industry) rises, the move implies a higher present worth for expected future earnings.

Statistical evidence demonstrates the correlation between stock prices and capital outlays, not only for industry as a whole, but also within major industry groups. Moreover, the time between the fluctuations of stock prices and the corresponding fluctuations of capital expenditures is rather short, a fact which implies that the process of relating new capital investments to profit expectations is relatively fast. If such a correlation works as well as it does, considering today's governmental impediments to the free movement of capital, one must conclude that in a completely free market the process would be much more efficient.

The churning of a nation's capital, in a fully free economy, would be continuously pushing capital into profitable areas—and this would effectively control the competitive price and

production policies of business firms, making a coercive monopoly impossible to maintain. It is only in a so-called mixed economy that a coercive monopoly can flourish, protected from the discipline of the capital markets by franchises, subsidies, and special privileges from governmental regulators.

To sum up: The entire structure of antitrust statutes in this country is a jumble of economic irrationality and ignorance. It is the product: (a) of a gross misinterpretation of history, and (b) of rather naive, and certainly unrealistic, economic theories.

As a last resort, some people argue that at least the antitrust laws haven't done any harm. They assert that even though the competitive process itself inhibits coercive monopolies, there is no harm in making doubly sure by declaring certain economic actions to be illegal.

But the very existence of those undefinable statutes and contradictory case law inhibits businessmen from undertaking what would otherwise be sound productive ventures. No one will ever know what new products, processes, machines, and cost-saving mergers failed to come into existence, killed by the Sherman Act before they were born. No one can ever compute the price that all of us have paid for that Act which, by inducing less effective use of capital, has kept our standard of living lower than would otherwise have been possible.

No speculation, however, is required to assess the injustice and the damage to the careers, reputations, and lives of business executives jailed under the antitrust laws. Those who allege that the purpose of the antitrust laws is to protect competition, enterprise, and efficiency, need to be reminded of the following quotation from Judge Learned Hand's indictment of ALCOA's so-called monopolistic practices:

It was not inevitable that it should always anticipate increases in the demand for ingot and be prepared to supply them. Nothing compelled it to keep doubling and redoubling its capacity before others entered the field. It insists that it never excluded competitors; but we can think of no more effective exclusion than progressively to embrace each new opportunity as it opened, and to face every newcomer with new capacity already geared into a great organization, having the advantage of experience, trade connections and the elite of personnel.

ALCOA is being condemned for being too successful, too efficient, and too good a competitor. Whatever damage the antitrust laws may have done to our economy, whatever distortions of the structure of the nation's capital they may have created, these are less disastrous than the fact that the effective purpose, the hidden intent, and the actual practice of the antitrust laws in the United States have led to the condemnation of the productive and efficient members of our society because they are productive and efficient.

Antitrust

By Fred S. McChesney

ORIGINS

BEFORE 1890, THE only "antitrust" law was the common law. Contracts that allegedly restrained trade (e.g., price-fixing agreements) often were not legally enforceable, but they did not subject the parties to any legal sanctions, either. Nor were monopolies illegal. Economists generally believe that monopolies and other restraints of trade are bad because they usually reduce total output, and therefore the overall economic well-being for producers and consumers (see monopoly). Indeed, the term "restraint of trade" indicates exactly why economists dislike monopolies and cartels. But the law itself did not penalize monopolies. The Sherman Act of 1890 changed all that by outlawing cartelization (every "contract, combination … or conspiracy" that was "in restraint of trade") and monopolization (including attempts to monopolize).

The Sherman Act defines neither the practices that constitute restraints of trade nor monopolization. The second important antitrust statute, the Clayton Act, passed in 1914, is somewhat more specific. It outlaws, for example, certain types of price discrimination (charging different prices to different buyers), "tying" (making someone who wants to buy good A buy good B as well), and mergers—but only when the effects of these practices "may be substantially to lessen competition or to tend to create a monopoly." The Clayton Act also authorizes private antitrust suits and triple damages, and exempts labor organizations from the antitrust laws.

Economists did not lobby for, or even support, the antitrust statutes. Rather, the passage of such laws is generally ascribed to the influence of populist "muckrakers" such as Ida Tarbell, who frequently decried the supposed ability of emerging corporate giants ("the trusts") to increase prices and exploit customers by reducing production. One reason most economists were indifferent to the law was their belief that any higher prices achieved by the supposed anticompetitive acts were more than outweighed by the price reducing effects of greater operating efficiency and lower costs. Interestingly, Tarbell herself conceded, as did "trustbuster" Teddy Roosevelt, that the trusts might be more efficient producers.

Only recently have economists looked at the empirical evidence (what has happened in the real world) to see whether the antitrust laws were needed. The popular view that cartels and monopolies were rampant at the turn of the century now seems incorrect to most economists.

Thomas DiLorenzo (1985) has shown that the trusts against which the Sherman Act supposedly was directed were, in fact, expanding output many times faster than overall production was increasing nationwide; likewise, the trusts' prices were falling faster than those of all enterprises nationally. In other words, the trusts were doing exactly the opposite of what economic theory says a monopoly or cartel must do to reap monopoly profits.

ANTICOMPETITIVE PRACTICES

In referring to contracts "in restraint of trade," or to arrangements whose effects "may be substantially to lessen competition or to tend to create a monopoly," the principal antitrust statutes are relatively vague. There is little statutory guidance for distinguishing benign from malign practices. Thus, judges have been left to decide which practices run afoul of the antitrust laws.

An important judicial question has been whether a practice should be treated as "per se illegal" (i.e., devoid of redeeming justification, and thus automatically outlawed) or whether it should be judged by a "rule of reason" (its legality depends on how it is used and on its effects in particular situations).

To answer such questions, judges sometimes have turned to economists for guidance. In the early years of antitrust, though, economists were of little help. They had not extensively analyzed arrangements such as tying, information sharing, resale price maintenance, and other commercial practices challenged in antitrust suits. But as the cases exposed areas of economic ignorance or confusion about different commercial arrangements, economists turned to solving the various puzzles.

Indeed, analyzing the efficiency rationale for practices attacked in antitrust litigation has dominated the intellectual agenda of economists who study what is called industrial organization. Initially, economists concluded that unfamiliar commercial arrangements that were not explicable in a model of perfect competition must be anticompetitive. In the past forty years, however, economic evaluations of various practices have changed. Economists now see that the perfect competition model relies on assumptions—such as everyone having perfect information and zero transaction costs—that are inappropriate for analyzing real-world production and distribution problems.

The use of more sophisticated assumptions in their models has led economists to conclude that many practices previously deemed suspect are not typically anticompetitive. This change in evaluations has been reflected in the courts. Per se liability has increasingly been superseded by rule-of-reason analysis reflecting the procompetitive potential of a given practice. Under the rule of reason, courts have become increasingly sophisticated in analyzing information and transaction costs and the ways that contested commercial practices can reduce them. Economists and judges alike are more sophisticated in several important areas.

VERTICAL CONTRACTS

Most antitrust practitioners once believed that vertical mergers (i.e., one company acquiring another that is either a supplier or a customer) reduced competition. Today, most antitrust experts believe that vertical integration usually is not anticompetitive.

Progress in this area began in the 1950s with work by Aaron Director and the Antitrust Project at the University of Chicago. Robert Bork, a scholar involved with this project (and later the federal judge whose unsuccessful nomination to the U.S. Supreme Court caused much controversy), showed that if firm A has monopoly power, vertically integrating with firm B (or acquiring B) does not increase A's monopoly power in its own industry. Nor does it give A monopoly power in B's industry if that industry was competitive in the first place.

Lester Telser, also of the University of Chicago, showed in a famous 1960 article that manufacturers used resale price maintenance ("fair trade") not to create monopoly at the retail level, but to stimulate nonprice competition among retailers. Since retailers operating under fair trade agreements could not compete by cutting price, noted Telser, they instead competed by demonstrating the product to uninformed buyers. If the product is a sophisticated one that requires explaining to prospective buyers, resale price maintenance can be a rational—and competitive—action by a manufacturer. The same rationale can account for manufacturers' use of exclusive sales territories. This new knowledge about vertical contracts has had a large impact on judicial antitrust rulings.

HORIZONTAL CONTRACTS

Changes in the assessment of horizontal contracts (agreements among competing sellers in the same industry) have come more slowly. Economists remain almost unanimous in condemning all horizontal price-fixing. Many, however (e.g., Donald Dewey), have indicated that price-fixing may actually be procompetitive in some situations, a conclusion bolstered by Michael Sproul's empirical finding that in industries where the government successfully sues against price-fixing, prices increase, rather than decrease, after the suit. At a minimum, Peter Asch and Joseph Seneca have shown empirically, price-fixers have not earned higher than normal profits. Other practices that some people believed made it easier for competitors to fix prices have been shown to have procompetitive explanations. Sharing of information among competitors, for example, may not necessarily be a prelude to price-fixing; it can instead have an independent efficiency rationale.

Perhaps the most important change in economists' understanding has occurred in the area of mergers. Particularly with the work of Joe Bain and George Stigler in the 1950s, economists (and courts) inferred a lack of competition in markets simply from the fact that an industry had a high four-firm concentration ratio (the percentage of sales accounted for by the four largest firms in the industry). But later work by economists such as Yale Brozen and Harold Demsetz demonstrated that correlations between concentration and profits either were transitory or were due more to superior efficiency than to anticompetitive conduct. Their work followed that of Oliver Williamson, who showed that even if merger caused a large increase in monopoly power, it would be efficient if it produced only slight cost reductions. As a result of this new evidence and new thinking, economists and judges no longer assume that concentration alone indicates monopoly. The various versions of the Department of Justice/Federal Trade Commission Merger Guidelines promulgated in the 1980s and revised in the 1990s have de-emphasized concentration as a factor inviting government challenge of a merger.

NONMERGER MONOPOLIZATION

Perhaps the most publicized monopolization case of recent years is the government's case against Microsoft, which (see Liebowitz and Margolis 2001) rested on questionable empirical claims and resulted ultimately in victory for Microsoft on most of the government's allegations. The failure of the government's case reflects a general recent decline in the importance of monopolization cases. Worries about monopoly have progressively diminished with the realization that various practices traditionally thought to be monopolizing devices (including vertical contracts, as discussed above) actually have procompetitive explanations. Likewise, belief in the efficacy of predatory pricing—cutting price below cost—as a monopolization device has diminished. Work begun by John McGee in the late 1950s (also an outgrowth of the Chicago Antitrust Project) showed that firms are highly unlikely to use predatory pricing to create monopoly. That work is reflected in several recent Supreme Court opinions, such as that in *Matsushita Electric Industrial Co. v. Zenith Radio Corp.*, where the Court wrote, "There is a consensus among commentators that predatory pricing schemes are rarely tried, and even more rarely successful."

As older theories of monopolization have died, newer ones have been hatched. In the 1980s, economists began to lay out new monopolization models based on strategic behavior, often relying on game-theory constructs. They postulated that companies could monopolize markets by raising rivals' costs (sometimes called "cost predation"). For example, if firm A competes with firm B and supplies inputs to both itself and to B, A could raise B's costs by charging B a higher price. It remains to be seen whether economists will ultimately accept the proposition that raising a rival's costs can be a viable monopolizing strategy, or how the practice will be treated in the courts. But courts have sometimes imposed antitrust liability on firms possessing supposedly "essential facilities" when they deny competitors access to those facilities.

The recent era of antitrust reassessment has resulted in general agreement among economists that the most successful instances of cartelization and monopoly pricing have involved companies that enjoy the protection of government regulation of prices and government control of entry by new competitors. Occupational licensing and trucking regulation, for example, have allowed competitors to alter terms of competition and legally prevent entry into the market. Unfortunately, monopolies created by the federal government are almost always exempt from antitrust laws, and those created by state governments frequently are exempt as well. Municipal monopolies (e.g., taxicabs, utilities) may be subject to antitrust action but often are protected by statute.

THE EFFECTS OF ANTITRUST

With the hindsight of better economic understanding, economists now realize that one undeniable effect of antitrust has been to penalize numerous economically benign practices. Horizontal and especially vertical agreements that are clearly useful, particularly in reducing transaction costs, have been (or for many years were) effectively banned. A leading example is the continued per se illegality of resale price maintenance. Antitrust also increases transaction costs because firms must hire lawyers and often must litigate to avoid antitrust liability.

One of the most worrisome statistics in antitrust is that for every case brought by government, private plaintiffs bring ten. The majority of cases are filed to hinder, not help, competition. According to Steven Salop, formerly an antitrust official in the Carter administration, and Lawrence J. White, an economist at New York University, most private antitrust actions are filed by members of one of two groups. The most numerous private actions are brought by parties who are in a vertical arrangement with the defendant (e.g., dealers or franchisees) and who therefore are unlikely to have suffered from any truly anticompetitive offense. Usually, such cases are attempts to convert simple contract disputes (compensable by ordinary damages) into triple-damage payoffs under the Clayton Act.

The second most frequent private case is that brought by competitors. Because competitors are hurt only when a rival is acting procompetitively by increasing its sales and decreasing its price, the desire to hobble the defendant's efficient practices must motivate at least some antitrust suits by competitors. Thus, case statistics suggest that the anticompetitive costs from "abuse of antitrust," as New York University economists William Baumol and Janusz Ordover (1985) referred to it, may actually exceed any procompetitive benefits of antitrust laws.

The case for antitrust gets no stronger when economists examine the kinds of antitrust cases brought by government. As George Stigler (1982, p. 7), often a strong defender of antitrust, summarized, "Economists have their glories, but I do not believe that antitrust law is one of them." In a series of studies done in the early 1970s, economists assumed that important losses to consumers from limits on competition existed, and constructed models to identify the markets where these losses would be greatest. Then they compared the markets where government was enforcing antitrust laws with the markets where governments should enforce the laws if consumer well-being was the government's paramount concern. The studies concluded unanimously that the size of consumer losses from monopoly played little or no role in government enforcement of the law. Economists have also examined particular kinds of antitrust cases brought by the government to see whether anticompetitive acts in these cases were likely. The empirical answer usually is no. This is true even in price-fixing cases, where the evidence indicates that the companies targeted by the government either were not fixing prices or were doing so unsuccessfully. Similar conclusions arise from studies of merger cases and of various antitrust remedies obtained by government; in both instances, results are inconsistent with antitrust's supposed goal of consumer well-being.

If public-interest rationales do not explain antitrust, what does? A final set of studies has shown empirically that patterns of antitrust enforcement are motivated at least in part by political pressures unrelated to aggregate economic welfare. For example, antitrust is useful to politicians in stopping mergers that would result in plant closings or job transfers in their home districts. As Paul Rubin documented, economists do not see antitrust cases as driven by a search for economic improvement. Rubin reviewed all articles written by economists that were cited in a leading industrial organization textbook (Scherer and Ross 1990) generally favorable to antitrust law. Per economists' evaluations, more bad than good cases were brought. "In other words," wrote Rubin, "it is highly unlikely that the net effect of actual antitrust policy is to deter inefficient behavior … Factors other than a search for efficiency must be driving antitrust policy" (Rubin 1995, p. 61). What might those factors be? Pursuing a point suggested by Nobel laureate Ronald Coase (1972, 1988), William Shughart argued that economists' support for antitrust derives considerably from their ability to profit personally, in the form of full-time jobs and lucrative part-time work as experts in antitrust matters: "Far from contributing to improved antitrust enforcement, economists have for reasons of self-interest actively aided and abetted the public law enforcement bureaus and private plaintiffs in using the Sherman, Clayton and FTC Acts to subvert competitive market forces" (Shughart 1998, p. 151).

ABOUT THE AUTHOR

Fred S. McChesney is the Class of 1967 James B. Haddad Professor of Law at Northwestern University School of Law and a professor in the Kellogg School of Management at Northwestern.

FURTHER READING

Asch, Peter, and J. J. Seneca. "Is Collusion Profitable?" *Review of Economics and Statistics* 53 (February 1976): 1–12.

Baumol, William J., and Janusz A. Ordover. "Use of Antitrust to Subvert Competition." *Journal of Law and Economics* 28 (May 1985): 247–265.

Bittlingmayer, George. "Decreasing Average Cost and Competition: A New Look at the Addyston Pipe Case." *Journal of Law and Economics* 25 (October 1982): 201–229.

Bork, Robert H. *The Antitrust Paradox: A Policy at War with Itself.* New York: Basic Books, 1978.

Bork, Robert H. "Vertical Integration and the Sherman Act: The Legal History of an Economic Misconception." *University of Chicago Law Review* 22 (Autumn 1954): 157–201.

Brozen, Yale. "The Antitrust Task Force Deconcentration Recommendation." *Journal of Law and Economics 13* (October 1970): 279–292.

Coase, R. H. "Industrial Organization: A Proposal for Research." In V. Fuchs, ed., *Economic Research: Retrospective and Prospect.* Vol. 3. Cambridge, Mass.: National Bureau of Economic Research. Reprinted in R. H. Coase, *The Firm, the Market and the Law.* Chicago: University of Chicago Press, 1988.

Coate, Malcolm B., Richard S. Higgins, and Fred S. McChesney. "Bureaucracy and Politics in FTC Merger Challenges." *Journal of Law and Economics* 33 (October 1990): 463–482.

Crandall, Robert W., and Clifford Winston. "Does Antitrust Policy Improve Consumer Welfare? Assessing the Evidence." *Journal of Economic Perspectives* 17, no. 4 (2003): 3–26.

Demsetz, Harold. "Industry Structure, Market Rivalry, and Public Policy." *Journal of Law and Economics* 16 (April 1973): 1–9.

Dewey, Donald. "Information, Entry and Welfare: The Case for Collusion." *American Economic Review* 69 (September 1979): 588–593.

DiLorenzo, Thomas J. "The Origins of Antitrust: An Interest-Group Perspective." *International Review of Law and Economics* 5 (June 1985): 73–90.

Liebowitz, Stan J., and Stephen E. Margolis. *Winners, Losers and Microsoft.* Rev. ed. Oakland, Calif.: Independent Institute, 2001.

McGee, John S. "Predatory Price Cutting: The Standard Oil (N.J.) Case." *Journal of Law and Economics* 1 (1958): 137–169.

Rubin, Paul H. "What Do Economists Think About Antitrust? A Random Walk down Pennsylvania Avenue." In Fred S. McChesney and William F. Shughart II, eds., *The Causes and Consequences of Antitrust: The Public-Choice Perspective.* Chicago: University of Chicago Press, 1995.

Scherer, F. M., and David Ross. *Industrial Market Structure and Economic Performance.* 3d ed. Boston: Houghton Mifflin, 1990.

Shughart, William F. II. "Monopoly and the Problem of the Economists." In Fred S. McChesney, ed., Economic Inputs, *Legal Outputs: The Role of Economists in Modern Antitrust.* New York: Wiley, 1998.

Shughart, William F. II, and Robert D. Tollison. "The Positive Economics of Antitrust Policy: A Survey Article." *International Review of Law and Economics* 5 (June 1985): 39–57.

Sproul, Michael F. "Antitrust and Prices." *Journal of Political Economy* 101 (1993): 741–754.

Stigler, George J. "The Economists and the Problem of Monopoly." In Stigler, *The Economist as Preacher and Other Essays.* Chicago: University of Chicago Press, 1982. pp. 38–54.

Stigler, George J. "The Economists and the Problem of Monopoly." *American Economic Review Papers and Proceedings* 72 (May 1982): 1–11.

Telser, Lester G. "Why Should Manufacturers Want Fair Trade?" *Journal of Law and Economics* 3 (October 1960): 86–105.

Williamson, Oliver E. "Economies as an Antitrust Defense: The Welfare Tradeoffs." *American Economic Review* 58 (March 1968): 18–35.

John D. Rockefeller
and the Oil Industry

By Burton Folsom

I N 1885 JOHN D. Rockefeller wrote one of his partners, "Let the good work go on. We must ever remember we are refining oil for the poor man and he must have it cheap and good." Or as he put it to another partner: "Hope we can continue to hold out with the best illuminator in the world at the *lowest* price." Even after twenty years in the oil business, "the best ... at the lowest price" was still Rockefeller's goal; his Standard Oil Company had already captured 90 percent of America's oil refining and had pushed the price down from 58 cents to eight cents a gallon. His well-groomed horses delivered blue barrels of oil throughout America's cities and were already symbols of excellence and efficiency. Consumers were not only choosing Standard Oil over that of his competitors; they were also preferring it to coal oil, whale oil, and electricity. Millions of Americans illuminated their homes with Standard Oil for one cent per hour; and in doing so, they made Rockefeller the wealthiest man in American history.

Rockefeller's early life hardly seemed the making of a near billionaire. His father was a peddler who often struggled to make ends meet. His mother stayed at home to raise their six children. They moved around upstate New York—from Richford to Moravia to Owego—and eventually settled in Cleveland, Ohio. John D. was the oldest son. Although he didn't have new suits or a fashionable home, his family life was stable. From his father he learned how to earn money and hold on to it; from his mother he learned to put God first in his life, to be honest, and help others.

"From the beginning," Rockefeller said, "I was trained to work, to save, and to give." He did all three of these things shortly after he graduated from the Cleveland public high school. He always remembered the "momentous day" in 1855, when he began work at age sixteen as an assistant bookkeeper for 50 cents per day.

On the job Rockefeller had a fixation for honest business. He later said, "I had learned the underlying principles of business as well as many men acquire them by the time they are forty." His first partner, Maurice Clark, said that Rockefeller "was methodical to an extreme, careful as to details and exacting to a fraction. If there was a cent due us he wanted it. If there was a cent due a customer he wanted the customer to have it." Such precision irritated some debtors, but it won him the confidence of many Cleveland businessmen; at age nineteen Rockefeller went into the grain shipping business on Lake Erie and soon began dealing in thousands of dollars.

Rockefeller so enjoyed business that he dreamed about it at night. Where he really felt at ease, though, was with his family and at church. His wife Laura was also a strong Christian and they spent many hours a week attending church services, picnics, or socials at the Erie Street Baptist Church. Rockefeller saw a strong spiritual life as crucial to an effective business life. He tithed from his first paycheck and gave to his church, a foreign mission, and the poor. He sought Christians as business partners and later as employees. One of his fellow churchmen, Samuel Andrews, was investing in oil refining; and this new frontier appealed to young John. He joined forces with Andrews in 1865 and would apply his same precision and honesty to the booming oil industry.

The discovery of large quantities of crude oil in northwest Pennsylvania soon changed the lives of millions of Americans. For centuries, people had known of the existence of crude oil scattered about America and the world. They just didn't know what to do with it. Farmers thought it a nuisance and tried to plow around it; others bottled it and sold it as medicine.

In 1855, Benjamin Silliman, Jr., a professor of chemistry at Yale, analyzed a batch of crude oil; after distilling and purifying it, he found that it yielded kerosene—a better illuminant than the popular whale oil. Other by-products of distilling included lubricating oil, gasoline, and paraffin, which made excellent candles. The only problem was cost: it was too expensive to haul the small deposits of crude from northwest Pennsylvania to markets elsewhere. Silliman and others, however, formed an oil company and sent "Colonel" Edwin L. Drake, a jovial railroad conductor, to Titusville to drill for oil.

"Nonsense," said local skeptics. "You can't pump oil out of the ground as you pump water." Drake had faith that he could; in 1859, when he built a thirty-foot derrick and drilled seventy feet into the ground, all the locals scoffed. When he hit oil, however, they quickly converted and preached oil drilling as the salvation of the region. There were few barriers to entering the oil business: drilling equipment cost less than $1,000, and oil land seemed abundant. By the early 1860s, speculators were swarming northwest Pennsylvania, cluttering it with derricks, pipes, tanks, and barrels. "Good news for whales," concluded one newspaper. America had become hooked on kerosene.

Cleveland was a mere hundred miles from the oil region, and Rockefeller was fascinated with the prospects of refining oil into kerosene. He may have visited the region as early as 1862. By 1863 he was talking oil with Samuel Andrews and two years later they built a refinery together. Two things about the oil industry, however, bothered Rockefeller right from the start: the appalling waste and the fluctuating prices.

The overproducing of oil and the developing of new markets caused the price of oil to fluctuate wildly. In 1862 a barrel (42 gallons) of oil dropped in value from $4.00 to $.35. Later, when President Lincoln bought oil to fight the Civil War, the price jumped back to $4.00, then to $13.75. A blacksmith took $200 worth of drilling equipment and drilled a well worth $100,000. Others, with better drills and richer holes, dug four wells worth $200,000. Alongside the new millionaires of the moment were the thousands of fortune hunters who came from all over to lease land and kick down shafts into it with cheap foot drills. Most failed.

Even Colonel Drake died in poverty. As J. W. Trowbridge wrote, "Almost everybody you meet has been suddenly enriched or suddenly ruined (perhaps both within a short space of time), or knows plenty of people who have."

Those few who struck oil often wasted more than they earned. Thousands of barrels of oil poured into Oil Creek, not into tanks. Local creek bottoms were often flooded with runaway oil; the Allegheny River smelled of oil and glistened with it for many miles toward Pittsburgh. Gushers of wasted oil were bad enough; sometimes a careless smoker would turn a spouting well into a killing inferno. Other wasters would torpedo holes with nitroglycerine, sometimes losing the oil and their lives.

Rockefeller was intrigued with the future of the oil industry, but was repelled by its past. He shunned the drills and derricks and chose the refining end instead. Refining eventually became very costly, but in the 1860s the main supplies were only barrels, a trough, a tank, and a still in which to boil the oil. The yield would usually be about 60 percent kerosene, 10 percent gasoline, 5 to 10 percent benzol or naphtha, with the rest being tar and wastes. High prices and dreams of quick riches brought many into refining; and this attracted Rockefeller, too. But right from the start, he believed that the path to success was to cut waste and produce the best product at the lowest price. Sam Andrews, his partner, worked on getting more kerosene per barrel of crude. Both men searched for uses for the by-products: they used the gasoline for fuel, some of the tars for paving, and shipped the naphtha to gas plants. They also sold lubricating oil, vaseline, and paraffin for making candles. Other Cleveland refiners, by contrast, were wasteful: they dumped their gasoline into the Cuyahoga River, they threw out other by-products, and they spilled oil throughout the city.

Rockefeller was constantly looking for ways to save. For example, he built his refineries well and bought no insurance. He also employed his own plumber and almost halved the cost on labor, pipes, and plumbing materials. Coopers charged $2.50 per barrel; Rockefeller cut this to $.96 when he bought his own tracts of white oak timber, his own kilns to dry the wood, and his own wagons and horses to haul it to Cleveland. There with machines he made the barrels, then hooped them, glued them, and painted them blue. Rockefeller and Andrews soon became the largest refiners in Cleveland. In 1870, they reorganized with Rockefeller's brother William, and Henry Flagler, the son of a Presbyterian minister. They renamed their enterprise Standard Oil.

Under Rockefeller's leadership they plowed the profits into bigger and better equipment; and, as their volume increased, they hired chemists and developed three hundred by-products from each barrel of oil. They ranged from paint and varnish to dozens of lubricating oils to anesthetics. As for the main product, kerosene, Rockefeller made it so cheaply that whale oil, coal oil, and, for a while, electricity lost out in the race to light American homes, factories, and streets. "We had vision," Rockefeller later said. "We saw the vast possibilities of the oil industry, stood at the center of it, and brought our knowledge and imagination and business experience to bear in a dozen, in twenty, in thirty directions."

Another area of savings came from rebates from railroads. The major eastern railroads—the New York Central, the Erie, and Pennsylvania—all wanted to ship oil and were willing to give discounts, or rebates, to large shippers. These rebates were customary and dated back to the first shipments of oil. As the largest oil refiner in America, Rockefeller was in a good position to save money for himself and for the railroad as well. He promised to ship 60 carloads of oil daily and provide all the loading and unloading services. All the railroads had to do was to ship it east. Commodore Vanderbilt of the New York Central was delighted to give Rockefeller the largest rebate he gave any shipper for the chance to have the most regular, quick and efficient deliveries. When smaller oil men screamed about rate discrimination, Vanderbilt's spokesmen gladly promised the same rebate to anyone else who would give him the same volume of business. Since no other refiner was as efficient as Rockefeller, no one else got Standard Oil's discount.

Many of Rockefeller's competitors condemned him for receiving such large rebates. But Rockefeller would never have gotten them had he not been the largest shipper of oil. These rebates, on top of his remarkable efficiency, meant that most refiners could not compete. From 1865 to 1870, the price of kerosene dropped from 58 to 26 cents per gallon. Rockefeller made profits during every one of these years, but most of Cleveland's refiners disappeared. Naturally, there were hard feelings. Henry Demarest Lloyd, whose cousin was an unhappy oil man, wrote *Wealth Against Commonwealth* in 1894 to denounce Rockefeller. Ida Tarbell, whose father was a Pennsylvania oil producer, attacked Rockefeller in a series of articles for *McClure's* magazine.

Some of the oil producers were unhappy, but American consumers were pleased that Rockefeller was selling cheap oil. Before 1870, only the rich could afford whale oil and candles. The rest had to go to bed early to save money. By the 1870s, with the drop in the price of kerosene, middle and working class people all over the nation could afford the one cent an hour that it cost to light their homes at night. Working and reading became after-dark activities new to most Americans in the 1870s.

Rockefeller quickly learned that he couldn't please everyone by making cheap oil. He pleased no one, though, when he briefly turned to political entrepreneurship in 1872. He joined a pool called the South Improvement Company and it turned out to be one of the biggest mistakes in his life. This scheme was hatched by Tom Scott of the Pennsylvania Railroad. Scott was nervous about low oil prices and falling railroad rates. He thought that if the large refiners and railroads got together they could artificially fix high prices for themselves. Rockefeller decided to join because he would get not only large rebates, but also drawbacks, which were discounts on that oil which his competitors, not he, shipped. The small producers and refiners bitterly attacked Rockefeller and forced the Pennsylvania Legislature to revoke the charter of the South Improvement Company. No oil was ever shipped under this pool, but Rockefeller got bad publicity from it and later admitted that he had been wrong.

At first, the idea of a pool appealed to Rockefeller because it might stop the glut, the waste, the inefficiency, and the fluctuating prices of oil. The South Improvement Company showed him that this would not work, so he turned to market entrepreneurship instead. He decided to become the biggest and best refiner in the world. First, he put his chemists to work trying to extract even more from each barrel of crude. More important, he tried to integrate Standard Oil vertically and horizontally by getting dozens of other refiners to join him. Rockefeller bought their plants and talent; he gave the owners cash or stock in Standard Oil.

From Rockefeller's standpoint, a few large vertically integrated oil companies could survive and prosper, but dozens of smaller companies could not. Improve or perish was Rockefeller's approach. "We will take your burden," Rockefeller said. "We will utilize your ability; we will give you representation; we will all unite together and build a substantial structure on the basis of cooperation." Many oil men rejected Rockefeller's offer, but dozens of others all over America sold out to Standard Oil. When they did, Rockefeller simply shut down the inefficient companies and used what he needed from the good ones. Officers Oliver Payne, H. H. Rogers, and President John Archbold came to Standard Oil from these merged firms.

Buying out competitors was a tricky business. Rockefeller's approach was to pay what the property was worth at the time he bought it. Outmoded equipment was worth little, but good personnel and even good will were worth a lot. Rockefeller had a tendency to be generous because he wanted the future good will of his new partners and employees. "He treated everybody fairly," concluded one oil man. "When we sold out he gave us a fair price. Some refiners tried to impose on him and when they found they could not do it, they abused him. I remember one man whose refinery was worth $6,000, or at most $8,000. His friends told him, 'Mr. Rockefeller ought to give you $100,000 for that.' Of course Mr. Rockefeller refused to pay more than the refinery was worth, and the man … abused Mr. Rockefeller."

Bigness was not Rockefeller's real goal. It was just a means of cutting costs. During the 1870s, the price of kerosene dropped from 26 to eight cents a gallon and Rockefeller captured about 90 percent of the American market. This percentage remained steady for years. Rockefeller never wanted to oust all of his rivals, just the ones who were wasteful and those who tarnished the whole trade by selling defective oil. "Competitors we must have, we must have," said Rockefeller's partner Charles Pratt. "If we absorb them, be sure it will bring up another."

Just as Rockefeller reached the top, many predicted his demise. During the early 1880s, the entire oil industry was in jeopardy. The Pennsylvania oil fields were running dry and electricity was beginning to compete with lamps for lighting homes. No one knew about the oil fields out west and few suspected that the gasoline engine would be made the power source of the future. Meanwhile, the Russians had begun drilling and selling their abundant oil, and they raced to capture Standard Oil's foreign markets. Some experts predicted the imminent death of the American oil industry; even Standard Oil's loyal officers began selling some of their stock.
Rockefeller's solution to these problems was to stake the future of his company on new oil discoveries near Lima, Ohio. Drillers found oil in this Ohio-Indiana region in 1885, but they could not market it. It had a sulphur base and stank like rotten eggs. Even touching this oil meant a long, soapy bath or social ostracism. No one wanted to sell or buy it and no city even wanted it shipped there. Only Rockefeller seemed interested in it. According to Joseph Seep, chief oil buyer for Standard Oil.

Mr. Rockefeller went on buying leases in the Lima field in spite of the coolness of the rest of the directors, until he had accumulated more than 40 million barrels of that sulphurous oil in tanks. He must have invested millions of dollars in buying and storing and holding the sour oil for two years, when everyone else thought that it was no good.

Rockefeller had hired two chemists, Herman Frasch and William Burton, to figure out how to purify the oil; he counted on them to make it usable. Rockefeller's partners were skeptical, however, and sought to stanch the flood of money invested in tanks, pipelines, and land in the Lima area. They "held up their hands in holy horror" at Rockefeller's gamble and even outvoted him at a meeting of Standard's Board of Directors. "Very well, gentlemen," said Rockefeller. "At my own personal risk, I will put up the money to care for this product: $2 million—$3 million, if necessary." Rockefeller told what then happened:

> This ended the discussion, and we carried the Board with us and we continued to use the funds of the company in what was regarded as a very hazardous investment of money. But we persevered, and two or three of our practical men stood firmly with me and constantly occupied themselves with the chemists until at last, after millions of dollars had been expended in the tankage and buying the oil and constructing the pipelines and tank cars to draw it away to the markets where we could sell it for fuel, one of our German chemists cried 'Eureka!' We … at last found ourselves able to clarify the oil.

The "worthless" Lima oil that Rockefeller had stockpiled suddenly became valuable; Standard Oil would be able to supply cheap kerosene for years to come. Rockefeller's exploit had come none too soon: the Russians struck oil at Baku, four square miles of the deepest and richest oil land in the world. They hired European experts to help Russia conquer the oil markets of the world. In 1882, the year before Baku oil was first exported, America refined 85 percent of the world's oil; six years later this dropped to 53 percent. Since most of Standard's oil was exported, and since Standard accounted for 90 percent of America's exported oil, the Baku threat had to be met.

At first glance, Standard Oil seemed certain to lose. First, the Baku oil was centralized in one small area: this made it economical to drill, refine, and ship from a single location. Second, the Baku oil was more plentiful: its average yield was over 280 barrels per well per day, compared with 4.5 barrels per day from American wells. Third, Baku oil was highly viscous: it made a better lubricant (though not necessarily a better illuminant) than oil in Pennsylvania or Ohio.

Fourth, Russia was closer to European and Asian markets: Standard Oil had to bear the costs of building huge tankers and crossing the ocean with them. One independent expert estimated that Russia's costs of oil exporting were one-third to one-half of those of the United States. Finally, Russia and other countries slapped high protective tariffs on American oil; this allowed inefficient foreign drillers to compete with Standard Oil. The Austro-Hungarian empire, for example, imported over half a million barrels of American oil in 1882; but they bought none by 1890. What was worse, local refiners there marketed a low-grade oil in barrels labeled "Standard Oil Company." This allowed the Austro-Hungarians to dump their cheap oil and damage Standard's reputation at the same time.

Rockefeller pulled out all stops to meet the Russian challenge. No small refinery would have had a chance; even a large vertically integrated company like Standard Oil was at a great disadvantage. Rockefeller never lost his vision, though, of conquering the oil markets of the world. First, he relied on his research team to help him out. William Burton, who helped clarify the Lima oil, invented "cracking," a method of heating oil to higher temperatures to get more use of the product out of each barrel. Engineers at Standard Oil helped by perfecting large steamship tankers, which cut down on the costs of shipping oil overseas.

Second, Rockefeller made Standard Oil even more efficient. He used less iron in making barrel hoops and less solder in sealing oil cans. In a classic move, he used the waste (culm) from coal heaps to fuel his refineries; even the sweepings from his factory he sorted through for tin shavings and solder drops.

Third, Rockefeller studied the foreign markets and learned how to beat the Russians in their part of the world. He sent Standard agents into dozens of countries to figure out how to sell oil up the Hwang Ho River in China, along the North Road in India, to the east coast of Sumatra, and to the huts of tribal chieftains in Malaya. He even used spies, often foreign diplomats, to help him sell oil and tell him what the Russians were doing. He used different strategies in different areas. Europeans, for example, wanted to buy kerosene only in small quantities, so Rockefeller supplied tank wagons to sell them oil street by street. As Allan Nevins notes:

> The [foreign] stations were kept in the same beautiful order as in the United States. Everywhere the steel storage tanks, as in America, were protected from fire by proper spacing and excellent fire-fighting apparatus. Everywhere the familiar blue barrels were of the best quality. Everywhere a meticulous neatness was evident. Pumps, buckets, and tools were all clean and under constant inspection, no litter being tolerated … The oil itself was of the best quality. Nothing was left undone, in accordance with Rockefeller's long-standing policy, to make the Standard products and Standard ministrations, abroad as at home, attractive to the customer.

Rockefeller's focus on quality meant that, in an evenly balanced price war with Russia, Standard Oil would win.

The Russian-American oil war was hotly contested for almost thirty years after 1885. In most markets, Standard's known reliability would prevail, if it could just get its price close to that of the Russians. In some years this meant that Rockefeller had to sell oil for 5.2 cents a gallon—leaving almost no profit margin—if he hoped to win the world. This he did; and Standard often captured two-thirds of the world's oil trade from 1882 to 1891 and a somewhat smaller portion in the decade after this.

Rockefeller and his partners always knew that their victory was a narrow triumph of efficiency over superior natural advantages. "If" as John Archbold said in 1899, "there had been as prompt and energetic action on the part of the Russian oil industry as was taken by the Standard Oil Company, the Russians would have dominated many of the world markets … "

At one level, Standard's ability to sell oil at close to a nickel a gallon meant hundreds of thousands of jobs for Americans in general and Standard Oil in particular. Rockefeller's margin of victory in this competition was always narrow. Even a rise of one cent a gallon would have cost Rockefeller much of his foreign market. A rise of three cents a gallon would have cost Rockefeller his American markets as well.

At another level, oil at almost a nickel a gallon opened new possibilities for people around the world. William H. Libby, Standard's foreign agent, saw this change and marveled at it. To the governor general of India he said:

I may claim for petroleum that it is something of a civilizer, as promoting among the poorest classes of these countries a host of evening occupations, industrial, educational, and recreative, not feasible prior to its introduction; and if it has brought a fair reward to the capital ventured in its development, it has also carried more cheap comfort into more poor homes than almost any discovery of modern times

In Standard Oil, Rockefeller arguably built the most successful business in American history. In running it, he showed the precision of a bookkeeper and the imagination of an entrepreneur. Yet, in day-to-day operations, he led quietly and inspired loyalty by example. Rockefeller displayed none of the tantrums of a Vanderbilt or a Hill, and none of the flamboyance of a Schwab. At board meetings, he would sit and patiently listen to all arguments. Until the end, he would often say nothing. But his fellow directors all testified to his genius for sorting out the relevant details and pushing the right decision, even when it was shockingly bold and unpopular. "You ask me what makes Rockefeller the unquestioned leader in our group," said John Archbold, later a president of Standard Oil. "Well, it is simple. In business we all try to look ahead as far as possible. Some of us think we are pretty able. But Rockefeller always sees a little further ahead than any of us—and then he sees around the corner."

Some of these peeks around the corner helped Rockefeller pick the right people for the right jobs. He had to delegate a great deal of responsibility, and he always gave credit—and sometimes large bonuses—for work well done. Paying higher than market wages was Rockefeller's controversial policy: he believed it helped slash costs in the long run. For example, Standard was rarely hurt by strikes or labor unrest. Also, he could recruit and keep the top talent and command their future loyalty. Rockefeller approached the ideal of the "Standard Oil family" and tried to get each member to work for the good of the whole. As Thomas Wheeler said, "He managed somehow to get everybody interested in saving, in cutting out a detail here and there … " He sometimes joined the men in their work, and urged them on. At 6:30 in the morning there was Rockefeller "rolling barrels, piling hoops, and wheeling out shavings." In the oil fields, there was Rockefeller trying to fit nine barrels on a eight-barrel wagon. He came to know the oil business inside out and won the respect of his workers. Praise he would give; rebukes he would avoid. "Very well kept-very indeed," said Rockefeller to an accountant about his books before pointing out a minor error and leaving. One time a new accountant moved into a room where Rockefeller kept an exercise machine. Not knowing what Rockefeller looked like, the accountant saw him and ordered him to remove it. *"All* right," said Rockefeller, and he politely took it away. Later, when the embarrassed accountant found out whom he had chided, he expected to be fired; but Rockefeller never mentioned it.

Rockefeller treated his top managers as conquering heroes and gave them praise, rest, and comfort. He knew that good ideas were almost priceless: they were the foundation for the future of Standard Oil. To one of his oil buyers, Rockefeller wrote, "I trust you will not worry about the business. Your health is more important to you and to us than the business." Long vacations at full pay were Rockfeller's antidotes for his weary leaders. After Johnson N. Camden consolidated the West Virginia and Maryland refineries for Standard Oil, Rockefeller said, "Please feel at perfect liberty to break away three, six, nine, twelve, fifteen months, more or less … Your salary will not cease, however long you decide to remain away from business." But neither Camden nor the others rested long. They were too anxious to succeed in what they were doing and to please the leader who trusted them so. Thomas Wheeler, an oil buyer for Rockefeller, said, "I have never heard of his equal in getting together a lot of the very best men in one team and inspiring each man to do his best for the enterprise."

Not just Rockefeller's managers, his fellow entrepreneurs thought he was remarkable. In 1873, the prescient Commodore Vanderbilt said, "That Rockefeller! He will be the richest man in the country." Twenty years later, Charles Schwab learned of Rockefeller's versatility when Rockefeller invested almost $40 million in the controversial ore of the Mesabi iron range near the Great Lakes. Schwab said, "Our experts in the Carnegie Company did not believe in the Mesabi ore fields. They thought the ore was poor … They ridiculed Rockefeller's investments in the Mesabi." But by 1901, Carnegie, Schwab, and J. P. Morgan had changed their minds and offered Rockefeller almost $90 million for his ore investments.

That Rockefeller was a genius is widely admitted. What is puzzling is his philosophy of life. He was a practicing Christian and believed in doing what the Bible said to do. Therefore, he organized his life in the following way: he put God first, his family second, and career third. This is the puzzle: how could someone put his career third and wind up with $900 million, which made him the wealthiest man in American history. This is not something that can be easily explained (at least not by conventional historical methods), but it can be studied.

Rockefeller always said the best things he had done in life were to make Jesus his savior and to make Laura Spelman his wife. He prayed daily the first thing in the morning and went to church for prayer meetings with his family at least twice a week. He often said he felt most at home in church and in regular need of "spiritual food;" he and his wife also taught Bible classes and had ministers and evangelists regularly in their home.

Going to church, of course, is not necessarily a sign of a practicing Christian. Ivan the Terrible regularly prayed and went to church before and after torturing and killing his fellow men. Even Commodore Vanderbilt sang hymns out of one side of his mouth and out of the other he spewed a stream of obscenities.

Rockefeller, by contrast, read the Bible and tried to practice its teachings in his everyday life. Therefore, he tithed, rested on the Sabbath, and gave valuable time to his family. This made his life hard to understand for his fellow businessmen. But it explains why he sometimes gave tens of thousands of dollars to Christian groups, while, at the same time, he was trying to borrow over a million dollars to expand his business. It explains why he rested on Sunday, even as the Russians were mobilizing to knock him out of European markets. It explains why he calmly rocked his daughter to sleep at night, even though oil prices may have dropped to an all-time low that day. Others panicked, but Rockefeller believed that God would pull him through if only he would follow His commandments. He worked to the best of his ability, then turned his problems over to God and tried not to worry. This is what he often said:

> Early I learned to work and to play.
> I dropped the worry on the way.
> God was good to me every day.

Those who heard him say this may have thought that he was mouthing platitudes, but the key to understanding Rockefeller is to recognize that he said it because he believed it.

When the Russians sold their oil in Standard's blue barrels, Rockefeller did not get into strife. He knew that the book of James said, "Where strife is there is confusion and every evil work." He fought the Russians, using his spies and his authority to stop them and outsell them; but he never slandered them or threatened them. No matter what, Rockefeller never lost his temper, either. This was one of the remarkable findings of Allan Nevins in his meticulous research on Rockefeller. During the 1930s, Nevins interviewed dozens of people who worked with Rockefeller and knew him intimately.

Not one—son, daughter, friend, or foe—could ever recall Rockefeller losing his temper or even being perturbed. He was always calm.

The most famous example is the time Judge K. M. Landis fined Standard Oil of Indiana over $29 million. The charge was taking rebates; and Landis, an advocate of government intervention, publicly read the verdict of "guilty" for Standard Oil. *Railway World* was shocked that "Standard Oil Company of Indiana was fined an amount equal to seven or eight times the value of its entire property because its traffic department did not verify the statement of the Alton rate clerk that the six-cent commodity rate on oil had been properly filed with the Interstate Commerce Commission." The New York *Times* called this decision a bad law and "a manifestation of that spirit of vindictive savagery toward corporations ... " But Rockefeller, who had testified at the trial was unruffled.

On the day of the verdict, he chose to play golf with friends. In the middle of their game, a frantic messenger came running through the fairways to deliver the bad news to Rockefeller. He calmly looked at the telegram, put it away, and said, "Well, shall we go on, gentlemen?" Then he hit his ball a convincing 160 yards. At the next hole, someone sheepishly asked Rockefeller, "How much is it?" Rockefeller said, "Twenty-nine million two hundred forty thousand dollars," and added "the maximum penalty, I believe. Will you gentlemen drive?" He ended the nine holes with a respectable score of 53, as though he hadn't a care in the world.

Landis's decision was eventually overruled, but Rockefeller was not so lucky in his fight against the Sherman Anti-trust Act. Rockefeller had set up a trust system at Standard Oil merely to allow his many oil businesses in different states to be headed by the same board of directors. Some states, like Pennsylvania, had laws permitting it to tax all of the property of any corporation located within state borders. Under these conditions, Rockefeller found it convenient to establish separate Standard Oil corporations in many different states, but have them directed in harmony, or in trust, by the same group of men. The Supreme Court struck this system down in 1911 and forced Standard Oil to break up into separate state companies with separate boards of directors.

This decision was puzzling to Rockefeller and his supporters. The Sherman Act was supposed to prevent monopolies and those companies "in restraint of trade." Yet Standard Oil had no monopoly and certainly was not restraining trade. The Russians, with the help of their government, had been gaining ground on Standard in the international oil trade. In America, competition in the oil industry was more intense than ever. Over one hundred oil companies-from Gulf Oil in Texas to Associated Oil in California-competed with Standard. Standard's share of the United States and world markets had been steadily declining from 1900 to 1910. Rockefeller, however, took the decision calmly and promised to obey it.

Even more remarkable than Rockefeller's serenity was his diligence in tithing. From the time of his first job, where he earned 50 cents a day, the sixteen-year-old Rockefeller gave to his local Baptist church, to missions in New York City and abroad, and to the poor—black or white. As his salary increased, so did his giving. By the time he was 45, he was up to $100,000 per year; at age 53, he topped the $1,000,000 mark in his annual giving. His eightieth year was his most generous: $138,000,000 he happily have away.

The more he earned the more he gave, and the more he gave the more he earned. To Rockefeller, it was the true fulfillment of the Biblical law: "Give, and it shall be given unto you; good measure, pressed down, and shaken together, and running over, shall men give unto your bosom." Not "money" itself but "the love of money" was "the root of all evil." And Rockefeller loved God much more than his money. He learned what the prophet Malachi meant when he said, "Bring the whole tithe into the storehouse, … and see if I will not throw open the floodgates of heaven and pour out so much blessing that you will not have room enough for it." He learned what Jesus meant when he said, "With the measure you use, it will be measured to you." So when Rockefeller proclaimed: "God gave me my money," he did so in humility and in awe of the way he believed God worked.

Some historians haven't liked the way Rockefeller made his money, but few have quibbled with the way he spent it. Before he died, he had given away about $550,000,000, more than any other American before him had ever possessed. It wasn't so much the amount that he gave as it was the amazing results that his giving produced. At one level he built schools and churches and supported evangelists and missionaries all over the world. After all, Jesus said, "Go ye into all the world, and preach the gospel to every creature."

Healing the sick and feeding the poor was also part of Rockefeller's Christian mission. Not state aid, but Rockefeller philanthropy paid teams of scientists who found cures for yellow fever, meningitis, and hookworm. The boll weevil was also a Rockefeller target, and the aid he gave in fighting it improved farming throughout the South.

Rockefeller attacked social and medical problems the same way he attacked the Russians—with efficiency and innovation. To get both of these, Rockefeller gave scores of millions of dollars to higher education. The University of Chicago alone got over $35,000,000. Black schools, Southern schools, and Baptist schools also reaped what Rockefeller had sown. His guide for giving was a variation of the Biblical principle-"If any would not work, neither should he eat." Those schools, cities, or scientists who weren't anxious to produce or improve didn't get Rockefeller money. Those who did and showed results got more. As in the parable of the talents, to him who has, more (responsibility and trust) shall be given by the Rockefeller Foundation.

At about age sixty, Rockefeller began to wind down his remarkable business career to focus more on philanthropy, his family, and leisure. He took up gardening, started riding more on his horses, and began playing golf. Yale University might ban the tango, but Rockefeller hired an instructor to teach him how to do it. Even in recreation, Rockefeller wanted to discipline his actions for the best result. In golf, he hired a caddy to say "Hold your head down," before each of his swings. He even strapped his left foot down with croquet wickets to keep it steady during his drives.

In a way, Rockefeller's life was a paradox. He was fascinated with human nature and enjoyed studying people. Yet his unparalleled success in business made friendships awkward and forced him to shut out much of the world. To his children Rockefeller was the man who played blind man's bluff with great gusto, balanced dinner plates on his nose, and taught them how to swim and to ride bicycles. But from the world he had to keep his distance: he was a target for fortune hunters, fawners, chiselers, mountebank preachers, and hundreds of hard-luck letters written to him each week.

Retirement, however, liberated him more to enjoy people and nature. On his estate in New York, he studied plants and flowers. Sometimes he would drive out into the countryside just to admire a wheat field. Down in Florida, he liked to watch all the people who passed his house and guess at what they did in life. He handed out dimes to the neighborhood children and urged them to work and to save.

Competition
(Except Where Prohibited by Law)

By Thomas J. DiLorenzo

The antitrust laws don't promote competition—they stifle it. But then, consider their source.

S
UCCESSFUL BUSINESSES ARE routinely taken to court for offering great products at low prices, having thus become "dominant firms" in their industries. Cutting prices to meet the competition is a boon to consumers—but has been condemned by government authorities as "price discrimination" and "predatory pricing." When ready-to-eat cereal producers perceived that consumers want more than just plain corn flakes in the morning, they were accused of "sharing" a monopoly through the dubious tactic of "brand proliferation." The list of absurdities perpetrated in this country in the name of "antitrust" could go on and on.

The first antimonopoly law, the Sherman Antitrust Act, was passed nearly a century ago, and others have been added over the years. But disenchantment with these laws has been growing lately, for economists are finding plenty of evidence that they often suppress competition rather than encourage it.

Yale Brozen of the University of Chicago concludes that the antitrust laws "are themselves restraining output and the growth of productivity." Dominick Armentano of the University of Hartford offers even sharper criticism, charging that historical evidence shows the antitrust laws to be a major *source* of monopoly power, routinely used to protect inefficient firms. And Harold Demsetz of the University of California at Los Angeles says that if certain antitrust policies were continued, he would favor outright repeal of the Sherman Act. In fact, recent research has given rise to what Brozen calls "a revolution in economics—in that part of the field called industrial organization—which is nearly complete in the professional journals."

Despite all the evidence, however, economists are still generally inclined to have great faith in the necessity of antitrust laws in a competitive economy. They may admit that mistakes have been made, but the antitrust laws in general and the Sherman Antitrust Act in particular are still widely held as the guarantors of a competitive economy. There is a strongly held belief that there once was a "golden age of antitrust" in which these laws were implemented to brush back a "rising tide of monopoly power."

This is odd. In other domains, when a pattern of perverse economic behavior—in this case, the suppression of competitive activity in the name of antitrust—persists over several decades, economists usually ascribe it to something inherent in the institution itself. But not with antitrust. In one popular industrial organization textbook,

F. M. Sherer proclaims that "in the United States ... the enforcement of the antitrust laws is the main weapon wielded by government in its effort to harmonize the profit-seeking behavior of private enterprise with the public interest." Likewise Kenneth Clarkson and Roger L. Miller, in another well-known text, say that "antitrust laws have been legislated and enforced in order to keep business behavior and markets competitive." And another textbook author, Marshall Howard, praises the Sherman Antitrust Act as the "Magna Carta of free enterprise."

These economists are not rare in hailing the antitrust laws. In a recent survey of a sample of 600 economists, 85 percent agreed with the statement that "antitrust laws should be used vigorously to reduce monopoly power from its current level."

So despite mounting evidence that antitrust is *anti*competitive in its effects, there is strong sentiment in favor of even wider application of the antitrust laws! This apparent paradox, however, may have an explanation that is also quite revealing. The Sherman Act, considered by some to be the "Magna Carta of free enterprise," was probably never intended to promote competition! Instead, there is strong evidence that it was basically a legislative response to protectionist pressures in the late 19th century, much akin to the current clamor for an "industrial policy" designed to prop up the fortunes of US businesses that are under competitive pressure.

Contrary to popular mythology, the Sherman Act was never intended to promote competition but to protect (some) competitors.

Like most government regulation, then, the Sherman Act was not designed to advance the "public interest" but benefited well-organized private interests, including 19th-century farmers, small businesses, and politicians. In short, it is a myth that the Sherman Act of 1890 was passed to promote and protect competition among businesses.

MAJOR POLITICAL SUPPORT for the Sherman Act was first led by farmers' Grangers and the Agricultural Alliance, who were among the most potent political forces of the day. As historian Sanford D. Gordon recounts:

Perhaps the most violent reaction of any single special interest group came from farmers. Besides their active participation in the early anti-monopoly movement ... the

Agricultural Alliance ... regularly denounced trusts. They singled out the jute bagging and alleged binder twine trust, and sent petitions to both their state legislators and to Congress demanding some relief. Cotton was suggested as a good substitute for jute to cover their cotton bales. In Georgia, Mississippi, and Tennessee the Alliances passed resolutions condemning the jute bagging trust and recommended the use of cotton cloth.

When cotton cloth, produced by southern farmers, was being replaced by jute, they sought legislation that would dissipate their competition.

Gordon found this to be characteristic of the farm lobby. During the 51st Congress, which passed the Sherman Act,

> 64 petitions and memorials were recorded in the *Congressional Record*, all calling for action against combinations. These were almost exclusively from farm groups ... Not a single voice spoke up either in favor of, or expressing any neutrality toward trusts ... The greatest vehemence was expressed by representatives from the Mid-West.

Many other groups soon joined in the antitrust coalition—small business organizations, academics, and especially "progressive" journalists. The *Congressional Record* of the 51st Congress is replete with examples of legislators voicing the complaints of small businesses in their districts that were being subjected to "unfair" competition from the trusts.

To this day, farmers and small-business owners are among the most effective special interest groups, for there are still large numbers of them in a majority of congressional districts. Needless to say, their interests do not necessarily coincide with the interests of the vast majority of consumers.

Urged on by these interest groups, Sen. John Sherman and his colleagues claimed that combinations of businesses—or trusts—restricted output, and this drove prices up. As legal expert Robert Bork concluded in an exhaustive review of the *Congressional Record* of the 51st Congress:

> Sherman demonstrated more than once that he understood that higher prices were brought about by a restriction of output ... Sherman and his colleagues identified the phrase "restraint of commerce" or "restraint of trade" with "restriction of output."

If Sherman's claims were true, a look at the record should show a restriction of output in industries that were allegedly being monopolized by trusts. By contrast, if the tendency to combine into trusts was part of an evolutionary process of competitive markets responding to the rapid technological changes of the time, one might expect an *expansion* of trade or output in these industries.

Being curious about this, I compiled from the *Congressional Record* of the 51st Congress a list of industries that were accused of being monopolized by trusts. The graph on page 36 shows the industries for which data on output from 1880 to 1900 are available. The striking thing about this list is that of the 17 industries, there were *increases* in output not only from 1880 to 1890, the year the Sherman Act was passed, but also to the turn of the century in all but two industries, matches and castor oil. These last two are hardly items that would warrant a national furor, even if they were monopolized.

In addition, output in these industries generally expanded more rapidly than output in other industries during the 10 years leading up to the first trust-busting legislation. For some industries, there are records only of nominal output, while measures of real output are available for others.

In the nine industries for which nominal output is known, output increased on average by 62 percent almost four times the 16 percent increase in nominal GNP (gross national product) during that period. Several of the industries expanded output by more than 10 times the overall increase in nominal GNP.

Real GNP (adjusted for changes in the price level) increased by approximately 24 percent from 1880 to 1890. Meanwhile, the allegedly monopolized industries for which some measure of real output is available grew on average by 175 percent—seven times faster than all other industries.

Furthermore, these trends continued to the turn of the century. Output expanded in each industry except castor oil, and on average, output in these industries grew at a faster rate than the rest of the economy. Industries for which nominal output data are available expanded by 99 percent compared to a 43 percent increase in nominal GNP from 1890 to 1900, while the other industries increased real output by 76 percent compared to a 46 percent rise in real GNP.

In summary, this evidence undermines the notion that the industries singled out by Senator Sherman and his congressional colleagues were creating a "rising tide of monopoly power," if one judges by Senator Sherman's own measuring rod of monopoly power: output restriction. These industries were expanding much faster than the economy as a whole—some at 10 times the rate.

And predictably, prices in these industries were generally *falling*, not rising even when compared to the declining general price level For example, the average price of steel rails fell from $58 to $32 between 1880 and 1890, or by 53 percent. The price of refined sugar fell from 9 cents per pound in 1880 to 7 cents in 1890 and to 4.5 cents in 1900; the price of lead dropped from $5.04 per pound in 1880 to $4.41 in 1890; and zinc fell from $5.51 per pound to $4.40. Although the general price level also fell by seven percent from 1880 to 1890, it fell proportionately less than all of these items.

It turns out that the great beneficiary of competition—the consumer—was not the object of antitrust concern at all.

Perhaps the most widely attacked trusts were those in the sugar and petroleum industries. But there is evidence that the effect of these combinations or mergers was to *reduce* the prices of sugar and petroleum. In fact, even Congress clearly recognized this!

Rep. William Mason admitted during the House debates over the Sherman Act that "trusts have made products cheaper, have reduced prices." The objection lay elsewhere. "If the price of oil for instance, were reduced to one cent a barrel," declared Mason, "it would not right the wrong done to the people of this country by the 'trusts' which have destroyed legitimate competition and driven honest men from legitimate business enterprises." Likewise, Sen. John Edwards, who played a key role in the debate, insisted that the lowering of sugar and oil prices "does not alter the wrong of the principle of any trust."

It turns out that the great beneficiary of competition—the consumer—was not the object of antitrust concern at all. Instead, it was less-efficient, "honest businessmen" who were being priced out of the market. It is surely not insignificant that these and other business owners were in a position to contribute to political campaigns.

SENATOR SHERMAN AND his were right in one respect—there certainly was monopoly power in American industry during the late 19th century. It appears, however, that one function of the Sherman Act was to divert public attention from the real *source* of monopoly power—the government itself. Tariffs imposed by Congress were probably the major restraint of trade in the late 19th century, but the Sherman Act made no provision whatsoever for dismantling these.

In a particularly revealing statement, Sherman attacked the trusts during the Senate debates over his bill on the basis that they "subverted the tariff system; they undermined the policy of government to protect ... American industries by levying duties on imported goods." It's an odd statement for a reputed "champion of free enterprise." It is perfectly consistent, however, with an alternative picture: that Sherman was a protectionist, not a free-trader. With output expanding and prices falling in the industries attacked by Sherman, monopoly profits previously secured through protective tariffs were being dissipated. This was not to the liking of the protected industries and their legislative allies such as Senator Sherman.

Indeed, Sherman's true colors were in clear view just three months after the act was passed, when, as chairman of the Senate Finance Committee, he sponsored a tariff bill. This was so transparently a piece of special-interest legislation that the *New York Times* dubbed it the "Campaign Contributors' Tariff Bill." It "now goes to the president for his signature, which will speedily be affixed to it," reported the *Times* on October 1, 1890, "and the favored manufacturers, many of whom ... proposed and made the [tariff] rates which affect their products, will begin to enjoy the profits of this legislation."

The *Times* noted that Sherman's speech in support of the bill "should not be overlooked, for it was one of confession." Senator Sherman had withdrawn this speech from the *Congressional Record* for "revision," but not before a *Times* reporter had obtained an unabridged copy of the original. As the reporter wrote:

> We direct attention to those passages relating to combinations of protected manufacturers designed to take full advantage of high tariff duties by exacting from consumers prices fixed by agreement after competition has been suppressed ... Mr. Sherman closed his speech with some words of warning and advice to the beneficiaries of the new

tariff. He was earnest enough in his manner to indicate that he is not at all confident as to the out-come of the law. The great thing that stood in the way of the success of the bill, he said, was whether or not the manufacturers of this country would permit free competition in the American market. The danger was that the beneficiaries of the bill would combine and cheat the people out of the benefits of the law. They were now given reasonable and ample protection, and if they would resist the temptation attaching to great aggregations of capital to combine and advance prices, they might hope for a season of great prosperity … He did hope, the Senator concluded, that the manufacturers would open the doors to fair competition and give its benefits to the people … He hoped the manufacturers would agree to compete one with another and would refuse to take the high prices that are so easily obtained.

For Senator Sherman to say that a protective tariff would not harm consumers if only manufacturers would not raise prices is contradictory, to put it mildly. Sherman's intention was clearly to isolate American manufacturers from international competition and then, when the protected industries raised prices, to blame it on "dangerous combinations of capital."

Such hypocrisy led to a complete reversal of the editorial position of the New York Times. For years the Times had been a foremost proponent of antitrust legislation. After observing the

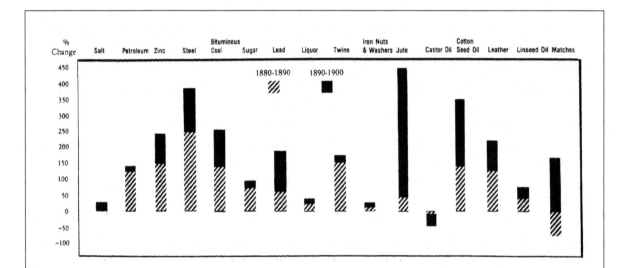

Nineteenth-century politicians claimed that monopolized industries would restrict output to drive up prices. In fact, from 1880 to 1890 (when the Sherman Act was passed) and from 1890 to 1900, the output in 15 out of 17 allegedly monopolized industries actually *increased*.

SOURCES: US BUREAU OF THE CENSUS: *STATISTICAL ABSTRACT OF THE UNITED STATES (VARIOUS YEARS) AND HISTORICAL STATISTICS OF THE UNITED STATES.*

behavior of Sherman and his congressional colleagues during the months following the passage of the Sherman Act, the editors concluded:

> That so-called Anti-Trust law was passed to deceive the people and to clear the way for the enactment of this … law relating to the tariff. It was projected in order that the party organs might say to the opponents of tariff extortion and protected combinations, "Behold! We have attacked the Trusts. The Republican party is the enemy of all such rings." And now the author of it can-only "hope" that the rings will dissolve of their own accord.

For centuries, monopoly has been associated with governmentally imposed barriers to free trade such as tariffs, import quotas, professional licenses, and monopoly franchises. But all of this is immune from antitrust law. It appears that the Sherman Act was passed to help draw public attention away from the actual process of monopolization in the economy, among the major beneficiaries of which have always been the legislators themselves. By interfering with the competitive process, Congress became perhaps the one interest group to benefit most from the Sherman Act.

One function of the Sherman Act was to divert public attention from the real source of monopoly power—the government.

WHERE WERE ECONOMISTS during all this? They were not even asked their opinions of the proposed antitrust law, and it is easy to understand why; they were nearly unanimously opposed to it. The historian Sanford D. Gordon has surveyed all articles and books written by economists on the topic of antitrust prior to the Sherman Act. A large majority, he found, conceded that the combination movement was to be expected, that high fixed costs made large scale enterprises economical, that competition under these new circumstances frequently resulted in cutthroat competition, that agreements among producers was a natural consequence, and the stability of prices usually brought more benefit than harm to the society. They seemed to reject the idea that competition was declining, or showed no fear of decline.

One of the best younger economists, John Bates Clark, said this about trusts:

> Combinations have their roots in the nature of social industry and are normal in their origin, their development, and their practical working. They are neither to be deprecated by scientists nor suppressed by legislators … A successful attempt to suppress them by law would involve the reversion of industrial systems to a cast-off type, the renewal of abuses from which society has escaped by a step in development.

Economists' opposition to antitrust legislation was so universal that even Richard T. Ely, who founded the American Economic Association and who believed that "the doctrine of laissez-faire is unsafe in politics and unsound in morals," was opposed to it.

So it should really come as no surprise that antitrust law, for the past 90 years, has been anti-competitive in its effects. Contrary to popular mythology, the Sherman Act was never intended to promote competition. Instead, its sole purpose was to protect (some) competitors.

When the aging Senator Sherman, who was about to retire, became involved in the antitrust issue, he had just gone through an exhausting and unsuccessful attempt to secure his party's presidential nomination, and perhaps he saw the antitrust issue as his final claim to political fame. Whatever else may be said of the Sherman Antitrust Act, one thing it did accomplish was to make Sen. John Sherman at least as famous as his elder brother, Gen. William Tecumseh Sherman, of Civil War notoriety. But like slavery, antitrust laws should be abolished.

Occupational Licensure

By Milton Friedman

THE OVERTHROW OF the medieval guild system was an indispensable early step in the rise of freedom in the Western world. It was a sign of the triumph of liberal ideas, and widely recognized as such, that by the mid-nineteenth century, in Britain, the United States, and to a lesser extent on the continent of Europe, men could pursue whatever trade or occupation they wished without the by-your-leave of any governmental or quasi-governmental authority. In more recent decades, there has been a retrogression, an increasing tendency for particular occupations to be restricted to individuals licensed to practice them by the state.

These restrictions on the freedom of individuals to use their resources as they wish are important in their own right. In addition, they provide still a different class of problems to which we can apply the principles developed in the first two chapters.

I shall discuss first the general problem and then a particular example, restrictions on the practice of medicine. The reason for choosing medicine is that it seems desirable to discuss the restrictions for which the strongest case can be made—there is not much to be learned by knocking down straw men. I suspect that most people, possibly even most liberals, believe that it is desirable to restrict the practice of medicine to people who are licensed by the state. I agree that the case for licensure is stronger for medicine than for most other fields. Yet the conclusions I shall reach are that liberal principles do not justify licensure even in medicine and that in practice the results of state licensure in medicine have been undesirable.

UBIQUITY OF GOVERNMENTAL RESTRICTIONS ON ECONOMIC ACTIVITIES MEN MAY ENGAGE IN

Licensure is a special case of a much more general and exceedingly widespread phenomenon, namely, edicts that individuals may not engage in particular economic activities except under conditions laid down by a constituted authority of the state. Medieval guilds were a particular example of an explicit system for specifying which individuals should be permitted to follow particular pursuits. The Indian caste system is another example. To a considerable extent in the caste system, to a lesser extent in the guilds, the restrictions were enforced by general social customs rather than explicitly by government.

A widespread notion about the caste system is that every person's occupation is completely determined by the caste into which he is born. It is obvious to an economist that this is an impossible system, since it prescribes a rigid distribution of persons among occupations determined entirely by birthrates and not at all by conditions of demand. Of course, this is not the way the system worked. What was true, and to some measure still is, was that a limited number of occupations were reserved to members of certain castes, but not every member of those castes followed those occupations. There were some general occupations, such as general agricultural work, which members of various castes might engage in. These permitted an adjustment of the supply of people in different occupations to the demand for their services.

Currently, tariffs, fair-trade laws, import quotas, production quotas, trade union restrictions on employment and so on are examples of similar phenomena. In all these cases, governmental authority determines the conditions under which particular individuals can engage in particular activities, which is to say, the terms on which some individuals are permitted to make arrangements with others. The common feature of these examples, as well as of licensure, is that the legislation is enacted on behalf of a producer group. For licensure, the producer group is generally a craft. For the other examples, it may be a group producing a particular product which wants a tariff a group of small retailers who would like to be protected from competition by the "chiseling" chain stores, or a group of oil producers, of farmers, or of steel workers.

Occupational licensure is by now very widespread. According to Walter Gellhorn[1], who has written the best brief survey I know, "By 1952 more than 80 separate occupations exclusive of 'owner-businesses,' like restaurants and taxicab companies, had been licensed by state law; and in addition to the state laws there are municipal ordinances in abundance, not to mention the federal statutes that require the licensing of such diverse occupations as radio operators and stockyard commission agents. As long ago as 1938 a single state, North Carolina, had extended its law to 60 occupations. One may not be surprised to learn that pharmacists, accountants, and dentists have been reached by state law as have sanitarians and psychologists, assayers and architects, veterinarians and librarians. But with what joy of discovery does one learn about the licensing of threshing machine operators and dealers in scrap tobacco? What of egg graders and guide dog trainers, pest controllers and yacht salesmen, tree surgeons and well diggers, tile layers and potato growers? And what of the hypertrichologists who are licensed in Connecticut, where they remove excessive and unsightly hair with the solemnity appropriate to their high sounding title?"[1] In the arguments that seek to persuade legislatures to enact such licensure provisions, the justification is always said to be the necessity of protecting the public interest. However, the pressure on the legislature to license an occupation rarely comes from the members of the public who have been mulcted or in other ways abused by members of the occupation. On the contrary, the pressure invariably comes from members of the occupation itself. Of course, they are more aware than others of how much they exploit the customer and so perhaps they can lay claim to expert knowledge.

---

1   Walter Gellhorn, *Individual Freedom and Governmental Restraints* (Baton Rouge: Louisiana State University Press, 1956). Chapter entitled "The Right to Make a Living," p. 106.

Similarly, the arrangements made for licensure almost invariably involve control by members of the occupation which is to be licensed. Again, this is in some ways quite natural. If the occupation of plumbing is to be restricted to those who have the requisite capacity and skills to provide good service for their customers, clearly only plumbers are capable of judging who should be licensed. Consequently, the board or other body that grants licenses is almost invariably made up largely of plumbers or pharmacists or physicians or whatever may be the particular occupation licensed.

Gellhorn points out that "Seventy-five percent of the occupational licensing boards at work in this country today are composed exclusively of licensed practitioners in the respective occupations. These men and women, most of whom are only part-time officials, may have a direct economic interest in many of the decisions they make concerning admission requirements and the definition of standards to be observed by licensees. More importantly, they are as a rule directly representative of organized groups within the occupations. Ordinarily they are nominated by these groups as a step toward a gubernatorial or other appointment that is frequently a mere formality. Often the formality is dispensed with entirely, appointment being made directly by the occupational association—as happens, for example, with the embalmers in North Carolina, the dentist in Alabama, the psychologists in Virginia, the physicians in Maryland, and die attorneys in Washington."[2]

Licensure therefore frequently establishes essentially the medieval guild kind of regulation in which the state assigns power to the members of the profession. In practice, the considerations taken into account in determining who shall get a license often involve matters that, so far as a layman can see, have no relation whatsoever to professional competence. This is not surprising. If a few individuals are going to decide whether other individuals may pursue an occupation, all sorts of irrelevant considerations are likely to enter. Just what the irrelevant considerations will be, will depend on the personalities of the members of the licensing board and the mood of the time. Gellhorn notes the extent to which a loyalty oath was required of various occupations when the fear of communist subversion was sweeping the country. He writes, "A Texas statute of 1952 requires each applicant for a pharmacist's license to swear that 'he is not a member of the Communist Party or affiliated with such party, and that he does not believe in and is neither a member of nor supports any group or organization that believes in, furthers or teaches the overthrow of the United States Government by force or any illegal or unconstitutional methods.' The relationship between this oath on the one hand and, on the other, the public health which is the interest purportedly protected by the licensing of pharmacists, is somewhat obscure. No more apparent is the justification for requiring professional boxers and wrestlers in Indiana to swear that they are not subversive ... A junior high school teacher of music, having been forced to resign after being identified as a Communist, had difficulty becoming a piano tuner in the District of Columbia because, forsooth, he was 'under Communist discipline.' Veterinarians in the state of Washington may not minister to an ailing cow or cat unless they have first signed a non-Communist oath."[3]

---

2 *Ibid.*, pp. 140–41.

3 *Ibid.*, pp. 129–30.

Whatever one's attitude towards communism, any relationship between the requirements imposed and the qualities which the licensure is intended to assure is rather far-fetched. The extent to which such requirements go is sometimes little short of ludicrous. A few more quotations from Gellhorn may provide a touch of comic relief.[4]

One of the most amusing sets of regulations is that laid down for barbers, a trade that is licensed in many places. Here is an example from a law which was declared invalid by Maryland courts, though similar language can be found in statutes of other states which were declared legal. "The court was depressed rather than impressed by a legislative command that neophyte barbers must receive formal instruction in the 'scientific fundamentals for barbering, hygiene, bacteriology, histology of the hair, skin, nails, muscles and nerves, structure of the head, face and neck, elementary chemistry relating to sterilization and antiseptics, disease of the skin, hair, glands and nails, haircutting, shaving and arranging, dressing, coloring, bleaching, and tinting of the hair.'"[5] One more quotation on the barbers: "Of eighteen representative states included in a study of barbering regulations in 1929, not one then commanded an aspirant to be a graduate of a 'barber college,' though apprenticeship was necessary in all. Today, the states typically insist upon graduation from a barbering school that provides not less (and often much more) than one thousand hours of instruction in 'theoretical subjects' such as sterilization of instruments, and this must still be followed by apprenticeship."[6] I trust these quotations make it clear that the problem of licensing of occupations is something more than a trivial illustration of the problem of state intervention, that it is already in this country a serious infringement on the freedom of individuals to pursue activities of their own choice, and that it threatens to become a much more serious one with the continual pressure upon legislatures to extend it.

Before discussing the advantages and disadvantages of licensing, it is worth noting why we have it and what general political problem is revealed by the tendency for such special legislation to be enacted. The declaration by a large number of different state legislatures that barbers must be approved by a committee of other barbers is hardly persuasive evidence that there is in fact a public interest in having such legislation. Surely the explanation is different; it is that a producer group tends to be more concentrated politically than a consumer group. This is an obvious point often made and yet one whose importance cannot be over-stressed.[7] Each of us is a producer and also a consumer. However, we are much more specialized and devote a much larger fraction of our attention to our activity as a producer than as a consumer. We consume literally thousands if not millions of items. The result is that people in the same trade, like barbers or physicians, all have an intense interest in the specific problems of this trade and

---

4 In fairness to Walter Gellhorn, I should note that he does not share my view that the correct solution to these problems is to abandon licensing. On the contrary, he thinks that while licensing has gone much too far, it has some real functions to perform. He suggests procedural reforms and changes that in his view would limit the abuse of licensure arrangements.

5 *Ibid.*, pp.121–22.

6 *Ibid.*, p.146.

7 See, for example, Wesley Mitchell's famous article on the "Backward Art of Spending Money," reprinted in his book of essays carrying that title (New York: McGraw-Hill, 1937), pp. 3–19.

are willing to devote considerable energy to doing something about them. On the other hand, those of us who use barbers at all get barbered infrequently and spend only a minor fraction of our income in barber shops. Our interest is casual. Hardly any of us are willing to devote much time going to the legislature in order to testify against the iniquity of restricting the practice of barbering. The same point holds for tariffs. The groups that think they have a special interest in particular tariffs are concentrated groups to whom the issue makes a great deal of difference. The public interest is widely dispersed. In consequence, in the absence of any general arrangements to offset the pressure of special interests, producer groups will invariably have a much stronger influence on legislative action and the powers that be than will the diverse, widely spread consumer interest. Indeed from this point of view, the puzzle is not why we have so many silly licensure laws, but why we don't have far more The puzzle is how we ever succeeded in getting the relative freedom from government controls over the productive activities of individuals that we have had and still have in this country, and that other countries have had as well.

The only way that I can see to offset special producer groups is to establish a general presumption against the state undertaking certain kinds of activities. Only if there is a general recognition that governmental activities should be severely limited with respect to a class of cases, can the burden of proof be put strongly enough on those who would depart from this general presumption to give a reasonable hope of limiting the spread of special measures to further special interests. This point is one we have adverted to time and again. It is of a piece with the argument for the Bill of Rights and for a rule to govern monetary policy and fiscal policy.

POLICY ISSUES RAISED BY LICENSURE

It is important to distinguish three different levels of control: first, registration; second, certification; third, licensing.

By registration, I mean an arrangement under which individuals are required to list their names in some official register if they engage in certain kinds of activities. There is no provision for denying the right to engage in the activity to anyone who is willing to list his name. He may be charged a fee, either as a registration fee or as a scheme of taxation.

The second level is certification. The governmental agency may certify that an individual has certain skills but may not prevent, in any way, the practice of any occupation using these skills by people who do not have such a certificate. One example is accountancy. In most states, anybody can be an accountant, whether he is a certified public accountant or not, but only those people who have passed a particular test can put the title CPA after their names or can put a sign in their offices saying they are certified public accountants. Certification is frequently only an intermediate stage. In many states, there has been a tendency to restrict an increasing range of activities to certified public accountants. With respect to such activities there is licensure, not certification. In some states, "architect" is a title which can be used only by those who have passed a specified examination. This is certification. It does not prevent anyone else from going into the business of advising people for a fee how to build houses.

The third stage is licensing proper. This is an arrangement under which one must obtain a license from a recognized authority in order to engage in the occupation. The license is more than a formality. It requires some demonstration of competence or the meeting of some tests ostensibly designed to insure competence, and anyone who does not have a license is not authorized to practice and is subject to a fine or a jail sentence if he does engage in practice.

The question I want to consider is this: under what circumstances, if any, can we justify the one or the other of these steps? There are three different grounds on which it seems to me registration can be justified consistently with liberal principles.

First, it may assist in the pursuit of other aims. Let me illustrate. The police are often concerned with acts of violence. After the event, it is desirable to find out who had access to firearms. Before the events it is desirable to prevent firearms from getting into the hands of people who are likely to use them for criminal purposes. It may assist in the pursuit of this aim to register stores selling firearms. Of course, if I may revert to a point made several times In earlier chapters, It is never enough to say that there *might* be a justification along these lines, in order to conclude that there *is* justification. It is necessary to set up a balance sheet of the advantages and disadvantages in the light of liberal principles. All I am now saying is that this consideration might in some cases justify overriding the general presumption against requiring the registration of people.

Second, registration is sometimes a device to facilitate taxation and nothing more. The questions at issue then become whether the particular tax is an appropriate method to raise revenue for financing government services regarded as necessary, and whether registration facilitates the collection of taxes. It may do so either because a tax is imposed on the person who registers, or because the person who registers is used as a tax collector. For example, in collecting a sales tax imposed on various items of consumption, it is necessary to have a register or list of all the places selling goods subject to the tax.

Third, and this is the one possible justification for registration which is close to our main interest, registration may be a means to protect consumers against fraud. In general, liberal principles assign to the state the power to enforce contracts, and fraud involves the violation of a contract. It is, of course, dubious that one should go very far to protect in advance against fraud because of the interference with voluntary contracts involved in doing so. But I do not think that one can rule out on grounds of principle the possibility that there may be certain activities that are so likely to give rise to fraud as to render it desirable to have in advance a list of people known to be pursuing this activity. Perhaps one example along these lines is the registration of taxicab drivers. A taxicab driver picking up a person at night may be in a particularly good position to steal from him. To inhibit such practices, it may be desirable to have a list of names of people who are engaged in the taxicab business, to give each a number, and to require that this number be put in the cab so that anyone molested need only remember the number of the cab. This involves simply the use of the police power to protect individuals against violence on the part of other individuals and may be the most convenient method of doing so.

Certification is much more difficult to justify. The reason is that this is something the private market generally can do for itself. This problem is the same for products as for people's services. There are private certification agencies in many areas that certify the competence of a person or the quality of a particular product. The *Good Housekeeping* seal is a private certification arrangement. For industrial products there are private testing laboratories that will certify to the quality of a particular product. For consumer products, there are consumer testing agencies of which Consumer's Union and Consumer's Research are the best known in the United States. Better Business Bureaus are voluntary organizations that certify the quality of particular dealers. Technical schools, colleges, and universities certify the quality of their graduates. One function of retailers and department stores is to certify the quality of the many items they sell. The consumer develops confidence in the store, and the store in turn has an incentive to earn this confidence by investigating the quality of the items it sells.

One can however argue that in some cases, or perhaps even in many, voluntary certification will not be carried as far as individuals would be willing to pay for carrying it because of the difficulty of keeping the certification confidential. The issue is essentially the one involved in patents and copyrights, namely, whether individuals are in a position to capture the value of the services that they render to others. If I go into the business of certifying people, there may be no efficient way in which I can require you to pay for my certification. If I sell my certification information to one person, how can I keep him from passing it on to others? Consequently, it may not be possible to get effective voluntary exchange with respect to certification, even though this is a service that people would be willing to pay for if they had to. One way to get around this problem, as we get around other kinds of neighborhood effects, is to have governmental certification.

Another possible justification for certification is on monopoly grounds. There are some technical monopoly aspects to certification since the cost of making a certification is largely independent of the number of people to whom the information is transmitted. However, it is by no means clear that monopoly is inevitable.

Licensure seems to me still more difficult to justify. It goes still farther in the direction of trenching upon the rights of individuals to enter into voluntary contracts. Nonetheless, there are some justifications given for licensure that the liberal will have to recognize as within his own conception of appropriate government action, though, as always, the advantages have to be weighed against the disadvantages. The main argument that is relevant to a liberal is the existence of neighborhood effects. The simplest and most obvious example is the "incompetent" physician who produces an epidemic. Insofar as he harms only his patient, that is simply a question of voluntary contract and exchange between the patient and his physician. On this score, there is no ground for intervention. However, it can be argued that if the physician treats his patient badly, he may unleash an epidemic that will cause harm to third parties who are not involved in the immediate transaction. In such a case, it is conceivable that everybody, including even the potential patient and physician, would be willing to submit to the restriction of the practice of medicine to "competent" people in order to prevent such epidemics from occurring.

In practice, the major argument given for licensure by its proponents is not this one, which has some appeal to a liberal, but rather a strictly paternalistic argument that has little or no appeal. Individuals, it is said, are incapable of choosing their own servants adequately, their own physician or plumber or barber. In order for a man to choose a physician intelligently, he would have to be a physician himself. Most of us, it is said, are therefore incompetent and we must be protected against our own ignorance. This amounts to saying that we in our capacity as voters must protect ourselves in our capacity as consumers against our own ignorance, by seeing to it that people are not served by incompetent physicians or plumbers or barbers.

So far, I have been listing the arguments for registration, certification, and licensing. In all three cases, it is clear that there are also strong social costs to be set against any of these advantages. Some of these social costs have already been suggested and I shall illustrate them in more detail for medicine, but it may be worth recording them here in general form.

The most obvious social cost is that any one of these measures, whether it be registration certification, or licensure, almost inevitably becomes a tool in the hands of a special producer group to obtain a monopoly position at the expense of the rest of the public. There is no way to avoid this result. One can devise one or another set of procedural controls designed to avert this out-come, but none is likely to overcome the problem that arises out of the greater concentration of producer than of consumer interest. The people who are most concerned with any such, arrangement, who will press most for its enforcement and be most concerned with its administration, will be the people in the particular occupation or trade involved. They will inevitably press for the extension of registration to certification and of certification to licensure. Once licensure is attained, the people who might develop an interest in undermining the regulations are kept from exerting their influence. They don't get a license, must therefore go into other occupations, and will lose interest. The result is invariably control over entry by members of the occupation itself and hence the establishment of a monopoly position.

Certification is much less harmful in this respect. If the certified "abuse" their special certificates; if, in certifying new-comers, members of the trade impose unnecessarily stringent requirements and reduce the number of practitioners too much, the price differential between certified and non-certified will become sufficiently large to induce the public to use non-certified practitioners. In technical terms, the elasticity of demand for the services of certified practitioners will be fairly large, and the limits within which they can exploit the rest of the public by taking advantage of their special position will be rather narrow.

In consequence, certification without licensure is a half-way house that maintains a good deal of protection against monopolization. It also has its disadvantages, but it is worth noting that the usual arguments for licensure, and in particular the paternalistic arguments, are satisfied almost entirely by certification alone. If the argument is that we are too ignorant to judge good practitioners, all that is needed is to make the relevant information available. If, in full knowledge, we still want to go to someone who is not certified, that is our business; we cannot complain that we did not have the information. Since arguments for licensure made by people who are not members of the occupation can be satisfied so fully by certification, I personally find it difficult to see any case for which licensure rather than certification can be justified.

Even registration has significant social costs. It is an important first step in the direction of a system in which every individual has to carry an identity card, every individual has to inform authorities what he plans to do before he does it. Moreover, as already noted, registration tends to be the first step toward certification and licensure.

MEDICAL LICENSURE

The medical profession is one in which practice of the profession has for a long time been restricted to people with licenses. Offhand, the question, "Ought we to let incompetent physicians practice?" seems to admit of only a negative answer. But I want to urge that second thought may give pause.

In the first place, licensure is the key to the control that the medical profession can exercise over the number of physicians. To understand why this is so requires some discussion of the structure of the medical profession. The American Medical Association is perhaps the strongest trade union in the United States. The essence of the power of a trade union is its power to restrict the number who may engage in a particular occupation. This restriction may be exercised indirectly by being able to enforce a wage rate higher than would otherwise prevail. If such a wage rate can be enforced, it will reduce the number of people who can get jobs and thus indirectly the number of people pursuing the occupation. This technique of restriction has disadvantages. There is always a dissatisfied fringe of people who are trying to get into the occupation. A trade union is much better off if it can limit directly the number of people who enter the occupation—who ever try to get jobs in it. The disgruntled and dissatisfied are excluded at the outset, and the union does not have to worry about them.

The American Medical Association is in this position. It is a trade union that can limit the number of people who can enter. How can it do this? The essential control is at the stage of admission to medical school. The Council on Medical Education and Hospitals of the American Medical Association approves medical schools. In order for a medical school to get and stay on its list of approved schools it has to meet the standards of the Council. The power of the Council has been demonstrated at various times when there has been pressure to reduce numbers. For example, in the 1930's during the depression, the Council on Medical Education and Hospitals wrote a letter to the various medical schools saying the medical schools were admitting more students than could be given the proper kind of training. In the next year or two, every school reduced the number it was admitting, giving very strong presumptive evidence that the recommendation had some effect.

Why does the Council's approval matter so much? If it abuses its power, why don't unapproved medical schools arise? The answer is that in almost every state in the United States, a person must be licensed to practice medicine, and to get the license, he must be a graduate of an approved school. In almost every State, the list of approved schools is identical with the list of schools approved by the Council on Medical Education and Hospitals of the American Medical Association. That is why the licensure provision is the key to the effective control of admission. It has a dual effect. On the one hand, the members of the licensure commission are always physicians and hence have some control at the step at which men apply for a license. This control is more limited in effectiveness than control at the medical school level. In almost all professions requiring licensure, people may try to get admitted more than once. If a person tries long enough and in enough jurisdictions he is likely to get through sooner or later. Since he has already spent the money and time to get his trainings he has a strong incentive to keep trying. Licensure provisions that come into operation only after a man is trained therefore affect entry largely by raising the costs of getting into the occupation since it may take a longer time to get in and since there is always some uncertainty whether he will succeed. But this rise in cost is nothing like so effective in limiting entry as is preventing a man from getting started on his career. If he is eliminated at the stage of entering medical school, he never comes up as a candidate for examination; he can never be troublesome at that stage. The efficient way to get control over the number in a profession is therefore to get control of entry into professional schools.

Control over admission to medical school and later licensure enables the profession to limit entry in two ways. The obvious one is simply by turning down many applicants. The less obvious, but probably far more important one, is by establishing standards for admission and licensure that make entry so difficult as to discourage young people from ever trying to get admission. Though most state laws require only two years of college prior to medical school, nearly 100 percent of the entrants have had four years of college. Similarly, medical training proper has been lengthened, particularly through more stringent internship arrangements.

As an aside, the lawyers have never been as successful as the physicians in getting control at the point of admission to professional school, though they are moving in that direction. The reason is amusing. Almost every school on the American Bar Association's list of approved schools is a full time day school; almost no night schools are approved. Many state legislators, on the other hand, are graduates of night law schools. If they voted to restrict admission to the profession to graduates of approved schools, in effect they would be voting that they themselves were not qualified. Their reluctance to condemn their own competence has been the main factor that has tended to limit the extent to which law has been able to succeed in imitating medicine. I have not myself done any extensive work on requirements for admission to law for many years but I understand that this limitation is breaking down. The greater affluence of students means that a much larger fraction are going to full time law schools and this is changing the composition of the legislatures.

To return to medicine, it is the provision about graduation from approved schools that is the most important source of professional control over entry. The profession has used this control to limit numbers. To avoid misunderstanding let me emphasize that I am not saying that individual members of the medical profession, the leaders of the medical profession, or the people who are in charge of the Council on Medical Education and Hospitals deliberately go out of their way to limit entry in order to raise their own incomes. That is not the way it works. Even when such people explicitly comment on the desirability of limiting numbers to raise incomes, they will always justify the policy on the grounds that if "too" many people are let in, this will lower their incomes so that they will be driven to resort to unethical practices in order to earn a "proper" income. The only way, they argue, in which ethical practices can be maintained is by keeping people at a standard of income which is adequate to the merits and needs of the medical profession. I must confess that this has always seemed to me objectionable on both ethical and factual grounds. It is extraordinary that leaders of medicine should proclaim publicly that they and their colleagues must be paid to be ethical. And if it were so, I doubt that the price would have any limit. There seems little correlation between poverty and honesty. One would rather expect the opposite; dishonesty may not always pay but surely it sometimes does.

Control of entry is explicitly rationalized along these lines only at times like the Great Depression when there is much unemployment and relatively low incomes. In ordinary times, the rationalization for restriction is different. It is that the members of the medical profession want to raise what they regard as the standards of "quality" of the profession. The defect in this rationalization is a common one and one that is destructive of a proper understanding of the operation of an economic system, namely, the failure to distinguish between technical efficiency and economic efficiency.

A story about lawyers will perhaps illustrate the point. At a meeting of lawyers at which problems of admission were being discussed, a colleague of mine, arguing against restrictive admission standards, used an analogy from the automobile industry. Would it not, he said, be absurd if the automobile industry were to argue that no one should drive a low quality car and therefore that no automobile manufacturer should be permitted to produce a car that did not come up to the Cadillac standard. One member of the audience rose and approved the analogy, saying that, of course, the country cannot afford anything but Cadillac lawyers! This tends to be the professional attitude. The members look solely at technical standards of performance, and argue in effect that we must have only first-rate physicians even if this means that some people get no medical service—though of course they never put it that way. Nonetheless, the view that people should get only the "optimum" medical service always lead to a restrictive policy, a policy that keeps down the number of physicians. I would not, of course, want to argue that this is the only force at work, but only that this kind of consideration leads many well-meaning physicians to go along with policies that they would reject out-of-hand if they did not have this kind of comforting rationalization.

It is easy to demonstrate that quality is only a rationalization and not the underlying reason for restriction. The power of the Council on Medical Education and Hospitals of the American Medical Association has been used to limit numbers in ways that cannot possibly have any connection whatsoever with, quality. The simplest example is their recommendation to various states that citizenship be made a requirement for the practice of medicine. I find it inconceivable to see how this is relevant to medical performance. A similar requirement that they have tried to impose on occasion is that examination for licensure must be taken in English. A dramatic piece of evidence on the power and potency of the Association as well as on the lack of relation to quality is proved by one figure that I have always found striking. After 1933, when Hitler came to power in Germany, there was a tremendous outflow of professional people from Germany, Austria and so on, including of course, physicians who wanted to practice in the United States. The number of physicians trained abroad who were admitted to practice in the United States in the five years after 1933 was the same as in the five years before. This was clearly not the result of the natural course of events. The threat of these additional physicians led to a stringent tightening of requirements for foreign physicians that imposed extreme costs upon them.

It is clear that licensure is the key to the medical profession's ability to restrict the number of physicians who practice medicine. It is also the key to its ability to restrict technological and organizational changes in the way medicine is conducted. The American Medical Association has been consistently against the practice of group medicine, and against prepaid medical plans. These methods of practice may have good features and bad features, but they are technological innovations that people ought to be free to try out if they wish. There is no basis for saying conclusively that the optimum technical method of organizing medical practice is practice by an independent physician. Maybe it is group practice, maybe it is by corporations. One ought to have a system under which all varieties can be tried.

The American Medical Association has resisted such attempts and has been able effectively to inhibit them. It has been able to do so because licensure has indirectly given it control of admission to practice in hospitals. The Council on Medical Education and Hospitals approves hospitals as well as medical schools. In order for a physician to get admission to practice in an "approved" hospital, he must generally be approved by his county medical association or by the hospital board. Why can't unapproved hospitals be set up? Because, under present economic conditions, in order for a hospital to operate it must have a supply of interns. Under most state licensure laws, candidates must have some internship experience to be admitted to practice, and internship must be in an "approved" hospital. The list of "approved" hospitals is generally identical with that of the Council on Medical Education and Hospitals. Consequently, the licensure law gives the profession control over hospitals as well as over schools. This is the key to the AMA's largely successful opposition to various types of group practice. In a few cases, the groups have been able to survive. In the District of Columbia, they succeeded because they were able to bring suit against the American Medical Association under the federal Sherman antitrust laws, and won the suit. In a few other cases, they have succeeded for special reasons. There is, however, no doubt that the tendency toward group practice has been greatly retarded by the AMA's opposition.

It is interesting, and this is an aside, that the medical association is against only one type of group practice, namely, prepaid group practice. The economic reason seems to be that this eliminates the possibility of engaging in discriminatory pricing.[8]

It is clear that licensure has been at the core of the restriction of entry and that this involves a heavy social cost, both to the individuals who want to practice medicine but are prevented from doing so and to the public deprived of the medical care it wants to buy and is prevented from buying. Let me now ask the question: Does licensure have the good effects that it is said to have?

In the first place, does it really raise standards of competence? It is by no means clear that it does raise the standards of competence in the actual practice of the profession for several reasons. In the first place, whenever you establish a block to entry into any field, you establish an incentive to find ways of getting around it, and of course medicine is no exception. The rise of the professions of osteopathy and of chiropractic is not unrelated to the restriction of entry into medicine. On the contrary, each of these represented, to some extent, an attempt to find a way around restriction of entry. Each of these, in turn, is proceeding to get itself licensed, and to impose restrictions. The effect is to create different levels and kinds of practice, to distinguish between what is called medical practice and substitutes such as osteopathy, chiropractic, faith

---

8   See Reuben Kessel, "Price Discrimination in Medicine," *The Journal of Law and Economics*, Vol. I (October, 1958), 20–53.

healing and so on. These alternatives may well be of lower quality than medical practice would have been without the restrictions on entry into medicine.

More generally, if the number of physicians is less than it otherwise would be, and if they are all fully occupied, as they generally are, this means that there is a smaller total of medical practice by trained physicians—fewer medical man-hours of practice, as it were. The alternative is untrained practice by somebody; it may and in part must be by people who have no professional qualifications at all. Moreover, the situation is much more extreme. If "medical practice" is to be limited to licensed practitioners, it is necessary to define what medical practice is, and featherbedding is not something that is restricted to the railroads. Under the interpretation of the statutes forbidding unauthorized practice of medicine, many things are restricted to licensed physicians that could perfectly well be done by technicians, and other skilled people who do not have a Cadillac medical training. I am not enough of a technician to list the examples at all fully. I only know that those who have looked into the question say that the tendency is to include in "medical practice" a wider and wider range of activities that could perfectly well be performed by technicians. Trained physicians devote a considerable part of their time to things that might well be done by others. The result is to reduce drastically the amount of medical care. The relevant average quality of medical care, if one can at all conceive of the concept, cannot be obtained by simply averaging the quality of care that is given; that would be like judging the effectiveness of a medical treatment by considering only the survivors; one must also allow for the fact that the restrictions reduce the amount of care. The result may well be that the average level of competence in a meaningful sense has been reduced by the restrictions.

Even these comments do not go far enough, because they consider the situation at a point in time and do not allow for changes over time. Advances in any science or field often result from the work of one out of a large number of crackpots and quacks and people who have no standing in the profession. In the medical profession, under present circumstances, it is very difficult to engage in research or experimentation unless you are a member of the profession. If you are a member of the profession and want to stay in good standing in the profession, you are seriously limited in the kind of experimentation you can do. A "faith healer" may be just a quack who is imposing himself on credulous patients, but may be one in a thousand or in many thousands will produce an important improvement in medicine. There are many different routes to knowledge and learning and the effect of restricting the practice of what is called medicine and defining it as we tend to do to a particular group, who in the main have to conform to the prevailing orthodoxy, is certain to reduce the amount of experimentation that goes on and hence to reduce the rate of growth of knowledge in the area. What is true for the content of medicine is true also for its organization, as has already been suggested. I shall expand further on this point below.

There is still another way in which licensure, and the associated monopoly in the practice of medicine, tend to render standards of practice low. I have already suggested that it renders the average quality of practice low by reducing the number of physicians, by reducing the aggregate number of hours available from trained physicians for more rather than less important tasks, and by reducing the incentive for research and development. It renders it low also by making it much more difficult for private individuals to collect from physicians for malpractice. One of the protections of the individual citizen against incompetence is protection against fraud and the ability to bring suit in the court against malpractice. Some suits are brought, and physicians complain a great deal about how much they have to pay for malpractice insurance. Yet suits for malpractice are fewer and less successful than they would be were it not for the watchful eye of the medical associations. It is not easy to get a physician to testify against a fellow physician when he faces the sanction of being denied the right to practice in an "approved" hospital. The testimony generally has to come from members of panels set up by medical associations themselves, always, of course, in the alleged interest of the patients:

When these effects are taken into account, I am myself persuaded that licensure has reduced both the quantity and quality of medical practice; that it has reduced the opportunities available to people who would like to be physicians, forcing them to pursue occupations they regard as less attractive; that it has forced the public to pay more for less satisfactory medical service, and that it has retarded technological development both in medicine itself and in the organization of medical practice. I conclude that licensure should be eliminated as a requirement for the practice of medicine.

When all this is said, many a reader, I suspect, like many a person with whom I have discussed these issues, will say, "But still, how else would I get any evidence on the quality of a physician. Granted all that you say about costs, is not licensure the only way of providing the public with some assurance of at least minimum quality?" The answer is partly that people do not now choose physicians by picking names at random from a list of licensed physicians; partly, that a man's ability to pass an examination twenty or thirty years earlier is hardly assurance of quality now; hence, licensure is not now the main or even a major source of assurance of at least minimum quality. But the major answer is very different. It is that the question itself reveals the tyranny of the status quo and the poverty of our imagination in fields in which we are laymen, and even in those in which we have some competence, by comparison with the fertility of the market. Let me illustrate by speculating on how medicine might have developed and what assurances of quality would have emerged, if the profession had not exerted monopoly power.

Suppose that anyone had been free to practice medicine without restriction except for legal and financial responsibility for any harm done to others through fraud and negligence. I conjecture that the whole development of medicine would have been different. The present market for medical care, hampered as it has been, gives some hints of what the difference would have been. Group practice in conjunction with hospitals would have grown enormously. Instead of individual practice plus large institutional hospitals conducted by governments or eleemosynary institutions, there might have developed medical partnerships or corporations—medical teams. These would have provided central diagnostic and treatment facilities, including hospital facilities. Some presumably would have been prepaid, combining in one package present hospital insurance, health insurance, and group medical practice. Others would have charged separate fees for separate services. And of course, most might have used both methods of payment.

These medical teams—department stores of medicine, if you will—would be intermediaries between the patients and the physician. Being long-lived and immobile, they would have a great interest in establishing a reputation for reliability and quality. For the same reason, consumers would get to know their reputation. They would have the specialized skill to judge the quality of physicians; indeed, they would be the agent of the consumer in doing so, as the department store is now for many a product. In addition, they could organize medical care efficiently, combining medical men of different degrees of skill and training, using technicians with limited training for tasks for which they were suited, and reserving highly skilled and competent specialists for the tasks they alone could perform, The reader can add further flourishes for himself, drawing in part, as I have done, on what now goes on at the leading medical clinics.

Of course, not all medical practice would be done through such teams. Individual private practice would continue, just as the small store with a limited clientele exists alongside the department store, the individual lawyer alongside the great many-partnered firm. Men would establish individual reputations and some patients would prefer the privacy and intimacy of the individual practitioner. Some areas would be too small to be served by medical teams. And so on.

I would not even want to maintain that the medical teams would dominate the field. My aim is only to show by example that there are many alternatives to the present organization of practice. The impossibility of any individual or small group conceiving of all the possibilities, let alone evaluating their merits, is the great argument against central governmental planning and against arrangements such as professional monopolies that limit the possibilities of experimentation. On the other side, the great argument for the market is its tolerance of diversity; its ability to utilize a wide range of special knowledge and capacity. It renders special groups impotent to prevent experimentation and permits the customers and not the producers to decide what will serve the customers best.

SECTION EIGHT

Information/Middlemen/Speculators

Why Speculators?

By Percy L. Greaves, Jr.

B ACK IN FEBRUARY, 1871, a group of free enterprisers found a way to help cotton growers adjust their production to market demand. They organized the New Orleans Cotton Exchange. There, for 93 years, cotton growers, wholesalers, manufacturers, and profit-seeking speculators could buy and sell cotton at free market prices for present and future delivery.

The prices paid and offered were published in the press. No cotton grower or user was long in doubt about the state of the cotton market, present or future. For there is no better indicator of the state of a commodity market than the prices at which that commodity is bought and sold for various dates of delivery.

The prices of the New Orleans Cotton Exchange were long a valuable guide for farmers and manufacturers alike. For farmers, they indicated how much land should be planted in cotton and how much in other crops. Through the growing season, future prices indicated how much time, care, and expense should be spent in tending crops. When future prices were high, no expense was spared to bring every possible ounce to market. When future prices were low, farmers were warned not to waste too much time and expense cultivating and picking that last possible ounce.

For manufacturers and other cotton buyers, the Cotton Exchange quotations provided a base for estimating or determining their future raw material costs. This in turn helped them calculate the prices on which they bid for future business. On orders accepted for delivery over long periods of time, they could always make sure of their raw material costs by immediately buying contracts for delivery of cotton on the dates they would need it.

COTTON PRICES CONTROLLED

On July 9, 1964, the New Orleans Cotton Exchange closed its doors to trading in "cotton futures," as contracts for future delivery are known. For years such sales have been fading away. With cotton prices more and more controlled by the government, neither farmers nor manufacturers need the information or insurance of a futures market.

When demand for cotton drops off, the government advances the subsidized price to farmers and stores all unsold cotton. When demand for cotton rises, cotton pours out of government subsidized warehouses and sells at the government set price. Either way, the taxpayers lose. Until present laws change or break down, cotton prices will be set by the government, cotton acreage will be guided by bureaucrats, and valuable men, materials, and tax money will continue to be wasted in nonproductive enterprise.

This situation reflects a complete lack of understanding of the rules of human behavior and the role of speculators in a free market society. It substitutes the wisdom of a few striving to stay in political power for the wisdom of those who spend their lives studying every facet of supply and demand before pledging their names and fortunes in support of their considered judgment.

It is human nature for men to try to improve their future conditions. That is the aim of every conscious human action. Men make mistakes, but they always aim at success in providing a better future for themselves or their loved ones. Free market transactions are merely the attempts of men to improve their own situations by social actions which also improve the situation of others. Barring force, fraud, or human error, all voluntary market transactions must improve the situations of all participants.

HOW MEN ACT

Actually, there are only three basic principles of human action. Men can act as gamblers, scientists, or speculators. Few acts fall entirely within any one classification. For every human action is confronted by elements of future uncertainty, such as those that exist in life itself.

Men act as gamblers when they know nothing in advance about the results except that some will win and others lose. There is nothing a man can know, study, learn, or experience that will help him to become a winner. When men gamble, the desired results depend upon pure chance. No skill whatsoever is involved.

Men act as scientists when they know in advance the results their actions will produce. Scientists deal only with solvable problems where conditions can be controlled and where identical actions in identical situations will always produce identical results. Automation is a modern example of scientifically directed action. In all scientific action, the repetition of prescribed procedure will always produce the same results. So, the more that scientists know about the laws of nature, the more they can undertake with prior certainty as to the actual results.

Men act as speculators when they have only partial knowledge and understanding of the results their actions are likely to produce. The more speculators know and understand, the better they can predict the future results of their actions. But they never can be certain of the actual results.

Most speculations involve people and how they will react to given situations. Since we can never know with certainty the future reactions of others, every action which involves others is a speculative action. Thus, all voluntary actions, including market actions, are speculative.

WHY MEN SPECIALIZE

The best way to increase the probability that speculative actions will produce the desired results is to increase our knowledge and understanding of all pertinent data, including the thoughts and ideas that motivate the actions and reactions of others. This takes time, study, experience, and economic analysis.

Men have found that the best way to gain more of the needed knowledge, experience, and understanding is for each one to select some limited area of human activity and then specialize in it.

Out of this division-of-labor principle the whole market system has developed. In a market society, everyone specializes and then trades the products of his specialty for the products of other specialists, his partners in total social production.

This system permits scientists to specialize in the automatic mass production of inanimate objects of wealth with certainty as to the physical results. However, men cannot plan or plot the market value of their products with scientific certainty. All such values are relative and speculative. They depend on the ever-changing ideas of buying men as to which of the many things offered for sale will give them the most satisfaction for the sums they have to spend.

Specialization can and does help men engaged in marketing and other speculative social actions. It permits them to learn more about what they sell and also more about the needs and wants of those to whom they seek to sell. Thus they become wiser and more efficient speculators, wasting less time trying to sell the wrong things to the wrong people.

Perfect results depend on the perfect prediction of future conditions. Because of human fallibility, this is rarely possible. However, better predictions and thus better results are often achievable. Greater specialization tends to reduce errors and help men achieve better results.

Many men prefer the relative security of a reasonably assured steady income to the insecurity of a wholly speculative income—an income that may turn out to be very high, very low, or even a net loss. Such security-seeking people tend to become employees.

Others prefer the lure and excitement of speculation. Such people are the investors, employers, business promoters, and professional speculators. They assume responsibility for the uncertainty of a business venture's future success or failure. Their likelihood of success depends largely on their ability to predict the future wants of buyers.

BETTER FORESIGHT PAYS

In a mass production market economy, the function of prediction and speculation falls primarily on investors, business promoters, and specialists rather than on consumers. When producers seek to act as scientists only, creating wealth by relying on the known laws of the physical sciences, they must find others to undertake the predictions and speculations as to the future conditions of the market.

Such specialists must estimate, at the time production starts, what consumer demand, competitive supplies, and other market conditions are likely to be at the time of sale. Such speculators then assume the responsibility that the planned production will meet the whims and wishes of consumers. Their income will depend on how correct their early predictions of future conditions prove to be.

As the division of labor has progressed, men and firms have tried to reduce their predictive and speculative functions to limited areas in which they become specialists with a better understanding than most other men. They concentrate on making or marketing certain goods and, in doing so, pay little attention to the market conditions of other goods, including their raw materials which may come from faraway sources with which they are unfamiliar.

Of course, the future prices they can get for their finished goods are in part dependent upon the ever-changing prices of the raw materials with which they are made. So, to protect themselves against future price fluctuations in their raw materials, businessmen sometimes engage in "hedging." By "hedging," they transfer the hazards resulting from the uncertainty of future prices to professional speculators in those products.

HOW HEDGING WORKS

A good example of "hedging" is the case of the cotton shirt manufacturer. He is a specialist in making and selling shirts. He knows that the selling price of cotton shirts is largely dependent upon the price of raw cotton. He has little time to study the cotton-growing conditions around the world or the other prospective demands on the raw cotton supply. He is fully occupied with his own problems in the shirt business. However, he would like to avoid the consequences of unforeseen changes in the prices of raw cotton.

Under free market conditions, he can hedge by contracting to sell at current prices raw cotton which he need not buy or deliver until the date he expects to sell the shirts he is making. Then, if the price for shirts has fallen, due to a drop in raw cotton prices, he would buy raw cotton at the lower price to meet his hedging contract. The profit on his raw cotton transaction would offset his loss on the shirts.

On the other hand, if the prices of both raw cotton and cotton shirts have risen, the extra profits from his shirt sales will be offset by his losses on the hedging transaction in raw cotton. By hedging he can protect himself against all possible fluctuations in raw cotton prices which might affect the prices of the shirts he sells. He rids his mind of this worry so that he can concentrate on the details of the shirt business at which he is a specialist.

The man who takes his hedge is usually a professional cotton speculator. He is a specialist who studies and interprets all the available data and conditions that are likely to affect future raw cotton prices. He trades in cotton a thousand times for every once or twice by the average cotton manufacturer. He knows how much has been planted in the many cotton-growing countries. He studies the rainfall and other weather conditions which may affect the size of the various crops. He keeps up-to-date on laws and proposed laws that may affect raw cotton prices. He follows the ups and downs in foreign exchange and transportation costs.

He also keeps an eye open for changes in demand for each type of cotton. He has informed ideas about increased demands arising from new uses for cotton, as well as any decreases due to the substitution of synthetics. He watches developments in mass purchasing power, production, and consumption in faraway lands like India. In short, he learns all he can about anything that might affect the supply of, or demand for, cotton and thus bring about a change in future raw cotton prices.

As a well-informed specialist, the speculator is much better able to predict future cotton prices than is the man who specializes in growing cotton or manufacturing cotton shirts. Competition among speculators trading on a commodity exchange forces them to share the benefits of their knowledge with their customers.

Businessmen can protect themselves from some speculative losses by taking out insurance. However, customary insurance can only be bought for risks which are largely known or predictable. Losses from fire, death, theft, or transportation accidents are thus distributed over all those insured, instead of falling entirely on the ones who suffer a specific disaster. Future price changes do not fall in this category. They are the same for everyone. Only the well-informed specialist is equipped to speculate successfully and "insure" others against losses from price changes.

A FALSE POPULAR NOTION OF THE SPECULATOR'S ROLE

In popular thinking, the speculator is a bold, bad man who makes money at the expense of others. Many people believe he gains his livelihood by luck, gambling, or inside manipulation. There are, of course, a few dishonest speculators who lie and cheat, as do some in all occupations, but the honest speculator is a serious specialist who serves mankind. He constantly strives to obtain a better understanding of future market conditions. He then places this better understanding at the service of all interested parties. Whenever his predictions are wrong, it is he who loses. When he is right, he and everyone who trades with him benefit. For if they did not expect to benefit, they would not trade with him.

The service of a speculator is to smooth out some of the gaps between supply and demand and some of the extreme ups and downs in prices. He tries to buy when and where a commodity is plentiful and the price is low and to sell when and where the commodity is in short supply and the price is high. When he does this wisely and successfully, he tends to raise extremely low prices and reduce extremely high prices.

Frequently, the speculator is the first to foresee a future scarcity. When he does, he buys while prices are still low. His buying bids up prices, and consumption is thus more quickly adjusted to future conditions than if no one had foreseen the approaching scarcity. A larger quantity is then stored for future use and serves to reduce the hardships when the shortage becomes evident to all.

Since a price rise tends to encourage increased production, the sooner prices rise, the sooner new and additional production will be started and become available. So a successful speculator reduces both the time and the intensity of shortages as well as the hardships which always accompany shortages.

Likewise, speculators are often the first to foresee an increase in future supplies. When they do, they hasten to sell contracts for future delivery. This in turn drives down future prices earlier than would otherwise be the case. This tends to discourage new production that could only be sold at a loss. It also gives manufacturers a better idea of what future prices will actually be. So, here again the speculator tends to smooth out production and consumption to the benefit of all concerned.

SPECULATORS SPREAD SUPPLIES

A good example of how speculators serve society was provided in the coffee market a few years ago. A small newspaper item reported a sudden unexpected frost blight in Brazil. Speculators immediately realized that such a frost must have killed large numbers of coffee bushes. This meant much smaller future supplies for the United States. So the speculators promptly bought all the coffee they could below the price they thought would prevail when consumers became fully aware of the approaching shortage. This tended to raise coffee prices immediately.

The effect of this was to reduce consumption and stretch some of the existing supply into the shortage period. It likewise alerted coffee growers in other areas to be more careful in their picking and handling of coffee so that there was less waste. Higher prices encouraged them to get to market every last bean, which at lower prices would not have been worth the trouble. Higher prices also speeded up the planting of new bushes. Since it takes five years for a new coffee bush to bear berries, the sooner new planting was undertaken the shorter the period of shortage.

The speculators who first acted on this development served every coffee consumer. If these speculators had not driven up prices immediately, consumers would have continued drinking coffee at cheap prices for a time. Then, suddenly, they would have faced a still greater shortage and still higher prices than those that actually prevailed.

By buying when coffee supplies were still relatively plentiful and selling later when the shortage was known to all, speculators helped to level out the available supply and reduce the extreme height to which prices would otherwise have risen. Speculators make money only when they serve society by better distributing a limited supply over a period of time in such a manner that it gives greater satisfaction to consumers. They thus permit other businessmen and consumers to proceed with greater safety and less speculation in their own actions.

SPECULATORS CAN LOSE

If a speculator buys a product thinking its price will rise and it later falls, he loses money for the simple reason that he has acted against the general welfare. He has sent out false indicators to producers and consumers alike. That happened just recently in the case of a large sugar importer. The firm bought large quantities of sugar when it was selling at 11¢ a pound. Its purchases were not hedged. In six months or so the price of sugar fell below 5¢ a pound and the importer was forced to file a petition under the National Bankruptcy Act.

Hedging with a professional speculator would have prevented that loss. Of course, if the speculator had made no better estimate about future sugar prices than the importer did, it might have been the speculator who filed under the bankruptcy law. But as a rule, speculators are the specialists who are best informed on what future prices are likely to be.

FRUITS OF INTERVENTION

When governments set prices, quotas, acreage limits, or other hampering restrictions on the honorable activities of men, they countermand the checks and balances that the free market places on supply and demand. The result is always surpluses and shortages: the former, where producers' rewards are set too high; the latter, where they are set too low. Where there are surpluses of some things, there will always be shortages of others. For the men and materials subsidized to produce surpluses have been lured from producing those things which free market conditions would indicate that consumers prefer.

Political interference with free market processes can only burden the taxpayer and weaken the human impulses of free men which tend to bring demand and supply into balance at the point which provides the greatest consumer satisfaction. With the passage of time, each such intervention can only make matters worse. Then, if people still believe the remedy for every economic ill is more intervention, political interventions will increase further until the police state is reached.

In any such trend toward a police state, the speculators are among the first to be eliminated. They are the specialists who study world-wide markets in order to reduce the uncertainties that face all farmers and businessmen. Without the services of speculators, bottlenecks of production—a symptom of socialism—soon develop.

Men and materials are then wasted in the production of surpluses. As a result there are ever-increasing shortages in the things people want most but can't have because the means to produce them have been misdirected by government decree. The recent end to trading in cotton futures on the New Orleans Cotton Exchange is an omen that should make thoughtful men reflect on the road we are now traveling.

Schools Brief:
Pennies from Hell

By Uncredited, *The Economist* Staff

FINANCIAL SPECULATORS ARE often accused of earning outrageous sums while contributing nothing to economic well-being. Not true, says the seventh in our series on economic misconceptions

"PAPER profits." This term captures perfectly the disdain with which the average citizen views the fruits of speculation. Unlike the good folk who labour to provide real goods and services, the "punters", in most people's eyes, add no value to the economy. At best, they are simply overdressed gamblers, who make a fortune whenever lady luck happens to smile their way. At worst, they are the outright enemies of ordinary workers.

In this view, the greed of bond traders drives up interest rates, and so harms output and jobs. Stockmarkets punish companies that invest in their workers instead of boosting profits. The managers of pension and mutual funds flood emerging markets with capital, then pull the plug on a whim. Even governments quail before the might of speculators. When they try to boost output by borrowing more, bond markets revolt. When they set their exchange rate at a vulnerable level, speculators sell the currency, forcing them to devalue.

At the root of this caricature is a belief that financial markets are somehow divorced from the rest of the economy. The language used to discuss them is full of "speculative bubbles", the "herd instinct" or "market psychology". Such phrases imply that speculators act in concert, behaving irrationally and yet becoming fabulously rich.

It is true that speculators are people, and therefore prey to the usual human infirmities. But the notion that they make up a uniform group is just wrong. Worse, it ignores the most important fact about financial speculation: that it takes two to gamble. For every buyer convinced that markets will rise, there has to be a seller. When they place their bets, speculators are trying to profit from one another, not from some innocent bystander. In the process, their opposing views about the value of a financial asset such as a share, a bond or a currency are embedded in its price. That is a valuable economic service.

BENEVOLENT DICTATORS

As Friedrich von Hayek, an Austrian economist, once pointed out, the beauty of markets is their ability to handle information. By condensing all the relevant facts about a product into a single price, market forces make it easier for people to make good decisions. If pests descend on Brazil's coffee crop, for example, shoppers need not learn about how badly this will affect the coffee supply. They simply need to know by how much coffee prices have risen, and trim their purchases accordingly.

In non-financial markets there are other factors (such as the existence of monopolies, or the costs of buying and selling) that make prices slow to adjust to changing conditions. Financial markets are much more efficient. Since there are many buyers and sellers, and trading costs are low, the prices of financial assets can react immediately to new information.

How does this help anyone? The prices upon which speculators have the biggest impact— share prices, interest rates, exchange rates—are precisely the ones that matter most for people taking economic decisions.

A firm's share price, for example, tells its managers how much the market thinks its future profits are worth. If a firm's share price is falling, it is because speculators think that its future prospects have grown bleaker. But a falling share price also makes it more expensive for the company to raise new capital in stockmarkets. This leads firms with diminishing prospects to do exactly what is best for the economy: make fewer investments. The capital that they do not use can then be reallocated to firms with brighter outlooks.

The prices of other financial assets, such as the return that lenders demand when they buy government bonds, perform the same signalling function. The yield (the percentage return to the investor) on long-term bonds changes in response to new information about the rate of inflation and the risk that the borrower will default.

Chart 1 shows that investors demand higher real interest rates from governments which run big budget deficits or tolerate high inflation. Bond yields can thus provide a useful signal to governments about the soundness of their policies (though whether governments heed these signals is another matter).

YOUR HELPFUL ARB

Sending signals is all very well. But what if the guesses of the speculators are wrong? This goes to the heart of the controversy about speculation. It is partly because many people doubt their divining powers that speculators are held in such low esteem.

It helps here to distinguish between two different types of "speculator". The first, the "arbitrageur" is not really a speculator at all. True arbitrageurs do not take any risks or make any bets: they simply exploit price differences between two related assets. They might notice, for instance, that a share trades for a lower price on one exchange than on another. By simultaneously buying on the first exchange and selling on the second, the arbitrageur can pocket the price difference without ever having to own the share.

The arbitrageur's job is usually more complicated. Instead of exploiting differences across exchanges, he often must seek out less obvious gaps between loosely related prices, such as the prices of financial derivatives (futures, swaps and options) and the assets on which they are based.

By finding these discrepancies, arbitrageurs not only earn a profit, but also eliminate the discrepancy. By making prices consistent they improve the market's efficiency. Although often maligned in the financial press, arbitrageurs are more akin to middlemen in product and service industries than to true speculators (see box on next page).

The true speculator, unlike the arbitrageur, is indeed constantly taking risks, placing bets and thereby sending signals into the economy. Needless to say, their guesses are sometimes wrong, and in these cases their signals can cause bad economic decisions. But even if their guesswork is not perfect, speculators are far more rational than they are often made out to be.

One common criticism, for example, is that they care too much about the short term, focusing on a firm's current profits and damaging the outlook of companies that take a more patient approach to business.

This criticism is flawed. Shares derive their worth from a firm's underlying assets. If the market in which these shares are traded "undervalued" them, anyone who bought such a share would be getting a bargain: they would receive a windfall in the future when the firm's long-term investment paid off. It would then be easy for a few clever investors to exploit the market's shortsightedness. For example, if it were true, as it is sometimes said, that the market attaches too little value to corporate R&D, a few investors could make a bundle by buying shares in firms with large R&D budgets. In the process, of course, these firms' prices would rise until they were no longer undervalued.

If this sounds abstract, consider the concrete evidence that investors care about the long term. The shares of many biotechnology or software firms, some of which have never made a profit, continue to fetch dizzying prices in the stockmarket. Indeed, a common criticism of stockmarket speculators is that they push the prices of high-tech firms too high. In other words, they seem to care too much, not too little, about the long term.

If speculators are so good at making guesses, why do prices rise and fall so spikily? To incorporate all relevant information, prices must move whenever markets learn anything new. But many people say that prices in financial markets are far more volatile than changes in fundamentals warrant. The blame for this is commonly put on the emergence of complicated new financial instruments such as derivatives, and a big rise in the volume of financial trading.

However, table 2 shows that although exchange rates and bond yields in the big industrial economies are more volatile than they were in the 1960s, a time when exchange rates were fixed within narrow bands and capital markets were tightly controlled, volatility has not increased much during the past two decades. If anything, bond yields and exchange rates have been more stable in the 1990s than in the 1980s; and stockmarkets have been even less flighty than in the 1960s.

AN UNFAIR EXCHANGE?

The most damning criticisms levelled at speculators involve their impact on currencies. The amount changing hands on foreign-exchange markets every day jumped from $60 billion in

1983 to more than $1.2 trillion in 1995. And in 1992 one famous speculator, George Soros, was credited with (or blamed for) shoving the pound out of Europe's exchange-rate mechanism (ERM), which had tried to keep European currency trading within a narrow band. The following year speculators forced the ERM to shift to wider bands.

French politicians like to blame the ERM debacles on a conspiracy by Anglo-Saxon speculators. The truth is that when speculators pounce they tend to have good reasons. In the case of the ERM, they were responding to perceived inconsistencies in economic policy. Germany's fiscal burden following unification required it to raise interest rates at a time when recession in the rest of Europe demanded lower interest rates. The higher rates needed to defend currencies against the D-mark therefore became politically untenable.

Large movements in exchange rates are often the symptoms, not the causes, of economic problems. Still, financial markets can be erratic in the way they judge economies. One example is Mexico's boom and bust in the 1990s. The country's overly loose monetary policy and a widening current-account deficit were largely to blame for its dramatic devaluation in December 1994. But in this case, investors were criticised for being too slow to blow the whistle, thereby failing to discipline the wayward government soon enough.

Even in such cases it is hard to think of a better alternative to letting the speculators place their bets. They may be fallible, but there are reasons to expect governments to make even bigger mistakes. Financial markets have a big incentive to get it right: they are, after all, betting with their own (or their investors') money. Also, financial markets tend to be quicker than governments to admit that they were wrong.

More to the point, any attempts to clamp down on speculators could make matters worse. Some politicians favour a financial-transactions tax to discourage currency speculators. But this would be hard to enforce, and would increase the cost of capital by discouraging good capital flows (eg, to finance trade) as well as bad ones. And, in cases where attacks on currencies really did signal errors in economic policy, it would muffle the signals and allow governments to delay urgent policy shifts for even longer. The inevitable adjustment, when it came, would be more painful.

The verdict on speculators? Their guesses are not always right. But the inconsistent criticisms thrown at them show what an impossible standard this is. They are alternately blamed for caring too much about the short term, and (often unwittingly) too much about the long term; for being too quick to mete out punishment and for taking too long.

However, because financial prices represent the collective best guess of millions of speculators, who often fiercely disagree, they are also the best gauge that society has available, and therefore the best ones for guiding decisions. Politicians and pundits may say they know better. But to trust them, instead of the market, would truly be a reckless gamble.

MARKET MOTIONS

Financial market volatility*

	Exchange rates	Bond yields	Share prices
1960-69	0.4	0.2	5.3
1070-70	1.3	0.3	4.4
1980-85	1.7	0.5	4.1
1986-89	1.7	0.4	5.0
1990-94	1.6	0.3	4.0

*Standard deviation of monthly % changes
Source: OECD
GRAPH: Sending signals: Real long-term interest rates and selected economic variables—Budget deficit
GRAPH: Sending signals: Real long-term interest rates and selected economic variables—Inflation

Middlemen

By Frédéric Bastiat

SOCIETY IS THE aggregate of all the services that men perform for one another by compulsion or voluntarily, that is to say, *public services* and *private services.*

The first, imposed and regulated by the law, which is not always easy to change when necessary, can long outlive their usefulness and still retain the name of *public services,* even when they are no longer anything but public nuisances. The second are in the domain of the voluntary, i.e., of individual responsibility. Each gives and receives what he wishes, or what he can, after bargaining. These services are always presumed to have a real utility, exactly measured by their comparative value.

That is why the former are so often static, while the latter obey the law of progress.

While the exaggerated development of public services, with the waste of energies that it entails, tends to create a disastrous parasitism in society, it is rather strange that many modern schools of economic thought, attributing this characteristic to voluntary, private services, seek to transform the functions performed by the various occupations.

These schools of thought are vehement in their attack on those they call middlemen. They would willingly eliminate the capitalist, the banker, the speculator, the entrepreneur, the businessman, and the merchant, accusing them of interposing themselves between producer and consumer in order to fleece them both, without giving them anything of value. Or rather, the reformers would like to transfer to the state the work of the middlemen, for this work cannot be eliminated.

The sophism of the socialists on this point consists in showing the public what it pays to the *middlemen* for their services and in concealing what would have to be paid to the state. Once again we have the conflict between what strikes the eye and what is evidenced only to the mind, between *what is seen and what is not seen.*

It was especially in 1847 and on the occasion of the famine[1] that the socialist schools succeeded in popularizing their disastrous theory. They knew well that the most absurd propaganda always has some chance with men who are suffering; *malesuada fames.*[2]

---

1 [Failures in the grain and potato crops in northern and western Europe in 1846 resulted in a rise of food prices in 1847, the year of "dear bread" and of agricultural, industrial, and financial depressions.—Translator.]

2 ["Hunger is an evil counsellor." *Virgil's Aeneid VI, 276.*—Translator]

Then, with the aid of those high-sounding words: *Exploitation of man by man, speculation in hunger, monopoly,* they set themselves to blackening the name of business and throwing a veil over its benefits.

"Why," they said, "leave to merchants the task of getting foodstuffs from the United States and the Crimea? Why cannot the state, the departments, and the municipalities organize a provisioning service and set up warehouses for stockpiling? They would sell at *net cost,* and the people, the poor people, would be relieved of the tribute that they pay to free, i.e., selfish, individualistic, anarchical trade."

The tribute that the people pay to business, *is what is seen.* The tribute that the people would have to pay to the state or to its agents in the socialist system, *is what is not seen.*

What is this so-called tribute that people pay to business? It is this: that two men render each other a service in full freedom under the pressure of competition and at a price agreed on after bargaining.

When the stomach that is hungry is in Paris and the wheat that can satisfy it is in Odessa, the suffering will not cease until the wheat reaches the stomach. There are three ways to accomplish this: the hungry men can go themselves to find the wheat; they can put their trust in those who engage in this kind of business; or they can levy an assessment on themselves and charge public officials with the task.

Of these three methods, which is the most advantageous?

In all times, in all countries, the freer, the more enlightened, the more experienced men have been, the oftener have they *voluntarily* chosen the second. I confess that this is enough in my eyes to give the advantage to it. My mind refuses to admit that mankind at large deceives itself on a point that touches it so closely.[3]

However, let us examine the question.

For thirty-six million citizens to depart for Odessa to get the wheat that they need is obviously impracticable. The first means is of no avail. The consumers cannot act by themselves; they are compelled to turn to middlemen, whether public officials or merchants.

However, let us observe that the first means would be the most natural. Fundamentally, it is the responsibility of whoever is hungry to get his own wheat. It is a *task* that concerns him; it is a *service* that he owes to himself. If someone else, whoever he may be, performs this *service* for him and takes the task on himself, this other person has a right to compensation. What I am saying here is that the services of *middlemen* involve a right to remuneration.

However that may be, since we must turn to what the socialists call a parasite, which of the two—the merchant or the public official—is the less demanding parasite?

Business (I assume it to be free, or else what point would there be in my argument?) is forced, by its own self-interest, to study the seasons, to ascertain day by day the condition of the crops, to receive reports from all parts of the world, to foresee needs, to take precautions. It has ships all ready, associates everywhere, and its immediate self-interest is to buy at the lowest

---

3 [The author has often invoked the presumption of truth which is connected with the *universal assent* manifested by the practice of all men. See especially chap. 13 of *Economic Sophisms*, the end of chap. 6 of the *Essays* (in the French edition), and in *Economic Harmonies* the appendix to chap. 6 entitled "Morality of Wealth."—Editor.]

possible price, to economize on all details of operation, and to attain the greatest results with the least effort. Not only French merchants, but merchants the whole world over are busy with provisioning France for the day of need; and if self-interest compels them to fulfill their task at the least expense, competition among them no less compels them to let the consumers profit from all the economies realized. Once the wheat has arrived, the businessman has an interest in selling it as soon as possible to cover his risks, realize his profits, and begin all over again, if there is an opportunity. Guided by the comparison of prices, private enterprise distributes food all over the world, always beginning at the point of greatest scarcity, that is, where the need is felt the most. It is thus impossible to imagine an *organization* better calculated to serve the interests of the hungry, and the beauty of this organization, not perceived by the socialists, comes precisely from the fact that it is free, i.e., voluntary. True, the consumer must pay the businessman for his expenses of cartage, of trans-shipment, of storage, of commissions, etc.; but under what system does the one who consumes the wheat avoid paying the expenses of shipping it to him? There is, besides, the necessity of paying also for *service rendered*; but, so far as the share of the middleman is concerned, it is reduced to a *minimum* by competition; and as to its justice, it would be strange for the artisans of Paris not to work for the merchants of Marseilles, when the merchants of Marseilles work for the artisans of Paris.

If, according to the socialist plan, the state takes the place of private businessmen in these transactions, what will happen? Pray, show me where there will be any economy for the public. Will it be in the retail price? But imagine the representatives of forty thousand municipalities arriving at Odessa on a given day, the day when the wheat is needed; imagine the effect on the price. Will the economy be effected in the shipping expenses? But will fewer ships, fewer sailors, fewer trans-shipments, fewer warehouses be needed, or are we to be relieved of the necessity for paying for all these things? Will the saving be effected in the profits of the businessmen? But did your representatives and public officials go to Odessa for nothing? Are they going to make the journey out of brotherly love? Will they not have to live? Will not their time have to be paid for? And do you think that this will not exceed a thousand times the two or three percent that the merchant earns, a rate that he is prepared to guarantee?

And then, think of the difficulty of levying so many taxes to distribute so much food. Think of the injustices and abuses inseparable from such an enterprise. Think of the burden of responsibility that the government would have to bear.

The socialists who have invented these follies, and who in days of distress plant them in the minds of the masses, generously confer on themselves the title of "forward-looking" men, and there is a real danger that usage, that tyrant of language, will ratify both the word and the judgment it implies. "Forward-looking" assumes that these gentlemen can see ahead much further than ordinary people; that their only fault is to be too much in advance of their century; and that, if the time has not yet arrived when certain private services, allegedly parasitical, can be eliminated, the fault is with the public, which is far behind socialism. To *my* mind and knowledge, it is the contrary that is true, and I do not know to what barbaric century we should have to return to find on this point a level of understanding comparable to that of the socialists.

The modern socialist factions ceaselessly oppose free association in present-day society. They do not realize that a free society is a true association much superior to any of those that they concoct out of their fertile imaginations.

Let us elucidate this point with an example:

> For a man, when he gets up in the morning, to be able to put on a suit of clothes, a piece of land has had to be enclosed, fertilized, drained, cultivated, planted with a certain kind of vegetation; flocks of sheep have had to feed on it; they have had to give their wool; this wool has had to be spun, woven, dyed, and converted into cloth; this cloth has had to be cut, sewn, and fashioned into a garment. And this series of operations implies a host of others; for it presupposes the use of farming implements, of sheepfolds, of factories, of coal, of machines, of carriages, etc.

If society were not a very real association, anyone who wanted a suit of clothes would be reduced to working in isolation, that is, to performing himself the innumerable operations in this series, from the first blow of the pickaxe that initiates it right down to the last thrust of the needle that terminates it.

But thanks to that readiness to associate which is the distinctive characteristic of our species, these operations have been distributed among a multitude of workers, and they keep subdividing themselves more and more for the common good to the point where, as consumption increases, a single specialized operation can support a new industry. Then comes the distribution of the proceeds, according to the portion of value each one has contributed to the total work. If this is not association, I should like to know what is.

Note that, since not one of the workers has produced the smallest particle of raw material from nothing, they are confined to rendering each other mutual services, to aiding each other for a common end; and that all can be considered, each group in relation to the others, as *middlemen*. If, for example, in the course of the operation, transportation becomes important enough to employ one person; spinning, a second; weaving, a third; why should the first one be considered more of a *parasite* than the others? Is there no need for transportation? Does not someone devote time and trouble to the task? Does he not spare his associates this time and trouble? Are they doing more than he, or just something different? Are they not all equally subject, in regard to their pay, that is, their share of the proceeds, to the law that restricts it to the *price agreed upon after bargaining?* Do not this division of labor and these arrangements, decided upon in full liberty, serve the common good? Do we, then, need a socialist, under the pretext of planning, to come and despotically destroy our voluntary arrangements, put an end to the division of labor, substitute isolated efforts for cooperative efforts, and reverse the progress of civilization?

Is association as I describe it here any the less association because everyone enters and leaves it voluntarily, chooses his place in it, judges and bargains for himself, under his own responsibility, and brings to it the force and the assurance of his own self-interest? For association to deserve the name, does a so-called reformer have to come and impose his formula and his will on us and concentrate within himself, so to speak, all of mankind?

The more one examines these "forward-looking" schools of thought, the more one is convinced that at bottom they rest on nothing but ignorance proclaiming itself infallible and demanding despotic power in the name of this infallibility.

I hope that the reader will excuse this digression. It is perhaps not entirely useless at the moment when, coming straight from the books of the Saint-Simonians, of the advocates of phalansteries, and of the admirers of Icaria,[4] tirades against the middlemen fill the press and the Assembly and seriously menace the freedom of labor and exchange.

---

4 [References to Claude Henri de Rouvroy, Comte de Saint-Simon (1760-1825), historic founder of French socialism; to the phalanstères, or common buildings, proposed by Francois Marie Charles Fourier in 1832 in his newspaper *Le Phalanstère* to house "phalanges" of sixteen hundred persons each as part of a socialistic scheme; and to *Voyage to Icaria*, a utopian book by Étienne Cabet (1788-1856).—Translator.]

Advertising

By Israel M. Kirzner

ADVERTISING HAS BEEN badly treated by many scholars who should know better. Not only Marxists and liberals, but even conservatives have given advertising a bad press. Let us examine some of the criticisms.

- First, many advertising messages are said to be offensive—by esthetic or ethical and moral standards. Unfettered, unhampered, laissez-faire capitalism, it is contended, would propagate such messages in a way that could very well demoralize and offend the tastes and morals of members of society.

- Second, advertising, it is argued, is deceitful, fraudulent, full of lies. Misinformation is spread by advertising, in print, on the airwaves, and this does harm to the members of society; for that reason advertising should be controlled, limited, taxed away.

- Third, it is argued that where advertising is not deceitful, it is at best persuasive. That is, it attempts to change people's tastes. It attempts not to fulfill the desires of man but to change his desires to fit that which has been produced. The claim of the market economist has always been that the free market generates the flow of production along the lines that satisfy consumer tastes; their tastes determine what shall be produced—briefly, consumer sovereignty. On the contrary, the critics of advertising argue, capital ism has developed into a system where producers produce and then mold men's minds to buy that which has been produced. Rather than production being governed by consumer sovereignty, quite the reverse: the consumer is governed by producer sovereignty.

- A fourth criticism has been that advertising propagates monopoly and is antithetical to competition. In a competitive economy, it is pointed out, there would be no advertising; each seller would sell as much as he would like to sell without having to convince consumers to buy that which they would not otherwise have bought. So, advertising is made possible by imperfections in the market. More seriously, it is contended, advertising leads toward monopoly by building up a wall of good will, a protective wall of loyalty among consumers which renders a particular product immune to outside competition.

Competing products, which do not share in the fruits of the advertising campaign, find themselves on the outside. This barrier to entry may gradually lead a particular producer to control a share of the market which is rendered invulnerable to the winds of outside competition.

- Finally—and this in a way sums up all of these criticisms—advertising is condemned as wasteful. The consumer pays a price for a product which covers a very large sum of money spent on advertising. Advertising does not change the commodity that has been purchased; it could have been produced and sold at a much lower price without the advertising. In other words, resources are being used and paid for by the consumer without his receiving anything that he could not have received in their absence.

These are serious criticisms. We have learned to expect them to be emphasized by contemporary liberal economists. To Marxist thinkers, again, advertising is essential for capitalism; it is seen as a socially useless device necessary in order to get excess production sold. They see no positive elements in advertising at all. But even conservative thinkers and economists have pointed out some apparent limitations, weaknesses, criticisms of advertising.

THE FREE ECONOMY AND HOW IT FUNCTIONS

It is not my purpose here to defend each and every advertising message. I would rather discuss a free economy, a laissez-faire economy, pure capitalism. I would like to show that in such a world, advertising would emerge with a positive role to play; that it would add to the efficiency with which consumer wants are satisfied; and that, while the real world is far from perfect, a large volume of the criticism would fade away were it understood what role advertising, in fact, has to play in a pure market economy.

Let me imagine a world, a free market, in which there are no deceitful men at all. All the messages beamed to consumers and prospective consumers would be, as far as the advertisers themselves believe, the strict truth. We will consider later the implications of the fact that men are imperfect and that men succumb to the temptation in selling something to say a little bit less, a little bit more, than the exact truth. In the meantime, let us talk about a world of honest men, men who do not try to deceive.

Further, let us imagine a pure market economy with government intervention kept to the absolute minimum—the night watchman role. The government stands to the sidelines and ensures the protection of private property rights, the enforcement of contracts freely entered into. Everyone then proceeds to play the game of the free market economy with producers producing that which they believe can be sold to the consumers at the highest possible money price. Entrepreneur producers, who detect where resources are currently being used in less than optimum fashion, take these resources and transfer them to other uses in the economy where they will serve consumer wants which the entrepreneurs believe are more urgently desired, as measured by the amounts of money consumers are willing to pay for various products.

We will assume that there is freedom of entry into all industries. No entrepreneur has sole control over any resource that is uniquely necessary for the production of a given product. No government licenses are required in order to enter into the practice of a given profession or to introduce a particular product. All entrepreneurs are free to produce what they believe to be profitable. All resource owners are free to sell their resources, whether labor, natural resources, capital goods. They are free to sell or rent these resources to the highest bidder. In this way the agitation of the market gradually shuffles resources around until they begin to be used to produce those products which consumers value most highly. Consumers arrange their spending to buy the commodities they believe to be most urgently needed by themselves. And the market flows on in the way that we understand it.

OPEN COMPETITION

We say this is a free market, a laissez-faire, competitive system. But we do not mean a *perfectly* competitive market, as this notion has been developed by the neo-classical economists. In a perfectly competitive market, each seller faces a demand curve which is perfectly horizontal. That is to say, each seller believes that he can sell as much as he would like to sell without having to lower the price. Each buyer faces a perfectly horizontal supply curve and each buyer believes that he can buy as much as he would like to buy of anything without having to offer a higher price. In such a world of "perfect competition," we have what we call an "equilibrium" situation, that is a situation where all things have already been fully adjusted to one another. All activities, all decisions have been fully coordinated by the market so that there are no disappointments. No participant in the economy discovers that he could have done something better. No participant in the economy discovers that he has made plans to do something which it turns out he cannot do.

In this model of the perfectly competitive economy, there would in fact be no competition in the sense in which the layman, or the businessman, understands the term. The term "competition" to the businessman, the layman, means an activity designed to outstrip one's competitors, a rivalrous activity designed to get ahead of one's colleagues, or those with whom one is competing. In a world of equilibrium, a world of "perfect competition," there would be no room for further rivalry. There would be no reason to attempt to do something better than is currently being done. There would, in fact, be no competition in the everyday sense of the term.

When we describe the laissez-faire economy as competitive, we mean something quite different. We mean an economy in which there is complete freedom of entry; if anyone believes that he can produce something that can serve consumers' wants more faithfully, he can try to do it. If anyone believes that the current producers are producing at a price which is too high, then he is free to try to produce and sell at a lower price. This is what competition means. It does not mean that the market has already attained the "equilibrium" situation, which goes under the very embarrassing technical name of "perfectly competitive economy."

Now, economists and others understand generally that competition means price competition: offering to sell at a lower price than your competitors are asking, or offering to buy at a higher price than your competitors are bidding. Entrepreneurs will offer higher prices than others are offering for scarce labor. They will offer to sell a product at lower prices than the competing store is asking. This is what price competition means. This is the most obvious form in which competition manifests itself.

However, we must remember that there is another kind of competition, sometimes called "non-price competition," sometimes called "quality competition." Competition takes the form not only of producing the identical product which your competitors are producing and selling it at a lower price, not only in buying the identical resource which your competitors are buying and offering a higher price. Competition means sometimes offering a better product, or perhaps an inferior product, a product which is more in line with what the entrepreneur believes consumers are in fact desirous of purchasing. It means producing a different model of a product, a different quality, putting it in a different package, selling it in a store with a different kind of lighting, selling it along with an offer of free parking, selling through salesmen who smile more genuinely, more sincerely. It means competing in many, many ways besides the pure price which is asked of the consumer in monetary terms.

With freedom of entry, every entrepreneur is free to choose the exact package, the exact opportunity which he will lay before the public. Each opportunity, each package has many dimensions. He can choose the specifications for his package by changing many, many of these variables. The precise opportunity that he will lay before the public will be that which, in his opinion, is more urgently desired by the consumer as compared with that which happens to be produced by others. So long as there's freedom of entry, the fact that my product is different from his does not mean that I am a monopolist.

The late Professor Edward H. Chamberlin of Harvard did economics a great disservice in arguing that because a producer is producing a unique product, slightly different from what the fellow across the street is producing, in some sense he is a monopolist. So long as there's freedom of entry, so long as the man across the road *can* do exactly what I'm doing, the fact that he is *not* doing exactly what I'm doing is simply the result of his different entrepreneurial judgment. He believes that he can do better with *his* model. I believe I can do better with *mine*. I believe that free parking is more important to consumers than fancy lighting in the store. He gives a different package than I do. Not because he couldn't do what I'm doing, not because I couldn't do what he's doing, but because each believes that he knows better what the consumer is most anxious to acquire. This is what we mean by competition in the broadest sense, not merely price competition, but quality competition in its manifold possible manifestations.

Professor Chamberlin popularized a distinction which was not original with him but which owes its present widely circulated popularity primarily to his work. That is a distinction between "production costs" and "selling costs." In his book of almost forty years ago, *The Theory of Monopolistic Competition*, Chamberlin argued that there are two kinds of costs which manufacturers, producers, sellers, suppliers incur. First, they incur the fabrication costs, the costs of producing what it is they want to sell. Second, they incur additional expenditures that do not produce the product or change it or improve it, but merely get it sold. Advertising, of course, is the most obvious example which Chamberlin cited. But "selling costs" of all kinds were considered by him to be sharply different from "production costs." In his original formulation, Chamberlin argued that "production costs" are costs incurred to produce the product for a given Demand Curve while "selling costs" simply shift the Demand Curve over to the right.

That is to say, the same product is now purchased in greater quantities at a given price but the product is the same.

A FALSE DISTINCTION

The fallacy in the distinction between production costs and selling costs is fairly easy to notice. In fact, it is impossible for the outside observer—except as he resorts to arbitrary judgments of value—to distinguish between expenditures which do, and expenditures which do not, alter the product. We know as economists that a product is not an objective quantity of steel or paper. A product is that which is perceived, understood, desired by a consumer. If there are two products otherwise similar to the outside eye which happen to be considered to be different products by the consumer, then to the economist these *are* different products.

Ludwig von Mises gives the example, which cannot be improved upon, of eating in a restaurant. A man has a choice of two restaurants, serving identical meals, identical food. But in one restaurant they haven't swept the floor for six weeks. The meals are the same. The food is the same. How shall we describe the money spent by the other restaurant in sweeping the floor? "Production costs" or "selling costs"? Does sweeping change the food? No. Surely, then, it could be argued that this is strictly a "selling cost." It is like advertising. The food remains the same; but, because you have a man sweeping out the floor, more people come to this restaurant than to that. But this is nonsense. What you buy when you enter a restaurant is not the food alone. What you buy is a meal, served in certain surroundings. If the surroundings are more desirable, it's a different meal, it's a different package. That which has been spent to change the package is as much production cost as the salary paid to the cook; no difference.

Another example that I recall was the case of the coal being run out of Newcastle and traveling along the railroad toward London. Every mile that coal travels nearer the London drawing room, the Demand Curve shifts over to the right. How shall we describe that transportation cost? "Production cost" or "selling cost"? Of course, it's "production cost." In fact, it's "selling cost" too. All "production costs" are "selling costs." All costs of production are incurred in order to produce something which will be more desirable than the raw materials.

You take raw meat and turn it into cooked steak. The act of changing the raw meat into cooked steak is to make the consumer desire it more eagerly. Does this simply shift the Demand Curve over to the right? Of course, it does that. It does it by changing the product.

Another example supposes there are two identical pieces of steel, except that one piece has been blessed, while the other piece is subject to a spiritual taint, which to the scientist is not there but which is very vivid and vital to the consumer. How shall we describe the expenditure on the commodities? Shall we describe the difference between them as nonexistent? Or should we not recognize that, if something is spiritually tainted to the consumer—in his view, not necessarily in mine or yours or the economist's or other than in the mind of the consumer—then he will not buy the tainted item, even though to the objective laboratory scientist there's no difference between the items? The economist has recognized these as two different commodities. There'll be two Demand Curves. The fact that the scientist doesn't see any difference—they look the same, they smell the same, if you touch them they feel the same—is irrelevant. We know, as

economists, that what we find in a commodity is not the objective matter that is inside it, but how it is received by the consumer.

Clearly then, the distinction between a so-called "selling cost" and "production cost" is quite arbitrary. It depends entirely on the value judgments of the outside observer. The outside observer can say that this particular selling effort does not change the product, but in that situation he is arrogating to himself the prerogative of pronouncing what is and what is not a product. That is something which violates our fundamental notions of individual consumer freedom: that a consumer's needs are defined by no one else other than himself. This may seem quite a detour from advertising and yet it is all relevant to the question of what role advertising has to play.

THE PROVISION OF INFORMATION

Let us consider how some of these notions apply to the matter of information. One of the standard defenses for advertising is that it provides a service which consumers value: the provision of knowledge, the provision of information. People buy books. People go to college. People enroll in all kinds of courses. Advertising is simply another way of providing information. To be sure, it would seem that the information provided by suppliers comes from a tainted source, but don't forget that we are imagining for the meantime a world without deceitful people.

We can even relax that assumption for a moment. It may be cheaper for the consumer to get his information from the supplier or the producer than from an outside source. In other words, if you, a consumer, have the choice of acquiring information about a particular product—either more cheaply from the producer or more expensively from an outside, "objective" source—you may decide that, on balance, you're likely to get a better deal, penny-for-penny, information-wise, by reading the information of the producer, scanning it perhaps with some skepticism, but nonetheless relying on that rather than buying it from an outside source. Technically, this involves what is known as the problem of transactions costs. It may be more economical for the information to be packaged together with the product, or at least to be produced jointly with the product, than to have the information produced and communicated by an outside source. This is a possibility not to be ignored.

Advertising provides information, and this goes a long way to explain the role which advertising and other kinds of selling efforts must play. Does this not seem to contradict the point just made, that there is no distinction between "production costs" and "selling costs"? Surely information about a product is distinct from the product. Surely the costs incurred to provide information are a different kind of costs than the costs incurred to produce the product. The answer is clearly, no. Information is produced; it is desired; it is a product; it is purchased jointly with the product itself; it is a part of the package; and it is something which consumers value. Its provision is not something performed on the outside that makes people consume something which they would not have consumed before. It is something for which people are willing to pay; it is a service.

You can distinguish different parts of a service. You can distinguish between four wheels and a car. But the four wheels are complementary commodities. That is to say, the usefulness of the one is virtually nil without the availability of the other. The car and gasoline are two separate products, to be sure, and yet they are purchased jointly, perhaps from different producers, different suppliers, but they are nonetheless parts of a total package, a total product. If it happens that the information is produced and sold jointly with the product itself, then we have no reason to question the characteristics of the costs of providing information as true "production costs," not producing necessarily the physical commodity about which information is produced, but producing information which is independently desired by consumers, independently but jointly demanded, complementarily used together with the "product" itself. In other words, the service of providing information is the service of providing something which is needed just as importantly as the "product" itself.

There is another aspect of advertising which is often overlooked. Information is exceedingly important. But, surely, it is argued, information can be provided without the characteristics of advertising that we know, without the color, without the emotion, without the offensive aspects of advertising. Surely information can be provided in simple straightforward terms. The address of this and this store is this and this place. These and these qualities of commodities are available at these and these prices. Why do illustrated advertising messages have to be projected? Why do all kinds of obviously uninformative matter have to be introduced into advertising messages? This is what renders the information aspects of advertising so suspect. The Marxists simply laugh it away. They say it is ridiculous to contend that advertising provides any kind of genuine information. If one rests the defense of advertising on its informative role, then one has a lot of explaining to do. One has to explain why information that could be provided in clear cut, straightforward terms is provided in such garish and loud forms, in the way that we know it

The answer, I think, is that advertising does much more than provide information which the consumer wishes to have. This is something which is often overlooked, even by economists. Suppose I set up a gas station. I buy gasoline and I have it poured into my cellar, my tanks. I have a pump carefully hidden behind some bushes, and cars that come down the road can buy gas if they know that I'm here. But I don't go to the effort to let them know I'm here. I don't put out a sign. Well, gas without information is like a car without gas. Information is a service required complementarily with the gas.

Supposing, then, I take a piece of paper, type very neatly in capital letters, "GAS," and stick it on my door. Cars speed down the road in need of gas, but they don't stop to read my sign. What is missing here? Information is missing. Don't people want information? Yes. They would like to know where the gas station is, but it's a well kept secret. Now, people *are* looking for that information. It's my task as an entrepreneur not only to have gas available but to have it in a form which is known to consumers. It is my task to supply gas-which-is-known-about, not to provide gas *and* information.

I have not only to produce opportunities which are available to consumers; I have to make consumers aware of these opportunities. This is a point which is often overlooked. An opportunity which is not known, an opportunity to which a consumer is not fully awakened, is simply not an opportunity. I am not fulfilling my entrepreneurial task unless I project to the consumer the awareness of the opportunity. How do I do that? I do that, not with a little sign on my door, but with a big neon sign, saying GAS; and better than that I chalk up the price; and better

 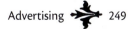

than that I make sure that the price is lower than the price at nearby stations; and I do all the other things that are necessary to *make* the consumer *fully* aware of the opportunity that I am in fact prepared to put before him. In other words, the final package consists not only of abstract academic information but in having the final product placed in front of the consumer in such a form that he cannot miss it.

FREE $10 BILLS!

The strange thing about the world in which we live is that it is a world in which $10 bills are floating around, free $10 bills! The problem is that very few of us notice these $10 bills. It is the role of the entrepreneur to notice the existence of $10 bills. An entrepreneur buys resources for $10 and he sells the product for $20. He is aware that resources available for $10 are currently being used in less than optimum fashion, that commodities for which consumers are willing to pay $20 are not being produced, and he puts these things together. He sees the $10 bill and makes the combination which other people do not see. Anybody might do it—freedom of entry. The entrepreneur notices the $10 bill, gets it for himself by placing in front of the consumer something which he had not noticed. If the consumer knew where he could buy resources for $10 and get the product that is worth $20, he wouldn't buy from the entrepreneur. He would do it himself. Since he doesn't know, I, as entrepreneur, have to create this opportunity and make the consumer aware.

It is not enough to buy gas and put it in the ground. The entrepreneur puts it in the ground in a form that the consumer recognizes. To do this requires much more than fabrication. It requires communication. It requires more than simple information. It requires more than writing a book, publishing it, and having it on a library shelf. It requires more than putting something in a newspaper in a classified ad and expecting the consumer to see it. You have to put it in front of the consumer in a form that he *will* see. Otherwise, you're not performing your entrepreneurial task.

Advertising has grown. Compare the volume of advertising today with the volume of 100 years ago and it has grown tremendously. More! Consider the price of a commodity that you buy in a drug store or in a supermarket. Find out what portion of that price can be attributed to advertising costs and it turns out that a much larger percentage of the final cost to the consumer can be attributed to advertising today than could have been attributed 50 years ago, 70 years ago, 100 years ago. Why is this? Why has advertising expenditure grown in proportion to total value of output? Why has advertising expenditure grown in proportion to the price of a finished commodity? Why has advertising apparently grown more offensive, more loud, more shrill? It's fairly easy to understand.

I give, as example, the lobby walls of a college building that I know very well. At one time this was a handsome lobby with walls of thick marble; you could walk from one end of the building to the other and the walls would be clear. Some years ago an enterprising entrepreneur decided to use some free advertising space. He pasted up a sign. It was the only sign on the wall; everybody looked at it, saw the message. I don't remember what the message was or whether it was torn down, but I do remember that soon afterward those walls were full of signs. As you walked down the passage, you could read all kinds of messages, all kinds of student activities, non-student activities, student non-activities. It was fairly easy to learn about what was going on simply by reading the signs.

At first, the signs did not have to be big. But as advertisers saw the opportunity, the free space gradually filled up. The Ricardian rent theory came into play; all the free land was in use. And as the free land or space was taken, of course, it became more and more important to get up early to paste up your sign. That was the "rent," the high price, getting up early. But more than that, it became necessary now to arouse all kinds of interest in me in order to get me to read these signs. In other words, the variety and multiplicity of messages make it harder and harder to get a hearing.

THE PRICE OF AFFLUENCE

We live in a world which is often described as an "affluent society." An affluent society is one in which there are many, many opportunities placed before consumers. The consumer enters a supermarket and if he is to make a sensible, intelligent decision he is going to have to spend several hours calculating very carefully, reading, rereading everything that's on the packages and doing a complete research job before feeding all the information into the computer and waiting for the optimum package to be read off. It's a tough job to be a consumer. And the multiplicity of opportunities makes it necessary for advertisers, for producers, to project more and more provocative messages if they want to be heard. This is a cost of affluence. It is a cost, certainly; something that we'd much rather do without, if we could; but we can't.

The number of commodities that have been produced is so great that in order for any one particular product to be brought to the attention of the consumer a large volume of advertising is necessary. And we can expect to get more and more. Is it part of production costs? Very definitely, yes. It is completely arbitrary for anyone to argue that, whether or not the consumer knows it, the commodity is there anyway, so that when he pays the price which includes the advertising communication he is paying *more* than is necessary for the opportunity made available. For an opportunity to be made available, it must be in a form which it is impossible to miss. And this is what advertising is all about.

One more word about the offensiveness of advertising. Ultimately in a free market, consumers tend to get what they want. The kinds of products produced will reflect the desires of the consumer. A society which wants moral objects will get moral objects. A society which wants immoral objects will tend to get immoral objects. Advertised communication is part of the total package produced and made available to consumers. The kind of advertising we get, sad to say, is what we deserve. The kind of advertising we get reflects the kind of people that we are. No doubt, a different kind of advertising would be better, more moral, more ethical in many respects; but I'm afraid we have no one to blame but ourselves, as in all cases where one deplores that which is produced by a market society.

A final word about deceit. Of course, deceitful advertising is to be condemned on both moral and economic grounds. But we have to put it in perspective. Let me read from one very eminent economist who writes as follows:

"The formation of wants is a complex process. No doubt wants are modified by Madison Avenue.

They are modified by Washington, by the university faculties and by churches. And it is not at all clear that Madison Avenue has the advantage when it comes to false claims and exaggerations."[1]

TAKE WITH A GRAIN OF SALT

In other words, we live in a world where you have to be careful what you read, to whom you listen, whom to believe. And it's true of everything, every aspect of life. If one were to believe everything projected at him, he would be in a sorry state.

It is very easy to pick out the wrong messages to believe. Now, this doesn't in any way condone or justify deceitful messages of any kind. We have to recognize, however, while particular producers may have a short-run interest in projecting a message to consumers of doubtful veracity, that so long as there's freedom of competition the consumer has his choice not only of which product to buy but whom to believe. And notice what is the alternative in this world of imperfect human beings. The alternative, of course, is government control—still by imperfect human beings. So there is no way to render oneself invulnerable to the possibility of false, fraudulent, deceitful messages.

It would be nice to live in a world where no deceitful men were present. It would be cheaper. You could believe any message received. You wouldn't have to check out the credentials of every advertiser. But that is not the world in which we live. You check out the credit standing of individuals, the character of people with whom you deal; and this is an unavoidable, necessary cost. To blame advertising for the imperfections and weaknesses of mankind is unfair. Advertising would exist under any type of free market system. Advertising would be less deceitful if men were less deceitful. It would be more ethical, less offensive, if men were less offensive and more ethical. But advertising itself is an integral, inescapable aspect of the market economy.

---

1   H. Demsetz, "The Technostructure, Forty-Six Years Later," (*Yale Law Journal*, 1968), p. 810.

Defeating Drug Lag

By Julie DeFalco

A T THE TURN OF the century, Upton Sinclair wrote of medicines that were poisonous, milk that was tainted, and, most alarmingly, sausages that were once humans. *The Jungle* so alarmed President Theodore Roosevelt that he urged the passing of the 1906 Food and Drug Act, which required labeling of contents on packages of foods and medicines.

Today, we are content with the safety of our food and medicines. However, the Food and Drug Administration (FDA), whose power grew slowly over the course of the century, is now hiding a danger that is just as real, but far less obvious, than toxic "snake oil." This phenomenon is known as drug lag, the time between submission of a new drug application and its approval, and it can be just as deadly.

DRUG LAG

The 1938 Food, Drug, and Cosmetic Act gave the FDA the power to test these products for safety. In this way, consumers were protected against poisonous products, and, at the same time, enjoyed a boom in drug production. In contrast, the 1962 amendments, enacted after the United States' near-encounter with thalidomide, required that efficacy be proven as well. While there was very little change in the quality or safety of drugs, there was a great reduction in the availability of new drugs.

For the past few decades, the scientific difficulties in creating a new drug have been matched only by the bureaucratic complications of the FDA. Even after tens of thousands of pages of data are submitted, the FDA often requests that even more tests be completed. For example, Dr. William Summers, inventor of an effective Alzheimer's drug, noted that "after positive publicity about the discovery, the FDA then severely restricted access to our study; conducted a two-and-a-half year investigation; and awarded further research to others. Our ten years of experience with Tacrine was largely wasted." The entire process can take from two to ten years, and during that time the only people who can have access to the drug are the lucky few who are admitted to clinical trials, or who have the means to travel abroad.

Thus, when the FDA announces the approval of a new drug, and proudly estimates how many lives it will save per year, it begs the question of how many lives were lost because of a lack of access to the drug. Any delay in approval of a life-saving drug is a deadly delay.

Economists Henry Grabowski and John Vernon note that there are reasons for the FDA's delays:

> An FDA official who approves a drug subsequently shown to be not safe or effective stands to bear heavy personal costs. Such an outcome, even if it occurs very infrequently, tends to be highly visible and is one for which both the FDA and the regulatory official are held politically accountable. The costs of rejecting a good drug are borne largely by outside-parties (drug manufacturers and sick patients who might benefit from it).

The people with AIDS who petitioned the FDA in the 1980s for access to AZT and other experimental drugs were unusually visible victims. Not only were they suffering from a singular disease, they were politically organized. Most drug lag victims have not been as unified or as active, and certainly not as conspicuous.

After submission to FDA advisory committees, new drug applications can languish for years. However, these drugs often become available in Europe with no difference in degree of safety. The Competitive Enterprise Institute has attempted to illustrate this human cost. For example, Interleukin-2, a therapy for a fatal form of kidney cancer, was submitted in 1988 for approval. It was approved in France, Denmark, and seven other European countries before finally receiving an OK from the FDA three and a-half years later.

The FDA's own figures support the conclusion that up to 3,500 kidney cancer victims died waiting for IL-2 (see chart). "The odds of being helped by IL-2 are about one out of four," said Eugene Schoenfeld, PhD., President of the National Kidney Cancer Association. "The odds of dying from the therapy are about one out of twenty-five. As gambles go, these are not bad odds, particularly when there is almost certainty of death if no risk is taken."

In addition to denying therapeutic benefits, drug lag also affects the development of new drugs. "By virtually any measure," wrote economist Sam Peltzman in his ground-breaking 1974 study of drug regulation, "the rate of new drug introductions to the U.S. market has declined substantially since the passage of the 1962 amendments." However, there has not been any corresponding increase in safety or efficacy of the drugs that have been approved. Even after companies spend millions of dollars on testing, there is always the possibility that the drug or device will be sent back two or three times.

Consequently, large drug companies have an advantage over smaller companies with less cash and less ability to wait for several years. Biotech companies are often the most affected. and they are increasingly taking their operations, and their creative research, overseas. "American leadership in biotechnology cannot be sustained in the face of FDA's 'zero risk' requirements for the approval of new biologics," says George Rathmann, head of ICOS Corporation. "It cannot survive the incredibly slow pace of approvals today."

The FDA's stranglehold on the availability of new drugs and devices extends to dissemination of information as well. The FDA manipulates the contents of drug package inserts and in advertising in medical journals. Copies of medical studies indicating previously unknown therapeutic benefits are off limits to drug companies wishing to distribute them. Even information about off-label uses, such as aspirin's beneficial effect on the heart, is impeded by FDA regulation of medical texts. The FDA clearly believes that ignorance is bliss, even if it costs lives.

WHAT ABOUT THALIDOMIDE?

To date, the answer to any question about changing the FDA has been a single word: thalidomide. This sedative, briefly used in Europe in the early 1960s, conjures images of deformed babies, hapless mothers, and John Kennedy awarding the President's Gold Medal of Distinguished Service to FDA staffer Frances Kelsey, the woman who "saved" America by sending thalidomide back for more tests. It single-handedly seems to justify the need for a strong FDA.

However, the facts are often lost in the hysteria. The side-effects of thalidomide were unquestionably a tragedy. However, it was rejected by the FDA under the 1938 "safety" standard. The 1962 "efficacy" standard was part of an unrelated multi-year effort of a small group of senators who wished to increase the power of the FDA. Even though a weaker FDA had been sufficient to keep the drug out of the United States, thalidomide provided both an initial justification for strengthening the agency, and, later, an excuse for its ever more stringent regulations.

What are the human costs of drug lag? Using the FDA's own numbers, it is possible to compute a rough estimate of how many people were victims of the FDA's overcautiousness.

NAME OF DRUG (AILMENT)	APPROV. DATE	DEATHS/ YEAR	% WHO BENEFIT	TIME OF DRUG LAG	ESTIMATED VICTIMS
Misoprostol (*Gastric ulcer bleeding*)	12/88	10,000 -20,000	94%	9 months•	8,000-15,000
Streptokinase (*Blood clots in heart attack victims*)	11/87	63,000	18%	2 years	22,000
Interleukin-2 (*Kidney cancer*)	5/92	10,000	15-20%	3.5 years••	3,500

• Available in Europe since 1985
•• Available in Europe in 1992

There is no question that other countries sometimes approve bad drugs. However, "important drugs still become available later in the United States, some much later, than the United Kingdom," says Dr. Kenneth Kaitin of Tufts University. "Moreover, the small difference in safety discontinuations in the two countries does not support the argument that delay protects the public from serious unforeseen adverse effects."

A MODEST PROPOSAL

The FDA's mission, to improve and protect public health, has been overshadowed by the FDA's institutional bias against approving drugs quickly. Past attempts to streamline the FDA's function, such as the Prescription Drug User Fee Act of 1992, have not fared well, nor can they as long as the FDA remains essentially the same.

CEI proposes that the FDA's current veto power over new drugs and devices be changed to one of certification. The FDA's safety and efficacy standards would remain the same, but experimental drugs and devices would be available to those in need through prescriptions from their doctors. All such drugs and devices would have clear warning of their unapproved status. For those who trust the FDA, life will not change; for those who are willing to take a risk on an experimental but potentially lifesaving drug, a new choice will be available.

BETTER LATE THAN NEVER
The FDA's record in approving life-saving "priority" drugs is dismal. Here are just a Few drugs which were available in other countries before the U.S.

NAME OF DRUG (AILMENT)	AVAILABLE ELSEWHERE	APPROVED IN UNITED STATES	LENGTH OF DRUG LAG
Tacrine (Alzheimer's disease)	1988, Bahamas	12193	5 Years
Navelbine (Lung cancer)	1989 France •	12194	5 Years
Lamictal (Epileptic seizures)	1990, Ireland ••	12194	4 Years

• Also available in 30 other countries
•• Also available in 12 other countries

Meanwhile, institutions such as medical schools, laboratories and hospitals would begin to evaluate unapproved drugs and devices with increasing frequency. Certain foreign approvals would also be meaningful; the United Kingdom's approval of cardiovascular drugs, for example, might be a credible indicator of a new drug's worth to an American cardiologist. Peer-reviewed medical journals have long had an impact on the practice of medicine. Thus, under CEI's proposal, these and other entities could compete with the FDA. The main beneficiary would be the consumer-patient. At a minimum, CEI believes that the FDA, on its own, could undertake post-approval audits to help estimate the costs to society of its deadly overcaution. Perhaps it will also encourage the FDA to reaffirm its official purpose, the health of the public. After all, isn't that why Congress authorized the FDA in the first place?

Theory, Evidence, and Examples
of FDA Harm

By The Independent Institute

To obtain permission to market a drug, the manufacturer must satisfy the FDA that the drug is both safe and effective. Additional testing often enhances safety and effectiveness, but requiring a lot of testing has at least two negative effects. First, it delays the arrival of superior drugs. During the delay, some people who would have lived end up dying. Second, additional testing requirements raise the costs of bringing a new drug to market; hence, many drugs that would have been developed are not, and all the people who would have been helped, even saved, are not.

In addition, because FDA approval is mandatory, industry and medicine must heed FDA standards regardless of their relevance, efficiency, and appropriateness. Not all testing is equally beneficial. The FDA apparatus mandates testing that, in some cases, is not useful or not appropriately designed. The case against the FDA is not that premarket testing is unnecessary but that the costs and benefits of premarket testing would be better evaluated and the trade-offs better navigated in a voluntary, competitive system of drug development.

Three bodies of evidence indicate that the costs o FDA requirements exceed the benefits. In other words, three bodies of evidence suggest that the FDA kills and harms, on net. First, we compare pre-1962 drug approval times and rates of drug introduction with post-1962 approval times and rates of introduction. Second, we compare drug availability and safety in the United States with the same in other countries. Third, we compare the relatively unregulated market of off-label drug uses in the United States with the on-label market. In the final section, before turning to reform opitions we also discuss the evidence showing that the costs of FDA advertising restrictions exceed the benefits.

COMPARISON OF PRE- AND POST-1962

Sam Peltzman (1973) wrote the first serious cost-benefit study of the FDA. He focused his attention on the 1962 Kefauver-Harris Amendments to the Food, Drug, and Cosmetics Act of 1938, which significantly enhanced FDA powers. The amendments added a proof-of-efficacy requirement to the existing proof-of-safety requirement, removed time constraints on the FDA disposition of NDAs, and gave the FDA extensive powers over the clinical testing procedures drug companies used to support their applications.

Using data from 1948 to 1962, Peltzman created a statistical model to predict the yearly number of new drug introductions. The model is based on three variables, the most important of which is the size of the prescription drug market, lagged two years. The idea is that if the prescription drug market were large two years ago, manufacturers would invest more money in research and development, which would pay off two years later in a new drug. (Prior to 1962, it took approximately two years to develop a new drug.) Despite the model's simplicity, it tracks the actual number of new drug introductions quite well, as indicated by figure 2.

FIGURE 2

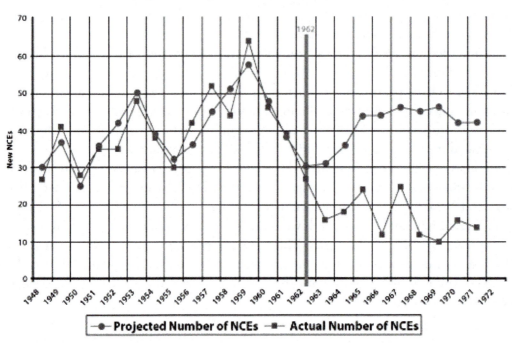

PELTZMAN 1973

Because Peltzman's model tracks the pre-1962 drug market quite well, we have some confidence that if all else had remained equal, the model also should have roughly tracked the post-1962 drug market. Peltzman's model, in other words, estimates the number of new drugs that would have been produced if the FDA's powers had not been increased in 1962. Thus, by comparing the model results with the actual number of new drugs, we can draw an estimate of the effect of the 1962 amendments. The model predicts a probable post-1962 average of forty-one new chemical entities (NCEs, or new drugs) approved per year.

The average number of new drugs introduced pre-1962 (forty) was also much larger than the post-1962 average (sixteen). Thus, whether one compares pre- and post-1962 averages or compares the results from a forecast with the actual results, the conclusions are the same: the 1962 Amendments caused a significant drop in the introduction of new drugs. Using data of longer span, Wiggins (1981) also found that increased FDA regulations raised costs and reduced the number of new drugs.

Even if FDA regulations have not improved safety, they might be redeemed if they have reduced the proportion of inefficacious drugs on the market. Using a variety of tests, however, Peltzman (1973) found little evidence to suggest a decline in the proportion of inefficacious drugs reaching the market since 1962. Thus, he concluded, "(the) penalties imposed by the marketplace on sellers of ineffective drugs prior to 1962 seem to have been enough of a deterrent to have left little room for improvement by a regulatory agency" (1086). Similarly, in their survey of the literature, Grabowski and Vernon (1983) conclude, "In sum, the hypothesis that the observed decline in new product introductions has largely been concentrated in marginal or ineffective drugs is not generally supported by empirical analyses" (34).

The costs of FDA regulations do not vary with the number of potential users of the drug, so the decline in drug development has been especially important in the treatment of rare diseases. By definition, each rare disease afflicts only a small number of people, but there are thousands of rare diseases. In aggregate, rare diseases afflict millions of Americans: according to an AMA estimate (AMA 1995), as many as 10 percent of the population. Thus, millions of Americans have few or no therapies available to treat their diseases because of increased costs of drug development brought about by stringent FDA "safety and efficacy" requirements. In response to this problem, in 1983 the Orphan Drug Act was passed to provide tax relief and exclusive privileges to firms developing drugs for diseases affecting two hundred thousand or fewer Americans (AMA 1995). It would be better to reduce or eliminate FDA regulations for all drugs and patient populations.

THE GRISLY COMPARISON

The delay and large reduction in the total number of new drugs has had terrible consequences. It is difficult to estimate how many lives the post-1962 FDA controls have cost, but the number is likely to be substantial; Gieringer (1985) estimates the loss of life from delay alone to be in the hundreds of thousands (not to mention millions of patients who endured unnecessary morbidity). When we look back to the pre-1962 period, do we find anything like this tragedy? The historical record—decades of a relatively free market up to 1962—shows that voluntary institutions, the tort system, and the pre-1962 FDA succeeded in keeping unsafe drugs to a low level. The Elixir Sulfanilamide tragedy, in which 107 people died, was the worst of those decades. Every life lost is important, but the grisly comparison is necessary. The number of victims of Elixir Sulfanilamide tragedy and of all other drug tragedies prior to 1962 is very small compared to the death toll of the post-1962 FDA.

COMPARISON WITH OTHER COUNTRIES

The second source of evidence comes from comparing drug availability and safety in the United States with the same in other countries. Prior to the Kefauver-Harris Bill of 1962, the average time from the filing of an IND to approval was seven months. By 1967, however, the average time to approval had increased to thirty months. Time to approval continued to rise through the late 1970s, when on average a successful drug took more than ten years to get approved. In the late 1980s and 1990s, times to approval decreased somewhat, but are still eight years on average, far higher than in the 1960s (Peltzman 1974; Thomas 1990; Tufts Center for the Study of Drug Development 1998).

Time to approval has historically been shorter by years in Europe than in the United States. Drugs are usually available in Europe before they are available in the United States. The difference between the time of a drug's availability in Europe and that in the United States has come to be called the drug lag (Grabowski 1980; Kaitin et al. 1989; Wardell 1973, 1978a,1978b; Wardell and Lasagna 1975). In recent years, however, the FDA has improved. In the latest data, covering 1996–98, the average time from filing the IND to submitting the NDA was 5.9 years and average NDA approval time was 1.4 years, for a total of 7.3 years, the quickest approval times in decades (Kaitin and Healy 2000). Researchers have suggested that the drug lag may be disappearing (Healy and Kaitin 1999).

What is significant for our purposes is that from approximately 1970 to 1993 the FDA clearly lagged significantly behind its counterparts in the United Kingdom, France, Spain, and Germany (Kaitin and Brown 1995). This fact gives us a basis for comparison: During the period of consistent drug lag, did the delay correspond to greater safety? Put another way: Did speedier drug approval in Europe lead to a scourge of unsafe drugs?

If the U.S. system resulted in appreciably safer drugs, we would expect to see far fewer postmarket safety withdrawals in the United States than in other countries. Bakke et al. (1995) compared safety withdrawals in the United States with those in Great Britain and Spain, each of which approved more drugs than the United States during the same time period. Yet, approximately 3 percent of all drug approvals were withdrawn for safety reasons in the United States, approximately 3 percent in Spain, and approximately 4 percent in Great Britain. There is no evidence that the U.S. drug lag brings greater safety. Wardell and Lasagna (1975) concluded their comparison of drug approvals in the United States and Great Britain by noting: "In view of the clear benefits demonstrable [*sic*] from some of the drugs introduced into Britain, it appears that the United States has lost more than it has gained from adopting a more conservative approach" (105).

Deaths owing to drug lag have been numbered in the hundreds of thousands. Wardell (1978a) estimated that practolol, a drug in the beta-blocking family, could save ten thousand lives a year if allowed in the United States. Although the FDA allowed a first beta-blocker, propranolol, in 1968, three years after that drug had been available in Europe, it waited until 1978 to allow the use of propranolol for the treatment of hypertension and angina pectoris, its most important indications. Despite clinical evidence as early as 1974, only in 1981 did the FDA allow a second beta-blocker, timolol, for prevention of a second heart attack. The agency's withholding of beta-blockers was alone responsible for probably tens of thousands of deaths (on this general issue see Gieringer 1985; Kazman 1990).

A chief source of information about drug delay is the Tufts Center for the Study of Drug Development, a scholarly, not too outspoken research center funded chiefly by pharmaceutical companies. Their information is often mined by researchers at the Competitive Enterprise Institute (CEI). The CEI has noted that in recent years thousands of patients have died because the FDA has delayed the arrival of new drugs and devices, including interleukin-2, taxotere, vasoseal, ancrod, glucophage, navelbine, lamictal, ethyol, photofrin, rilutek, citicoline, panorex, femara, prostar, omnicath, and transform. Prior to FDA approval, most of these drugs and devices had already been available in other countries for a year or longer.

Gieringer (1985) used data on drug disasters in countries with less-stringent drug regulations than the United States to create a ballpark estimate of the number of lives saved by the extra scrutiny induced by FDA requirements. He then computed a similar ballpark figure for the number of lives lost owing to drug delay:

> [T]he benefits of FDA regulation relative to that in foreign countries could reasonably be put at some 5,000 casualties per decade or 10,000 per decade for worst-case scenarios. In comparison, it has been argued above that the cost of FDA delay can be estimated at anywhere from 21,000 to 120,000 lives per decade ... Given the uncertainties of the data, these results must be interpreted with caution, although it seems clear that the costs of regulation are substantial when compared to benefits. (196)

Note three things about the foregoing passage. (1) The comparison is between the FDA and the foreign systems of drug control. (2) The relative benefits of the FDA are expressed in number of *casualties*, whereas the relative costs are in number of *lives*. (3) In addressing the costs, Gieringer estimated the costs only from drug delay; he does not attempt to quantify the costs associated with drug loss. Nevertheless, his conclusion is clear: the FDA is responsible for more lives *lost* than lives *saved*.

FDA INCENTIVES

Even if the FDA required only the most relevant clinical trials and worked at peak efficiency to evaluate new drugs, the trade-off between more testing and delayed drugs would still exist. We cannot escape this trade-off. The only question is whether a centralized bureaucracy should decide on these trade-offs for everyone or patients and doctors should make such decisions. Much of the FDA's delay, however, is not owing to useful—albeit not necessarily optimal—testing. Much of the delay is pure waste. The cause is not laziness but incentives. (Read the sidebar Why the FDA Has an Incentive to Delay the Introduction of New Drugs for an explanation.)

COMPARISON OF ON-LABEL AND OFF-LABEL USAGE

The third sort of evidence on the costs of FDA regulations comes from comparing the utilization of drugs for their on-label uses with their utilization for off-label uses. The hidden lesson of off-label usage is that, even in today's highly regimented setting, there functions a realm of efficacy testing and assurance quite apart from the FDA.

When the FDA evaluates the safety and efficacy of a drug, the evaluation is made with respect to a specified use of the drug. Once a drug has been approved for some use, however, doctors may legally prescribe the drug for other uses. Approved uses are known as on-label uses, and other uses are considered off-label uses. Amoxicillin, for example, has an on-label use for treating respiratory tract infections and an off-label use for treating stomach ulcers.

For the on-label treatment of respiratory tract infections, amoxicillin has been tested and passed muster in all three phases of the IND clinical study; phase I trials for basic safety and phase II and phase III trials for efficacy. For the treatment of stomach ulcers, however, amoxicillin has not gone through FDA-mandated phase II and phase III trials and thus is not FDA approved for this use. Indeed, amoxicillin will probably never go through FDA efficacy trials for the treatment of stomach ulcers because the basic formulation is no longer under patent. Yet any textbook or medical guide discussing stomach ulcers will mention amoxicillin as a potential treatment, and a doctor who did not consider prescribing amoxicillin or other antibiotic for the treatment of stomach ulcers would today be considered highly negligent. Off-label uses are in effect regulated according to the FDA's pre-1962 rules (which required only safety, not efficacy), whereas on-label uses are regulated according to the post-1962 rules.

FDA defenders suggest that an unregulated market for drugs would be a medical disaster. Do patients and doctors shrink in fear from uses not certified by the FDA?

Not at all! Most hospital patients are given drugs that are not FDA approved for prescribed use. In a large number of fields, a majority of patients are prescribed at least one drug off-label. Off-label prescriptions are especially common for AIDS, cancer, and pediatric patients, but are also common throughout medicine.

Doctors learn of off-label uses from extensive medical research, testing, peer-reviewed publications, newsletters, lecture presentations, conferences, advertising, Internet sources, and trusted colleagues. Scientists and doctors, working through professional associations and organizations, make official determinations of "best practice" and certify off-label uses in standard reference compendia such as *AMA Drug Evaluations, American Hospital Formulary Service Drug Information,* and *U.S. Pharmacopoeia Drug Indications.* Doctors use this information to try to make the best decisions for their patients. Medical decisions are most often made under uncertainty and partial ignorance, so there is rarely a single best decision, and different doctors and different patients choose different treatments. New information constantly flows into this system as outcomes accumulate, epidemiological studies reveal new correlations, scientists propose theoretical explanations, researchers design and embark on new clinical studies, scientific institutions arrive at new judgments, and pharmaceutical companies create new drugs. As this medical knowledge grows and develops, information flows in a decentralized fashion, and doctors adjust their decisions accordingly.

Economist J. Howard Beales (1996) found that off-label uses appeared in the Pharmacopoeia on average 2.5 years earlier than the FDA recognized those uses. The difference between the on-label and off-label markets is not that the off-label market is "unregulated" but that it is unregulated by the FDA, a centralized and coercive authority. In approving or rejecting a new drug, the FDA makes a decision everyone must obey. It's as if the Department of Transport unilaterally decided what vehicles Americans could and could not purchase. Heterogeneity among patients in both preferences and circumstances is great. A drug that can save the life of A may be dangerous to B even if A and B have the same disease. An athlete and a college professor with the same disease may choose different courses of treatment. The FDA's "one size fits all" policy is not appropriate for every patient.

The off-label market is regulated by thousands of doctors and patients acting in a decentralized manner. Compared to the FDA, this market adjusts quickly to new information, shows less sign of biased incentives, and allows a more precise adjusting of treatment decisions to preferences and the conditions of time and place. The evidence indicates that these benefits are not offset by significantly greater risk (Tabarrok 2000). The off-label market operates with much less government intervention than the on-label market and provides a good idea of the benefits to be had from reducing FDA control over approval decisions.

By their actions, doctors tell us that they believe in off-label prescribing. Getting the FDA to approve a new use for an old drug requires an expensive and lengthy process. In many cases, the costs to the sponsor of the required testing exceed the benefits of approval. It is clear that if the FDA prohibited off-label prescribing, current practices would have to change significantly. No one would be foolish enough to suggest that the FDA prohibit off-label prescribing.

But there is a logical inconsistency in allowing off-label prescribing and requiring proof of efficacy for the drug's initial use (Tabarrok 2000). Logical consistency would require us *either* (1) to oppose off-label prescribing and favor initial proof of efficacy, *or* (2) to favor off-label prescribing and oppose initial proof of efficacy. Experience recommends the second option. Efficacy requirements should be dropped altogether!

SUMMARY OF THE THREE BODIES OF EVIDENCE: FDA-CAUSED MORTALITY AND MORBIDITY ARE UNREDEEMED

Evidence from the pre-1962 market shows that FDA restrictions have greatly reduced the number of new drugs, and because there was little or no corresponding gain in drug quality, the concomitant mortality and morbidity were unredeemed. The international evidence shows that there has long been a drug lag in the United States, and because Americans have not benefited from the extra "precaution," the concomitant mortality and morbidity are unredeemed. Finally, the off-label evidence indicates that the network of doctors, patients, pharmaceutical firms, hospitals, universities, rating organizations, and so forth is really in charge of defining and judging efficacy and that it functions smoothly and successfully in the realm of uses not approved by the FDA; hence, the mortality and morbidity that result from proof-of-efficacy requirements are unredeemed. All the systematic evidence goes against the coercive FDA apparatus.

FDA ADVERTISING RESTRICTIONS: IGNORANCE IS DEATH

In addition to permitting drugs on the market, the FDA controls advertising and promotion. The costs of such control parallel the costs of restricting drugs. They include (1) reducing the speed at which consumers learn of and adopt important new therapies; (2) reducing the size of the market for drugs, thereby reducing the incentive to research and develop new drugs; and (3) reducing the number of treatment options, making it more difficult for physicians to provide therapies tailored to each individual patient (Rubin 1995; Tabarrok 2000).

In numerous instances, the FDA has reduced the speed at which patients and their agents have learned of and adopted new drugs or new uses of old drugs. The most important example is aspirin.

The FDA prevented aspirin manufacturers from advertising that clinical studies had shown that the use of aspirin during and after heart attacks might prevent death. When, years after the clinical studies had been completed, the FDA finally sanctioned aspirin for heart-attack patients, Dr. Carl Pepine, codirector of cardiovascular medicine at the University of Florida College of Medicine, estimated that as many as ten thousand lives annually could be saved. In other words, Dr. Pepine thought that the FDA restrictions preventing the advertising and promotion of aspirin for heart attack patients were responsible for the deaths of tens of thousands of people. Noting that the decision should have come years earlier, Dr. Pepine said, "I'm disappointed that something that has such potential to save so many lives took so long. But it's better late than never" (quoted in Ross 1996). Paul Rubin (1995), whose paper on FDA advertising restrictions provides the title for this section, wrote that "the banning of advertising of aspirin for first heart attack prevention, may be the single most harmful regulatory policy currently pursued by any agency of the U.S. government" (48). (Keith [1995] reaches a similar, though less pointed, conclusion.) Despite studies showing benefits, the FDA still does not allow aspirin manufacturers to advertise the benefits of aspirin as a preventive measure for people at high risk for a first heart attack.

Another example: In 1992, the federal Centers for Disease Control and Prevention (CDC) recommended that women of childbearing age take folic acid supplements. Studies showed that taking folic acid reduced risks of babies suffering neural-tube birth defects such as anencephaly and spina bifida. The FDA immediately announced, however, that it would prosecute any food or vitamin manufacturer that placed the CDC recommendation in its advertising or product labeling (Calfee 1997). The public did not learn of the importance of folic acid until Congress passed the Dietary Supplement Health and Education Act of 1994, which loosened the FDA's vise on the advertising of vitamins and other dietary supplements. Within only a few years of its ban on publicizing the CDC recommendation, the FDA made a complete turnabout. Since 1998, the agency has required manufacturers to fortify a variety of grain products with folic acid—that which is not prohibited is mandatory!

The FDA has also restricted how manufacturers can promote the off-label uses of drugs (these restrictions were in part ruled unconstitutional in *Washington Legal Foundation v. Friedman*). Such restrictions make it more difficult for doctors to best match patient with treatment. In a survey, 79 percent of neurologists and neurosurgeons, 67 percent of cardiologists, and 76 percent of oncologists said that the FDA should not restrict information about off-label uses.

In response to a follow-up question, similar numbers indicated that the FDA policy of limiting information had made it more difficult for them to learn about new uses of drugs and devices (Conko 1998).

(On government control of advertising more generally, see Calfee 1997; Kaplar 1993; Masson and Rubin 1985; Rubin 1991a, 1991b, 1994; and Tabarrok 2000; they evaluate FDA restrictions on advertising and promotion in more detail.)

In recent years, the courts have found First Amendment limits on the FDA's power to restrict commercial speech. In *Washington Legal Foundation v. Friedman*, the Federal Appeals Court for the District of Columbia ruled that the FDA may not prohibit drug manufacturers from providing practitioners and others with independent publications such as off-prints of scientific articles, or from organizing medical education programs about off-label uses of their products. The court's ruling contained strong and decisive language:

"In asserting that any and all scientific claims about the safety, effectiveness, contradictions, side effects, and the like regarding prescription drugs are presumptively untruthful or misleading until the FDA has had the opportunity to evaluate them, FDA exaggerates its overall place in the universe ... the conclusions reached by a laboratory scientist or university academic and presented in a peer-reviewed journal or textbook, or the findings presented by a physician at a CME seminar are not "untruthful" or "inherently misleading" merely because the FDA has not yet had the opportunity to evaluate the claim. As two commentators astutely stated, 'the FDA is not a peer review mechanism for the scientific community.'"

In *Pearson v. Shalala* the Federal appeals court for the District of Columbia followed this reasoning and ruled that dietary supplements can be labeled with health claims so long as they bear a disclaimer that such claims have not received FDA approval.

SECTION NINE

Income Determination

Introduction:
The Heroic Enterprise

By John Hood

IN 1947, A SLIM volume written by a relatively obscure General Motors corporate executive was issued by a small publishing house under the title *The Mainspring of Human Progress.* The book began with an intriguing chapter entitled "Puzzling Questions of Vital Concern to 2,155,000,000 Individuals" led off with this curious paragraph:

> For 60 known centuries, this planet that we call Earth has been inhibited by human beings not much different from ourselves. Their desire to live has been just as strong as ours. They have had at least as much physical strength as the average person of today, and among them have been men and women of great intelligence. But down through the ages, most human beings have gone hungry, and many have always starved.[1]

The author, Henry Grady Weaver, served as director of customer research for GM. Blind in one eye, he nevertheless spent much of his lift peering over data, He was a number-cruncher, not a philosopher or polemicist; his writing experience had consisted mainly of penning articles on psychological research. But *The Mainspring of Human Progress, an amateur's paean to freedom and individual ingenuity, remains one of the finest discussions of the impact of business on society that has ever been written.*

Weaver was writing to an American public that had just endured almost two decades of desperate economic hardship, social upheaval, and war. There was a sense of euphoria after the surrender of Germany and Japan in 1945, a commonly held belief that the United States had managed to extricate itself from turmoil and disaster to achieve unparalleled strength and influence around the world. At the same time, however, doubts were beginning to surface about some of America's traditional institutions and principles. The apparent vitality of the Soviet Union, which had itself fought back from the brink of destruction to a glorious victory, was unsettling. The lingering economic controversies from the New Deal—about the role of the federal government in society, and the ability of capitalism to provide jobs and opportunities for the common man—had been left unresolved during a half decade of world war. Indeed, the growth of the federal government during World War II and the unprecedented role it assumed of directing and managing the wartime economy was just being recognized and debated.

Weaver was a practical man as well as vigorous defender of American business. He understood that in order to persuade his readers that the free enterprise system was worth preserving, he would have to eschew elaborate theory and focus instead on historic fact and common sense. So he began his book with a discussion of the state shared by most human beings throughout most of human history: hunger. The ancient civilizations extolled by historians and philosophers, Weaver pointed out, consistently failed to keep their people fed. Egyptians and Greeks sometimes killed their babies because they couldn't feed them. The Roman Empire collapsed in famine. French peasants were dying of hunger when Thomas Jefferson bought Louisiana from Napoleon Bonaparte. As late as 1846, the Irish were starving to death from a potato famine. In Weaver's day, famines continued to plague significant portions of Asia and Africa, but in the United Stated there were only periodic, geographically limited episodes of hunger.[2] And after Weaver's time (he died in 1949), the "green revolution" of unparalleled agricultural productivity in the 1960s essentially eradicated hunger as serious problem not only in the United States but throughout much of the developed and developing world (except in those regions where war or politics disrupts agriculture and commerce).[3]

Weaver was fascinated with the sudden, amazing productivity of agriculture, as well as with other pleasant surprises of modern life. "Why did men, women, and children eke out their meager existence for 6,000 years [of recorded history], toiling desperately from dawn to dark—barefoot, half-naked, unwashed, unshaved, uncombed, with lousy hair, mangy skins, and rotting teeth—then suddenly, in one place on Earth there is an abundance of such things as rayon underwear, nylon hose, shower baths, safety razors ice cream sodas, lipsticks, and permanent waves?" he asked.[4] Imagine what Weaver might think of American society today, where a family of modest means might have access to a cornucopia of foods and treats, dozens of television channels, thousands of movies, inexpensive clothes and cosmetics, a luxurious (by the standards of 1947) home with air conditioning, microwave ovens, digital stereo, a medicine chest full of lifesaving or pain-alleviating drugs, several reliable automobiles, and a magical desktop machine capable of balancing a checkbook, drawing a picture, publishing a newspaper, playing a game, and sending a letter instantaneously to another city or even another country. Indeed, the average American now consumes about twice as many goods and services as families did in Weaver's day—and he thought his contemporaries enjoyed and extremely high and unprecedented standard of living! (We might well say the same today: Studies of household consumption show that poor families today live very much like middle-income families did in the 1950s in terms of housing and amenities.[5])

A devout Southern Baptist, husband, and father of two, Weaver was no materialist. He would not (nor should anyone) interpret the mere possession of conveniences and luxuries as proof of social well-being. At the same time, however, Weaver lacked the elitist's disdain for the importance of material comfort. He carefully studied human nature—specifically, consumer preferences—and understood the revolutionary impact of economic progress on the lives of the middle class and poor. Nor did Weaver have much patience for those who tried to interpret American progress in ethnic or racial terms. "That sounds fine in after-dinner oratory and goes over big at election time," he wrote perceptively, "but the argument is difficult to support. Our own ancestors, including the Anglo-Saxons, have starved right along with everyone else."[6] Instead, Weaver Argued, the mainspring of human progress was freedom itself. The United States, by allowing the most individual freedom to produce goods and services and sell them to consumers for profit, had unleashed the greatest degree of invention and ingenuity, resulting in social benefits for all.

In Weaver's time, this simple statement of the virtues of a capitalist economy, while increasingly rare in the ivory towers of American academia, was hardly incongruent with public sentiment. During the 1940s and 1950s most Americans held business as an institution in high esteem (as well as, it should be noted, such other institutions as government, organized religion, and the press). The media, too, often viewed business and corporate leaders with at least equanimity, if not actual approval. Media analysts Robert Lichter, Linda Lichter, and Stanley Rothman point out that many television and motion-picture plots of the 1950s featured businessmen in positive, sometimes heroic roles. Wise, honest, and trustworthy fathers Jim Anderson of "Father Knows Best" and Ward Cleaver of "Leave It To Beaver" were an insurance salesman and an accountant, respectively. Nick Charles, "The Thin Man," was a publisher. Herbert Philbrick, the hero of the popular 1950s TV adventure series "I Led Three Lives," was a pipe-smoking advertising executive, a Communist Party worker, and an FBI counterspy. Bruce Wayne (also known as Batman) was a wealthy industrialist. Even into the 1960s, television series continues to portray those in business as "good guys." Westerns were a surprising source of positive images about business; Ben Cartwright of "Bonanza," after all, ran a sprawling ranching and mining empire on the family's thousand-acre Ponderosa estate.[7]

In most cases, however, while these business characters were portrayed positively, they were rarely portrayed in the actual practice of doing business. The Beaver spent little time at his father's accounting firm. Bruce Wayne even donned a mask and fought crime at night so as to distinguish Batman from the CEO of Wayne Enterprises. There were some notable exceptions. The hit 1954 film *Sabrina*—in which brothers played by Humphrey Bogart and William Holden vied for the affections of Audrey Hepburn—has several memorable scenes with both major and minor characters bouncing up and down on a new plastic, to be manufactured out of sugar cane and sold by Bogart's and Holden's family firm. Holden, a hedonist with little interest in business, asks his workaholic brother why he was spending so much time dabbling with plastic rather than having fun. "What will that prove?" be demands, pointing to the strip of plastic. Bogart replies *as* follows:

> Prove? Nothing much. A new product has been found, something of use to the world. So a new industry moves into an underdeveloped area … People who never saw a dime before suddenly have a dollar, and barefoot kids wear shoes and have their teeth fixed and their faces washed. What's wrong with the kind of an urge that gives people hospitals, libraries, baseball diamonds, and movies on a Saturday night? [8]

Needless to say, if Weaver had lived long enough to see Sabrina, he would have rooted for Bogart's crusty but insightful businessman over Holder's irresponsible playboy. Nor would he have been alone: Movie audiences were supposed to root for Bogart who gets the girl in the end (while Holden learns responsibility and prepares to shoulder his weight in the family business).

THE BACKLASH AGAINST BUSINESS

But even in the comparatively conservative 1950s, there was significant undercurrent of skepticism and revisionist thinking about the role of business in society. These ideas flowed through universities, then bubbled up through the legal system in a series of court decisions that redefined the purpose and responsibilities of the American corporation. Social movements, responding to problems such as racial injustice and environmental degradation, began to view business as a corrupt, amoral institution in which a few greedy individuals profited at the expense of the broader community. By the 1960s and 1970s, the undercurrent of revisionism about business became a raging river of criticism, protests, and hostility.

The mass media both reflected and influenced these public perceptions. Investigative journalism became an heroic, even romantic, calling, with the name of the game being to catch greedy corporations in the act polluting the water, selling shoddy and overpriced products, exploiting workers and families, and sacrificing the public's health, safety, and welfare to make a quick buck. On television and in the movies, business executives increasingly became the villains, to be challenged by heroic lawyers, policemen, reporters, and activists. In a study of the hundred highest-grossing films (selected from Variety listings), researchers found that nearly nine out of ten business characters were portrayed positively before 1965, but two out of three were portrayed negatively thereafter. After 1975, the proportion of negative business characters rose to three out of four.[9] Such films as *The China Syndrome, Norma Rae, Silkwood,* and *Wall Street* are examples of this trend, in which antisocial or even criminal corporate behavior could be challenged only by the heroic actions of crusading lawyers and journalists or brave whistle-blowers. Lichter, Lichter, and Rothman found the same pattern for television characters. While small-business owners were treated about the same over the decades, the percentage of big-business characters portrayed as villains rose from 31 percent before 1965 to 58 percent afterward. The authors compared, for example, the positive portrayals of the Cartwright family in "Bonanza" to the largely corrupt and immoral Ewing family of "Dallas."[10]

Public sentiment toward business, influenced by social activism and media images, also began to change. In 1965 almost 60 percent of Americans believed that businesses made a "reasonable profit" whereas 24 percent thought businesses made too much. By 1975 the trend lines had reversed, with more Americans calling profits excessive rather than reasonable.[11] Even in 1939, as the economic stagnation of the Great Depression lingered, 56 percent of Americans said that the interests of employers and employees were "basically the same," while only 25 percent said they were opposed. But by 1994, more Americans thought the interests of the two groups clashed than thought they coincided.[12] Much of the cringe has occurred in public perception of big business; in one 1992 poll, 64 percent of Americans rated the moral and ethical standards of small-business owners as excellent or good, while only 31 percent said the same about "business executives."[13]

It was during this same period of social upheaval and changing media images about business that a movement began among business scholars, journalists, issue-oriented activist groups, and some corporate executives to shift the goals and principles of American business away from profits and return to shareholders and toward the interests of a broader constituency of so-called stakeholders—workers, customers, neighbors, and society at large.[14] Variously called "corporate social responsibility" or "socially responsible business," the modern movement is dated by many of its adherents to 1953, with publications of *Social Responsibilities of the Businessman* by Howard Bowen. In 1963 came *Business and Society*, a textbook for colleges and universities by business professor Joseph McGuire, and by 1970s the field was a full-fledged academic discipline that could boast programs in major business schools and dozens of important books.[15] Today corporate social responsibility is not only an academic field of inquiry and a guiding philosophy for many social activists but a major issue among corporate managers whose deep concerns about corporate image, public relations, environmental liability, lawsuits, relations with governments, and worker morale—and, it should be said, about the many lingering problems in American society often spotlighted by business critics—have melded into a search for a coherent set of ethical and managerial principles to guide economic enterprises in the 1990s and beyond.

Of course, corporate social responsibility as a late twentieth-century American movement is only a modern manifestation of an ancient debate among philosophers and theologians in many lands and cultures about the morality of commerce itself. Is economic competition the enemy of compassion and community? Is commercial activity a necessary evil or a desirable good? To whom do traders and merchants owe their loyalty? Do capitalists exploit their workers and the poor? Is it moral to sell basic human necessities at a profit? The greatest thinkers of human history have wrestled with these questions. Aristotle wrote about trading and business profits in his *Nicomachean Ethics and Politics*. Major portions of Old Testament books such as Deuteronomy contain rules for ethical business practice. Adam Smith's *The Wealth of Nations* is usually thought of as a treatise on economics, but it also discusses in depth the social context and impact of commercial activity. Smith was, after all, a theologian and ethicist, not a businessman or economist. Karl Marx was no economist either, and had never set foot in a factory, but his critical analysis of business behavior changed the course of history.

In the United States of the late nineteenth century, the issue sharpened as defenders and critics of the "robber barons" clashed over the role of profit exploitation, and immoral business practices in the development of the West, the growth of industry, and the accumulation of vast fortunes. Over the next century the debate about such controversial businessmen as Cornelius Vanderbilt, Leland Stanford, Jay Gould, J. J. Hill, J. P. Morgan, and John D. Rockefeller raged on. Were these men exemplars of the evils of unfettered, greedy capitalism, or were they instead great innovators whose impact on society justified their wealth? (In actuality, the story of the "robber baron" period is more complicated than either of these propositions would allow, as described in such works is *Entrepreneurs vs. the State* by Burton W. Folsom Jr.[16])

In the modern corporate social responsibility movement, the key issues of contention include the following:

- The supposedly declining prospects of American workers (in terms of wages, job satisfaction, and leisure time)
- Worker access to health insurance and other benefits
- Health and safety issues for both workers and consumers
- Corporate discrimination against minorities, women, the disabled, and other aggrieved groups
- The impact of business on families and children
- The relationship between business and other social institutions such as schools and charities
- Environmental degradation

An example of how activists of the 1990s critique corporate behavior can be found in *Absence of the Sacred*, written by former advertising executive and business analyst Jerry Mander and published by Sierra Club Books in 1991. Corporations, Mander argued, are essentially amoral institutions who sacrifice the common good in pursuit of mindless profits. While this occurs across a range of corporate actions, the most serious problem is ecological. In modern industrial production, he said, "metals from the ground are converted into cars. Trees are converted into boards and then into houses, furniture, and paper products. Oil is converted into energy. In all such activity, a piece of nature is taken from where it belongs and processed into a new form." Mander even resurrected the old "labor theory of value" to indict the concept of corporate profit itself:

> All corporate profit is obtained by a simple formula: Profit equals the difference between the amount paid to an employee and the economic value of the employee's output, and/or the difference between the amount paid for raw materials used in product (including costs of processing) and the ultimate sales price of the processed raw materials. Karl Marx was right: A worker is not compensated for the full value of his or her labor, [and] neither is the raw material supplier. The owners of capital skim off part of the value as profit. Profit is based on underpayment … this is called exploitation.[17]

One might view Minder's attack on corporate behavior in America as extreme and atypical of business critics. But allegations of corporate misbehavior, irresponsibility, exploitation, and greed are commonplace in the mainstream media of the 1990s: in morning newspapers, in evening TV newsmagazines, in movies and popular music, and even in children's cartoon programs like "Captain Planet and the Planeteers." Just to take one example, during early 1995 there were a spate of stories on TV newscasts and in major newspapers and magazines about the "overworked American." The cover story for the March 6 *Newsweek*, entitled "Breaking Point," chronicled the supposed inability of American workers to keep up with the demands of their downsizing, profit-chasing employers while also trying to rear families and enjoy leisure time. "We are fast becoming the nation of the quick, or the dead-tired," the magazine proclaimed.[18] Yet in actuality the average workweek of Americans has been falling for decades; leisure time, as well as participation in a wide variety of leisure and recreational activities, has been increasing.[19] In opinion polls, most Americans express satisfaction with both their jobs and their family lives, and few say they would be willing to work fewer hours if it would mean less income.[20]

In a cover story in the April 1992 issue of *Inc. Magazine*, a popular publication among entrepreneurs and business owners, Paul Hawken—the founder of Smith & Hawken, a garden catalog company, and a prominent activist and hero in the corporate social responsibility movement—called for new "Ecology of Commerce." He wrote matter-of-factly that "we can say in no uncertain terms that business is destroying the world." This catastrophe could be averted, Hawken continued, if business would work to reduce consumption, raise wages, and reduce its impact on the world environment. "Either we see business as a restorative undertaking, or we, as businesspeople, will march the entire race to the undertaker."[21] What was amazing about Hawken's polemic was not its ideology but the fact that the editors of a business magazine apparently thought his views to be both serious and of interest to a business audience. After all, *Inc.* presumably is no less concerned than its competitors about maintaining and expanding its readership (those greedy profiteers!). Are America's entrepreneurs likely to agree, "in no uncertain terms," that business is destroying the world?

The situation is hardly bleak. The corporate social responsibility movement has its critics and combatants, both within business and without. Corporate public relations, a massive industry in its own right, has made social responsibility a major theme in advertising, promotions, article placements, and events. In economics, free-market thinkers from Smith to Milton Friedman have argued that the pursuit of profit by economic enterprises generated tremendous social benefits. And in politics, impassioned arguments against heavy regulation and in favor of business freedom and competitiveness seem to have found an audience among many policymakers and voters, who still view business with greater respect than other institutions such as government or the press.

But this public respect for business is abstract in nature; it doesn't extend to all the complaints of the social responsibility movement. A Roper Organization poll in 1991 asked respondents to rank the responsibilities of business. At the top of the list, were both tasks Americans believed corporations were doing well (such as producing good-quality products and services, and protecting the health and safety of workers) and tasks Americans believed corporations were doing poorly (such as cleaning up pollution). Lower on the list of perceived business responsibilities were "developing new products and services" and "keeping profits at reasonable levels." Neither omission is surprising. The innovation and invention inherent in business, and so crucial to social progress, rarely gets much press or public attention. And on the latter point, Americans have for many years exaggerated the size of corporate profits, telling pollsters that they believe the average profit of U.S. firms is 34 percent when in reality it is only about 4 percent.[22]

A DIFFERENT APPROACH

I approach the issues surrounding business behavior and the common good in a very different way than have most analysts of corporate social responsibility. First and foremost, I spend very little time on theoretical discussion; I merely summarize the major viewpoints and disagreements in the corporate social responsibility debate. Nor is this book primarily an analysis of the history of business, since such analyses can already be found in numerous works of scholarship and journalism. Instead, this book describes the conduct and social effects of business in America today. It examines many areas of greater concern to scholars, business executives, and the general public, but it does so through the lens of actual experience. Interviews with business executives and case studies of how businesses address and solve problems help to define the issue of corporate social responsibility more sharply, leading to several clear (and to some, no doubt, surprising) conclusions about the moral and ethical aspects of commerce and the key tenets of the corporate social responsibility movement.

One of the fundamental distinctions in philosophy and ethics is the "is-ought" dichotomy. To describe what *is* does not necessarily describe what *ought* to be; however, sometimes a descriptive discussion can lead to normative conclusions. Most philosophers and ethicists give at least some attention to tradition—to the bundle of beliefs and behaviors that evolve in a particular society or institution over time, as human beings struggle to understand and cope with the problems they face in their everyday lives. I contend in this book that corporate social responsibility can be judged by examining in detail how actual companies, in their day-to-day operations, confer broad and measurable benefits to the society in which they operate. In this approach I borrow from the technique of Weaver and of Adam Smith, who introduced his subject in The Wealth of Nations in descriptive terms and discussed at length the actual operation of capital markets and foreign trade in eighteenth-century Europe. His views about what we would today call corporate social responsibility are expressed as the lesson not of ethical reasoning but of his own experience: "I have never known much good done by those who affected to trade for the public good."[23]

My purpose is simply to update and revise this discussion in the context of late twentieth-century American commerce, providing students of corporate social responsibility—in the academy, in the boardroom, in the newsroom, or in the legislative chamber—with specific examples, of how businesses can and do serve society through me pursuit of excellence, worker performance competitiveness, innovation, and profit.[24] Whether business, due to its demonstrable contributions to the common good, can and will be viewed as "heroic" as are other professions or callings is a matter of great importance if free enterprise is to survive and thrive. Henry Grady Weaver, in the heady and unsettling days after World War II, understood this well. Writing about great American entrepreneurs such as Eli Whitney (the father of not only the cotton gin but much of mass production itself), John Deere, Thomas Edison, and Henry Ford, Weaver argued that their contributions to American society were greater, in his judgment, than those of many political or military leaders who were better known to the public. Indeed, even such early American political heroes as Benjamin Franklin, Thomas Jefferson, and Thomas Paine were important inventors and entrepreneurs in their own right.[25]

Americans were and are an inventive people, Weaver wrote, because of the very system of free economic competition based on profit and reward. "No matter how much money John Deere may have made," he observed, "it would be insignificant in comparison with the tremendous overall benefits shared by millions of people" from his innovative steel plow that made prairie agriculture, and thus westward expansion, viable. 'It's just possible that good old John Deere wouldn't have bothered his head about the plowing problem if he hadn't been living in a free country, where an ambitious blacksmith had a chance to became a prosperous manufacturer."[26]

In reality the business world is populated more by heroes like John Deere than by the villains who make the morning newspapers, are vilified on the evening newsmagazines, or appear in Hollywood's unrealistic and silly fantasies about American society. Few tasks are more important than exploring this world and trying to explain how it actually works.

Entrepreneurs Are the Heroes of the World

By Johan Norberg

I THINK OF A paragraph in Ludwig von Mises' book *Human Action*, where he says that the market economy does not need apologists or propagandists. The best argument for the market economy can be found in the epitaph of Sir Christopher Wren, the architect who built and is buried in St. Paul's Cathedral: "si monumentum requiris, circumspice" (if you are looking for a monument, look around you). Look at what he built. Look at his vision. You are standing in it right now.

That, I think is the best defense that the market economy can ever hop for—that people look around and ponder the amazing things and opportunities that entrepreneurs and business have given the world during the last 200 years. Just look around at the health, the wealth, the technologies, the opportunities, and the food on your plates. Could any of that have been possible for a king or a queen 200 years ago?

THE AMAZING FACT is that entrepreneurs and innovators and businesses have turned luxuries that not even kings could afford into low-priced everyday items at your local store. That is the best defense of capitalism.

In a very short time, the world has experienced an extreme makeover. And that is what my recent book, *When Man Created the World,* is about. The interesting thing is that history shows us that freedom works. During 1,000 years of absolute monarchy, feudalism, and slavery, mankind's average income increased by about 50 percent. In the 180 years since 1820, mankind's average income has increased by almost 1,000 percent.

During the last 100 years, we have created more wealth, reduced poverty more, and increased life expectancy more than in the previous 100,000 years. And that happened because of people like you—entrepreneurs, thinkers, creators, innovators—who had new ideas, who traveled geographical distances and, more important, mental distances to create new things and who saw to it that old traditions, which would have stopped new creations, would not stop them for long.

That is why we have all this wealth. That is why our son, who will be born in January, has a greater chance of reaching retirement age than children in all previous eras had of experiencing their first birthday.

GLOBAL SPREAD

In the last few decades of globalization, when new opportunities, technologies, and means of communicating and producing have spread across the world, we have witnessed an amazing phenomenon: developing countries are growing faster than the richest countries on the planet. It took us something like 40 years to double our average income. It takes 10 to 15 years today for China, India, Bangladesh, and Vietnam to do the same thing. They can use the ideas and technologies that it took us generations to develop right away. That is why poverty in the world has been cut in half in the last 20 years.

Every minute I speak, 13 children go from work, toil, and sweat on farms or in factories into schools for education, to have a better life later on and to increase their opportunities.

And every minute I speak, your life expectancy is increasing by about 15 seconds because of the increase of wealth and new medical technologies. All of this is dependent on innovators and entrepreneurs. The entrepreneur is an explorer who travels into uncharted territory and opens up new routes along which we will all be traveling pretty soon. Nothing has existed "from the beginning." Not even natural resources are natural in any meaningful sense—something that a lot of governments have realized when they have nationalized oil and gas resources and other things. They had failed to understand that we also need the entrepreneurial spirit—the ability to see how to use a resource and how to invest in it in a positive way to make sure that it is used efficiently.

The OPEC countries grew by about 4 percent every year because of their oil resources until 1973, when most of them had nationalized their oil industries. Since then, they have grown poorer by about 1 percent every year.

Fifty years ago a North Carolinian truck driver, Malcolm McLean, thought that there must be a more efficient way of transporting goods and components all over the world. Back then, people would take their trucks down to the harbor. The boat would sit there for a week or so while the unionized work force slowly and steadily loaded every single piece of cargo on the boat. The reverse would happen in the destination harbor.

McLean thought, "What if I use wheel-less boxes and just put all the goods in the boxes and hoist them onto the trucks, drive down to the harbor, and then just put the unopened boxes on the ship?"

In one night, McLean created modern container traffic. He reduced the cost of sending goods and components across the oceans by something like 97 percent. It is possible for us to have a particular kind of computer, with components from all major continents on the planet, the clothes we wear, the food on our plates because of one man and his dream and a culture that did not try to stop him but instead encouraged his dreams and his visions. And developing countries all around the world suddenly have use for their talent and their hard work—to produce what they can produce best, put it into containers, and send it somewhere else.

But technology is not enough. We also need freedom for new technology. Unless governments step out of the way and allow entrepreneurs to do their thing, none of this will happen. We know that, because there are places where modern technologies are not used because of regulations, corruption, and government intervention.

If you are sending one truckload of fruit from South Africa to Zimbabwe, it costs you more in time, bribes, fees to the government, and taxes than it would cost to send the same truckload of fruit from South Africa all the way to the United States.

OUR HEROES

There is a classic work by Joseph Campbell, a book on cultural history called *The Hero with a Thousand Faces,* about heroes in different cultures. Because Campbell traveled the world by reading books from other continents, he could see that there are heroes in all cultures, in all books, in all eras. We need heroes, because they say something about what our values are, what is good, what is great, what is bad, what we should strive for, and what we should try to avoid.

He saw a common pattern. He thought that in most cultures and in most eras the same kinds of things are seen as heroic.

Something big happens, and our hero is forced to go on a journey to fight hostile enemies against all odds with a lack of knowledge of what to do and when and how. But along the way he makes some friends who help him along and give him the knowledge and the inspiration to do what is right.

Think about that heroic journey once again, and think of the persons I just talked about—people like you, thinkers, innovators, entrepreneurs. What makes it possible for us to buy equipment and goods from the other side of the world? Entrepreneurs face ancient traditions, political obstacles, taxes, and regulations, but they also have friends—people with access to capital, to knowledge, to other businesses. If they are lucky, entrepreneurs succeed. If not, they learn something new, make it even better the next time, and bring to the community something new that changes lives forever.

That is the heroic epic. The entrepreneur is the hero of our world. We do not really need the Frodos, the Luke Skywalkers, or the Buffy the Vampire Slayers. We have the Malcolm McLeans of the world.

But as you all know, that is not really what popular culture thinks of capitalists and entrepreneurs today. If you go to an average Hollywood movie, the hero is someone quite different.

The scientist and the capitalist are the enemies in most Hollywood productions. That is a bit ironic, because we would not have film technology if there were no scientists, and we would not have a film industry if it were not for the capitalists. But they are presented as villains.

Some anti-globalists and people opposed to free trade are now well-paid consultants who sit on the boards of big companies and tell them that what they do is really a bad thing and that they must accept much more corporate social responsibility. In their terms, corporate social responsibility means that what you have done so far is not social. It is not enough to create goods, services, and technologies that increase our life expectancies and save the lives of our children. No, you need to do something more. After making your profit, you need to give something back to society.

Give something back to society? As if the entrepreneurs and capitalists had stolen something that belonged to society that they have to give back!

Profit is not something that we have to apologize for. Profit is proof that the capitalist has given something to society that it cherishes more than the material wealth it has given to the businessman.

I must emphasize that entrepreneurs should never be grateful for a society that gives them license to act, to dream, to innovate, and to create. I think that we, the society, should be grateful to the entrepreneur and to the businessman for what they do. Entrepreneurs are the heroes of our world—that despite the risks, the hard work, the hostility from society, the envy from neighbors, and state regulations, they keep on creating, they keep on producing and trading. Without them, nothing would be there.

MAGIC IS ALIVE

Max Weber, the German sociologist, thought that the modern world experienced a demystification that was very problematic. There was no magic left in the world, with science explaining everything—life, nature, disease.

Excuse me very much. No magic? That is nonsense. I flew here. In 1901 we heard from a very insightful commentator who said that that was impossible. We could not fly. We wouldn't be able do something like that for at least the next 50 years. That commentator was Wilbur Wright, one of the two Wright brothers, who two years later took the first flight, because he wanted to explore. He took that risk and made it all happen. That is magic.

I have in my computer more power of calculation than existed in most countries 40 years ago. My thoughts are being turned into ones and zeroes that are transmitted through fiber optics, optic cables of glass, thin as a hair, and they come to the other side of the planet a tenth of a second later. And by the click of the mouse, I can order just about any kind of knowledge that exists anywhere in the world.

Above us there are satellites that guide our navigation. And beneath us we have robots that mine metal from rock. We have traveled out in space, and we have read the genetic code within us. We have conquered hunger and disease. So I will say to you: we live in an enchanted world, in a magic world, and it is even more enchanted because the creators and the innovators make it so.

There is vision. There are intelligence, ingenuity, and hard work in every good, in every service, and in every technology that we use every day. And we are just barely getting started. We have more scientists alive today than existed in all previous eras combined.

Imagine what free individuals and creators can do with the new breakthroughs in nanotechnology, biotechnology, and robotics. I am sure it will surprise us just as much as flight and computers would have surprised our forefathers. If people take these things for granted, it is only because our everyday lives have become fantastic.

WELL OF FREEDOM

You know the old proverb, "He that has satisfied his thirst turns his back to the well." Well, that is why we meet and that is why we share lunch. That is why we work and that is why we fight—to remind people of that well of freedom and of individualism, to keep that well from running dry, and to remind people of the reasons more people live longer lives and richer lives than ever, in countries that are freer than ever.

It is customary at the end of a talk to say thank you to signal that it is the end of the talk. I do it when I speak to anti-globalist and Marxists and so on. But this time I really mean it.

I must say thank you for creating this fantastic world. And thank you so very much for your support for the ideas that make it possible.

Job Safety

By W. Kip Viscusi

MANY PEOPLE BELIEVE that employers do not care about workplace safety. If the government were not regulating job safety, they contend, workplaces would be unsafe. In fact, employers have many incentives to make workplaces safe. Since the time of Adam Smith, economists have observed that workers demand "compensating differentials" (i.e., wage premiums) for the risks they face. The extra pay for job hazards, in effect, establishes the price employers must pay for an unsafe workplace. Wage premiums paid to U.S. workers for risking injury are huge; they amount to about $245 billion annually (in 2004 dollars), more than 2 percent of the gross domestic product and 5 percent of total wages paid. These wage premiums give firms an incentive to invest in job safety because an employer who makes the workplace safer can reduce the wages he pays.

Employers have a second incentive because they must pay higher premiums for workers' compensation if accident rates are high. And the threat of lawsuits over products used in the workplace gives sellers of these products another reason to reduce risks. Of course, the threat of lawsuits gives employers an incentive to care about safety only if they anticipate the lawsuits. In the case of asbestos litigation, for example, liability was deferred by several decades after the initial exposure to asbestos. Even if firms had been cognizant of the extent of the health risk—and many were not—none of them could have anticipated the shift in legal doctrine that, in effect, imposed liability retroactively. Thus, it is for acute accidents rather than unanticipated diseases that the tort liability system bolsters the safety incentives generated by the market for safety.

How well does the safety market work? For it to work well, workers must have some knowledge of the risks they face. And they do. One study of how 496 workers perceived job hazards found that the greater the risk of injury in an industry, the higher the proportion of workers in that industry who saw their job as dangerous. In industries with five or fewer disabling injuries per million hours worked, such as women's outerwear manufacturing and the communication equipment industry, only 24 percent of surveyed workers considered their jobs dangerous. But in industries with forty or more disabling injuries per million hours, such as the logging and meat products industries, 100 percent of the workers knew that their jobs were dangerous. That workers know the dangers makes sense. Many hazards, such as visible safety risks, can be readily monitored. Moreover, some dimly understood health risks are often linked to noxious

W. Kip Viscusi, "Job Safety," from *The Concise Encyclopedia of Economics*, ed. David R. Henderson, 2008, pp. 311–313. Copyright © 2008 The Liberty Fund, Inc. Permission to reprint granted by the publisher.

exposures and dust levels that workers can monitor. Also, symptoms sometimes flag the onset of some more serious ailment. Byssinosis, for example, a disease that afflicts workers exposed to cotton dust, proceeds in stages.

Even when workers are not well informed, they do not necessarily assume that risks are zero. According to a large body of research, people systematically overestimate small risks and underestimate large ones. If workers overestimate the probability of an injury that occurs infrequently—for example, exposure to a highly publicized potential carcinogen, such as secondhand smoke—then employers will have too great an incentive to reduce this hazard. The opposite is also true: when workers underestimate the likelihood of more frequent kinds of injuries, such as falls and motor vehicle accidents on the job, employers may invest too little in preventing those injuries.

The bottom line is that market forces have a powerful influence on job safety. The $245 billion in annual wage premiums referred to earlier is in addition to the value of workers' compensation. Workers on moderately risky blue-collar jobs, whose annual risk of getting killed is 1 in 25,000, earn a premium of $280 per year. The imputed compensation per "statistical death" (25,000 times $280) is therefore $7 million. Even workers such as coal miners and firemen, who are not strongly averse to risk and who have knowingly chosen extremely risky jobs, receive compensation on the order of $1 million per statistical death.

These wage premiums are the amount workers insist on being paid for taking risks—that is, the amount workers would willingly forgo to avoid the risk. Employers will eliminate hazards only when it costs them less than what they will save in the form of lower wage premiums. For example, the employer will spend $10,000 to eliminate a risk if doing so allows the employer to pay $11,000 less in wages. Costlier reductions in risk are not worthwhile to employees (since they would rather take the risk and get the higher pay) and are not voluntarily undertaken by employers.

Other evidence that the safety market works comes from the decrease in the riskiness of jobs throughout the century. One would predict that, as workers become wealthier, they will be less desperate to earn money and will therefore demand more safety. The historical data show that this is what employees have done and that employers have responded by providing more safety. As per capita disposable income per year rose from $1,085 (in 1970 prices) in 1933 to $3,376 in 1970, death rates on the job dropped from 37 per 100,000 workers to 18 per 100,000. Since 1997, fatality rates have been less than 4 per 100,000.

The impetus for these improvements has been increased societal wealth. Every 10 percent increase in people's income leads them to increase by 6 percent the price they charge employers for bearing risk. That is, their value of statistical life increases, boosting the wages required to attract workers to risky jobs.

Despite this strong evidence that the market for safety works, not all workers are fully informed about the risks they face. They may be uninformed about little-understood health hazards that have not yet been called to their attention. But even where workers' information is imperfect, additional market forces are at work. Survey results indicate that of all workers who quit manufacturing jobs, more than one-third do so when they discover that the hazards are greater than they initially believed. Losing employees costs money. Production suffers while companies train replacements. Companies, therefore, have an incentive to provide a safe work environment, or at least to inform prospective workers of the dangers. Although the net effect of these market processes does not always ensure the optimal amount of safety, the incentives for safety are substantial.

Beginning with the passage of the Occupational Safety and Health Act of 1970, the federal government has attempted to augment these safety incentives, primarily by specifying technological standards for workplace design. These government attempts to influence safety decisions formerly made by companies generated substantial controversy and, in some cases, imposed huge costs. A particularly extreme example is the 1987 OSHA formaldehyde standard, which imposed costs of $78 billion for each life that the regulation is expected to save. Because the U.S. Supreme Court has ruled that OSHA regulations cannot be subject to a formal cost-benefit test, there is no legal prohibition against regulatory excesses. However, OSHA sometimes takes account of costs while designing regulations. For example, OSHA set the cotton dust standard at a level beyond which compliance costs would have grown explosively.

Increases in safety from OSHA's activities have fallen short of expectations. According to some economists' estimates, OSHA regulations have reduced workplace injuries by, at most, 2–4 percent. Why such a modest impact on risks? One reason is that the financial incentives for safety imposed by OSHA are comparatively small. Although total penalties have increased dramatically since 1986, they averaged less than $10 million per year for many years of the agency's operation. By 2002, the total annual OSHA penalties levied had reached $149 million. The $245 billion wage premium that workers "charge" for risk is more than sixteen hundred times as large.

The workers' compensation system that has been in place in the United States since the early twentieth century also gives companies strong incentives to make workplaces safe. Premiums for workers' compensation, which employers pay, totaled $26 billion annually as of 2001. Particularly for large firms, these premiums are strongly linked to their injury performance. Statistical studies indicate that in the absence of the workers' compensation system, workplace death rates would rise by 27 percent. This estimate assumes, however, that workers' compensation would not be replaced by tort liability or higher market wage premiums. The strong performance of workers' compensation, particularly when contrasted with the command-and-control approach of OSHA regulation, has led many economists to suggest that an injury tax be instituted as an alternative to the current regulatory standards.

The main implication of economists' analysis of job safety is that financial incentives matter and that the market for job safety is alive and well.

ABOUT THE AUTHOR

W. Kip Viscusi is the University Distinguished Professor of Law, Economics, and Management at Vanderbilt University. He is the founding editor of the *Journal of Risk and Uncertainty*. Viscusi was also deputy director of President Jimmy Carter's Council on Wage and Price Stability, which was responsible for White House oversight of new regulations.

FURTHER READING

Morrall, John F. "Saving Lives: A Review of the Record." *Journal of Risk and Uncertainty* 27, no. 3 (2003): 221–237.

Viscusi, W. Kip. *Rational Risk Policy: The 1996 Arne Ryde Memorial Lectures.* New York: Oxford University Press, 1998.

Viscusi, W. Kip, and Joseph E. Aldy. "The Value of a Statistical Life: A Critical Review of Market Estimates Throughout the World." *Journal of Risk and Uncertainty* 27, no. 1 (2003): 5–76.

Puzzling Questions of Vital Concern for 2,155,000,000 Individuals

By Henry Grady Weaver

FOR 60 KNOWN centuries, this planet that we call Earth has been inhabited by human beings not much different from ourselves. Their desire to live has been just as strong as ours. They have had at least as much physical strength as the average person of today, and among them have been men and women of great intelligence. But down through the ages, most human beings have gone hungry, and many have always starved.

The ancient Assyrians, Persians, Egyptians, and Greeks were intelligent people; but in spite of their intelligence and their fertile lands, they were never able to get enough to eat. They often killed their babies because they couldn't feed them.

The Roman Empire collapsed in famine. The French were dying of hunger when Thomas Jefferson was President of the United States. As late as 1846, the Irish were starving to death; and no one was particularly surprised because famines in the Old World were the rule rather than the exception. It is only within the last century that western Europeans have had enough food to keep them alive—soup and bread in France, fish in Scandinavia, beef in England.

Hunger has always been normal. Even to this day,

famines kill multitudes in China, India, Africa; and in the 1930's, thousands upon thousands starved to death on the richest farmlands of the Soviet Union.

Down through the ages, countless millions, struggling unsuccessfully to keep bare life in wretched bodies, have died young in misery and squalor. Then suddenly, in one spot on this planet, people eat so abundantly that the pangs of hunger are forgotten.

THE QUESTIONS

Why did men die of starvation for 6,000 years? Why is it that we in America have never had a famine?

Why did men walk and carry goods (and other men) on their straining backs for 6,000 years—then suddenly, on only a small part of the earth's surface, the forces of nature are harnessed to do the bidding of the humblest citizen?

289

Why did families live for 6,000 years in caves and floor-less hovels, without windows or chimneys—then within a few generations, we in America take floors, rugs, chairs, tables, windows, and chimneys for granted and regard electric lights, refrigerators, running water, porcelain baths, and toilets as common necessities?

Why did men, women, and children eke out their meager existence for 6,000 years, toiling desperately from dawn to dark—barefoot, half-naked, unwashed, unshaved, uncombed, with lousy hair, mangy skins, and rotting teeth—then suddenly, in one place on earth there is an abundance of such things as rayon underwear, nylon hose, shower baths, safety razors, ice cream sodas, lipsticks, and permanent waves?

WHAT ARE THE ANSWERS?

It's incredible, if we would but pause to reflect! Swiftly, in less than a hundred years, Americans have conquered the darkness of night—from pine knots and candles to kerosene lamps, to gas jets; then to electric bulbs, neon lights, fluorescent tubes.

We have created wholly new and astounding defenses against weather—from fireplaces to stoves, furnaces, automatic burners, insulation, air conditioning.

We are conquering pain and disease, prolonging life, and resisting death itself—with anesthetics, surgery, sanitation, hygiene, dietetics.

We have made stupendous attacks on space—from oxcarts, rafts, and canoes to railroads, steamboats, streetcars, subways, automobiles, trucks, busses, airplanes—and attacks on time through telegraph, telephone, and radio.

We have moved from backbreaking drudgery into the modern age of power, substituting steam, electricity, and gasoline for the brawn of man; and today the nuclear physicist is taking over and finding ways for subduing to human uses the infinitesimally tiny atom—tapping a new source of power so vast that it bids fair to dwarf anything that has gone before.

It is true that many of these developments originated in other countries. But new ideas are of little value in raising standards of living unless and until something is done about them. The plain fact is that we in America have outdistanced the world in extending the benefits of inventions and discoveries to the vast majority of people in all walks of life.

HOW DID IT HAPPEN?

Three generations—grandfather to grandson—have created these wonders which surpass the utmost imaginings of all previous time. How did it come about? How can it be explained? Just what has been responsible for this unprecedented burst of progress, which has so quickly transformed a hostile wilderness into the most prosperous and advanced country that the world has ever known?

Perhaps the best way to find the answer is first to rule out some of the factors that were *not* responsible.

To say that it is because of our natural resources is hardly enough. The same rich resources were here when the mound builders held forth. Americans have had no monopoly on iron, coal, copper, aluminum, zinc, lead, or other materials. Such things have always been available to human beings. China, India, Russia, Africa—all have great natural resources. Crude oil oozed from the earth in Baku 4,000 years ago; and when Julius Caesar marched west into Gaul, Europe was a rich and virgin wilderness inhabited by a few roving savages, much as America was when the Pilgrim Fathers landed at Plymouth.[1]

Is it because we work harder? Again the answer is "No" because in most countries the people work much harder, on the average, than we do.

Can it be that we are a people of inherent superiority? That sounds fine in after-dinner oratory and goes over big at election time, but the argument is difficult to support. Our own ancestors, including the Anglo-Saxons, have starved right along with everyone else.

Can it be that we have more energy than other peoples of the world? That's not the answer either, but it's getting pretty close. We are not endowed with any superior energy—mental or physical—but it is a fact that we, in the United States of America, have made more effective use of our human energies than have any other people on the face of the globe—anywhere or at any time.

THE REAL ANSWER

That's the answer—the real answer—the only answer. It's a very simple answer, perhaps too simple to be readily accepted. So it is the purpose of this book to dig beneath the surface and to seek the reasons underlying the reason.

In other words, just why does human energy work better here than anywhere else? And answering that question leads us into a whole string of questions, such as:

1. What is the nature of human energy?
2. How does it differ from other forms of energy?
3. What makes it work?
4. What are the things that keep it from working?
5. How can it be made to work better? More efficiently? More effectively?

The answers, even the partial answers, to these questions should be extremely helpful in contributing to future progress.

In the last analysis, poverty, famine, and the devastations of war are all traceable to a lack of understanding of human energy and to a failure to use it to the best advantage.

---

1   Really, when you come right down to it, nothing is a "natural resource" until after men have made it useful to human beings. Coal was not a natural resource to Julius Caesar, nor crude oil to Alexander the Great, nor aluminum to Ben Franklin, nor the atom to anyone until 1945. Men may discover uses for any substance. Nobody can know today what may be a natural resource tomorrow. It is not natural resources, but the uses men make of them that really count.

History affords abundant evidence in support of that statement; but the evidence is somewhat obscured because most of the textbooks stress war and conflict, rather than the causes of war and what might be done to prevent war.[2]

In later chapters, well attempt to reverse the usual procedure. In other words, we'll try to see what can be learned from history as bearing upon the effective use of human energy, which advances progress—as against the misuse of human energy, which retards progress and leads to the destruction of life as well as wealth. But as a background for the main text of this book, it seems necessary, first of all, to review a few elementary facts—including a lot of things which we already know but which we are inclined to overlook.

ENERGY

First, let's consider the general subject of energy—human versus nonhuman. This entire planet is made up of energy. The atoms of air surrounding it are energy. The sun pours energy upon this air and upon this earth. Life depends on energy; in fact, life *is* energy.

Every living thing must struggle for its existence, and human beings are no exception. The thin defenses of civilization tend to obscure the stark realities; but men and women survive on this earth only because their energies constantly convert other forms of energy to satisfy human needs, and constantly attack the nonhuman energies that are dangerous to human existence.

Some people are keenly aware of this: doctors and nurses, farmers, sailors, construction engineers, weather forecasters, telephone linemen, airplane pilots, railroad men, "sand hogs," miners—all the fighters who protect human life and keep the modern world existing. Such people stand the brunt of the struggle and enable the rest of us to forget.

But it is important that we do not forget. When we do forget, there is the temptation to indulge in wishful thinking—to build imaginative Utopias on the basis of things as we might like them to be, instead of facing the real human situation and reckoning with things as they are. In the last analysis, there can be no progress except through the more effective use of our individual energies, personal initiatives, and imaginative abilities—applied to the things and forces of nature.

ENERGY AT WORK

But let's get away from broad generalities for a moment and take a closer look at human energy at work.

Right now you are reading this book. Let's say you want to turn a page. You are the dynamo that generates the energy to turn the page. Your brain-energy makes the decision and controls the movement of the muscle-pulleys and bone-levers of your arm, your hand, and your fingers; and you turn the page.

---

2   From a standpoint of military history, I suppose it's important to know that the Battle of Bull Run came ahead of Vicksburg, but Margaret Mitchell's *Gone With the Wind* is far more revealing as bearing upon the causes and effects of the War Between the States.

The energy that you used to turn the page is the same kind of energy that created this book. Down through centuries of time and across space, from the first maker of paper, of ink, of type, every act of the innumerable minds and hands that created this book and delivered it to you—miners digging coal and iron in Pennsylvania, woodsmen sinking their axes into spruce in Norway and Oregon, chemists in laboratories, workers in factories and foundries, mechanics, printers, binders—was an operation of human energy generated and controlled by the person who performed the act.

And that's really shortchanging the story. To make it complete, we would have to go back to the thousands of people who invented the tools—not just the paper-making machinery and the printing presses and binding equipment, but the tools that were used to make all these things, plus the tools that were used to make the tools.

As a result of modern equipment and facilities, the amount of human time required to produce this book and deliver it to you was less than an hour, whereas a few hundred years ago it would have taken months.

It all comes back to the effective use of human energy; and human energy, like any other energy, operates according to certain natural laws. For one thing, it works only under its own natural control. Your decision to turn the page released the energy to turn it. It was your will which controlled the use of that energy. Nothing else *can* control it.

It is true, of course, that many of your actions are prompted by suggestions and requests or orders and commands from others; but that doesn't change the fact that the decision to act and the action itself are always under your own control.

FREEDOM AND RESPONSIBILITY

Let's take an extreme case. A robber breaks into your house and threatens you at the point of a gun. Discretion being the better part of valor, you give in and tell him where your valuables are hidden. But *you* make the decision, and *you* do the telling.

If, instead of a robber, it were a kidnaper after your child, it would be a different story. But in either case, your thoughts and acts are under your own control. Thousands of men and women have suffered torture and even death without speaking a word that their persecutors tried to make them speak.

Your freedom of action may be forbidden, restricted, or prevented by force. The robber, kidnaper, or jailer may bind your hands and feet and put a gag in your mouth. But the fact remains that no amount of force can *make* you act unless you agree—perhaps with hesitation and regret—to do so.

I know this all sounds hairsplitting and academic, but it leads to a very important point—in fact, to two important points:

1. Individual freedom is the natural heritage of each living person.
2. Freedom cannot be separated from responsibility.

Your natural freedom—your control over your own life-energy—was born in you along with life itself. It is a part of life itself. No one can give it to you, nor can you give it to someone else. Nor can you hold any other person responsible for your acts. Control simply can't be separated from responsibility; control *is* responsibility.

RESULTS VERSUS DESIRES

A steam engine will not run on gasoline, nor will a gasoline engine run on steam.

To use any kind of energy effectively, it is first necessary to understand the nature of the energy and then to set up conditions that will permit it to work to the best advantage.

To make the most effective use of steam energy, it is necessary to reckon with the nature of steam. To make the most effective use of human energy, it is necessary to reckon with the nature of man. And there's no escaping the fact that human energy operates very differently from any other energy.

Steam energy always acts in exactly the same way, so long as the conditions are the same ditto gasoline energy and electrical energy.

Insects and animals follow certain patterns of action. Honeybees, for example, all make the same hexagonal cells of wax. Beavers all build the same form of dam, and the same kinds of birds make the same kinds of nests. Generation after generation, they continue to follow their changeless routines—always doing the same things in the same ways.

But a man is different because he is a human being; and as a human being, he has the power of reason, the power of imagination, the ability to capitalize on the experiences

of the past and the present as bearing on the problems of the future. He has the ability to change *himself* as well as his environment. He has the ability to progress and to keep on progressing.

Plants occupy space and contend with each other for it. Animals defend their possession of places and things. But man has enormous powers, of unknown extent, to make new things and to change old things into new forms. He not only owns property, but he also actually creates property.

In the last analysis, a thing is not property unless it is owned; and without ownership, there is little incentive to improve it.

Three Myths About Labor Unions

By Isaac DiIanni

INTRODUCTION

MANY PEOPLE VIEW labor unions in a positive light. They believe that unions represent worker solidarity, that they raise workers' wages, and that they protect workers against exploitation by profit-driven employers. But a closer examination reveals that all three of these are myths.

WHAT IS A LABOR UNION?

Perhaps the most fundamental myth about labor unions concerns the definition of the term *labor union*. The AFL-CIO, a federation of labor unions that represents over 11 million workers, describes a labor union as: "a group of workers who form an organization" who "decide they want to come together to improve their jobs," and it describes workers "exercising their freedom to improve their lives."

None of this sounds objectionable, of course. But unfortunately, this image of a union as a group of workers who voluntarily join together is not consistent with reality.

Under the National Labor Relations Act (NLRA), passed in 1935, any union that gains the consent of the majority of employees in a work site automatically becomes the legal representative of all employees at that work site. In other words: if you're a worker, and you want to be represented by a union of your choice, or you prefer to have no union at all, and bargain directly with your employer, you may be denied that freedom. If a majority of your co-workers votes for a certain union, you are forced by law to accept that union as your representative.

At many work sites workers are required to join the union as a condition of employment. At other worksites even non-members may be required to pay dues to the union, and are not allowed to bargain with their employer on their own about pay or working conditions. They are forced to accept whatever bargain the union and employer reach.

At the same time, employers are legally required to bargain with that union as well. The federal government, through the National Labor Relations Board, has the power to decide whether a company has bargained "in good faith" with that union, and can impose legal penalties if the company behaves in a way of which the Board disapproves.

In sum, unions are not voluntary organizations. They are political entities. In the worksites where they operate, unions restrict the freedom of workers to bargain voluntarily for their own wages and working conditions, they restrict the freedom of employers to decide the terms under which they will hire workers, and they eliminate freedom of contract between workers and employers, and replace it with a political process.

DO LABOR UNIONS RAISE WORKERS' WAGES?

Labor union advocates argue that unions raise workers' wages and improve their working conditions. For example, the AFL-CIO claims that: "through unions, workers win better wages, benefits and a voice on the job" and "unions have made life better for all working Americans."

But let's take a closer look. It is true that labor unions generally do increase the wages of their members. However, the way they achieve this goal is by restricting job market competition from other (non-union) workers. Labor unions are labor cartels.

The traditional symbol of union power is the strike, in which workers join together and refuse to work until employers meet their demands for higher pay or improved working conditions. But a strike, on its own, cannot accomplish much. If the workers at a worksite are being paid below the competitive wage level for the type and quality of labor that they are providing, they can simply quit and work elsewhere, saving themselves the cost of lost wages and benefits during a strike. If they choose to strike, this implies that better opportunities are not available elsewhere—in other words: that they are demanding wages and benefits higher than the competitive level. But in that case, the employer could simply hire new workers to replace them.

This is why strikes have traditionally been accompanied by picket lines, in which striking employees line up in front of their work sites to prevent other workers (pejoratively called "scabs") from working in their place.

Contrary to the impression created by labor union advocates, workers do not all share a common anti-employer agenda. "Labor" and "Capital" are not homogeneous groups, within which individual interests coincide, and between which conflict is inevitable. Workers are not in competition with their employers; they are in competition with other workers. When strikes turn violent, "scabs" are not just accidental victims. On the contrary, competing workers have often been the intended target of union violence and intimidation.

The NLRA has made picket lines and union street violence less prevalent than in the past, because the law makes it illegal for companies to fire workers for engaging in union activities, such as going on strike. The National Labor Relations Board has the power to prohibit companies from firing its union workers and replacing them with new workers, and to punish those companies if they don't comply.

One stated purpose of the NLRA was to reduce "industrial strife or unrest." But the law has not resolved the basic conflict, it has only replaced union violence with government violence. Instead of union workers coercing competing workers to prevent them from accepting jobs, the National Labor Relations Board coerces employers to prevent them from offering jobs.

The principle is the same: non-union workers are coercively restricted from competing with unionized workers. As a result of this monopoly power, union members are able to achieve wages and working conditions above the competitive level.

This has implications for non-union workers as well. When employment opportunities are restricted in unionized industries, workers who might have held those jobs instead look for jobs in non-unionized industries. The increased supply of workers seeking non-union jobs drives down wages in those industries. So labor unions may raise the wages of their own members, but only at the expense of other workers, whose wages are lower than they otherwise would be.

WHAT WOULD WORKERS DO WITHOUT LABOR UNIONS?

It is sometimes argued that without unions, workers would be at a disadvantage relative to employers; that greedy employers, in the pursuit of profits, will try to pay workers as little as possible, and that workers have too little bargaining power to successfully oppose them. For example, the AFL-CIO writes that unions provide "a counterbalance to the unchecked power of employers."

The problem with this argument is that wages are not determined by bargaining power; they are determined by labor productivity. Employers have an incentive to pay workers according to their marginal product. This is not a matter of employer generosity, but of market competition. Employers compete for workers just like they compete for customers.

If you are running a business, and you learn that one of your rivals has an employee who is earning only $10 per hour, but who is producing $20 per hour worth of value, what do you have an incentive to do? Lure that employee away with an offer of a higher wage! For profit-hungry employers, underpaid workers represent a profit opportunity waiting to be seized. Any employer foolish enough to systematically underpay its employees is effectively sending its most productive workers away to work for its rivals—hardly a winning business strategy.

Just as an employer cannot long remain successful while underpaying its workers, it also must avoid overpaying them. Paying workers more than they are worth is a losing proposition. A firm that insists on doing so must eventually either change its policy or go out of business.

Unionized work sites have been learning this lesson over the past sixty years. In 1945, the proportion of the private sector labor force that was in unions was 35%. Since then, the number of union jobs has fallen steadily such that by 2008 only 7.5% of private sector workers were union members. Despite various forms of government assistance and protectionist legislation, large unionized industries such as steel and automobile manufacturing have had great difficulty staying competitive against foreign producers who need not contend with American unions. The result has been a steady erosion of jobs in unionized industries.

As over 92% of American private sector workers already know, and the rest are now learning, being in a union does not guarantee you a good job—or any job at all.

CONCLUSION

While the benefits created for union members are widely recognized and celebrated, the harm imposed on other workers, employers, and unionized sectors of the economy usually goes unnoticed by the general public. A look at the facts reveals that the positive image of unions that many people hold contains more myth than reality.

The author is Assistant Professor of Economics at Northeastern State University in Tahlequah, Oklahoma.

All quotes from the AFL-CIO come from the internet article "Unions 101," retrieved on 7/10/2009 from http://www.aflcio.org/joinaunion/union101.cfm.

Outrageous CEO Pay

By Hans Sennholz

Nothing sharpens the sight like envy. Some legislators who are enjoying six-figure remunerations and seven-figure benefits are dismayed about CEO compensation. They resent the fact that top executives are earning multimillion-dollar-pay packages while lawmakers subsist on such meager fare. CEOs, in their judgment, are greedy executives who thrive on corporate profits when times are good and when times are bad. Similarly, media commentators and journalists never tire of pointing at apparent excesses of executive compensation practices. One business magazine recently lamented especially about Apple Corporation's issue of a stock-option package valued at more than $500 million, calling it "The Great CEO Pay Heist."

CEO compensation usually is pay-for-performance, consisting of a base pay plus equity-based incentives such as bonuses, stock options, and other equity vehicles. CEO income rises and falls with performance. The market way to measure his or her performance is by the size of company profits and the price of the company stock. Numerous stockholders continually judge the efficiency and profitability of a corporation and set stock prices by buying and selling shares. They love and acclaim a CEO who improves the profitability of their company and thereby may add millions of dollars to the value of the company. They offer multimillion-dollar incentives to management so that it may identify with the interests of the owners.

Irate critics of high CEO pay often base their charges on the notion that corporate boards of directors and compensation consultants who make such astonishing recommendations are cozy and "cushy" with management. Cronyism, they charge, is a strong and habitual business inclination to promote the interests of one another. We may agree that it is a human constant, not only in business, but it may also conflict with the interests of the cronies. In fact, U.S. corporations probably are the most share-holder-responsive in the world because the shareholders themselves may be judged by the price of the corporate stock.

The U.S. stock market is driven by powerful institutional investors such as mutuals and pension funds which force management to maximize shareholder returns and profits. Institutional investors have assumed the role which wealthy families used to play before the age of confiscatory estate taxation; they have the financial clout and resolve to unseat managements of poorly performing companies. They replaced the heads of IBM, General Motors, K-Mart, and American Express with new talent. They may force CEOs to restructure corporate operations and trim their payrolls to the bone—a tactic that was unheard of and unthinkable in the past.

Institutional investors are forcing management to search for the best possible combination of capital and labor, that is, the optimum investment of capital with the optimum number of workers assuring most profitable operation. To employ fewer workers than the optimum is to fail to utilize fully the capital equipment; to employ more is to reduce labor productivity and raise costs. In short, if the number of workers is too small, company profitability demands the hiring of more workers; if the number of workers is too large, profitability requires that excess labor be discharged.

Giant corporations consist of numerous company divisions, departments, branches, and affiliates. Some are more profitable than others; some may even suffer losses and rely on the earnings and subsidies of the profitable branches. An alert CEO is quick to recognize the situation, to reorganize the loss-inflicting activity or terminate it. He does not permit some departments to inflict losses on the owners. To tolerate such failures would soon lead to his dismissal or early retirement.

CEOs may reap unearned windfalls when the Federal Reserve engages in inflationary policies that drive up stock prices. They may pocket undeserved bonuses and exercise stock options which the Fed made profitable. Throughout the 1990s the Fed managed to create the greatest and longest economic boom in American history, which drove stock prices to unprecedented heights and some executive pay to astonishing levels. Even mediocre CEOs could reap unearned option profits as the boom boosted company profits and raised stock prices.

When boom conditions finally turn into economic recessions, CEO income falls as company profits may turn into losses and stock options lose their value. During boom periods option profits may rise to 80 or 90 percent of CEO compensation; during recessions they tend to vanish. Companies may then readjust management options to make up for the fall in stock prices. They have no choice but to create incentives in good times and especially when times are bad. Capable CEOs may choose to work somewhere else if their options are hopelessly out of the money.

Executive stock options impose no costs to the company; they are not paid out of earnings. But they grant ownership to management which dilutes the ownership of all other stockholders. It dilutes the earnings and book value per share whenever the stock options are exercised. Profit and loss statements usually reveal the "fully diluted earnings per share," if and when the options claim three percent or more of company earnings. But stockholders rarely complain because the options granted become valuable only when stock prices rise to the exercise price, which benefits not only the option owners but also the stockholders.

Options aim to keep CEO eyes on company growth and share prices, which in this age of political correctness is no easy task. Powerful political and social forces continually demand the attention of management. There are the environmentalists, civil rightists, racists, protectionists, tax collectors, and last but not least, labor unionists who lay claim to company earnings. Million-dollar stock options fostering individual self-interest constitute a powerful defense against all special interests. Yet many managements fall prey to militant demands.

The extraordinary height of some executive compensation reflects not only the stockholders' attempt to overcome the countervailing forces but also some institutional obstacles to corporate takeovers and management competition. Until well into the 1980s corporations that were led astray by political pressures and consequently languished in growth and earnings became the favorite targets of takeover entrepreneurs. But during the early 1990s many corporations succeeded in practically closing this avenue of corporate control by adopting poison pills and other antitakeover defenses. Their primary aim was the preservation of the firm's current managers' jobs and income regardless of their performance in leading the corporation.

The defensive tactics now include "greenmail," "poison pills," and "golden parachutes." *Greenmail* is the premium payment to a raider trying to take over a company. By accepting the payment, the raider agrees not to buy any more shares or pursue the takeover any further. *Poison pills* are various management moves to make a stock less attractive to an acquirer. For instance, it may allow all existing stockholders to buy additional shares at a bargain price after a takeover. *Golden parachutes* are lucrative employment contracts to provide lavish benefits in case of company takeover resulting in the loss of a job. They may include generous severance pay, stock options, or huge bonuses. All such measures raise the costs of an acquisition and cause dilution which, hopefully, will deter a takeover bid and keep the newcomers out.

Resuscitation of the takeover market would not lower executive pay overnight, but it would expose all compensation packages to the fresh air of market competition. It would surely redress the imbalance of power and compensation. But it is unlikely that it would appease the social critics and concerned politicians. They resent most what they envy most.

The 59¢ Fallacy

By Jennifer Roback

T HIS BEING AN election year, you have probably been seeing people wearing every sort of campaign pin imaginable—the standards like Reagan and Bush, Mondale, and Hart, not to mention all of the more-localized varieties. But you may also have seen a pin that says simply "59¢."

There is nobody with that surname running for office. It is a pin distributed by the National Organization for Women (NOW), and according to a recent fundraising letter signed by NOW president Judy Goldsmith, it symbolizes "the plain, frightening fact … that most women are paid just over half as much as men for the very same work—to be exact, 59¢ every $1 earned by a man." She continues, "Today, nothing better illustrates the economic plight of American women than NOW's 59¢ campaign button."

What Goldsmith is keying into is the much-discussed "earnings gap." It is an article of orthodox feminist faith that this earnings gap requires aggressive intervention by the government. The argument runs something like this: Earnings differences between men and women are evidence of discrimination in the free market. The earnings gap widened between 1955, when women's earnings averaged 64 percent of men's, and 1977, when women's earning level dropped to 59 percent. Therefore, it is concluded, discrimination against women has increased. Since this discrimination takes place in the free market, the government needs to intervene to protect women.

However, there is a large gap in this earnings-gap argument, as becomes clear if several key questions are considered. Is the earnings gap really due to discrimination? What other factors might account for the earnings gap? And, most important, is it even possible to distinguish discrimination from some of these other factors?

Surely the most striking change concerning women in the labor market since 1955 is that there are so many more of us now than there were then. The labor force participation rate of women the percentage of women who are working or seeking work jumped from 31 percent to 52 percent from 1952 to 1982, which translates into nearly three times as many working women. This huge increase in the number of women working outside the home is important because increases in the supply of something are usually associated with decreases in its price. In this case, the supply of women workers increased in comparison with men, so it should not be surprising to find the wages of women falling in comparison to those of men between 1955 and 1977.

Suppose, though, that the labor market doesn't really work like the market for apples or houses, and therefore a supply increase could not cause that large a wage change. It's a fair enough question. But then consider a different example that can't possibly be explained by discrimination. The baby boom created a huge increase in the supply of young workers in comparison with the number of older workers in the late 1960s. Did the earnings of the baby-boom new workers fall in comparison with prime or middle-aged workers? The answer is a resounding yes. The earnings of young workers fell from 63 percent of the earnings of middle-aged workers in 1968 to 54 percent in 1974.

This supply increase actually caused a larger fall in earnings than the one that women have experienced. And the baby boomers' financial bust happened over a shorter period of time. In fact, some economists have been surprised that the earnings gap between men and women didn't widen even more than it did! Probably the reason is that not all the women entering the labor force went into "female" jobs. Many entered jobs and professions formerly closed to women, in which they compete primarily with men and not with other women. Because they were not increasing the supply of female-job workers, the women who pioneered in the fields of banking, medicine, construction, and law did not lower the average wages of women.

Even so, a disproportionate number of women *did* enter traditionally female jobs such as clerical and service work. Clerical jobs actually account for a larger fraction of jobs held by women now than in 1960. The wages in these occupations have not kept pace with wages in other sectors of the economy, at least in part because of the flood of new women workers entering these fields for the first time. Since these are the jobs in which women are most heavily concentrated, it is not surprising that women's average wages have fallen in comparison with men's.

Another characteristic of the newly working woman is that she is likely to be an older person, either returning to work after child rearing or entering the labor market for the first time. This means that she very likely has limited experience in the job market, In fact, women have 10 to 15 years less labor-force experience on average than do men of the same age. Naturally, the wages that inexperienced women can command will usually be lower than those of men or of other women who have worked longer or more continuously. So the average earnings of women have fallen in part because so many women are relatively inexperienced.

This is not to conclude that there is no discrimination against women. That would be silly. But it is equally silly to conclude that discrimination has increased since 1955 *because* the difference in earnings between men and women has increased over that time. There are many plausible explanations for that fact.

Anyone who has had his or her eyes open at all has noticed that women have opportunities today that were unheard of in our mothers' time. Women who would have been afraid to risk the wrath of society and family are venturing into the workplace for the first time. Others of us are breaking into male-dominated fields and finding a degree of success and acceptance that astounds our mothers. (The percentage of lawyers and judges who are female jumped from 4 percent in 1972 to 15 percent in 1982. The percentage of physicians who are women increased from 10 to 15 percent in the same period. And the percentage of women on college and university faculties has risen from 22 to 37 percent just since 1967.) Still others of us are taking even greater risks and starting businesses of our own. We still have some

distance to travel in the job market, but it is difficult to take seriously the idea that women face *more* discrimination today than they did in the 1950s.

Of course, feminists usually don't come right out and claim that women are worse off economically today than they were 30 years ago. That would be too obviously absurd. So NOW president Judy Goldsmith, for example, talks in a fund-raising letter of "the economic plight of American women" and urges the 59¢ button on women as "a symbol that vividly demonstrates the intolerable economic discrimination against the status of women in our society."

The insidious thing is that an argument is implied here rather than stated directly. If Goldsmith were to come right out and say, "The earnings gap is *totally* caused by discrimination," she would have to draw the absurd conclusion that women face more discrimination today than they did in the 1950s. More to the point, her readers might draw that conclusion themselves and then question her initial premise.

On the other hand, it would be an important concession if Goldsmith were to acknowledge that the earnings gap might be caused by something other than male or market malevolence. NOW's symbol, the 59¢ button, would lose some of its point. More importantly, though, the plain fact of the matter is that it is extraordinarily difficult to establish a linkage between discrimination and a difference in wages. The 59¢ logic sidesteps that problem by placing the wage differential on the defensive. It presumes that an earnings difference is prima facie evidence of discrimination.

Actually, many of the factors that contribute to the earnings gap are the result of personal choices made by women themselves, not decisions thrust on them by bosses. The most important example is marriage.

Married women often are unable to relocate to further their careers as much as they would like. Many married women drop out of the labor force to raise children. As a result of both of these factors, married women tend to choose occupations with easily transferable skills that do not deteriorate when unused. This is why many women traditionally have chosen elementary-school teaching more often than college teaching, nursing more often than doctoring, and humanities more often than technical subjects.

These differences between married women and single women (and between married women and men, for that matter) contribute dramatically to reducing the earnings of married women. Thus we find, in a comparison of the earnings of never-married women and those of never-married men, that the women's earnings in 1980 were 89 percent of men's. This figure has been essentially unchanged since the 1960 census. So if one is looking for a "culprit" for the earnings gap, it is far more plausible to pin the blame on *marital status* than on *gender*.

Some people might argue that these figures simply reflect the oppressiveness of marriage and the need for radical changes in this institution. There is some merit in this argument. Nevertheless, it is undeniable that many women do choose to get married. Perhaps a large number believe that the pleasures of intimate companionship and raising children are worth some financial sacrifice. We might wish that marriage did not require that women make this sacrifice, and we might work very hard to promote better options. But it is entirely unfair to blame employer discrimination for earnings differences that are essentially the result of choices made by individual women.

Moreover, while marriage may often mean a disadvantage in the job market, that has been changing for the better. Women are now less likely to drop out of the labor force to raise their children. More women are training themselves in technical fields. And in many households, the wife's career needs are determining the family's next move.

So why don't married women have higher relative earnings now? This is certainly a valid question. But these different lifestyles have become widespread only over the last 10 to 15 years. The earnings gap is based on aggregate data that include women ranging in age from 25 to 64 years, most of whom have not really been affected by these lifestyle changes. Among full-time workers 25 to 34 years old, women's earnings were 70 percent of men's in 1980.

So there are a number of differences between men and women in the job market that may account for their earnings differences. Taken altogether, these very reasonable and understandable factors cannot, it is true, account for the entire earnings gap. But when the gap *is* corrected for these factors, it is not 59 percent but more like 66-87 percent, depending on the study.

It is often claimed that the difference that still remains after all the economic factors have been accounted for must be due to discrimination. That is, discrimination is measured as the residual, or leftover, difference, after all other factors have been taken into account. But this attempt to gauge discrimination is dubious.

The residual actually measures our ignorance. It includes everything that has not been directly measured but that influences a person's wage. The residual includes things as diverse as good luck and personality as well as discrimination. Common sense tells us that personality makes a huge difference to a person's career success. Ambition, aggressiveness, willingness to take risks, ability to get along with and motivate others, commitment to the job, willingness to assume responsibility—all of these factors contribute to higher wages. In fact, many career magazines for women advise their readers to develop exactly these traits. But none of these factors can be measured, and the residual earnings difference could just as easily be due to differences in these factors as well as to discrimination. The point is that we can not distinguish discrimination from these other, unmeasurable factors.

Do we really know that women are on average so much less aggressive and less ambitious that their earnings would be 87 percent of men's? The answer is that we don't know and we can't know. We cannot rule it out as a possibility, though, because our ignorance of what does generate a person's earnings is so great.

Clearly, neither feminist fund raisers nor the average well-informed citizen knows this stunning fact: only 40 percent of the earnings of white men can be accounted for by measurable factors. That is, if we look at a population of white men, a full *60 percent* of the differences in earnings among them cannot be explained by anything we can measure. Conventional discrimination cannot possibly be an issue in this particular population. Yet the unexplained residual earnings difference within this group swamps the largest difference in male-female earnings that could possibly be due to discrimination.

This is why we cannot rule out the possibility that the entire earnings gap between men and women is due to real personal productivity differences that cannot be measured. The upshot is that the *presence of discrimination can be neither proven nor disproven with statistical tests.*

Despite these technical problems, which are well known among economists, statistical tests are often introduced as evidence in discrimination lawsuits. An unexplained earnings gap is usually accepted as evidence of discrimination. And if it is accepted as evidence, the plaintiff will almost always win. In effect, this means that there is a presumption of guilt rather than innocence on the part of the employer accused of sex bias. It is true that the earnings difference in a specific employer's work force could be due to the employer's discrimination. But it could instead be the result of something equally unmeasurable. Mere statistics are not enough to tell.

A few years ago, an economist named George Borjas wrote an article in which he examined the salaries at the Department of Health, Education and Welfare (HEW), now Health and Human Services. He subjected HEW's salaries to the same statistical procedure that HEW itself used to demonstrate that universities were discriminating in their employment practices. Lo and behold, he found that HEW discriminated at least as much and sometimes more than the institutions they were charged with regulating. Many people interpreted this study as an attack on HEW salary and promotions policies. Actually, the point was to attack the methodology that HEW used in its attempts to ferret out discrimination in academia. Unfortunately, these procedures are still widely used in court cases.

So the 59¢ button is not really a very good symbol of women's economic plight. It is much more a symbol of a flawed method of correcting some very real problems that exist for some women in the workplace. It is a symbol of the misuse of statistics, both to make a dramatic point in the arena of public opinion and to win in court. It is a symbol of the faith that much of the women's movement places in government intervention as a solution to women's problems.

Unfortunately for that faith, many women are liberating themselves without the help of the law. They are finding their own path through the maze of the world of work and devising their own way to balance all of their financial, personal, and emotional needs. And the movement's loss is the individual's gain; for many of the problems that some women face today will best be solved by the individuals themselves and not by government action.

Profit and Loss

By Ludwig Von Mises

A. THE ECONOMIC NATURE OF PROFIT AND LOSS

1. The Emergence of Profit and Loss

In the capitalist system of society's economic organization the entrepreneurs determine the course of production. In the performance of this function they are unconditionally and totally subject to the sovereignty of the buying public, the consumers. If they fail to produce in the cheapest and best possible way those commodities which the consumers are asking for most urgently, they suffer losses and are finally eliminated from their entrepreneurial position. Other men who know better how to serve the consumers replace them.

If all people were to anticipate correctly the future state of the market, the entrepreneurs would neither earn any profits nor suffer any losses. They would have to buy the complementary factors of production at prices which would, already at the instant of the purchase, fully reflect the future prices of the products. No room would be left either for profit or for loss. What makes profit emerge is the fact that the entrepreneur who judges the future prices of the products more correctly than other people do buys some or all of the factors of production at prices which, seen from the point of view of the future state of the market, are too low. Thus the total costs of production—including interest on the capital invested—lag behind the prices which the entrepreneur receives for the product. This difference is entrepreneurial profit.

On the other hand, the entrepreneur who misjudges the future prices of the products allows for the factors of production prices which, seen from the point of view of the future state of the market, are too high. His total cost of production exceeds the prices at which he can sell the product. This difference is entrepreneurial loss.

Thus profit and loss are generated by success or failure in adjusting the course of production activities to the most urgent demand of the consumers. Once this adjustment is achieved, they disappear. The prices of the complementary factors of production reach a height at which total costs of production coincide with the price of the product. Profit and loss are ever-present features only on account of the fact that ceaseless change in the economic data makes again and again new discrepancies, and consequently the need for new adjustments originates.

2. The Distinction Between Profits and Other Proceeds

Many errors concerning the nature of profit and loss were caused by the practice of applying the term profit to the totality of the residual proceeds of an entrepreneur.

Interest on the capital employed is not a component part of profit. The dividends of a corporation are not profit. They are interest on the capital invested plus profit or minus loss.

The market equivalent of work performed by the entrepreneur in the conduct of the enterprise's affairs is entrepreneurial quasi-wages but not profit.

If the enterprise owns a factor on which it can earn monopoly prices, it makes a monopoly gain. If this enterprise is a corporation, such gains increase the dividend. Yet they are not profit proper.

Still more serious are the errors due to the confusion of entrepreneurial activity and technological innovation and improvement.

The maladjustment the removal of which is the essential function of entrepreneurship may often consist in the fact that new technological methods have not yet been utilized to the full extent to which they should be in order to bring about the best possible satisfaction of consumers' demand. But this is not necessarily always the case. Changes in the data, especially in consumers' demand, may require adjustments which have no reference at all to technological innovations and improvements. The entrepreneur who simply increases the production of an article by adding to the existing production facilities a new outfit without any change in the technological method of production is no less an entrepreneur than the man who inaugurates a new way of producing. The business of the entrepreneur is not merely to experiment with new technological methods, but to select from the multitude of technologically feasible methods those which are best fit to supply the public in the cheapest way with the things they are asking for most urgently. Whether a new technological procedure is or is not fit for this purpose is to be provisionally decided by the entrepreneur and will be finally decided by the conduct of the buying public. The question is not whether a new method is to be considered as a more "elegant" solution of a technological problem. It is whether, under the given state of economic data, it is the best possible method of supplying the consumers in the cheapest way.

The activities of the entrepreneur consist in making decisions. He determines for what purpose the factors of production should be employed. Any other acts which an entrepreneur may perform are merely accidental to his entrepreneurial function. It is this that laymen often fail to realize. They confuse the entrepreneurial activities with the conduct of the technological and administrative affairs of a plant. In their eyes not the stockholders, the promoters and speculators, but hired employees are the real entrepreneurs. The former are merely idle parasites who pocket the dividends.

Now nobody ever contended that one could produce without working. But neither is it possible to produce without capital goods, the previously produced factors of further production. These capital goods are scarce, i.e., they do not suffice for the production of all things which one would like to have produced. Hence the economic problem arises: to employ them in such a way that only those goods should be produced which are fit to satisfy the most urgent demands of the consumers. No good should remain unproduced on account of the fact that the factors required for its production were used—wasted—for the production of another good for which the demand of the public is less intense. To achieve this is under capitalism the function of entrepreneurship that determines the allocation of capital to the various branches of production. Under socialism it would be a function of the state, the social apparatus of coercion and oppression. The problem of whether a socialist directorate, lacking any method of economic calculation, could fulfill this function is not to be dealt with in this essay.

There is a simple rule of thumb to tell entrepreneurs from non-entrepreneurs. The entrepreneurs are those on whom the incidence of losses on the capital employed falls. Amateur-economists may confuse profits with other kinds of intakes. But it is impossible to fail to recognize losses on the capital employed.

3. Non-Profit Conduct of Affairs

What has been called the democracy of the market manifests itself in the fact that profit-seeking business is unconditionally subject to the supremacy of the buying public.

Non-profit organizations are sovereign unto themselves. They are, within the limits drawn by the amount of capital at their disposal, in a position to defy the wishes of the public.

A special case is that of the conduct of government affairs, the administration of the social apparatus of coercion and oppression, viz. the police power. The objectives of government, the protection of the inviolability of the individuals' lives and health and of their efforts to improve the material conditions of their existence, are indispensable. They benefit all and are the necessary prerequisite of social cooperation and civilization. But they cannot be sold and bought in the way merchandise is sold and bought; they have therefore no price on the market. With regard to them there cannot be any economic calculation. The costs expended for their conduct cannot be confronted with a price received for the product. This state of affairs would make the officers entrusted with the administration of governmental activities irresponsible despots if they were not curbed by the budget system. Under this system the administrators are forced to comply with detailed instructions enjoined upon them by the sovereign, be it a self-appointed autocrat or the whole people acting through elected representatives. To the officers limited funds are assigned which they are bound to spend only for those purposes which the sovereign has ordered. Thus the management of public administration becomes bureaucratic, i.e., dependent on definite detailed rules and regulations.

Bureaucratic management is the only alternative available where there is no profit and loss management.[1]

---

1   Cf. Ludwig von Mises, Human Action: A Treatise on Economics (New Haven, Conn.: Yale University Press, 1949), pp. 306–07; *Bureaucracy*, (New Haven, Conn.: Yale University Press, 1944), pp. 40–73.

4. The Ballot of the Market

The consumers by their buying and abstention from buying elect the entrepreneurs in a daily repeated plebiscite as it were. They determine who should own and who not, and how much each owner should own.

As is the case with all acts of choosing a person—choosing holders of public office, employees, friends, or a consort—the decisions of the consumers are made on the ground of experience and thus necessarily always refers to the past. There is no experience of the future. The ballot of the market elevates those who in the immediate past have best served the consumers. However, the choice is not unalterable and can daily be corrected. The elected who disappoints the electorate is speedily reduced to the ranks.

Each ballot of the consumers adds only a little to the elected man's sphere of action. To reach the upper levels of entrepreneurship he needs a great number of votes, repeated again and again over a long period of time, a protracted series of successful strokes. He must stand every day a new trial, must submit anew to reelection as it were.

It is the same with his heirs. They can retain their eminent position only by receiving again and again confirmation on the part of the public. Their office is revocable. If they retain it, it is not on account of the deserts of their predecessor, but on account of their own ability to employ the capital for the best possible satisfaction of the consumers.

The entrepreneurs are neither perfect nor good in any metaphysical sense. They owe their position exclusively to the fact that they are better fit for the performance of the functions incumbent upon them than other people are. They earn profit not because they are clever in performing their tasks, but because they are more clever or less clumsy than other people are. They are not infallible and often blunder. But they are less liable to error and blunder less than other people do. Nobody has the right to take offense at the errors made by the entrepreneurs in the conduct of affairs and to stress the point that people would have been better supplied if the entrepreneurs had been more skillful and prescient. If the grumbler knew better, why did he not himself fill the gap and seize the opportunity to earn profits? It is easy indeed to display foresight after the event. In retrospect all fools become wise.

A popular chain of reasoning runs this way: The entrepreneur earns profit not only on account of the fact that other people were less successful than he in anticipating correctly the future state of the market. He himself contributed to the emergence of profit by not producing more of the article concerned; but for intentional restriction of output on his part, the supply of this article would have been so ample that the price would have dropped to a point at which no surplus of proceeds over costs of production expended would have emerged. This reasoning is at the bottom of the spurious doctrines of imperfect and monopolistic competition. It was resorted to a short time ago by the American Administration when it blamed the enterprises of the steel industry for the fact that the steel production capacity of the United States was not greater than it really was.

Certainly those engaged in the production of steel are not responsible for the fact that other people did not likewise enter this field of production. The reproach on the part of the authorities would have been sensible if they had conferred on the existing steel corporations the monopoly of steel production. But in the absence of such a privilege, the reprimand given to the operating mills is not more justified than it would be to censure the nation's poets and musicians for the fact that there are not more and better poets and musicians. If somebody is to blame for the fact that the number of people who joined the voluntary civilian defense organization is not larger, then it is not those who have already joined but only those who have not.

That the production of a commodity p is not larger than it really is, is due to the fact that the complementary factors of production required for an expansion were employed for the production of other commodities. To speak of an insufficiency of the supply of p is empty rhetoric if it does not indicate the various products m which were produced in too large quantities with the effect that their production appears now, i.e., after the event, as a waste of scarce factors of production. We may assume that the entrepreneurs who instead of producing additional quantities of p turned to the production of excessive amounts of m and consequently suffered losses, did not intentionally make their mistake.

Neither did the producers of p intentionally restrict the production of p. Every entrepreneur's capital is limited; he employs it for those projects which, he expects, will, by filling the most urgent demand of the public, yield the highest profit.

An entrepreneur at whose disposal are 100 units of capital employs, for instance, 50 units for the production of p and 50 units for the production of q. If both lines are profitable, it is odd to blame him for not having employed more, e.g., 75 units, for the production of p. He could increase the production of p only by curtailing correspondingly the production of q. But with regard to q the same fault could be found by the grumblers. If one blames the entrepreneur for not having produced more p, one must blame him also for not having produced more q. This means: one blames the entrepreneur for the facts that there is a scarcity of the factors of production and that the earth is not a land of Cockaigne.

Perhaps the grumbler will object on the ground that he considers p a vital commodity, much more important than q, and that therefore the production of p should be expanded and that of q restricted. If this is really the meaning of his criticism, he is at variance with the valuations of the consumers. He throws off his mask and shows his dictatorial aspirations. Production should not be directed by the wishes of the public but by his own despotic discretion.

But if our entrepreneur's production of q involves a loss, it is obvious that his fault was poor foresight and not intentional.

Entrance into the ranks of the entrepreneurs in a market society, not sabotaged by the interference of government or other agencies resorting to violence, is open to everybody. Those who know how to take advantage of any business opportunity cropping up will always find the capital required. For the market is always full of capitalists anxious to find the most promising employment for their funds and in search of the ingenious newcomers, in partnership with whom they could execute the most remunerative projects.

People often failed to realize this inherent feature of capitalism because they did not grasp the meaning and the effects of capital scarcity. The task of the entrepreneur is to select from the multitude of technologically feasible projects those which will satisfy the most urgent of the not yet satisfied needs of the public. Those projects for the execution of which the capital supply does not suffice must not be carried out. The market is always crammed with visionaries who want to float such impracticable and unworkable schemes. It is these dreamers who always complain about the blindness of the capitalists who are too stupid to look after their own interests. Of course, the investors often err in the choice of their investments. But these faults consist precisely in the fact that they preferred an unsuitable project to another that would have satisfied more urgent needs of the buying public.

People often err very lamentably in estimating the work of the creative genius. Only a minority of men are appreciative enough to attach the right value to the achievement of poets, artists, and thinkers. It may happen that the indifference of his contemporaries makes it impossible for a genius to accomplish what he would have accomplished if his fellow men had displayed better judgment. The way in which the poet laureate and the philosopher *à la mode* are selected is certainly questionable.

But it is impermissible to question the free market's choice of the entrepreneurs. The consumers' preference for definite articles may be open to condemnation from the point of view of a philosopher's judgment. But judgments of value are necessarily always personal and subjective. The consumer chooses what, as he thinks, satisfies him best. Nobody is called upon to determine what could make another man happier or less unhappy. The popularity of motor cars, television sets, and nylon stockings may be criticized from a "higher" point of view. But these are the things that people are asking for. They cast their ballots for those entrepreneurs who offer them this merchandise of the best quality at the cheapest price.

In choosing between various political parties and programs for the commonwealth's social and economic organization most people are uninformed and groping in the dark. The average voter lacks the insight to distinguish between policies suitable to attain the ends he is aiming at and those unsuitable. He is at a loss to examine the long chains of aprioristic reasoning which constitute the philosophy of a comprehensive social program. He may at best form some opinion about the short-run effects of the policies concerned. He is helpless in dealing with the long-run effects. The socialists and communists in principle often assert the infallibility of majority decisions. However, they belie their own words in criticizing parliamentary majorities rejecting their creed, and in denying to the people, under the one-party system, the opportunity to choose between different parties.

But in buying a commodity or abstaining from its purchase there is nothing else involved than the consumer's longing for the best possible satisfaction of his instantaneous wishes. The consumer does not—like the voter in political voting—choose between different means whose effects appear only later. He chooses between things which immediately provide satisfaction. His decision is final.

An entrepreneur earns profit by serving the consumers, the people, as they are and not as they should be according to the fancies of some grumbler or potential dictator.

5. The Social Function of Profit and Loss

Profits are never normal. They appear only where there is a maladjustment, a divergence between actual production and production as it should be in order to utilize the available material and mental resources for the best possible satisfaction of the wishes of the public. They are the prize of those who remove this maladjustment; they disappear as soon as the maladjustment is entirely removed. In the imaginary construction of an evenly rotating economy there are no profits. There the sum of the prices of the complementary factors of production, due allowance being made for time preference, coincides with the price of the product.

The greater the preceding maladjustments, the greater the profit earned by their removal. Maladjustments may sometimes be called excessive. But it is inappropriate to apply the epithet "excessive" to profits.

People arrive at the idea of excessive profits by confronting the profit earned with the capital employed in the enterprise and measuring the profit as a percentage of the capital. This method is suggested by the customary procedure applied in partnerships and corporations for the assignment of quotas of the total profit to the individual partners and shareholders. These men have contributed to a different extent to the realization of the project and share in the profits and losses according to the extent of their contribution.

But it is not the capital employed that creates profits and losses. Capital does not "beget profit" as Marx thought. The capital goods as such are dead things that in themselves do not accomplish anything. If they are utilized according to a good idea, profit results. If they are utilized according to a mistaken idea, no profit or losses result. It is the entrepreneurial decision that creates either profit or loss. It is mental acts, the mind of the entrepreneur, from which profits ultimately originate. Profit is a product of the mind, of success in anticipating the future state of the market. It is a spiritual and intellectual phenomenon.

The absurdity of condemning any profits as excessive can easily be shown. An enterprise with a capital of the amount c produced a definite quantity of p which it sold at prices that brought a surplus of proceeds over costs of s and consequently a profit of n percent. If the entrepreneur had been less capable, he would have needed a capital of $2c$ for the production of the same quantity of p. For the sake of argument we may even neglect the fact that this would have necessarily increased costs of production as it would have doubled the interest on the capital employed, and we may assume that s would have remained unchanged. But at any rate s would have been confronted with $2c$ instead of c and thus the profit would have been only $n/2$ percent of the capital employed. The "excessive" profit would have been reduced to a "fair" level. Why? Because the entrepreneur was less efficient and because his lack of efficiency deprived his fellow men of all the advantages they could have got if an amount c of capital goods had been left available for the production of other merchandise.

In branding profits as excessive and penalizing the efficient entrepreneurs by discriminatory taxation, people are injuring themselves. Taxing profits is tantamount to taxing success in best serving the public. The only goal of all production activities is to employ the factors of production in such a way that they render the highest possible output. The smaller the input required for the production of an article becomes, the more of the scarce factors of production are left for the production of other articles. But the better an entrepreneur succeeds in this regard, the more is he vilified and the more is he soaked by taxation. Increasing costs per unit of output, that is, waste, is praised as a virtue.

The most amazing manifestation of this complete failure to grasp the task of production and the nature and functions of profit and loss is shown in the popular superstition that profit is an addendum to the costs of production, the height of which depends uniquely on the discretion of the seller. It is this belief that guides governments in controlling prices. It is the same belief that has prompted many governments to make arrangements with their contractors according to which the price to be paid for an article delivered is to equal costs of production expended by the seller increased by a definite percentage. The effect was that the purveyor got a surplus the higher, the less he succeeded in avoiding superfluous costs. Contracts of this type enhanced considerably the sums the United States had to expend in the two World Wars. But the bureaucrats, first of all the professors of economics who served in the various war agencies, boasted of their clever handling of the matter.

All people, entrepreneurs as well as non-entrepreneurs, look askance upon any profits earned by other people. Envy is a common weakness of men. People are loath to acknowledge the fact that they themselves could have earned profits if they had displayed the same foresight and judgment the successful businessman did. Their resentment is the more violent, the more they are subconsciously aware of this fact.

There would not be any profits but for the eagerness of the public to acquire the merchandise offered for sale by the successful entrepreneur. But the same people who scramble for these articles vilify the businessman and call his profit ill-got.

The semantic expression of this enviousness is the distinction between earned and unearned income. It permeates the textbooks, the language of the laws and administrative procedure. Thus, for instance, the official Form 201 for the New York State Income Tax Return calls "Earnings" only the compensation received by employees and, by implication, all other income, also that resulting from the exercise of a profession, unearned income. Such is the terminology of a state whose governor is a Republican and whose state assembly has a Republican majority.

Public opinion condones profits only as far as they do not exceed the salary paid to an employee. All surplus is rejected as unfair. The objective of taxation is, under the ability-to-pay principle, to confiscate this surplus.

Now one of the main functions of profits is to shift the control of capital to those who know how to employ it in the best possible way for the satisfaction of the public. The more profits a man earns, the greater his wealth consequently becomes, the more influential does he become in the conduct of business affairs. Profit and loss are the instruments by means of which the consumers pass the direction of production activities into the hands of those who are best fit to serve them. Whatever is undertaken to curtail or to confiscate profits impairs this function. The result of such measures is to loosen the grip the consumers hold over the course of production. The economic machine becomes, from the point of view of the people, less efficient and less responsive.

The jealousy of the common man looks upon the profits of the entrepreneurs as if they were totally used for consumption. A part of them is, of course, consumed. But only those entrepreneurs attain wealth and influence in the realm of business who consume merely a fraction of their proceeds and plough back the much greater part into their enterprises. What makes small business develop into big business is not spending, but saving and capital accumulation.

6. Profit and Loss in the Progressing and in the Retrogressing Economy

We call a stationary economy an economy in which the per head quota of the income and wealth of the individuals remains unchanged. In such an economy what the consumers spend more for the purchase of some articles must be equal to what they spend less for other articles. The total amount of the profits earned by one part of the entrepreneurs equals the total amount of losses suffered by other entrepreneurs.

A surplus of the sum of all profits earned in the whole economy above the sum of all losses suffered emerges only in a progressing economy, that is in an economy in which the per head quota of capital increases. This increment is an effect of saving that adds new capital goods to the quantity already previously available. The increase of capital available creates maladjustments insofar as it brings about a discrepancy between the actual state of production and that state which the additional capital makes possible. Thanks to the emergence of additional capital, certain projects which hitherto could not be executed become feasible. In directing the new capital into those channels in which it satisfies the most urgent among the previously not satisfied wants of the consumers, the entrepreneurs earn profits which are not counterbalanced by the losses of other entrepreneurs.

The enrichment which the additional capital generates goes only in part to those who have created it by saving. The rest goes, by raising the marginal productivity of labor and thereby wage rates, to the earners of wages and salaries and, by raising the prices of definite raw materials and food stuffs, to the owners of land, and, finally, to the entrepreneurs who integrate this new capital into the most economical production processes. But while the gain of the wage earners and of the landowners is permanent, the profits of the entrepreneurs disappear once this integration is accomplished. Profits of the entrepreneurs are, as has been mentioned already, a permanent phenomenon only on account of the fact that maladjustments appear daily anew by the elimination of which profits are earned.

Let us for the sake of argument resort to the concept of national income as employed in popular economics. Then it is obvious that in a stationary economy no part of the national income goes into profits. Only in a progressing economy is there a surplus of total profits over total losses. The popular belief that profits are a deduction from the income of workers and consumers is entirely fallacious. If we want to apply the term deduction to the issue, we have to say that this surplus of profits over losses as well as the increments of the wage earners and the landowners is deducted from the gains of those whose saving brought about the additional capital. It is their saving that is the vehicle of economic improvement, that makes the employment of technological innovations possible and raises productivity and the standard of living. It is the entrepreneurs whose activity takes care of the most economical employment of the additional capital. As far as they themselves do not save, neither the workers nor the landowners contribute anything to the emergence of the circumstances which generate what is called economic progress and improvement. They are benefited by other peoples' saving that creates additional capital on the one hand and by the entrepreneurial action that directs this additional capital toward the satisfaction of the most urgent wants on the other hand. A retrogressing economy is an economy in which the per head quota of capital invested is decreasing. In such an economy the total amount of losses incurred by entrepreneurs exceeds the total amount of profits earned by other entrepreneurs.

7. The Computation of Profit and Loss

The originary praxeological categories of profit and loss are psychic qualities and not reducible to any interpersonal description in quantitative terms. They are intensive magnitudes. The difference between the value of the end attained and that of the means applied for its attainment is profit if it is positive and loss if it is negative.

Where there are social division of efforts and cooperation as well as private ownership of the means of production, economic calculation in terms of monetary units becomes feasible and necessary. Profit and loss are computable as social phenomena. The psychic phenomena of profit and loss, from which they are ultimately derived, remain, of course, incalculable intensive magnitudes.

The fact that in the frame of the market economy entrepreneurial profit and loss are determined by arithmetical operations has misled many people. They fail to see that essential items that enter into this calculation are estimates emanating from the entrepreneur's specific understanding of the future state of the market. They think that these computations are open to examination and verification or alteration on the part of a disinterested expert. They ignore the fact that such computations are as a rule an inherent part of the entrepreneur's speculative anticipation of uncertain future conditions.

For the task of this essay it suffices to refer to one of the problems of cost accounting. One of the items of a bill of costs is the establishment of the difference between the price paid for the acquisition of what is commonly called durable production equipment and its present value. This present value is the money equivalent of the contribution this equipment will make to future earnings. There is no certainty about the future state of the market and about the height of these earnings. They can only be determined by a speculative anticipation on the part of the entrepreneur. It is preposterous to call in an expert and to substitute his arbitrary judgment for that of the entrepreneur. The expert is objective insofar as he is not affected by an error made. But the entrepreneur exposes his own material well-being.

Of course, the law determines magnitudes which it calls profit and loss. But these magnitudes are not identical with the economic concepts of profit and loss and must not be confused with them. If a tax law calls a magnitude profit, it in effect determines the height of taxes due. It calls this magnitude profit because it wants to justify its tax policy in the eyes of the public. It would be more correct for the legislator to omit the term profit and simply to speak of the basis for the computation of the tax due.

The tendency of the tax laws is to compute what they call profit as high as possible in order to increase immediate public revenue. But there are other laws which are committed to the tendency to restrict the magnitude they call profit. The commercial codes of many nations were and are guided by the endeavor to protect the rights of creditors. They aimed at restricting what they called profit in order to prevent the entrepreneur from withdrawing to the prejudice of creditors too much from the firm or corporation for his own benefit. It was these tendencies which were operative in the evolution of the commercial usages concerning the customary height of depreciation quotas.

There is no need today to dwell upon the problem of the falsification of economic calculation under inflationary conditions. All people begin to comprehend the phenomenon of illusory profits, the offshoot of the great inflations of our age.

Failure to grasp the effects of inflation upon the customary methods of computing profits originated the modern concept of *profiteering*. An entrepreneur is dubbed a profiteer if his profit and loss statement, calculated in terms of a currency subject to a rapidly progressing inflation, shows profits which other people deem "excessive." It has happened very often in many countries that the profit and loss statement of such a profiteer, when calculated in terms of a noninflated or less inflated currency, showed not only no profit at all but considerable losses.

Even if we neglect for the sake of argument any reference to the phenomenon of merely inflation-induced illusory profits, it is obvious that the epithet profiteer is the expression of an arbitrary judgment of value. There is no other standard available for the distinction between profiteering and earning fair profits than that provided by the censor's personal envy and resentment.

It is strange indeed that an eminent logician, the late L. Susan Stebbing, entirely failed to perceive the issue involved. Professor Stebbing equated the concept of profiteering to concepts which refer to a clear distinction of such a nature that no sharp line can be drawn between extremes. The distinction between excess profits or profiteering, and "legitimate profits," she declared, is clear, although it is not a sharp distinction.[2] Now this distinction is clear only in reference to an act of legislation that defines the term excess profits as used in its context. But this is not what Stebbing had in mind. She explicitly emphasized that such legal definitions are made "in an arbitrary manner for the practical purposes of administration." She used the term *legitimate* without any reference to legal statutes and their definitions. But is it permissible to employ the term legitimate without reference to any standard from the point of view of which the thing in question is to be considered as legitimate? And is there any other standard available for the distinction between profiteering and legitimate profits than one provided by personal judgments of value?

Professor Stebbing referred to the famous *acervus* and *calvus* arguments of the old logicians. Many words are vague insofar as they apply to characteristics which may be possessed in varying degrees. It is impossible to draw a sharp line between those who are bald and those who are not. It is impossible to define precisely the concept of baldness. But what Professor Stebbing failed to notice is that the characteristic according to which people distinguish between those who are bald and those who are not is open to a precise definition. It is the presence or the absence of hair on the head of a person. This is a clear and unambiguous mark of which the presence or absence is to be established by observation and to be expressed by propositions about existence. What is vague is merely the determination of the point at which non-baldness turns into baldness. People may disagree with regard to the determination of this point. But their disagreements refer to the interpretation of the convention that attaches a certain meaning

---

2   Cf. L. Susan Stebbing, *Thinking to Some Purpose* (New York: Pelican Books, 1939), pp. 185–87

 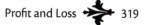

to the word baldness. No judgments of value are implied. It may, of course, happen that the difference of opinion is in a concrete case caused by bias. But this is another thing.

The vagueness of words like bald is the same that is inherent in the indefinite numerals and pronouns. Language needs such terms, as for many purposes of daily communication between men, an exact arithmetical establishment of quantities is superfluous and too bothersome. Logicians are badly mistaken in attempting to attach to such words, whose vagueness is intentional and serves definite purposes, the precision of the definite numerals. For an individual who plans to visit Seattle the information that there are many hotels in this city is sufficient. A committee that plans to hold a convention in Seattle needs precise information about the number of hotel beds available.

Professor Stebbing's error consisted in the confusion of existential propositions with judgments of value. Her unfamiliarity with the problems of economics, which all her otherwise valuable writings display, led her astray. She would not have made such a blunder in a field that was better known to her. She would not have declared that there is a clear distinction between an author's "legitimate royalties" and "illegitimate royalties." She would have comprehended that the height of the royalties depends on the public's appreciation of a book and that an observer who criticizes the height of royalties merely expresses his personal judgment of value.

B. THE CONDEMNATION OF PROFIT

1. Economics and the Abolition of Profit

Those who spurn entrepreneurial profit as "unearned" mean that it is lucre unfairly withheld either from the workers or from the consumers or from both. Such is the idea underlying the alleged "right to the whole produce of labor" and the Marxian doctrine of exploitation. It can be said that most governments—if not all—and the immense majority of our contemporaries by and large endorse this opinion although some of them are generous enough to acquiesce in the suggestion that a fraction of profits should be left to the "exploiters."

There is no use in arguing about the adequacy of ethical precepts. They are derived from intuition; they are arbitrary and subjective. There is no objective standard available with regard to which they could be judged. Ultimate ends are chosen by the individual's judgments of value. They cannot be determined by scientific inquiry and logical reasoning. If a man says, "This is what I am aiming at whatever the consequences of my conduct and the price I shall have to pay for it may be," nobody is in a position to oppose any arguments against him. But the question is whether it is really true that this man is ready to pay any price for the attainment of the end concerned. If this latter question is answered in the negative, it becomes possible to enter into an examination of the issue involved.

If there were really people who are prepared to put up with all the consequences of the abolition of profit, however detrimental they may be, it would not be possible for economics to deal with the problem. But this is not the case. Those who want to abolish profit are guided by the idea that this confiscation would improve the material well-being of all non-entrepreneurs. In their eyes the abolition of profit is not an ultimate end but a means for the attainment of a definite end, viz., the enrichment of the non-entrepreneurs. Whether this end can really be attained by the employment of this means and whether the employment of this means does not perhaps bring about some other effects which may to some or to all people appear more undesirable than conditions before the employment of this means, these are questions which economics is called upon to examine.

2. The Consequences of the Abolition of Profit

The idea to abolish profit for the advantage of the consumers involves that the entrepreneur should be forced to sell the products at prices not exceeding the costs of production expended. As such prices are, for all articles the sale of which would have brought profit, below the potential market price, the available supply is not sufficient to make it possible for all those who want to buy at these prices to acquire the articles. The market is paralyzed by the maximum price decree. It can no longer allocate the products to the consumers. A system of rationing must be adopted.

The suggestion to abolish the entrepreneur's profit for the benefit of the employees aims not at the abolition of profit. It aims at wresting it from the hands of the entrepreneur and handing it over to his employees.

Under such a scheme the incidence of losses incurred falls upon the entrepreneur, while profits go to the employees. It is probable that the effect of this arrangement would consist in making losses increase and profits dwindle. At any rate, a greater part of the profits would be consumed and less would be saved and ploughed back into the enterprise. No capital would be available for the establishment of new branches of production and for the transfer of capital from branches which—in compliance with the demand of the customers—should shrink into branches which should expand. For it would harm the interests of those employed in a definite enterprise or branch to restrict the capital employed in it and to transfer it into another enterprise or branch. If such a scheme had been adopted half a century ago, all the innovations accomplished in this period would have been rendered impossible. If, for the sake of argument, we were prepared to neglect any reference to the problem of capital accumulation, we would still have to realize that giving profit to the employees must result in rigidity of the once attained state of production and preclude any adjustment, improvement, and progress.

In fact, the scheme would transfer ownership of the capital invested into the hands of the employees. It would be tantamount to the establishment of syndicalism and would generate all the effects of syndicalism, a system which no author or reformer ever had the courage to advocate openly.

A third solution of the problem would be to confiscate all the profits earned by the entrepreneurs for the benefit of the state. A one hundred percent tax on profits would accomplish this task. It would transform the entrepreneurs into irresponsible administrators of all plants and workshops. They would no longer be subject to the supremacy of the buying public. They would just be people who have the power to deal with production as it pleases them.

The policies of all contemporary governments which have not adopted outright socialism apply all these three schemes jointly. They confiscate by various measures of price control a part of the potential profits for the alleged benefit of the consumers. They support the labor unions in their endeavors to wrest, under the ability-to-pay principle of wage determination, a part of the profits from the entrepreneurs. And, last but not least, they are intent upon confiscating, by progressive income taxes, special taxes on corporation income and "excess profits" taxes, an ever increasing part of profits for public revenue. It can easily be seen that these policies if continued will very soon succeed in abolishing entrepreneurial profit altogether.

The joint effect of the application of these policies is already today rising chaos. The final effect will be the full realization of socialism by smoking out the entrepreneurs. Capitalism cannot survive the abolition of profit. It is profit and loss that force the capitalists to employ their capital for the best possible service to the consumers. It is profit and loss that make those people supreme in the conduct of business who are best fit to satisfy the public. If profit is abolished, chaos results.

3. The Anti-Profit Arguments

All the reasons advanced in favor of an anti-profit policy are the outcome of an erroneous interpretation of the operation of the market economy.

The tycoons are too powerful, too rich, and too big. They abuse their power for their own enrichment. They are irresponsible tyrants. Bigness of an enterprise is in itself an evil. There is no reason why some men should own millions while others are poor. The wealth of the few is the cause of the poverty of the masses.

Each word of these passionate denunciations is false. The businessmen are not irresponsible tyrants. It is precisely the necessity of making profits and avoiding losses that gives to the consumers a firm hold over the entrepreneurs and forces them to comply with the wishes of the people. What makes a firm big is its success in best filling the demands of the buyers. If the bigger enterprise did not better serve the people than a smaller one, it would long since have been reduced to smallness. There is no harm in a businessman's endeavors to enrich himself by increasing his profits. The businessman has in his capacity as a businessman only one task: to strive after the highest possible profit. Huge profits are the proof of good service rendered in supplying the consumers. Losses are the proof of blunders committed, of failure to perform satisfactorily the tasks incumbent upon an entrepreneur. The riches of successful entrepreneurs are not the cause of anybody's poverty; it is the consequence of the fact that the consumers are better supplied than they would have been in the absence of the entrepreneur's effort. The penury of millions in the backward countries is not caused by anybody's opulence; it is the correlative of the fact that their country lacks entrepreneurs who have acquired riches. The standard of living of the common man is highest in those countries which have the greatest number of wealthy entrepreneurs. It is to the foremost material interest of everybody that control of the factors of production should be concentrated in the hands of those who know how to utilize them in the most efficient way.

It is the avowed objective of the policies of all present-day governments and political parties to prevent the emergence of new millionaires. If this policy had been adopted in the United States fifty years ago the growth of the industries producing new articles would have been stunted. Motorcars, refrigerators, radio sets, and a hundred other less spectacular but even more useful innovations would not have become standard equipment in most of the American family households.

The average wage earner thinks that nothing else is needed to keep the social apparatus of production running and to improve and to increase output than the comparatively simple routine work assigned to him. He does not realize that the mere toil and trouble of the routinist is not sufficient. Sedulousness and skill are spent in vain if they are not directed toward the most important goal by the entrepreneur's foresight and are not aided by the capital accumulated by capitalists. The American worker is badly mistaken when he believes that his high standard of living is due to his own excellence. He is neither more industrious nor more skillful than the workers of Western Europe. He owes his superior income to the fact that his country clung to "rugged individualism" much longer than Europe. It was his luck that the United States turned to an anticapitalistic policy as much as forty or fifty years later than Germany. His wages are higher than those of the workers of the rest of the world because the capital equipment per head of the employee is highest in America and because the American entrepreneur was not so much restricted by crippling regimentation as his colleagues in other areas. The comparatively greater prosperity of the United States is an outcome of the fact that the New Deal did not come in 1900 or 1910, but only in 1933.

If one wants to study the reasons for Europe's backwardness, it would be necessary to examine the manifold laws and regulations that prevented in Europe the establishment of an equivalent of the American drug store and crippled the evolution of chain stores, department stores, super markets, and kindred outfits. It would be important to investigate the German Reich's effort to protect the inefficient methods of traditional *Handwerk* (handicraft) against the competition of capitalist business. Still more revealing would be an examination of the Austrian *Gewerbepolitik*, a policy that from the early eighties on aimed at preserving the economic structure of the ages preceding the Industrial Revolution.

The worst menace to prosperity and civilization and to the material well-being of the wage earners is the inability of union bosses, of "union economists" and of the less intelligent strata of the workers themselves to appreciate the role entrepreneurs play in production. This lack of insight has found a classical expression in the writings of Lenin. As Lenin saw it all that production requires besides the manual work of the laborer and the designing of the engineers is "control of production and distribution," a task that can easily be accomplished "by the armed workers." For this accounting and control "have been *simplified* by capitalism to the utmost, till they have become the extraordinarily simple operations of watching, recording and issuing receipts, within the reach of everybody who can read and write and knows the first four rules of arithmetic."[3] No further comment is needed.

---

3   V.I. Lenin, *State and Revolution* (New York: Edition by International Publishers, 1917), pp. 83–84). The italics are Lenin's (or the communist translator's)

4. The Equality Argument

In the eyes of the parties who style themselves progressive and leftist the main vice of capitalism is the inequality of incomes and wealth. The ultimate end of their policies is to establish equality. The moderates want to attain this goal step by step; the radicals plan to attain it at one stroke, by a revolutionary overthrow of the capitalist mode of production.

However, in talking about equality and asking vehemently for its realization, nobody advocates a curtailment of his own present income. The term equality as employed in contemporary political language always means upward leveling of one's income, never downward leveling. It means getting more, not sharing one's own affluence with people who have less.

If the American automobile worker, railroadman, or compositor says equality, he means expropriating the holders of shares and bonds for his own benefit. He does not consider sharing with the unskilled workers who earn less. At best, he thinks of equality of all American citizens. It never occurs to him that the peoples of Latin America, Asia, and Africa may interpret the postulate of equality as world equality and not as national equality.

The political labor movement as well as the labor union movement flamboyantly advertise their internationalism. But this internationalism is a mere rhetorical gesture without any substantial meaning. In every country in which average wage rates are higher than in any other area, the unions advocate insurmountable immigration barriers in order to prevent foreign "comrades" and "brothers" from competing with their own members. Compared with the anti-immigration laws of the European nations, the immigration legislation of the American republics is mild indeed because it permits the immigration of a limited number of people. No such normal quotas are provided in most of the European laws.

All the arguments advanced in favor of income equalization within a country can with the same justification or lack of justification also be advanced in favor of world equalization. An American worker has no better title to claim the savings of the American capitalist than has any foreigner. That a man has earned profits by serving the consumers and has not entirely consumed his funds but ploughed back the greater part of them into industrial equipment does not give anybody a valid title to expropriate this capital for his own benefit. But if one maintains the opinion to the contrary, there is certainly no reason to ascribe to anybody a better right to expropriate than to anybody else. There is no reason to assert that only Americans have the right to expropriate other Americans. The big shots of American business are the scions of people who immigrated to the United States from England, Scotland, Ireland, France, Germany, and other European countries. The people of their country of origin contend that they have the same title to seize the property acquired by these men as the American people have. The American radicals are badly mistaken in believing that their social program is identical or at least compatible with the objectives of the radicals of other countries. It is not. The foreign radicals will not acquiesce in leaving to the Americans, a minority of less than 7 percent of the world's total population, what they think is a privileged position. A world government of the kind the American radicals are asking for would try to confiscate by a world income tax all the surplus an average American earns above the average income of a Chinese or Indian worker. Those who question the correctness of this statement, would drop their doubts after a conversation with any of the intellectual leaders of Asia.

There is hardly any Iranian who would qualify the objections raised by the British Labour Government against the confiscation of the oil wells as anything else but a manifestation of the most reactionary spirit of capitalist exploitation. Today governments abstain from virtually expropriating—by foreign exchange control, discriminatory taxation and similar devices—foreign investments only if they expect to get in the next years more foreign capital and thus to be able in the future to expropriate a greater amount.

The disintegration of the international capital market is one of the most important effects of the anti-profit mentality of our age. But no less disastrous is the fact that the greater part of the world's population looks upon the United States—not only upon the American capitalists but also upon the American workers—with the same feelings of envy, hatred, and hostility with which, stimulated by the socialist and communist doctrines, the masses everywhere look upon the capitalists of their own nation.

5. Communism and Poverty

A customary method of dealing with political programs and movements is to explain and to justify their popularity by referring to the conditions which people found unsatisfactory and to the goals they wanted to attain by the realization of these programs.

However, the only thing that matters is whether or not the program concerned is fit to attain the ends sought. A bad program and a bad policy can never be explained, still less justified by pointing to the unsatisfactory conditions of its originators and supporters. The sole question that counts is whether or not these policies can remove or alleviate the evils which they are designed to remedy.

Yet almost all our contemporaries declare again and again: If you want to succeed in fighting communism, socialism, and interventionism, you must first of all improve peoples' material conditions. The policy of *laissez faire* aims precisely at making people more prosperous. But it cannot succeed as long as want is worsened more and more by socialist and interventionist measures.

In the very short run the conditions of a part of the people can be improved by expropriating entrepreneurs and capitalists and by distributing the booty. But such predatory inroads, which even the *Communist Manifesto* described as "despotic" and as "economically insufficient and untenable," sabotage the operation of the market economy, impair very soon the conditions of all the people and frustrate the endeavors of entrepreneurs and capitalists to make the masses more prosperous. What is good for a quickly vanishing instant, (i.e., in the shortest run) may very soon (i.e., in the long run) result in most detrimental consequences.

Historians are mistaken in explaining the rise of Nazism by referring to real or imaginary adversities and hardships of the German people. What made the Germans support almost unanimously the twenty-five points of the "unalterable" Hitler program was not some conditions which they deemed unsatisfactory, but their expectation that the execution of this program would remove their complaints and render them happier. They turned to Nazism because they lacked common sense and intelligence. They were not judicious enough to recognize in time the disasters that Nazism was bound to bring upon them.

The immense majority of the world's population is extremely poor when compared with the average standard of living of the capitalist nations. But this poverty does not explain their propensity to adopt the communist program. They are anti-capitalistic because they are blinded by envy, ignorance, and too dull to appreciate correctly the causes of their distress. There is but one means to improve their material conditions, namely, to convince them that only capitalism can render them more prosperous.

The worst method to fight communism is that of the Marshall Plan. It gives to the recipients the impression that the United States alone is interested in the preservation of the profit system while their own concerns require a communist regime. The United States, they think, is aiding them because its people have a bad conscience. They themselves pocket this bribe but their sympathies go to the socialist system. The American subsidies make it possible for their governments to conceal partially the disastrous effects of the various socialist measures they have adopted.

Not poverty is the source of socialism, but spurious ideological prepossessions. Most of our contemporaries reject beforehand, without having ever studied them, all the teachings of economics as aprioristic nonsense. Only experience, they maintain, is to be relied upon. But is there any experience that would speak in favor of socialism?

Retorts the socialist: But capitalism creates poverty; look at India and China. The objection is vain. Neither India nor China has ever established capitalism. Their poverty is the result of the absence of capitalism.

What happened in these and other underdeveloped countries was that they were benefited from abroad by some of the fruits of capitalism without having adopted the capitalist mode of production. European, and in more recent years also American, capitalists invested capital in their areas and thereby increased the marginal productivity of labor and wage rates. At the same time these peoples received from abroad the means to fight contagious diseases, medications developed in the capitalist countries. Consequently mortality rates, especially infant mortality, dropped considerably. In the capitalist countries this prolongation of the average length of life was partially compensated by a drop in the birth rate. As capital accumulation increased more quickly than population, the per head quota of capital invested grew continuously. The result was progressing prosperity. It was different in the countries which enjoyed some of the effects of capitalism without turning to capitalism. There the birth rate did not decline at all or not to the extent required to make the per head quota of capital invested rise. These nations prevent by their policies both the importation of foreign capital and the accumulation of domestic capital. The joint effect of the high birth rate and the absence of an increase in capital is, of course, increasing poverty.

There is but one means to improve the material well-being of men, viz., to accelerate the increase in capital accumulated as against population. No psychological lucubrations, however sophisticated, can alter this fact. There is no excuse whatever for the pursuit of policies which not only fail to attain the ends sought, but even seriously impair conditions.

6. The Moral Condemnation of the Profit Motive

As soon as the problem of profits is raised, people shift it from the praxeological sphere into the sphere of ethical judgments of value. Then everybody glories in the aureole of a saint and an ascetic. He himself does not care for money and material well-being. He serves his fellow men to the best of his abilities unselfishly. He strives after higher and nobler things than wealth. Thank God, he is not one of those egoistic profiteers.

The businessmen are blamed because the only thing they have in mind is to succeed. Yet everybody—without any exception—in acting aims at the attainment of a definite end. The only alternative to success is failure; nobody ever wants to fail. It is the very essence of human nature that man consciously aims at substituting a more satisfactory state of affairs for a less satisfactory. What distinguishes the decent man from the crook is the different goals they are aiming at and the different means they are resorting to in order to attain the ends chosen. But they both want to succeed in their sense. It is logically impermissible to distinguish between people who aim at success and those who do not.

Practically everybody aims at improving the material conditions of his existence. Public opinion takes no offense at the endeavors of farmers, workers, clerks, teachers, doctors, ministers, and people from many other callings to earn as much as they can. But it censures the capitalists and entrepreneurs for their greed.

While enjoying without any scruples all the goods business delivers, the consumer sharply condemns the selfishness of the purveyors of this merchandise. He does not realize that he himself creates their profits by scrambling for the things they have to sell.

Neither does the average man comprehend that profits are indispensable in order to direct the activities of business into those channels in which they serve him best. He looks upon profits as if their only function were to enable the recipients to consume more than he himself does. He fails to realize that their main function is to convey control of the factors of production into the hands of those who best utilize them for his own purposes. He did not, as he thinks, renounce becoming an entrepreneur out of moral scruples. He chose a position with a more modest yield because he lacked the abilities required for entrepreneurship or, in rare cases indeed, because his inclinations prompted him to enter upon another career.

Mankind ought to be grateful to those exceptional men who out of scientific zeal, humanitarian enthusiasm, or religious faith sacrificed their lives, health, and wealth, in the service of their fellow men. But the philistines practice self-deception in comparing themselves with the pioneers of medical X-ray application or with nuns who attend people afflicted with the plague. It is not self-denial that makes the average physician choose a medical career, but the expectation of attaining a respected social position and a suitable income.

Everybody is eager to charge for his services and accomplishments as much as the traffic can bear. In this regard there is no difference between the workers, whether unionized or not, the ministers, and teachers on the one hand and the entrepreneurs on the other hand. None of them has the right to talk as if he were Francis d'Assisi.

There is no other standard of what is morally good and morally bad than the effects produced by conduct upon social cooperation. A—hypothetical—isolated and self-sufficient individual would not in acting have to take into account anything else than his own wellbeing. Social man must in all his actions avoid indulging in any conduct that would jeopardize the smooth working of the system of social cooperation. In complying with the moral law, man does not sacrifice his own concerns to those of a mythical higher entity, whether it is called class, state, nation, race, or humanity. He curbs some of his own instinctive urges, appetites and greed, that is his short-run concerns, in order to serve best his own—rightly understood or long-run—interests. He forgoes a small gain that he could reap instantly lest he miss a greater but later satisfaction. For the attainment of all human ends, whatever they may be, is conditioned by the preservation and further development of social bonds and interhuman cooperation. What is an indispensable means to intensify social cooperation and to make it possible for more people to survive and to enjoy a higher standard of living is morally good and socially desirable. Those who reject this principle as unchristian ought to ponder over the text: "That thy days may be long upon the land which the Lord thy God giveth thee." They can certainly not deny that capitalism has made man's days longer than they were in the precapitalistic ages.

There is no reason why capitalists and entrepreneurs should be ashamed of earning profits. It is silly that some people try to defend American capitalism by declaring: "The record of American business is good; profits are not too high." The function of entrepreneurs is to make profits; high profits are the proof that they have well performed their task of removing maladjustments of production.

Of course, as a rule capitalists and entrepreneurs are not saints excelling in the virtue of self-denial. But neither are their critics saintly. And with all the regard due to the sublime self-effacement of saints, we cannot help stating the fact that the world would be in a rather desolate condition if it were peopled exclusively by men not interested in the pursuit of material well-being.

7. The Static Mentality

The average man lacks the imagination to realize that the conditions of life and action are in a continual flux. As he sees it, there is no change in the external objects that constitute his well-being. His world view is static and stationary. It mirrors a stagnating environment. He knows neither that the past differed from the present nor that there prevails uncertainty about future things. He is at a complete loss to conceive the function of entrepreneurship because he is unaware of this uncertainty. Like children who take all the things the parents give them without asking any questions, he takes all the goods business offers him. He is unaware of the efforts that supply him with all he needs. He ignores the role of capital accumulation and of entrepreneurial decisions. He simply takes it for granted that a magic table appears at a moment's notice laden with all he wants to enjoy.

This mentality is reflected in the popular idea of socialization. Once the parasitic capitalists and entrepreneurs are thrown out, he himself will get all that they used to consume. It is but the minor error of this expectation that it grotesquely overrates the increment in income, if any, each individual could receive from such a distribution. Much more serious is the fact that it assumes that the only thing required is to continue in the various plants production of those goods they are producing at the moment of the socialization in the ways they were hitherto produced. No account is taken of the necessity to adjust production daily anew to perpetually changing conditions. The dilettante-socialist does not comprehend that a socialization effected fifty years ago would not have socialized the structure of business as it exists today but a very different structure. He does not give a thought to the enormous effort that is needed in order to transform business again and again to render the best possible service.

This dilettantish inability to comprehend the essential issues of the conduct of production affairs is not only manifested in the writings of Marx and Engels. It permeates no less the contributions of contemporary psuedo-economics.

The imaginary construction of an evenly rotating economy is an indispensable mental tool of economic thinking. In order to conceive the function of profit and loss, the economist constructs the image of a hypothetical, although unrealizable, state of affairs in which nothing changes, in which tomorrow does not differ at all from today and in which consequently no maladjustments can arise and no need for any alteration in the conduct of business emerges. In the frame of this imaginary construction there are no entrepreneurs and no entrepreneurial profits and losses. The wheels turn spontaneously as it were. But the real world in which men live and have to work can never duplicate the hypothetical world of this mental makeshift.

Now one of the main shortcomings of the mathematical economists is that they deal with this evenly rotating economy—they call it the static state—as if it were something really existing. Prepossessed by the fallacy that economics is to be treated with mathematical methods, they concentrate their efforts upon the analysis of static states which, of course, allow a description in sets of simultaneous differential equations. But this mathematical treatment virtually avoids any reference to the real problems of economics. It indulges in quite useless mathematical play without adding anything to the comprehension of the problems of human acting and producing. It creates the misunderstanding as if the analysis of static states were the main concern of economics. It confuses a merely ancillary tool of thinking with reality.

The mathematical economist is so blinded by his epistemological prejudice that he simply fails to see what the tasks of economics are. He is anxious to show us that socialism is realizable under static conditions. As static conditions, as he himself admits, are unrealizable, this amounts merely to the assertion that in an unrealizable state of the world socialism would be realizable. A very valuable result, indeed, of a hundred years of the joint work of hundreds of authors, taught at all universities, publicized in innumerable textbooks and monographs and in scores of allegedly scientific magazines!

There is no such thing as a static economy. All the conclusions derived from preoccupation with the image of static states and static equilibrium are of no avail for the description of the world as it is and will always be.

C. THE ALTERNATIVE

A social order based on private control of the means of production cannot work without entrepreneurial action and entrepreneurial profit and, of course, entrepreneurial loss. The elimination of profit, whatever methods may be resorted to for its execution, must transform society into a senseless jumble. It would create poverty for all.

In a socialist system there are neither entrepreneurs nor entrepreneurial profit and loss. The supreme director of the socialist commonwealth would, however, have to strive in the same way after a surplus of proceeds over costs as the entrepreneurs do under capitalism. It is not the task of this essay to deal with socialism. Therefore it is not necessary to stress the point that, not being able to apply any kind of economic calculation, the socialist chief would never know what the costs and what the proceeds of his operations are.

What matters in this context is merely the fact that there is no third system feasible. There cannot be any such thing as a non-socialist system without entrepreneurial profit and loss. The endeavors to eliminate profits from the capitalist system are merely destructive. They disintegrate capitalism without putting anything in its place. It is this that we have in mind in maintaining that they result in chaos.

Men must choose between capitalism and socialism. They cannot avoid this dilemma by resorting to a capitalist system without entrepreneurial profit. Every step toward the elimination of profit is progress on the way toward social disintegration.

In choosing between capitalism and socialism people are implicitly also choosing between all the social institutions which are the necessary accompaniment of each of these systems, its "superstructure" as Marx said. If control of production is shifted from the hands of entrepreneurs, daily anew elected by a plebiscite of the consumers, into the hands of the supreme commander of the "industrial armies" (Marx and Engels) or of the "armed workers" (Lenin), neither representative government nor any civil liberties can survive. Wall Street, against which the self-styled idealists are battling, is merely a symbol. But the walls of the Soviet prisons within which all dissenters disappear forever are a hard fact.

Gumball Now or Ice Cream Later?
The Formation of Interest Rates by Subjective Time Preference

By Nathanael D. Snow

THE FORMATION OF INTEREST RATES BY SUBJECTIVE TIME PREFERENCE

"May we have a gumball please, Papa?"

I pushed the cart of groceries toward the store exit. "You may either have the gumball now or some ice cream when we get home."

"As *soon* as we get home?" Two sets of pleading blues eyes looked up into mine.

"No, after you eat your dinner. We're having eggplant parmesan," their least favorite dish.

I could see the girls mulling it over in their minds.

"Okay," my eldest, Micah, murmured.

"I want the gumball," replied Rachael, the younger.

"You should have to wait to have the gumball after dinner, too!" exclaimed Micah.

"Then I'll have the ice cream."

"Well, what will it be, Rachael?" I asked.

It can be hard to wait. No one likes to postpone satisfaction. It is only human nature to want to have things as soon as possible, and the longer we must wait, the less we like it.

But it can also be good to plan for the future. Some people like to save large portions of their income, though in order to do so they must live more frugally today. Others prefer to live in the present, "*Carpe diem*! Seize the day!" they say, and perhaps only save a little—in case of emergencies. We often call the first *misers*, mocking that they might not live until tomorrow to enjoy their savings, and the second *spendthrifts*, recalling the parable of the grasshopper and the ants. But these are all matters of opinion, **normative** questions, as we say in the sciences.

Economics can't really answer normative questions. This is because people have different preferences, *subjective* preferences. You may prefer action movies to dramas. Your friend may prefer comedies to either. No ranking of preferences is right or wrong, and it is extremely difficult (I'd say impossible) to try to say *how much* more we like one thing over another.

The only way to find an intermediate preference level is to introduce another choice, perhaps adventure movies in our example above. Whichever movie you end up watching together most closely reflects a *coincidence of preferences*. Economics can help describe the way people with different preferences come to cooperate with one another without one person taking advantage of the other.

Among the ways people can cooperate is in their preference for *time*. The miser may lend to the spendthrift and get her money back later, with *interest*, which pleases her greatly. The spendthrift is also happier than he was before because he has more to spend now. This double satisfaction of wants is the magic of exchange, and it applies to markets for loanable funds just as much as to any other market.

In other markets we show the double satisfaction of wants on a supply and demand graph.

Figure 1

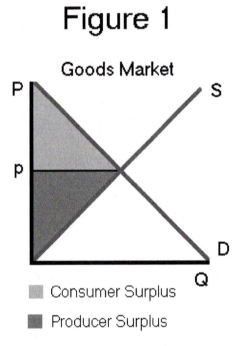

Goods Market

■ Consumer Surplus

■ Producer Surplus

The marginal unit exchanged determines the exchange rate, or relative price, of the goods traded. Since in a market economy we usually are just trading money for goods, *price* implies the money price. The area under the demand curve and above the price line is our consumer surplus, and the area above the supply curve and below the price line is our producer surplus. In the loanable funds market it works the same way.

Both girls wanted a gumball, but Rachael wanted one more than Micah did, at least in comparison to ice cream. She revealed this by her willingness to give up the opportunity of having ice cream after dinner for a gumball right away. Let's show this in Table 1.

Table 1

Rachael's Preference Ranking	
1	Ice Cream Now
2	Gumball Now
3	Ice Cream After Dinner
4	Gumball After Dinner

Micah's Preference Ranking	
1	Ice Cream Now
2	Ice Cream After Dinner
3	Gumball Now
4	Gumball After Dinner

What is different between these two rankings? Both prefer ice cream to gumballs. Both prefer either now to the same item later. But, Rachael is willing to give up the opportunity for ice cream later in order to have a gumball now, while Micah is not. Does this seem unreasonable? To Micah maybe, but to an objective observer it is entirely plausible. What then motivates Rachael to be willing to exchange the ice cream later for the gumball now? *Time.* She does not want to wait. And she is willing to give up something she likes more than gumballs—ice cream to have the gumball now. We might say her impatience costs her something. It costs her the difference between her desire for ice cream and her desire for gumballs. If Rachael had to wait to have the gumball, as Micah suggested she should, she would rather have the ice cream.

This difference, *interest,* is hard to measure without a schedule of intermediate goods, especially when we are talking about ice cream and gumballs, but such a distinction is more readily realized in the market for loanable funds through the interest rate.

There are a great many elements which can influence the market interest rate. Among these are expectations about the amount of money in the economy (inflation), expectations about the amount of goods in the economy (productivity or rent), expectations about the uncertainty of the future (risk premiums), and many other factors.

None of these elements can explain the formation of a market for loanable funds, however. To get at the real formative force behind the emergence of interest rates we have to hold all these other elements constant for all market participants. If we do this we can see that *subjective time preference* alone is a necessary and sufficient condition for the formation of interest rates. Rachael was not considering inflation, productivity, or rent in making her decision. She was only thinking about her preferences over time.

With interest rates we have a continuous schedule of intermediate possibilities along which we can map individuals' preferences over time. In other words, we can graph the supply and demand curves of the market for loanable funds with interest rates as the price.

Figure 2

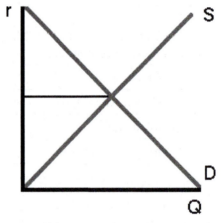

Loanable Funds Market

Here we see that at a given interest rate, borrowers are willing to "buy" a certain quantity of loaned funds. If the interest rate goes down they will be willing to borrow more. Similarly, lenders are willing to part with their money if the interest rate is attractive enough to them. The higher the interest rate the more willing they are to forego the use of the money today, which is their opportunity cost of lending.

With enough participants willing to borrow and lend, a market interest rate will emerge, where the last (marginal) borrower's preferred interest rate is just a bit greater than the last lender's preferred interest rate. All the other borrowers and lenders have realized a surplus, just like the surpluses afforded to consumers and producers in goods markets. Wealth has been created.

Although the economic (subjective) values of these surpluses are impossible to measure, we can at least calculate the monetary, or accounting returns to investment.

Let's think about how this might work. We could take $1,000 today and invest it at 6% interest for two years. After the first year we would have the $1,000 plus 6% interest, which would be $1,060. To find this we multiply the principle, the original amount, by (1+the interest rate). 6% is the same as 6/100, or 0.06. Then $1,000 x 1.06 = $1060. If we reinvest the whole $1,060 for another year we use the same method: $1060 x 1.06 = $1123.60. Let's look at what we have done: we took the principal and multiplied it by (1 + the interest rate), and for a second year we multiplied it by 1 plus the interest rate again. For a third year we would multiply it by one plus the interest rate a third time, and so on.

So we have a formula:

$$Return = Principle * (1 + interest\ rate)^{(number\ of\ years)}$$
Or,

$$R = P(1+r)^n$$

Now we can do this in reverse. We can take a certain amount we want in the future, divide it by 1 plus the interest rate however many years into the future we want to get it, and then discover how much it is worth to us today.

We use the formula:

$$PV = \frac{Amount}{(1+r)^n}$$

where PV is the present value, n is the number of periods, and r is the interest rate.

This says that the present value of some future amount is discounted by the interest rate raised to the power of the number of periods into the future.

For example: the value today of $1,000 two years from now at 6% interest is

$$\frac{\$1000}{(1+.06)^2} = \$890.00$$

This means a person with a subjective interest rate of 6% would be indifferent between $890.00 now, or $1,000.00 two years from now.

Consider another individual with a subjective interest rate of 3%.

$$\frac{\$1000}{(1+.03)^2} = \$942.60$$

This means a person with a subjective interest rate of 3% would be indifferent between $942.60 now, or $1,000.00 two years from now.

Let's put the two of these next to each other in a table.

Table 2

Subjective Interest Rate	6%	3%
Amount in two years	$1000	$1000
Present Value (PV)	$890	$942.60
Difference (Amount – PV)	$110	$57.40

Note that the difference between the two differences ($110 - $57.40) is $52.60.

Remember, the good in question here is the rights to $1000 two years from now. If the person with the 6% subjective interest rate held those rights, the person with the 3% interest rate would be willing to pay up to $52.60, the difference between the respective present valuations, for those rights. Similarly, if he had $942.60, he might lend the $890 in exchange for repayment of $1000 two years from now, and keep the difference, $52.60, for himself as surplus. The differences in subjective interest rates allow a market for loanable funds to emerge.

Let's see this on a graph:

Figure 3

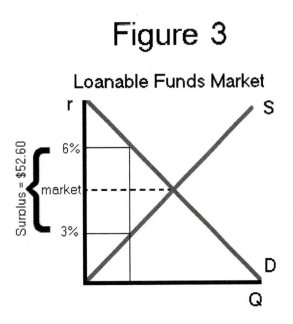

Notice the demander has the higher willingness to pay, while the supplier is willing to wait. It is important to remember that in this analysis we have held numerous other factors constant, all of which may influence the market interest rate, yet none of which contradict its subjective time preference origins.

I let Rachael have the gumball when we got in the car, and Micah gloated a little over her ice cream after dinner. When I asked Rachael if she would choose the gumball again, she said maybe, we'd have to see the next time we go to the grocery. The suspense is killing me.

SECTION TEN

Environmental Economics

Nature's Entrepreneurs

By Terry Anderson

"We have our idealists, inventors, innovators and organizers
all around us, and in a vast mechanism of economic and
social change there is work for all kinds to do ..."
—Jonathan Hughes, *The Vital Few*

IN HIS BOOK *THE Vital Few*, Jonathan Hughes describes the entrepreneurs of the late nineteenth and twentieth centuries who unleashed America's industrial power. Names like Rockefeller, Vanderbilt, Carnegie, Ford, and Morgan lead the cast of characters. In some cases these "vital few" invented new products or production techniques, but mostly they amassed capital, contracted with other input owners, and developed marketing strategies that lowered the cost of products and increased profits. In recent times, industrialists may have fallen from the list of the vital few, replaced by electronic-information gurus like Bill Gates or media moguls like Ted Turner, but the required entrepreneurial skills remain basically the same.

It is impossible to predict the frontiers on which the next wave of entrepreneurs will leave their mark. One possibility is the environment.

It is worth asking what it takes to be a successful entrepreneur in the environmental arena. If we were to compile a list of the vital few from the environmental history books, it might be headed with names like Audubon, Leopold, and Muir. As entrepreneurs, these men recognized the value of the natural world at a time when most people saw nature's frontier as a wilderness to be tamed. Of these early entrepreneurs, however, only Aldo Leopold saw the importance of linking the conservation movement to entrepreneurship, with all the trappings of finance, contracting, marketing, and even profits.

Unfortunately, many of today's environmentalists have not picked up where Leopold left off. His entrepreneurial spirit has given way to political opportunism. Instead of business acumen, the vital few in the environmental movement understand politics, lobbying, and fund-raising as the tools to achieve their political objectives. The headquarters for most major groups are located in Washington, D.C., and the personnel spend their time in the halls of Congress rather than in the wilds of nature.

The campaign to "save" the African elephant illustrates how political and financial agendas can overtake environmental realism. Though more than one million elephants roam southern Africa, environmental leaders of groups such as the Humane Society of the United States and the World Wildlife Fund declared elephants an endangered species and instituted fund-raising campaigns, publicized with vivid pictures of slaughtered elephants, tusks removed by chain saws. They raised millions of dollars to promote a ban on trade in ivory, although many African conservationists believed this would only further drive up the price of ivory and increase poaching. Rather than channeling their efforts into the direct protection of elephant habitat, these leaders politicized the elephant issue and motivated politicians and bureaucrats to ban trade in elephant products through CITES (Convention on International Trade in Endangered Species). They gave little consideration to the incentives faced by African natives who directly bear the costs of living with the elephants. These people, many of whom live at subsistence levels, are being asked to preserve habitat, let their crops be destroyed, and perhaps even be killed to save elephants because Westerners living in comfort thousands of miles across the ocean think it is a good idea. These political entrepreneurs demand the protection of elephants but place the burden of their protection on the backs of those who can least afford it. In the end, the campaign to "save" African elephants by banning trade in ivory filled the coffers of Western environmental groups. Unfortunately, it reduced the potential for Africans to live in harmony with elephants because it prevented the indigenous population from profiting from good stewardship.

ENVIRO-CAPITALISM

There is an alternative approach—enviro-capitalism—that begins when environmental entrepreneurs discover new opportunities for improving environmental quality and then figure out how to produce it in the private sector. Enviro-capitalists are entrepreneurs using business tools to preserve open space, develop wildlife habitat, save endangered species, and generally improve environmental quality. These entrepreneurs are meeting the growing demand for recreational and environmental amenities. To do this, enviro-capitalists must invent new products, attract venture capital, contract with resource owners, and market their products. The enviro-capitalist encourages fee hunting to reward landowners for bearing the cost of providing habitat for wild animals; buys endangered-species habitat instead of lobbying for regulations that restrict the use of private lands; and leases water to increase instream flows, rather than seeking legislation to limit water use by irrigators. In meeting each of these human demands, enviro-capitalists also benefit the environment.

People are beginning to realize that markets can be a powerful force in the environmental movement. Market-based incentives have become a common approach in both the private and public sectors. Corporations are searching for ways to increase profits in environmentally friendly ways. Policymakers are facing the reality that a cleaner environment comes at an increasingly higher cost. By harnessing market forces as enviro-capitalists do, we can achieve environmental ends at a lower cost.

With rising incomes, the demand for environmental amenities grows. The question is who will meet those demands, politicians or enviro-capitalists.

MORE THAN PAPER PROFITS

Tom Bourland, wildlife biologist and entrepreneur, preaches that the market can be wildlife's best ally. He believes that the growing demand for wildlife and recreation provides landowners with powerful incentives to produce more wildlife habitat and more recreational opportunities. And he should know, having turned wildlife into a money-maker for International Paper (IP), one of the largest timber producers in the United States.

In the early 1980s, Bourland became a wildlife manger of 1.2 million acres of IP's timber-producing land in its mid-south region, including parts of Texas, Louisiana, and Arkansas. When he joined the company, its wildlife and recreation program was not designed to generate income but rather to keep neighbors happy, appease environmentalists, and stem the rising tide of government regulations placed on private timber owners. Bourland was hired as a token wildlife biologist to operate within this agenda, but he was quickly frustrated—the bottom line on the financial statement was driven by timber production.

Recognizing the importance of the profit motive, Bourland locked his entrepreneurial radar onto the relationship between wildlife and IP's financial statements. He noted the growing demand for hunting, fishing, and recreation, as well as the consumers' willingness to pay for quality experiences. But he also saw that the company was receiving nothing for the use of these amenities. Bourland's environmental agenda had to give way to new realities. To respond to these realities, the company's wildlife and recreation program had to earn its way by charging user fees of those enjoying the amenities on IP's lands.

Charging fees for recreation represented a bold move for a timber company because it was bucking tradition. In the rural townships of Louisiana, Bourland's home state, local people were accustomed to hunting, fishing, and camping for free on IP's lands. Some did not take kindly to having to pay. Indeed, some regional managers at IP worried that they would be the ones facing the wrath of a disgruntled public. According to IP's then-chairman and chief executive, John Georges, "There were times when some executives were asking, 'Is it worth it—should we be doing this?'"

Despite local objections, IP proceeded with the change, spurred by several factors. Besides evidence of growing recreational demand, increasing abuse on IP's open lands was costing the company dearly. Litter, arson, and off-road traffic were major problems. Also, wildlife populations were declining from years of poaching and excessive legal hunting. Hunters were complaining about too little game and too many people.

Bourland and other supporters of fees at IP argued that revenues from wildlife and recreation would more than offset the additional costs of monitoring IP's lands and improving conditions for wildlife. They believed that fees for land use provided an effective strategy that would create stronger incentives for users to care for the land. A major part of the fee program included selling multiyear land leases to hunting clubs. Under the lease arrangement, clubs have a personal stake in stewardship of "their" areas. Bourland believed that clubs would monitor land use, limit hunting pressure, and cooperate with wildlife managers, all of which would add to the members' enjoyment of the recreation on IP property and lower the company's costs.

IP had already made substantial investments in experimental wildlife management programs and knew the potential for integrating wildlife management with timber programs. In 1957 the company established its 16,000-acre Southlands Experimental Forest near Bainbridge, Georgia. This forest served as a proving ground for management techniques that harmonize timber production and the needs of wildlife while earning profits from recreation. Exemplifying the innovative techniques pioneered at Southlands were experiments with prescribed burning.

Fire is an important tool in the management of southern pine forests. Because the pines are fire-resistant, periodic burning reduces competitive undergrowth and thereby enhances timber production. Prescribed burning also benefits wildlife by promoting the growth of browse essential to white-tailed deer and bobwhite quail. Prior to the Southlands burning projects, deer, turkey, quail, and rabbit populations in the experimental forest were low. By the early 1980s, however, prescribed burning had dramatically increased populations of these species. After visiting Southlands, outdoor writer Richard Starnes concluded, "Experiments with whitetails, turkey, quail, dove, rabbits, and a host of other game and nongame species are proving that it is practical—and profitable—to manage continuous-yield tree plantations in a way that ensures the healthy proliferation of wildlife."

HUNTING CLUB LEASES

Under Bourland's direction, IP launched its fee-based wildlife and recreation program in 1983, emphasizing three sources for revenues: hunting club leases, daily-use permits, and seasonal family permits. By 1986, the program had made dramatic strides. Revenues from recreational sales in Arkansas, Louisiana, and Texas had tripled to $2 million, and corresponding profits were an impressive 25 percent of total profits in IP's mid-south region. Fourteen hundred hunting clubs had leased one million acres of IP lands, more than double the amount leased by the end of 1983. The results convinced the skeptics.

"Managed fee hunting programs are gaining acceptance among hunters seeking exclusivity, safer conditions, and abundant game," Bourland said. He pointed out that the hunting clubs are an integral part of wildlife management because they "can provide wildlife protection, control harvest pressure, and accomplish habitat improvements to a degree not generally possible through other arrangements." In addition, a new partnership, or "contract," between recreational users and the company was being formed among a growing number of clubs that gave new meaning to wildlife management. At a club's request, company biologists provided members with wildlife-management guidance, survey assistance, harvest analysis, and food-plot material. In return, club members restricted their hunting techniques, recorded harvests, and followed company-imposed restrictions on harvests. By 1986, new contracts had been adopted by nearly one-third of the clubs that leased IP land.

The company also began experimenting with other recreational packages. At the upper end of the scale, IP opened the 3,000-acre Big Oak Club in East Texas. In 1986, hunters at the club paid $200 per day for lodging and guides and for the opportunity to take one buck and two doe white-tailed deer. Farther down the price scale was the 1985 opening of the 4,000-acre San Patricio Bowhunting Area. Bowhunters using the area paid $200 per season or $100 for a three-day hunt and enjoyed a success rate of 61 percent. Services provided by the company included a walk-in cooler and campsites furnished with electricity, water, tables, grills, and bathroom facilities.

Most importantly, as revenues from IP's recreational program grew, regional forest managers began managing their forests differently. In 1988, speaking to congressional staff members in Big Sky, Montana, Bourland described the new behavior of the timber owners: "Because the status of wildlife affected the bottom line, the landowner bent over backwards to provide habitat for white-tailed deer, wild turkey, fox, squirrel, and bobwhite quail, as well as endangered bald eagles and red-cockaded woodpeckers." They left corridors of trees 100 yards wide between harvested areas through which wildlife could travel safely. They left clumps of trees uncut while younger stands next to them grew, thus creating greater age diversity. They reduced the size of cut areas and made their perimeters more irregular and therefore more attractive to a greater variety of wildlife. They did not harvest large strips of trees and shrubs along either side of streams, and they planted food plots.

These and other efforts have paid big dividends to wildlife as well as stockholders. Ten years after the inception of the program, game surveys showed that populations of deer, turkey, fox, quail, and ducks had increased substantially. Eastern wild turkey and white-tailed deer had exhibited the largest gains, increasing tenfold and fivefold, respectively. According to company biologists, the main reasons are better habitat and less hunting pressure. Nongame populations have also benefited. Company biologists carry out an assortment of projects to improve habitat for these species, from putting up bluebird boxes to protecting heron rookeries. Even though nongame species have no explicit market, hunters, campers, anglers, and hikers are willing to pay more for a diversified recreational experience. IP's biologists continue to explore other options that would provide additional revenue for nongame species.

The 1990s have been a time of change and continued success for the program. Bourland has left IP to form a flourishing business, providing wildlife and forest management consulting for private, nonindustrial (that is, small) timber owners in the South. In this new venture, Bourland is helping hundreds of private forest owners benefit from the years of wildlife research carried out at IP. Meanwhile, IP's wildlife and recreation program continues to grow. Nearly two-thirds of the company's more than 6 million acres in the United States are now managed profitably for wildlife and recreation. Revenues from the program reached $10 million in 1990 and are expected to double rapidly. Thirty-five thousand hunting and recreational customers now use IP lands in Arkansas, Louisiana, and Texas, and another 25,000 pay to use IP lands elsewhere in the country. On the company's timber lands in northern Maine, for example, the public pays daily fees of $3 to $6 and seasonal fees of $15 to $90 for camping, hiking, fishing, and canoeing. In the Adirondack region of New York, people lease cabin sites, paying $700 to $1,000 per year.

The International Paper Company's wildlife and recreation program indicates a growing trend. In the South and the East, where most of the land base is privately owned, fee-based wildlife recreation is becoming firmly established. In addition, environmental entrepreneurs are coming up with new products and services to meet new markets. Texas ranches such as the King Ranch near Corpus Christi, the Fennessey Ranch near Baytown, and the Selah Ranch near San Antonio are providing nature hikes and bird-watching tours. In the West, where there is so much free access to public lands, it is tougher for the private landowners to compete, but the fee-recreation market is beginning to develop even there. Enviro-capitalists such as Tom Bourland are leading the way for new land management techniques.

This example illustrates how entrepreneurial skills can be successfully used to improve the environment. Entrepreneurial approaches that capitalize on profits in the marketplace offer an important alternative for producing environmental quality in a world where acrimony and tight budgets dominate most policy debates.

To Drill, or Not to Drill,
Let the Environment Decide

By Dwight R. Lee

IGH PRICES OF gasoline and heating oil have made drilling for oil in Alaska's Arctic National Wildlife Refuge (ANWR) an important issue. ANWR is the largest of Alaska's sixteen national wildlife refuges, containing 19.6 million acres. It also contains significant deposits of petroleum. The question is, should oil companies be allowed to drill for that petroleum?

The case for drilling is straightforward. Alaskan oil would help to reduce U.S. dependence on foreign sources subject to disruptions caused by the volatile politics of the Middle East. Also, most of the infrastructure necessary for transporting the oil from nearby Prudhoe Bay to major U.S. markets is already in place. Furthermore, because of the experience gained at Prudhoe Bay, much has already been learned about how to mitigate the risks of recovering oil in the Arctic environment.

No one denies the environmental risks of drilling for oil in ANWR. No matter how careful the oil companies are, accidents that damage the environment at least temporarily might happen. Environmental groups consider such risks unacceptable; they argue that the value of the wilderness and natural beauty that would be spoiled by drilling in ANWR far exceeds the value of the oil that would be recovered. For example, the National Audubon Society characterizes opening ANWR to oil drilling as a threat "that will destroy the integrity" of the refuge (see statement at www.audubon.org/campaign/refuge).

So, which is more valuable, drilling for oil in ANWR or protecting it as an untouched wilderness and wildlife refuge? Are the benefits of the additional oil really less than the costs of bearing the environmental risks of recovering that oil? Obviously, answering this question with great confidence is difficult because the answer depends on subjective values. Just how do we compare the convenience value of using more petroleum with the almost spiritual value of maintaining the "integrity" of a remote and pristine wilderness area? Although such comparisons are difficult, we should recognize that they can be made. Indeed, we make them all the time.

We constantly make decisions that sacrifice environmental values for what many consider more mundane values, such as comfort, convenience, and material well-being. There is nothing wrong with making such sacrifices because up to some point the additional benefits we realize from sacrificing a little more environmental "integrity" are worth more than the necessary sacrifice. Ideally, we would somehow acquire the information necessary to determine where that point is and then motivate people with different perspectives and preferences to respond appropriately to that information.

Achieving this ideal is not as utopian as it might seem; in fact, such an achievement has been reached in situations very similar to the one at issue in ANWR. In this article, I discuss cases in which the appropriate sacrifice of wilderness protection for petroleum production has been responsibly determined and harmoniously implemented. Based on this discussion, I conclude that we should let the Audubon Society decide whether to allow drilling in ANWR. That conclusion may seem to recommend a foregone decision on the issue because the society has already said that drilling for oil in ANWR is unacceptable. But actions speak louder than words, and under certain conditions I am willing to accept the actions of environmental groups such as the Audubon Society as the best evidence of how they truly prefer to answer the question: To drill or not to drill in ANWR?

PRIVATE PROPERTY CHANGES ONE'S PERSPECTIVE

What a difference private property makes when it comes to managing multiuse resources. When people make decisions about the use of property they own, they take into account many more alternatives than they do when advocating decisions about the use of property owned by others. This straightforward principle explains why environmental groups' *statements* about oil drilling in ANWR (and in other publicly owned areas) and their *actions* in wildlife areas they own are two very different things.

For example, the Audubon Society owns the Rainey Wildlife Sanctuary, a 26,000-acre preserve in Louisiana that provides a home for fish, shrimp, crab, deer, ducks, and wading birds, and is a resting and feeding stopover for more than 100,000 migrating snow geese each year. By all accounts, it is a beautiful wilderness area and provides exactly the type of wildlife habitat that the Audubon Society seeks to preserve. But, as elsewhere in our world of scarcity, the use of the Rainey Sanctuary as a wildlife preserve competes with other valuable uses.

Besides being ideally suited for wildlife, the sanctuary contains commercially valuable reserves of natural gas and oil, which attracted the attention of energy companies when they were discovered in the 1940s. Clearly, the interests served by fossil fuels do not have high priority for the Audubon Society. No doubt, the society regards additional petroleum use as a social problem rather than a social benefit. Of course, most people have different priorities: they place a much higher value on keeping down the cost of energy than they do on bird-watching and on protecting what many regard as little more than mosquito-breeding swamps. One might suppose that members of the Audubon Society have no reason to consider such "anti-environmental" values when deciding how to use their own land. Because the society owns the Rainey Sanctuary, it can ignore interests antithetical to its own and refuse to allow drilling. Yet, precisely because the society owns the land, it has been willing to accommodate the interests of those whose priorities are different and has allowed thirty-seven wells to pump gas and oil from the Rainey Sanctuary.

In return, it has received royalties of more than $25 million (Baden and Stroup 1981; Snyder and Shaw 1995).

One should not conclude that the Audubon Society has acted hypocritically by putting crass monetary considerations above its stated concerns for protecting wilderness and wildlife. In a wider context, one sees that because of its ownership of the Rainey Sanctuary, the Audubon Society is part of an extensive network of market communication and cooperation that allows it to do a better job of promoting its objectives by helping others promote theirs. Consumers communicate the value they receive from additional gas and oil to petroleum companies through the prices they willingly pay for those products, and this communication is transmitted to owners of oil-producing land through the prices the companies are willing to pay to drill on that land. Money really does "talk" when it takes the form of market prices. The money offered for drilling rights in the Rainey Sanctuary can be viewed as the most effective way for millions of people to tell the Audubon Society how much they value the gas and oil its property can provide.

By responding to the price communication from consumers and by allowing the drilling, the Audubon Society has not sacrificed its environmental values in some debased lust for lucre. Instead, allowing the drilling has served to reaffirm and promote those values in a way that helps others, many of whom have different values, achieve their own purposes. Because of private ownership, the valuations of others for the oil and gas in the Rainey Sanctuary create an opportunity for the Audubon Society to purchase additional sanctuaries to be preserved as habitats for the wildlife it values. So the society has a strong incentive to consider the benefits as well as the costs of drilling on its property. Certainly, environmental risks exist, and the society considers them, but it also responsibly weighs the costs of those risks against the benefits as measured by the income derived from drilling. Obviously, the Audubon Society appraises the benefits from drilling as greater than the costs, and it acts in accordance with that appraisal.

COOPERATION BETWEEN BIRD-WATCHERS AND HOT-RODDERS

The advantage of private ownership is not just that it allows people with different interests to interact in mutually beneficial ways. It also creates harmony between those whose interests would otherwise be antagonistic. For example, most members of the Audubon Society surely see the large sport utility vehicles and high-powered cars encouraged by abundant petroleum supplies as environmentally harmful. That perception, along with the environmental risks associated with oil recovery, helps explain why the Audubon Society vehemently opposes drilling for oil in the ANWR as well as in the continental shelves in the Atlantic, the Pacific, and the Gulf of Mexico. Although oil companies promise to take extraordinary precautions to prevent oil spills when drilling in these areas, the Audubon Society's position is *no* off-shore drilling, *none*. One might expect to find Audubon Society members completely unsympathetic with hot-rodding enthusiasts, NASCAR racing fans, arid drivers of Chevy Suburbans. Yet, as we have seen, by allowing drilling for gas and oil in the Rainey Sanctuary, the society is accommodating the interests of those with gas-guzzling lifestyles, risking the "integrity" of its prized wildlife sanctuary to make more gasoline available to those whose energy consumption it verbally condemns as excessive.

The incentives provided by private property and market prices not only motivate the Audubon Society to cooperate with NASCAR racing fans, but also motivate those racing enthusiasts to cooperate with the Audubon Society. Imagine the reaction you would get if you went to a stock-car race and tried to convince the spectators to skip the race and go bird-watching instead. Be prepared for some beer bottles tossed your way. Yet by purchasing tickets to their favorite sport, racing fans contribute to the purchase of gasoline that allows the Audubon Society to obtain additional wildlife habitat and to promote bird-watching. Many members of the Audubon Society may feel contempt for racing fans, and most racing fans may laugh at bird-watchers, but because of private property and market prices, they nevertheless act to promote one another's interests.

The Audubon Society is not the only environmental group that, because of the incentives of private ownership, promotes its environmental objectives by serving the interests of those with different objectives. The Nature Conservancy accepts land and monetary contributions for the purpose of maintaining natural areas for wildlife habitat and ecological preservation. It currently owns thousands of acres and has a well-deserved reputation for preventing development in environmentally sensitive areas. Because it owns the land, it has also a strong incentive to use that land wisely to achieve its objectives, which sometimes means recognizing the value of developing the land.

For example, soon after the Wisconsin chapter received title to 40 acres of beachfront land on St. Croix in the Virgin Islands, it was offered a much larger parcel of land in northern Wisconsin in exchange for its beach land. The Wisconsin chapter made this trade (with some covenants on development of the beach land) because owning the Wisconsin land allowed it to protect an entire watershed containing endangered plants that it considered of greater environmental value than what was sacrificed by allowing the beach to be developed (Anderson and Leal 1991, chap. 1).

Thanks to a gift from the Mobil Oil Company, the Nature Conservancy of Texas owns the Galveston Bay Prairie Preserve in Texas City, a 2,263-acre refuge that is home to the Attwater's prairie chicken, a highly endangered species (once numbering almost a million, its population had fallen to fewer than ten by the early 1990s). The conservancy has entered into an agreement with Galveston Bay Resources of Houston and Aspects Resources, LLC, of Denver to drill for oil and natural gas in the preserve. Clearly some risks attend oil drilling in the habitat of a fragile endangered species, and the conservancy has considered them, but it considers the gains sufficient to justify bearing the risks. According to Ray Johnson, East County program manager for the Nature Conservancy of Texas, "We believe this could provide a tremendous opportunity to raise funds to acquire additional habitat for the Attwater's prairie chicken, one of the most threatened birds in North America." Obviously the primary concern is to protect the endangered species, but the demand for gas and oil is helping achieve that objective. Johnson is quick to point out, "We have taken every precaution to minimize the impact of the drilling on the prairie chickens and to ensure their continued health and safety."

BACK TO ANWR

Without private ownership, the incentive to take a balanced and accommodating view toward competing land-use values disappears. So, it is hardly surprising that the Audubon Society and other major environmental groups categorically oppose drilling in ANWR. Because ANWR is publicly owned, the environmental groups have no incentive to take into account the benefits of drilling. The Audubon Society does not capture any of the benefits if drilling is allowed, as it does at the Rainey Sanctuary; in ANWR, it sacrifices nothing if drilling is prevented. In opposing drilling in ANWR, despite the fact that the precautions to be taken there would be greater than those required of companies operating in the Rainey Sanctuary, the Audubon Society is completely unaccountable for the sacrificed value of the recoverable petroleum.

Obviously, my recommendation to "let the environmentalists decide" whether to allow oil to be recovered from ANWR makes no sense if they are not accountable for any of the costs (sacrificed benefits) of preventing drilling. I am confident, however, that environmentalists would immediately see the advantages of drilling in ANWR if they were responsible for both the costs and the benefits of that drilling. As a thought experiment about how incentives work, imagine that a consortium of environmental organizations is given veto power over drilling, but is also given a portion (say, 10 percent) of what energy companies are willing, to pay for the right to recover oil in ANWR. These organizations could capture tens of millions of dollars by giving their permission to drill. Suddenly the opportunity to realize important environmental objectives by favorably considering the benefits others gain from more energy consumption would come into sharp focus. The environmentalists might easily conclude that although ANWR is an "environmental treasure," other environmental treasures in other parts of the country (or the world) are even more valuable; moreover, with just a portion of the petroleum value of the ANWR, efforts might be made to reduce the risks to other natural habitats, more than compensating for the risks to the Arctic wilderness associated with recovering that value.

Some people who are deeply concerned with protecting the environment see the concentration on "saving" ANWR from any development as misguided even without a vested claim on the oil wealth it contains. For example, according to Craig Medred, the outdoor writer for the *Anchorage Daily News* and a self-described "development-phobic wilderness lover,"

> That people would fight to keep the scar of clearcut logging from the spectacular and productive rain-forests of Southeast Alaska is easily understandable to a shopper in Seattle or a farmer in Nebraska. That people would argue against sinking a few holes through the surface of a frozen wasteland, however, can prove more than a little baffling even to development-phobic, wilderness lovers like me. Truth be known, I'd trade the preservation rights to any 100 acres on the [ANWR] slope for similar rights to any acre of central California wetlands … It would seem of far more environmental concern that Alaska's ducks and geese have a place to winter in overcrowded, overdeveloped California than that California's ducks and geese have a place to breed each summer in uncrowded and undeveloped Alaska. (1996, C1)

Even a small share of the petroleum wealth in ANWR would dramatically reverse the trade-off Medred is willing to make because it would allow environmental groups to afford easily a hundred acres of central California wetlands in exchange for what they would receive for each acre of ANWR released to drilling.

We need not agree with Medred's characterization of the ANWR as "a frozen wasteland" to suspect that environmentalists are overstating the environmental amenities that drilling would put at risk. With the incentives provided by private property, environmental groups would quickly reevaluate the costs of drilling in wilderness refuges and soften their rhetoric about how drilling would "destroy the integrity" of these places. Such hyperbolic rhetoric is to be expected when drilling is being considered on public land because environmentalists can go to the bank with it. It is easier to get contributions by depicting decisions about oil drilling on public land as righteous crusades against evil corporations out to destroy our priceless environment for short-run profit than it is to work toward minimizing drilling costs to accommodate better the interests of others. Environmentalists are concerned about protecting wildlife and wilderness areas in which they have ownership interest, but the debate over any threat from drilling and development in those areas is far more productive and less acrimonious than in the case of ANWR and other publicly owned wilderness areas.

The evidence is overwhelming that the risks of oil drilling to the arctic environment are far less than commonly claimed. The experience gained in Prudhoe Bay has both demonstrated and increased the oil companies' ability to recover oil while leaving a "light footprint" on arctic tundra and wildlife. Oil-recovery operations are now sited on gravel pads providing foundations that protect the underlying permafrost.

Instead of using pits to contain the residual mud and other waste from drilling, techniques are now available for pumping the waste back into the well in ways that help maintain well pressure and reduce the risks of spills on the tundra. Improvements in arctic road construction have eliminated the need for the gravel access roads used in the development of the Prudhoe Bay oil fields. Roads are now made from ocean water pumped onto the tundra, where it freezes to form a road surface. Such roads melt without a trace during the short summers. The oversize rubber tires used on the roads further minimize any impact on the land.

Improvements in technology now permit horizontal drilling to recover oil that is far from directly below the wellhead. This technique reduces further the already small amount of land directly affected by drilling operations. Of the more than 19 million acres contained in ANWR, almost 18 million acres have been set aside by Congress—somewhat more than 8 million as wilderness and 9.5 million as wildlife refuge. Oil companies estimate that only 2,000 acres would be needed to develop the coastal plain (Murkowski 2000).

This carefully conducted and closely confined activity hardly sounds like a sufficient threat to justify the rhetoric of a righteous crusade to prevent the destruction of ANWR, so the environmentalists warn of a detrimental effect on arctic wildlife that cannot be gauged by the limited acreage directly affected. Given the experience at Prudhoe Bay, however, such warnings are difficult to take seriously. The oil companies have gone to great lengths and spent tens of millions of dollars to reduce any harm to the fish, fowl, and mammals that live and breed on Alaska's North Slope. The protections they have provided for wildlife at Prudhoe Bay have been every bit as serious and effective as those the Audubon Society and the Nature Conservancy find acceptable in the Rainey Sanctuary and the Galveston Bay Prairie Preserve. As the numbers of various wildlife species show, many have thrived better since the drilling than they did before.

Before drilling began at Prudhoe Bay, a good deal of concern was expressed about its effect on caribou herds. As with many wildlife species, the population of the caribou on Alaska's North Slope fluctuates (often substantially) from year to year for completely natural reasons, so it is difficult to determine with confidence the effect of development on the caribou population. It is noteworthy, however, that the caribou population in the area around Prudhoe Bay has increased greatly since that oil field was developed, from approximately 3,000 to a high of some 23,400. Some argue that the increase has occurred because the caribou's natural predators have avoided the area—some of these predators are shot, whereas the caribou are not. But even if this argument explains some or even all of the increase in the population, the increase still casts doubt on claims that the drilling threatens the caribou. Nor has it been shown that the viability of any other species has been genuinely threatened by oil drilling at Prudhoe Bay.

CARIBOU VERSUS HUMANS

Although consistency in government policy may be too much to hope for, it is interesting to contrast the federal government's refusal to open ANWR with some of its other oil-related policies. While opposing drilling in ANWR, ostensibly because we should not put caribou and other Alaskan wildlife at risk for the sake of getting more petroleum, we are exposing humans to far greater risks because of federal policies motivated by concern over petroleum supplies.

For example, the United States maintains a military presence in the Middle East in large part because of the petroleum reserves there. It is doubtful that the U.S. government would have mounted a large military action and sacrificed American lives to prevent Iraq from taking over the tiny sheikdom of Kuwait except to allay the threat to a major oil supplier. Nor would the United States have lost the nineteen military personnel in the barracks blown up in Saudi Arabia in 1996 or the seventeen killed onboard the *USS Cole* in a Yemeni harbor in 2000. I am not arguing against maintaining a military presence in the Middle East, but if it is worthwhile to sacrifice Americans' lives to protect oil supplies in the Middle East, is it not worthwhile to take a small (perhaps nonexistent) risk of sacrificing the lives of a few caribou to recover oil in Alaska?

Domestic energy policy also entails the sacrifice of human lives for oil. To save gasoline, the federal government imposes Corporate Average Fuel Economy (CAFE) standards on automobile producers. These standards now require all new cars to average 27.5 miles per gallon and new light trucks to average 20.5 miles per gallon. The one thing that is not controversial about the CAFE standards is that they cost lives by inducing manufacturers to reduce the weight of vehicles. Even Ralph Nader has acknowledged that "larger cars are safer—there is more bulk to protect the occupant"(qtd. in Peters and Burnet 1997). An interesting question is, How many lives might be saved by using more (ANWR) oil and driving heavier cars rather than using less oil and driving lighter, more dangerous cars?

It has been estimated that increasing the average weight of passenger cars by 100 pounds would reduce U.S. highway fatalities by 200 a year (Klein, Hertz, and Borener 1991). By determining how much additional gas would be consumed each year if all passenger cars were 100 pounds heavier, and then estimating how much gas might be recovered from ANWR oil, we can arrive at a rough estimate of how many human lives potentially might be saved by that oil. To make this estimate, I first used data for the technical specifications of fifty-four randomly selected 2001 model passenger cars to obtain a simple regression of car weight on miles per gallon. This regression equation indicates that every additional 100 pounds decreases mileage by 0.85 miles per gallon. So 200 lives a year could be saved by relaxing the CAFE standards to allow a 0.85 miles per gallon reduction in the average mileage of passenger cars. How much gasoline would be required to compensate for this decrease of average mileage? Some 135 million passenger cars are currently in use, being driven roughly 10,000 miles per year on average (1994–95 data from U.S. Bureau of the Census 1997, 843).[1] Assuming these vehicles travel 24 miles per gallon on average, the annual consumption of gasoline by passenger cars is 56.25 billion gallons (=135 million X 10,000/24). If instead of an average of 24 miles per gallon the average were reduced to 23.15 miles per gallon, the annual consumption of gasoline by passenger cars would be 58.32 billion gallons (= 135 million X 10,000/23.15). So, 200 lives could be saved annually by an extra 2.07 billion gallons of gas. It is estimated that ANWR contains from 3 to 16 billion barrels of recoverable petroleum. Let us take the midpoint in this estimated range, or 9.5 billion barrels. Given that on average each barrel of petroleum is refined into 19.5 gallons of gasoline, the ANWR oil could be turned into 185.25 billion additional gallons of gas, or enough to save 200 lives a year for almost ninety years (185.25/2.07 = 89.5). Hence, in total almost 18,000 lives could be saved by opening up ANWR to drilling and using the fuel made available to compensate for increasing the weight of passenger cars.

I claim no great precision for this estimate. There may be less petroleum in ANWR than the midpoint estimate indicates, and the study I have relied on may have overestimated the number of lives saved by heavier passenger cars. Still, any reasonable estimate will lead to the conclusion that preventing the recovery of ANWR oil and its use in heavier passenger cars entails the loss of thousands of lives on the highways. Are we willing to bear such a cost in order to avoid the risks, if any, to ANWR and its caribou?

CONCLUSION

I am not recommending that ANWR actually be given to some consortium of environmental groups. In thinking about whether to drill for oil in ANWR, however, it is instructive to consider seriously what such a group would do *if* it owned ANWR and therefore bore the costs as

---

1   According to data from the Federal Highway Administration, as shown in the *Statistical Abstract* for 1997, average annual vehicle miles was 11,372 for passenger cars and for other two-axle, four-tire vehicles; presumably, the "other" category includes many commercial vehicles that raise the average substantially, making 10,000 a reasonable figure for passenger cars alone.

well as enjoyed the benefits of preventing drilling. Those costs are measured by what people are willing to pay for the additional comfort, convenience, and safety that could be derived from the use of ANWR oil. Unfortunately, without the price communication that is possible only by means of private property and voluntary exchange, we cannot be sure what those costs are or how private owners would evaluate either the costs or the benefits of preventing drilling in ANWR. However, the willingness of environmental groups such as the Audubon Society and the Nature Conservancy to allow drilling for oil on environmentally sensitive land they own suggests strongly that their adamant verbal opposition to drilling in ANWR is a poor reflection of what they would do if they owned even a small fraction of the ANWR territory containing oil.

REFERENCES

Anderson, Terry L., and Donald R. Leal. 1991. *Free Market Environmentalism*. Boulder, Colo.: Westview.

Baden, John, and Richard Stroup. 1981. Saving the Wilderness. *Reason* (July): 28–36.

Klein, Terry M., E. Hertz, and S. Borener. 1991. *A Collection of Recent Analyses of Vehicle Weight and Safety*. Washington, D.C.: U.S. Department of Transportation, DOT HS 807 *677*, May.

Medred, Craig. 1996. Heated Emotions in So Cold a Place. *Anchorage Daily News*, November 5, C1.

Murkowski, Frank H. 2000. Drilling Won't Make It Less of a Refuge. *Washington Post*, December 10.

Peters, Eric, and H. Sterling Burnet. 1997. *Will Minivans Become an Endangered Species?* Brief Analysis No. 232. Dallas, Tex.: National Center for Policy Analysis, June 4.

Snyder, Pamela S., and Jane S. Shaw. 1995. PC Drilling the a Wildlife Refuge. *Wall Street Journal*, September 7.

U.S. Bureau of the Census. 1997. *Statistical Abstract of the United States*. 117th ed. Washington, D.C.: U.S. Government Printing Office.

ACKNOWLEDGMENT:

The author began work on this article when he was a visiting scholar at the Federal Reserve Bank of Dallas during the summer of 2000.

The Endangered Species Act:
Making Innocent Species the Enemy

By Richard Stroup

"The red-cockaded woodpecker is closer to extinction today than it was a quarter century ago when the protection began."
—Michael Bean Environmental Defense Fund

"I am convinced that more habitat for the black-capped vireo, and especially the golden-cheeked warbler, has been lost in those areas of Texas since the listing of these birds than would have been lost without the Endangered Species Act at all."
—Larry McKinney Texas Parks and Wildlife Department

INTRODUCTION

"IT IS INCREASINGLY CLEAR that Congress will amend the Endangered Species Act. For one thing, property rights groups, who are important constituents of the new Republican Congress, are outraged at the power the Act gives federal agents to control landowners' use of their property. For another, the Act isn't working well to save species.

Although many improvements could be made, the Endangered Species Act does not need massive changes; rather, it needs a few fundamental ones. "Takings" legislation that requires compensation when the federal government takes control of landowners' property, already embodied in a bill passed by the House, would go a long way toward correcting the ESA's major flaws. It would reduce the animosity of landowners, encourage cooperation, and force the government agencies that administer the Act to weigh their priorities. Such a law would probably spur Congress to make additional changes in the Act, but, even without further legislation, it would change the way the Act is administered.

To understand why change is needed, and why a few changes will have multiple benefits, we need to understand why the Endangered Species Act has aroused such hostility. That is the chief purpose of this paper.

THE PARADOX OF THE ACT

The Endangered Species Act, which was passed in 1973, poses a paradox. On the one hand, it is enormously powerful. "In other laws," writes Rocky Barker in his book *Saving All the Parts*,[1] "federal agencies are required to provide protection 'where practicable.'" But the Endangered Species Act "elevated protection of all species to one of the U.S. government's highest priorities." This protection is "absolute. No equivocation." Others agree with Barker's description. The Act is "widely regarded by its proponents as one of this country's most important and powerful environmental laws and an international model," wrote M. Lynne Corn in a Congressional Research Service report.[2]

Yet evidence of its effectiveness is weak. Only 27 species have been taken off the endangered or threatened list ("threatened" species are those that are likely to become endangered; their treatment under the Act is about the same). Some of these delistings were for errors in the original listings.[3]

At most, only eight species can be described as recovered: the brown pelican, three Palau Island birds, the American alligator, the Rydberg milk-vetch, the gray whale, and the Arctic peregrine falcon, although some others that remain listed are doing well. In his 1993 book, Rocky Barker refers to five "official success stories," but discusses at length only two successes: bald eagles and peregrine falcons (not the Arctic peregrine falcon but the Eastern peregrine falcon, which is still on the list but largely recovered).

And it is difficult to give the credit for these recoveries to the ESA. Most people believe that the ban on the pesticide DDT has helped large raptors such as the bald eagles, the brown pelican, and the peregrine falcon. Furthermore, the falcon's recovery was accomplished almost singlehandedly by Tom Cade and the private organization he created, The Peregrine Fund (now called the World Center for Birds of Prey). Using techniques developed by falconers, Cade painstakingly bred peregrines in captivity. The gray whale, another apparent success, has been increasing in numbers ever since 1946, when an international treaty prohibited commercial hunting for that species of whale. It is doubtful that the Endangered Species Act had an important role. The few successes should be compared with a total of more than 1400 plant and animal species on the endangered or threatened list.[4]

How can such a powerful tool have such inadequate results? The answer is that the Endangered Species Act ignores the fundamental economic problem, the problem of scarcity. Resources for saving species are inevitably limited. They are scarce. For example, it is obvious that we can't set aside the entire acreage of the United States for wildlife habitat, and we can't set aside even a large part of that acreage without interfering with other uses. But the current Endangered Species Act, as it is now interpreted, represents an effort to avoid or disregard this fact. Government agents—primarily the U.S. Fish and Wildlife Service—have too often acted as though there are no limits, as though they are exempt from the problem of scarcity. Their actions have had perverse results.

The ESA, as interpreted by the Fish and Wildlife Service, calls for FWS biologists to control how land is used any time they consider it important for listed species. They decide whether farming, or logging, or building or even walking the land will be allowed. On such land, private or public, the FWS biologists become, in effect, land managers on behalf of the listed species. (The National Marine Fisheries Service has the responsibility for ocean-going fish.)

When a northern spotted owl, red-cockaded woodpecker, or other species listed as endangered or threatened is found on private property, the owners are required to meet the demands of the Fish and Wildlife Service biologists. Yet the biologists have no economic incentive to limit their demands. Since they have no requirement to compensate the owners of the land they control, other people's land has no budgetary cost to them; it is available free of charge.

In fact, however, land *is* a scarce good. The landowner who has listed species on his or her land, or who has habitat that might attract listed species, may not willingly offer it up free simply because Fish and Wildlife Service officials think they need it. Yet according to the law, the government has no obligation to consider the wishes of the owner or compensate the owner for taking control away.

The result is not only animosity on the part of landowners, animosity that is fully justified. It is also damage to the species that the biologists want to protect. This ability to control how property is used makes an enemy out of even the most harmless of birds or other listed species. In other words, by focusing the enormous power of the federal government on the supposed protection of rare species, the Act has made rare species unwanted and has even encouraged some people to get rid of them. This explains the paradox of the Act's enormous power and minimal results.

Like other dedicated people, Fish and Wildlife officials would like to believe that their mission transcends all others. And, at least as currently interpreted, the law appears to support them. It appears to authorize the protection of endangered species as "trumping" all other missions. But until the conflict between the fact of scarcity and the apparent ability to disregard scarcity is resolved, the ESA will not work effectively to save species.

AN ILLUSTRATION OF THE PARADOX

The case of Ben Cone illustrates what happens when the government ignores the fact of scarcity.[5] In 1982, Benjamin Cone, Jr., inherited 7200 acres of land in Pender County, North Carolina. He has managed the land primarily for wildlife. He has planted chuffa and rye for wild turkey, for example, and the wild turkey has made a comeback in Pender County partly due to his efforts. He has also frequently conducted controlled burns of the property to improve the habitat for quail and deer.

In the 1970s, Ben Cone and his caretaker noted a couple of red-cockaded woodpeckers on the property. Red-cockaded woodpeckers are listed as an endangered species. They nest in the cavities of very old trees and are apparently attracted to places that have both old trees and a clear understory. By clearing the understory to protect quail and deer and by selectively cutting small amounts of timber, Cone may have helped attract the woodpecker. In the 1970s, however, the birds posed no obvious problem, because Cone did not want to log their habitat at that time.

In 1991, when Cone did intend to sell some timber from his land, the presence of the birds was formally recorded. Cone hired a wildlife biologist to determine the number of birds, which is now believed to be 29 birds in 12 colonies. According to the Fish and Wildlife Service's guidelines then in effect for the red-cockaded woodpecker, a circle with a half-mile radius had to be drawn around each colony, within which no timber could be harvested. If Cone harvested the timber, he would be subject to a severe fine, and/or imprisonment under the Endangered Species Act.

Based on biologists' estimates of the presence of the birds and the Fish and Wildlife rules, it appears that 1560.8 acres of Cone's land are now under the control of the Fish and Wildlife Service. But Cone is still required by law to pay taxes on the land's previous value.

Cone has made several changes in the way he manages the wildlife and timber. In the past, he clearcut a 50-acre block every five to ten years. That created edge for the wildlife and roughly simulated the effect of a small, intense fire, the kind that would start the cycle of succession again every five to ten years. The whole of his property was thus attractive to a variety of wildlife on a sustained basis.

But since the woodpeckers were found, and the logging stopped on more than 1560 acres to help them, Cone has clearcut 300-500 acres every year on the rest of his land. He told an investigator, "I cannot afford to let those woodpeckers take over the rest of the property. I'm going to start massive clear-cutting. I'm going to a 40-year rotation, instead of a 75- to 80-year rotation."[6] Cone's new rotation will do away with old trees on the areas he can still harvest, preventing the woodpecker from nesting in the tree cavities that would have appeared there. Eventually, the acres that have been set aside for the woodpecker will rot or burn, and his land will be free of the woodpecker.

Ben Cone is a relatively wealthy man, and to many people may not be a sympathetic figure. But we don't have to have sympathy for him personally to see that he faces a genuine problem and that his experience teaches a lesson to all landowners who learn about his situation. They may be in for similar treatment unless they do something about it. Indeed, after Cone informed the owner of neighboring land about possible liabilities in connection with the red-cockaded woodpecker, he noticed that the owner, a firm, clearcut the property.[7]

THE RIVERSIDE FIRES

Many other people have been affected by the ESA, some more dramatically than others. For example, in 1992 in Riverside County, California, the Fish and Wildlife Service told homeowners that they could not create firebreaks around their homes by discing the land (that is, plowing the land, although they were allowed to mow the grass). Why? Because the area had been designated as habitat of the Stephens' kangaroo rat. The Fish and Wildlife Service told them that discing could lead to criminal and civil penalties, including going to federal prison or being fined up to $100,000.

Yshmael Garcia had a house in Riverside County. He followed the instructions of the Fish and Wildlife Service and mowed, rather than disced, his property. Unfortunately, when serious fires developed in Riverside in October 1993, his home was one of 29 that were destroyed.

One of those who violated the Fish and Wildlife Service's instructions was Michael Rowe. When he saw the fire approaching about 1 a.m. on October 27, he got into his tractor and made a firebreak. He disced and saved his house.

Ike Sugg wrote about Michael Rowe in *The Wall Street Journal*,[8] and his story was subsequently featured in an ABC television show "20/20." And in March 1995, a CBS program, "Eye to Eye with Connie Chung," also highlighted the connection between the ESA rules against firebreaks and the California fires.

Sugg pointed out that the Riverside fires were not the only fires affected by such strictures. The fire chief of Orange County, California, said that if residents had been able to clear brush around Laguna Beach, that fire could have been stopped. But the brush was protected habitat for a bird called the California gnatcatcher. (In 1994, a federal judge took the gnatcatcher off the threatened species list on the grounds that the proper listing process hadn't been followed.)

Experiences like Ben Cone's and Michael Rowe's encourage landowners around the country to prevent their land from harboring listed species. Some landowners are managing their land now in a way that almost assures that it will not be suitable for listed species. Others may even be going to the extreme of "shoot, shovel, and shut up," a term that has become popular to describe the attitude of some. No one knows for sure that "shooting, shoveling, and shutting up" has happened, but the takeover of land for the sake of protected species is having a perverse effect. An official of the Texas Parks and Wildlife Department wrote in 1993 that more habitat for the black-capped vireo and the golden-checked warbler has been lost in Texas since they were listed under the Endangered Species Act than would have been lost if the ESA had not applied at all to them.[9]

Some environmentalists argue that examples like Cone's and Rowe's are merely anecdotes or isolated instances that exaggerate the negative impact of the ESA. Or they paint these individuals as placing their wealth above their social responsibilities. The National Wildlife Federation simply calls them false. In a briefing paper called "Fairy Tales & Facts About Environmental Protection,"[10] the Federation disputes the facts of some well-known cases, including Ben Cone's. It contends, for example, that Cone was offered "two practical alternatives" that "would permit him full use of his land," but he turned them down.

The brief report doesn't say what those alternatives were, but they probably included the creation of a habitat conservation plan or the use of a revised draft of the Fish and Wildlife Service's guidelines for management of red-cockaded woodpecker habitat. Preparing a habitat conservation plan would be quite costly, and the guidelines, which are still in draft form, establish very strict criteria for thinning around bird clusters. In either case, Cone would still have had to place his land under the control of the Fish and Wildlife Service, and it is difficult to see how he would have had "full use of his land."

The story of the Riverside fires has come under criticism as well. In fact, it has evoked a storm of controversy, as environmentalists, upset by the message, have challenged every aspect of the story. Congressmen hostile to changing the Endangered Species Act even brought in the Government Accounting Office to investigate the story.[11] This report confirmed that the Fish and Wildlife Service did not allow discing, but disputed Michael Rowe's claim that by discing he saved his home. The Competitive Enterprise Institute has rebutted the major premises of the GAO report.[12]

The dispute, however, is largely irrelevant. Clearly, the Fish and Wildlife Service used the authority of the ESA to place its goals above fire protection goals. At some levels of fire and wind intensity, the prohibited discing would have protected the houses, and potentially even human lives. The message is clear to landowners: If you want freedom to use your land, avoid endangered species. Perhaps simply by managing your land differently you can avoid attracting red-cockaded woodpeckers or northern spotted owls. While Ben Cone may lose the ability to harvest some of his timber, over time he can get rid of the woodpeckers by failing to burn the understory. When the buildup of brush gets too great, the woodpeckers will go away. (In fact, however, Cone continues to conduct prescribed burns to provide quail and deer habitat.)

THE PROBLEM IN A NUTSHELL

Some environmental leaders recognize that a real problem exists. Michael Bean, an Environmental Defense Fund attorney who is often informally credited with authorship of the Endangered Species Act, told a group that included Fish and Wildlife Service officials that there is "increasing evidence that at least some private landowners are actively managing their land so as to avoid potential endangered species problems." He emphasized that these actions are "not the result of malice toward the environment" but "fairly rational decisions, motivated by a desire to avoid potentially significant economic constraints." He called them a "predictable response to the familiar perverse incentives that sometimes accompany regulatory programs, not just the endangered species program but others."[13]

It is ironic that the Constitution explicitly forbids the U.S. Army, even in the name of national defense, from requiring that a citizen quarter a soldier (that is, provide food and shelter for a soldier). Yet the government can require the same citizen to quarter a grizzly bear, a spotted owl, or any other member of a threatened or endangered species, at the landowner's expense.

If the Army had the same power to demand the billeting of soldiers as the Fish and Wildlife Service does now for endangered species we could expect to see soldiers feared, despised, and perhaps even ambushed, as listed species reportedly are today. Yet, in fact, the armed forces are nearly always welcome. The reason is that the military pays their way. The current battles over base closures are fights by communities to *keep* the soldiers, not to make others take them. Thanks to the policy of compensation, it is truly difficult for the Pentagon to close a base.

HOW TO CHANGE A SPECIES FROM AN ENEMY TO A FRIEND

To make the Endangered Species Act effective on private land, it will be necessary to change the status of endangered species from the landowner's enemy to the landowner's friend. One way in which this might happen is for the courts to recognize that when government takes control of habitat under the ESA, a property right has been taken. If such recognition occurs, the Fish and Wildlife Service will have to follow the clause in the Fifth Amendment of the Constitution that requires compensation when the government takes property. So far, no actions of the Fish and Wildlife Service under the ESA have been judged to be "takings" of property rights.

However, this may change. Recent Supreme Court decisions such as *Dolan vs. Tigard*[14] suggest that the Supreme Court is concerned about regulatory takings. In that case, the government of Tigard, Oregon, had told Florence Dolan that she must donate land for a bicycle path to be allowed to expand her plumbing-supply business. The city claimed that the path was needed to relieve traffic congestion that the expansion would bring. But the Supreme Court said that the city's demand was out of proportion to the problem, and thus was an unconstitutional taking of Dolan's property. This and a few other recent cases suggest that the Supreme Court recognizes that arbitrary control of land through regulation can require compensation. Actions under the Endangered Species Act could qualify as takings.

Change may come through the courts in an entirely different way. The Supreme Court has agreed to reconsider whether the Fish and Wildlife Service correctly interprets the Act as requiring it to tell landowners how to use their land. In the case of *Sweet Home Chapter of Communities for a Greater Oregon v. Babbitt*,[15] the U.S. Appeals Court for the District of Columbia rejected this interpretation of the Act. It stated that Congress did not intend to grant authority to the FWS to prohibit habitat modification on private land except where there is a federal role in the land use. If the Supreme Court agrees with this decision, the power of the Fish and Wildlife Service will be dramatically curtailed. So will takings, and their anti-species effects.

Even if these changes do not occur, however, we can expect congressional action. The more generalized takings legislation that passed the House of Representatives in early March would apply to the Endangered Species Act. Although final legislation may take a quite different form, that bill now would require compensation if a regulation takes away 20% or more of a property's value. Regulation that simply stopped a polluter from harming others would not be affected.

A number of groups have been trying to come up with modifications of the Endangered Species Act that would provide incentives for landowner cooperation. One suggestion is to provide property tax credits for landowners who commit themselves to long-range habitat protection.[16] Another is to pay landowners "bounties" or "rewards" for endangered species found on their land.[17] Still another is to "rent" the land that is to be used for endangered species.

All these approaches are worth considering. But the key change must be to remove the ability of the Fish and Wildlife Service to seize control of land without compensation. This may happen through court action or legislative action.

This change would have two benefits: Landowners would no longer fear finding endangered species on their property, and the Fish and Wildlife Service would have to consider costs, and thus would have to recognize the goals of others, since it would depend on funding through the normal congressional budget process. Furthermore, the Fish and Wildlife Service would find that its incentives had changed. Once the agency had to pay for what it used, its staff would begin to search for cost-effective ways of preserving species.

Now, wildlife habitat devoted exclusively to nurturing listed species is essentially costless to the Fish and Wildlife Service, and its officials have an incentive to overuse it—that is, they rely on direct control of habitat as the chief way of protecting species. Yet there may be ways of protecting wildlife that don't exclude so many other uses of the land. The captive breeding that brought back the peregrine falcon requires little or no habitat specifically for the falcon. Specially designed boxes for red-cockaded woodpeckers, replacing the cavities of old trees, might be a cost-effective alternative. (Companies such as International Paper are already using such boxes, and many more landowners could be persuaded to do so if that did not increase the danger of draconian controls should the woodpeckers nest there.)

LARGE SUCCESSES ON SMALL BUDGETS

Putting the Fish and Wildlife Service "on budget" does not mean that protection would disappear or even diminish. There will be little incentive for covert habitat or animal destruction, and landowners will be far more amenable to cooperation. Equally important, if the penalties are removed, there is plenty of evidence that individuals and organizations will take action on their own to protect species. Private organizations, both for-profit and non-profit, have for many decades developed highly effective, low-cost habitat preservation. Removing landowner penalties will make it easier for them to gain landowner help in doing so.

Here are a few examples of what to expect. (For information about these and other groups, contact them at the addresses listed in the Appendix.) The Delta Waterfowl Foundation has an "adopt-a-pothole" program, which pays farmers who protect prairie potholes (depressions in the land that harbor nesting areas for ducks). The Montana Land Reliance keeps large stretches of agricultural land from development through voluntary donations of conservation easements. Many private refuges protect birds and other species; some of them "pay for themselves" by oil or gas drilling. The Pine Butte Preserve in Montana, owned by The Nature Conservancy, provides "eco-tourist" facilities for interested environmentalists, helping to support the preserve, which protects lowland habitat for the threatened grizzly bear. The managers of this preserve have actually created habitat for the bear by burning grasslands in the spring to allow for vegetation to grow and by planting chokecherries, a prized food of the grizzly.

REASONS FOR OPTIMISM

Not everyone, of course, will act to protect endangered species simply because the penalties are removed. But in a diverse country where there is plenty of freedom and thus growing amounts of wealth, we can expect ever more protection of the environment. There are concrete reasons to believe this.

Economists have begun to document a link between economic growth and interest in environmental protection. One reason is that people with higher incomes are willing to pay more for environmental quality. Economist Donald Coursey finds that in the United States and in other industrial nations, citizens' support for measures to improve environmental quality is highly sensitive to income changes.[18] In economic terms, the "income elasticity of demand" for environmental quality is 2.5, he says. That means that a 10 percent increase in income leads to a 25 percent increase in citizens' willingness and ability to pay for environmental measures.

Similarly, a 10 percent decline in a community's income leads to a 25 percent decline in that community's support for costly environmental measures.

According to Coursey, the demand for environmental quality has approximately the same income responsiveness as the demand for luxury automobiles like the BMW and Mercedes-Benz. Environment, it turns out, is a BMW!

There are other indications of this link between economic growth and environmental protection. Gene M. Grossman and Alan Krueger studied several environmental measures for many countries and found that while economic growth in very poor countries "may be associated with worsening environmental conditions," once a "critical level of income has been reached," air and water quality improves. (They found the critical level to be an annual per capita gross domestic product of less than $8,000 in 1985 dollars, or about $11,200 today; the U.S. per capita GDP today is about $26,000).[19] The relationship between economic growth and concern for the environment is also illustrated by the fact that the incomes of Sierra Club members are far higher than average incomes.[20] Simply improving our economy will spur more people to take action to protect the environment, and protecting endangered species is one such action.

But the Endangered Species Act in its current form is a roadblock to creative environmental protection. It not only imposes unnecessarily high costs on landowners; it has also created animosity between environmental groups and landowner groups. In the political arena (unlike the market), discrediting another group or individual can be advantageous. So each group castigates the other, taking advantage of every opportunity to undermine the other's claims. The bitter conflict over the role of the Endangered Species Act in the California fires is just one sign of this deep division. Environmentalists are doing everything possible to discredit the property rights movement; the property rights movement is doing the same to environmentalists.

Thus, today protection of species is a political football. That is because landowners' rights are up for grabs. The landowner fears the Fish and Wildlife Service because it is allowed to take away property rights, while environmental groups fear that property rights legislation will take away the discretionary power of the Fish and Wildlife Service.

Only when rights are explicit and well-defended can landowners and environmentalists work together. Just as good fences make good neighbors (because they clearly define property rights), protection of property rights fosters sensitivity to the desires of others. One of the best examples of such cooperation is the long history at Rainey Preserve, where major oil and gas companies operate natural gas wells under controls worked out with the owners, the National Audubon Society.

ENDANGERED SPECIES ON PUBLIC LAND

Our discussion so far has dealt primarily with the effect of the Endangered Species Act on private land. The effects are important because perhaps half of all the endangered species are found on private land.[21] But the most publicized and hostile conflicts have occurred over the application of the Act to federal land. Land-use decisions following the 1990 designation of the northern spotted owl as a threatened subspecies are the most recent example. Logging was halted on millions of acres of federally-owned national forests in Washington and Oregon.

Just as the mission of the Endangered Species Act trumps all other goals on private land, it trumps the other goals of federal agencies, including the Forest Service's goal of harvesting and selling timber. Agencies like the Forest Service must bend to the wishes of the Fish and Wildlife Service, just as private landowners do, even when less disruptive actions could solve the problem equally well.

To correct this imbalance, some means of deciding how land should be managed is needed. It would be possible to require the Fish and Wildlife Service to compensate another federal agency when its mission reduces the ability of that agency to use land to pursue its goals. However, since all federal land is owned by the taxpayer and its management overseen by Congress, another approach may be more feasible. The Fish and Wildlife Service could be required to go to Congress when it believes that a parcel of land managed by another agency is necessary to protect a listed species. Congress could explicitly debate the transfer of control over any sizeable tract of federal land. In this way, the goals of all citizens could be considered; one single goal would not automatically triumph without discussion. Such debate could be triggered by the quantity of land that the Fish and Wildlife Service wants to control; perhaps the transfer of control over any parcel over 100 acres should be made only when Congress concurs.

Another reform could enlist the help of the private sector to protect endangered species on federal lands. A number of federal laws could be changed to allow environmental groups to bid for the lease or purchase of federal lands to protect endangered species habitat (or pursue other environmental goals). For example, today only someone willing to cut down timber can bid on Forest Service timber sales; it is illegal to purchase timber and not harvest. But the law could be changed so that Defenders of Wildlife or The Wilderness Society could bid for parcels and then be allowed not to log, preserving the habitat for endangered species. (Concerns over disease and fire control, however, would have to be addressed.)

CONCLUSION

In summary, any reform of the Endangered Species Act should have as its goal making endangered species the friend, not the enemy, of landowners. This can be largely accomplished by ending the Fish and Wildlife Service's power to control land without compensation.

Several results will stem from such a change. Landowners will no longer fear finding endangered species on their property and will become much more cooperative. The Fish and Wildlife Service will go "on budget." Its goals will be weighed against other desirable goals, and it will have an incentive to husband its resources, try out creative approaches, and establish priorities.

To achieve these outcomes, either judicial or legislative change is required. The Supreme Court may decide that the control of land to protect endangered species is a taking, and require compensation under the Constitution's Fifth Amendment.

Or, the Supreme Court may uphold the *Sweet Home* decision that the Act does not normally authorize habitat restrictions on private land.

Or, without any judicial action, Congress may, through broad "takings" legislation, require that a reduction in property value requires compensation.

Or, Congress may amend the Act itself to require compensation. This would give Congress an opportunity to specify the way in which the Fish and Wildlife Service could compensate landowners and encourage mutually beneficial land uses.

On public land, other goals than endangered species protection must be considered, too. Inter-agency compensation is one approach; a more feasible one may be to let Congress decide which goal has priority when the Fish and Wildlife Service wants to control a significant amount of federal acreage.

These changes, however they come about, will end the tragic situation that is now occurring as landowners learn that they will lose their freedom and their property if they find endangered species on their land. If property rights are respected, both landowners and species will benefit.

Richard Stroup has a doctorate in economics from the University of Washington. He is an adjunct professor at North Carolina State University in Raleigh, NC, and a Senior Associate at PERC in Bozeman, MT. He is the author of many scholarly articles and co-authored with James D. Gwartney *Economics: Private and Public Choice.*

NOTES

1. Rocky Barker, *Saving All the Parts: Reconciling the Endangered Species Act* (Washington, DC: Island Press, 1993), p. 19, 137.

2. M. Lynne Corn, *Endangered Species Act Issues* (Washington, DC: Congressional Research Service, May 27, 1992), p. 1.

3. U.S. Fish and Wildlife Service, "Endangered and Threatened Wildlife and Plants," 50 CFR 17.11 & 17.12 (special reprint, August 20, 1994). This annual list included 20 delistings. Since then, seven additional species have been delisted, reports the Competitive Enterprise Institute (Washington, DC), in "Delisted Endangered and Threatened Species," March 9, 1995.

4. U.S. Fish and Wildlife Service, "Endangered and Threatened Wildlife and Plants," 50 CFR 17.11 & 17.12 (Special reprint, August 20, 1994).

5. Lee Ann Welch, "Property Rights Conflicts under the Endangered Species Act: Protection of the Red-Cockaded Woodpecker," PERC Working Paper No. 94-12, Bozeman, MT, 1994.

6. Ike C. Sugg, "Ecosystem Babbitt-Babble," *The Wall Street Journal*, April 2, 1993, p. A12.

7. Welch, p. 47.

8. Ike Sugg, "California Fires—Losing Houses, Saving Rats," *The Wall Street Journal*, November 10, 1993.

9. Larry McKinney, "Reauthorizing the Endangered Species Act—Incentives for Rural Landowners," in *Building Economic Incentives Into the Endangered Species Act* (Washington, DC: Defenders of Wildlife, May 1994), p. 74.

10. National Wildlife Federation, "Fairy Tales & Facts About Environmental Protection" (Washington, DC, February 1994), p. 4.

11. General Accounting Office, "Endangered Species Act: Impact of Species Protection Efforts on the 1993 California Fire," GAO/RCED-94-224, July 8, 1994.

12. Ike C. Sugg, "Rats, Lies and the GAO" (Washington, DC: Competitive Enterprise Institute), August 1994.

13. Transcript of a talk by Michael Bean at a U.S. Fish and Wildlife Service seminar, November 3, 1994, Marymount University, Arlington, VA.

14. *Dolan v. City of Tigard*, Supreme Court Reporter, Vol. 114, p. 2309 (1994).

15. *Sweet Home v. Babbitt*, 17 Federal Reporter 3rd., Vol. 17, p. 1463 (D.C. Cir. 1994).

16. Jim McKinney, Mark Shaffer, Jeff Olson, "Economic Incentives to Preserve Endangered Species Habitat and Biodiversity on Private Land," in *Building Economic Incentives Into the Endangered Species Act* (Washington, DC: Defenders of Wildlife, May 1994), p. 1.

17. Terry L. Anderson and Jody J Olsen, "Positive Incentives for Saving Endangered Species," in *Building Economic Incentives Into the Endangered Species Act* (Washington, DC: Defenders of Wildlife, May 1994), p. 110.

18. Donald Coursey discussed this topic in "The Demand for Environmental Quality," a paper presented January 1993 at the annual meeting of the American Economic Association in Anaheim, California.

19. Gene M. Grossman and Alan B. Krueger, "Economic Growth and the Environment," *NBER Working Paper Series* (National Bureau of Economic Research, Cambridge, MA, 1994), p. 19.

20. 1992 Reader Survey prepared by *Sierra* (San Francisco, CA: Sierra Club), p. 1.

21. Hank Fischer, Bill Snape, and Wendy Hudson, "Building Economic Incentives Into the Endangered Species Act," *Endangered Species Technical Bulletin* (U.S. Fish and Wildlife Service, 1994), Vol. XIX, No. 2, p. 4.

Chemicals and Witches:
Standards of Evidence in Regulation

By Robert Nelson

WHY DO BAD things happen? Why does a child die? Judeo-Christian theology instructs its followers to trust that God has a purpose, however difficult it may be to understand.

That answer has not been fully satisfactory for many people. Before the Enlightenment, many in the European religious world explained disasters through evil spirits, witches, and other agents of the devil, which undermined true faith, spread injury and disease, and caused many bad things to happen.

Our modern and scientific age—a time when most people no longer believe in the active presence of the devil in the world—confronts a similar problem. Science tells us that our fate is a matter of the workings of the laws of nature: Cancer is an accident of cell biology; a high death rate in one town is simply the random statistical consequence of the workings of probabilities in a nation with many thousands of communities. Yet secular thought today is as filled with devils, and bad things are as attributed to evil influences, as in the European world of 500 years ago.

The many parallels were developed in a remarkable article—still known mainly to environmental specialists—that appeared in 1980 on "Witches, Floods and Wonder Drugs."[1] The author, William C. Clark, then at a prestigious international think tank, the International Institute for Applied Systems Analysis in Vienna, Austria, is today a member of the science, technology, and public policy program at the Kennedy School of Government at Harvard University.

Clark begins by noting that "for several centuries spanning the Renaissance and Reformation, societal risk assessment meant witch hunting." Indeed, people found in "'witches' a convenient label for their fears of the unknown." It was their way of dealing with "the inevitable misfortunes which befell one's crops, health and happiness." Although the Catholic Church did not aggressively persecute witches for many centuries, the publication in 1486 of *The Hammer of*

---

1 William C. Clark, "Witches, Floods, and Wonder Drugs," in Societal Risk Assessment: How Safe is Safe Enough? edited by Richard C. Schwing and Walter A. Albers, Jr. (New York: Plenum Press, 1980), pp. 287–313..

the Witches proved, as Clark writes, a "collective consciousness watershed." Witch hunting rose to fever pitch in the sixteenth and seventeenth centuries, as public panics came and went, and many tens of thousands of alleged witches were executed throughout Europe.

WITCHES AND CHEMICALS

Clark sees similar phenomena underlying our modern chemical panics, although the hapless victims are no longer executed; instead, they lose their jobs, businesses, and communities. The governing authorities today are often just as craven in capitulating to public fears.

He notes that a key question is "the kind of evidence we admit in our attempts to answer" questions of cause and effect, of guilt and innocence. In both witch hunting and contemporary chemical hunting, there is no "conceivable empirical observation which could logically force an answer 'No.' In neither case is there a 'stopping rule' which can logically terminate the investigation short of a revelation of guilt."

In the witch hunts of the sixteenth and seventeenth centuries, "the Inquisition's principal tool for identifying witches was torture ... If she said no, what else would you expect of a witch? So she was tortured until she confessed the truth." And in our current chemical inquisitions, Clark notes, something that is not a risk with a parts-per-trillion test "can always be exposed to a parts-per-billion examination ... The only stopping rule is discovery of the sought-for effect, or exhaustion of the investigator (or his funds)."

Environmental investigators, for example, proclaimed a decade ago that dioxin was among the most carcinogenic chemicals ever seen. The occupants of Times Beach, Missouri, were relocated in haste after dioxin was found in its streets. Yet, by the 1990s, the scientist who had called for this evacuation had recanted. Workers heavily exposed to dioxin in a 1970s industrial accident in Italy were showing few of the dire effects predicted. Michael Gough, formerly director of the Center for Risk Management at Resources for the Future, and past coordinator of a major dioxin study for the Congressional Office of Technology Assessment, wrote in 1993 that all credible studies "have concluded that dioxin exposure has not caused elevated levels of cancer."[2]

In response to such challenges, the Environmental Protection Agency initiated a new dioxin study in 1991. Yet when the EPA finally released its study in 1994, dioxin was not exonerated. The EPA grudgingly acknowledged that the original cancer concerns might still be unproven by any direct epidemiological evidence, but now dioxin was charged with a new litany of sins. It was as Gough had commented: "No experiment or study can prove the negative ... As each postulated connection dissolves, new ones can be proposed."[3]

Perhaps dioxin will eventually be proven a great menace. The full scientific truth will not be known for some time to come. What is obvious is that, like the witch hunters of the sixteenth

---

2   Michael Gough, "Dioxin, Perceptions, Estimates, and Measures," in Kenneth R. Foster, David E. Bernstein, and Peter Huber, eds., *Phantom Risk: Scientific Interference and the Law* (Cambridge, Mass.: MIT Press, 1993), p. 268.

3   Michael Gough, p. 272

and seventeenth centuries, the members of government bureaucracies have a large personal stake in the outcome—as large as the chemical manufacturers whose scientific reports are routinely dismissed by many people. As Clark noted, "there was certainly an element of opportunistic careerism in the Inquisition, and there is almost certainly an element of opportunistic careerism in the present risk assessment movement."

Arousing public fears is an ancient bureaucratic strategy, practiced effectively early in this century, for example, by the founder of the Forest Service, Gifford Pinchot. He warned constantly—and altogether baselessly, as matters turned out—that the nation would soon run out of wood, that there would be a dire "timber famine."

Witch hunting was not limited to any one religion or country. Indeed, while the Inquisition was Roman Catholic, about 4,000 witches were executed in Calvinist Scotland between 1590 and 1680. Paul Johnson reports in his *History of Christianity*[4] that "wherever Calvinism became strong, witches were systematically hunted."

THE SALEM EXPERIENCE

The execution of 19 witches in Salem in 1692, backed by leading members of the Massachusetts Puritan branch of Calvinism, was no great anomaly, although it came near the close of the witch hunting craze. The Salem court that heard the case consisted of seven prominent citizens, including the lieutenant governor of the Massachusetts colony. The victims were convicted largely by "spectral" evidence supplemented by the confessions of other supposed witches. Spectral evidence consisted of testimony in which a vision of the alleged witch—the "spectre"—was said to have appeared before the witness and tempted that person to evil deeds. The appearance of such a spectre was attributed by the court to the witch, and was considered to be decisive evidence of the possession of witchcraft powers.

(By the way, no one who confessed was executed at Salem. Execution was reserved for people who refused to admit their guilt and thus continued in defiance of God and the court—hardly an incentive to resist confession.)

Today, risks of chemicals are assessed from animal tests based on the "maximum tolerable dose." A sample of rats, for example, will be exposed to the chemical at the highest dose that the rats can accept and still continue to live. This dose will often be many hundreds or thousands of times the equivalent doses to which humans are exposed. If the rats then show abnormal rates of cancer or other health problems, the chemical stands convicted.

The standard of proof here is not much higher than the spectral evidence and the "voluntary" confessions accepted by the Salem court. Normal human health requires many chemicals that would be very harmful in the body at much higher concentrations. There are large numbers of "natural" chemicals that have been present in the food supply for thousands of years and that today show positive carcinogenic results under current testing methods.

Science magazine found the existing standards of scientific evidence so lacking that it called editorially in 1990 for an end to chemical witch hunting: "Resultant stringent regulations and

---

4   Paul Johnson, *A History of Christianity* (New York: Atheneum, 1987), p. 310.

attendant frightening publicity have led to public anxiety and chemophobia," said the editorial. "If current ill-based regulatory levels continue to be imposed, the cost of cleaning up phantom hazards will be in the hundreds of billions of dollars with minimal benefit to human health. In the meantime, real hazards are not receiving adequate attention."[5]

Bruce Ames, an early developer of tests for carcinogenic impact and Professor of Biochemistry and Molecular Biology at the University of California at Berkeley as well as a member of the National Academy of Sciences, writes with Lois Gold that existing maximum tolerable dose methods of testing, even though they are a main method used by the government for assessing cancer risk, are of little worth. They "cannot predict the cancer risk to humans at the much lower levels to which [humans] are typically exposed."[6]

The Massachusetts executions of witches came to an end when charges started being hurled not only against the social outcasts and the poor but against the governing officials, the relatives of clergy, and other prominent members of the Massachusetts colony. The turning point was a public statement issued in the fall of 1692 by Increase Mather and other leading Puritan ministers rejecting the use of spectral evidence. Similarly, Clark reports that a critical event in the winding down of the witch trials in Europe was the publication by Inquisitor Alonso Salazar y Fras of a detailed analysis of witch burnings at Logroño, Navarre. The analysis by this well-respected member of the church showed that "most of the original accusations had been false, that torture had created witches where none existed, and that there was not a single case of actual witchcraft to show for all the preaching, hunting, and burning which had been carried out in the name of the church." Perhaps Bruce Ames and the small band of other scientists who have had the courage in recent years to insist on firm evidence in the face of today's environmental panics will eventually find a similar place in history.

ENVIRONMENTALISTS AS PURITANS

Environmental witch hunting is only one of several ways in which the more radical segments of the present environmental movement have revived the seventeenth-century heritage of Puritan Massachusetts. When radical environmentalists such as David Brower and David Foreman refer to mankind as the "cancer" or "AIDS" of the earth, they are repeating once again the old Calvinist message of doom and gloom—that mankind has fallen into a deep and fundamental state of depravity and that the earth is headed for divine retribution unless human beings mend their corrupt ways.[7]

In his classic study of the New England mind of the seventeenth century, the Harvard historian Perry Miller observed that the Puritans were "obsessed with" the "theology of nature."

---

5 "Testing for Carcinogens with Rodents," editorial, *Science*, September 21, 1990, p. 1357.

6 Bruce N. Ames and Lois Swirsky Gold, "Environmental Pollution and Cancer: Some Misconceptions," in Foster, Bernstein, and Huber, *Phantom Risk*, p. 154.

7 See Robert H. Nelson, "Environmental Calvinism: The Judeo-Christian Roots of Eco-Theology," in Roger E. Meiners and Bruce Yandle, eds., *Taking the Environment Seriously* (Lanham, Md.: Rowman and Littlefield Publishers, Inc., 1993).

They had a "reverence" for nature reflecting their belief that "the creatures … are subordinate arguments and testimonies of the most wise God, pages of the book of nature, ministers and apostles of God, the vehicles and the way by which we are carried to God."[8] Environmentalism today, in essence, secularizes this theology.

In Nature it is possible to experience directly the Creation; in theological terms, it is possible to encounter a work of God free of the corruptions introduced by sinful humanity. Indeed, intellectual historians such as Miller have traced a path from the Puritans through the New England transcendentalists of the nineteenth century to current environmentalism. The founder of the Sierra Club, John Muir, followed in the footsteps of Ralph Waldo Emerson; the late Edward Abbey, a writer who lamented the loss of the pristine West, was an intellectual descendant of Henry David Thoreau.

The Judeo-Christian heritage is the bearer of many of the glories of Western civilization. American Puritanism helped to spur abolitionism and women's rights, and is the great source of much of the reform impetus in American history. Yet Western religion has also fallen into moments of persecution and fanaticism.

Such moments come when trust in reason erodes. The persecution of witches arose at about the same time as the Protestant Reformation. The Roman Catholic church became increasingly defensive as Luther, Calvin, and other Protestants contested its authority. Reason was called into question as the Reformation challenged the natural law theology of the medieval Roman Catholic church. Similarly today, trust in reason is fading as science faces growing numbers of doubters. This paves the way for hysterical reactions.

As environmentalism undertakes the worthy task of further developing the religious grounds for the stewardship of the earth, it will be well to recall these lessons of the past. In matters of environmental regulation of chemicals, the future credibility of the environmental movement rests on demanding strict standards of proof before taking actions that displace many people and spend many tens of billions of hard-earned citizen dollars. […]

---

8   Perry Miller, The New England Mind: The Seventeenth Century (Cambridge, Mass.: Harvard University Press, 1954), pp. 208–209

Enclosing the Environmental Commons

By Fred Smith

ECO-MYTHS DEBUNKED

- *Nearly all environmental problems-air and water pollution, declining fisheries, extinctions, rainforest destruction, coral reef degradation occur in open-access commons.*
- *In a commons, no one is in charge, no one protects the resource, so people have an incentive to exploit a resource before someone else beats them to it, leading to environmental damage.*
- *Political management of a commons has proven to be costly and ineffective and merely slows the damage caused to the natural world by the misdirected incentives in a commons. Politicizing the environment does not resolve the tragedy of the commons. Rather, it institutionalizes it.*
- *Enclosure—that is, assigning owners to environmental goods—will integrate those goods into the private sector and reveal their true values and help protect and preserve them.*

OWNERSHIP OF THE COMMONS CAN PREVENT THE TRAGEDY OF THE COMMONS-A PARADIGM FOR ENVIRONMENTAL PROBLEMS

FEW THINGS PROVE as depressing as reading the conventional environmentalist lore. Fertile topsoil is being blown off our farms. Not only are our waters unsafe to drink, but there is less available every year. Elephants in Africa, tigers in Asia, parrots in Brazil, the spotted owl in the Pacific Northwest-indeed, ever more species on our planet are threatened with extinction. The Amazon forests are disappearing like rain in the desert-and the deserts are encroaching on arable land. Around the world, coral reefs are dying, while increasingly fishermen return home with empty holds. Growing quantities of hazardous substances contaminate airsheds in our urban centers. And, of course, we face a global warming catastrophe. While it is now becoming more widely understood that ideological environmentalists have exaggerated the extent of such problems, most of us believe we can and should do better.

But to do better, one must know why environmental problems arise in the first place, and here ideological environmentalists have seriously misdiagnosed the causes of environmental degradation. Lacking knowledge of the historical response to industrial pollution and disdainful of private property and markets, environmentalists have accepted unthinkingly the market failure explanation for pollution. Pollution and its impacts, they believe, are external to the market and, therefore, ignored. Thus government intervention is necessary.

Their indictment goes further. Since mankind enjoys the fruits of industry, environmental controls must extend to the population itself, our demand for goods and services, and our reliance on new and inadequately tested technologies. Environmentalists see the world in "terrible toos" terms: There are *too* many of us, we consume *too* much, and we rely *too* heavily on technology that we understand *too* little about. These factors, they argue, stress our planet and explain environmental woes. Since private action has created the problem, only political action-population control, consumption restrictions, and prior approval of technology—offer any hope of reducing the stress our insatiable demands are placing on the carrying capacity of our all too finite Earth.

An alternative explanation of pollution is found in the work of Garrett Hardin in his oft-cited *Science* article "The Tragedy of the Commons." Hardin describes an open-access resource, a pasture, that inevitably experiences environmental degradation. His example deals with a village surrounding a pasturage open to all. Initially, there are few villagers and the pasture is adequate for their cattle. However, as the village grows, so also do the number of cows. Self-interest motivates the first villager to place one more cow on the commons, the second to follow suit, and so on, reducing the availability of forage and degrading the pasture with accumulating animal waste. However, while each villager gains the full value of the additional cow, he bears only a fraction of the costs. The calculus is clear: The gains of an additional cow accrue to the individual; the costs of the lower quality pasturage are borne by all. Eventually, the carrying capacity of the pasture is exceeded, resulting in the tragedy of the commons, a degraded pasture providing little value to anyone. Hardin summarized the result: "Ruin is the destination toward which all men rush, each pursuing his own best interest in a society which believes in the freedom of the commons. Freedom in a commons brings ruin to all."

The problem, it should be noted, is not that demand per se is excessive, but rather that there is no gatekeeper to moderate such demands by reducing the number of cattle or by adopting ways to use the pasture more intensively. Environmental problems reflect the lack of stewardship arrangements. Factories belch smoke into the air because the people in the affected regions cannot legally stop them. The degradation of rivers and estuaries by municipal sewage reflects the fact that downstream groups-lacking any property rights in the harmed resource-have no right to block such pollution. The depletion of rain forests and fisheries results from their open access, their common property status-not from any excessive demands. To realize how these problems reflect the lack of property rights, note that steel mills do not dump slag in people's backyards (where ownership protections are explicit) but do dump soot and acid residuals into the airsheds and waterways (where private ownership is absent).

The *market failure* explanation for environmental problems ignores the basic fact that markets without property rights are a grand illusion. Without the institutional framework of property rights, no goods can be protected or valued. Environmental goods and values are at risk because they have not been integrated into and the market system of property rights. No market exists and thus cannot have failed. Tragedies of the commons are not observed where property rights exist and are protected. To see this, consider a few examples. Groundwater is increasingly scarce, while oil is becoming ever more abundant (in the relevant metric of the hours of human work needed to purchase this substance). Greater demands for quality air in the indoor spaces (cars, offices, malls, workplaces) where we spend an increasing fraction of our lives are met readily; yet despite the expenditure of many billions of dollars, the air in many urban areas remains smoggy. Note also that while many species of wildlife are threatened, domesticated species-pets as well as livestock-are prospering. None of this is surprising. The late Julian Simon liked to quote the 19th-century American economist Henry George: "Both the jayhawk and the man eat chickens, but the more jayhawks, the fewer chickens, while the more men, the more chickens." The point is that people own chickens and have an incentive to produce more as demand increases.

Simon's key observation is that environmental resources are endangered-not because of the market, but rather because environmental resources have been left out in the cold. Lacking any property right protections, they are vulnerable. The resources noted above-wildlife, groundwater, urban air-all are common property resources. Everyone can use these resources-no one owns them and has a direct interest in protecting them. The result is the tragedy of the commons. But tragedy is not inevitable. It can be resolved by the creation of property rights in the resource at risk. Private ownership arrangements are pervasive in our society, allowing individuals to nurture and protect many things they care about. People can protect their backyards and their pets, so why not water or wildlife? From this perspective, the problem is not that too much of the planet is privately controlled, but rather that too little is. Our goal should be to allow more of the planet to become the moral equivalent of someone's backyard or pet and, thereby, to empower people to play a direct and immediate role in environmental protection.

The problem is not that people lack ecological consciousness; that problem can be addressed by value education. Indeed, Hardin argues, it would be wrong to "browbeat a free man in the commons into acting against his own interests." Moral suasion in the commons situation is worse than useless. Any sacrifice that the ecologically conscious individual might make would be pointless because the less-sensitive villager would simply take advantage of his sacrifice to place his additional cow on the commons. The pasture would still degrade, and the altruist would lose vis-a-vis his neighbors. For such reasons, the ecologically sensitive individual is disadvantaged in open-access situations.

Resolving the tragedy, Hardin argues, required institutional change: Either the resource must be privatized or the resource must come under political control. Let us consider the implications of each choice. First, if we go down the political path, we would create a regulatory control agency, call it the Pasture Protection Agency (PPA), and appoint a PPA Administrator. If we take the privatization path, we would divide the pasture into plots and grant each villager a deed to a portion. In either situation, similar problems must be addressed: How many cattle can the pasture accommodate? Who will be allowed to graze their cattle and how many cows will they be allowed? How can we ensure that the allocations granted are observed? How should we respond to changes-a drought, a bountiful year, requests to graze sheep or to build a lawn tennis court? How do we improve the pasture over time? Let's see how well these tasks will be performed under each alternative.

In the private property option, each villager would decide the number of cows to graze on his field. He would be free to place as many or as few as he wished. He would, of course, also have to decide whether to fence his plot or not. If not, he would have to decide how to protect his pasture from wandering cows from other farms. The initial decisions are likely to be wrong, but the farmers will have every incentive to gain knowledge quickly to improve management through trial and error. Too few cows will yield too Iowa return; too many may damage the pasturage. Some villagers will garner this knowledge more quickly than others, and their practices will soon be emulated by everyone. One environmentally beneficial aspect of the privatization option is the variety of experimentation it encourages.

The PPA Administrator will also seek to determine the number of cattle that can safely graze on the pasture. He may well hire an analyst to calculate that number. But again mistakes will happen. However, the Administrator operates in a political environment, and mistakes are likely to be viewed as malfeasance. If the estimate turns out to be too low, the Administrator will be criticized for depriving the village of the additional value. If the estimate is too high, the Administrator will be criticized for allowing the pasture to deteriorate. The analyst hired by the PPA has every professional reason to determine the correct number, but neither the analyst nor the PPA administration are directly affected by success or failure. Indeed, a bad decision by the PPA may even mean that the agency will be awarded a larger budget.

Note that pasture management entails gathering information on the quality and quantity of the grass, the stress placed by the cattle or other animals allowed to graze, the value of the various species grazing, and how these values would change with alternative grazing policies. The individual villagers will experiment with various strategies. Mistakes will be noted by other villagers, as will successes. The variety of approaches exercised under private management is likely to result in much faster acquisition of knowledge than under the centralized PPA approach. And again, the fact that the PPA employees do not directly lose or profit argues for slower learning. The creative bureaucrat may well garner commendation and perhaps a merit award, but those incentives are far weaker than if he were an owner who would capture the full ecological and economic value of a successful innovation.

In either case, the hope is that, over time, we will learn how to do more with less. Innovations are critical for sustainable pasture management. Along the private path, the desire for improvements creates a market. Note that incentives exist for people who have no direct linkage to the pasture to provide such innovations. Markets link the broader society to the challenge of improving pasture management. The individual villager will be eager to compensate those able to increase his profits. The PPA Administrator will seek funds to conduct similar research, but his budget may not permit extensive research. Note that any gains that such research might yield would not accrue to his budget. Bureaucracies, as a result, are slow to innovate.

Adapting to changing conditions and tastes poses further management problems. Should, for example, only cows be allowed or should we also allow sheep and goats and geese? Should the pasture be preserved for grazing only or would it be permissible to allow some to create a lawn tennis court? Should the pasture be used continuously or would it be better to put it in fallow every few years? Each villager may also face the problem of adjusting his policies in the event of a drought or a year of plenty. The private manager has every incentive to find ways to accommodate such diverse demands-the greater the demand for his land, the greater the potential profits. Problems arising from inappropriate mixes will strongly signal the villager to rethink any mismanagement.

Political resource managers are subject to political pressures. Powerful political interests are likely to be favored over political pariahs. Election concerns may well lead the PPA Administrator to ease up on restrictions, even if that would create long-term problems for the pasture. Moreover, changes in administration may cause changes in policy. The sheep contingent may prevail at the polls over the cattlemen with destabilizing impact on pasture management. Changes in stocking patterns will also occur in the private example, but the dispersal of control would normally lead to a wider variety of responses and a lowering of overall harm to the pasturage.

The foregoing discussion suggests the reasons why private ownership of grazing lands (or its equivalent in long-term leases for politically controlled areas) has become so dominant. Ownership rights create incentives for wise management today and for creative innovations over time. Political controls are likely to prove superior to open access common property arrangements. However, a political management system lacks the reward structure essential to good management and innovation. Ultimately, the political approach does not really resolve the tragedy of the commons, but rather it institutionalizes it. Nonetheless, modern environmental policy has relied almost totally on political controls to address environmental concerns.

PROGRESSIVES INSTITUTIONALIZE THE TRAGEDY OF THE COMMONS

If the environmental tragedy of the commons can be better resolved by privatization, why then has the Pasture Protection Administration path so often been selected? The answer is that the market's ability to address environmental concerns had been so weakened prior to the dawn of the modern environmental age (dated roughly as April 22, 1970, the first Earth Day) that almost everyone perceived environmental problems as the inevitable result of industrial activity. Markets were seen as causing environmental problems, not solving them.

Let us briefly examine the historical record. First note these resources (minerals, food, oil) integrated (via property rights) into the market have become more abundant, not less, over the last century. Moreover, historical record suggests that market forces in both England and the United States were beginning to address environmental concerns in the early days of the Industrial Revolution (the latter half of the 19th century) far before the environmental concerns became prominent. The Industrial Revolution did pose serious and novel environmental problems. Industrial wastes were often more noxious and greater in quantity than the effluents of the preindustrial age. Early mills produced vast quantities of liquid effluents; trains belched forth vast quantities of smoke and soot. Yet the initial inclination of the courts was not to stand idle but rather to regard these nuisances as actionable. Property owners expected that their property rights would be protected-that industrial corporations could not mar private owners' rights to enjoy their properties peacefully.

Nobel Prize-winning economist Ronald Coase documents a number of those examples in his article "The Problem of Social Cost." Coase describes offices disturbed by vibration from adjoining industrial operations, odors arising from distilling operations, smoke coming from railroad locomotives, and dams flooding upstream properties. The courts sought to integrate these concerns into the established property rights system. The question was whether one had created an actionable nuisance or whether one's actions constituted trespass. If so, then the individual could stop the enterprise or, at least, obtain restitution for damages. For example, early mills built dams that sometimes flooded upstream properties. That flooding, an early form of pollution, was treated as a trespass, and the dam builder was forced to reach accommodation with upstream parties or else lower the dam. Similarly, early steam locomotives spewed forth not only smoke but also sparks. Those sparks sometimes ignited grain fields near the rail tracks. Again, that action was treated as trespass and the railroad was held responsible for damages.

Thus the Industrial Revolution did not inevitably mean the destruction of the natural environment, but rather prompted a response by the courts that promised to "housebreak" these newer enterprises, subjecting them to the same restraints imposed on traditional enterprises. Unfortunately, that process was short-circuited. The belief that private property was critical, that society was responsible for protecting private property, lost favor to the belief that property was a social construct to be used for the public good.

In America, this negative attitude toward private property was chiefly championed by the growing Progressive movement of the late 19th and early 20th centuries. Progressives, of course, held disparate views; however, the government's intervention in the economy, collective action, via politics was, they believed, more likely to advance the public interest, to ensure that resources were used for their greatest value. The Progressive shift brought about changes in the way courts came to view externalities and property rights. Property rights were weakened as the courts moved from common law trespass and nuisance concepts to utilitarian concepts of balancing "social" gains and losses. The language of a 1911 Georgia Supreme Court is telling: "The pollution of the air, so far as reasonably necessary to the *enjoyment* of life and indispensable to the progress of society, is not actionable" (emphasis added). Coase details this transformation, noting that in both Britain and the United States, legislatures authorized activities that were known to create environmental problems. The courts heeded these legislative acts by offering less protection against such environmental harms. Coase notes a number of cases-consider the language of one court decision: "Legislative sanction makes that lawful which otherwise might be a nuisance. Examples of this are damages to adjacent land arising from smoke, vibration and noise in the operation of a railroad … unpleasant odors connected with sewers, oil refining and storage of naphtha."

This Progressive bias for economic growth over ecological values is neatly captured in the phrase: Excuse our dust, but grow we must! In that political climate, it is not surprising that people came to associate economic activities with pollution.

Progressives viewed the world in utilitarian terms-resources were placed on this Earth to be used! People who held their land idle, who failed to develop resources, were squandering a precious heritage. Indeed, to gain ownership of land one often needed to demonstrate that one had put it to use-plowing the land, building a house, catching the fish, digging the mine, grazing the cattle, cutting the timber. Forests were to be logged to produce housing, fuel, paper, and wealth. Rivers were to be channeled to improve America's transportation infrastructure and to provide power to light our homes. Even "environmental agencies" such as the Department of the Interior's National Park Service viewed their mission in developmental (maximizing the number of visitor days) rather than in preservation terms. Most Americans, of course, agreed with these policies at the time.

Given this orientation, the surprise is that there wasn't even more pollution, more environmental damage. The primary reason is that markets encourage efficient use of energy and raw materials, and efficiency is not only good business, but it also reduces pollution. Pollution, after all, is that fraction of material and energy input that does not find its way into the final product. The phrase "industrial ecology" hadn't yet been coined, but industrialists, nonetheless, continually found ways of doing more with less. An excellent example was the invention of the Kraft process for papermaking. That, process not only allowed the use of pines and other lower-cost woods, but also burning the noncellulose component of the wood pile provided most of the energy required to make paper. The result was less waste per unit of paper produced. Moreover, firms desired to have good relations with their neighbors and thus to some degree sought to reduce the nuisances attendant to their activities.

Still, the utilitarian bias of the Progressive Era that undermined property protections reduced the incentives for industry to proceed along a more ecologically sensitive path. After all, if a manufacturer could not be held responsible for his pollution, why expend monies to reduce it? Why purchase buffer zones around a facility? Why purchase pollution control equipment or install settling ponds?

Perhaps the most serious consequence of this weakening of common law property protections was that it reduced the amount of social experimentation that would have occurred. Even a century ago, there were some people who valued the environment highly. In a world where property rights were respected, companies would have found themselves forced to adjust their operations to accommodate these concerns. Firms would have learned to negotiate with adjoining property owners prior to locating a plant. Consider railroads. Had property rights been honored, firms might well have purchased buffer zones or noise easements adjacent to their tracks. Spark and smoke suppression technologies would probably have been introduced earlier. Tracks and loading yards would, more likely, have been located in nonresidential areas. The need to respect the property rights of the environmentally sensitive minority would have encouraged firms to reduce their environmental footprint during the era when few have placed high value on the environment. The result would have been that environmental management strategies would have been introduced in a few locations at an early date. As America grew wealthier and environmental concerns increased accordingly, there would have been a smoother transition to the environmentally conscious world of today, with less damage to the natural world.

Another legacy of the Progressive Era, antitrust regulation, has made it difficult to develop cooperative conservation agreements. As but one example, Gulf Coast shrimpers organized to reduce their catch and thus conserve shrimp stocks. That arrangement was disallowed by the federal antitrust authorities.

The work of Ronald Coase regarding the way laws were changed during the industrialization era suggests we rethink the path along which environmental policy has proceeded for the last few decades. As discussed above, Coase examined the legal and legislative records and found that, rather than markets failing, it would be more accurate to say that markets had been blocked from operating in ways that would have better protected the natural world. Legislative bodies deliberately weakened the defenses available to property owners (specifically nuisance and trespass claims), leaving industry free to develop along a more polluting path. Environmental policy makers today remain largely unaware of this fact. Commenting on that point, Coase notes,

> *Most economists seem to be unaware of [the role played by laws weakening property defenses] … When they are prevented from sleeping at night by the roar of jet planes overhead (publicly authorized and perhaps publicly operated), are unable to think(or rest} in the day because of the noise and vibration from passing trains (publicly authorized and perhaps publicly operated), find it difficult to breathe because of the odour from the local sewage farm (publicly authorized and perhaps publicly operated), and are unable to escape because their driveways are blocked by a road obstruction (without any doubt, publicly devised), their nerves frayed and mental balance disturbed, they proceed to declaim about the disadvantages of private enterprise and the need for government regulation.*

Coase's point is that property rights once had linked economic concerns to environmental concerns. Had property rights remained secure, environmental policy might well have taken a very different course. First, development would have proceeded in ways that created less environmental harm. Also, many more innovative options for addressing environmental concerns would have been explored over the last century. Pollution-minimizing technologies would have been developed and adopted much earlier. Activities that are inherently disturbing would have been sited in more remote locations; firms would have organized their work year to minimize operations in times when they would have had the greatest negative effect on the environment. Firms would have purchased larger buffer zones around their plants and negotiated in advance with neighboring property owners. Communities might well have gained the right to police their airsheds, allowing use for consideration (possibly payments by firms and adjoining jurisdictions affecting the community that would permit lower taxes, for example). Pollution-reducing technology would have a ready market. Unfortunately, when environmental activists emerged as major players in the policy arena after the first Earth Day in 1970, they had no knowledge of the role that private property had once played, nor its potential for addressing their concerns.

THE MODERN ENVIRONMENTAL AGE AND ITS PROBLEMS

Tragically Earth Day activists knew little history, so from their limited perspective, markets were inherently antagonistic to environmental values. They sought immediate action to address what they viewed as pervasive and dangerous ecological problems. They gave little consideration to extending property rights to environmental resources (indeed, that idea would have seemed blasphemous to those environmental activists espousing a "This land is your land, this land is my land" ideology). The result was the rapid enactment of an array of laws governing air, water, and land pollution. The aim was to control the flow of energy and materials through the economy to prevent environmental harm. The complexity of such a cradle-to-gravemonitoring and control system is incredible. Moreover, federal environmental laws in the United States generally preempt state and local government rules. As a result, environmental policy became largely federalized and thoroughly politicized. The environmental slogan "Think globally, act locally!" has never been realized.

For example, the regulatory powers of the Environmental Protection Agency (EPA) are vast, with the power to control any activity that might pollute. Since, however, every process that converts energy or material into more human-friendly forms leaves some residue, this rule literally allows the EPA to regulate every economic activity. In effect, the EPA has become America's national economic planning agency, exercising more power than almost any other agency of government. Central planning, however, does not work. That point is now well understood in the economic world; it has yet to be realized in the environmental area. That is somewhat surprising, because ecological central planning is, if anything, an even more complex task. After all, the economic planner does have a metric to determine whether focusing on one sector or another is more likely to yield higher returns. Money provides a metric for evaluating alternative policies. There is no such metric in the environmental field. Not surprisingly, therefore, the EPA has encountered serious problems.

The EPA's problems are akin to those discussed earlier in the pasture example. The EPA has no ready means of establishing priorities. The EPA's priorities are based on ephemeral political concerns, and it makes little use of science and analysis.

Consider the problem of setting priorities. The EPA faces many claimants, none of whom can be ignored. Moreover, since there is no market for the various environmental resources being protected, there is no way for the claimants to bid among themselves to determine which goals should receive greatest emphasis. What is more important, African elephants or the ozone layer, recycling or population control, reducing trace elements in our water supply or increasing fuel efficiency? Priorities vary widely among individuals in the ecological area just as they do in the economic area. One of the chief virtues of the private economy is that it permits people to set priorities without any central planning agency. The challenge is to create a mechanism that would permit people to express their choices in the ecological sphere as well as they now do in the economic sphere. Absent property rights, this becomes incredibly complex.

Moreover, like all political entities, the EPA is subject to special interest lobbying. Most people lack the direct interest (the economic gains) needed to invest much time in environmental policy. Those active in such matters tend to be groups having an unusual economic or ideological stake in the outcome. The pressure groups that influence the EPA represent only a fraction of the diverse interests characterizing our complex society. The EPA will encounter primarily ideological environmentalists, along with business groups who find regulations a useful tool to tilt the playing field against their competitors. The likelihood that their combined voices are representative of the public interest is minimal. Nonetheless, the EPA listens to them and often heeds their advice. The current system clearly advances special interests not those of the public. Again, in effect, politicizing the environment does not resolve the tragedy of the commons. Rather, it institutionalizes it.

THE PATH NOT TAKEN: ASSESSING THE PRIVATIZATION OPTION

Some within the environmentalist community would agree with all of the above and, yet, still doubt whether private property approaches would prove superior in protecting environmental values. How, they ask, would extending private property advance environmental goals?

Wildlife ownership illustrates the rich potential of the privatization approach. Several African nations have realized that conservation laws were failing to protect their wildlife. Elephants, for example, were protected by national laws. But the enforcement of these laws given the value of ivory-was difficult. Moreover, many in the rural regions viewed poaching as a fully legitimate activity (recall that Robin Hood was a "poacher" after all). For rural Africans, elephants provided no positive gains; yet they often cost local villagers dearly, destroying crops and even killing people. Responding to this reality, several African nations elected to grant management responsibilities (a partial "ownership right") for the elephants to the local villagers. In effect, the local jurisdictions would decide (within limits) whether elephants should be killed or protected. Communities received money from the sale of ivory and meat, from the sale of limited licenses to hunt elephants, and from the tourism trade. They now had a direct financial incentive to manage elephant herds effectively, and that change brought about dramatic gains in elephant populations. Rather than complaints about "your" elephants creating damage, the tribes began to speak of "our" elephants needing protection. The countries that adopted this private management saw their elephant populations expand dramatically, while those that continued with the old central planning model of wildlife protection suffered further severe declines in their elephant herds.

To generalize from this example, we should make it possible for individuals and groups to come forward with their ideas on providing stewardship responsibilities for some valued environmental resource. That is, we should devise an "ecological adoption" statute to encourage the transfer of environmental resources to private hands. Adoption, after all, is the procedure by which individuals volunteer to become protectors—"parents"—of an abandoned child. The adoption process involves a review procedure to ensure that the prospective parents are qualified; if the petitioners are deemed worthy, then the parents become the stewards of the child. In effect, the child is transferred from state to private control.

Something akin to this could work to protect many environmental goods and values. Government agencies are stressed; they find it difficult to do all that is expected of them. A process allowing private citizens and groups to take some of the burden would be a valued step and would also allow some changes. The local community has greater knowledge and is better positioned to determine how best to manage the resource to ensure sustainable development. Steps to allow hunting and fishing clubs or shellfish or commercial fishing cooperatives to seek title over stretches of forests, rivers, and bays should be encouraged. In these cases, we should also ensure that the groups are granted the power to protect their property in the courts.

The second principle is that environmental issues should be resolved locally whenever possible. Uniform national rules result in spending far too much on controlling some emissions that create little problem-for example, controlling water pollution in periods when river flows are high and thus assimilative capacity great, and spending too little on controls during low flow periods, when emissions are likely to have a much greater impact. Local groups have greater knowledge about such trade-offs and are better positioned to monitor compliance. Each region should be free to make its own decisions on the appropriate trade-off between environmental and developmental matters.

The third principle emphasizes efforts to simplify the task of determining which polluters are damaging which regions of the country. A property rights-oriented approach would focus on ways to unravel the complex sequence of events that relate economic activities in one place to environmental damage in another.

The fourth feature focuses on the way in which privatization creates improved fencing and trespass enforcement technology. One example-barbed wire fences separating cattle-is indicative of the innovations needed. "Beepers" or computer chip implants that would signal the location of larger wildlife (manatees, whales, Siberian tigers) might well have value. Technologies also exist making it possible to determine the quantity and types of air pollution entering a region. Lasimetrics, for example, is a technology that can map atmospheric chemical concentrations from orbit. In time, that science might provide a sophisticated means of tracking transnational pollution flows. Most nations label high explosives manufactured in their countries as part of a worldwide antiterrorist program.

An excellent example of how private property better reconciles environmental and economic values is the Rainey Wildlife Refuge. This preserve, owned by a major environmental group, is located in the midst of vast natural gas and oil fields. Since the refuge was privately owned, development was at the discretion of its owner, the National Audubon Society. A "purist," no-development attitude would have lost the royalty payment of producing wells. Instead, the society elected to permit drilling under careful guidelines to reduce environmental damage. Economic and environmental gains to both parties resulted. The drillers obtained a valuable natural resource. The Audubon Society obtained revenue that could be used to better manage Rainey and other refuges. In contrast, the Audubon Society, along with most other U.S. environmental organizations, vigorously opposes energy development in the politically controlled Arctic National Wildlife Refuge. Absent a property stake in rational development, there is little reason to be rational.

The example of the English fishing club, the Pride of Derby (a river) illustrates how property rights can prevent stream pollution. In England, clubs own the right to fish along some rivers and are quick to respond to pollution threats. In the Derby case, a fishing club brought an action to stop an upstream municipality from polluting the stream. The courts viewed the issue from the property rights perspective; the municipality was harming the property of the fishing club and was required to modify its behavior. The court did not "balance the interests" of the fishing club against those of the city; rather, it enforced property rights.

In the United States, the ability of private parties such as fishing clubs to restrain municipal polluters is more limited. Under the Clean Water Act, the political authorities are told to "balance the interests" to decide what standards each polluter must meet. Not surprisingly, municipalities have been treated far more leniently than corporations. City cleanup targets are less stringent than those assigned industrial polluters; moreover, the cities are granted more lenient compliance schedules. In the political world, the status of the polluter determines the severity of the regulation. Politically preferred polluters are treated more leniently than are pariah polluters. Yet to the river and the fish, pollution is pollution.

Ownership of a pollution-sensitive species or area is a key strategy for environmental protection. By protecting privately owned fishing spots from pollution, the owners protect not only their portion of the river but also downstream areas. Similar ownership rights in oyster or shellfish beds, like those at Willapa Bay in Washington state, protect larger lakes and bays. As these examples suggest, partial ownership rights might suffice; even if only upstream or shoreline areas are privatized, the whole region can be protected.

Private ownership acts like a trip wire protecting the larger environmental commons because owners, by protecting their property, also incidentally act to protect downstream and offshore areas. For example, an owner who protects a species also protects its habitat.

Environmentalists sometimes talk about the "canary in the coal mine" safety rule. However, the canary is a far better warning signal when it has an owner that cares about it. Privatizing the commons creates multiple protections. This adoption strategy would do much to augment environmental protection efforts.

Note that the protection and conservation of groundwater is increasingly important. An advantage of the property rights approach is its flexibility. If the initial division of the property makes proper management difficult, the owner can restructure the property boundary. More than half of all drinking water now comes from aquifers. The problem is that aquifers are a classic commons. Each well drilled into the common pool benefits that owner but depletes the shared resource. Each surface property owner has a right to drill on her property. Exercising that right leads to excessive depletion and contamination.

However, new principles do not have to be devised from scratch since a similar problem has been solved routinely by the oil industry. Like an aquifer, an oil pool is an underground liquid resource subject to depletion and quality deterioration. To address this problem, the oil industry has developed a property rights restructuring program called *unitization,* which entails the assignment of all individual ownership rights in the common pool to a new entity (the unit). The unit manager then operates the field in an integrated fashion for the duration of production. Each owner receives a share of the income of the pool. Unitization illustrates the restructuring of already-existing property rights to allow more efficient management. Such reassignments of rights can be important for protecting and enhancing a resource. Unitization is not always easy. Still, it has been used successfully by the oil industry for many years. As groundwater becomes more valuable, the unitization approach might well be extended to management of groundwater.

Although many agree that command-and-control regulatory approaches to handling the problems found in environmental commons are costly and rarely achieve optimal goals, most still reject a property rights approach. For example, Harvard economist Robert Stavins states:

> *Does anyone really believe that acid rain can be efficiently controlled by assigning private property rights for U.S. airshed and then effecting negotiations among all affected parties? Economic-incentive mechanisms, on the other hand, avoid the impracticalities of the pure,*

private property approach, while retaining the merits of decentralized, market-driven policies.

Stavins is right that urban air pollution control poses one of the most difficult problems to advocates of enclosing environmental commons. But he minimizes the problems associated with "green" tax and quota programs and neglects the role that private property rights could play to control air pollutants. Conceptually, one can envision a town or political jurisdiction "owning" its airshed (much as many communities do own their watershed). Practically, there has been little examination of how such properties might be "fenced" or how "trespass" might be detected and prevented. Such problems have led most environmentalists to favor political airshed management. Note, however, that these technical difficulties are not made any easier by resorting to political management. Nor has the performance of the EPA in this area been brilliant. Still, a property rights scheme suggests some directions for reforming the management of pollutants in airsheds.

One approach would involve the use of automobile emissions charges. The municipalities in which pollution is a problem could test each car to determine its emission profile. This profile could be based on emissions per kilometer, and a windshield or bumper sticker (a red, yellow, or green circle, for example) indicating the emission class of that car could be required. The owner would pay an annual fee based on the miles driven in his pollution classification. Since, however, the data suggest that many of the cars fall out of tune, there should also be monitoring sites throughout the city (some mobile to catch evaders) to detect any car emitting outside its pollution classification. Violators would pay a fine and move to a higher annual fee category.

This program would encourage owners to maintain their cars more carefully. Moreover, emission performance would become one of the features sought when buyers are choosing among vehicles to purchase. If one drives mostly outside of cities, this emissions performance would not be important; if one were driving largely in cities, one might purchase a tightly controlled vehicle in order to avoid the pollution fees.

The most difficult environmental issues are global, such as the alleged greenhouse warming and ozone depletion. How serious these problems are is unclear. For many years into the future, the evidence will be ambiguous, but this is unlikely to make much difference to the policy debate. Despite the evidence to the contrary, many people are convinced that the Earth is warming, that such changes will have disastrous consequences, and that urgent global political action is needed to save Mother Earth (see chapter 1 on global warming). The major risk today is less global warming than it is that politicians might adopt antigrowth, antienergy policies.

A new layer of global regulation would be foolish. There is no reason to adopt solutions that will not work—and there is no prospect that international environmental bureaucracies will prove even as effective and reliable as their national counterparts.

How might the property rights approach be extended to the atmosphere? How might it be protected under the relatively weak rules of international property and liability law? Feasible answers are illusive. One approach is to consider the gradual evolution of private law into the international realm. In many areas, today one can make damage claims against foreign tortfeasors. Commercial liability treaties dealing with airlines, oil spills, and satellite disasters are examples of such arrangements.

Prevention, however, is not the only response to any postulated greenhouse warming. Given the uncertainties inherent in this area, the possibility that this effect might even prove beneficial on balance, and the difficulty in preventing a warming (were it valid), it would be wise to adopt a policy of resilience rather than avoidance. After all, the Earth is known to have thrived during warmer periods such as the Medieval Climatic Optimum, which occurred some 1,000 years ago. Besides, even substantial efforts to cut energy use are only likely to delay rather than prevent these changes. Rather than spend trillions of dollars that might, at best, delay inevitable changes, a better move would be to deregulate and privatize the economies of the world, reduce the barriers to wealth creation, and thereby make the world more prosperous, more technologically adept, and better able to weather whatever harms that might emerge. Greater wealth and more advanced technologies would make possible many measures that would make whatever climate change that occurs less onerous in any event.

CONCLUSION

In a world of private property, unpopular values can be protected. In the political world, an airshed, a fishery, or a rain forest can be protected only if it garners sufficient political support. The extent of environmental values and goods at risk in the modern world is vast. Yet there are fewer than 200 governments, many of which now find it hard even to protect their own citizens. There are, however, more than 6 billion people on this globe. Only if the collective instincts of these peoples-their interests, skills, and wealth-are enlisted in the environmental cause is any appreciable fraction of the natural environment likely to receive adequate protection. The best way to enlist them is by giving them a stake in the fate of the Earth, by enclosing the environmental commons and deeding them a portion of those resources.

The challenge then is not to restrict markets, or to segregate the natural world from the global economy, but rather to integrate the ecology and the economy. By extending the institutions of markets and private property throughout the world, humanity will gain the proper incentives to save nature and better ability to do so. Ocean reefs in the South Pacific, Andean mountaintops, elephants in Africa, the shoreline of Lake Baikal—all deserve stewards, property owners, who can protect them from misuse.

Enclosing the environmental commons will not be easy. To many, open-access rules appear more just, more equitable, even when such rules pose serious threats to a sustainable ecology and society. In part, this reflects humanity's tribal prehistory—we instinctually find it hard to reject communal management approaches that served us well for many hundreds of thousands of years. Moreover, corporations have vested interests in the status quo. Current environmental rules create a complex array of penalties and subsidies. Economic actors, while unsure about the fairness or justness of the current balance, will still fear that change might make things worse. Enclosing airsheds and rivers would mean that corporations would have to pay for services (disposing of residuals) that they now get for free.

Such antiprivatization values make it hard even to move purely economic resources into the private sector. It is especially difficult to convert an informal (communal, custom-based, extra-legal) system to a modern, formal legal system. Nothing is feasible if the change is not viewed as legitimate. Yet today, many would view such a shift toward property rights as immoral, whether it was effective in protecting the resource in question or not. For example, politics has stalled efforts to privatize resources like the electromagnetic spectrum and many declining fisheries. Peruvian economist Hernando De Soto has noted the strong cultural opposition to any efforts to legitimize informal property rights in land and structures in less-developed countries.

Since we have had far less experience with ecological privatization, opposition is even more fierce. The history of the past century, where environmental values were first overridden and then supposedly advanced by massive central political intervention in the economy, has created a difficult situation. Since most people do not understand the creative role of private action, their naive view is Malthusian: If there were only fewer of us, if we only consumed less, if only we innovated less rapidly, then our footprints would be lighter, our threat to the planet less severe. Such views in a world of more than 6 billion people, where many still lack basic necessities, are immoral and impractical.

Some ideological environmentalists might object that attempts to integrate people and nature further are inherently suspect and denigrating to nature itself. Nature should be wild and free—not fenced and owned. This is a vision left over from humanity's open-access, tribal prehistory. Environmental enclosure is the path not yet taken, but both practice and theory show that it offers the best way to protect and preserve nature while building sustainable societies.

Bootleggers and Baptists—
The Education of a Regulatory Economist

By Bruce Yandle

T HE SEARCH FOR regulatory relief is as young as the Reagan administration, and as old as man. When the American Medical Association chafes under Federal Trade Commission oversight, it feels the same frustration Adam must have felt at the menu regulations he faced in Eden. But often people want relief not from regulation but through the protections regulation can provide. Today, some airline executives want succor from the uncertainties they confront in a world without regulated (uniform) pricing. The London weavers felt that same way about their trade in the thirteenth century and obtained relief through a provision in the Magna Carta requiring all cloth woven in the realm to be of uniform dimensions-conforming to the London standard. Nothing is new under the sun.

Economists from Adam Smith on (and including Karl Marx) have realized that government regulation is a sword that cuts in both directions, and all have called for reforms to improve the good regulations and prune the bad. But desiring reform and achieving it are obviously two different things. What we want to find out here is under what circumstances they can coincide. When can we achieve regulatory reform?

REGULATION AND MURPHY'S LAW

In my studies of the relationships between governments and business, my attention was first attracted to the unbelievably costly things that governments do when attempting to control

Bruce Yandle is executive director of the Federal Trade Commission. The views expressed here are his own. It seemed, as Murphy might have said, that if there was a wrong way of doing something, the regulators would adopt it. I found countless cases where rules and regulations imposed tremendous costs while delivering little if any benefit.

- Freight rates for one class of shippers were subsidized by another class of shippers. As a result, factories were located on the basis of false signals, real costs were hidden, and goods were shipped great distances at lower fares to be processed in higher-cost plants.

- Catalytic converters were installed on automobiles for the purpose of reducing emissions. But, for the converters to operate properly, unleaded gas had to be used—and it is more expensive than regular. So cost-conscious drivers put leaded gas in their tanks, which turned the converters into so much junk and added more emissions to the environment than there would have been had engines been even slightly modified or some other plan introduced.
- Petrochemical plants were required to reduce emissions at each and every stack by the same percentage. If instead managers had been given plant-wide targets and left free to attain them efficiently, the same degree of pollution control could have been achieved at much lower cost.
- Petroleum companies that found oil on Alaska's North Slope and sought to bring it to the lower forty-eight states by way of the West Coast were barred from doing so by complex environmental rules. Logic would then have dictated that the oil be shipped to Japanese re-fineries, which could have returned the refined product to the United States. But that was against federal law too. Instead, the crude oil is being shipped from Alaska to Texas, where it is unloaded and refined, all at considerable extra cost.
- Precise fuel economy standards were prescribed for automakers, to prod them into building the kind of cars that probably would have been produced and purchased voluntarily if the price of gasoline had been higher. But the price of gasoline was regulated so it could not rise; and the automakers had to ration their larger cars, which U.S. buyers wanted, while forcing smaller cars into the market. Eventually, the price of gasoline was deregulated and the effects of the mandated fuel-economy scheme tended to evaporate-for the time being, at least.

The list could go on and on. Not only does government rarely accomplish its stated goals at lowest cost, but often its regulators seem dedicated to choosing the highest-cost approach they can find. Because of all this, I and others in academia became convinced years ago that a massive program in economic education was needed to save the world from regulation. If we economists could just teach the regulators a little supply and demand, countless billions of dollars would be saved.

BOOTLEGGERS AND BAPTISTS

My views began to change after I joined the Council on Wage and Price Stability in 1976. There my assignment was to review proposed regulations from the Environmental Protection Agency (EPA), the Federal Trade Commission (FTC), the Department of Transportation (DOT), and parts of the Department of Health, Education, and Welfare (HEW). The field was white unto the harvest, and I was ready to educate the regulators. But then I began to talk with some of them, and I began to hear from people in the industries affected by the rules. To my surprise, many regulators knew quite a bit about economics. Even more surprising was that industry representatives were not always opposed to the costly rules and occasionally were even fearful that we would succeed in getting rid of some of them. It was in considerable confusion that I returned later to my university post, still unable to explain what I had observed and square it with the economics I thought I understood.

That marked the beginning of a new approach to my research on regulation. First, instead of assuming that regulators really intended to minimize costs but somehow proceeded to make crazy mistakes, I began to assume that they were not trying to minimize costs at all—at least not the costs I had been concerned with. They were trying to minimize *their* costs, just as most sensible people do. And what are some of those costs that keep regulators from choosing efficient ways of, say, reducing emissions of hydrocarbons?

- *The cost of making a mistake.* Simple rules applied across the board require fewer decisions where mistakes can be made.
- *The cost of enforcement.* Again, simple rules requiring uniform behavior are easier to monitor and enforce than complex ones, and they also have a false ring of fairness.
- *Political costs.* A legislator is likely to be unhappy with regulators who fail to behave in politically prudent ways—who fail, in the legislator's view, to remember the industries and the workers in his area.

Second, I asked myself, what do industry and labor want from the regulators? They want protection from competition, from technological change, and from losses that threaten profits and jobs. A carefully constructed regulation can accomplish all kinds of anticompetitive goals of this sort, while giving the citizenry the impression that the only goal is to serve the public interest.

> ... What do industry and labor want from
> the regulators ? They want protection from
> competition, from technological change,
> and from losses that threaten profits and
> jobs.

Indeed, the pages of history are full of episodes best explained by a theory of regulation I call "bootleggers and Baptists." Bootleggers, you will remember, support Sunday closing laws that shut down all the local bars and liquor stores. Baptists support the same laws and lobby vigorously for them. Both parties gain, while the regulators are content because the law is easy to administer. Of course, this theory is not new. In a democratic society, economic forces will always play through the political mechanism in ways determined by the voting mechanism employed. Politicians need resources in order to get elected. Selected members of the public can gain resources through the political process, and highly organized groups can do that quite handily. The most successful ventures of this sort occur where there is an overarching public concern to be addressed (like the problem of alcohol) whose "solution" allows resources to be distributed from the public purse to particular groups or from one group to another (as from bartenders to bootleggers).

> ... The challenges of regulatory reform
> are institutional ... The fact that a regulation

has come into being as a result of a costly
political exchange means that reform
can hardly be gained easily.

What all this implies is that the challenges of regulatory reform are institutional. Regulation is relief for some and a burden for others, so that reform is a burden for some and a re-lief for others. The fact that a regulation has come into being as a result of a costly political exchange means that reform can hardly be gained easily. This is not to suggest that all is for naught, that there are no opportunities for reducing net (overall) regulatory costs or re-moving the protective regulatory cocoons woven so tightly and carefully around this activity and that. But it is to say that we can scarcely expect full-scale deregulation to occur often. Not when the Baptists and the bootleggers vote together.

SHOCKING THE SYSTEM: PARETO-PAPERWORK

Let us accept for the moment the proposition that all regulation produced in a given period has value at least sufficient to justify the direct costs borne by those supporting it. Since those who opposed a given regulation most probably fought it, rather than allowing it to proceed by default, we will not assume that the value of the regulation exceeds the total costs incurred by the winners, losers, and regulators.

Now consider an equilibrium state in which the political-economic market has produced a given quantity of regulation and will continue to maintain it unless there is an out-side shock to the system. Imagine that you are regulatory czar, subject to all the economic forces at play in the system (other activities and actions being held constant) and with a free rein to reform the regulatory process. Finally, to make the situation more interesting (and more illuminating), imagine also that you are a long-suffering student of the regulatory system, with a long list of regulations you are convinced cannot be justified at all, or at least not in their present form. What would you do?

Regulatory paperwork would likely be your best candidate for reform-for it is an area where you might be able to reduce costs for both the regulated and the regulators (making both better off, no one worse off, in a kind of Pareto move), without disturbing the equilibrium state established by the interplay of rules and regulations. Of course, reducing paperwork is not nearly so dramatic as deregulating the airlines, speeding up new drug approvals, or re-moving import quotas (supposing any of these appealed to you). Still, it would not be a minor ac-complishment. The cumulative savings from paperwork reduction for the years 1981 through 1983 are expected to reach 300 million hours. If you managed that as czar, we might well rise up and call your name blessed.

Unfortunately, other reforms would be much more difficult. Remember that you must act within the existing political forces, that the actors in the drama are all well-informed, and that the existing equilibrium is the product of a massive struggle.

Changes in the Demand for Regulation.

So, let us ask, how might you upset that equilibrium by creating new players or causing the current players to acquire an interest in deregulation. Put differently, what factors might shift the demand for regulation?

- *Technological change.* A technology protected or even induced by regulation can nonetheless become obsolete, and the regulated businesses can find themselves hamstrung by the very rules that protected them.
- *Demographic change.* With migration and population growth, patterns of production and distribution supported by regulation can become So costly over time that the producer chooses to throw back the protective blanket.
- *Significant changes in factor costs.* Regulated firms generally seek regulations that fit production arrangements based on predicted prices for labor, materials, and capital-which means that unpredicted changes in those prices can alter the amount and incidence of the benefits of regulation.
- *New information.* With increasing scholarly and press attention to regulatory issues, voter/taxpayer/consumer groups might discover that their benefits from regulation are less than their costs.

Looking down the roster of successful regulatory reforms, it is not difficult to find cases that can be explained in part or as a whole by some combination of the above factors. For example, take the impact of technological change on the AT&T monopoly. Microwave, computer, and satellite technology outstripped the basic "hard-wire" systems used in Bell's telephone operations, creating competitive opportunities and weakening the demand for monopoly privilege. The field of action that had been created partly by inventions of the major telephone companies, yet barred to them, came to offer greater opportunities for growth and profit than the older regulated field. Technological change was also a crucial factor in banking and finance. The electronic transmission of funds, coupled with the Federal Reserve Board's dominant position in the check-clearing process, contributed significantly to a new technical base for financial institutions. This development, along with the unexpectedly high interest rates that commercial banks and savings and loans were barred from paying, made the old regulatory structure obsolete.

Changes in two other demand factors arguably undermined the traditional regulatory framework in trucking and other surface transportation. The unexpected increase in the price of energy magnified the costs associated with circuitous routes and empty backhauls, and changing population patterns made old route structures less desirable. Both developments fueled the demand for reform. Finally, take air-line deregulation. In this case, it was rising energy prices, changing patterns of equipment utilization, and population shifts-combined with the development of new aircraft and intensive reporting of research on the effects of these changes-that shifted the demand for regulation.

As for future reforms, what might we predict on this same basis? Two come to mind. First, like AT&T, the U.S. Postal Service has stuck to an obsolete technology. With electronic transmission of messages, arguments about natural monopoly status have lost any credibility they may have once had and, for that reason among others, the statutes barring competition in the delivery of first class mail are under increasing fire. Energy regulation is another likely candidate for reform. Technical change and rapidly shifting relative prices have placed enormous pressures on existing regulatory structures, so that producers and consumers are now seeking greater flexibility than the present "public utility" status of much of the industry will allow. For example, the need for appropriate incentives to increase the amount of natural gas delivered to the market is widely recognized, and alternative systems for pricing and arranging the distribution of electricity are being explored. (Here, at least, we may have found one beneficial aftereffect of OPEC and its works.)

Changes in the Supply of Regulation.

The supply side of regulation, like the demand side, helps determine the quantity of regulation produced in political-economic markets. Among the variables here are the bureaucracy and the electoral and legislative process.

- *Bureaucratic incentives and structure.* If lawyers and economists can improve their expected lifetime earnings by filing enforcement actions against specific industries, for example, those actions will tend to be filed. More broadly, how agencies are organized (whether they are independent commissions or headed by a single administrator), what voting rules are applied in making decisions, to what extent the agency specializes in an industry or product, and whether there is competition from other agencies for jurisdiction are traditionally thought to affect the supply of regulation.
- *Congressional oversight.* The legislative component of the supply side is closely related to demand, since elected officials also represent special interests who seek regulatory benefits. But, even so, the competition among legislators, their voting rules, and their committee organization are supply characteristics.

Assuming that demand is held constant, to what extent will changes in these supply-side characteristics affect the quantity or quality of regulations produced? For example, will a reduction in the number of commissioners (as is happening now at the FCC) , or a shift in the party mix of agency oversight committees, cause regulation to change?

Empirical research suggests strongly that the supply side matters. For example, Barry Weingast and Mark Moran report that, contrary to some opinions, the FTC's regulatory behavior mirrors the conservative-liberal makeup of the agency's key congressional committees: in other words, the agency is hardly ever "out of control" (Regulation, May/June 1982). Roger Faith, Donald R. Leavens, and Robert Tollison find that the FTC has been less likely to take actions against firms headquartered in the districts of congressmen who sit on the FTC's congressional committees than against firms not so favorably situated (*Journal of Law and Economics*, October 1982). My recent research on the FTC suggests that the agency's behavior is influenced not only by shifts in the chairman-ship from a Democrat to a Republican and vice versa, but also by shifts in how the chairman is chosen (in 1950 the method was changed from rotation to presidential designation).

… There are strong possibilities for regulatory reform when the institutions involved are changing for other reasons …

Putting all this together, we may say that there are strong possibilities for regulatory re-form when the institutions involved are changing for other reasons anyway. Such changes would help explain the flurry of deregulation initiatives at the FCC, especially those dealing with broadcasting, as well as the shift away from industry-wide rulemaking and structural antitrust investigations at the FTC. Moreover, the cautious attitude now shown by the Justice Department and the FTC when considering price discrimination, resale price maintenance, and vertical combinations, along with the probing economic analysis applied in such investigations, reflect new learning in law and economics and changes in the structure of the two agencies. Indeed, the significant overall reduction in new regulatory initiatives across the entire federal government reflects a coordinated effort that draws on each of the items mentioned.

OTHER AGENTS OF CHANGE

So far I have hardly mentioned yet another interest group: those who gain special satisfaction from participating in the regulatory process in ways that will improve economic efficiency. While some might conclude that students of the process can only observe, record, and analyze, I have a more sanguine view: simply put, people and their ideas do make a difference.

Some individuals, for example, make a difference by continuing to raise questions about grand principles-overall social efficiency, the appropriate role of government, economic freedom, the virtues of the price system. The more articulate and informed of these point out the compromises being made by the rest of us. Of equal importance are those whose goal is to understand how the regulatory process works, what interests are driving it, and how its out-come might be predicted. These are the academic researchers, the public policy analysts, the economists with private firms and in government, who struggle to bring about marginal adjustments. Their task is the creative application of economic logic. At yet a third level, there is active participation in decision making itself. When I observed the effect of an Alfred Kahn at the CAB, a Darius Gaskins at the ICC, and a James Miller at the FTC—to say nothing of the less visible but nonetheless significant work performed by scores of others in the arena where decisions are made—I must believe they make a difference, a very great difference.

Finally, one should not expect to see sudden and widespread transformation in regulation. Like all market processes, the market for regulation is relatively stable, the result of thousands of transactions and years of institutional development. Yet, also like other markets, the forces of supply and demand do change, and the agents for change can and do have marginal but significant impact on political demand and regulatory supply. Bootleggers and Baptists may have been agitating for a century or more, but the saloon is still with us-and usually on Sundays, too.

Resolving the Tragedy of the Commons by Creating Private Property Rights in Wildlife

By Robert J. Smith

DURING MAN'S RELATIVELY brief existence on this planet, he has relied on the bounty of its flora and fauna for his existence. He has harvested wildlife for food, clothing, shelter, medicines, beasts of burden, pets, and companionship. Over most of this period, this harvesting and exploitation had little impact on those resources. Human population was very low, and most animal and plant populations were relatively large. Animal and plant communities, populations, and species that became extinct did so from other than human causes. Only in recent centuries has man's exploitation of wildlife begun to have a deleterious effect. This was the result of rapid population growth, more efficient means of capture and kill, and expansion into new continents, especially islands and tropical areas where many species of wildlife had evolved with small, localized populations and without contact with man or his camp followers, such as dogs, cats, and rats. Western exploration and colonization quickly created serious problems of overharvesting and over-exploitation of wildlife and led to a slow development of human-caused extinctions.

However, there is increasing evidence that primitive man also had a profound impact on many species. Humans did not live in the idyllic harmony with nature that has been so rapturously portrayed by the more romantic environmentalists who question the direction of modern life and call for a new environmental ethic. At least some of the large mammals, such as mammoths and mastodons, that roamed the earth during the Pleistocene Epoch and immediately thereafter and whose disappearance has been attributed to natural causes, were forced into extinction by primitive men with primitive tools. They drove herds over cliffs, into swamps, or into box canyons, often setting massive grassland fires to assist in the drive.

It would appear that precivilized, or at least preindustrial, man exploited wildlife just as carelessly and as effectively as does modern man. The mythologized American Indians also used wasteful and ecologically unsound methods of hunting and killing. Regarding the Plains Indians' exploitation of the buffalo, Baden, Stroup, and Thurman point out that it is generally held that these highly diverse groups shared a common reverence for the land and the interdependencies of nature that provided man his niche ... The actual behavior attributed to these cultures reads like an admonition from Francis of Assisi, the patron saint of the ecology movement.

Prior to the introduction of the horse, the hunting of bison was uncertain, and relatively unproductive. In the pre-horse period the capture of a buffalo was comparatively rare. Its biomass was highly valued and hence fully utilized.

In effect, the introduction of the horse, steel tools and later firearms lowered the price of the animal. As the price fell due to technological adaptation, patterns of utilization changed dramatically. During this period many buffalo were killed by Indians merely for the tongue and the two strips of back strap. By 1840 the Indian had driven the buffalo from portions of its original habitat.

It is not true, however, that the Indians' "wasteful" use of wildlife occurred after the introduction of white man's tools. There is abundant evidence that the Indians engaged in wasteful harvesting methods whenever the opportunity arose. Long before they had horses and rifles, the Plains tribes regularly set vast prairie fires in the late summer and fall in order to stampede buffalo herds over cliffs or bluffs. "A successful drive produced a large number of carcasses, often more than could be used before the meat spoiled ... At a large kill much of the meat spoiled before it could be processed." Fires were so commonly used that millions of acres were blackened each year. The Washo tribe of the Great Basin lived in an extremely hostile environment, barely eking out a precarious existence, yet, during the fall they would drive such enormous numbers of jackrabbits into their nets that after the skins were taken, the meat was left to rot.

Over-exploitation of wildlife is not a peculiar characteristic of Western man, nor is it a consequence of some form of the modern economic system or the much maligned "commerce" so frequently condemned by environmentalists. Whenever and wherever there have been incentives to overharvest or deplete wildlife it has taken place, whether by primitive or modern man.

While the environmental movement comprises a diverse amalgamation of different groups, with concerns ranging from visual "pollution" such as clear-cuts, to chemical- and smoke-induced damage to human health, the glue that binds the groups is wildlife conservation and preservation. Even here there is a wide and growing chasm among organizations. The more "conservative" groups are interested in wildlife management, such as increasing the numbers of commonly hunted species of fish and game. The "middle-of-the-roaders" are interested in developing sustained-yield management programs for species where it is clear that wise management and international cooperation can achieve better results than ending all harvesting. The "liberals" push for an end to the exploitation of most species and a complete ban on all trade in most threatened wildlife. Finally, there are the animal rights groups, the "radicals," who value the rights of animals to life and liberty at least as highly as human rights.

The growth, influence, and public support of these organizations has increased rapidly over the past two decades. Since 1970, conservationists have painted a dismal picture of an increasing struggle for survival of wildlife, with one species after another being pushed to the brink of extinction. There is no doubt that human-caused extinctions are occurring at an increasing rate and generating momentum for the environmental movement.

Norman Myers treats the problem of disappearing species in considerable detail and emphasizes the accelerated rate of extinction:

> At least 90% of all species that have existed have disappeared. But almost all of them have gone under by virtue of natural processes. Only in the recent past, perhaps from around 50,000 years ago, has man exerted much influence. As a primitive hunter, man probably proved himself capable of eliminating species, albeit as a relatively rare occurrence. From the year A.D. 1600, however, he became able, through advancing technology, to overhunt animals to extinction in just a few years, and to disrupt extensive environments just as rapidly. Between the years 1600 and 1900, man eliminated around seventy-five known species ... Since 1900 man has eliminated around another seventy-five known species ... The rate from the year 1600 to 1900, roughly one species every 4 years, and the rate during most of the present century, about one species per year, are to be compared with a rate of possibly one per 1,000 years during the "great dying" of the dinosaurs.

Since 1960, human population growth and worldwide development have greatly accelerated the extinction rate, which may have reached 1,000 species per year by 1975. Myers projects that by the late 1980s it may reach one species per hour.[2] This is, indeed, a dismal picture, and it is important to recognize that it is not merely small and local populations of wildlife that have suffered. Many animal species that have disappeared or have been drastically reduced were at one time found in truly enormous numbers.

The passenger pigeon, which was native to North America, was once probably the most numerous species of bird on earth. At its peak, its population may have numbered around 3 billion. Its migrating flocks darkened the skies over towns and cities and sounded like an approaching tornado, yet they were extinct by 1914, mainly because of massive market-hunting. A similar fate befell the great auk, a large, flightless seabird that nested in vast numbers on islands in the North Atlantic. It was exterminated by whalers and fishermen who slaughtered it for food, eggs, feathers, and oil.

Many other species that survived over-exploitation, although often only barely so, were slaughtered in equally staggering numbers. The Spanish explorers described the buffalo herds as a limitless "brown sea." At one time, 75 million roamed the western plains, but by 1895 there were little more than 800 left, most in captivity or on private ranches. Vast flocks of ducks, geese, prairie chickens, and shorebirds were decimated by market hunters to provide relatively inexpensive meat for the large cities. Naturalist Frank Graham, Jr., points out:

> In 1873 Chicago markets bought 600,000 prairie chickens at $3.25 a dozen. Frank M. Chapman, the ornithologist, recalled as a boy in the 1870s the glut of prairie

chickens in the butcher shops … By the end of the century he had to travel to the sand hills of Nebraska to find them in any numbers.

It is obvious, however, that not all natural resources or wildlife have disappeared or even been seriously depleted. Environmentalists, journalists, and writers draw our attention to the most shocking cases. But there are many species that are more common today than they were at any previous time. Many plant and animal species exist in large numbers today that were not present in North America before the arrival of the white man. Furthermore, certain animals and plants are thriving under some specific ownership and management conditions but vanishing under other conditions. It is extremely important to examine these cases in order to understand why over-exploitation of some resources and wildlife takes place and why other living or renewable resources are managed on a self-sustaining basis.

Why are some species disappearing and others thriving? First, we can examine what is disappearing and what is not. Apparently, few environmentalists have taken the time to do this in their haste to catalog extinct and vanishing species. It is true that the prairie chicken nearly vanished—the heath hen is extinct, the Atwater's greater prairie chicken has been reduced to endangered species status, and the rest are uncommon, localized, and greatly reduced in numbers—but what about other chickens? Why is the Atwater's greater prairie chicken on the endangered species list but not the Rhode Island Red, the Leghorn, or the Barred Rock? These chickens are not even native American birds. They came to this continent with the first European settlers, and the small flocks at the settlement in Jamestown, Virginia, in 1607 became the basis for a broiler industry that produces 3 billion birds a year.

Similar questions can be asked: Why was the American buffalo nearly exterminated but not the Hereford, the Angus, or the Jersey cow? Why are salmon and trout habitually overfished in the nation's lakes, rivers, and streams, often to the point of endangering the species, while the same species thrive in fish farms and privately owned lakes and ponds? Why do cattle and sheep ranchers overgraze the public lands but maintain lush pastures on their own property? Why are rare birds and mammals taken from the wild in a manner that often harms them and depletes the population, but carefully raised and nurtured in aviaries, game ranches, and hunting preserves? Which would be picked at the optimum ripeness, blackberries along a roadside or blackberries in a farmer's garden? In all of these cases, it is clear that the problem of over-exploitation or overharvesting is a result of the resource's being under public rather than private ownership. The difference in their management is a direct result of two totally different forms of property rights and ownership: public, communal, or common property vs. private property. Wherever we have public ownership we find overuse, waste, and extinction; but private ownership results in sustained-yield use and preservation. Although it may be philosophically or emotionally pleasing to environmentalists to persist in maintaining that wildlife, the oceans, and natural resources belong to mankind, the inevitable result of such thinking is the opposite of what they desire.

Harold Demsetz defines communal ownership as

a right which can be exercised by all members of the community … The community denies … to individual citizens the right to interfere with any person's exercise of communally-owned rights. Private ownership implies that the community recognizes the right of the owner to exclude others from exercising the owner's private rights ... Suppose that land is communally owned ... If a person seeks to maximize the value of his communal rights, he will tend to overhunt and overwork the land because some of the costs of his doing so are borne by others. The stock of game and the richness of the soil will be diminished too quickly ...

If a single person owns the land, he will attempt to maximize its present value by taking into account alternative future time streams of benefits and costs and selecting that one which he believes will maximize the present value of his privately-owned land rights ... It is very difficult to see how the existing communal owners can reach an agreement that takes account of these costs.

It is important to recognize that this distinction between the destructive overuse of common property resources and careful sustained-yield use of private property resources does not merely apply to a comparison of wild with domesticated populations of plants and animals.

Common property problems involving wildlife have been especially prevalent in America, and they continue to be extremely vexing precisely because of American wildlife law. The President's Council on Environmental Quality has stressed that "under U.S. law, native wildlife belongs to the people; it is not private property, even on private land." Victor B. Scheffer points out that

wildlife in the United States is the property of the people ... No animal may be reduced to private ownership except by permission of the state. Wild animals do not belong to the owner of the land upon which the animals live, though the owner can post his land against entry and thus restrain the public from using its property.

In Europe, native wildlife often belongs to private landowners or is managed under a combination of private and public property. Some European countries have fewer problems of over-exploitation of wildlife, regardless of population pressures and economic and political systems. In other words, we find precisely what economic analysis has predicted about the treatment of common property and private property wildlife resources.

The salmon fishery provides a nearly perfect example of the differences between private and common property management. Salmon are anadromous fish. They hatch in the clear, shallow waters of the upper reaches of rivers, go downstream to the sea where they grow to maturity, and then return upstream to spawn another generation in the same rivers where they were hatched. Management of a fishery should be a relatively low-cost operation because the only requirements are to maintain a high-quality spawning environment and to prevent overfishing. The fish don't need to be fed because they grow to maturity in the sea and return as a highly valuable source of protein.

Yet most of the salmon in the United States have either disappeared from their ancestral rivers or are being rapidly depleted precisely as a result of their being treated as part of the common heritage. As a common property resource, they belong to everyone, can be caught by everyone, and essentially belong to no one. They run a gantlet of competing users at every stage of their migration. They are sought at sea by commercial fishing boats, off the river mouths by sports fishermen, in the rivers by netting operations, and upstream by rod fishermen and Indians, all of whom are interested in taking all the salmon they can before others do. In addition, foreign fishing fleets take all the salmon they can beyond the 200-mile limit. Furthermore, the rivers are also common property; dams and logging operations often make them impassable, and pollution makes them uninhabitable.

Because no one owns the salmon, each user is pitted against all other users, and the result has been a rapid depletion of the stock. As each group catches fewer fish, they turn to the government for special legislation that will limit, control, and regulate the catch and the fishing techniques used by their competitors. As a result, fishing techniques have become increasingly inefficient and costly. But this still does not prevent overfishing.

Douglass C. North and Roger LeRoy Miller have commented on the alarming decline of the Bristol Bay salmon fishery in Alaska.

> In an attempt to reverse the trend, regulations over the season, fishing hours, boats, and gear increased in complexity.

> Naturally, the results in real life are more like a nightmare than a fairy tale. Fishermen are poor because they are forced to use inefficient equipment and to fish only a small fraction of the time, and of course there are far too many of them. The consumer pays a much higher price for red salmon than would be necessary if efficient methods were used. Despite the ever-growing intertwining bonds of regulations, the preservation of the salmon run is still not assured.

> The root of the problem lies in the current non-ownership arrangement. It is not in the interests of any individual fisherman to concern himself with perpetuation of the salmon run. Quite the contrary: It is rather in his interests to catch as many fish as he can during any one season.

The consequence of treating the salmon as common property has been to destroy the salmon resource and to waste economic resources through regulations. John Baden describes the results:

> The regulatiors are such that it is increasingly more difficult and more expensive to obtain salmon ... The state and federal regulations are now such that salmon ... have a negative social value, if one includes the cost of government management of the industry. Given current institutions, society would be better off if the salmon disappeared; it costs society more to get a salmon than it is worth for food.

The environmental literature has reported at length on the sad plight of the salmon fisheries; but many authors appear either to be unaware of common property theory or, worse, to ignore it because it clashes with their philosophical view that wildlife should belong to everyone. So we continue to read their attacks on profit-seekers, free enterprise, big business, and a consumptionist lifestyle. And we continue to watch the salmon disappear.

Fortunately, salmon are a highly desirable fish, and American entrepreneurs are attempting to remove them from the common property trap, even though they generally run afoul of our wildlife laws, which act to prevent private property solutions. Obviously, under a common property system, there is no incentive for any user to restock the fishery by creating a private hatchery because everyone else would merely receive a cost-free benefit from his investment. But attempts at salmon mariculture or farming are being made where private owners can avoid the problem of having their fish migrate along common property rivers.

One such effort is being made by Bay Center Mariculture Company in Washington State. Until recently, raising salmon in ponds in order to market them for profit was not permitted in Washington, although taxpayer-supported state fish hatcheries were used to help alleviate over-exploitation. Bay Center reports:

> It has been discovered in recent years that salmon go through their early development and growth much faster in brackish water than in the fresh water we are accustomed to expect them in during their early life … We take advantage of this by both sea-farming salmon and raising them to market size in controlled ponds. Because of the specificity of salmon to return to the spot of their birth, it is possible to release them at an early age and allow them to mature in the sea and return to the hatchery site a year earlier than they would if raised in nature in freshwater streams. The expected return is a very small percentage, but still very profitable.

In 1977 Weyerhauser initiated a similar system in southern Oregon, where the young salmon will be raised in ponds at the head of a bay and then released into the bay, whence they will go out to sea. They will not be able to prevent fishermen from catching the returning salmon at the mouth of the bay, but Weyerhauser expects to make a profit if one percent of the adult salmon return to the company's fish ladders. In the wild, approximately 2 to 5 percent of the salmon survive to return to their spawning grounds.

Such programs not only solve wildlife conservation problems at private rather than at taxpayer expense, but they reduce the take on the wild common property populations and, as a positive externality, provide food for the wild food chain.

Outside the United States we find a strikingly different situation. In Iceland and in some northern European countries, the salmon fishery is in much healthier shape because the rights to the salmon or the salmon rivers are privately owned. Some of the finest stretches of rivers are owned or leased by individuals, groups of fishermen, or fishing lodges, and the salmon are not overfished. It is in the economic self-interest of the resource owners to conserve the salmon. Limits are effectively placed on the number of fish that can be caught, enough fish are released to maintain a healthy population, and the owners carefully protect their streams and see that agricultural and grazing activities do not adversely affect the quality of the water.

In Iceland private property rights have also been extended to the common eider, a large sea-dwelling duck of the North Atlantic. The eider supplies meat, eggs, and especially eiderdown (a brownish down under the breast feathers of the female that she plucks for her nest to insulate the eggs) for the farmers and local populations. As early as 1281, the civil and ecclesiastical codes stated that the eiders "belong to the occupiers of the lands where they occurred." The farmers have protected the eider nesting colonies for centuries and actually farm them. Robin W. Doughty writes:

> Skuli Magnusson, pioneer agriculturalist and industrialist, and others, who protected and farmed the nesting places of wild eiders for down and eggs, promoted the concept of farming. In the 1770s, Magnusson protected a very large colony on the island of Videy, where reportedly he gathered and cleaned about 90 pounds of down from his "favorite" birds. On a visit to the same place in 1810, Sir George MacKenzie noted that eider ducks were "assembled in great numbers to nestle," and that severe penalties were imposed on persons killing them.

The number of such farming operations grew during the nineteenth century and peaked during the 1920s, when there were more than 250 farms. Because many farmers have moved into towns, the number of farms has declined, currently totaling about 200, and eiderdown production is now about half of its peak figures. One result of this decline has been an increase in predation on the eiders by gulls, ravens, and feral mink and fox. Even though the number of wild predators has increased, the eider are still carefully protected on the existing farms, where property owners shoot and poison predators.

Iceland's management of the wild eider as a private property resource has been a great success. The private eider farms have benefited both the property owners and the eider population. The farmers have protected the birds from over-exploitation, from poachers, and from natural predators. They have also created artificial nesting sites in which the female will nest. The combined provision of protected nesting areas and artificial nesting sites has served to maintain a thriving population.

The individual self-interest of private property owners has caused them to protect and carefully manage a valuable wildlife resource. Because private property rights were extended to the wild eider, the harvesters of eiderdown and eider eggs were allowed to manage the resource in a nonconsumptive and nondestructive manner. If they had killed the eider to obtain the down, they would have been killing the fabled golden goose. Instead, they harvested the resource on a sustained-yield basis and realized a far greater return.

If the eider had been treated as a common property resource, the only way the Icelanders could have captured any economic value from the resource would have been to take all they could before other users did the same. It would not have been profitable to wait for the eider to line their nests with down; someone else might have collected it first. The rational course of action for each user would have been to kill the eider and immediately appropriate all of the down. It also would not have been in anyone's self-interest to invest in conservation programs, such as nest site construction or predator control. All of the other down collectors would have benefited from the actions of the conservationist. We would have seen the creation of a new fable: "Who killed the eider that provided the golden down?"

It is also instructive to compare wildlife ownership and management in Great Britain with that in the United States. Throughout much of British history, the right to harvest wildlife belonged to owners of the land. For centuries landowners in England were entitled by law to the wildlife on their lands. This was supported by "qualification statutes," which determined the amount of land or income that was necessary in order to have the right to own and harvest game. The landowner owned the game, and he had the right to what was supported by his land. It was recognized that the economic incentives engendered by the right to own wildlife often led the landowners not to use their land for agricultural purposes that would be harmful to wildlife. To the extent that wildlife was valued as a source of economic gain, or even of hunting pleasure, wildlife would be protected, and it would be hunted on a sustained-yield basis to ensure the preservation of breeding stock and the continuous replenishment of the population. Landowners even employed gamekeepers who managed the game, protecting it against predators, preserving habitat, and guarding against poachers.

The evidence indicates that there have been far fewer problems of vanishing wildlife in Britain than in the United States. We can still witness the benefits of the private ownership system in the management of Britain's most famous game bird, the red grouse. The opening of grouse season each August is reverently referred to as the "Glorious Twelfth." So highly prized and desired are the grouse that restaurants throughout the London area compete to see which can deliver the first meal of grouse. Commercial airlines, private jets, and even helicopters are used in the race, and the resulting roast grouse may cost $85.

The grouse are clearly a valuable resource, and they provide a substantial income to the landowners of the great estates in Scotland, where wealthy hunters gather to participate in the hunts. Reservations for the shoots are required well in advance, and social status and wealth may be necessary in order to hunt on the best and most productive lands. Landowners obviously have incentives to carefully manage the grouse on a sustained-yield basis, to keep the habitat in prime condition, to prevent the heather from being burned, to control predators, and to keep out poachers. As a result, the birds are not overexploited, in spite of heavy shooting and even though commercial marketing is allowed. Compare the results of this system with the over-exploitation of the American prairie chicken.

Unfortunately, because so much of the ownership of land in Britain, especially the great estates, was based on government grants of privilege, the landowner's property right to wildlife increasingly came under attack as a special privilege accorded to the wealthy. In the eighteenth century, the great egalitarian and democratic debates over property rights in land and wildlife resulted in America's rejection of the English system. Private property rights in wildlife and game were viewed as part of an undemocratic system emanating from government grants to the ruling classes. But in rejecting them, Americans threw out the baby with the bath water. The English system was attacked because it supposedly benefited the rich at the expense of the poor, and it was held that wildlife in America should belong to all. From the earliest time American law adopted a policy of "free taking," which recognized everyone's right to take game. Only the law of trespass kept anyone from entering another's property, and its efficacy was severely restricted by the requirement that the land be posted against hunting if the owner wanted exclusive use of it.

Thomas A. Lund essentially approves of the egalitarian approach to wildlife law. Nevertheless, he states:

> Early American law sought to dispatch the antidemocratic vices of its legacy while at the same time to preserve the system's virtues ... Following these seemingly harmless improvements to the English system, American wildlife populations fell as if afflicted by a plague. While the incursion of new settlers into habitat played a role in this decline, subsequent proof that wildlife can coexist and even thrive alongside agricultural development shows that the spread of primitive farming and ranching does not bear principal responsibility. Instead the affliction upon wildlife must be attributed to a surprising source: those democratic policies that were injected into wildlife law. Their unforeseen impact was to undercut totally the bases upon which English wildlife law had been so effective.

Another especially illustrative example of private property rights in wildlife appears in the Montagnais Indians of Quebec and Labrador. The Montagnais dwelled in the forests of the Labrador Peninsula, hunting such fur-bearing animals as caribou, deer, and beaver. They treated wildlife as a common property resource, with everyone sharing in the bounty of the hunt. Because game was plentiful and the Indian population was relatively low, the common property resource system was able to work. "The externality was clearly present. Hunting could be practiced freely and was carried on without assessing its impact on other hunters. But these external effects were of such small significance that it did not pay anyone to take them into account."

However, with the arrival of the French fur traders in the 1600s, the demand for beaver began to rise rapidly. As the value of the furs rose, there was a corresponding increase in the exploitation of the resource. Increasing use of the common property resource would have led to over-exploitation of the beaver. However,

> With the beaver increasing in value, scarcity, depletion, and localized extinction could be predicted under the existing system of property rights. But unlike the buffalo, virtually condemned to extinction as common property, the beaver were protected by the evolution of private property rights among the hunters. By the early to mid-18th century, the transition to private hunting grounds was almost complete and the Montagnais were managing the beaver on a sustained-yield basis.

It was a highly sophisticated system. The Montagnais blazed trees with their family crests to delineate their hunting grounds, practiced retaliation against poachers and trespassers, developed a seasonal allotment system, and marked beaver houses.

Animal resources were husbanded. Sometimes conservation practices were carried on extensively. Family hunting territories were divided into quarters. Each year the family hunted in a different quarter in rotation, leaving a tract in the center as a sort of bank, not to be hunted over unless forced to do so by a shortage in the regular tract.

This remarkably advanced system lasted for over a century and certainly served to prevent the extinction of the beaver. Unfortunately, more whites entered the region and began to treat the beaver as a common property resource, trapping them themselves rather than trading with the Indians, and the beaver began to disappear. Finally, the Indians were forced to abandon their private property system and joined the whites in a rapid over-exploitation of the beaver. Baden, Stroup, and Thurman sum up this sorry return to a common property system:

> With the significant intrusion of the white trapper in the 19th century, the Indians property rights were violated. Because the Indian could not exclude the white trapper from the benefits of conservation both joined in trapping out the beaver … In essence, the Indians lost their ability to enforce property rights and rationally stopped practicing resource conservation.

Another example of how private ownership can successfully preserve wildlife is found on game ranches, hunting preserves, safari parks, and animal and bird farms. Many of these private ventures, especially the game ranches, were established to generate profits from private hunting. Consequently, there has been a tremendous outcry from environmentalists and conservationists because the animals are raised for profit and some of them are killed. Yet, if emotional responses can be put aside, it seems clear that these game ranches produce many positive results. Many of the animals they stock are rapidly disappearing in their native countries because of pressures resulting from a rapidly expanding human population. Native habitats are disappearing through the encroachment of agriculture, cattle grazing, timber harvesting, and desertification arising from over-exploitation of common property water resources, overgrazing of grasslands, and over-utilization of brush, scrub, and trees for firewood and shelter. So serious are these problems and so insoluble under a common property system that there is little hope of saving many species of wildlife in the developing countries. Indeed, some of the more spectacular and most sought-after big-game mammals may now have healthier and more stable populations on some of the game ranches than in their native countries.

As human population growth accelerates throughout the Third World, as annual incomes hover at the subsistence level, and as rising costs of petroleum and agricultural fertilizers and chemicals continue to compound the misery, fewer and fewer internal resources will be available to preserve wildlife. In spite of the noble intentions of India and some African and South American nations to preserve their vanishing wildlife, there are few signs of any real accomplishments. Impoverished people have little patience with elephants rampaging through their meager crops or with lions, cheetahs, and leopards preying on their livestock. Poachers take a terrible toll, for food as well as for ivory and spotted cat skins that bring high prices on the black market. And there is ready evidence that government officials in many of these countries, while publicly showing great concern for wildlife, are profiting handsomely from the illegal trade. If these common property resources are going to be depleted anyway, what incentives do they have to act otherwise?

Many environmentalists bemoan the fact that the once free-roaming animal herds of the African continent are now kept in captivity for the benefit of American hunters and safari park visitors. But free-roaming is a relative concept. These animals are certainly free-roaming within the boundaries of the game ranches, and many of these ranches are enormous. Furthermore, as the African plains are increasingly delimited with hostile political boundaries and with warring armies and starving populations, there seems little point in mounting campaigns against so-called immoral game ranches and preserves. The growth of agriculture and cattle ranching in these countries is also restricting the free-roaming nature of the wildlife herds.

If the profits gained by giving hunters access to exotic game can provide the economic incentive for these landowners to manage the animals on a sustained-yield basis, some species will be saved. The same holds for the profits to be derived from visitors to game parks and preserves. In fact, the protection provided at some of the parks, preserves, and gardens has actually produced a glut of some animals. There have been well-publicized efforts by some preserves to return their surplus animals to Africa. Lions from America have even been taken to Africa to appear in movies that were filmed there. While we read of zoological parks attempting to discover reversible birth control techniques in order to control their tiger populations, we continue to read about the never-ending difficulties of preserving the remaining tigers in the wild.

Perhaps we should judge all of these activities by their achievements rather than by their motives, for it may turn out that in the future the developing countries will be restocked with their native fauna from specimens now thriving on game ranches and preserves.

It is important not to cloud the issue of common vs. private property resources with philosophical judgments regarding competing economic systems or with attacks on a free-market system or profit-seeking activities. The books on disappearing wildlife abound with stories of captive breeding of birds and mammals and the successful preservation of species that have either become extremely rare or have disappeared entirely in the wild.

Among the many mammals in this category are Père David's deer , which does not exist in the wild and was "discovered" living in the royal zoological park in Peking. It has been saved from extinction by breeding in zoos and private parks. The European bison, or wisent, was reduced to three animals in 1927 and now survives in preserves in Poland. There are similar stories for the Asiatic lion, Prsewalski's Mongolian wild horse, the Arabian oryx, the wild ass or onager, and the Bactrian camel.

Private waterfowl breeders exist widely in many countries, and perhaps the most notable success story has been the preservation of the Hawaiian goose, or nene. Once they numbered over 25,000 in the wild, but under common property management the population had plummeted to 20 to 30 birds by 1949. Fortunately, they had been bred by aviculturists as early as 1824. A Hawaiian rancher had many on his farm, and there was a flock at the Wildfowl Trust at Slimbridge, England. Through the combined efforts of many interested parties, an intensive captive breeding program was begun in the United States and Europe, and thousands of young nenes were produced. Beginning in the 1960s, they were reintroduced to the wild in Hawaii, and by the mid-1970s there were as many as 600 in their native habitat. Many species of pheasant have always had small and local populations and would not have survived long under common property pressures. Many of the rarest species have been preserved in private aviaries and ornamental collections, with at least six endangered species being raised in captivity in the United States.

The same is true for many members of the parrot family. The familiar budgerigar, or budgie, is commonly kept as a pet in the United States and is bred in enormous numbers by thousands of breeders. Practically the entire trade is supplied by captive-bred birds. This demonstrates another conservation aspect of extending private property rights to wildlife, as captive breeding can supply the market demand for the birds and reduce or eliminate the demand on wild populations.

In all of these examples it is clear that the single most important element in wildlife survival was their removal from common property ownership. Under private property ownership, others were prevented from exploiting the resource, and there were incentives for the owners to preserve them. Furthermore, these incentives were not solely motivated by the possibility of economic gain. With the exception of game ranches, economic gain has seldom been the primary motivation behind most captive breeding projects. Many of these examples were fostered for the pleasure of owning and breeding attractive or rare wildlife, as well as for more "altruistic" reasons, such as a deep commitment to the preservation of vanishing wildlife. Private ownership includes not only hunting preserves, commercial bird breeders, parrot jungles, and safari parks, it also includes wildlife sanctuaries, Audubon Society refuges, World Wildlife Fund preserves, and a multitude of private, nonprofit conservation and preservation projects.

The problems of environmental degradation, over-exploitation of natural resources, and depletion of wildlife all derive from their existence as common property resources. Wherever we find an approach to the extension of private property rights in these areas, we find superior results. Wherever we have exclusive private ownership, whether it is organized around a profit-seeking or nonprofit undertaking, there are incentives for the private owners to preserve the resource. Self-interest drives the private property owners to careful management and protection of their resource.

It is important not to fall into the trap of believing that the different results arising from these two forms of resource management can be changed through education or persuasion. The methods of using or exploiting the resources are inherent in the incentives that are necessarily a part of each system. The overuse of common property resources and the preservation of private property resources are both examples of rational behavior by resource users. It is not a case of irrational vs. rational behavior. In both cases we are witnessing rational behavior, for resource users are acting in the only manner available to them to obtain any economic or psychological value from the resource.

It has nothing to do with the need for a new environmental ethic. Asking people to revere resources and wildlife won't bring about the peaceable kingdom when the only way a person can survive is to use up the resource before someone else does. Adopting a property system that directs and channels man's innate self-interest into behavior that preserves natural resources and wildlife will cause people to act as *if* they were motivated by a new conservationist ethic.

Any resource held in common—whether land, air, the upper atmosphere and outer space, the oceans, lakes, streams, outdoor recreational resources, fisheries, wildlife, or game—can be used simultaneously by more than one individual or group for more than one purpose with many of the multiple uses conflicting. No one has exclusive rights to the resource, nor can any one prevent others from using it for either the same or any noncompatible use. By its very nature a common property resource is owned by everyone and owned by no one. Since everyone uses it there is overuse, waste, and extinction. No one has an incentive to maintain or preserve it. The only way any of the users can capture any value, economic or otherwise, is to exploit the resource as rapidly as possible before someone else does.

But private ownership allows the owner to capture the full capital value of the resource, and self-interest and economic incentive drive the owner to maintain its long-term capital value. The owner of the resource wants to enjoy the benefits of the resource today, tomorrow, and ten years from now, and therefore he will attempt to manage it on a sustained-yield basis.

Given the nature of man and the motivating forces of self-interest and economic incentive, we can see why the buffalo nearly vanished, but not the Hereford; why the Atwater's greater prairie chicken is endangered, but not the red grouse; why the common salmon fisheries of the United States are overfished, but not the private salmon streams of Europe.

It should be equally clear that the analysis applies to broader environmental issues. Many of the most beautiful national parks are suffering from severe overuse and a near destruction of their recreational values, but most private parks are maintained in far better condition. The National Audubon Society does a better job of preserving its wildlife refuges and protecting wildlife than do many federal wildlife refuges. The public grazing lands have been repeatedly over-grazed, while lush private grazing lands are maintained by private ranchers. National forests are carelessly logged and overharvested, but private forests are carefully managed and cut on a sustained-yield basis, and costly nursery tree farms have been developed. In addition, the basic concept of self-interest explains why people don't litter their own yards but do litter public parks and streets, and why people don't dump old refrigerators and tires in their own farm ponds or swimming pools, but repeatedly dump them in the unowned streams, rivers, and swamps.

Perhaps the most important treatment of the common property syndrome was that of the noted biologist and environmentalist, Garrett Hardin:

> Picture a pasture open to all. It is to be expected that each herdsman will try to keep as many cattle as possible on the commons. Such an arrangement may work reasonably satisfactorily for centuries because tribal wars, poaching, and disease keep the numbers of both man and beast well below the carrying capacity of the land. Finally, however, comes the day of reckoning, that is, the day when the long-desired goal of social stability becomes a reality. At this point, the inherent logic of the commons remorselessly generates tragedy.
>
> As a rational being, each herdsman seeks to maximize his gain. Explicitly or implicitly, more or less consciously, he asks, "What is the utility *to me* of adding one more animal to my herd?" The utility has one negative and one positive component.

1. The positive component is a function of the increment of one animal. Since the herdsman receives all the proceeds from the sale of the additional animal, the positive utility is nearly + 1.
2. The negative component is a function of the additional overgrazing created by one more animal. Since, however, the effects of overgrazing are shared by all the herdsmen, the negative utility for any particular decision-making herdsman is only a fraction of -1.

Adding together the component partial utilities, the rational herdsman concludes that the only sensible course for him to pursue is to add another animal to his herd. And another; and another ... But this is the conclusion reached by each and every rational herdsman sharing a commons. Therein is the tragedy. Each man is locked into a system that compels him to increase his herd without limit-in a world that is limited. Ruin is the destination toward which all men rush, each pursuing his own best interest in a society that believes in the freedom of the commons. Freedom in a commons brings ruin to all.

Unfortunately, environmentalists have either overlooked the economic analysis of common property resources or they have deliberately ignored it because of the profound difficulties it raises for a philosophy that is opposed to private ownership of natural resources and wildlife. Certainly, the former is true, but there is also evidence of the latter, since some of the more scholarly treatments of wildlife problems refer rather fleetingly to the problems of common property resources and to Hardin's analysis. But they mainly refer to Hardin when they are following his proposals for limiting human population growth to preserve the natural world. Meanwhile, the logic of the commons continues to generate a remorseless loss of the world's wildlife.

Where, then, do most environmentalists place the blame for our environmental problems? Most environmental literature and treatments by the public media consistently repeat attacks on man's greed, self-interest, consumerism, piggishness, the profit system, the market economy, and Western political, legal, economic, religious, and property institutions and beliefs. *Newsweek* points to "entrepreneurial greed." The *New York Times* mentions "commercial exploitation." Michael Satchell writes, "The road ahead seems to lead to more extinctions on the altar of consumerism.

This level of thinking is especially prevalent in popular magazines published by the major wildlife, conservation, and environmental organizations, ranging from the Audubon Society to the World Wildlife Fund. A typical example, written by the editor, John Strohm, appeared in a recent issue of *International Wildlife*. He asked why there were growing problems of overfishing, overcutting, overgrazing, overplowing, and disappearing species of plants and animals. Following a discussion of too many people, too many wasteful demands, and the haves vs. the have-nots, he wrote: "We must eliminate waste ... and adopt a more frugal lifestyle. You cut a tree, you plant a tree. You catch a fish, you leave some behind so you can fish tomorrow."

But even the most serious, scholarly books on wildlife conservation fail to rise much above this level. Norman Myers, in *The Sinking Ark,* writes about how we like hamburgers, our consumerist lifestyle, our desire to be consumers and fat cats, and our love of inexpensive foreign beef. David Ehrenfeld, in *Conserving Life on Earth*, finds the problem to be economic success and increases in consumption. He calls for the disassociation of progress from growth, blames the pet trade, attacks private land ownership as unplanned, and points out that one of his students had discovered that people believe that China is the only country that has successfully coped with environmental problems. Ehrenfeld calls for the creation of a radically altered economic system that would produce labor-intensive and nonpolluting goods, such as guitars, rather than goods that are capital-intensive and highly polluting, such as snowmobiles.

These examples make one wonder whether the intellectual leaders of the environmental movement are more interested in a visionary society patterned after Rousseau and Thoreau than in grappling with the difficult problems of finding a method of conserving life on earth.

Two major themes repeatedly appear in the environmental literature as the source of all our problems with environmental preservation and conservation: commerce and the free-enterprise or free-market economic system. We find emotional references to the role of commerce in the overexploitation of wildlife. Victor Scheffer has written:

> By market hunting I mean the trapping and clubbing of fur-bearers, the shooting of animals for the pet-food industry, the live-capturing of rabbits for coursing, the capturing of hawks for sale to falconers, and similar pursuits of wild birds and mammals for commercial ends. The Friends of the Earth organization has already taken the position that the use of wild animal products as objects of commerce should be discouraged.

In *Time of the Turtle*, Jack Rudloe describes a conversation with Dr. Archie Carr, widely recognized as the world's foremost sea turtle scientist:

> Inevitably a discussion on the morality of eating this heavenly tasting, but nearly extinct creature arose. Was it wrong to eat it when we knew the endangered status of the green turtle?

> "That touches on a very deep and fundamental problem" said Archie in a defensive tone. "If we had gone out and bought it, paid cash for it, and encouraged its commercial sale, then we would have been wrong. More than anything else, the commercialization of turtle meat and products has pushed the species to extinction. It isn't the Indian eating a few turtles on the beach for subsistence. At least five thousand turtles each year are being slaughtered in Nicaragua right up the coast from us. Thousands used to be shipped into the Keys for soup. And last year thirty thousand pounds of meat came in from Colombia, Mexico, and even from the Middle East to the United States. It isn't coastal people sharing the meat among themselves in the village that's the problem, it's that mass marketing that's going on in the world trade that is."

However, it seems totally inappropriate to refer to the harvesting of unowned wild populations as commerce. Environmentalists and scientists make exceptions for wildlife harvesting by native populations and Indians, whether it is for food, clothing, medicine, ornamentation, religious rites and ceremonies, or for pets. Yet, when European exploration and settlement began to affect wildlife populations by providing food, clothing, and ornamentation for growing settlements, it was referred to as commerce. It is somehow suggested that exchanging wildlife for money is somehow immoral.

The overharvesting of the earth's wildlife can no more be labeled commerce than the primitive gathering of wild fruits, vegetables, and grains can be called agriculture—even if those products are subsequently sold in the marketplace. Jacques-Yves Cousteau has written: "Unlike livestock rearing and fish farming, fishing and hunting are really sheer pillaging of the environment and quickly lead to the destruction of the very resources they seek to cull."

The disappearance of wildlife has nothing to do with commerce or a lack of reverence for wildlife. The more rapid disappearance of common property wildlife during the past century is due to the fact that much larger human populations are using it, more efficient means of capture and kill are employed, and a larger number of uses have been found for the resources. Furthermore, many of the most populous species of wildlife had been reduced to a severely depleted state long before the development of modern business and commerce. This is especially true regarding sea turtles.

Sea turtles have been on earth for up to 100 million years and were probably one of the first wildlife foods used by man. They abounded in the warm water between the Tropics of Cancer and Capricorn. The green turtle, *Chelonia mydas,* has been called the world's most valuable species of reptile. Before Europeans arrived in the Caribbean its population was as high as 50 million. On Columbus's fourth voyage to the New World he recorded that on May 10, 1503, his ship "raised two small islands full of turtles" and the surrounding sea "seethed with turtles." He named the islands Las Tortugas.

By the time the British renamed their colony the Cayman Islands the turtles were a valuable source of meat and eggs for seamen and early colonists. One scientist noted that the green turtle was the most valuable dietary factor in opening up the Caribbean, although at a heavy cost to the species. Originally their numbers were so great that mariners lost in the fog could navigate by following the sound of the turtles swimming toward their breeding beaches. But decades of over-exploitation rapidly depleted the population. As early as 1620 the Bermuda turtle population was so reduced that the assembly passed an act prohibiting their killing. Today there are not more than a few thousand green turtles in the Caribbean and possibly no more than 400,000 worldwide. The appearance of a wild turtle in Caymanian waters is now a rarity.

The logic of the commons worked its inexorable tragedy for the green turtle long before the development of any modern commercial trade in sea turtles and turtle products, and thus it is all the more inappropriate for so excellent a scientist as Professor Carr to single out commerce as the cause of the turtles' depletion and to state: "Turtles aren't feeding protein-poor Indians, but rich gringos in high-rise hotels." Clearly, the current plight of the sea turtles has nothing to do with rich gringos in high-rise hotels. Common property exploitation had nearly doomed the turtles long before Miami Beach was developed.

Many farsighted scientists and conservationists have supported the development of commercial sea turtle farms in an effort to reduce the exploitation of the remaining wild turtles. Even Archie Carr wrote:

> The one move that appears most promising as a way to accomplish the dual aim of feeding people and saving natural turtle populations is to set up turtle farms. If the teeming people of the future are to have turtle products—tortoise-shell, calipee, meat, soup, hides—they should come from captive stock. They cannot keep coming from the small, shrinking, natural populations of the world ... Turtle farming will be commercially profitable, however, only when it is done on a big scale.

Unfortunately, following the successful development of Cayman Turtle Farm, Ltd., many American environmentalists and some scientists launched an attack on farming. Essentially they were opposed to commercial use of sea turtles and the profit-seeking nature of the farm. They also argued that it was likely to stimulate trade in sea turtles. In spite of strong support for the farm from other sea turtle experts, scientists, and conservationists, the antifarmers ultimately persuaded the United States government to ban the import of farm-bred turtle products. This followed an earlier ban on the importation of endangered wild turtle products.

The predictable result has been the increased exploitation and smuggling of a rapidly dwindling wild population. The demand for turtle products is now being met through illicit channels, that is, black market smuggling. It is a sad irony that while the Cayman Turtle Farm is being forced to reduce the size of its captive stock because its American markets are closed, the *Washington Star* reports that two huge shipments of illegal wild sea turtle meat have recently been seized by United States agents. These shipments contained fifty-three tons of wild olive ridley meat, the results of the slaughter of nearly nine thousand irreplaceable wild sea turtles.

For some perplexing reason Archie Carr reversed his position on turtle farms, and he, David Ehrenfeld, and some of their associates have been leading the fight against farming. Rudloes conversation with Carr concluded:

> "That's absolutely correct," Archie rationalized as we ate the last piece. "No money exchanged hands. The meat was not swapped for dollars. The soldiers divided the meat up among the villagers, themselves, their major, and ourselves. If a turtle is going to be butchered, that's the only way it should be done. That's why I'm against turtle farming. It isn't increasing the species, all it's doing is putting more commercial pressure on an already endangered species."

Farming was, of course, doing precisely the opposite. The species was increased because the pressure on the remaining wild population was reduced. Further, the Cayman Turtle Farm became a closed-cycle operation and no longer needed to collect breeding stock eggs from the wild, most of which were "doomed" eggs that would not have hatched anyway because of beach erosion, harvesting by natives, or predation. The Cayman Turtle Farm achieved the first recorded instance of captive sea turtle breeding and served as a living laboratory for scientific research on sea turtle biology. Yet the more successful the farm became, the more vocal its opponents were. The farm's major markets are closed, and economic survival is in doubt. Scientists still visit the farm to carry on research, but the future of the green turtle and of all sea turtles is now dim. One of the most disheartening aspects of the antifarm campaign is that the farm has been forced to reduce its captive stock by an amount considerably larger than all the remaining wild green turtles in the Caribbean.

We can see just how counterproductive the emotional and philosophical opposition to turtle farming has been. By successfully halting the development of private farming and the extension of private property rights into the wildlife commons, environmentalists and antifarming scientists are subjecting sea turtles to the tragedy of the commons. Unless there is a rapid turnaround in their views or in the United States laws, the worldwide demand for turtle products will soon drive the remaining wild turtles to near extinction.

The second common theme used by most environmentalists is the private enterprise system and the free market. Myers has written at length about the evils of the system:

> But within the American system, with its emphasis on private profit to be derived from private property, common property of society's heritage gets short shrift; farmers' interests are allowed precedence over the nation's needs.

> The guts of the issue are that private interests do not necessarily run parallel with public interests. In certain circumstances, private interests undermine public interests. This runs counter to much conventional wisdom concerning a free-market economy, as exemplified by Adam Smith's dictum that, through pursuing his own interests, an individual is "led by an invisible hand to promote the public interest."

In the concluding section of Myers's book, he develops his strategy for conservation:

> Much decline of species is due to the deficiencies and failures of the market-place system, which sometimes favors the here-and-now needs of private individuals to the detriment of long-term needs of the community in general. Moreover, the market-place tends to ignore the value of resources without a price tag ... Governments should step in to take account of the fact that the open market-place does not cater for all economic needs of society, and especially that the market-place ignores and even depletes the common heritage Species.

Ehrenfeld argues from a nearly identical position:

> The greatest barrier to the implementation of a strong and unified conservation policy is the difficulty of protecting those parts of the public domain that have traditionally been exploited by private interests. Both Keynes and later Hardin have explained that there is no logically consistent reason why an individual, corporation, or nation acting in self-interest should voluntarily abstain from exploiting the public domain even

when the result will be certain destruction of the valuable features of that domain. Hardin, in fact, goes somewhat farther in "The Tragedy of the Commons" by asserting that it is usually damaging to private interests (at least in the short run) to act for the collective good as far as the commons are concerned.

If private interests cannot be expected to protect the public domain, then external regulation by public agencies, governments, or international authorities is needed. If that regulation is effective, the commons will be managed to provide the maximum *sustained* yield of natural products, which in turn will ultimately maximize the sum total of the profits for the various interests that rely on the commons. This concept, simple in theory, is difficult to put into practice.

It is difficult to decide how to deal with Myers's and Ehrenfeld's critiques of free enterprise and the tragedy of the commons. One can understand their philosophical objection to private ownership of property and to the free-market economy, yet it is difficult to deal with their analyses of the tragedy of the commons. Nowhere does Hardin state that the tragedy of the commons is the result of free enterprise, the profit system, or the existence of private property. Since common property is the antithesis of private property, there is simply no way in which private property can be the cause of the tragedy. Hardin clearly stresses that it is by treating a resource as common property that we become locked in its inexorable destruction. The conservationist-minded common property resource user has no more incentive to restrain his over-exploitation of the resource than the most shortsighted and greedy common property resource user has. That is precisely why such a system remorselessly generates tragedy.

Regarding the whaling industry in the ocean commons, Hardin mentions the Japanese and the Russians. But the ocean's common property resources are being overexploited by the ships of all nations, regardless of economic and political systems. It is certainly true that ships sailing out from the United States are seeking to take all the fish they can, but ships from socialist and communist nations are following a similar course. Indeed, because individual profit-and-loss calculations play such a small role in the economic activities of socialist nations, there is less incentive for their fleets to desist in their over-exploitation when it becomes economically unprofitable than there is for a private American fishing boat. One can only conclude that writers like Myers and Ehrenfeld have either completely failed to grasp the concept of the commons or they have deliberately misrepresented it in order to support their philosophical positions.

It is true that Hardin is somewhat ambiguous in recommending a solution to the tragedy of the commons. He points out that there is no technological solution and that a political solution must be found that will create some form of ownership for the earth's resources. While he does not explicitly recommend private property rights, he appears to lean in that direction in his discussion of parks as commons:

What shall we do? We have several options. We might sell them off as private property. We might keep them as public property, but allocate the right to enter them. The allocation might be on the basis of wealth, by the use of an auction system. It might be on the basis of merit, as defined by some agreed-upon standards. It might be by lottery. Or it might be on a first-come, first-served basis, administered to long queues. These, I think, are all the reasonable possibilities. They are all objectionable. But we must choose-or acquiesce in the destruction of the commons that we call our National Parks.

At least in certain areas Hardin views the creation of private property rights as a solution: "The tragedy of the commons as a food basket is averted by private property, or something formally like it."

Unfortunately Hardin swings in the other direction in his treatment of the ocean commons:

> Faced with the tragedy of the commons, we can have only one rational response: change the system. To what? Basically, there are only two possibilities: free enterprise and socialism. Free enterprise in the oceans would require some sort of fences, real or figurative. It is doubtful if we can create territories in the ocean by fencing. If not, we must-if we have the will to do it-adopt the other alternative and socialize the oceans: create an international agency *with teeth*. Such an agency must issue not recommendations but directives; and enforce them.

It is possible that in perceiving the difficulties involved in solving the intricate boundary problems Hardin seems to acquiesce to some form of state or socialist ownership and control of ocean resources. Hardin does stress that our experience with the League of Nations and the United Nations gives us little hope that a system of state ownership would succeed. Indeed, the decade-long debates at the Law of the Seas conferences have repeatedly been mired over the establishment of suprastate authority over the manganese nodules carpeting vast areas of the ocean bottom—a far more tractable problem than managing the highly fugitive wildlife resources of the oceans. However, the problem of "fencing" the seas may not be as difficult to solve as Hardin imagined. North and Miller have written:

> Notice that, until recently, it would have been immeasurably difficult, or even impossible, to maintain and enforce private rights in the ocean, but the invention of modern electronic sensing equipment has now made the policing of large bodies of water relatively cheap and easy. Through the centuries it has often become feasible for common property to give way to private property precisely because technology has made possible the enforcement of private rights (exclusivity). We are not saying that making the oceans into private property is "good." We are saying that doing so would lead to more output and fewer ecological disasters ...

The problems of over-exploitation and extinction of wildlife appear to derive consistently from their being treated as a common property resource. Example after example bears this out. It is also predicted by the economic analysis of common property resources. Both the economic analysis of common property resources and Hardin's treatment of the tragedy of the commons suggest that the only way to avoid the tragedy of the commons in natural resources and wildlife is to end the common property system by creating a system of private property rights.

Private property rights have worked successfully in a broad array of cases to preserve wildlife and resolve the tragedy of the commons. Experience and the logical implications of common property resource theory suggest that private property rights are far superior to state or public property rights partly because of the unambiguous exclusivity of private property rights and the difficult problem of preventing too many from using the public domain under a system of state ownership. Furthermore, private property owners have a direct and immediate incentive not to mismanage their own property, while government owners or managers do not have the same incentives, nor are there many incentives that prevent all of the public from overusing the resources held in the public domain.

It seems that Hardin's proposal that resolution of the tragedy of the commons comes down to a choice between private ownership or government ownership is insufficient. State ownership appears to be little more than a more regulated commons. We witness the same overuse and destruction of the public domain as we do in the purest commons.

The proper path toward resolving the vexing issues of wildlife conservation lies in removing wildlife from common property resource treatment and creating private property rights. This entails an outright rejection of the concept that wildlife should be viewed as the common heritage of all mankind. It also poses a direct challenge to the basic philosophical beliefs of many environmentalists. But if we are to resolve the tragedy of the commons and preserve our natural resources and wildlife, we must create a new paradigm for the environmental movement: private property rights in natural resources and wildlife.

NOTES:

1. John Baden, Richard L. Stroup, and Walter Thurman, "Good Intentions and Self-interest: Lessons from the American Indian," in *Earth Day Reconsidered*, ed. John Baden (Washington, D.C.: The Heritage Foundation, 1980), pp. 7–9.

2. Francis Haines, *The Buffalo* (New York: Thomas Y. Crowell, 1970), p. 20.

3. James F. Downs, *The Two Worlds of the Washo: An Indian Tribe of California and Nevada* (New York: Holt, Rinehart and Winston, 1966).

4. Norman Myers, *The Sinking Ark* (Oxford: Pergamon Press, 1979), p. 4. The distinction between natural and human-caused extinction seems to be a philosophically loaded one. Once we make human beings some special type of causative agent apart from the rest of nature, it is very easy to begin to single out specific groups of humans as "good" or "bad," e.g., conservation organizations are good and multinational timber companies are bad. What does it matter to the species whether its extinction results from natural or human causes?-it is just as dead.

5. Ibid., pp. 4–5.

6. Frank Graham, Jr., *Man's Dominion: The Story of Conservation in America* (NewYork: M. Evans and Co., 1971), pp. 23–24.

7. Robert E. Cook, Harvey L. Bumgardner, and William E. Shaklee, "How Chicken on Sunday Became an Anyday Treat," in *The 1975 Yearbook of Agriculture: That We May Eat* (Washington, D.C.: Government Printing Office, 1975), p. 125.

8. Harokl Demsetz, "Toward a Theory of Property Rights," *American Economic Review* 57 (May 1967): 354–56.

9. Council on Environmental Quality, *The Sixth Annual Report of the Council on Environmental Quality* (Washington, D.C.: Government Printing Office, 1975), p. 257.

10. Victor B. Scheffer, *A Voice for Wildlife: A Call for a New Ethic in Conservation* (New York: Charles Scribner's Sons, 1974), p. 138.

11. Douglass C. North and Roger LeRoy Miller, *The Economics of Public Issues,* 2d ed. (New York: Harper & Row, 1973), pp. 109–11.

12. John Baden, "Persona Grata: An Interview with John Baden," *World Research Ink* (November-December 1979), p. 22.

13. Bay Center Mariculture Company brochure, Bay City (Willapa Bay), Wash., n.d.

14. Another interesting experiment is being conducted by Maine Sea Farms, where the common property problem has been eliminated by raising the salmon in a fenced sea-water cove. They are fed a special diet of ground shrimp and crab, achieve a nearly 50 percent survival rate, and are marketed twenty months later as 9- to 12-ounce "yearlings" in the luxury fresh fish markets of the Northeast.

15. Robin W. Doughty, "Farming Iceland's Seafowl: The Eider Duck," *Sea Frontiers* (November-December 1979), p. 346.

16. For an important discussion of British and American wildlife laws, see Thomas A. Lund, *American Wildlife Law* (Berkeley and Los Angeles: University of California Press, 1980.).

17. Opponents of private ownership of wildlife have occasionally used the example of overzealous attempts by English gamekeepers to destroy all predatory species of birds and mammals as an argument against the system. However, much of that happened long before the enlightened understanding of the role of predators in the ecosystem. Furthermore, this hardly seems a convincing argument in view of the incalculable loss of predators in the United States resulting from three centuries of shooting, poisoning, and trapping of predators by local, county, state, and federal government agents, as well as an enormous payout in bounty fees by the government to private citizens for eliminating predators and "nuisance" animals.

18. Lund, *American Wildlife Law,* p. 103.

19. This remarkable development of private property rights in land and especially in wildlife by an aboriginal people was first treated by anthropologists Frank Speck and Eleanor Leacock. More recently it has been subjected to economic analysis by Harold Demsetz and by John Baden, Richard Stroup, and Walter Thurman. See Frank G. Speck, "The Basis of American Indian Ownership of Land," *Old Penn Weekly Review* (January 16, 1915); idem, "A Report on Tribal Boundaries and Hunting Areas of the Malechite Indians of New Brunswick," *American Anthropologist* 48 (1946); Eleanor B. Leacock, "The Montagnais 'Hunting Territory' and the Fur Trade," *American Anthropologist* 56, no. 5, pt. 2, memoir no. 78 (October 1954); Demsetz, "Toward a Theory of Property Rights"; and Baden, Stroup, and Thurman, "Good Intentions and Self-Interest."

20. Demsetz, "Toward a Theory of Property Rights," pp. 351–52.

21. Baden, Stroup, and Thurman, "Good Intentions and Self-Interest," p. 10.

22. Demsetz, "Toward a Theory of Property Rights," p. 353.

23. Baden, Stroup, and Thurman, "Good Intentions and Self-Interest," pp. 10–11.

24. See David R. Zimmerman, *To Save a Bird in Peril* (New York: Coward McCann & Geoghegan, 1975), pp. 113–29.

25. Garrett Hardin, "The Tragedy of the Commons," *Science* 162 (December 13, 1968): 1244.

26. Michael Satchell, "How the Smuggling Trade Is Wiping Out Wildlife," *Parade* (December 3,1978), p. 25.

27. John Strohm, "An Open Letter to Colleen," *International Wildlife* September-October 1978), p. 19.

28. Myers, *The Sinking Ark.*

29. David W. Ehrenfeld, *Conserving Life on Earth* (New York: Oxford University Press, 1972).

30. Scheffer, *A Voice for Wildlife,* p. 210.

31. Jack Rudloe, *Time of the Turtle* (New York: Penguin Books, 1980), pp. 251–52.

32. Jacques-Yves Cousteau, "The Endangered Sea," *Vision* (July-August 1974), p. 53.

33. Quoted in Sir Alan S. Parkes, "Captive Breeding: A Double Landmark," a Mariculture, Ltd. (which later became the Cayman Turtle Farm), supplement to *The Cayman Islands Northwester,* October 1973, p. 17.

34. Ibid., p. 7.

35. Quoted in Sharon Begley and Mary Hager, "The Plight of the Turtle," *Newsweek* (January 14, 1980), p. 56.

36. Archie Carr, *The Turtle: A Natural History* (London: Cassell & Co., 1967), pp. 234–35.

37. Boris Weintraub, "The Lowly Sea Turtle vs. Man," *Washington Star,* September 16, 1980, pp. C1–2.

38. Rudloe, *Time of the Turtle,* p. 253.

39. The full story of this controversy is still to be discovered. The carefully orchestrated attack on the Cayman Turtle Farm as well as the apparent campaign of abuse against its supporters raise a number of disturbing questions regarding the true motives of the antifarming people. What do they have to gain by closing the farm and encouraging rapid exploitation of the few remaining wild turtles? Most people who have heard only the official antifarm party line are usually astounded when they learn the facts. Scientific objectivity has vanished in a biopolitical debate in which philosophical and personal considerations carry more importance than the facts surrounding the achievements of the turtle farm. This may prove to be a scientific scandal: America's own version of Lysenkoism.

40. Myers, *The Sinking Ark,* pp. 88–89.

41. Ibid., pp. 235-36.

42. Ehrenfeld, *Conserving Life on Earth,* p. 322.

43. Discussing pollution of the commons, Hardin does say, "We are locked into a system of 'fouling our own nest,' so long as we behave as independent, rational freeenterprisers." See Hardin, "Tragedy of the Commons," p. 1245. However, it is evident that socialist and communist nations have been even less successful in solving pollution problems. See Robert J. Smith, "The Environment under Socialism," *Policy Review 2* (Fall 1977): 113-18, for a brief review of the Soviet experience with environmental degradation.

44. Garrett Hardin, *Exploring New Ethics for Survival: The Voyage of the Spaceship Beagle* (New York: The Viking Press, 1972), p. 121.

45. Hardin, "The Tragedy of the Commons," p. 1245.

46. Ibid.

47. Hardin, *Exploring New Ethics,* p. 121.

48. North and Miller, *The Economics of Public Issues,* p. 112.

SECTION ELEVEN

Public Choice/Government

School Brief:
State and Market

By Uncredited, *The Economist* Staff

People are quick to assume that "market failure" justifies action by the government. This final brief in our series on economic fallacies argues for a strong presumption in favour of markets—not because they always work perfectly (they never do) but because the alternative is usually worse

ACCORDING TO THE central deduction of economic theory, under certain conditions markets allocate resources efficiently. "Efficiency" has a special meaning in this context. The theory says that markets will produce an outcome such that, given the economy's scarce resources, it is impossible to make anybody better-off without making somebody else worse-off.

Economic theory, in other words, offers a proof of Adam Smith's big idea. In a market economy, if certain conditions are met, an invisible hand guides countless apparently uncoordinated individuals to a result that is, in one plausible sense, the best that can be done.

In rich countries, markets are too familiar to attract attention. Yet a certain awe is appropriate. When Soviet planners visited a vegetable market in London during the early days of perestroika, they were impressed to find no queues, shortages, or mountains of spoiled and unwanted vegetables. They took their hosts aside and said: "We understand, you have to say it's all done by supply and demand. But can't you tell us what's really going on? Where are your planners, and what are their methods?"

The essence of the market mechanism is indeed captured by the supply-and-demand diagram shown in chart 1. The supply curve measures the cost to sellers, at any level of output, of selling one more unit of their good. As output grows, the law of diminishing returns forces this extra (or marginal) cost higher, so the supply curve slopes upwards. In the same way, the demand curve measures the benefit to consumers of consuming one more unit. As consumption grows, the benefit from extra consumption falls, so the demand curve slopes downwards.

At the place where the curves cross, a price is set such that demand equals supply. There, and only there, the benefit from consuming one more unit exactly matches the cost of producing it. If output were less, the benefit from consuming more would exceed the cost of producing it.

If output were higher, the cost of producing the extra units would exceed the extra benefits. So the point where supply equals demand is "efficient".

The shaded area in chart 2 shows the "surplus" created by the market. The upper part is the consumers' surplus: the benefit from consumption (i.e., the total area under the demand curve) less what consumers have to pay for it. In the same way, the lower part measures the producers' surplus: revenues received, less the cost of production (the area under the supply curve).

This gain in welfare is at its greatest if consumption and production happen where the lines cross. If, for some reason, consumption and production are less than that, the surplus is smaller and the economy suffers what economists call a deadweight loss, as shown in chart 3. If production and consumption are more than the efficient amount, the same is true. Producers' surplus is smaller because the extra output has cost more to make than it brings in revenues; consumers' surplus is reduced because the extra consumption has cost buyers more than the benefits it brings. Again, as shown in chart 4, the economy suffers a dead-weight loss.

FINE ON PAPER

However, the conditions for market efficiency are extremely demanding—far too demanding ever to be met in the real world. The theory requires "perfect competition": there must be many buyers and sellers; goods from competing suppliers must be indistinguishable; buyers and sellers must be fully informed; and markets must be complete that is, there must be markets not just for bread here and now, but for bread in any state of the world. (What is the price today for a loaf to be delivered in Timbuktu on the second Tuesday in December 2014 if it rains?)

In other words, market failure is pervasive. It comes in four main varieties:

- **Monopoly.** By reducing his sales, a monopolist can drive up the price of his good. His sales will fall but his profits will rise. Consumption and production are less than the efficient amount, causing a dead-weight loss in welfare.
- **Public goods.** Some goods cannot be supplied by markets. If you refuse to pay for a new coat, the seller will refuse to supply you. If you refuse to pay for national defence, the "good" cannot easily be withheld. You might be tempted to let others pay. The same reasoning applies to other "non-excludable" goods such as law and order, clean air, and so on. Since private sellers cannot expect to recover the costs of producing such goods, they will fail to supply them.
- **Externalities.** Making some goods causes pollution: the cost is borne by people with no say in deciding how much to produce. Consuming some goods (education, anti-lock brakes) spreads benefits beyond the buyer; again, this will be ignored when the market decides how much to produce. In the case of "good" externalities, markets will supply too little; in the case of "bads," too much.
- **Information.** In some ways a special kind of externality, this deserves to be mentioned separately because of the emphasis placed upon it in recent economic theory. To see why information matters, consider the market for used cars. A buyer, lacking reliable informa-

tion, may see the price as providing clues about a car's condition. This puts sellers in a quandary: if they cut prices, they may only convince people that their cars are rubbish.

The labour market, many economists believe, is another such "market for lemons". This may help to explain why it is so difficult for the unemployed to price themselves into work.

HOW HARMFUL?

When markets fail, there is a case for intervention. But two questions need to be answered first. How much does market failure matter in practice? And can governments put the failure right? The rest of this article deals with the first question. For a brief response to the second, see the box on the next page.

Markets often correct their own failures. In other cases, an apparent failure does nobody any harm. In general, market failure matters less in practice than is often supposed.

Monopoly, for instance, may seem to preclude an efficient market. This is wrong. The mere fact of monopoly does not establish that any economic harm is being done. If a monopoly is protected from would-be competitors by high barriers to entry, it can raise its prices and earn excessive profits. If that happens, the monopoly is undeniably harmful. But if barriers to entry are low, lack of actual (as opposed to potential) competitors does not prove that the monopoly is damaging: the threat of competition may be enough to make it behave as though it were a competitive firm.

That is why economists are no longer so interested in concentration ratios (the output of an industry's biggest firm or firms as a proportion of the industry's total output). Judging whether markets are "contestable"-that is, whether barriers to entry are high-is thought to be more important.

Many economists would accept that Microsoft, for instance, is a near-monopolist in some parts of the personal-computer software business-yet would argue that the firm is doing no harm to consumers because its markets remain highly contestable. Because of that persistent threat of competition, the company prices its products keenly. In this and in other ways it behaves as though it were a smaller firm in a competitive market.

Suppose, on the other hand, that a "natural monopoly" (a firm not subject to the law of diminishing returns, whose costs fall indefinitely as it increases its output) is successfully collecting excessive profits. Then would-be competitors would spare no effort to make the market contestable, through innovation or by other means.

Telecommunications was once considered a natural monopoly. Today, thanks to new technology and deregulation, it is an intensely competitive business-and in many countries would be more so if not for remaining government restrictions. Economists used to see natural monopolies wherever they looked. Now, thanks mainly to innovation-inspired chiefly by the private pursuit of profit, these beasts are sighted much less often.

Economists have also changed their thinking on public goods. Almost all economists accept that there are such things: national defence and law and order remain the most straightforward examples. But it was once taken for granted that many other products also qualify (if not by being pure public goods, at least by having some of the relevant characteristics). This is no longer so.

The classical example of a public good is a lighthouse. Its services are both non-excludable and "non-rivalrous in consumption", meaning that extra ships can consume its output without the existing users having to consume less. This implies that lighthouses are a pure public good: only the state can provide them. Such a neat example, cited by economists from John Stuart Mill to Paul Samuelson—yet it is at odds with the facts.

As Ronald Coase pointed out in a celebrated paper, from the 17th century many of Britain's lighthouses were privately built and run. Payment to cover costs (and provide a profit) was extracted through fees collected in local ports. The government's role was confined to authorizing this collection, exactly as a modern government might provide for a private road-builder to collect a toll.

On the face of it, television broadcasting is another pure public good-again, both non-excludable and non-rivalrous in consumption. Now, thanks to technology, it is straightforwardly excludable: satellite broadcasters collect a subscription, and in return provide a card that unscrambles their signal. With cable and pay-per-view, excludability works with even finer discrimination. And these market-strengthening innovations were not necessary for privately provided television to succeed, despite its public-good appearance. Non-excludable television was and is financed through advertising (another kind of innovation).

FABLE OF THE BEES

The same Ronald Coase who attacked the lighthouse myth is better known (and won a Nobel prize) for his work on externalities-the third species of market failure discussed earlier. He argued that, so long as property rights are clearly established, externalities will not cause an inefficient allocation of resources. In fact, few economists would agree: in many cases, unavoidably high costs will prevent the necessary transactions from taking place. Even so, MrCoase's insight was fruitful. Markets find ways to take account of externalities—ways to "internalize" them, as economists say—more often than you might think.

Bees are to externalities as lighthouses are to public goods. For years they served as a favorite textbook example. Bee-keepers are not rewarded for the pollination services they provide to nearby plant-growers, so they and their bees must be inefficiently few in number. Again, however, the world proved cleverer than the textbooks. Steven Cheung studied the apple growers of Washington state and discovered a long history of contracts between growers and beekeepers. The supposed market failure had been effectively—and privately—dealt with.

As for lack of information, the final main source of market failure discussed earlier, here too economists have discovered all manner of private remedies. Recall the used-car example. An easy way round the difficulty is to buy from a seller with a good reputation (one worth protecting), or who offers guarantees. In ways such as this, the information gap can often be filled, albeit at a cost, and sometimes only partially.

More broadly, the new thinking on information in economics sees the institutions of capitalism largely as attempts to solve this very problem. The fact that firms, banks and other institutions exist, and are organized as they are, reflects society's efforts to make best use of scarce information.

Even on economic grounds (never mind other considerations), there is no tidy answer to the question of where the boundary between state and market should lie. Markets do fail-because of monopoly, public goods, externalities, lack of information and for other reasons. But, more than critics allow, markets find ways to mitigate the harm-and that is a task at which governments have often been strikingly unsuccessful.

All in all, a strong presumption in favour of markets seems wise. This is not because classical economic theory says so, but because experience seems to agree.

The Federalist No. 51

By James Madison

The Structure of the Government Must Furnish the Proper Checks and Balances Between the Different Departments

To the People of the State of New York:

TO WHAT EXPEDIENT, THEN, shall we finally resort, for maintaining in practice the necessary partition of power among the several departments, as laid down in the Constitution? The only answer that can be given is, that as all these exterior provisions are found to be inadequate, the defect must be supplied, by so contriving the interior structure of the government as that its several constituent parts may, by their mutual relations, be the means of keeping each other in their proper places. Without presuming to undertake a full development of this important idea, I will hazard a few general observations, which may perhaps place it in a clearer light, and enable us to form a more correct judgment of the principles and structure of the government planned by the convention.

In order to lay a due foundation for that separate and distinct exercise of the different powers of government, which to a certain extent is admitted on all hands to be essential to the preservation of liberty, it is evident that each department should have a will of its own; and consequently should be so constituted that the members of each should have as little agency as possible in the appointment of the members of the others. Were this principle rigorously adhered to, it would require that all the appointments for the supreme executive, legislative, and judiciary magistracies should be drawn from the same fountain of authority, the people, through channels having no communication whatever with one another. Perhaps such a plan of constructing the several departments would be less difficult in practice than it may in contemplation appear. Some difficulties, however, and some additional expense would attend the execution of it. Some deviations, therefore, from the principle must be admitted. In the constitution of the judiciary department in particular, it might be inexpedient to insist rigorously on the principle: first, because peculiar qualifications being essential in the members, the primary consideration ought to be to select that mode of choice which best secures these qualifications; secondly, because the permanent tenure by which the appointments are held in that department, must soon destroy all sense of dependence on the authority conferring them.

James Madison, "The Federalist No. 51," from <http://www.constitution.org/fed/federa51.htm>.

It is equally evident, that the members of each department should be as little dependent as possible on those of the others, for the emoluments annexed to their offices. Were the executive magistrate, or the judges, not independent of the legislature in this particular, their independence in every other would be merely nominal.

But the great security against a gradual concentration of the several powers in the same department, consists in giving to those who administer each department the necessary constitutional means and personal motives to resist encroachments of the others. The provision for defense must in this, as in all other cases, be made commensurate to the danger of attack. Ambition must be made to counteract ambition. The interest of the man must be connected with the constitutional rights of the place. It may be a reflection on human nature, that such devices should be necessary to control the abuses of government. But what is government itself, but the greatest of all reflections on human nature? If men were angels, no government would be necessary. If angels were to govern men, neither external nor internal controls on government would be necessary. In framing a government which is to be administered by men over men, the great difficulty lies in this: you must first enable the government to control the governed; and in the next place oblige it to control itself. A dependence on the people is, no doubt, the primary control on the government; but experience has taught mankind the necessity of auxiliary precautions.

This policy of supplying, by opposite and rival interests, the defect of better motives, might be traced through the whole system of human affairs, private as well as public. We see it particularly displayed in all the subordinate distributions of power, where the constant aim is to divide and arrange the several offices in such a manner as that each may be a check on the other—that the private interest of every individual may be a sentinel over the public rights. These inventions of prudence cannot be less requisite in the distribution of the supreme powers of the State.

But it is not possible to give to each department an equal power of self-defense. In republican government, the legislative authority necessarily predominates. The remedy for this inconveniency is to divide the legislature into different branches; and to render them, by different modes of election and different principles of action, as little connected with each other as the nature of their common functions and their common dependence on the society will admit. It may even be necessary to guard against dangerous encroachments by still further precautions. As the weight of the legislative authority requires that it should be thus divided, the weakness of the executive may require, on the other hand, that it should be fortified. An absolute negative on the legislature appears, at first view, to be the natural defense with which the executive magistrate should be armed. But perhaps it would be neither altogether safe nor alone sufficient. On ordinary occasions it might not be exerted with the requisite firmness, and on extraordinary occasions it might be perfidiously abused. May not this defect of an absolute negative be supplied by some qualified connection between this weaker department and the weaker branch of the stronger department, by which the latter may be led to support the constitutional rights of the former, without being too much detached from the rights of its own department?

If the principles on which these observations are founded be just, as I persuade myself they are, and they be applied as a criterion to the several State constitutions, and to the federal

Constitution it will be found that if the latter does not perfectly correspond with them, the former are infinitely less able to bear such a test.

There are, moreover, two considerations particularly applicable to the federal system of America, which place that system in a very interesting point of view.

First. In a single republic, all the power surrendered by the people is submitted to the administration of a single government; and the usurpations are guarded against by a division of the government into distinct and separate departments. In the compound republic of America, the power surrendered by the people is first divided between two distinct governments, and then the portion allotted to each subdivided among distinct and separate departments. Hence a double security arises to the rights of the people. The different governments will control each other, at the same time that each will be controlled by itself.

Second. It is of great importance in a republic not only to guard the society against the oppression of its rulers, but to guard one part of the society against the injustice of the other part. Different interests necessarily exist in different classes of citizens. If a majority be united by a common interest, the rights of the minority will be insecure. There are but two methods of providing against this evil: the one by creating a will in the community independent of the majority—that is, of the society itself; the other, by comprehending in the society so many separate descriptions of citizens as will render an unjust combination of a majority of the whole very improbable, if not impracticable. The first method prevails in all governments possessing an hereditary or self-appointed authority. This, at best, is but a precarious security; because a power independent of the society may as well espouse the unjust views of the major, as the rightful interests of the minor party, and may possibly be turned against both parties. The second method will be exemplified in the federal republic of the United States. Whilst all authority in it will be derived from and dependent on the society, the society itself will be broken into so many parts, interests, and classes of citizens, that the rights of individuals, or of the minority, will be in little danger from interested combinations of the majority. In a free government the security for civil rights must be the same as that for religious rights. It consists in the one case in the multiplicity of interests, and in the other in the multiplicity of sects. The degree of security in both cases will depend on the number of interests and sects; and this may be presumed to depend on the extent of country and number of people comprehended under the same government. This view of the subject must particularly recommend a proper federal system to all the sincere and considerate friends of republican government, since it shows that in exact proportion as the territory of the Union may be formed into more circumscribed Confederacies, or States oppressive combinations of a majority will be facilitated: the best security, under the republican forms, for the rights of every class of citizens, will be diminished: and consequently the stability and independence of some member of the government, the only other security, must be proportionately increased. Justice is the end of government. It is the end of civil society. It ever has been and ever will be pursued until it be obtained, or until liberty be lost in the pursuit. In a society under the forms of which the stronger faction can readily unite and oppress the weaker, anarchy may as truly be said to reign as in a state of nature, where the weaker individual is not secured against the violence of the stronger; and as, in the latter state, even the stronger individuals are prompted, by the uncertainty of their condition, to submit to a government which may protect the weak as well as themselves; so, in the former state, will the more powerful factions or parties be gradually induced, by a like motive, to wish for a government which will protect all parties, the weaker as well as the more powerful. It can be little doubted that if the State of Rhode Island was separated from the Confederacy and left to itself, the insecurity of rights under the popular form of government within such narrow limits would be displayed by such reiterated oppressions of factious majorities that some power altogether independent of the people would soon be called for by the voice of the very factions whose misrule had proved the necessity of it. In the extended republic of the United States, and among the great variety of interests, parties, and sects which it embraces, a coalition of a majority of the whole society could seldom take place on any other principles than those of justice and the general good; whilst there being thus less danger to a minor from the will of a major party, there must be less pretext, also, to provide for the security of the former, by introducing into the government a will not dependent on the latter, or, in other words, a will independent of the society itself. It is no less certain than it is important, notwithstanding the contrary opinions which have been entertained, that the larger the society, provided it lie within a practical sphere, the more duly capable it will be of self-government. And happily for the *republican cause*, the practicable sphere may be carried to a very great extent, by a judicious modification and mixture of the *federal principle*.

PUBLIUS

Loot

By Leonard E. Read

He sins as much who holds the sack as he who fills it.—Gabriel Meurier

RICHARD WEAVER WROTE a book titled *Ideas Have Consequences*. Ideas do indeed shape our way of life and mold our very being. However, we think in words; and what we mean by the words we use, and what others think we mean by them, may range from the bright lights of creativity to the dark shadows of destruction. The scholarly authors of *The Meaning of Meaning* (Charles Ogden and Ivor Richards) referred to "the tyranny of words," meaning, of course, their misuse and thee consequent misunderstanding and confusion. As someone phrased it years ago:

> I know you believe you understand what you think I said. But I am not sure you realize that what you heard is not what I meant.

Not only do we need to know the ideas and practice the ways, we also need the words to explain how freedom works its wonders. And what words will best describe and explain freedom's opposite? How does one make it clear that accepting coercively confiscated "benefits" is just as sinful as the confiscation itself? It would seem self-evident that if no one would accept Social Security payments there would be no governmental plundering to finance the program. And the same is true of thousands of other ignoble schemes.

"He sins as much who holds the sack as he who fills it." The acceptance of plunder is as sinful as the plundering itself. But where are the words to portray the sinful nature of plunder?

Many of us, over the years, have used the words "special privilege" to describe freedom's opposite—the plundering way of life. But these words no longer serve to describe the undesirable; they have lost their derogatory impact. So widespread is the practice of plunder that what were at one time devised as special grants of political power—and were more or less clearly recognized as such—are now claimed as the inalienable rights of the special class spawned by such privileges. Among pigs at the trough there is no stigma attached to the specialist; he may indeed be considered more saint than sinner.

So, why not use another word that has a chance of clarifying our meaning? Let's try an acronym—the first letters of several truly definitive words: **L**iving **O**ff **O**thers **T**houghtlessly—**LOOT!**

Looting is an accurate synonym for plundering and still carries a sharp verbal sting which most of us would rather avoid. Nevertheless, many of us today are *thoughtlessly* living off the labor of others.

Throughout history there have been looters of this or that variety. But we seem now to be confronted with a *progression* of such harmful behavior. As more and more people have abandoned more scruples—feathering their nests at the expense of others—looting in its countless forms has more and more become a way of life.

Emerson wrote, "Thought is the seed of action." Honest, moral, and sound economic thought results in commendable and creative action; each person serves himself through serving others. But if dishonest, immoral, and uneconomic thinking prevails, the results must be harmful, not only to others but to the self as well. Such thoughtlessness, then—rather than careful thoughts—is the seed of actions which presently bedevil us. And the seeds, more often than not, are words with garbled meanings, such as the twisted meaning of "special privilege"—warped from bad to good. The tyranny of words!

It is increasingly evident that countless millions in all walks of life thoughtlessly "live" off others; they loot and they don't know it. They are the unwitting victims of their own naïveté, stumbling along the devolutionary road.

Does a professional thief think of himself as a looter? No, he probably thinks of himself as a professional. He has only a primitive or stunted mentality, like the tribesmen of yore who raided distant tribes and made off with what they thoughtlessly regarded as theirs. Economically illiterate—but innocent!

So, we have in the professional crook an unconscious looter suffering no mental pains but glorying in his "gains." Exceptional? No, tens of millions fall into this identical category, and with pride instead of guilt.

Frédéric Bastiat helps us to see through this shameful practice:

> See if the law [government] takes from some persons what belongs to them, and gives it to other persons to whom it does not belong. See if the law benefits one citizen at the expense of another *by doing what the citizen himself cannot do without committing a crime.*

It is obvious that government would not take from some and give to others were the others to reject the loot. It follows then, that the recipients of ill-gotten gains are as sinful as the government which effects the transfer by force.

Only the hardened professional criminals—a fraction of the population—would personally so indulge themselves. The vast majority would refrain from immoral action were it a you-and-me relationship. Honesty would prevail.

However, when government does the coercive taking and handing out, most citizens—those who do no thinking for themselves—are relieved of any sense of indulging in crimes. Instead they experience a false sense of absolution. Their lack of vision obscures reality!

In compiling a list of looters, let us take care not to confine it just to the "beneficiaries" of food stamps, Medicare, rent control, federal housing projects, workers paid not to work or farmers paid not to farm, and countless thousands of others engaged in more or less obvious forms of looting. In fairness, we must label all looting as such, and much of it is far from obvious. We must include all instances where coercion, be it private or public, is employed to "benefit" some at the expense of others. The list is too long to count, let alone explain, so a few samplings must suffice.

- In St. Louis it was a Gateway Arch that taxpayers from every state were compelled to help finance. Elsewhere, a school, library, park, dam, housing project, or whatever. Is there a community in the U.S.A. without one more such monuments to looting?
- Minimum-wage laws coercively invoked, with strong support from labor unions, cause large-scale unemployment, the burdens of which all taxpayers are compelled to share. This, too, is a form of looting.
- Strikers by the thousands quit their jobs, and the law makes it impossible for others to accept the jobs the strikers have vacated. More unemployment, less productivity, higher prices and taxes—consumers and taxpayers looted!
- Businessmen and their associations obtain legal prohibitions of free exchange, such as tariffs, embargoes, and quotas. They are no less looters than are the striking workmen. How is this looting done? All others are deprived of the opportunity to produce in those fields—the looting or limitation of their livelihood and their lives.

At this point, let us be mindful of that old adage, "the pot calling the kettle black." For we critics of looting may be looters ourselves. Plundering is so rampant that everyone is involved more or less—unconsciously participating or trapped beyond escape. Doubtless you are trapped in the Social Security "lootery." I am trapped in the socialist mail "system." Examples abound. This predicament poses the final question: What should we critics of looting do? What might the right tactic be?

Perhaps another acronym may help to clarify the creative force: **Living In Good High Thought: LIGHT!**

To see the **LIGHT** we need what I would call intellectual binoculars. We should see, not with just one, but with both eyes.

The vast majority see with one eye only and, as a consequence, observe merely surface or false appearances. Being half-blind results in discouragement and frustration; it lacks any creative stimulus—life's mission abandoned.

Fortunately, there are those who see with one eye the falseness of **LOOT**, and with the other observe the true **LIGHT**. To thus see beneath the surface brings enlightenment—encouragement. Such persons are aware of the growing numbers who are beginning to see the destructiveness of plunder and how freedom works its unbelievable wonders.

The half-blind see only the shadows. Those with "intellectual binoculars" can share the insight of Goethe:

> Where the light is brightest,
> The shadows are darkest.

The Federalist No. 10

By James Madison

The Utility of the Union as a Safeguard Against Domestic Faction and Insurrection (continued)

To the People of the State of New York:

AMONG THE NUMEROUS advantages promised by a well constructed Union, none deserves to be more accurately developed than its tendency to break and control the violence of faction. The friend of popular governments never finds himself so much alarmed for their character and fate, as when he contemplates their propensity to this dangerous vice. He will not fail, therefore, to set a due value on any plan which, without violating the principles to which he is attached, provides a proper cure for it. The instability, injustice, and confusion introduced into the public councils, have, in truth, been the mortal diseases under which popular governments have everywhere perished; as they continue to be the favorite and fruitful topics from which the adversaries to liberty derive their most specious declamations. The valuable improvements made by the American constitutions on the popular models, both ancient and modern, cannot certainly be too much admired; but it would be an unwarrantable partiality, to contend that they have as effectually obviated the danger on this side, as was wished and expected. Complaints are everywhere heard from our most considerate and virtuous citizens, equally the friends of public and private faith, and of public and personal liberty, that our governments are too unstable, that the public good is disregarded in the conflicts of rival parties, and that measures are too often decided, not according to the rules of justice and the rights of the minor party, but by the superior force of an interested and overbearing majority. However anxiously we may wish that these complaints had no foundation, the evidence, of known facts will not permit us to deny that they are in some degree true. It will be found, indeed, on a candid review of our situation, that some of the distresses under which we labor have been erroneously charged on the operation of our governments; but it will be found, at the same time, that other causes will not alone account for many of our heaviest misfortunes; and, particularly, for that prevailing and increasing distrust of public engagements, and alarm for private rights, which are echoed

James Madison, "The Federalist No. 10," from <http://www.constitution.org/fed/federa10.htm>.

from one end of the continent to the other. These must be chiefly, if not wholly, effects of the unsteadiness and injustice with which a factious spirit has tainted our public administrations.

By a faction, I understand a number of citizens, whether amounting to a majority or a minority of the whole, who are united and actuated by some common impulse of passion, or of interest, adversed to the rights of other citizens, or to the permanent and aggregate interests of the community.

There are two methods of curing the mischiefs of faction: the one, by removing its causes; the other, by controlling its effects.

There are again two methods of removing the causes of faction: the one, by destroying the liberty which is essential to its existence; the other, by giving to every citizen the same opinions, the same passions, and the same interests.

It could never be more truly said than of the first remedy, that it was worse than the disease. Liberty is to faction what air is to fire, an aliment without which it instantly expires. But it could not be less folly to abolish liberty, which is essential to political life, because it nourishes faction, than it would be to wish the annihilation of air, which is essential to animal life, because it imparts to fire its destructive agency.

The second expedient is as impracticable as the first would be unwise. As long as the reason of man continues fallible, and he is at liberty to exercise it, different opinions will be formed. As long as the connection subsists between his reason and his self-love, his opinions and his passions will have a reciprocal influence on each other; and the former will be objects to which the latter will attach themselves. The diversity in the faculties of men, from which the rights of property originate, is not less an insuperable obstacle to a uniformity of interests. The protection of these faculties is the first object of government. From the protection of different and unequal faculties of acquiring property, the possession of different degrees and kinds of property immediately results; and from the influence of these on the sentiments and views of the respective proprietors, ensues a division of the society into different interests and parties.

The latent causes of faction are thus sown in the nature of man; and we see them everywhere brought into different degrees of activity, according to the different circumstances of civil society. A zeal for different opinions concerning religion, concerning government, and many other points, as well of speculation as of practice; an attachment to different leaders ambitiously contending for pre-eminence and power; or to persons of other descriptions whose fortunes have been interesting to the human passions, have, in turn, divided mankind into parties, inflamed them with mutual animosity, and rendered them much more disposed to vex and oppress each other than to cooperate for their common good. So strong is this propensity of mankind to fall into mutual animosities, that where no substantial occasion presents itself, the most frivolous and fanciful distinctions have been sufficient to kindle their unfriendly passions and excite their most violent conflicts. But the most common and durable source of factions has been the various and unequal distribution of property. Those who hold and those who are without property have ever formed distinct interests in society. Those who are creditors, and those who are debtors, fall under a like discrimination. A landed interest, a manufacturing interest, a mercantile interest, a moneyed interest, with many lesser interests, grow up of necessity in civilized nations, and divide them into different classes, actuated by different sentiments and views. The regulation of these various and interfering interests forms the principal task of modern legislation, and involves the spirit of party and faction in the necessary and ordinary operations of the government.

No man is allowed to be a judge in his own cause, because his interest would certainly bias his judgment, and, not improbably, corrupt his integrity. With equal, nay with greater reason, a body of men are unfit to be both judges and parties at the same time; yet what are many of the most important acts of legislation, but so many judicial determinations, not indeed concerning the rights of single persons, but concerning the rights of large bodies of citizens? And what are the different classes of legislators but advocates and parties to the causes which they determine? Is a law proposed concerning private debts? It is a question to which the creditors are parties on one side and the debtors on the other. Justice ought to hold the balance between them. Yet the parties are, and must be, themselves the judges; and the most numerous party, or, in other words, the most powerful faction must be expected to prevail. Shall domestic manufactures be encouraged, and in what degree, by restrictions on foreign manufactures? are questions which would be differently decided by the landed and the manufacturing classes, and probably by neither with a sole regard to justice and the public good. The apportionment of taxes on the various descriptions of property is an act which seems to require the most exact impartiality; yet there is, perhaps, no legislative act in which greater opportunity and temptation are given to a predominant party to trample on the rules of justice. Every shilling with which they overburden the inferior number, is a shilling saved to their own pockets.

It is in vain to say that enlightened statesmen will be able to adjust these clashing interests, and render them all subservient to the public good. Enlightened statesmen will not always be at the helm. Nor, in many cases, can such an adjustment be made at all without taking into view indirect and remote considerations, which will rarely prevail over the immediate interest which one party may find in disregarding the rights of another or the good of the whole.

The inference to which we are brought is, that the *causes* of faction cannot be removed, and that relief is only to be sought in the means of controlling its *effects*.

If a faction consists of less than a majority, relief is supplied by the republican principle, which enables the majority to defeat its sinister views by regular vote. It may clog the administration, it may convulse the society; but it will be unable to execute and mask its violence under the forms of the Constitution. When a majority is included in a faction, the form of popular government, on the other hand, enables it to sacrifice to its ruling passion or interest both the public good and the rights of other citizens. To secure the public good and private rights against the danger of such a faction, and at the same time to preserve the spirit and the form of popular government, is then the great object to which our inquiries are directed. Let me add that it is the great desideratum by which this form of government can be rescued from the opprobrium under which it has so long labored, and be recommended to the esteem and adoption of mankind.

By what means is this object attainable? Evidently by one of two only. Either the existence of the same passion or interest in a majority at the same time must be prevented, or the majority, having such coexistent passion or interest, must be rendered, by their number and local situation, unable to concert and carry into effect schemes of oppression. If the impulse and the opportunity be suffered to coincide, we well know that neither moral nor religious motives can be relied on as an adequate control. They are not found to be such on the injustice and violence of individuals, and lose their efficacy in proportion to the number combined together, that is, in proportion as their efficacy becomes needful.

From this view of the subject it may be concluded that a pure democracy, by which I mean a society consisting of a small number of citizens, who assemble and administer the government in person, can admit of no cure for the mischiefs of faction. A common passion or interest will, in almost every case, be felt by a majority of the whole; a communication and concert result from the form of government itself; and there is nothing to check the inducements to sacrifice the weaker party or an obnoxious individual. Hence it is that such democracies have ever been spectacles of turbulence and contention; have ever been found incompatible with personal security or the rights of property; and have in general been as short in their lives as they have been violent in their deaths. Theoretic politicians, who have patronized this species of government, have erroneously supposed that by reducing mankind to a perfect equality in their political rights, they would, at the same time, be perfectly equalized and assimilated in their possessions, their opinions, and their passions.

A republic, by which I mean a government in which the scheme of representation takes place, opens a different prospect, and promises the cure for which we are seeking. Let us examine the points in which it varies from pure democracy, and we shall comprehend both the nature of the cure and the efficacy which it must derive from the Union.

The two great points of difference between a democracy and a republic are: first, the delegation of the government, in the latter, to a small number of citizens elected by the rest; secondly, the greater number of citizens, and greater sphere of country, over which the latter may be extended.

The effect of the first difference is, on the one hand, to refine and enlarge the public views, by passing them through the medium of a chosen body of citizens, whose wisdom may best discern the true interest of their country, and whose patriotism and love of justice will be least likely to sacrifice it to temporary or partial considerations. Under such a regulation, it may well happen that the public voice, pronounced by the representatives of the people, will be more consonant to the public good than if pronounced by the people themselves, convened for the purpose. On the other hand, the effect may be inverted. Men of factious tempers, of local prejudices, or of sinister designs, may, by intrigue, by corruption, or by other means, first obtain the suffrages, and then betray the interests, of the people. The question resulting is, whether small or extensive republics are more favorable to the election of proper guardians of the public weal; and it is clearly decided in favor of the latter by two obvious considerations:

In the first place, it is to be remarked that, however small the republic may be, the representatives must be raised to a certain number, in order to guard against the cabals of a few; and that, however large it may be, they must be limited to a certain number, in order to guard against the confusion of a multitude. Hence, the number of representatives in the two cases not being in proportion to that of the two constituents, and being proportionally greater in the small republic, it follows that, if the proportion of fit characters be not less in the large than in the small republic, the former will present a greater option, and consequently a greater probability of a fit choice.

In the next place, as each representative will be chosen by a greater number of citizens in the large than in the small republic, it will be more difficult for unworthy candidates to practice with success the vicious arts by which elections are too often carried; and the suffrages of the people being more free, will be more likely to centre in men who possess the most attractive merit and the most diffusive and established characters.

It must be confessed that in this, as in most other cases, there is a mean, on both sides of which inconveniences will be found to lie. By enlarging too much the number of electors, you render the representatives too little acquainted with all their local circumstances and lesser interests; as by reducing it too much, you render him unduly attached to these, and too little fit to comprehend and pursue great and national objects. The federal Constitution forms a happy combination in this respect; the great and aggregate interests being referred to the national, the local and particular to the State legislatures.

The other point of difference is, the greater number of citizens and extent of territory which may be brought within the compass of republican than of democratic government; and it is this circumstance principally which renders factious combinations less to be dreaded in the former than in the latter. The smaller the society, the fewer probably will be the distinct parties and interests composing it; the fewer the distinct parties and interests, the more frequently will a majority be found of the same party; and the smaller the number of individuals composing a majority, and the smaller the compass within which they are placed, the more easily will they concert and execute their plans of oppression. Extend the sphere, and you take in a greater variety of parties and interests; you make it less probable that a majority of the whole will have a common motive to invade the rights of other citizens; or if such a common motive exists, it will be more difficult for all who feel it to discover their own strength, and to act in unison with each other. Besides other impediments, it may be remarked that, where there is a consciousness of unjust or dishonorable purposes, communication is always checked by distrust in proportion to the number whose concurrence is necessary.

Hence, it clearly appears, that the same advantage which a republic has over a democracy, in controlling the effects of faction, is enjoyed by a large over a small republic,—is enjoyed by the Union over the States composing it. Does the advantage consist in the substitution of representatives whose enlightened views and virtuous sentiments render them superior to local prejudices and schemes of injustice? It will not be denied that the representation of the Union will be most likely to possess these requisite endowments. Does it consist in the greater security afforded by a greater variety of parties, against the event of any one party being able to out-number and oppress the rest? In an equal degree does the increased variety of parties comprised within the Union, increase this security. Does it, in fine, consist in the greater obstacles opposed to the concert and accomplishment of the secret wishes of an unjust and interested majority? Here, again, the extent of the Union gives it the most palpable advantage.

The influence of factious leaders may kindle a flame within their particular States, but will be unable to spread a general conflagration through the other States. A religious sect may degenerate into a political faction in a part of the Confederacy; but the variety of sects dispersed over the entire face of it must secure the national councils against any danger from that source. A rage for paper money, for an abolition of debts, for an equal division of property, or for any other improper or wicked project, will be less apt to pervade the whole body of the Union than a particular member of it; in the same proportion as such a malady is more likely to taint a particular county or district, than an entire State.

In the extent and proper structure of the Union, therefore, we behold a republican remedy for the diseases most incident to republican government. And according to the degree of pleasure and pride we feel in being republicans, ought to be our zeal in cherishing the spirit and supporting the character of Federalists.

PUBLIUS

Not Yours to Give

By Davy Crockett

In this tale an unidentified narrator relates Davy Crockett's experience when he was a member of Congress (1827–31, 1832–1835). The story is slightly condensed from The Life of Colonel David Crockett *compiled by Edward S. Ellis (Philadelphia: Porter & Coates, 1884).*

First published as "A Sockdolager" in The Freeman, *August 1961, "Not Yours to Give" has been a FEE favorite for more than 40 years, second in popularity only to "I, Pencil."*

Holders of political office are but reflections of the dominant leadership—good or bad—among the electorate. Horatio Bunce is a striking example of responsible citizenship. Were his kind to multiply, we would see many new faces in public office; or as in the case of Davy Crockett, a new Crockett.

ONE DAY IN the House of Representatives, a bill was taken up appropriating money for the benefit of a widow of a distinguished naval officer. Several beautiful speeches had been made in its support. The Speaker was just about to put the question when Crockett arose:

"Mr. Speaker—I have as much respect for the memory of the deceased, and as much sympathy for the sufferings of the living, if suffering there be, as any man in this House, but we must not permit our respect for the dead or our sympathy for a part of the living to lead us into an act of injustice to the balance of the living. I will not go into an argument to prove that Congress has no power to appropriate this money as an act of charity. Every member upon this floor knows it. We have the right, as individuals, to give away as much of our own money as we please in charity; but as members of Congress we have no right so to appropriate a dollar of the public money. Some eloquent appeals have been made to us upon the ground that it is a debt due the deceased. Mr. Speaker, the deceased lived long after the close of the war; he was in office to the day of his death, and I have never heard that the government was in arrears to him.

"Every man in this House knows it is not a debt. We cannot, without the grossest corruption, appropriate this money as the payment of a debt. We have not the semblance of authority to appropriate it as a charity. Mr. Speaker, I have said we have the right to give as much money

Davy Crockett, "Not Yours to Give," from <http://fee.org/nff/not-yours-to-give/>.

of our own as we please. I am the poorest man on this floor. I cannot vote for this bill, but I will give one week's pay to the object, and if every member of Congress will do the same, it will amount to more than the bill asks."

He took his seat. Nobody replied. The bill was put upon its passage, and, instead of passing unanimously, as was generally supposed, and as, no doubt, it would, but for that speech, it received but few votes, and, of course, was lost.

Later, when asked by a friend why he had opposed the appropriation, Crockett gave this explanation:

"Several years ago I was one evening standing on the steps of the Capitol with some other members of Congress, when our attention was attracted by a great light over in Georgetown. It was evidently a large fire. We jumped into a hack and drove over as fast as we could. In spite of all that could be done, many houses were burned and many families made houseless, and, besides, some of them had lost all but the clothes they had on. The weather was very cold, and when I saw so many women and children suffering, I felt that something ought to be done for them. The next morning a bill was introduced appropriating $20,000 for their relief. We put aside all other business and rushed it through as soon as it could be done.

"The next summer, when it began to be time to think about the election, I concluded I would take a scout around among the boys of my district. I had no opposition there, but, as the election was some time off, I did not know what might turn up. When riding one day in a part of my district in which I was more of a stranger than any other, I saw a man in a field plowing and coming toward the road. I gauged my gait so that we should meet as he came up to the fence. As he came up, I spoke to the man. He replied politely, but, as I thought, rather coldly.

I began: "Well, friend, I am one of those unfortunate beings called candidates, and—"

"Yes I know you; you are Colonel Crockett. I have seen you once before, and voted for you the last time you were elected. I suppose you are out electioneering now, but you had better not waste your time or mine. I shall not vote for you again."

"This was a sockdolager ... I begged him to tell me what was the matter."

"'Well, Colonel, it is hardly worth-while to waste time or words upon it. I do not see how it can be mended, but you gave a vote last winter which shows that either you have not capacity to understand the Constitution, or that you are wanting in the honesty and firmness to be guided by it. In either case you are not the man to represent me. But I beg your pardon for expressing it in that way. I did not intend to avail myself of the privilege of the constituent to speak plainly to a candidate for the purpose of insulting or wounding you. I intend by it only to say that your understanding of the Constitution is very different from mine; and I will say to you what, but for my rudeness, I should not have said, that I believe you to be honest ... But an understanding of the Constitution different from mine I cannot overlook, because the Constitution, to be worth anything, must be held sacred, and rigidly observed in all its provisions. The man who wields power and misinterprets it is the more dangerous the more honest he is."

"'I admit the truth of all you say, but there must be some mistake about it, for I do not remember that I gave any vote last winter upon any constitutional question.'

"No, Colonel, there's no mistake. Though I live here in the backwoods and seldom go from home, I take the papers from Washington and read very carefully all the proceedings of

Congress. My papers say that last winter you voted for a bill to appropriate $20,000 to some sufferers by a fire in Georgetown. Is that true?"

"Well, my friend; I may as well own up. You have got me there. But certainly nobody will complain that a great and rich country like ours should give the insignificant sum of $20,000 to relieve its suffering women and children, particularly with a full and overflowing Treasury, and I am sure, if you had been there, you would have done just as I did."

"It is not the amount, Colonel, that I complain of; it is the principle. In the first place, the government ought to have in the Treasury no more than enough for its legitimate purposes. But that has nothing to do with the question. The power of collecting and disbursing money at pleasure is the most dangerous power that can be entrusted to man, particularly under our system of collecting revenue by a tariff, which reaches every man in the country, no matter how poor he may be, and the poorer he is the more he pays in proportion to his means. What is worse, it presses upon him without his knowledge where the weight centers, for there is not a man in the United States who can ever guess how much he pays to the government. So you see, that while you are contributing to relieve one, you are drawing it from thousands who are even worse off than he. If you had the right to give anything, the amount was simply a matter of discretion with you, and you had as much right to give $20,000,000 as $20,000. If you have the right to give to one, you have the right to give to all; and, as the Constitution neither defines charity nor stipulates the amount, you are at liberty to give to any and everything which you may believe, or profess to believe, is a charity, and to any amount you may think proper. You will very easily perceive what a wide door this would open for fraud and corruption and favoritism, on the one hand, and for robbing the people on the other. No, Colonel, Congress has no right to give charity. Individual members may give as much of their own money as they please, but they have no right to touch a dollar of the public money for that purpose. If twice as many houses had been burned in this county as in Georgetown, neither you nor any other member of Congress would have thought of appropriating a dollar for our relief. There are about two hundred and forty members of Congress. If they had shown their sympathy for the sufferers by contributing each one week's pay, it would have made over $13,000. There are plenty of wealthy men in and around Washington who could have given $20,000 without depriving themselves of even a luxury of life. The congressmen chose to keep their own money, which, if reports be true, some of them spend not very creditably; and the people about Washington, no doubt, applauded you for relieving them from the necessity of giving what was not yours to give. The people have delegated to Congress, by the Constitution, the power to do certain things. To do these, it is authorized to collect and pay moneys, and for nothing else. Everything beyond this is usurpation, and a violation of the Constitution.

"So you see, Colonel, you have violated the Constitution in what I consider a vital point. It is a precedent fraught with danger to the country, for when Congress once begins to stretch its power beyond the limits of the Constitution, there is no limit to it, and no security for the people. I have no doubt you acted honestly, but that does not make it any better, except as far as you are personally concerned, and you see that I cannot vote for you."

"I tell you I felt streaked. I saw if I should have opposition, and this man should go to talking, he would set others to talking, and in that district I was a gone fawn-skin. I could not answer him, and the fact is, I was so fully convinced that he was right, I did not want to. But I must satisfy him, and I said to him:

"Well, my friend, you hit the nail upon the head when you said I had not sense enough to understand the Constitution. I intended to be guided by it, and thought I had studied it fully. I have heard many speeches in Congress about the powers of Congress, but what you have said here at your plow has got more hard, sound sense in it than all the fine speeches I ever heard. If I had ever taken the view of it that you have, I would have put my head into the fire before I would have given that vote; and if you will forgive me and vote for me again, if I ever vote for another unconstitutional law I wish I may be shot."

"He laughingly replied; 'Yes, Colonel, you have sworn to that once before, but I will trust you again upon one condition. You say that you are convinced that your vote was wrong. Your acknowledgment of it will do more good than beating you for it. If, as you go around the district, you will tell people about this vote, and that you are satisfied it was wrong, I will not only vote for you, but will do what I can to keep down opposition, and, perhaps, I may exert some little influence in that way."

"If I don't," said I, "I wish I may be shot; and to convince you that I am in earnest in what I say I will come back this way in a week or ten days, and if you will get up a gathering of the people, I will make a speech to them. Get up a barbecue, and I will pay for it."

"No, Colonel, we are not rich people in this section, but we have plenty of provisions to contribute for a barbecue, and some to spare for those who have none. The push of crops will be over in a few days, and we can then afford a day for a barbecue. This is Thursday; I will see to getting it up on Saturday week. Come to my house on Friday, and we will go together, and I promise you a very respectable crowd to see and hear you."

"Well, I will be here. But one thing more before I say good-by. I must know your name."

"My name is Bunce."

"Not Horatio Bunce?"

"Yes."

"Well, Mr. Bunce, I never saw you before, though you say you have seen me, but I know you very well. I am glad I have met you, and very proud that I may hope to have you for my friend."

"It was one of the luckiest hits of my life that I met him. He mingled but little with the public, but was widely known for his remarkable intelligence and incorruptible integrity, and for a heart brimfull and running over with kindness and benevolence, which showed themselves not only in words but in acts. He was the oracle of the whole country around him, and his fame had extended far beyond the circle of his immediate acquaintance. Though I had never met him before, I had heard much of him, and but for this meeting it is very likely I should have had opposition, and had been beaten. One thing is very certain, no man could now stand up in that district under such a vote.

"At the appointed time I was at his house, having told our conversation to every crowd I had met, and to every man I stayed all night with, and I found that it gave the people an interest and a confidence in me stronger than I had ever seen manifested before.

"Though I was considerably fatigued when I reached his house, and, under ordinary cir-cumstances, should have gone early to bed, I kept him up until midnight, talking about the principles and affairs of government, and got more real, true knowledge of them than I had got all my life before.

"I have known and seen much of him since, for I respect him—no, that is not the word—I reverence and love him more than any living man, and I go to see him two or three times every year; and I will tell you, sir, if every one who professes to be a Christian lived and acted and enjoyed it as he does, the religion of Christ would take the world by storm.

"But to return to my story. The next morning we went to the barbecue, and, to my surprise, found about a thousand men there. I met a good many whom I had not known before, and they and my friend introduced me around until I had got pretty well acquainted—at least, they all knew me.

"In due time notice was given that I would speak to them. They gathered up around a stand that had been erected. I opened my speech by saying:

'Fellow-citizens—I present myself before you today feeling like a new man. My eyes have lately been opened to truths which ignorance or prejudice, or both, had heretofore hidden from my view. I feel that I can today offer you the ability to render you more valuable service than I have ever been able to render before. I am here today more for the purpose of acknowledging my error than to seek your votes. That I should make this acknowledgment is due to myself as well as to you. Whether you will vote for me is a matter for your consideration only.'

"I went on to tell them about the fire and my vote for the appropriation and then told them why I was satisfied it was wrong. I closed by saying:

'And now, fellow-citizens, it remains only for me to tell you that the most of the speech you have listened to with so much interest was simply a repetition of the arguments by which your neighbor, Mr. Bunce, convinced me of my error.

'It is the best speech I ever made in my life, but he is entitled to the credit for it. And now I hope he is satisfied with his convert and that he will get up here and tell you so.'

"He came upon the stand and said:

"Fellow citizens—It affords me great pleasure to comply with the request of Colonel Crockett. I have always considered him a thoroughly honest man, and I am satisfied that he will faithfully perform all that he has promised you today."

"He went down, and there went up from that crowd such a shout for Davy Crockett as his name never called forth before.

"I am not much given to tears, but I was taken with a choking then and felt some big drops rolling down my cheeks. And I tell you now that the remembrance of those few words spoken by such a man, and the honest, hearty shout they produced, is worth more to me than all the honors I have received and all the reputation I have ever made, or ever shall make, as a member of Congress."

"Now, sir," concluded Crockett, "you know why I made that speech yesterday.

"There is one thing now to which I will call your attention. You remember that I proposed to give a week's pay. There are in that House many very wealthy men—men who think nothing of spending a week's pay, or a dozen of them, for a dinner or a wine party when they have something to accomplish by it. Some of those same men made beautiful speeches upon the great debt of gratitude which the country owed the deceased—a debt which could not be paid by money—and the insignificance and worthlessness of money, particularly so insignificant a sum as $10,000, when weighed against the honor of the nation. Yet not one of them responded to my proposition. Money with them is nothing but trash when it is to come out of the people. But it is the one great thing for which most of them are striving, and many of them sacrifice honor, integrity, and justice to obtain it."

Cloaking the State's Dagger

By Robert Nisbet

WHAT WE CALL political philosophy is so overladen in the West with euphemism, panegyric, and idealization that anyone might be forgiven for occasionally failing to remember just what this philosophy's true subject is: the political state, unique among major institutions in its claim of absolute power over human lives. Euphemisms for the state drawn from kinship, religion, nature, reason, mechanics, biology, the people, and other essentially nonpolitical sources have been ascendant for so long in Western history that it is downright difficult to keep in mind that the state's origin and essential function is, as philosopher David Hume pointed out in the 18th century, in and of force—above all, military force. What procreation is to kinship and propitiation of gods is to religion, monopolization of power is to the state.

There is no political order known to us in history, from ancient Egypt to contemporary Israel, that has not originated in war, its claimed sovereignty but an extension and ramification of what the Romans called the *imperium,* absolute military command. War is the origin of the state and, in Randolph Bourne's familiar phrasing, is the health of the state. Modern war, grounded as it usually is in the kinds of political and moral ideals, or claimed ideals, which can justify almost limitless expansion of the state at the expense of society, is very healthful indeed to any form of state.

The essence of the state, then, is its unique possession of sovereignty—absolute and unconditional power over all individuals and their associations and possessions within a given area. And at the basis of the state's sovereignty is the contingent power to use the military to compel obedience to its rule. This is as true of democratic as of despotic states.

The most democratic of contemporary states claims a monopoly of power within its borders, exclusive possession of and control over the military and police, and the right to declare war and peace, to conscript life and appropriate income and property, to levy taxes, to supervise the family and even, when necessary, the church, to grant selective entitlements, to administer justice, and to define crime and set punishment. The political state is the only association whose freedom to act cannot be limited by the state. With all respect to differences among types of government, there is not, in strict theory, any difference between the powers available to the democratic and to the totalitarian state. We may pride ourselves in the democracies on bills or other expressions of individual rights against the state, but in fact they are rights against a given government and in history and practice have been obliterated or sharply diminished when deemed necessary, as in the United States and other Western-democratic powers in the two world wars.

It is not strange, then, that the history of the state should be accompanied by the rich embroidery of euphemism. Any institution born of war, that thrives in war, and that claims unique absoluteness of power over all individuals within its borders requires all the symbolic assistance it can get. Such assistance has for a very long time been the offering of the political clerisy. Like the church, the state must have its defenders, rationalizers, and justifiers, its scribes and prophets. Also like the church, the state must have its dogmas and rituals, its feast days, its saints and martyrs, and its sacred objects.

FAMILY

The oldest of euphemisms for the state's distinctive military power is drawn from the realm of kinship, which is natural, given the age and universality of family, clan, and kindred in mankind's history. Thus early kings or chiefs might claim themselves patriarchs. Recurrently in history, kings have been rulers of *peoples* rather than territories; they were this in the early Middle Ages. *King* is a derivative of Old English *cyng,* meaning kinship.

The patriarchal image of the state was nourished by a good deal of theology during the Middle Ages: and feudalism itself, as we find it at its height, was an ingenious fusion of military substance and kinship symbol. Patriarchalism survived the decline of medieval society, its enduring appeal well illustrated in the modern world by the popularity everywhere of such words and phrases as *fatherland, mother country, sister-nations,* and the like. Mario Cuomo, the keynote speaker at the 1984 Democratic convention, used the word *family* to describe the American nation just under two dozen times. It was with a keen sense of the antiquity of kinship metaphors in politics that George Orwell chose to give his horrifying totalitarian government the label of Big Brother. But in many ways the most telling example of the power of a euphemism in thought is the argument in political and social philosophy—extending from Aristotle to modern political ethnology—that the state is but the natural development through time of kinship. It assuredly is not, but the myth appears to be ineradicable by now.

RELIGION

Religion is second only to family in its fecundity of euphemism for the war-born state. Prepolitical man was as saturated by religious as by kinship influences upon his thinking. Almost as hoary as the patriarch is the prophet in mankind's annals. How better to give root to a military conqueror's acceptance by the conquered than to sanctify, even deify, him; to make him at worst an indispensable voice of the gods, at best one of the gods himself. Egyptian kings were addressed in rescript and inscription as Aton, Horus, Re, and so on in the order to give expression to their claimed identities as sun-gods.

The speed with which passage from the human to the divine could occur, and much later than the age of Egyptian pharaohs, is well illustrated by the careers of Alexander in the Hellenistic world and of Octavian, conqueror of Mark Antony at Actium, in the Roman. The latter was obliged by still-respected republican tradition to be more subtle than had been Alexander, but even so not a great deal of time passed before Octavian became officially *Imperator Caesar divi filus Augustus,* a title that artfully fused military, divine, and kinship.

> **The history of political thought is a history of one euphemism after another to disguise the naked power of the state.** —Robert Nisbet

Christianity was born in a setting of emperor-worship, and from the beginning its teachers and missionaries sought to nullify as far as possible the influence of the imperial religion upon Christian minds. But taking the long history of Christianity into account, it is impossible to overlook the readiness with which Christian faith and dogma could include acceptance of the sacredness of royal office if not personage. The crowning of Charlemagne by the Pope as *holy* Roman emperor suggests first the claim of suzerainty by church over state, including power of investiture of king, but second the allowance by church of sacred character into the kingship. Even the most powerful and assertive of popes in the Middle Ages did not deny to kingships their holy, if derivative, status.

It was, however, in the Reformation that the unqualified divinity of kings was once again proclaimed in the West. As Luther, Calvin, and others saw the matter, elevation of kings to divine status in their rule—directly divine status, unmediated by church—was as powerful a blow as could be struck at the hated and feared papacy. We tend to associate James I of England most prominently with the Divine Right of Kings because of his early-manifest fascination with the theology of the subject. It was under Charles I, though, in 1640, that what must be the all-time high in English belief in royal divinity was expressed. The statement begins: "The most high and sacred order of kings is of Divine Right, being the ordinance of God Himself, founded in the Prime laws of nature, and clearly established by express texts both of the Old and new Testaments."

Despite the numerous rationalist criticisms to which the divine-right panegyric was subjected in the next two centuries, it survived healthily. It was the influential German philosopher Hegel who, during the 19th century, declared the state—with the Prussian state foremost in mind—"the march of God on earth." And even when the German political idealists chose to retreat God to the background, obvious surrogates for God abounded: Dialectic, World-Spirit, and so on. ...

THE PEOPLE

Very probably the most fateful concept of the late 18th century in politics was "the people." Not the numerical aggregate of all who lived within a given set of boundaries, for this could include rabble on the one hand and tyrants and exploiters on the other. Rather, those individuals who could free their minds of sectarian prejudices and loyalties, who could in a rational way make their individual ways to comprehension of the general good and who acted virtuously in political matters—these were "the people," properly understood. If government were based in them, it would be inherently incapable of tyranny, for the people would never tyrannize itself.

Jean-Jacques Rousseau's momentous idea of the general will epitomized perfectly this vision of the people in contrast to a mere multitude. The vision has made its way uninterruptedly through 19th-century ideas of plebiscitary dictatorship to 20th century totalitarianisms, none of the latter would use *totalitarian* as a label. For that matter even *communism* tends to be eschewed in favor of, say, *people's democratic republic.* ...

SOCIAL WELFARE

During the 20th century, yet another euphemism for political power has made its way into popular usage: the social welfare state. It is one of history's ironies that the word *social* should have been so easily appropriated by the political clerisy. When this word achieved popularity in the West in the early 19th century, the context was overwhelmingly the *nonpolitical* spheres of society—family, neighborhood, local community, and voluntary cooperative association foremost. To French sociologists and radical anarchists alike, the state and the political were in bad odor after the totalitarianism of the Revolution. Auguste Comte, founder of sociology, led the way in seeking to repudiate the political and to exalt the social as the only feasible alternative to the political. Alas for Comte's hopes, the political clerisy was already at work seizing upon the "social" before he died.

It is not difficult to understand the attractiveness of the "social" in place of the "political", for the latter had inevitably become somewhat stained in the public imagination. There were too many citizens for whom the state was still a reminder of war and taxes, and, in any event, there were simply limits to what could be done with the word *political.* Such neologisms as *politicization* and, worse, *politicalization* didn't recommend themselves when reference was being made to the political state's ownership and control of increasingly large areas of economy and society. Such words may have told the truth, but it is the function of language to be able to conceal, as well as reveal, the truth.

Social was made to order as a beguiling prefix. "Social reform," "social security," and "social budget"' were so much better as labels for what governments were actually doing than would have been any of these with the word *political* used instead of *social.* Similarly, for those who could dream of an ever more state-dominated future, *socialism* was much to be preferred to *politicism.* And who is to say the clerisy is wrong? How, for instance, could the now-mammoth and always near-bankrupting "social security" system in the United States have ever reached its eminence and load of close to 40 million people it if had been called in the beginning "political security" or something so mercilessly exact as "state charity ..."

AFTERWORD

It is almost too much to bear. More than 2,000 years of political euphemism and panegyric, and with what result? The state, born of war and nourished by war, has become, all euphemism notwithstanding, more powerful, more inquisitorial in human lives, than at any time in its history. It is almost as if Mars, god of war, were exacting tribute from us for having sought for thousands of years to conceal with euphemism the union of war and state. For, in our century the state has reached a pinnacle of force never before known in history, and warfare has taken more lives in devastation, killing, and mutilation than in all previous centuries put together.

The Economic View of Regulation

By Robert Rush

REGULATION, OR GOVERNMENT intervention in the market place, is a large component of modern economies. The amount of regulation in America has been ballooning since the Great Depression, and the trend appears to be an increasing one. As such, understanding why regulations come into existence becomes progressively more vital for understanding the effect of the political sphere on the economy.

Figure One illustrates the growth in regulation by reporting the per decade increase in Federal Register pages. As can be clearly seen, recent decades have experienced an enormous increase the numbers of pages of regulation. This translates into a combination of an increasing number of regulations, and an increasing complexity of new regulations. To see if this is to be welcomed or feared, we need to be aware of the nature of regulation.

FIGURE ONE: NEW FEDERAL REGISTER PAGES PER DECADE

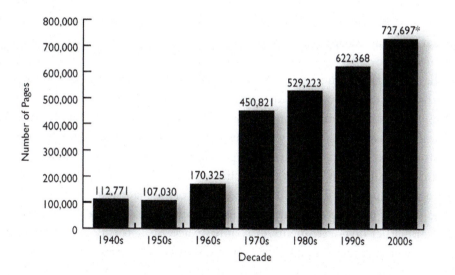

* PROJECTION BASED ON EIGHT-YEAR AVERAGE.
SOURCE: TEN THOUSAND COMMANDMENTS, CLYDE WAYNE CREWS JR..

Robert Rush, "The Economic View of Regulation." Permission to reprint granted by the author.

There are two basic camps on the origins of regulation and regulation's effectiveness in improving economic efficiency. The old theory of regulation, often referred to as the *public interest* view, sees regulations as efficient outcomes, stemming from voters' demands for protection against the abuses of businesses. The more refined of these theorists typically see regulation as bringing markets closer to their ideal competitive levels. The other is the *interest group* theory, where regulations are generated from businesses themselves and serve their interests, not that of the consumer or average voter.

There are four assumptions stated, whether explicitly or implicitly, in the public interest view of regulation. First, markets must have the capability to be inefficient. There has been a large literature generated discussing real and hypothetical market failures. However, how many of these failures actually exist, and their importance, is less clear. Secondly, there must be a mechanism where markets can become more efficient through use of coercive power. This, too, is theoretically possible in the form of Pigovian taxes and subsidies, as well as some more complicated schemes for natural monopoly regulation. Thirdly, the process of regulation must be less expensive than the problem it is fixing. Often times this is glazed over with an assumption of costless or near costless regulation.[1] The fourth assumption they made is that regulators actually attempt to reach an optimal result. All of these assumptions must hold in order for regulation to be efficient. Whether any of these fundamentals have drastically changed since the 1960s when regulation started to grow rapidly is questionable.

For a theory to be a theory it must have testable predictions, if it is to be true they must sync with the world around us. If the public interest theory were correct, we would expect to see regulation primarily in industries where externalities arguably exist, and we would also see existing regulations that are optimal responses to these problems. An externality is simply a cost or benefit that does not affect the decision makers and thus, is either over or under produced. We should then see that the industries that are regulated are those with the most pollution or other uncontrolled externalities. This also means we should primarily see taxes and subsidies with few, if any, quotas or requirements. Instead, what we see is licensing restrictions for interior decorators, and quotas for sugar. We would expect antitrust legislation to be used primarily in highly concentrated industries with rising prices, which nearly all evidence discredits. We would expect many things that are not true to life.

It can be agreed upon by nearly all in the regulatory debate that markets do not always operate at the highest possible efficiency. The main contribution of *public choice* economics is to illustrate that neither do governments. It is only by accepting this point that we can begin to explain the various regulatory puzzles. For example if ethanol is argued to be under produced, tariffs which reduce the quantity instead of increasing it would be among the last things that we would want. And yet a politician picked at random would probably groan in dismay over the lack of ethanol and then vote to place a restrictive tariff on its import.

Public choice theory sees regulation as a product purchased by industry from governmental organizations for the benefit of industry. It states that industries which otherwise would be

---

1   Richard A. Posner, "Theories of Economic Regulation" , The Bell Journal of Economics and Management Science, Vol. 5 No. 2 (Autumn, 1974),pp. 335-358

unable to form stable cartels, but can do so through the coercive force of government, are primarily those that seek to be regulated. And that regulation benefits the regulated, or at least some of those who are regulated. This however, begs the question of why, in a democracy, interest groups can generate legislation that is against the interest of the vast majority of people.

The answer to this lies in rational ignorance. Information is not costless to obtain for voters, and since they will cast a decisive vote with a near zero probability they consume little information. In addition, the cost of any one regulation to a voter is typically small, further diluting voter incentives. Those within industries, on the other hand, receive large gains from legislation, and therefore, are not only informed as to political positions, but are also willing to vote in mass almost solely based on the issue. Perhaps, more importantly, they can lobby for regulations by providing political resources. Through this process the politicians are unlikely to lose many votes, and gain voting blocks and campaign resources. Domestic corn growers can lobby to keep out foreign ethanol, and politicians are unlikely to lose votes, even if they, conflictingly, are proponents of ethanol subsidization as well.

But why, so often, like in the case of sugar, do we see quotas instead of tariffs and tariffs instead of subsidies? If interest groups can get government to take from the taxpayers and give to them, why should it be done through such inefficient means? The answer to this was first developed by Nobel Laureate economist George Stigler in his groundbreaking article *The Theory of Economic Regulation*.[2] The main idea is that subsidies have to be shared with everyone in the industry, including new entrants, so industries prefer regulations that help prevent future entrants instead. An interesting result from carrying Stigler's logic through is that it will typically be less concentrated industries that will opt for government to create large barriers to entry, as it creates effective cartels that would otherwise be impossible. Conversely, it is industries that have higher barriers to entry and higher concentrations that are more likely to get direct subsidies.

Judge Richard Posner, one of the founders of "law and economics," accepts much of this argument, but points out that it, by itself does not explain some other curious aspects of regulation.[3] Specifically, he was perplexed as to why, in so many cases, regulation creates forces that drive prices down and quantities higher than what would occur in a competitive market. Indeed, he notes that in many cases such as railways, regulation pushes prices down, even below marginal cost. Posner was able to solve this puzzle by viewing regulation as a form of taxation.

Regulation can be seen as performing redistributive tasks usually associated with the other powers of government. A clear example of this is cost structure regulation, regulation that specifies at what price varying quantities may be sold for in industries with fixed costs. This leads to the true cost of a product being shifted from one group of customers to another, which in turn helps certain firms in an industry while hurting others. As Posner notes, in this case groups of purchasers who benefit the most might be the ones who bring about the legislation, not just firms who might benefit from a cost structure regulation.

---

2   George Stigler, "The Theory of Economic Regulation", The Bell Journal of Economics and Management Science, Vol. 2, No. 1 (Spring, 1971), pp. 3-21

3   Richard A. Posner, "Taxation by Regulation", The Bell Journal of Economics and Management Science, Vol. 2, No. 1 (Spring, 1971), pp. 22-50

Pricing below marginal cost is inefficient, and indeed, in the presence of fixed costs, even charging at marginal cost can be inefficient.[4] This is because, as Ronald Coase pointed out, if the purchasers would not be willing to pay to cover the fixed costs necessary to provide the good in the first place, producing the good is a misallocation of resources. For if people would not be willing to pay the fixed costs, more resources would be spent than the social benefit generated from the goods existence. This creates misallocation as the true costs of production are not being taken into account.

Additionally politicians might prefer the use of regulation over regular taxation because of fiscal illusion. The general idea of fiscal illusion is that there are some forms of revenue generating behaviors that are not fully observed by voters. Thus, when policies are funded by these means, voters are aware of the benefits, but not all the costs, and are therefore biased towards too much spending. As a general principle of regulation, it tends to make some parties better off and some parties worse off, much as a tax and subsidization program does. However, since regulation tends to be complicated, often requiring an education in economics to understand, politicians will often prefer to use regulation rather than easier to see tax and subsidy systems.

If regulation is efficient then the benefit cost ratio should be the same, or at least roughly the same. To illustrate why this is, consider the following example, there are two industries that produce deadly side effects. For one, every million dollars in regulation prevents one person from dying, in the other every two million dollars prevents a person from dying. If a regulator could only regulate a certain amount, say three million dollars worth then he would be foolish to save one life in each industry. This is because the opportunity cost of saving one life for two million dollars is saving two lives. If we assume as is plausible that regulations tend to exhibit decreasing returns, then these two should eventually catch up but in the end they must have the same cost to benefit ratio. As seen in Table One, this far from the case.[5]

---

4   Ronald H. Coase, "The Marginal Cost Controversy" Economica, New Series, Vol. 13, No. 51 (Aug., 1946), pp. 169-182

5   For the second column of Table One, a normalized life saved is a life saved taking into account life expectancy, simply put if a regulation saves 80 year old lives it receives a lower weight than if it were to save 8 year old lives.

Table 1 The Costs and Benefits of Regulation

Regulation	Year	Agency	Cost per life saved, millions of 1990 dollars	Cost per normalized life saved, millons of 1995 dollars
Aircraft cabin fire protection standard	1985	FAA	0.1	0.1
Seat belt/air bag	1984	NHTSA	0.1	0.1
Steering column protection standards	1967	NHTSA	0.1	0.1
Underground construction standards	1989	OSHA	0.1	0.1
Trihalomethane in drinking water	1979	EPA	0.2	0.6
Aircraft seat cushion flammability	1984	FAA	0.5	0.6
Alcohol and drug controls	1985	FRA	0.5	0.6
Auto fuel-system integrity	1975	NHTSA	0.5	0.5
Aircraft floor emergency lighting	1984	FAA	0.7	0.9
Concrete and masonry construction	1988	OSHA	0.7	0.9
Crane suspended personnel platform	1988	OSHA	0.8	1
Passive restraints for trucks and buses	1989	NHTSA	0.8	0.8
Auto side-impact standards	1990	NHTSA	1	1
Children's sleepwear flammability ban	1973	CPSC	1	1.2
Auto side door supports	1970	NHTSA	1	1
Metal mine electrical equipment standards	1970	MSHA	1.7	2
Trenching and excavation standards	1989	OSHA	1.8	2.2
Traffic alert and collision avoidance systems	1988	FAA	1.8	2.2
Hazard communication standard	1983	OSHA	1.9	4.8
Trucks, buses and MPV side-impact	1989	NHTSA	2.6	2.6
Grain dust explosion prevention standards	1987	OSHA	3.3	4
Rear lap/shoulder belts for autos	1989	NHTSA	3.8	3.8
Stds for radionuclides in uranium mines	1984	EPA	4.1	10.1
Benzene NESHAP (original: fugitive emissions)	1984	EPA	4.1	10.1
Ethylene dibromide in drinking water	1991	EPA	6.8	17
Electrical equipment in coal mines	1970	MSHA	11	13.3
Arsenic emission standards for glass plants	1986	EPA	16.1	40.2
Ethylene oxide occupational exposure limit	1984	OSHA	24.4	61
Arsenic/copper NESHAP	1986	EPA	27.4	68.4
Hazardous waste listing of petroleum refining sludge	1990	EPA	32.9	82.1
Cover/move uranium mill tailings (inactive)	1983	EPA	37.7	94.3
Cover/move uranium mill tailings (active sites)	1983	EPA	53.6	133.8
Acrylonitrile occupational exposure limit	1978	OSHA	61.3	153.2
Asbestos occupational exposure limit	1986	OSHA	88.1	220.1
Arsenic occupational exposure limit	1978	OSHA	127.3	317.9
Asbestos ban	1989	EPA	131.8	329.2
Diethylstilbestrol (DES) cattlefeed ban	1979	FDA	148.6	371.2
Benzene NESHAP (revised: waste operations)	1990	EPA	200.2	500.2
1,2-Dichloropropane in drinking water	1991	EPA	777.4	1942.1
Hazardous waste land disposal ban	1988	EPA	4988.7	12462.7
Municipal solid waste landfills	1988	EPA	22746.8	56826.1
Formaldehyde occupational exposure limit	1987	OSHA	102622.8	256372.7
Atrazine/alachlor in drinking water	1991	EPA	109608.5	273824.4
Hazardous waste listing for wood-preserving chemicals	1990	EPA	6785822	16952364.9

Source: Measures of Mortality Risk, W. Kip Viscusi et al.

Though dollar per life saved is not a perfect measure for the benefit of a health or safety regulation, it is easy to obtain and a fairly good indicator. So small differences might be forgiven, large differences should be looked upon with great suspicion. In some of these cases the difference in cost per life saved is almost absurd, ranging from one hundred thousand dollars per normalized life saved to 16.9 trillion per normalized life saved. While it may be true that for the bans, if they are nearly perfectly followed there is little more that can be done. Things like trihalomethane in the drinking water can be changed quite easily, and should be changed before anything lower in the list is done. While this may seem cruel to some, we live in a world of scarcity, and scarcity necessitates choice, and clearly sixteen trillion dollars per normalized life saved is not a correct choice, if one's interests are to do anything other than to, perhaps, burn resources.

It is not a difficult task to show theoretically or empirically that the public interest view of regulation can not go very far in increasing understanding. Nearly all of its assumptions are rarely correct, if ever, and as has been shown following its logic leads to models that do not match reality at all. Instead of this, I argue that the economic approach to regulation is the only approach that can be taken if one wishes to gain an understanding of how the world works.

SECTION TWELVE

Markets and Liberty

Ungenerous Endowments

By Uncredited, *The Economist* Staff

It is natural to think of plentiful resources, such as oil, coal, minerals or fertile land, as good for a country. Natural, but usually wrong

IT HAS BECOME A familiar lament. Country X, now all but bankrupt, really ought to be rich—because it has such huge reserves of oil, of farmland or minerals. How could it have frittered away such natural advantages? And how could country Y, which lacks natural endowments, have overtaken it? Examples are legion: on one side stand Mexico, Nigeria, Argentina; on the other, South Korea, Taiwan, Japan.

Nor is this just bar-room talk. In September the World Bank, bowing to years of green pressure, published a report on environmentally sustainable development, in which it offered measures of economic performance that took account of the environment. One such is "wealth", based on an assessment of capital assets and human resources—and natural endowments. The Bank even produced a ranking of countries by this new measure (see table). Thanks to natural resources, the countries with the highest wealth per head are Australia and Canada; the top 15 include Iceland, Qatar, the United Arab Emirates and Kuwait. Germany scrapes in at 15th; Britain comes in 22nd place.

That may sound startling, but on reflection it appears to make sense. It is, after all, wonderful to be able to make money out of stuff lying in the ground, rather than having to work or build factories. And surely nobody would deny that Australians have benefited from their country's minerals; or that inhabitants of the Gulf states have been made rich by oil? Even before the 1973 and 1979 price shocks, oil in particular had a potent image, evoking as it did Texan and Californian oil millionaires, the tentacular global oil companies known as the "Seven Sisters", wealthy and abundantly confident Arab sheikhs.

It also seems obvious enough that natural resources have played a big part in economic success in the past. For a long time, indeed, natural resources, including agriculture, were almost the only source of income and wealth. Egyptian civilization flourished on the back of the fertile Nile valley. Wool and wheat produced the magnificent churches of East Anglia. Gold from the Americas propelled Spain to leadership of Europe in the 16th century.

Even when industry came, natural resources still seemed dominant. Cotton made white planters in the American South rich. The factories of the early industrial revolution in Britain,

Belgium and elsewhere depended on plentiful local deposits of iron ore and coal. At the turn of the century New Zealand and Argentina were among the world's richest countries (measured by income per head), thanks mainly to their farms. Something similar was true for Australia and South Africa, thanks to their mines.

A HARSHER REALITY

So natural resources, it appears, make you rich. Yet a closer look at both history and economics casts considerable doubt on this obvious-sounding conclusion. The value of natural resources is, indeed, clear—provided that other things are equal. The trouble is that other things never are equal. Even worse, it is precisely the existence of valuable natural resources that makes these other things unequal.

Consider the historical record. Surprisingly many economies that flourished on the back of natural resource booms then fell back and became fallow. When Spain's imported gold brought inflation and slow growth, resource-poor Holland overtook its erstwhile imperial master. In the 18th century Haiti's exports to Europe, mostly of sugar, were worth more than those of the 13 American colonies put together; shortly afterwards Haiti collapsed into the poverty that mires it still. The American South lost the civil war partly because the more industrial North had swept past it economically. Later in the 19th century, resource-rich Russia was overtaken (and later defeated in war) by apparently poorer Japan.

Recent trends are even more striking, partly because human and capital resources have become more significant than natural wealth. Still, it is notable that so many of the countries in the world with the highest incomes per head are notably poor in natural resources: examples include Japan, Switzerland and Denmark.

Australia, though still rich, has slipped relative to others for most of this century. And several countries with plentiful natural resources have relatively low incomes per head: Russia, Brazil and Argentina, for instance. A similar pattern is detectable inside countries. Louisiana and Texas, for instance, both hugely rich in natural resources, have significantly lower incomes per head than resource-poor Connecticut and Massachusetts.

Or consider developing countries. The star economic performers of the past 30 years have been resource-poor countries in East Asia such as South Korea, Taiwan, Hong Kong and, more recently, Thailand. Several of their resource-rich rivals such as Mexico, Venezuela, Ghana and Nigeria have gone spectacularly bust, some of them more than once. Many once-feared OPEC countries are now in serious economic or financial difficulty—even the most oil-rich of them all, Saudi Arabia.

A broad look at the experience of developing countries confirms that these are not odd anecdotes or isolated incidents. A recent paper by Jeffrey Sachs and Andrew Warner of Harvard University* assesses possession of natural resources and economic performance from 1971 to 1989 in a sample of 97 countries. Their regression analysis strongly suggests that growth was higher among less endowed countries than among those with abundant natural resources (see chart). Mr. Sachs and Mr. Warner also note that, of the top 18 developing countries ranked by growth rates during this period, only two-Malaysia and Mauritius—were rich in natural resources.

That result sounds surprising. Yet there are good economic reasons to expect a link between natural-resource wealth and slow economic growth. And, more recently, some economists have focused on a number of socio-political factors that help to explain why natural resources have so often been transformed from a blessing into a curse.

ILLS AND DISEASES

The best-known illness to afflict resource-rich economies is the "Dutch disease", a term coined to describe Holland's experience after its discovery of massive natural gas reserves in the late 1950s. There is disagreement about the exact diagnosis (and Holland is hardly a byword for economic or social disaster). But the general consensus is that the main symptom is the shrinkage of an economy's traded-goods sector, which often means its manufacturing capacity.

A couple of forces are to blame for this. One is that natural resources do not come for free. Exploiting them often requires considerable investment, which diverts capital and labour away from productive investments in traded goods, including manufacturing. This is especially important if, as some economists maintain, manufacturing plays a crucial role in generating economic growth. Another force at work is real exchange-rate appreciation, thanks to either a rise in resource exports or a cut in resource imports, which undermines the competitiveness of traded goods.

How serious is the Dutch disease? Enough to be a concern for British policy-makers in the late 1970s, as they pondered the probable effects of North Sea oil. The experience of the early 1980s, when sterling soared against other currencies and the British manufacturing base shrivelled, suggested that the Dutch disease had struck with a vengeance. Other countries have suffered too. In *Oil Windfalls: Blessing or Curse?* (published by Oxford University Press in 1988), Alan Gelb of the World Bank found that the average real effective exchange rate of a sample of six oil-exporting countries had risen by nearly 50% between 1970 and 1984, severely hampering nascent manufacturing sectors.

Yet fears about the Dutch disease can be exaggerated. Real exchange-rate appreciation brings benefits as well as costs, for instance making possible higher consumption or public investment. The share of manufacturing in most economies has declined, and few now attribute to it any special role in generating economic growth. Several countries have found ways to avoid the disease through fiscal and monetary policies. Indeed the bigger risk is often that attempted "cures" for the Dutch disease can prove harmful: in particular, protection or subsidies for manufacturing may themselves damage competitiveness.

If the Dutch disease is not necessarily catching, however, a second economic cause of the poor performance of resource-rich countries is less easily avoided. Because commodity prices swing far more than prices of goods and services, natural-resource economies are more vulnerable to external shocks. This applies both ways: that is, whether the shock sends price levels up or down. Highly volatile commodity prices make it hard for an economy to adjust smoothly whether they produce unexpected windfalls or shortfalls.

Two examples of the problems associated with volatility are provided by coffee in the late 1970s and by oil in 1979-82. Coffee prices rose by 216% between 1975 and 1977, only to fall back later; oil prices rose by 154% between 1977 and 1980 and then tumbled. One might have expected coffee exporters such as Costa Rica and Côte d'Ivoire to have done well from the first shock; and oil-producers such as Mexico and Nigeria to have gained from the oil-price hike. In fact they did terribly. In all four, the balance of payments deteriorated despite the massive terms-of-trade improvement brought about by the commodity-price rise. And in all four, growth rates were slower after the shock than they had been before. Both Mexico and Nigeria in effect went bust in the 1980s.

What these countries have found—as have so many lottery winners—is that it is exceedingly hard to spend a windfall wisely. You cannot (and should not)just consume the proceeds. But investing them is also tricky; financial markets may not be able to cope with huge sudden inflows, and direct capital investment is constrained as much by a shortage of projects with decent rates of return as by a shortage of money.

Hence, perhaps, a third economic problem that has, time and again, afflicted countries enjoying natural-resource booms: a sudden expansion of the public sector. All too often the proceeds of recent commodity windfalls have accrued to governments, either through taxes or because they have nationalized the companies involved. Naturally enough the governments have then instituted lavish spending programmes—for instance, sustaining a generous welfare state (Holland, Norway), building a new transport network (Trinidad), moving the country's capital (Nigeria) or improving health and education (everywhere).

Public spending is not always bad; indeed the right kind of public investment can be an important engine of economic growth. Inevitably, however, many of the public-spending programmes put in place by countries enjoying a resource boom have not been of this kind. Economists who have sought to measure the effectiveness of such spending, for instance after the 1973 oil shock, have found that it often yielded minimal, zero or, in a few cases, even negative rates of return.

There is a further problem with expanding public spending. Once started, it is hard to stop. Many countries have found themselves lumbered with budgetary burdens that have become untenable when the resources run out or their price falls. The necessary adjustment can be huge; in the past five years, the value of Venezuela's oil exports expressed in terms of the average cost of its imports has fallen by 75%. Figures such as these make the past decade's rash of current-account and budget deficits, or even bankruptcies, among oil-exporting countries look less surprising.

It could still be that, troublesome though natural resources often are, especially when they produce windfalls, the problems can be handled by the right government action. Yes, up to a point, they can be, as several examples have shown. Indonesia, for instance, has mostly used its oil resources wisely, developing a thriving and balanced economy. Malaysia has built a booming manufacturing sector. Botswana has diversified similarly. Kuwait has invested a big part of its oil wealth in foreign assets (as, to some extent, has Britain with North Sea oil revenues).

UNWORTHY OF THEIR RENTS

These examples suggest a few guiding principles for a country that either already has ample natural resources or experiences a sudden natural-resource boom. Do not indulge in breakneck, ill-considered fiscal expansion; instead, keep your public sector small. Do not treat temporary windfalls as permanent income gains. Invest the proceeds from natural resources cautiously and productively, that is in education or essential infrastructure. Keep your economy open to foreign competition and allow the free movement of capital. Build up foreign assets. These are all things that any country should do to increase its prosperity; so they ought not to be hard for one that is rich in natural resources.

Yet in practice they have often proved not just hard, but virtually impossible. Why? The answer lies in some socio-political factors that provide the clinching argument against those who persist in seeing natural-resource endowments as a blessing. The resource-rich fail to use their wealth wisely not because they are, coincidentally, run by cussed governments, or because they are short of good economic advisers. Their failure is not, in fact, coincidental at all: it arises precisely because they are resource-rich. An analogy is with a 21-year-old who inherits a fortune that she promptly dissipates-often leaving her more indebted and worse off than before.

A natural-resource endowment gives rise to what economists call "rent"—the difference between what is actually paid to the producer and the minimum price that he would have demanded to produce the stuff in the first place. For many countries that have enjoyed booming natural-resource incomes in the past few decades, especially those that have had sudden windfalls, these rents have been staggeringly large. Nice for the producers, it seems; by assumption, too, nice for the country's people.

The trouble is that the lure of those fat rents can be hard to resist. The upshot is routinely an outbreak of competitive rent-seeking. The power centres in any resource-rich country soon notice that the profits from capturing a slice of the rent from the natural resources beat those from any possible alternatives; and they act accordingly.

Behind the economic jargon is a simple enough proposition: give a group of people a big pot of money and they will spend their time arguing about how to share it out, not thinking of risky ways to make even more money by investing the original sum. Experience bears this out. In Mexico in the 1970s, politicians and firms battled over the state's oil revenues. So it was in Venezuela, Nigeria and several other big oil-exporting countries. Nor is the experience restricted to oil-exporters. Other resource-rich countries have blown the proceeds of their wealth in competitive rent-seeking: Australia and Brazil are outstanding examples.

In developed countries, such rent-seeking can damage other parts of the economy. Louisiana spent too much on its roads and hospitals; Alaskans concentrate too hard on their regular annual dividend from the state's oil fund. Too many people in such places also tend to ask why they should bother getting an education or working hard—or at all—when they can live off a natural endowment.

Idleness has its attractions, and if well-informed voters freely decide to live off natural-resource wealth, their choice cannot be gainsaid, imprudent though it may be. Rather worse is what happens when aggressive rent-seeking takes place in poorer countries, where liberal, democratic traditions are often weak, if they exist at all. There living off resources is all too likely to corrupt the business of government—and so the functioning of the entire economy.

Mexico, Venezuela and a slew of Middle Eastern and Asian oil-exporters all offer sorry examples of what goes wrong. Corruption in the natural-resource sector spreads across the whole public sector—and frequently suborns the government. Instability follows. When people bemoan the coincidence that oil is so often to be found in dangerously unstable countries, they overlook the obvious explanation: that it is the oil (and the rent-seeking it engenders) that has made the countries unstable.

Nowhere suffers more than Africa, the poorest continent of all. Civil wars in countries such as Angola and Zaire have frequently been driven (and often financed) by mineral or oil wealth. Successive governments in Sierra Leone have been bought by diamond traders. Governments in Côte d'Ivoire, Ghana, Cameroon and Gabon have all at different times been suborned by powerful groups fighting over their natural-resource wealth.

Most notorious of all is Nigeria, which "ought", on the basis of its massive oil reserves, to be rich. Since independence, Nigeria has had a civil war, a succession of military coups and corruption on a gargantuan scale—all paid for to a large extent by oil money. The troubles in Ogoniland that culminated in the recent execution of Ken Saro-Wiwa were largely about oil. On one estimate, nearly 75% of the money "invested" in large public-sector capital projects in 1970-85 was diverted—into officials' pockets, construction frauds and overseas bank accounts. Nigeria today is one of the most corrupt, most heavily indebted and slowest-growing of African countries.

It also offers no end of a lesson. Next time you hear of a poor country that has suddenly struck oil or discovered diamonds, do not sit back and give thanks that its future is assured. Tremble, rather, for its poor people—for they will be the last to benefit.

* "Natural Resource Abundance and Economic Growth." By Jeffrey Sachs and Andrew Warner. Harvard Institute for International Development, October 1995

TOP 15 COUNTRIES, RANKED BY WEALTH PER HEAD, 1990

	Wealth	Sources of wealth		% of total
	$'000 Per head	People	Capital assets	Natural resources
Australia	835	21	7	71
Canada	704	22	9	69
Luxembourg	658	83	12	4
Switzerland	647	78	19	3
Japan	565	81	18	2
Sweden	496	56	16	29
Iceland	486	23	16	61
Qatar	473	51	11	39
United Arab Emirates	471	65	14	21
Denmark	463	76	17	7
Norway	424	48	22	30
United States	421	59	16	25
France	413	77	17	7
Kuwait	405	79	17	4
Germany	399	79	17	4

Source: World Bank
Totals may not add due to rounding
GRAPH: Better without them: Natural resources and economic growth

Economic Freedom:
Of Liberty and Prosperity

❧ ━━━━━━━━━━━━━━━━━━━━━━━━━━━━━━━━━━━ ❧

By Uncredited, *The Economist* Staff

Does economic freedom help a country to grow more quickly? That it does (or does not) has been easy to assert, but harder to prove. Until now

WISDOM ABOUT WHETHER government intervention helps or hinders economic progress has often become conventional. But the wisdom that is conventional has varied over the past half century. After the second world war, some forms of intervention became fashionable in Europe, particularly "planning" and state ownership of many companies. At the same time, though, America led worldwide efforts to reduce tariffs and other barriers to trade that had been put up in the 1920s and 1930s. Yet in poorer countries in Africa, Latin America and Asia conventional wisdom often said that governments should "lead" development through state ownership and investment, behind high trade barriers.

The debate has moved on. But motion does not necessarily bring clarity. Central planning and state ownership may be out of fashion; and barriers to trade and capital flows have been lowered, especially in the developing world. But views still differ markedly about how, and how much, the state should interfere in the functioning of economies. Liberals, including The Economist, think that the demise of socialism and of old, state-led, import-substitution models of development will bring faster, more sustained growth to countries that keep their economies free. Others see evidence in the recent success of East Asia for the idea that state control can, when intelligently applied, boost growth.

This debate will never, it is safe to predict, be settled. But it has been bedevilled by two things. The first has been a lack of any clear definition of what is meant by economic freedom, and of how to measure that freedom. If this were agreed upon, at least people could be sure of what they were arguing over. The second problem has been a lack of data that applies this definition across a wide enough range of countries and over a long enough stretch of time to test credibly whether there is a correlation between freedom and prosperity. A new book[*], published on January 12th by 11 economic institutes around the world, goes a long way towards plugging both gaps.

The study is the outcome of a series of six conferences sponsored by the Fraser Institute of Vancouver and the Liberty Fund of Indianapolis between 1986 and 1993, which were attended by some of the world's top economists and which shaped research done by the book's three authors under the auspices of Florida State University. Quite apart from being the best attempt yet to define and measure economic freedom, the study also produces powerful evidence in support of the liberals' case.

Indeed, the conclusion from this research into 102 countries over 20 years could scarcely be more emphatic: the more economic freedom a country had in that period, the more economic growth it achieved and the richer its citizens became. Even if you read this article no further, it is worth looking at chart 1 to see how powerfully and plainly this relationship holds. The chart groups countries into bands from "A" to "F-", according to their 1995 economic-freedom ratings, and relates those bands to wealth and to growth rates of GDP per head. If you think that is too general, turn the page for a moment and try a more specific example: chart 3 contrasts the differing fortunes in 1975-95 of Chile, whose governments gradually increased their citizens' economic freedom, and Venezuela, whose governments gradually reduced it.

If it is that clear, why will this not end the debate? One reason is that correlation does not prove causation: some say that East Asian countries got rich first and then handed out freedoms, rather than the other way around. In part, this is a confusion of economic freedoms with political ones. Also, however, the sequence of change can be pointed to: China, for example, started to liberalise in 1978, and began to grow rapidly later. But more important still is the fact that East Asian countries have long been much freer than most people realise.

AN ELUSIVE THING, FREEDOM

This is one of the ways in which this new study is so helpful. By attempting both to define and to measure economic freedom, the economists show how subtle a concept such freedom is. It cannot be captured merely by looking at the size of public spending relative to GDP, say, or at the extent of state ownership of industry, or at the level of trade barriers. It is a combination of these and many other factors, which leaves lots of room for debate about different elements of the mix.

Stripped to its essentials, economic freedom is concerned with property rights and choice. Individuals are economically free if property that they have legally acquired is protected from invasions or intrusions by others, and if they are free to use, exchange or give away their property so long as their actions do not violate other people's similar rights. That sounds abstract, but it comes to life as soon as you think of how a government might restrict freedom. Failing to protect property rights would be one way. Others would be to confiscate property, to require individuals to give up their time through military conscription, or to lay down rules for what they may buy or sell and at what price. A more subtle, but just as destructive, way would be to pursue monetary policies that lead to hyperinflation, eroding the value of money.

To measure freedom, then, requires first some measures of the ways in which governments restrict it. The authors choose 17 such measures, in four broad areas:

Money and inflation. Does government protect money as a store of value and allow it to be used as a medium of exchange? This measure includes the volatility of inflation; monetary growth relative to the potential growth capacity of an economy; and citizens' rights to hold foreign-currency accounts at home and bank accounts abroad.

Government operations and regulations. Who decides what is produced and consumed? The measures of this include public spending as a share of GDP; the size of the state-controlled sector; price controls ; freedom to enter markets; and controls on borrowing and lending rates.

"Takings" and discriminatory taxation. Are you free to earn, and to keep your earnings? Measures of this include subsidies and transfer payments as a share of GDP; the level and impact of marginal tax rates; and whether there is conscription.

International exchange. Are you free to exchange goods and money with foreigners? Measures of this include taxes on international trade; any differences between an official exchange rate and a black-market one; the actual size of a country's trade relative to the size that might be expected; and restrictions on capital flows.

The economists rated 102 countries on each of these measures on a scale of 0-10, in which zero means that a country is completely unfree and ten means it is completely free. Such scores were given for 1975, 1980, 1985, 1990 and 1993-95 (depending on the latest figures available).

Having obtained such ratings, however, they had to decide what weight to apply to each. Do high marginal tax rates matter more for economic freedom than volatile inflation? Or do they all matter equally? There is no foolproof answer. The authors used three methods: 1) with each component having an equal impact; 2) with weights determined by a survey of "knowledgeable people", defined as economists who attended the final three conferences (!) and so were familiar with the topic; and 3) with weights derived from a survey of experts on specific countries.

Which method is best? The authors prefer the second, the survey of their fellow economists. That may be biased, but it would be implausible to assume that each component is equally important, and the authors' survey of country experts was incomplete. So the ratings in chart 2 show those rankings. To spice things up, and to provide an albeit imperfect way to evaluate these rankings, the box overleaf also gives the results of a poll conducted by The Economist, showing the scores that a panel of ten eminent people gave to 20 countries, as well as providing some statistics on how the countries vary on several measures of state involvement.

KEEP ON ARGUING

Chart 2 shows the ratings given for 1993–95 for all 102 countries included in the study. On average, the ratings show little change in overall economic freedom from 1975–85, but a gradual liberalization from 1985 onwards.

As noted in chart 1, taking the period since 1975 as a whole, the ratings reveal a strong correlation between economic freedom and wealth, especially for countries that maintained a high level of freedom for many years. Before individuals and companies will respond to new-won freedom, they must believe that it is likely to last. It is no coincidence that the six countries that had persistently high ratings throughout the 1975–95 period (Hong Kong, Switzerland, Singapore, the United States, Canada and Germany) were also all in the top ten in terms of GDP per head in 1993–95.

In contrast, no country with a persistently low rating was able even to achieve a middling income. For the 16 countries for which the index fell the most during this period, average real GDP per head fell at an annual rate of 0.6%. These were Nicaragua, Somalia, Iran, Honduras, Venezuela, Congo, Zambia, Tanzania, Algeria, Morocco, Panama, Syria, Greece, El Salvador, Sierra Leone and Brazil.

Most noteworthy, perhaps, are the ratings given to the fast-growing economies of East Asia, and to Japan, for many people assume that in these countries economic freedom is heavily curtailed. Yet Singapore comes in second place, Malaysia is sixth, Japan is ninth, and South Korea is 12th. (Sadly, China is not included because that country's data was incomplete.)

One possible explanation is that the measure is flawed: that it does not capture the ways in which East Asian governments control their economies. Japan, for instance, is alleged to block imports through unmeasurable non-tariff and institutional barriers. The authors have tried to deal with this criticism by including a score for whether a country's imports and exports are as large as other indications (mainly the country's size, level of development and proximity to potential trading partners) would suggest that they should be. Sure enough, Japan scores badly on this test, with this component's rating falling from three in 1975 (when total trade was 25.6% of GDP) to just one in 1993–95 (by when trade had fallen to 18% of GDP).

Yet what is striking is how well Japan scores on the other tests. Government consumption is low, and few companies are owned by the state. Inflation has been consistently low for 20 years. Capital transactions are free, and people can put their money wherever they wish. Freedom may be curtailed in one area (though one hardly need add that there is plenty of controversy over whether Japan's trade barriers are high or low), but that does not mean that choice is being restricted or distorted overall.

In the case of Singapore, one area of government intervention is entirely missing from the ratings (which the authors admit). The government's Central Provident Fund uses mandatory savings to fund pensions and other benefits. This omission probably means that Singapore's score is too high: this is not a free-market approach. But neither is this omission as serious as it seems. If you compare a mandatory savings scheme with the more typical use of taxation to fund state pensions, the Singapore system (see page 38) preserves incentives to work, as both the amount paid in and the amount eventually received as a pension are related to earnings. It may be unfree, but not as unfree as many governments' alternatives.

That, in the end, is one of the most important lessons of this study. Economic freedom is a coat of many colors. Rather than assessing it simply by the extent of state involvement, one needs to look at how the forms of involvement compare with alternative approaches, and how they affect the incentives faced by individuals. And it must be looked at over time, as the credibility of laws, policies and institutions is at least as important as their design. Just as ministers' promises to kill inflation require years of achievement before they become credible, so a general shift towards economic freedom will not transform growth or wealth overnight. These things take time.

* "Economic Freedom of the World: 1975-1995". By James Gwartney, Robert Lawson and Walter Block. Co-published by 11 institutes including the Fraser Institute in Vancouver, the Cato Institute in Washington, DC, and the Institute of Economic Affairs in London (C$29.95, $22.95, £15.00).

In the eye of the beholder statistics and rankings are important. But perceptions also matter, and often differ from the cold numbers. As a test of this, we sent a questionnaire to ten economists and politicians, asking them to rank 20 countries according to where the panelists thought they stood on a spectrum between liberalism (ten) and collectivism (one). We also asked them to say whether they thought these countries had become more liberal or more collectivist during the past five years, or whether they had stayed the same.

The table shows the results, along with a selection of statistical measures of state involvement in economic life, against which readers can compare some of their own perceptions. Our panel felt that the world is indeed becoming more liberal; hardly any thought that any of the 20 countries were becoming more collectivist. But the panelists differed widely in how liberal they felt certain countries already were.

They were broadly consistent in the ratings given to the United States: our voters' verdicts for America ranged from seven to nine. Panelists were also consistent in their praise for Chile, their suspicion of France, and their view of China and Russia as still highly collectivist.

Yet East Asia proved more controversial. While eight of the panelists gave Singapore a rating of between six and eight, two rated Lee Kuan Yew's city-state far more harshly, at two and three respectively. Japan, too, divided the panel: while no one gave it a better score than seven, one reckoned it deserved only two. South Korea drew scores varying from two to seven. All three of these East Asian economies fared worse with our panel than in the Fraser Institute's ratings.

The panelists were: Milton Friedman, of the Hoover Institution; Mervyn King, of the Bank of England; Shijuro Ogata, former deputy governor of the Bank of Japan; Jagdish Bhagwati, of Columbia University; Jaime Serra Puche, former finance minister of Mexico; David Hale, of the Kemper Financial Companies; Norbert Walter, of Deutsche Bank; Charles Goodhart, of the London School of Economics; Panayotis Thomopoulos, deputy governor of the Bank of Greece; and Sebastian Edwards, of the World Bank. We are grateful to them all.

Political Economy of the U.S. Constitution

By Dwight Lee

D URING THE BICENTENNIAL of the U.S. Constitution it is appropriate to reflect on the political wisdom of our Founding Fathers. No written constitution in history has established a more durable or successful democracy than has the U.S. Constitution. A full appreciation of the Founding Fathers, however, requires an understanding of the economic as well as the political consequences of our Constitution. Every economy is a political economy and the enormous success of the U.S. economy has been as dependent on our political system as on our economic system.

Indeed, many of the problems that currently plague the U.S. economy are the result of our failure to hold on to the political wisdom that guided our Founding Fathers. Economic knowledge is obviously important in the effort to promote economic growth and development. But no matter how sound our economic understanding, economic performance will continue to suffer until we once again recognize that political power is a force for progress only when tightly constrained and directed toward limited objectives.

The genesis of the political and economic wisdom of our Founding Fathers is found in the fact that they distrusted government while fully recognizing the necessity of government for a beneficent social order. The cautious embrace the Founders gave government is reflected in their view of democracy as necessary but not sufficient for the proper control of government.

The concerns that led to the colonists' break with Great Britain were very much in the public mind when the Constitutional Convention met in Philadelphia during the summer of 1787. The well known pre-revolution rallying cry, "No taxation without representation," reflected a clear understanding of the dangers that accompanied any exercise of government power not answerable to those who are governed. That the government established by the Constitution would be democratic in form was not in doubt. Unchecked democratic rule, however, was anathema to the most thoughtful of the Founding Fathers. A grievance against English rule rivaling that of "taxation without representation" concerned the sovereign authority assumed by the English Parliament in 1767. In that year Parliament decreed that, through its democratically elected members, it had the power to pass or strike down any law it desired. The colonists had brought with them the English political tradition, which dated back at least to the Magna Carta

Dwight Lee, "Political Economy of the U.S. Constitution," from *The Freeman, 37, 2,* February 1987, pp. 1–18.

of 1215: the people have certain rights that should be immune to political trespass regardless of momentary desires of a democratic majority. The concern was not only that the colonists were unrepresented in Parliament but, more fundamentally, that Parliament assumed unlimited power to meddle in the private lives of individuals whether represented or not:

Although the Founding Fathers were determined to establish a government that was democratic in the limited sense that political decisions could not ignore citizen input, they had no intention of creating a government that was fully responsive to majority interests. In many ways the Constitution is designed to frustrate the desire of political majorities to work their will through the exercise of government power. The most obvious example of this is the first ten amendments to the Constitution, or the Bill of Rights. These amendments guarantee certain individual freedoms against political infringement regardless of majority will. If, for example, freedom of speech and the press was dependent on majority vote many unpopular but potentially important ideas would never be disseminated. How effectively would a university education expose students to new and controversial ideas if professors had to submit their lectures for majority approval?

Other examples exist of the undemocratic nature of the government set up by the Constitution. There is very little that can be considered democratic about the Supreme Court. Its nine members are appointed for life, and their decision can nullify a law passed by the Congress and supported by the overwhelming majority of the American public. In a five to four decision one member of the court, insulated from the democratic process, can frustrate the political will of a nearly unanimous public. The arrangement whereby the President can reverse the will of the Congress through his veto power is certainly not a very democratic one. Neither is the Senate where the vote cast by a senator from Wyoming carries weight equal to the vote by the senator from California, even though the California senator represents a population fifty times larger than does the Wyoming senator. The senators from the twenty-six least populated states can prevent a bill from clearing Congress, even though it has incontestable popular support in the country at large. Congress is actually less democratic than just indicated once it is recognized that popular bills can be prevented from ever being considered in the full House of Representatives or Senate by a few representatives who serve on key congressional committees.

It is safe to say that the chief concern of the framers of the Constitution was not that of insuring a fully democratic political structure. Instead they were concerned with limiting government power in order to minimize the abuse of majority rule. In the words of R. A. Humphreys, "they [the Founding Fathers] were concerned not to make America safe for democracy, but to make democracy safe for America."[1]

PRELUDE TO THE CONSTITUTIONAL CONVENTION

Fear of the arbitrary power that could be exercised by a strong central government, democratically controlled or otherwise, was evident from the Articles of Confederation. The Articles of

---

1 R. A. Humphreys. "The Rule of Law and the American Revolution," *Law Quarterly Review* 11937). Also quoted in F. A. Hayek, *The Constitution of Liberty* {Chicago: University of Chicago Press, 1960). p. 474.

Confederation established the "national government" of the thirteen colonies after they declared their independence from England. There is some exaggeration in this use of the term national government, since the Articles did little more than formalize an association (or confederation) of thirteen independent and sovereign states. While the congress created by the Articles of Confederation was free to deliberate on important issues and pass laws, it had no means of enforcing them. The Articles did not even establish an executive branch of government, and congressional resolutions were nothing more than recommendations that the states could honor if they saw fit. The taxes that states were assessed to support the Revolutionary War effort were often ignored, and raising money to outfit and pay the American army was a frustrating business.

Because of the weakness of the national government, the state governments under the Article of Confederation were strong and often misused their power. Majority coalitions motivated by special interests found it relatively easy to control state legislatures and tramp on the interests of minorities. Questionable banking schemes were promoted by debtors, with legislative assistance, in order to reduce the real value of their debt obligations. States often resorted to the simple expedient of printing money to satisfy their debts. Trade restrictions between the states were commonplace as legislators responded to the interests of organized producers while ignoring the concerns of the general consumers. There was a 1786 meeting in Annapolis, Maryland of the five middle states to discuss ways to reduce trade barriers between the states. At this meeting the call was made for a larger meeting in Philadelphia in the following year to discuss more general problems with the Articles of Confederation. This meeting became the Constitutional Convention.

ACHIEVING WEAKNESS THROUGH STRENGTH

It was the desire of Madison, Hamilton, and other leaders at the Constitutional Convention to replace the government established by the Articles of Confederation with a central government that was more than an association of sovereign states. The new government would have to be strong enough to impose some uniformity to financial, commercial, and foreign policy and to establish some general protections for citizens against the power of state governments if the new nation was to be viable and prosperous. In the words of James Madison, we needed a "general government" sufficiently strong to protect "the rights of the minority," which are in jeopardy "in all cases where a majority are united by a common interest or passion."[2] But this position was not an easy one to defend. Many opponents to a genuine national government saw little merit in the desire to strengthen government power at one level in order to prevent the abuse of government power at another level. Was there any genuine way around this apparent conflict? Many thought not, short of giving up on the hope of a union of all the states. There were those who argued that the expanse and diversity of the thirteen states, much less that of the larger

---

2 *Records of the Federal Convention of 1787*, Max Ferrand. ed. (New Haven: Yale University Press. 1937) Vol. I, p. 57 and pp. 134–135.

continent, were simply too great to be united under one government without sacrificing the liberty that they had just fought to achieve.[3]

Madison, however, saw no conflict in strengthening the national government in order to control the abuses of government in general. In his view the best protection against arbitrary government authority was through centers of government power that were in effective com petition with one another. The control that one interest group, or faction, could realize through a state government would be largely nullified when political decisions resulted from the interaction of opposing factions within many states. Again quoting Madison,

The influence of factious leaders may kindle a flame within their particular States but will be unable to spread a general conflagration through the other States ... A rage for paper money, for an abolition of debts, for an equal division of property, or for any other improper or wicked project, will be less apt to pervade the whole body of the Union than a particular member of it ... [4]

A central government strong enough to unite a large and diverse set of states would weaken, rather than strengthen, the control that government in general could exercise.

To the framers of the Constitution weakening government in the sense just discussed meant making sure that government was unable to extend itself beyond a relatively limited role in the affairs of individuals. This does not imply, however, impotent government. The referees in a football game, for example, certainly are not the strongest participants on the field and have limited control over specific outcomes in the game. Yet in enforcing the general rules of the game the decisions of the referees are potent indeed. Government, in its role as referee, obviously cannot lack the authority to back up its decisions. In addition to performing its refereeing function, it is also desirable for government to provide certain public goods; goods such as national defense that will not be adequately provided by the private market. Again this is a duty which requires a measure of authority; in this case the authority to impose taxes up to the limit required to provide those public goods which are worth more than they cost.

HOW TO IMPOSE CONTROL?

In granting government the power to do those things government should do, the Founding Fathers knew they were creating a power that had to be carefully controlled. But how could this control be imposed? It could not be imposed by specifying a particular list of government do's and don'ts. Such a list would be impossibly detailed and even if it could be drafted it would need to be revised constantly in response to changes in such considerations as population size, age distribution, wealth, and the state of technology. Instead, government has to be controlled by a general set of constitutional rules within which governmental decisions are made, with specific government outcomes determined through the resulting political process. It was the hope of those at the Constitutional Convention to establish a political process, through con-

---

3   See Herbert J. Storing, *What the Anti-Federalists Were for: The Political Thought of the Opponents of the Constitution* (Chicago: The University of Chicago Press. 198])

4   Madison in Federalist 10. *The Federalist Papers* (New York: New American Library. Edition. 1961)

stitutional reform, that brought government power into action only when needed to serve the broad interests of the public.

This hope was not based on the naive, though tempting, notion that somehow individuals would ignore their personal advantages and concentrate on the general advantage when making political decisions. While noble motives are seldom completely absent in guiding individual behavior, whether private or public, the Founding Fathers took as a given that most people, most of the time, maintain a healthy regard for their private concerns. The only way to prevent self- seeking people from abusing government power was to structure the rules of the political game in such a way that it would be costly for them to do so. The objective of the framers was to create a government that was powerful enough to do those things that received political approval, but to establish a political process that made it exceedingly difficult to obtain political approval for any action that lacked broad public support.

There were, of course, some powers that the national government was not constitutionally permitted to exercise. The national government was created by the states, and until the Constitution all governmental power resided in the states. Through the Constitution the states relinquished some of their powers to the national government, e.g., the power to impose taxes on the citizens, establish uniform rules of naturalization, raise an army and navy, and declare war. In addition the states agreed to refrain from exercising certain powers; e.g., the power to coin money, pass laws impairing the obligation of contracts, and pass retroactive laws. Important government powers remained in the states, however, with some of them located in the local governments. Thus the powers that could be exercised by government were limited, and the powers that did exist were diffused over three levels of government. The Constitution further diffused power at the national level by spreading it horizontally over three branches of government, the power of each acting as a check and balance on the power of the others.

The intent of the Founding Fathers was to so fragment government power that it would be extremely difficult for any narrowly motivated faction to gain sufficient control to work its political will. Only those objectives widely shared and consistent with Constitutional limits would be realized through the use of government power. The beauty of the political process established by the Constitution is that it is cumbersome and inefficient. According to Forrest McDonald the process is "So cumbersome and inefficient … that the people, however virtuous or wicked, could not activate it. It could be activated through deals and deceit, through bargains and bribery, through logrolling and lobbying and trickery and trading, the tactics that go with man's baser attributes, most notably his greed and his love of power. And yet, in the broad range and on the average, these private tactics and motivations could operate effectively only when they were compatible with the public good, for they were braked by the massive inertia of society as a whole."[5] Or, as Clinton Rossiter has said of the Founding Fathers' motives in

---

5   Forrest McDonald, *E Pluribus Unum: The Formation of the American Republic 1776–1790* (Indianapolis: Liberty Press. 1979). p, 316.

creating the system of checks and balances, "Liberty rather than authority, protection rather than power, delay rather than efficiency were the concern of these constitution-makers."[6]

THE ECONOMIC SUCCESS OF THE CONSTITUTION

It is hard to argue with the success of the U.S. Constitution. The history of the United States in the decades after the ratification of the Constitution was one of limited government and individual liberty, major increases in the size of the U.S. in terms of population and geography, and unprecedented growth in economic well-being. With the major exception of (and to a large extent, in spite of) the unfortunate legacy of slavery and the Civil War, millions of diverse people were able to pursue their individual objectives through harmonious and productive interaction with one another. The opportunities created by the process of specialization and exchange made possible by limited and responsible government motivated an outpouring of productive effort that soon transformed a wilderness into one of the most prosperous nations in the world. The role the U.S. Constitution played in this transformation was an important one and can be explained in terms of both negative and positive incentives.

Broadly speaking there are two ways an individual can acquire Wealth: 1) capture existing wealth through nonproductive transfer activities, or 2) create new wealth through productive activities. A major strength of the Constitution is that it established positive incentives for the latter activities and negative incentives for the former.

The most obvious form of nonproductive transfer activity is private theft. The thief simply takes through force or stealth something that belongs to someone else. A primary purpose for establishing government is to outlaw private theft. But the power that government necessarily possesses if it is to enforce laws against private theft is a power that affords individuals or groups the opportunity to benefit through public "theft" (legal transfer activity to phrase it more gently). The more vague and ineffective the limits on government authority, the less difficult it is to acquire legal transfers through political activity, and the larger the number of people who will find this activity offering them the greatest profit opportunity.

While those who are successful at the transfer game can increase their personal wealth, in some cases significantly, it is obvious that the country at large cannot increase its wealth through transfer activity. What one person receives is what another person, or group, loses. No net wealth is created, and for this reason transfer activity is often referred to as a zero-sum game. In fact, it is more accurately described as a negative-sum game. The attempts of some to acquire transfers, and the predictable efforts of others to protect their wealth against transfers, require the use of real resources. These resources could be productively employed creating new wealth rather than wasted in activities that do nothing more than redistribute existing wealth. For every dollar that one person receives from a transfer activity the rest of the community sacrifices more than a dollar.

---

6 Clinton Rossiter, *Seedtime of the Republic: The Origin of the American Tradition of Political Liberty* (New York: Harcourt. Brace and World. 1953), p. 425.

INCENTIVES TO PRODUCE

A major virtue of the U.S. Constitution was that it discouraged people from playing the transfer game. By establishing a governmental apparatus that was very difficult to put in motion for narrowly motivated purposes, the Constitution dampened the incentive to use government as a means of acquiring the wealth of others. This is not to say that the government was not used as a vehicle for transfer in the early days of our Constitutional government. Every political decision results in some redistribution of wealth, and no governmental structure will ever completely insulate the political process against the transfer activities of some.[7] But the opportunity for personal enrichment through political activity was limited. Most people found that the best way to increase their wealth was through wealth producing activities.

It was here that the political structure established by the Constitution created positive incentives. Not only did the Constitution establish a climate in which it was difficult to profit from transfer activities, it also created a setting in which productive effort was rewarded. By providing protection against the arbitrary taking of private property (the Fifth Article of the Bill of Rights) people were given assurance that they would not be denied the value generated by their efforts. This provided people with strong incentives to apply themselves and their property diligently. In the words of M. Bruce Johnson, "America was a place where if you were ready to sow, then by God you could reap."[8]

But the motivation to work hard is not enough for a productive economy. Also needed is information on the objectives toward which effort and resources are best directed, as well as incentives to act on this information. It is the protection of private property that provides the foundation for a system of price communication and market interaction which serves to guide effort and resources into their most valuable employments. To complete this system the concept of private property rights has to be expanded to include the right to transfer one's property to others at terms regulated only by the mutual consent of those who are party to the exchange. The lower the cost of entering into transactions of this type, the more effectively the resulting market prices will allow people to communicate and coordinate with each other to the advantage of all. The U.S. Constitution lowered these transaction costs by reducing government's ability to interfere with mutually acceptable exchanges and by putting the weight of the national government behind the sanctity of the contracts that resulted from these exchanges.

In what has become known as the "contract clause" of the Constitution, the states are for bidden from passing any "law impairing the obligation of contracts ... " In the same clause the states are also forbidden from imposing tariff duties on imports or exports (unless absolutely necessary for enforcing inspection laws). In the "commerce clause" the national government was given the power to regulate commerce "among the several states." Though the commerce clause can be interpreted (and indeed has been in recent decades) as providing the central

---

7   For a discussion of the use of government to transfer wealth throughout American history), see Jonathan R. T. Hughes, *The Governmental Habit: Economic Controls from Colonial Times to the Present* (New York: Basic Books. 1977).

8   M. Bruce Johnson. ed., *Resolving the Housing Crisis: Government Policy, Decontrol. and the Public Interest* (San Francisco: Pacific Institute for Public Research. 1982). p. 3

government the authority to substitute political decisions for market decisions over interstate commerce, the U.S. Congress ignored this possibility until it passed the Interstate Commerce Act in 1887. Prior to the Civil War the commerce clause was used instead by the U.S. Supreme Court to rule unconstitutional state laws that attempted to regulate commerce. After 1868 the Supreme Court made use of the doctrine of due process as expressed in the fourteenth amendment to strike down many government attempts to violate the sanctity of contracts through their regulation of such things as prices, working hours, working conditions, and pay.

In summary, the Constitution created an environment in which private advantage was best Served by engaging in productive positive-sum activities. The specialization and exchange facilitated by the Constitutional rules of the game is a system in which individuals can improve their own position only by serving the interests of others. When private property is protected against confiscation, an individual becomes wealthy only by developing skills, creating new products, or innovating better technologies and thereby providing consumers with more attractive options than they would otherwise have. In a truly free enterprise economy, with the minimum government role envisioned by the framers of the Constitution, the rich are the benefactors of the masses, not the exploiters as commonly depicted. Wealth through exploitation becomes possible only when unrestricted government allows negative-sum transfer activity to become more profitable than positive-sum market activity.

CONSTITUTIONAL EROSION AND THE RISE OF POLITICAL PIRACY

The early success of the Constitution, and the economic system that developed under it, is reflected in the fact that relatively few people felt any urgency to worry about politics. Political activity offered little return as there was little chance to exploit others, and little need to prevent from being exploited by others, through political involvement. People could safely get on with their private affairs without having to worry about the machinations and intrigues of politicians and bureaucrats in faraway places. But this very success can, over time, undermine itself as a politically complacent public increases the opportunities for those who are politically involved to engage in political chicanery.

Motivating people to maintain the political vigilance necessary to protect themselves against government is always a difficult task. The individual who becomes involved in political activity incurs a direct cost. By devoting time and resources in attempting to realize political objectives he is sacrificing alternative objectives. The motivation to become politically active will be a compelling one only if the expected political outcome is worth more to the individual than the necessary personal sacrifices. This will typically not be the case when the objective is to prevent government from undermining the market process that it is government's proper role to protect. The benefits that are realized from limited government are general benefits. These benefits accrue to each individual in the community whether or not he personally works to constrain government.

Over the broad range of political issues, then, people quite rationally do not want to get involved. This is not to say, however, that everyone will be apathetic about all political issues. This clearly is not the case, and it is possible to predict the circumstances that will motivate political activism. Often a relatively small number of individuals will receive most of the benefit from a particular political decision, while the community at large bears the cost. Members of such a special interest group will find it relatively easy to organize for the purpose of exerting political influence. The number of people to organize is comparatively small; the group is probably already somewhat organized around a common interest, and the political issues that affect this common interest will be of significant importance to each member of the group.

Of course, the free rider problem exists in all organizational efforts, but the smaller the group and the narrower the objective the easier it is to get everyone to contribute his share. Also, the benefits of effective effort can be so great to particular individuals in the group that they will be motivated to work for the common objective even if some members of the group do free-ride. Not surprisingly then, narrowly focused groups commonly will have the motivation and ability to organize for the purpose of pursuing political objectives.[9] The result is political piracy in which the politically organized are able to capture ill-gotten gains from the politically unorganized.

The Constitutional limits on government imposed effective restraints on political piracy for many years after the Constitution was ratified. There are undoubtedly many explanations for this. The vast frontier rich in natural resources offered opportunities for wealth creation that, for most people, overwhelmed the opportunities for personal gain through government transfer activity. Also, it can take time for politically effective coalitions to form after the slate has been wiped clean, so to speak, by a social upheaval of the magnitude of first the Revolutionary War and then the Civil War.[10] Public attitudes were also an important consideration in the control of government.

Much has been written about how the pervasive distrust of government power among the American people shaped the framing of a Constitution that worked to limit government.[11] What might be more important is that the Constitution worked to limit government because the public had a healthy distrust of government power. For example, in the 1860s the Baltimore and Ohio railroad had its Harpers Ferry bridge blown up many times by both the Confederate and Union armies, and each time the railroad rebuilt the bridge with its own funds without any attempt to get the government to pick up part of the tab. Or consider the fact that in 1887 President Grover Cleveland vetoed an appropriation of $25,000 for seed corn to assist drought-stricken farmers with the statement, "It is not the duty of government to support the people."[12] There is little doubt that Cleveland's view on this matter was in keeping with broad public opinion.

---

9   According to Milton Friedman. "The most potent group in a democracy such as ours is a small minority that has a special interest which it values very highly, for which it is willing to give its vote regardless of what happens elsewhere, and about which the rest of the community does not care very strongly." See Milton Friedman, "Special Interest and His Law," *Chicago Bar Record* (June 1970)

10   Mancur Olson, *The Rise and Decline of Nations* (New Haven: Yale University Press, 1982).

11   Gordon S. Wood, *The Creation of the American Republic: 1776.1787* (Chapel Hill: The University of North Carolina Press. 1969), especially chapter 1.

12   Quoted in A, Nevins. *Grover Cleveland: A Study in Courage* (New York: Dodd Mead. 1932).

The Constitutional safeguards against government transfer activity unfortunately have lost much of their effectiveness over the years. The western frontier disappeared, and a long period of relative stability in the political order provided time for factions to become entrenched in the political process. Of more direct and crucial importance, however, in the move from productive activity to transfer activity has been the weakening judicial barrier to the use of government to advance special interests. The 1877 Supreme Court decision in *Munn v. Illinois* is often considered to be a watershed case. This decision upheld a lower court ruling that the Illinois state legislature had the authority to determine the rates that could be charged for storing grain. This decision, by sanctioning an expanded role for government in the determination of prices, increased the payoff to political activity relative to market activity and established an important precedent for future increases in that payoff.

In *Chicago, Milwaukee and St. Paul Railroad Co. v. Minnesota*, decided in 1890, the Supreme Court imposed what appeared to be limits on state regulation of economic activity by ruling that such regulation must be reasonable. Unfortunately, this reasonableness doctrine put the effectiveness of judicial restraint on government at the mercy of current fashion in social thought. What is considered unreasonable at one time may be considered quite reasonable at another.[13] It was unreasonable for the Baltimore and Ohio railroad to consider requesting government funds to repair its Harpers Ferry bridge, destroyed by government forces, during the Civil War. In the 1980s it was considered reasonable for Chrysler Corporation to request and receive a federal government bailout because Chrysler was not competing successfully for the consumer's dollar.

UNDERMINING CONSTITUTIONAL LAW

The idea of reasonable regulation significantly undermined the concept of a higher Constitutional law that established protections needed for the long-run viability of a free and productive social order. Once the notion of reasonable regulation stuck its nose into the judicial tent it was just a matter of time before the courts began seeing their task as that of judging particular outcomes rather than overseeing the general rules of the game. Illustrative of this changing emphasis was the legal brief submitted by Louis Brandeis, then an attorney for the state of Oregon, in the 1908 case *Muller v. Oregon*. At issue was the constitutionality of an Oregon law which regulated the working hours of women. The Brandeis brief contained only a few pages addressing constitutional considerations and well over one hundred pages of social economic data and argumentation attempting to establish the unfortunate consequences of women working long hours. It was a judgment on the reasonableness of a particular outcome, women working long hours, rather than constitutional considerations, which were considered of paramount

---

13   In spite of the two decisions just cited, between 1897 and 1937. the Supreme Court made use of the due process clause of the Fourteenth Amendment to reach decisions that served to protect the market process against political intrusions, See Bernard Siegan. *Economic Liberties and the Constitution* (Chicago: University of Chicago Press. 1981). Unfortunately, this pattern of judicial decisions was not solid enough to prevent these decisions from being ignored or overruled when the political climate and prevailing notions of reasonableness changed.

importance and led to a Supreme Court ruling in favor of Oregon.[14] When the constitutionality of legislation stands or falls on the "reasonableness" of the particular outcomes it hopes to achieve, opportunities increase for people to increase their wealth through nonproductive political activity.

In the 1911 case *United States v. Grimand*, the Supreme Court handed down a decision that significantly increased the private return to obtaining transfers through political influence. Prior to this decision, the U.S. Congress had increasingly moved toward granting administrative agencies the authority to promulgate specific rules in order to implement the general policy objectives outlined by Congress. In *United States v. Grimand* the high court empowered these administrative rulings with the full force of law. After this decision, the cost of successfully using government authority to transfer wealth decreased significantly as special interest groups seeking preferential treatment could concentrate their influence on a few key members of a particular administrative board or agency. The typical result of this has been the development of symbiotic relationships between bureaucratic agencies and their special interest clients. A special interest group can thrive on the benefits transferred to it by the ruling of a bureaucracy, and the bureaucracy's budget and prestige will depend on a thriving special interest group demanding its services.[15]

What we have observed over the years is a slow, somewhat erratic, but unmistakable breakdown in the protection the Constitution provides the public against arbitrary government power. Those who want to get on with the task of creating new wealth have much less assurance today then they did in the past that significant portions of the wealth they create will not be confiscated by government and transferred to those who have specialized in political influence.

Maintaining constitutional constraints on government transfer activity is a task requiting constant vigilance. Once a breakdown in these constraints begins, it can initiate a destructive dynamic of increasing government transfers that is difficult to control. Any change that makes it easier to obtain transfers through government will motivate some people to redirect their efforts away from productive enterprises and into transfer enterprises. As this is done, those who continue to create new wealth find the payoff from doing so is somewhat diminished as more of this wealth is being taken from them. This further reduction in the relative return to productive activity motivates yet more people to use government power to benefit at the expense of others.

---

14   For a brief but useful discussion of this case see Thomas K. McCraw, *Prophets of Regulation* (Cambridge: The Belknap Press of Harvard University Press. Cambridge. 19841. pp. 87–88.

15   The relationship between the U.S. Department of Agriculture and the farm bloc is but one of many illustrative examples that could be cited here. It is clear that those employed by the Department of Agriculture strongly support the agricultural price support and subsidy programs that transfer literally billions of dollars from the American consumer and taxpayer to the nation's farmers (most of this transfer goes to the largest and wealthiest farmers; see Bruce L. Gardner. *The Governing of Agriculture* [Lawrence: Regents Press of Kansas. 1981]). It is by expanding these programs that the Department of Agriculture can justify bigger budgets and more employees, something it has been quite successful at doing. In 1920 when the farm population was approximately 31 million, the Department of Agriculture employed 19,500 people. By 1975 the farm population had declined to less than 9 million, but the Department of Agriculture had increased its employment to 121,000 people. This trend toward fewer agricultural workers relative to agricultural bureaucrats has continued into the 1980s.

Furthermore, the burdens and inefficiencies created by one government program will be used as "justification" for yet additional government programs which will create new burdens and inefficiencies.[16] This dynamic can lead to what is best characterized as a "transfer society."[17]

POLITICAL PIRACY AND THE TRANSFER SOCIETY

Once we start down the road to the transfer society we can easily find ourselves trapped in a situation almost everyone will disapprove of, but which no one will be willing to change. The analogy of piracy is appropriate here. When all ships are productively employed shipping the goods, a large amount of wealth can be generated. But if sanctions against piracy are eased a few shippers may find it to their personal advantage to stop shipping and start pirating the merchandise being shipped by others, even though this reduces the total wealth available. This piracy by the few will reduce the return the others receive from shipping, and there will be an increase in the number finding the advantage in piracy. Eventually the point may be reached where everyone is sailing the seas looking for the booty that used to be shipped but is no longer. No one is doing well under these circumstances, and indeed, all would be much better off if everyone would return to shipping the goods. Yet who will be willing to return to productive shipping when everyone else is a pirate?

Obviously, we have not yet arrived at the point of being a full-blown transfer society; not everyone has become a political pirate. There are plenty of people who remain productive, and they still receive a measure of protection against the confiscation of the returns to their efforts by the constitutional limitations that remain on government power. But there can be no doubt that these limitations are less effective today than they were in the past. This erosion is in large measure due to a change in the prevailing attitude toward government. The fear of unrestrained government power that guided the Founding Fathers has been largely replaced with the view that discretionary government power is a force for social good. If there is a problem, government supposedly has the obligation and ability to solve it. Such public attitudes have a decisive influence on the effectiveness of constitutional limitations.

Simply writing something down on a document called the Constitution does not by itself make it so. And, because of this fact, Alexis de Tocqueville, writing in the 1830s, predicted that the U.S. Constitution would eventually cease to exercise effective restraint on government. According to Tocqueville, "The government of the Union depends almost entirely upon legal fictions." He continued that it would be difficult to "imagine that it is possible by the aid of

---

16 Our Federal farm programs are a perfect example of this process. See Gardner, *ibid*, Early on, James Madison recognized the possibility of this type of legislative chain reaction. In Federalist 44 Madison states, "that legislative interference, is but the first link of a long chain of repetitions; every subsequent interference being naturally produced by the effects of the preceding.

17 For a detailed and compelling analysis of how the breakdown in constitutional limitations on government activity has moved the U.S. away from positive-sum economic activity and toward negative-sum activity, see Terry L, Anderson and Peter J, Hill, *The Birth of a Transfer Society* (Stanford, California: Hoover Institution Press. 1980)

legal fictions to prevent men from finding out and employing those means of gratifying their passions which have been left open to them"[18]

But controlling our passions is what constitutional government is all about. In the absence of government we have the anarchy of the Hobbesian jungle in which those who control their passion for immediate gratification-and apply their efforts toward long-run objectives only increase their vulnerability to the predation of those who exercise no control or foresight. Granting government the power to enforce general rules of social interaction is surely a necessary condition if a productive social order is to emerge from a state of anarchy. But without strict constitutional limits on the scope of government activity, the existence of government power will only increase the scope of effective predation. The notion that government can solve all problems becomes a convenient pretense for those who would solve their problems, not in cooperation with others, but at the expense of others. Unlimited government reduces the personal advantage to the productive pursuit of long-run objectives just as surely as does anarchy. In such a case, government is little more than the means of moving from the anarchy of the Hobbesian jungle to the anarchy of the political jungle.

The American experience, however, demonstrates convincingly that with a healthy fear of government power and a realistic understanding of human nature, a constitution can be designed that, over a long period of time, will effectively constrain government to operate within the limits defined by the delicate balance between proper power and prudent restraint. All that is needed to restore the U.S. Constitution to its full effectiveness is a return to the political wisdom that guided our Founding Fathers 200 years ago.

CONCLUSION

The U.S. is a wealthy country today in large part because our Founding Fathers had what can be quite accurately described as a negative attitude toward government. They had little confidence in the ability of government to promote social well-being through the application of government power to achieve particular ends. In their view, the best that government can realistically hope to achieve is the establishment of a social setting in which individuals are free, within the limits of general laws, to productively pursue their own objectives.

This negative view of government contrasts sharply with the dominant view today; the view that government is the problem solver of last resort and has an obligation to provide a solution to any problem not resolved immediately in the private sector. Unfortunately, this positive view of government is less conducive to positive consequences than the negative view of the Founders. According to F. A. Hayek:

The first [positive view] gives us a sense of unlimited power to realize our wishes, while the second [negative view] leads to the insight that there are limitations to what we can deliberately bring about, and to the recognition that some of our present hopes are delusions. Yet the effect of allowing ourselves to be deluded by the first view has always been that man has actually

---

18   Quoted in Felix Morley, *Freedom and Federalism*, (Chicago: Regnery, 1959): pp. 138–139.

limited the scope of what he can achieve. For it has always been the recognition of the limits of the possible which has enabled man to make full use of his powers.[19]

The exercise of government can, without doubt, be used to accomplish particular ends. Neither can it be denied that many of the specific outcomes realized through government programs provide important benefits and advance worthy objectives. But, as is always the case, those accomplishments are only realized at a cost, and the pervasive truth about government accomplishments is that those who benefit from them are seldom those who pay the cost. Indeed, much of the motivation for engaging in political actions is to escape the discipline imposed by the market where individuals are accountable for the cost of their choices.

The escape from market discipline is the inevitable consequence of reducing the constitutional limits on the use of government power. The immediate and visible benefits that are generated by wide-ranging government discretion are paid for by a shift in the incentive structure that, over the long run, will reduce the amount of good that can be accomplished. More, much more, has been accomplished by the American people because our Founding Fathers had a strong sense of the limits on what can be accomplished by government.

---

19   Friedrich A. Hayek, *Law. Legislation and Liberty*, Vol. 1 *Rules and Order* (Chicago: University of Chicago Press. 1973). p. 8.

What Is Capitalism?

By Ayn Rand

THE DISINTEGRATION OF philosophy in the nineteenth century and its collapse in the twentieth have led to a similar, though much slower and less obvious, process in the course of modern science.

Today's frantic development in the field of technology has a quality reminiscent of the days preceding the economic crash of 1929: riding on the momentum of the past, on the unacknowledged remnants of an Aristotelian epistemology, it is a hectic, feverish expansion, heedless of the fact that its theoretical account is long since overdrawn—that in the field of scientific theory, unable to integrate or interpret their own data, scientists are abetting the resurgence of a primitive mysticism. In the humanities, however, the crash is past, the depression has set in, and the collapse of science is all but complete.

The clearest evidence of it may be seen in such comparatively young sciences as psychology and political economy. In psychology, one may observe the attempt to study human behavior without reference to the fact that man is conscious. In political economy, one may observe the attempt to study and to devise social systems without reference to *man*.

It is philosophy that defines and establishes the epistemological criteria to guide human knowledge in general and specific sciences in particular. Political economy came into prominence in the nineteenth century, in the era of philosophy's post-Kantian disintegration, and no one rose to check its premises or to challenge its base. Implicitly, uncritically, and by default, political economy accepted as its axioms the fundamental tenets of collectivism.

Political economists—including the advocates of capitalism—defined their science as the study of the management or direction or organization or manipulation of a "community's" or a nation's "resources." The nature of these "resources" was not defined; their communal ownership was taken for granted—and the goal of political economy was assumed to be the study of how to utilize these "resources" for "the common good."

The fact that the principal "resource" involved was man himself, that he was an entity of a specific nature with specific capacities and requirements, was given the most superficial attention, if any. Man was regarded simply as one of the factors of production along with land, forests, or mines—as one of the less significant factors, since more study was devoted to the influence and quality of these others than to *his* role or quality.

Political economy was, in effect, a science starting in midstream: it observed that men were producing and trading, it took for granted that they had always done so and always would—it accepted this fact as the given, requiring no further consideration—and it addressed itself to the problem of how to devise the best way for the "community" to dispose of human effort.

There were many reasons for this tribal view of man. The morality of altruism was one; the growing dominance of political statism among the intellectuals of the nineteenth century was another. Psychologically, the main reason was the soul-body dichotomy permeating European culture: material production was regarded as a demeaning task of a lower order, unrelated to the concerns of man's intellect, a task assigned to slaves or serfs since the beginning of recorded history. The institution of serfdom had lasted, in one form or another, till well into the nineteenth century; it was abolished, politically, only by the advent of capitalism; politically, but not intellectually.

The concept of man as a free, independent individual was profoundly alien to the culture of Europe. It was a tribal culture down to its roots; in European thinking, the tribe was the entity, the unit, and man was only one of its expendable cells. This applied to rulers and serfs alike: the rulers were believed to hold their privileges only by virtue of the services they rendered to the tribe, services regarded as of a noble order, namely, armed force or military defense. But a nobleman was as much chattel of the tribe as a serf: his life and property belonged to the king. It must be remembered that the institution of private property, in the full, legal meaning of the term, was brought into existence only by capitalism. In the pre-capitalist eras, private property existed *de facto,* but not *de jure, i.e.,* by custom and sufferance, not by right or by law. In law and in principle, all property belonged to the head of the tribe, the king, and was held only by his permission, which could be revoked at any time, at his pleasure. (The king could and did expropriate the estates of recalcitrant noblemen throughout the course of Europe's history.)

The American philosophy of the Rights of Man was never grasped fully by European intellectuals. Europe's predominant idea of emancipation consisted of changing the concept of man as a slave of the absolute state embodied by a king, to the concept of man as a slave of the absolute state embodied by "the people"—*i.e.,* switching from slavery to a tribal chief into slavery to the tribe A non-tribal view of existence could not penetrate the mentalities that regarded the privilege of ruling material producers by physical force as a badge of nobility.

Thus Europe's, thinkers did not notice the fact that during the nineteenth century, the galley slaves had been replaced by the inventors of steamboats, and the village blacksmiths by the owners of blast furnaces, and they went on thinking in such terms (such contradictions in terms) as "wage slavery" or "the antisocial selfishness of industrialists who take so much from society without giving anything in return"—on the unchallenged axiom that wealth is an anonymous, social, tribal product.

That notion has not been challenged to this day; it represents the implicit assumption and the base of contemporary political economy.

As an example of this view and its consequences, I shall cite the article on "Capitalism" in the *Encyclopaedia Britannica.* The article gives no definition of its subject; it opens as follows:

> CAPITALISM, a term used to denote the economic system that has been dominant in the western world since the breakup of feudalism. Fundamental to any system called

capitalist are the relations between private owners of nonpersonal means of production (land, mines, *industrial plants,* etc., collectively known as capital) [italics mine] and free but capitalless workers, who sell their labour services to employers ... The resulting wage bargains determine the proportion in which the total product of society will be shared between the class of labourers and the class of capitalist entrepreneurs.[1]

(I quote from Galt's speech in *Atlas Shrugged,* from a passage describing the tenets of collectivism: "An industrialist—blank-out—there is no such person. A factory is a 'natural resource,' like a tree, a rock or a mud-puddle.")

The success of capitalism is explained by the *Britannica* as follows:

> Productive use of the "social surplus" was the special virtue that enabled capitalism to outstrip all prior economic systems. Instead of building pyramids and cathedrals, those in command of the social surplus chose to invest in ships, warehouses, raw materials, finished goods and other material forms of wealth. The social surplus was thus converted into enlarged productive capacity.

This is said about a time when Europe's population subsisted in such poverty that child mortality approached fifty percent, and periodic famines wiped out the "surplus" *population* which the precapitalist economies were unable to feed. Yet, making no distinction between tax-expropriated and industrially produced wealth, the *Britannica* asserts that it was the *surplus wealth* of that time that the early capitalists "commanded" and "chose to invest"—and that this investment was the cause of the stupendous prosperity of the age that followed.

What is a "social surplus"? The article gives no definition or explanation. A "surplus" presupposes a norm; if subsistence on a chronic starvation level is above the implied norm, what is that norm? The article does not answer.

There is, of course, no such thing as a "social surplus." All wealth is produced by somebody and belongs to somebody. And "the special virtue that enabled capitalism to outstrip all prior economic systems" was *freedom* (a concept eloquently absent from the *Britannica's* account), which led, not to the expropriation, but to the *creation* of wealth.

I shall have more to say later about that disgraceful article (disgraceful on many counts, not the least of which is scholarship). At this point, I quoted it only as a succinct example of the tribal premise that underlies today's political economy. That premise is shared by the enemies and the champions of capitalism alike; it provides the former with a certain inner consistency, and disarms the latter by a subtle, yet devastating aura of moral hypocrisy—as witness, their attempts to justify capitalism on the ground of "the common good" or "service to the consumer" or "the best allocation of resources." (*Whose* resources?)

If capitalism is to be understood, it is this *tribal premise* that has to be checked—and challenged.

---

1 *Encyclopaedia Britannica,* 1964, Vol. IV, pp. 839–845.

Mankind is not an entity, an organism, or a coral bush. The entity involved in production and trade is *man*. It is with the study of man—not of the loose aggregate known as a "community"—that any science of the humanities has to begin.

This issue represents one of the epistemological differences between the humanities and the physical sciences, one of the causes of the former's well-earned inferiority complex in regard to the latter. A physical science would not permit itself (not yet, at least) to ignore or bypass the nature of its subject. Such an attempt would mean: a science of astronomy that gazed at the sky, but refused to study individual stars, planets, and satellites—or a science of medicine that studied disease, without any knowledge or criterion of health, and took, as its basic subject of study, a hospital as a whole, never focusing on individual patients.

A great deal may be learned about society by studying man; but this process cannot be reversed: nothing can be learned about man by studying society—by studying the inter-relationships of entities one has never identified or defined. Yet that is the methodology adopted by most political economists. Their attitude, in effect, amounts to the unstated, implicit postulate: "Man is that which fits economic equations." Since he obviously does not, this leads to the curious fact that in spite of the practical nature of their science, political economists are oddly unable to relate their abstractions to the concretes of actual existence.

It leads also to a baffling sort of double standard or double perspective in their way of viewing men and events: if they observe a shoemaker, they find no difficulty in concluding that he is working in order to make a living; but as political economists, on the tribal premise, they declare that his purpose (and duty) is to provide society with shoes. If they observe a panhandler on a street corner, they identify him as a bum; in political economy, he becomes "a sovereign consumer." If they hear the communist doctrine that all property should belong to the state, they reject it emphatically and feel, *sincerely*, that they would fight communism to the death; but in political economy, they speak of the government's duty to effect "a fair redistribution of wealth," and they speak of businessmen as the best, most efficient trustees of the nation's "natural resources."

This is what a basic premise (and philosophical negligence) will do; this is what the tribal premise has done.

To reject that premise and begin at the beginning—in one's approach to political economy and to the evaluation of various social systems—one must begin by identifying man's nature, *i.e.*, those essential characteristics which distinguish him from all other living species.

Man's essential characteristic is his rational faculty. Man's mind is his basic means of survival—his only means of gaining knowledge.

> Man cannot survive, as animals do, by the guidance of mere percepts … He cannot provide for his simplest physical needs without a process of thought. He needs a process of thought to discover how to plant and grow his food or how to make weapons for hunting. His percepts might lead him to a cave, if one is available—but to build the simplest shelter, he needs a process of thought. No percepts and no "instincts" will tell him how to light a fire, how to weave cloth, how to forge tools, how to make a wheel, how to make an airplane, how to perform an appendectomy, how to produce

an electric light bulb or an electronic tube or a cyclotron or a box of matches. Yet his life depends on such knowledge—and only a volitional act of his consciousness, a process of thought, can provide it.[2]

A process of thought is an enormously complex process of identification and integration, which only an individual mind can perform. There is no such thing as a collective brain. Men can learn from one another, but learning requires a process of thought on the part of every individual student. Men can cooperate in the discovery of new knowledge, but such cooperation requires the independent exercise of his rational faculty by every individual scientist. Man is the only living species that can transmit and expand his store of knowledge from generation to generation; but such transmission requires a process of thought on the part of the individual recipients. As witness, the breakdowns of civilization, the dark ages in the history of mankind's progress, when the accumulated knowledge of centuries vanished from the lives of men who were unable, unwilling, or forbidden to think.

In order to sustain its life, every living species has to follow a certain course of action required by its nature. The action required to sustain human life is primarily intellectual: everything man needs has to be discovered by his mind and produced by his effort. Production is the application of reason to the problem of survival.

If some men do not choose to think, they can survive only by imitating and repeating a routine of work discovered by others—but those others had to discover it, or none would have survived. If some men do not choose to think or to work, they can survive (temporarily) only by looting the goods produced by others—but those others had to produce them, or none would have survived. Regardless of what choice is made, in this issue, by any man or by any number of men, regardless of what blind, irrational, or evil course they may choose to pursue—the fact remains that reason is man's means of survival and that men prosper or fall, survive or perish in proportion to the degree of their rationality.

Since knowledge, thinking, and rational action are properties of the individual, since the choice to exercise his rational faculty or not depends on the individual, man's survival requires that those who think be free of the interference of those who don't. Since men are neither omniscient nor infallible, they must be free to agree or disagree, to cooperate or to pursue their own independent course, each according to his own rational judgment. Freedom is the fundamental requirement of man's mind.

A rational mind does not work under compulsion; it does not subordinate its grasp of reality to anyone's orders, directives, or controls; it does not sacrifice its knowledge, its view of the truth, to anyone's opinions, threats, wishes, plans, or "welfare." Such a mind may be hampered by others, it may be silenced, proscribed, imprisoned, or destroyed; it cannot be forced; a gun is not an argument. (An example and symbol of this attitude is Galileo.)

It is from the work and the inviolate integrity of such minds—from the intransigent innovators—that all of mankind's knowledge and achievements have come. (See *The Fountainhead*.) It is to such minds that mankind owes its survival. (See *Atlas Shrugged*.)

---

2   Ayn Rand, "The Objectivist Ethics," in *The Virtue of Selfishness*.

The same principle applies to all men, on every level of ability and ambition. To the extent that a man is guided by his rational judgment, he acts in accordance with the requirements of his nature and, to that extent, succeeds in achieving a human form of survival and well-being; to the extent that he acts irrationally, he acts as his own destroyer.

The social recognition of man's rational nature—of the connection between his survival and his use of reason—is the concept of *individual rights*.

I shall remind you that "rights" are a moral principle defining and sanctioning a man's freedom of action in a social context, that they are derived from man's nature as a rational being and represent a necessary condition of his particular mode of survival I shall remind you also that the right to life is the source of all rights, including the right to property.[3]

In regard to political economy, this last requires special emphasis: man has to work and produce in order to support his life. He has to support his life by his own effort and by the guidance of his own mind. If he cannot dispose of the product of his effort, he cannot dispose of his effort; if he cannot dispose of his effort, he cannot dispose of his life. Without property rights, no other rights can be practiced.

Now, bearing these facts in mind, consider the question of what social system is appropriate to man.

A social system is a set of moral-political-economic principles embodied in a society's laws, institutions, and government, which determine the relationships, the terms of association, among the men living in a given geographical area. It is obvious that these terms and relationships depend on an identification of man's nature, that they would be different if they pertain to a society of rational beings or to a colony of ants. It is obvious that they will be radically different if men deal with one another as free, independent individuals, on the premise that every man is an end in himself—or as members of a pack, each regarding the others as the means to *his* ends and to the ends of "the pack as a whole."

There are only two fundamental questions (or two aspects of the same question) that determine the nature of any social system: Does a social system recognize individual rights?—and: Does a social system ban physical force from human relationships? The answer to the second question is the practical implementation of the answer to the first.

Is man a sovereign individual who owns his person, his mind, his life, his work and its products—or is he the property of the tribe (the state, the society, the collective) that may dispose of him in any way it pleases, that may dictate his convictions, prescribe the course of his life, control his work and expropriate his products? Does man have the *right* to exist for his own sake—or is he born in bondage, as an indentured servant who must keep buying his life by serving the tribe but can never acquire it free and clear?

This is the first question to answer. The rest is consequences and practical implementations. The basic issue is only: Is man free?

In mankind's history, capitalism is the only system that answers: Yes.

---

3 For a fuller discussion of rights, I refer you to my articles "Man's Rights" in the appendix, and "Collectivized 'Rights'" in *The Virtue of Selfishness*.

Capitalism is a social system based on the recognition of individual rights, including property rights, in which all property is privately owned.

The recognition of individual rights entails the banishment of physical force from human relationships: basically, rights can be violated only by means of force. In a capitalist society, no man or group may *initiate* the use of physical force against others. The only function of the government, in such a society, is the task of protecting man's rights, *i.e.,* the task of protecting him from physical force; the government acts as the agent of man's right of self-defense, and may use force only in retaliation and only against those who initiate its use; thus the government is the means of placing the retaliatory use of force under *objective control.*[4]

It is the basic, metaphysical fact of man's nature—the connection between his survival and his use of reason—that capitalism recognizes and protects.

In a capitalist society, all human relationships are *voluntary.* Men are free to cooperate or not, to deal with one another or not, as their own individual judgments, convictions, and interests dictate. They can deal with one another only in terms of and by means of reason, *i.e.,* by means of discussion, persuasion, and *contractual* agreement, by voluntary choice to mutual benefit. The right to agree with others is not a problem in any society; it is *the right to disagree* that is crucial. It is the institution of private property that protects and implements the right to disagree—and thus keeps the road open to man's most valuable attribute (valuable personally, socially, and *objectively*): the creative mind.

This is the cardinal difference between capitalism and collectivism.

The power that determines the establishment, the changes, the evolution and the destruction of social systems is philosophy. The role of chance, accident, or tradition, in this context, is the same as their role in the life of an individual: their power stands in inverse ratio to the power of a culture's (or an individual's) philosophical equipment, and grows as philosophy collapses. It is, therefore, by reference to philosophy that the character of a social system has to be defined and evaluated. Corresponding to the four branches of philosophy, the four keystones of capitalism are: metaphysically, the requirements of man's nature and survival—epistemologically, reason—ethically, individual rights'—politically, freedom.

This, in substance, is the base of the proper approach to political economy and to an understanding of capitalism—not the tribal premise inherited from prehistoric traditions.

The "practical" justification of capitalism does not lie in the collectivist claim that it effects "the best allocation of national resources." Man is *not* a "national resource" and neither is his mind—and without the creative power of man's intelligence, raw materials remain just so many useless raw materials.

The *moral* justification of capitalism does not lie in the altruist claim that it represents the best way to achieve "the common good." It is true that capitalism does—if that catch-phrase has any meaning—but this is merely a secondary consequence. The moral justification of capitalism lies in the fact that it is the only system consonant with man's rational nature, that it protects man's survival *qua* man, and that its ruling principle is: *justice.*

---

4 For a fuller discussion of this subject, see my article "The Nature of Government" in the appendix.

Every social system is based, explicitly or implicitly, on some theory of ethics. The tribal notion of "the common good" has served as the moral justification of most social systems—and of all tyrannies—in history. The degree of a society's enslavement or freedom corresponded to the degree to which that tribal slogan was invoked or ignored.

"The common good" (or "the public interest") is an undefined and undefinable concept: there is no such entity as "the tribe" or "the public"; the tribe (or the public or society) is only a number of individual men. Nothing can be good for the tribe as such; "good" and "value" pertain *only* to a living organism—to an individual living organism—not to a disembodied aggregate of relationships.

"The common good" is a meaningless concept, unless taken literally, in which case its only possible meaning is: the sum of the good of *all* the individual men involved. But in that case, the concept is meaningless as a moral criterion: it leaves open the question of what *is* the good of individual men and how does one determine it?

It is not, however, in its literal meaning that that concept is generally used. It is accepted precisely for its elastic, undefinable, mystical character which serves, not as a moral guide, but as an escape from morality. Since the good is not applicable to the disembodied, it becomes a moral blank check for those who attempt to embody it.

When "the common good" of a society is regarded as something apart from and superior to the individual good of its members, it means that the good of *some* men takes precedence over the good of others, with those others consigned to the status of sacrificial animals. It is tacitly assumed, in such cases, that "the common good" means "the good of the *majority*" as against the minority or the individual. Observe the significant fact that that assumption is *tacit:* even the most collectivized mentalities seem to sense the impossibility of justifying it morally. But "the good of the majority," too, is only a pretense and a delusion: since, in fact, the violation of an individual's rights means the abrogation of all rights, it delivers the helpless majority into the power of any gang that proclaims itself to be "the voice of society" and proceeds to rule by means of physical force, until deposed by another gang employing the same means.

If one begins by defining the good of individual men, one will accept as proper only a society in which that good is achieved and *achievable.* But if one begins by accepting "the common good" as an axiom and regarding individual good as its possible but not necessary consequence (not necessary in any particular case), one ends up with such a gruesome absurdity as Soviet Russia, a country professedly dedicated to "the common good," where, with the exception of a minuscule clique of rulers, the entire population has existed in subhuman misery for over two generations.

What makes the victims and, worse, the observers accept this and other similar historical atrocities, and still cling to the myth of "the common good"? The answer lies in philosophy—in philosophical theories on the nature of moral values.

There are, in essence, three schools of thought on the nature of the good: the intrinsic, the subjective, and the objective. The *intrinsic* theory holds that the good is inherent in certain things or actions as such, regardless of their context and consequences, regardless of any benefit or injury they may cause to the actors and subjects involved. It is a theory that divorces the concept of "good" from beneficiaries, and the concept of "Value" from valuer and purpose—claiming that the good is good in, by, and of itself.

The *subjectivist* theory holds that the good bears no relation to the facts of reality, that it is the product of a man's consciousness, created by his feelings, desires, "intuitions," or whims, and that it is merely an "arbitrary postulate" or an "emotional commitment."

The intrinsic theory holds that the good resides in some sort of reality, independent of man's consciousness; the subjectivist theory holds that the good resides in man's consciousness, independent of reality.

The *objective* theory holds that the good is neither, an attribute of "things in themselves" nor of man's emotional states, but *an evaluation* of the facts of reality by man's consciousness according to a rational standard of value, (Rational, in this context, means: derived from the facts of reality and validated by a process of reason.) The objective theory holds that *the good is an aspect of reality in relation to man*—and that it must be discovered, not invented, by man. Fundamental to an objective theory of values is the question: Of value to whom and for what? An objective theory does not permit context-dropping or "concept-stealing"; it does not permit the separation of "value" from "purpose," of the good from beneficiaries, and of man's actions from reason.

Of all the social systems in mankind's history, *capitalism is the only system based on an objective theory of values.*

The intrinsic theory and the subjectivist theory (or a mixture of both) are the necessary base of every dictatorship, tyranny, or variant of the absolute state. Whether they are held consciously or subconsciously—in the explicit form of a philosopher's treatise or in the implicit chaos of its echoes in an average man's feelings—these theories make it possible for a man to believe that the good is independent of man's mind and can be achieved by physical force.

If a man believes that the good is intrinsic in certain actions, he will not hesitate to force others to perform them. If he believes that the human benefit or injury caused by such actions is of no significance, he will regard a sea of blood as of no significance. If he believes that the beneficiaries of such actions are irrelevant (or interchangeable), he will regard wholesale slaughter as his moral duty in the service of a "higher" good. It is the intrinsic theory of values that produces a Robespierre, a Lenin, a Stalin, or a Hitler. It is not an accident that Eichmann was a Kantian.

If a man believes that the good is a matter of arbitrary, subjective choice, the issue of good or evil becomes, for him, an issue of: *my* feelings or *theirs?* No bridge, understanding, or communication is possible to him. Reason is the only means of communication among men, and an objectively perceivable reality is their only common frame of reference; when these are invalidated (*i.e.,* held to be irrelevant) in the field of morality, force becomes men's only way of dealing with one another. If the subjectivist wants to pursue some social ideal of his own, he feels morally entitled to force men "for their own good," since he *feels* that he is right and that there is nothing to oppose him but their misguided feelings.

Thus, in practice, the proponents of the intrinsic and the subjectivist schools meet and blend. (They blend in terms of their psycho-epistemology as well: by what means do the moralists of the intrinsic school discover their transcendental "good," if not by means of special, non-rational intuitions and revelations, *i.e.,* by means of their feelings?) It is doubtful whether anyone can hold either of these theories as an actual, if mistaken, conviction. But both serve as a rationalization of power-lust and of rule by brute force, unleashing the potential dictator and disarming his victims.

The objective theory of values is the only moral theory incompatible with rule by force. Capitalism is the only system based implicitly on an objective theory of values—and the historic tragedy is that this has never been made explicit.

If one knows that the good is *objective*—*i.e.,* determined by the nature of reality, but to be discovered by man's mind—one knows that an attempt to achieve the good by physical force is a monstrous contradiction which negates morality at its root by destroying man's capacity to recognize the good, *i.e.,* his capacity to value. Force invalidates and paralyzes a man's judgment, demanding that he act against it, thus rendering him morally impotent. A value which one is forced to accept at the price of surrendering one's mind, is not a value to anyone; the forcibly mindless can neither judge nor choose nor value. An attempt to achieve the good by force is like an attempt to provide a man with a picture gallery at the price of cutting out his eyes. Values cannot exist (cannot be valued) outside the full context of a man's life, needs, goals, and *knowledge.*

The objective view of values permeates the entire structure of a capitalist society.

The recognition of individual rights implies the recognition of the fact that the good is not an ineffable abstraction in some supernatural dimension, but a value pertaining to reality, to this earth, to the lives of individual human beings (note the right to the pursuit of happiness). It implies that the good cannot be divorced from beneficiaries, that men are not to be regarded as interchangeable, and that no man or tribe may attempt to achieve the good of some at the price of the immolation of others.

The free market represents the *social* application of an objective theory of values. Since values are to be discovered by man's mind, men must be free to discover them—to think, to study, to translate their knowledge into physical form, to offer their products for trade, to judge them, and to choose, be it material goods or ideas, a loaf of bread or a philosophical treatise. Since values are established contextually, every man must judge for himself, in the context of his own knowledge, goals, and interests. Since values are determined by the nature of reality, it is reality that serves as men's ultimate arbiter: if a man's judgment is right, the rewards are his; if it is wrong, he is his only victim.

It is in regard to a free market that the distinction between an intrinsic, subjective, and objective view of values is particularly important to understand. The market value of a product is *not* an intrinsic value, not a "value in itself" hanging in a vacuum. A free market never loses sight of the question: Of value *to whom?* And, within the broad field of objectivity, the market value of a product does not reflect its *philosophically objective* value, but only its *socially objective* value.

By "philosophically objective," I mean a value estimated from the standpoint of the best possible to man, *i.e.,* by the criterion of the most rational mind possessing the greatest knowledge, in a given category, in a given period, and in a defined context (nothing can be estimated in an undefined context). For instance, it can be rationally proved that the airplane is *objectively* of immeasurably greater value to man (to *man at his best)* than the bicycle—and that the works of Victor Hugo are *objectively* of immeasurably greater value than true-confession magazines. But if a given man's intellectual potential can barely manage to enjoy true confessions, there is no reason why his meager earnings, the product of *his* effort, should be spent on books he cannot read—or on subsidizing the airplane industry, if his own transportation needs do not extend beyond the range of a bicycle. (Nor is there any reason why the rest of mankind should be held down to the level of his literary taste, his engineering capacity, and his income. Values are not determined by fiat nor by majority vote.)

Just as the number of its adherents is not a proof of an idea's truth or falsehood, of an art work's merit or demerit, of a product's efficacy or inefficacy—so the free-market value of goods or services does not necessarily represent their philosophically objective value, but only their *socially objective* value, *i.e.,* the sum of the individual judgments of all the men involved in trade at a given time, the sum of what *they* valued, each in the context of his own life.

Thus, a manufacturer of lipstick may well make a greater fortune than a manufacturer of microscopes—even though it can be rationally demonstrated that microscopes are scientifically more valuable than lipstick. But—valuable *to whom?*

A microscope is of no value to a little stenographer struggling to make a living; a lipstick is; a lipstick, to her, may mean the difference between self-confidence and self-doubt, between glamour and drudgery.

This does not mean, however, that the values ruling a free market are *subjective.* If the stenographer spends all her money on cosmetics and has none left to pay for the use of a microscope (for a visit to the doctor) *when she needs it,* she learns a better method of budgeting her income; the free market serves as her teacher: she has no way to penalize others for her mistakes. If she budgets rationally, the microscope is always available to serve her own specific needs *and no more,* as far as she is concerned: she is not taxed to support an entire hospital, a research laboratory, or a space ship's journey to the moon. Within her own productive power, she does pay a part of the cost of scientific achievements, *when and as she needs them.* She has no "social duty," her own life is her only responsibility—and the only thing that a capitalist system requires of her is the thing that *nature* requires: rationality, *i.e.,* that she live and act to the best of her own judgment.

Within every category of goods and services offered on a free market, it is the purveyor of the best product at the cheapest price who wins the greatest financial rewards *in that field*—not automatically nor immediately nor by fiat, but by virtue of the free market, which teaches every participant to look for the *objective* best within the category of his own competence, and penalizes those who act on irrational considerations.

Now observe that a free market does not level men down to some common denominator—that the intellectual criteria of the majority do not rule a free market or a free society—and that the exceptional men, the innovators, the intellectual giants, are not held down by the majority. In fact, it is the members of this exceptional minority who lift the whole of a free society to the level of their own achievements, while rising further and ever further.

A "free market is a *continuous process* that cannot be held still, an upward process that demands the best (the most rational) of every man and rewards him accordingly. While the majority have barely assimilated the value of the automobile, the creative minority introduces the airplane. The majority learn by demonstration, the minority is free to demonstrate. The "philosophically objective" value of a new product serves as the teacher for those who are willing to exercise their rational faculty, each to the extent of his ability. Those who are unwilling remain unrewarded— as well as those who aspire to more than their ability produces. The stagnant, the irrational, the subjectivist have no power to stop their betters.

(The small minority of adults who are *unable* rather than unwilling to work, have to rely on voluntary charity; misfortune is not a claim to slave labor; there is no such thing as the *right* to consume, control, and destroy those without whom one would be unable to survive. As to depressions and mass unemployment, they are not caused by the free market, but by government interference into the economy.)

The mental parasites—the imitators who attempt to cater to what they think is the public's known taste—are constantly being beaten by the innovators whose products raise the public's knowledge and taste to ever higher levels. It is in this sense that the free market is ruled, not by the consumers, but by the producers. The most successful ones are those who discover new fields of production, fields which had not been known to exist.

A given product may not be appreciated at once, particularly if it is too radical an innovation; but, barring irrelevant accidents, it wins in the long run. It is in this sense that the free market is not ruled by the intellectual criteria of the majority, which prevail only at and for any given moment; the free market is ruled by those who are able to see and plan long-range—and the better the mind, the longer the range.

The economic value of a man's work is determined, on a free market, by a single principle: by the voluntary consent of those who are willing to trade him their work or products in return. This is the moral meaning of the law of supply and demand; it represents the total rejection of two vicious doctrines: the tribal premise and altruism. It represents the recognition of the fact that man is not the property nor the servant of the tribe, that *a man works in order to support his own life*—as, by his nature, he must—that he has to be guided by his own rational self-interest, and if he wants to trade with others, he cannot expect sacrificial victims, *i.e.,* he cannot expect to receive values without trading commensurate values in return. The sole criterion of what is commensurate, in this context, is the free, voluntary, uncoerced judgment of the traders.

The tribal mentalities attack this principle from two seemingly opposite sides: they claim that the free market is "unfair" both to the genius and to the average man. The first objection is usually expressed by a question such as: "Why should Elvis Presley make more money than Einstein?" The answer is: Because men work in order to support and enjoy their own lives—and if many men find value in Elvis Presley, they are entitled to spend their money on their own pleasure. Presley's fortune is not taken from those who do not care for his work (I am one of them) nor from Einstein—nor does he stand in Einstein's way—nor does Einstein lack proper recognition and support in a free society, on an appropriate intellectual level.

As to the second objection, the claim that a man of average ability suffers an "unfair" disadvantage on a free market—

> Look past the range of the moment, you who cry that you fear to compete with men
> of superior intelligence, that their mind is a threat to your livelihood, that the strong

leave no chance to the weak in a market of voluntary trade … When you live in a rational society, where men are free to trade, you receive an incalculable bonus: the material value of your work is determined not only by your effort, but by the effort of the best productive minds who exist in the world around you …

The machine, the frozen form of a living intelligence, is the power that expands the potential of your life by raising the productivity of your time … Every man is free to rise as far as he's able or willing, but it's only the degree to which he thinks that determines the degree to which he'll rise. Physical labor as such can extend no further than the range of the moment. The man who does no more than physical labor, consumes the material value-equivalent of his own contribution to the process of production, and leaves no further value, neither for himself nor others. But the man who produces an idea in any field of rational endeavor—the man who discovers new knowledge—is the permanent benefactor of humanity … It is only the value of an idea that can be shared with unlimited numbers of men, making all sharers richer at no one's sacrifice or loss, raising the productive capacity of whatever labor they perform …

In proportion to the mental energy he spent, the man who creates a new invention receives but a small percentage of his value in terms of material payment, no matter what fortune he makes, no matter what millions he earns. But the man who works as a janitor in the factory producing that invention, receives an enormous payment in proportion to the mental effort that his job requires of *him*. And the same is true of all men between, on all levels of ambition and ability. The man at the top of the intellectual pyramid contributes the most to all those below him, but gets nothing except his material payment, receiving no intellectual bonus from others to add to the value of his time. The man at the bottom who, left to himself, would starve in his hopeless ineptitude, contributes nothing to those above him, but receives the bonus of all of their brains. Such is the nature of the "competition" between the strong and the weak of the intellect. Such is the pattern of "exploitation" for which you have damned the strong. *(Atlas Shrugged)*

And such is the relationship of capitalism to man's mind and to man's survival.

The magnificent progress achieved by capitalism in a brief span of time—the spectacular improvement in the conditions of man's existence on earth—is a matter of historical record. It is not to be hidden, evaded, or explained away by all the propaganda of capitalism's enemies. But what needs special emphasis is the fact that this progress was achieved by *non-sacrificial* means.

Progress cannot be achieved by forced privations, by squeezing a "social surplus" out of starving victims. Progress can come only out of *individual surplus, i.e.,* from the work, the energy, the creative over-abundance of those men whose ability produces more than their personal consumption requires, those who are intellectually and financially able to seek the new, to improve on the known, to move forward. In a capitalist society, where such men are free to function and to take their own risks, progress is not a matter of sacrificing to some distant future, it is part of the living present, it is the normal and natural, it is achieved as and while men live—and *enjoy*—their lives.

Now consider the alternative—the tribal society, where all men throw their efforts, values, ambitions, and goals into a tribal pool or common pot, then wait hungrily at its rim, while the leader of a clique of cooks stirs it with a bayonet in one hand and a blank check on all their lives in the other. The most consistent example of such a system is the Union of Soviet Socialist Republics.

Half a century ago, the Soviet rulers commanded their subjects to be patient, bear privations, and make sacrifices for the sake of "industrializing" the country, promising that this was only temporary, that industrialization would bring them abundance, and Soviet progress would surpass the capitalistic West.

Today, Soviet Russia is still unable to feed her people—while the rulers scramble to copy, borrow, or steal the technological achievements of the West. Industrialization is not a static goal; it is a dynamic process with a rapid rate of obsolescence. So the wretched serfs of a planned tribal economy, who starved while waiting for electric generators and tractors, are now starving while waiting for atomic power and interplanetary travel. Thus, in a "people's state," the progress of science is a threat to the people, and every advance is taken out of the people's shrinking hides.

This was not the history of capitalism.

America's abundance was not created by public sacrifices to "the common good," but by the productive genius of free men who pursued their own personal interests and the making of their own private fortunes. They did not starve the people to pay for America's industrialization. They gave the people better jobs, higher wages, and cheaper goods with every new machine they invented, with every scientific discovery or technological advance—and thus the whole country was moving forward and profiting, not suffering, every step of the way.

Do not, however, make the error of reversing cause and effect: the good of the country was made possible precisely by the fact that it was not forced on anyone as a moral goal or duty; it was merely an effect; the cause was a man's right to pursue his own good. It is this right—not its consequences—that represents the moral justification of capitalism.

But this right is incompatible with the intrinsic or the subjectivist theory of values, with the altruist morality and the tribal premise. It is obvious which human attribute one rejects when one rejects objectivity; and, in view of capitalism's record, it is obvious against which human attribute the altruist morality and the tribal premise stand united: against man's mind, against intelligence—particularly against intelligence applied to the problems of human survival, *i.e.,* productive ability.

While altruism seeks to rob intelligence of its rewards, by asserting that the moral duty of the competent is to serve the incompetent and sacrifice themselves to anyone's need—the tribal premise goes a step further: it denies the existence of intelligence and of its role in the production of wealth.

It is morally obscene to regard wealth as an anonymous, tribal product and to talk about "redistributing" it. The view that wealth is the result of some undifferentiated, collective process, that we all did something and it's impossible to tell who did what, therefore some sort of equalitarian "distribution" is necessary—might have been appropriate in a primordial jungle with a savage horde moving boulders by crude physical labor (though even there someone had to initiate and organize the moving). To hold that view in an industrial society—where individual achievements are a matter of public record—is so crass an evasion that even to give it the benefit of the doubt is an obscenity.

Anyone who has ever been an employer or an employee, or has observed men working, or has done an honest day's work himself, knows the crucial role of ability, of intelligence, of a focused, competent mind—in any and all lines of work, from the lowest to the highest. He knows that ability or the lack of it (whether the lack is actual or volitional) makes a difference of life-or-death in any productive process. The evidence is so overwhelming—theoretically and practically, logically and "empirically," in the events of history and in anyone's own daily grind—that no one can claim ignorance of it. Mistakes of this size are not made innocently.

When great industrialists made fortunes on a *free* market *(i.e.,* without the use of force, without government assistance or interference), they *created* new wealth—they did not take it from those who had *not* created it. If you doubt it, take a look at the "total social product"—and the standard of living—of those countries where such men are not permitted to exist.

Observe how seldom and how inadequately the issue of human intelligence is discussed in the writings of the tribal-statist-altruist theoreticians. Observe how carefully today's advocates of a mixed economy avoid and evade any mention of intelligence or ability in their approach to politico-economic issues, in their claims, demands, and pressure-group warfare over the looting of "the total social product."

It is often asked: Why was capitalism destroyed in spite of its incomparably beneficent record? The answer lies in the fact that the lifeline feeding any social system is a culture's dominant philosophy and that capitalism never had a philosophical base. It was the last and (theoretically) incomplete product of an Aristotelian influence. As a resurgent tide of mysticism engulfed philosophy in the nineteenth century, capitalism was left in an intellectual vacuum, its lifeline cut. Neither its moral nature nor even its political principles had ever been fully understood or defined. Its alleged defenders regarded it as compatible with government controls *(i.e.,* government interference into the economy), ignoring the meaning and implications of the concept of laissez-faire. Thus, what existed in practice, in the nineteenth century, was not pure capitalism, but variously mixed economies. Since controls necessitate and breed further controls, it was the statist element of the mixtures that wrecked them; it was the free, capitalist element that took the blame.

Capitalism could not survive in a culture dominated by mysticism and altruism, by the soul-body dichotomy and the tribal premise. No social system (and no human institution or activity of any kind) can survive without a moral base. On the basis of the altruist morality, capitalism had to be—and was—damned from the start.[5]

---

5 For a discussion of the philosophers' default in regard to capitalism, see the title essay in my book *For the New Intellectual*.

For those who do not fully understand the role philosophy in politico-economic issues, I offer—as the clearest example of today's intellectual state—some further quotations from the *Encyclopaedia Britannica's* article on capitalism.

> Few observers are inclined to find fault with capitalism as an engine of production. Criticism usually proceeds either from *moral* or *cultural* disapproval of certain features of the capitalist system, or from the short-run vicissitudes (crises and depressions) with which long-run improvement is interspersed. [Italics mine.]

The "crises and depressions" were caused by government interference, not by the capitalist system. But what was the nature of the "moral or cultural disapproval"? The article does not tell us explicitly, but gives one eloquent indication:

> Such as they were, however, both tendencies and realizations [of capitalism] bear the unmistakable stamp of the businessman's interests and still more the businessman's type of mind. Moreover it was not only policy but the philosophy of national and individual life, the scheme of cultural values, that bore that stamp. Its materialistic utilitarianism, its naive confidence in progress of a certain type, its actual achievements in the field of pure and applied science, the temper of its artistic creations, may all be traced to *the spirit of rationalism* that emanates from the businessman's office. [Italics mine.]

The author of the article, who is not "naive" enough to believe in a capitalistic (or *rational*) type of progress, holds, apparently, a different belief:

> At the end of the middle ages western Europe stood about where many underdeveloped countries stand in the 20th century. [This means that the culture of the Renaissance was about the equivalent of today's Congo; or else, it means that people's intellectual development has nothing to do with economics.] In underdeveloped economies the difficult task of statesmanship is to get under way a cumulative process of economic development, for once a certain momentum is attained, further advances appear to follow more or less automatically.

Some such notion underlies every theory of a planned economy. It is on some such "sophisticated" belief that two generations of Russians have perished, waiting for *automatic* progress.

The classical economists attempted a tribal justification of capitalism on the ground that it provides the best "allocation" of a community's "resources." Here are their chickens coming home to roost:

> The market theory of resource allocation within the private sector is the central theme of classical economics. The criterion for allocation between the public and private sectors is formally the same as in any other resource allocation, namely that the

community should receive equal satisfaction from a marginal increment of resources used in the public and private spheres ... Many economists have asserted that there is substantial, perhaps overwhelming, evidence that total welfare in capitalist United States, for example, would be increased by a reallocation of resources to the public sector—more schoolrooms and fewer shopping centers, more public libraries and fewer automobiles, more hospitals and fewer bowling alleys.

This means that some men must toil all their lives without adequate transportation (automobiles), without an adequate number of places to buy the goods they need (shopping centers), without the pleasures of relaxation (bowling alleys)—in order that other men may be provided with schools, libraries, and hospitals.

If you want to see the ultimate results and full meaning of the tribal view of wealth—the total obliteration of the distinction between private action and government action, between production and force, the total obliteration of the concept of "rights," of an individual human being's reality, and its replacement by a view of men as interchangeable beasts of burden or "factors of production"—study the following:

Capitalism has a bias against the public sector for two reasons. First, all products and income accrue [?] initially to the private sector while resources reach the public sector through the painful process of taxation. Public needs are met only by sufferance of consumers in their role as taxpayers [what about *producers?*], whose political representatives are acutely conscious of their constituents' tender feelings [!] about taxation. That people know better than governments what to do with their income is a notion more appealing than the contrary one, that people get more for their tax money than for other types of spending. [By what theory of values? By whose judgment?] ...

Second, the pressure of private business to sell leads to the formidable array of devices of modern salesmanship which influence consumer choice and bias consumer values toward private consumption ... [This means that your desire to spend the money you earn rather than have it taken away from you, is a mere *bias.*] Hence, much private expenditure goes for wants that are not very urgent in any fundamental sense. [Urgent—to whom? Which wants are "fundamental," beyond a cave, a bearskin, and a chunk of raw meat?] The corollary is that many public needs are neglected because these superficial private wants, artificially generated, compete successfully for the same resources, [*Whose* resources?] ...

A comparison of resource allocation to the public and private sectors under capitalism and under socialist collectivism is illuminating. [It is.] In a collective economy all resources operate in the public sector and are available for education, defense, health, welfare, and other public needs without any transfer through taxation. Private consumption is restricted to the claims that are *permitted* [by whom?] against the *social product,* much as public services in a capitalist economy are limited to the claims permitted against the private sector. [Italics mine.] In a collective economy public needs enjoy the same sort of built-in priority that private consumption enjoys in a capitalist economy. In the Soviet Union teachers are plentiful, but automobiles are scarce, whereas the opposite condition prevails in the United States.

Here is the conclusion of that article:

Predictions concerning the survival of capitalism are, in part, a matter of definition. One sees everywhere in capitalist countries a shifting of economic activity from the private to the public sphere ... At the same time [after World War II] private consumption appeared destined to increase in communist countries. [Such as the consumption of wheat?] The two economic systems seemed to be drawing closer together by changes converging from both directions. Yet significant differences in the economic structures still existed. It seemed reasonable to assume that the society which invested more in people would advance more rapidly and inherit the future. In this important respect capitalism, in the eyes of some economists, labours under a fundamental but not inescapable disadvantage in competition with collectivism.

The collectivization of Soviet agriculture was achieved by means of a government-planned famine—planned and carried out deliberately to force peasants into collective farms; Soviet Russia's enemies claim that fifteen million peasants died in that famine; the Soviet government admits the death of seven million.

At the end of World War II, Soviet Russia's enemies claimed that thirty million people were doing forced labor in Soviet concentration camps (and were dying of planned malnutrition, human lives being cheaper than food); Soviet Russia's apologists admit to the figure of twelve million people.

This is what the *Encyclopaedia Britannic a* refers to as "investment in people."

In a culture where such a statement is made with intellectual impunity and with an aura of moral righteousness, the guiltiest men are not the collectivists; the guiltiest men are those who, lacking the courage to challenge mysticism or altruism, attempt to bypass the issues of reason and morality and to defend the only rational and moral system in mankind's history—capitalism—on any grounds other than rational and moral.

SECTION THIRTEEN

Applied Economics

A Public Choice View
of the Minimum Wage

By Thomas Rustici

Why, when the economist gives advice to his society, is he so often coolly ignored? He never ceases to preach free trade … and protectionism is growing in the United States. He deplores the perverse effects of minimum wage laws, and the legal minimum is regularly raised each 3 or 5 years. He brands usury laws as a medieval superstition, but no state hurries to repeal its law.

—George Stigler

I. INTRODUCTION

Much of public policy is allegedly based on the implications of economic theory. However, economic analysis of government policy is often disregarded for political reasons. The minimum wage law is one such example. Every politician openly deplores the spectacle of double-digit teenage unemployment pervading modern society. But, when economists claim that scientific proof, a priori and empirical, dictates that minimum wage laws cause such a regretful outcome, their statements generally fall on deaf congressional ears. Economists too often assume that policymakers are interested in obtaining all the existing economic knowledge before deciding on a specific policy course. This view of the policy-formation process, however, is naive. In framing economic policy politicians will pay some attention to economists' advice, but such advice always will be rejected when it conflicts with the political reality of winning votes. At bottom, what is important in analyzing the course of economic policy is an understanding of the public choice aspects of the decision-making process in government. In such an undertaking, the incentive structure confronting governmental decision makers must be carefully examined.

This paper therefore takes a public-choice perspective of minimum wage laws, explaining their persistent political support by examining the underlying incentive structure. Although the unemployment effects of such laws have been public knowledge for decades, and despite nearly unanimous opposition to them within the economics profession, they are now as solidly in place as ever before. Some conflicting conclusions can be drawn from this paradox: (1) the majority of economists are completely wrong on this issue, and have been for decades; or (2) politicians who claim opposition to unemployment and then call on economists to testify about the minimum wage before voting to increase it are not really interested in what economists have to say; or (3) economists have not been able to convince the average voter that it is in his interest to reject the minimum wage.

If the first conclusion is true, economists need to reevaluate the quality of their evidence on the economic effects of the minimum wage. The second conclusion would indicate that economists have very little influence over the direction of public policy disputes in advising politicians, who are constrained by the incentive structure of the "political market." The final reason for the paradox would point to a needed change in the direction of emphasis taken by economists in dealing with the minimum wage.

The relevant question for this paper, therefore, is the following: If the minimum wage law has consequences deemed undesirable by those who implement it, and if evidence accumulated over the decades conclusively proves these consequences to be inevitable features of the law, then why does it continue to survive? To answer this question, the paper begins with an examination of the economic effects of the minimum wage in section II. The sources of political support for the minimum wage law are then explored in section III. Section IV looks at the minimum wage issue from a North-South perspective and discusses the beneficiaries and victims of the minimum wage. Given the political environment of past minimum wage legislation, section V considers the prospects of real reform, and section VI concludes with the proviso that economists ought to direct their reform efforts at educating the public on the adverse effects of the minimum wage rather than trying to influence legislators directly.

II. ECONOMIC EFFECTS OF THE MINIMUM WAGE

Economic analysis has demonstrated few things as clearly as the effects of the minimum wage law. It is well known that the minimum wage creates unemployment among the least skilled workers by raising wage rates above free market levels. Eight major effects of the minimum wage can be discussed: unemployment effects, employment effects in uncovered sectors of the economy, reduction in nonwage benefits, labor substitution effects, capital substitution effects, racial discrimination in hiring practices, human capital development, and distortion of the market process with respect to comparative advantage. Although the minimum wage has other effects, such as a reduction in hours of employment, these eight effects are the most significant ones for this paper.

Unemployment Effects

The first federal minimum wage laws were established under the provisions of the National Recovery Administration (NRA). The National Industrial Recovery Act, which became law on 16 June 1933, established industrial minimum wages for 515 classes of labor. Over 90 percent of the minimum wages were set at between 30 and 40 cents per hour.[1] Early empirical evidence attests to the unemployment effects of the minimum wage. Using the estimates of C. F. Roos, who was the director of research at the NRA, Benjamin Anderson states: "Roos estimates that, by reason of the minimum wage provisions of the codes, about 500,000 Negro workers were on relief in 1934. Roos adds that a minimum wage definitely causes the displacement of the young, inexperienced worker and the old worker."[2]

On 27 May 1935 the Supreme Court declared the NRA unconstitutional, burying the minimum wage codes with it. The minimum wage law reappeared at a later date, however, with the support of the Supreme Court. In what became the precedent for the constitutionality of future minimum wage legislation, the Court upheld the Washington State minimum wage law on 29 March 1937 in *West Coast Hotel v. Parrish*.[3] This declaration gave the Roosevelt administration and Labor Secretary Frances Perkins the green light to reestablish the federal minimum wage, which was achieved on 25 June 1938 when President Roosevelt signed into law the Fair Labor Standards Act (FLSA).

The FLSA included legislation affecting work-age requirements, the length of the workweek, pay rates for overtime work, as well as the national minimum wage provision. The law established minimum wage rates of 25 cents per hour the first year, 30 cents per hour for the next six years, and 40 cents per hour after seven years. The penalty for noncompliance was severe: violators faced a $10,000 fine, six months imprisonment, or both. In addition, an aggrieved employee could sue his employer for twice the difference between the statutory wage rate and his actual pay.[4]

With the passage of the FLSA, it became inevitable that major dislocations would result in labor markets, primarily those for low-skilled and low-wage workers. Although the act affected occupations covering only one-fifth of the labor force,[5] leaving a large uncovered sector to minimize the disemployment effects, the minimum wage was still extremely counterproductive. The Labor Department admitted that the new minimum wage had a disemployment effect, and one historian sympathetic to the minimum wage was forced to concede that "[t]he Department of Labor estimated that the 25-cents-an-hour minimum wage caused about 30,000 to 50,000 to lose their job. About 90% of these were in southern industries such as bagging, pecan shelling, and tobacco stemming."[6]

1   Leverett Lyon, et al. *The National Recovery Administration: An Analysis and Appraisal* (New York: Da Capo Press, 1972), pp. 318–19.

2   Benjamin M. Anderson, *Economics and the Public Welfare: A Financial and Economic History of the United States, 1914–1946* (Indianapolis: Liberty Press, 1979), p. 336.

3   Jonathan Grossman, "Fair Labor Standards Act of 1938: Maximum Struggle for a Minimum Wage," *Monthly Labor Review* 101 (June 1978): 23.

4   "Wage and Hours Law," *New York Times*, 24 October 1938, p. 2.

5   Grossman, "Fair Labor Standards Act," p. 29.

6   Ibid., p. 28.

These estimates seriously understate the actual magnitude of the damage. Since only 300,000 workers received an increase as a result of the minimum wage,[7] estimates of 30,000–50,000 lost jobs reveal that 10–13 percent of those covered by the law lost their jobs. But it is highly dubious that only 30,000–50,000 low-wage earners lost their jobs in the entire country; that many unemployed could have been found in the state of Texas alone, where labor authorities saw devastation wrought via the minimum wage on the pecan trade. The *New York Times* reported the following on 24 October 1938:

> Information received today by State labor authorities indicated that more than 40,000 employees of the pecan nut shelling plants in Texas would be thrown out of work tomorrow by the closing down of that industry, due to the new Wages and Hours Law. In San Antonio, sixty plants, employing ten thousand men and women, mostly Mexicans, will close … Plant owners assert that they cannot remain in business and pay the minimum wage of 25 cents an hour with a maximum working week of forty-four hours. Many garment factories in Texas will also close.[8]

It can reasonably be deduced that even if the Texas estimates had been wildly inaccurate, the national unemployment effect would still have exceeded the Department of Labor's estimates.

The greatest damage, however, did not come in Texas or in any other southern state, but in Puerto Rico. Since a minimum wage law has its greatest unemployment effect on low-wage earners, and since larger proportions of workers in poorer regions such as Puerto Rico tend to be at the lower end of the wage scale, Puerto Rico was disproportionately hard-hit. Subject to the same national 25-cents-per-hour rate as workers on the mainland, Puerto Rican workers suffered much more hardship from the minimum wage law. According to Anderson:

> It was thought by many that, in the first year, the provision would not affect many industries outside the South, though the framers of the law apparently forgot about Puerto Rico, and very grave disturbances came in that island … Immense unemployment resulted there through sheer inability of important industries to pay the 25 cents an hour.[9]

Simon Rottenberg likewise points out the tragic position in which Puerto Rico was placed by the enactment of the minimum wage:

When the Congress established a minimum wage of 25 cents per hour in 1938, the average hourly wage in the U.S. was 62.7 cents … It resulted in a mandatory increase for only some 300,000 workers out of a labor Force of more than 54 million. In Puerto Rico, in contrast … the

---

7   Ibid., p. 29.

8   "Report 40,000 Jobs Lost," *New York Times*, 24 October 1938, p. 2.

9   Anderson, *Economics and the Public Welfare*, p. 458.

new Federal minimum far exceeded the prevailing average hourly wage of the major portion of Puerto Rican workers. If a continuing serious attempt at enforcement ... had been made, it would have meant literal economic chaos for the island's economy.[10]

On 24 October 1938, a special cable from Puerto Rico was printed in the *New York Times* detailing the effects of the new wage law on Puerto Rican workers:

Wage payrolls estimated at approximately $1,000,000 monthly by the Chamber of Commerce will end tomorrow with the application of the Fair Labor Standards Act. Both labor and employers appear to be united in the position that the law applied to Puerto Rico ends employment for approximately 120,000 persons. It is also believed to terminate prospects for any possible further industrialization.

Recent conferences in Washington between Administrator Elmer F. Andrews and island representatives led to the conclusion that there was not any means of modifying the effects of the law in the island short of a Congressional amendment. With the unemployment resulting from the law's enforcement, the Chamber of Commerce study shows that the 230,000 normally unemployed, out of a total of 650,000 employables there, will be increased to 350,000, or more than half of Labor's ranks in the island ...

Much of labor is more than anxious to continue at the prevailing rates on the theory that half a loaf is better than none. Labor Commissioner Prudenceo Rivera Martinez, in a published statement today said: "The medicine is too strong for the patient."[11]

Puerto Rico's unemployment rate rose sharply due to the Fair Labor Standards Act. Tens of thousands lost their jobs in such industries as cigar and cigarette manufacturing, which all but disappeared.[12] The needlework industry, which employed over 40,000 workers in 1935, stagnated after the new act took effect. The value of needle-trade exports fell from over $20 million before the act in 1937 to barely $5 million in 1940.[13] Rafael Pico describes the plight of the needlework industry after the act took effect:

An industry which had been paying three or four cents per hour for work in homes could obviously not survive under the drastic mandatory increase. The effects of the law ... were catastrophic ... The industry would have disappeared entirely if a legislative appeal for special legislation on minimum wages had not been sent to the Congress of the U.S.[14]

After two years of economic disruption in Puerto Rico, Congress amended the minimum wage provisions.[15] The minimum wage was reduced to 12.5 cents per hour, but it was too late for many industries and for thousands of low-wage earners employed by them, who suddenly found unemployment the price they had to pay for the minimum wage.

---

10   Simon Rottenberg, "Minimum Wages in Puerto Rico," in *Economics of Legal Minimum Wages*, edited by Simon Rottenberg (Washington, D.C.: American Enterprise Institute, 1981), p. 330.

11   "Puerto Rico Hurt by Wage Hour Law," *New York Times*, 24 October 1938, p. 2.

12   Rafael Pico, *The Geography of Puerto Rico* (Chicago: Aldine Publishing, 1974), p. 293.

13   Ibid., p. 294.

14   Ihid,

15   Rottenberg, "Minimum Wages in Puerto Rico," p. 333.

In sum, the tragedy of the minimum wage laws during the NRA and the FLSA was not just textbook-theorizing by academic economists, but real-world disaster for the thousands who became the victims of the law. But these destructive effects have not caused the law to be repealed; to the contrary, it has been expanded in coverage and increased in amount.

Meanwhile, as can be seen from Table 1, the evidence for the unemployment effects of the minimum wage continues to mount. Many empirical studies since the early 1950s—from early research by Marshall Colberg and Yale Brozen to more recent work by Jacob Mincer and James Ragan—have validated the predictions of economic theory regarding the unemployment effects of the minimum wage law. In virtually every case it was found that the net employment effects and labor-force participation rates were negatively related to changes in the minimum wage, In the face of 50 years of evidence, the question is no longer *if* the minimum wage law creates unemployment, but *how much* current or future increases in the minimum wage will adversely affect the labor market.

Employment in Uncovered Sectors

The labor market can be divided into two sectors: that covered by the minimum wage law, and that not covered. In a partially covered market, the effects of the minimum wage are somewhat disguised. Increasing it disemploys workers in the covered sector, prompting them to search for work in the uncovered sector if they are trainable and mobile. This then drives down the wage rate in the uncovered sector, making it lower than it otherwise would have been. Since perfect knowledge and flexibility is not observed in real-world labor markets, substantial unemployment can occur during the transition period.

Employees in the covered sector who do not lose their jobs get a wage-rate increase through the higher minimum wage. But this comes only at the expense of (1) the disemployed workers who lose their jobs and suffer unemployment during the transition to employment in the uncovered sector, and (2) everyone in the uncovered sector, as their wage rate falls due to the influx of unemployed workers from the covered sector. While increasing the incomes of some low-wage earners, increasing the minimum wage tends to make the lowest wage earners in the uncovered sector even poorer than they otherwise would have been.

Yale Brozen has found that the uncovered household sector served to absorb the minimum wage-induced disemployed in the past.[16] But the "safety valve" of the uncovered portion of the economy is rapidly vanishing with the continual elimination of various exemptions.[17] Because of this trend we can expect to see the level of structural unemployment increase with escalation of the minimum wage.[18]

---

16   Yale Brozen, "Minimum Wage Rates and Household workers," *Journal of Law and Economics* 5 (October 1962): 103–10.

17   Finis Welch, "Minimum Wage Legislation in the United States," *Economic Inquiry* 12 (September 1974); 286.

18   Brozen "Minimum Wage Rates and Household Workers," pp. 107–08.

TABLE 1

UNEMPLOYMENT EFFECTS OF THE MINIMUM WAGE: A SURVEY

Author(s)	Source	Empirical Findings & Conclusions
Marshall Colberg	"Minimum Wage Effects on Florida's Economic Development," *Journal of Law and Economics* (October 1962)	The response to the increase in the minimum wage from $0.75 per hour to $1.00 per hour resulted in a 15.2 percent reduction in man-hours of employment for production workers in low-wage counties during January—April 1956. Weeks of unemployment compensation paid for low-wage counties increased 67.8 percent during the same period.
Yale Brozen	"Minimum Wage Rates and Household Workers," *Journal of Law and Economics* (April 1962)	Household employment, which usually moves contracyclically, failed to do so when the minimum wage was increased. The uncovered sector of the household labor market absorbed those workers who became displaced by the higher minimum wage.
Arthur Burns	*The Management of Prosperity* (New York: Columbia University Press, 1966)	An increase of $0.25 per hour in the minimum wage would raise the unemployment rate for nonwhite teenagers by 8 percent.
Yale Brozen	"The Effects of the Statutory Minimum Wage Increases on Teen-Age Unemployment," *Journal of Law and Economics* (April 1969)	Successive increases in the minimum wage were directly followed by increases in the teenage unemployment rate.
Finis Welch	"Minimum Wage Legislation in the United States," *Economic Inquiry* (September 1974)	The minimum wage reduced employment and heightened vulnerability of teenage employment over the course of the business cycle.

Author	Publication	Findings
Edward Gramlich	"Impact of Minimum Wage on Other Wages, Employment, and Family Income," *Brookings Papers on Economic Activity* 2 (1976)	The minimum wage creates unemployment, while the bulk of increased benefits tend to go to higher income families.
Jacob Mincer	"Unemployment Effects of Minimum Wages," *Journal of Political Economy* (August 1976)	The net effect of the minimum wage on labor force participation is negative, with the largest negative effect observed for nonwhite teenagers. The net employment effect is also negative, with the largest disemployment effect occurring in the nonwhite teenage group.
U.S. Chamber of Commerce	*The Congressional Record,* 6 October 1977, p. 32708	The estimated impact of the proposed increases in the minimum wage from $2.30 to $3.15 in three steps through January 1980 would lead to a national 1,977,000 job loss, and a 4.1 percent increase in labor costs.
James Ragan	"Minimum Wages and the Youth Labor Market," *Review of Economics and Statistics* (May 1977)	Had the 1966 amendment to increase the minimum wage not occurred, aggregate youth employment would have been 225,000 higher in 1972, and the youth unemployment rate 3.8 percent lower.
William Beranek	"The Illegal Alien Work Force, Demand for Unskilled Labor, and the Minimum Wage," *Journal of Labor Research* (Winter 1982)	"The abolition of minimum wage laws and alternative income support programs in 1978 could have increased employment levels of domestic unskilled workers from roughly 500,000 to 2 million." [a]
Robert H. Meyer & David A. Wise	"The Effects of the Minimum Wage on the Employment and Earnings of Youth," *Journal of Labor Economics* 1, no. 1 (1983)	"Among black youth with market wage rates below the minimum, nonemployment is increased from 25.3% without the minimum to 43.4% with the minimum." [a]

[a] Direct quotation from the author(s).

Nonwage Benefits

Wage rates are not the only costs associated with the employment of workers by firms. The effective labor cost a firm incurs is usually a package of pecuniary and nonpecuniary benefits. As such, contends Richard McKenzie,

> employers can be expected to respond to a minimum wage law by cutting back or eliminating altogether those fringe benefits and conditions of work, like the company parties, that increase the supply of labor but which do not affect the productivity of labor, By reducing such non-money benefits of employment, the employer reduces his labor costs from what they otherwise would have been and loses nothing in the way of reduced labor productivity."[19]

If one takes the view that employees desire both pecuniary and nonpecuniary income, then anything forcing them to accept another mix of benefits would clearly make them worse off. For example, suppose worker A desires his income in the form of $3.00 per hour in wages, an air-conditioned workplace, carpeted floors, safety precautions, and stereo music. If he *is forced* by the minimum wage law to accept $3.25 per hour and fewer nonpecuniary benefits, he is worse off than at the preminimum wage and the *higher* level of nonpecuniary income. A priori, the enactment of minimum wage laws must place the worker and employer in a less-than-optimal state. Thus it may not be the case that only unemployed workers suffer from the minimum wage; even workers who receive a higher wage and retain employment may be net losers if their nonpecuniary benefits are reduced.

Labor Substitution Effects

The economic world is characterized by a plethora of substitutes. In the labor market low-skill, low-wage earners are substitutes for high-skill, high-wage earners. As Walter Williams points out:

> Suppose a fence can be produced by using either one high skilled worker or by using three low skilled workers. If the wage of high skilled workers is $38 per day, and that of a low skilled worker is $13 per day, the firm employs the high skilled worker because costs would be less and profits higher ($38 versus $39). The high skilled worker would soon recognize that one of the ways to increase his wealth would be to advocate a minimum wage of, say, $20 per day in the fencing industry ... After enactment of the minimum wage laws, the high skilled worker can now demand any wage up to $60 per day ... and retain employment. Prior to the enactment of the minimum wage of $20 per day, a demand of $60 per day would have cost the high skilled worker his job. Thus the effect of the minimum wage is to price the high skilled worker's competition out of the market.[20]

---

19   Richard McKenzie, "The Labor Market Effects of Minimum Wage Laws: A New Perspective," *Journal of Labor Research* 1 (Fall 1980); 258–59.

20   Walter Williams, *The State Against Blacks* (New York; McGraw-Hill, 1982), pp. 44–45.

Labor competes against labor, not against management. Since low-skill labor competes with high-skill labor, the minimum wage works against the lower-skill, lower-paid worker in favor of higher-paid workers. Hence, the consequences of the law are exactly opposite its alleged purpose.

Capital Substitution Effects

To produce a given quantity of goods, some bundle of inputs is required. The ratio of inputs used to produce the desired output is not fixed by natural law but by the relative prices of inputs, which change continuously with new demand and supply conditions. Based on relative input prices, producers attempt to minimize costs for a given output. Since many inputs are substitutes for one another in the production process, a given output can be achieved by increasing the use of one and diminishing the use of another. The optimal mix will depend on the relative supply and demand for competing substitute inputs.

As a production input, low-skill labor is often in direct competition with highly technical machinery. A Whirlpool dishwasher can be substituted for low-skill manual dishwashers in the dishwashing process, and an automatic elevator can take the place of a nonautomatic elevator and a manual operator. This not to imply that automation "destroys jobs," a common Luddite myth. As Frederic Bastiat explained over a century ago, jobs are obstacles to be overcome.[21] Automation shifts the *kinds* of jobs to be done in society but does not reduce their total number. Low-skill jobs are done away with, but higher-skill jobs are created simultaneously. When the minimum wage raises the cost of employing low-skill workers, it makes the substitute of automated machinery an attractive option.

Racial Discrimination in Hiring Practices

At first glance the connection between the level of racial discrimination in hiring practices and the minimum wage may not seem evident. On closer examination, however, it is apparent that the minimum wage law gives employers strong incentives to exercise their existing racial preferences.[22] The minimum wage burdens minority groups in general and minority teenagers most specifically. Although outright racism has often been blamed as the sole cause of heavy minority teenage unemployment, it is clearly not the only factor. William Keyes informs us that

> In the late 1940's and early 1950's, young blacks had a lower unemployment rate than did whites of the same age group. But after the minimum wage increased significantly,

21   Frederic Bastiat, *Economic Sophisms* (Irvington-on-Hudson, N.Y.; Foundation for Economic Education, 1946), pp. 16–19.

22   Walter Williams, "Government Sanctioned Restraints That Reduce the Economic Opportunities for Minorities," *Policy Review* 22 (Fall 1977): 15.

especially in 1961, the black youth unemployment rate has increased to the extent that it is now a multiple of the white youth unemployment rate.[23]

To make the case that racism itself is the cause of the employment and unemployment disparity among blacks and whites, one would have to claim that America was more racially harmonious in the past than it is now. In fact, during the racially hostile times of the early 1900s 71 percent of blacks over nine years of age were employed, as compared with 51 percent for whites.[24] The minimum wage means that employers are not free to decide among low-wage workers on the basis of price differentials; hence, they face fewer disincentives to deciding according to some other (possibly racial) criteria.

To see the racial implications of minimum wage legislation, it is helpful to look at proponents of the law in a country where racial hostility is very strong, South Africa. Since minimum wage laws share characteristics in common with equal pay laws, white racist unions in South Africa continually support both minimum wage and equal-pay-for-equal-work laws for blacks. According to Williams:

> Right-wing white unions in the building trades have complained to the South African government that laws reserving skilled jobs for whites have been broken and should be abandoned in favor of equal pay for equal work laws ... The conservative building trades made it clear that they are not motivated by concern for black workers but had come to feel that legal job reservation had been so eroded by government exemptions that it no longer protected the white worker.[25]

The reason white trade unions are restless in South Africa is a $1.52-per-hour wage differential between black and white construction workers.[26] Although the owners of the construction firms are white, they cannot afford to restrict employment to whites when blacks are willing to work for $1.52 per hour less. As minimum wages eliminate the wage differential, the cost to employers of hiring workers with the skin color they prefer is reduced. As the cost of discrimination falls, and with all else remaining the same, the law of demand would dictate that more discrimination in employment practices will occur.

Markets frequently respond where they can, even to the obstacles the minimum wage presents minority groups. In fact, during the NRA blacks would frequently be advanced to the higher rank of "executives" in order to receive exemptions from the minimum wage.[27] The free market demands that firms remain color-blind in the conduct of business: profit, not racial preference, is the primary concern of the profit-maximizing firm. Those firms who fail the profit test get driven

---

23 William Keyes, "The Minimum Wage and the Davis Bacon Act: Employment Effects on Minorities and Youth," *Journal of Labor Research* 3 (Fall 1982): 402.

24 Williams, *State Against Blacks*, p. 41.

25 Ibid., p. 43.

26 Ibid., pp. 43–44.

27 Lyon, *National Recovery Administration*, p. 339.

out of business by those who put prejudice aside to maximize profits. When markets are restricted by such laws as the minimum wage, the prospects for eliminating racial discrimination in hiring practices and the shocking 40-50 percent rate of black teenage unemployment in our cities are bleak.

Human Capital Development

Minimum wage laws restrict the employment of low-skill workers when the wage rate exceeds the workers' marginal productivity. By doing so, the law prevents workers with the least skills from acquiring the marketable skills necessary for increasing their future productivity, that is, it keeps them from receiving on-the-job training.

It is an observable fact, true across ethnic groups, that income rises with age.[28] As human capital accumulates over time, it makes teenagers more valuable to employers than workers with no labor-market experience. But when teenagers are priced out of the labor market by the minimum wage, they lose their first and most crucial opportunity to accumulate the human capital that would make them more valuable to future employers. This stunting reduces their lifetime potential earnings. As Martin Feldstein has commented:

> [F]or the disadvantaged young worker, with few skills and below average education, producing enough to earn the minimum wage is incompatible with the opportunity for adequate on-the-job learning. For this group, the minimum wage implies high short-run unemployment and the chronic poverty of a life of low wage jobs.[29]

Feldstein also finds a significant irony in the minimum wage: "It is unfortunate and ironic that we encourage and subsidize expenditure on formal education while blocking the opportunity for individuals to 'buy' on-the-job training."[30] This is especially hard on teenagers from the poorest minority groups, such as blacks and hispanics—a truly sad state of affairs, since the law is instituted in the name of the poor.

Distortion of the Market Process

Relative prices provide the transmission mechanism by which information is delivered to participants in the market about the underlying relative scarcities of competing factor inputs. They serve as signals for people to substitute relatively less scarce resources for relatively more scarce resources, in many cases without their even being aware of it.[31]

Whenever relative price differentials exist for input substitutes in the production process, entrepreneurs will switch from higher-priced inputs to lower-priced inputs. In a dynamically

---

28 U.S., Department of Commerce, Bureau of the Census, *Statistical Abstract of the United States 1982–83*, p. 431.

29 Martin Feldstein, "The Economics of the New Unemployment," *The Public Interest*, no. 33 (Fall 1973):14–15.

30 Ibid., p. 15.

31 Thomas Sewell, *Knowledge and Decisions* (New York: Basic Books, 1980), p. 79.

changing economy, this switching occurs continually. But when prices are not allowed to transmit market information accurately, as in the case of prices artificially controlled by government, then distorted information skews the market and guides it to something clearly less than optimal.[32]

Minimum wages, being such a distortion of the price system, lead to the wrong factor input mix between labor and all other inputs. As a result, industry migrates to locations of greater labor supply more slowly, and labor-intensive industries tend to remain fixed in non-optimal areas, areas with greater labor scarcity. Large labor pools of labor-abundant geographical areas are not tapped because the controlled price of labor conveys the wrong information to all the parties involved. Thus, the existence of price differentials, as knowledge to be transmitted through relative prices, is hidden.[33] The slowdown of industrial migration keeps labor-abundant regions poorer than they otherwise would be because economic growth there is stifled. As Simon Rottenberg explains for the case of Puerto Rico:

> The aggregate effect of all these distortions was that Puerto Rico could be expected to produce fewer goods and services than would have otherwise been produced and that the rate at which insular per capita income rose toward mainland United States income standards could be expected to be dampened. In sum, the minimum wage law could be expected to reduce the rate of improvement in the standard of life of the Puerto Rican people and to intensify poverty in the island.[34]

In summary, the evidence is in on the minimum wage. All eight major effects of the minimum wage examined here make the poor, disadvantaged, or young in society worse off—the alleged beneficiaries turn out to be the law's major victims. So why does a law whose consequences its own designers would officially declare to be "bad" on all counts continue to survive decade after decade? Why, moreover, is it periodically expanded in scope and raised in amount? The answer is to be found by examining the actual beneficiaries of the law and the functioning of the political market.

III. SOURCES OF POLITICAL SUPPORT FOR THE MINIMUM WAGE

Unions and the Minimum Wage

Unions everywhere support the minimum wage, a fact that could be deduced from the above analysis of the labor substitution effect of the minimum wage law. Unions are labor cartels that attempt to restrict the supply of workers entering given occupations. Since nonunion labor is priced below the cartelized price of union labor, it is an attractive substitute for union workers. Because unionization of *all* potential competition to the cartel is impossible due to the high policing costs that would be involved, unions resort to the minimum wage. By artificially increasing

---

32   Ibid.
33   Ibid., pp. 167–68,
34   Rottenberg, "Minimum Wages in Puerto Rico," p. 329,

the wage rate of lower-skilled workers—who could substitute for union workers—the minimum wage increases the demand for union workers and hence their wage rates. Thus, government enforcement of a minimum wage allows unions to (1) keep a stronger cartel, raising their income; (2) incur no policing costs; and (3) have the government force low-skilled, nonunion workers out of the labor market.

It is important to note that unions unanimously supported the cartelization created by the NRA codes.[35] When the NRA and the minimum wage provisions were abolished in 1935 by the Supreme Court, unions scurried to reestablish wage floors everywhere. The recurrent phenomenon of firms with lower labor costs outcompeting unionized firms presented a serious problem for such labor unions as the International Ladies Garment Workers Union, which faced its fiercest competition from nonunion garment factories in the southern United States and in Puerto Rico. The efforts of major unions to equalize labor costs nationally were futile.[36] A substitute for the defunct NRA codes was needed by the unions and was found in the Fair Labor Standards Act. Former senator Paul Douglas notes the support of the FLSA by prominent union leaders:

> Sidney Hillman, president of the Amalgamated Clothing Workers, an important CIO union, who was in charge of the organization drive in the textile industry, testified, however, that he wanted this power of the Board retained, since he believed that legislation should not stop at an $800 full-time yearly wage. He, moreover, declared that such higher rates would aid rather than hinder collective bargaining by protecting the high wage firms from undue wage-cutting by competitors.[37]

On 19 July 1955, testimony was entered in the *Congressional Record* from the presidents of four major unions concerning the minimum wage in Puerto Rico. The union presidents demanded that the Puerto Rican minimum be increased in spite of the opposition of Governor Luis Munoz-Marin.[38] It is just not credible that the presidents of the Amalgamated Clothing Workers, International Ladies Garment Workers Union, United Hatters, Cap and Millinery Workers, and the Textile Workers Union were all sincerely misguided humanitarians who happened not to understand the economic effects of the law. To the contrary, they knew that Puerto Rican wage differentials spelled trouble for members of their unions.

> The question of the minimum wages to be required in Puerto Rico under the act is of special interest to the four unions [the four unions mentioned above], which have formed the Joint Minimum Wage Committee ... Yet, today, the wage gap between Puerto Rico

35 Jesse Thomas Carpenter, Competition *and Collective Bargaining in the Needle Trades 1910–1967* (New York; W. F. Humphrey Press, 1972), p 759.

36 Ibid., p. 815.

37 Paul Douglas, "Fair Labor Standards Act of 1938," *Political Science Quarterly* 53 (December 1938):501.

38 *Congressional Record*, 19 July 1955, p 10977.

and the mainland is wider, not narrower, than it was in 1949, and Puerto Rico enjoys greater, not less, competitive advantages over the mainland ... The lack of proper wage advances in Puerto Rico constitutes an increasingly unfair threat to the mainland. This is a situation which cannot be left unchallenged by your committee and the House of Representatives.[39]

In what must go down in history as a classic example of political double-talk, the union presidents said that "[t]he unions joining in this communication are all friends of Puerto Rico. If we were unconcerned about the island's economic welfare we would be urging uniform minimum wages for Puerto Rico and the mainland."[40]

The union presidents were declaring explicitly that they understood the economic effects of the law. They also understood their self-interest, however, and therefore denounced the wage differentials. What is so astounding is that they would first express their knowledge that elimination of the wage differential would harm the island, then demand an increase in the minimum wage, and then claim to be friends of Puerto Rico! Rottenberg sums up the unions' motivation in getting the law applied to Puerto Rico:

> It is clear that their intention is not to improve the conditions of Puerto Rican workers so much as to deprive those workers of employment opportunities by compelling them to offer their services at a high legally defined price. Their interest lies in influencing the spatial distribution of particular kinds of economic activity so that more of the kinds of goods produced by their members will be made on the mainland and less in Puerto Rico, They want to effect the distribution of wealth and income to the advantage of particular sets of mainland workers at the expense of Puerto Rican workers. The minimum wage law is an instrumental tactic employed by unions to achieve that purpose.[41]

Trade unions are highly organized institutions, and they do not take lightly the benefits that accrue to them through minimum wage laws. At their disposal are large numbers of highly organized voting members, as well as considerable financial/political clout.[42] Five of the ten largest political action committees in 1979–80 were unions.[43] The greatest concentration of benefits would, a priori, be thought to accrue to unions in such occupations as apparel, textiles, and agriculture, where direct competition with nonunion workers is greatest. And indeed, these are the unions we actually see consistently lobbying for higher minimum wages.

It is clear that unions have no intention of improving the lot of poorer workers through the minimum wage law, especially those in Puerto Rico and the Virgin Islands. Since there are no

---

39 Ibid.

40 Ibid.

41 Rottenberg, "Minimum Wages in Puerto Rico," p. 337.

42 Nornian J, Ornstein, et al., *Vital Statistics of Congress 1982* (Washington, D.C.; American Enterprise Institute, 1982), p. 77.

43 Ibid., p. 86.

official trade barriers between U.S. territories and the mainland, the minimum wage serves as a proxy for tariffs on goods imported from lower-wage territories. It is hard to believe that the supposedly benign intentions of unions are usually accepted at face value. Equally amazing is the fact that the alleged motives of a second major beneficiary, business, are also uncritically accepted.

Business Support for the Minimum Wage

At first glance it may seem strange that business would push for a higher minimum wage. On examination, however, we find that some businesses have the same motives for supporting the minimum wage as have labor unions. The economic self-interest of businesses that pay above the minimum wage dictates that they try to eliminate lower-cost rivals that pay below the minimum by forcing them to pay higher wage rates. That this is the case can be seen as far back as the time of the NRA codes.

Business interest groups definitely favored the minimum wage and price fixing of the NRA. In April 1935 the U.S. Chamber of Congress voted 1,495 to 419 in favor of continuation of the NRA.[44] After the Supreme Court declared the NRA unconstitutional, businesses collaborated with unions in lobbying for a substitute. The letter of C. R. Palmer, president of Cluett, Peabody and Co., to Rep. Arthur Healy (Mass.) on 25 March 1938 speaks for itself:

> When the present administration went into office, we wrote the Department of Labor, March 21, 1938, requesting that consideration be given to the possibility of establishing a minimum wage throughout the country. We realized that in many sections of the country wages were so low and hours so long that it made it impossible, or most difficult, to obtain business by companies that were paying good wages and working reasonable hours. So, when the N.R.A. provisions for wages and hours were adopted, we believed that objective had been obtained. Then when the N.R.A. collapsed, we were glad that many companies did not immediately increase their hours or reduce their wages. But now the situation is again difficult ... We had hopes that there would be a new bill controlling this situation within reasonable limits ... We are hoping that you agree with us, and that you will use your influence to see that something is done about it.[45]

Three months later, President Roosevelt signed the Fair Labor Standards Act into law.

When proposals to raise the minimum wage in the 1950s materialized, businesses were at the forefront of the lobbying effort.

On 19 July 1955, Representative Reuss from Milwaukee entered the following in the *Congressional Record*:

---

44   Carpenter, *Competition and Collective Bargaining*, p. 759.
45   *Congressional Record*, 28 March 1938, p, 1213.

I am proud of the fact that employers from my district have written me asking my support for the $1.25 minimum wage because they do not want sweatshop competition. Some of these letters from Milwaukee employers show a high level of social responsibility and business morality which I wish to quote for the Record;

Dear Congressman Reuss:
    This is to advise you that the Schmitt-Orlon Co. subscribes to the $1.25 minimum wage, as it will serve to bring closer the wage differentials between the low and high labor areas ...
    We, Wisconsin textile garment manufacturers, would then be placed on a better competitive basis.
    Yours very truly,
    Arthur J. Schmitt,
    Chairman of the Board.[46]

Businesses like the minimum wage for the same reason they like tariffs—to shut out lower-priced firms from free market competition. The minimum wage becomes a mechanism by which firms with high labor costs can force higher labor costs on their lower-cost competition. What makes it so seductive for businesses is that it can effectively close down their rivals, increase their incomes, and enable them to claim "social responsibility and business morality" in the process.

The Poverty Industry

The tragedy of the minimum wage is not only the 40–50 percent black teenage unemployment rates in our large cities, but that many drop out of the labor force altogether to become another poverty statistic or turn to criminal activity. If frustrated workers can end up as recipients of the generous welfare state, they may decide that receiving welfare is better than working productively. As Keith Leffler states:

The alternative implicitly in mind for disemployed workers is zero income. However, this is unlikely to be the relevant alternative in the 1970's since public relief programs are available for nearly all categories of citizens laid off due to a higher minimum wage. Minimum wages may therefore be a technique of lowering the costs of establishing eligibility for the increasingly generous public welfare programs.[47]

Examining the ratio of average income from work at the minimum wage to average income from Aid to Families with Dependent Children (AFDC) welfare payments, Leffler found that "[o]n the average, AFDC payments alone replace over 80 percent of work income. In addition, work

---

46   *Congressional Record*, 19 July 1955, p. 10984.

47   Keith Leffler, "Minimum Wages, Welfare, and Wealth Transfers to the Poor," *Journal of Law and Economics* 21 (October 1978): 346.

related expenses (excluding day care) averaged over 15 percent of earned income for those with minimum-wage income levels."[48]

Although increases in welfare payments tend to draw people away from work and onto the welfare rolls, it is not true that increases in the minimum wage necessarily draw people away from welfare.[49] Linda Leighton and Jacob Mincer make an analogous observation concerning the so-called inducement hypothesis, which describes the alleged incentive effects of the minimum wage on school enrollment: "It is clear now, given the evidence on labor force participation and on enrollment effects of minimum wages, that the inducement argument is not valid. Indeed, the logical conclusion is to the contrary: minimum wages induce welfare, not work."[50]

In this case, the disemployed workers who receive welfare are not the only vested interests; social workers and the entire "poverty industry" also benefit. If there are more poor because of the minimum wage, the demand for people to manage and take care of the poor also increases.[51] There is little incentive for social workers or poverty rights activists to advocate the repeal of the law that keeps them employed.

Politicians who "champion" a large poverty class are beneficiaries of the minimum wage as well. Since the law cuts off the first necessary condition for upward mobility (first-time employment), a permanent supporting constituency is preserved. A powerful triangle then emerges among the "poverty politician," social workers, and welfare recipients. Politicians who claim to represent the working poor can raise the minimum wage, throwing low-wage earners out of work. The modern welfare state can pick them up and provide them with greater benefits than what they could receive by working. Welfare recipients reward the politicians by voting for them, and the social workers and welfare bureaucrats find the demand for their services increased, entrenching their jobs. Each group in the political triangle of the minimum wage tends to benefit at the expense of the general taxpayer and the relatively low-skilled worker.

IV. BENEFICIARIES AND VICTIMS OF THE MINIMUM WAGE: A NORTH-SOUTH PERSPECTIVE

The beneficiaries and victims of the minimum wage are clearly visible when the historical attitudes of the Northern and Southern United States are compared. The North, tending to have higher wage rates due to earlier industrialization, would be the net beneficiary; the South, with lower wage rates, would be the major loser.

With the creation of the NRA, the United States had for the first time a national law for minimum wages. The minimum wage provisions of the NRA were not unified into a single wage for all classes of industrial labor; some were set differently.[52] Industries located in high-wage

---

48   Ibid., pp. 353–54.

49   Ibid., p. 350.

50   Linda Leighton and Jacob Mincer, "The Effects of Minimum Wages on Human Capital Formation," in Rottenberg, *Economics of Legal Minimum Wages*, p. 157.

51   Walter Williams, "Economist Addresses Racial and Economic Fallacies," *Laissez-Faire Society*, 11 April 1984, p. 2.

52   Lyon, *National Recovery Administration*, p. 317.

districts, in this case the North in general, desired an absence of wage differentials during the process of code formation.[53]

It has already been established that the minimum wage imposed by the NRA devastated the South and Puerto Rico. Benjamin Anderson summarizes the consequences of the NRA in the following observation:

> NRA created a great deal of unemployment in the South. Despite the differentials, the greatest percentage increase in wages, the greatest shortening of hours, and the greatest percentage increase in labor costs under NRA were in the South. In the lumber trade, for example, very little increase was made in western wages, while a very great increase was made in southern wages, even though they remained well below those of the West ... An interesting book by Charles Frederick Roos ... gives significant figures in connection with this point and says; "In view of these data, it is not surprising that lumber business was diverted from the South to the Pacific Northwest."[54]

With the demise of the NRA, textile, apparel, lumber, and other industrial sectors began to experience vigorous competition from the South. This occurred because geographical wage differentials reappeared, reflecting underlying free market comparative advantages of doing business in the South. Consequently, Northern unions (such as the International Ladies Garment Workers Union) and industrial associations (such as the National Dress Manufacturers Association) desired the protection of Northern industry.[55] During the period before the enactment of the ELSA, both unions and businesses in the North had begun to express a fear of Southern competition.[56]

In the needle trades, it became evident that the wage rates set by the NRA would not hold. Manufacturing associations attempted to re-create the NRA privately and failed completely, largely due to enforcement failures.[57] Such unions as the Amalgamated Clothing Workers of America attempted general organization drives with special emphasis on the South but also met with widespread failure.[58] Faced with these failures in attempting private cartelization to protect Northern from Southern industry, government cartelization became the logical alternative. This form of cartelization came in the form of the FLSA, as noted by Walter Boles: "There is evidence to show that some of the support behind the Act—a consequence of the interstate nature of markets—was based on the older industrial areas' fear of the growing industrialization of the South."[59]

The political-geographical background of the FLSA became sharply distinct. Northern senators and congressmen lined up to support the act, while representatives from the South opposed it. John F. Moloney observes that

---

53 Ibid, p. 324.

54 Anderson, *Economics and the Public Welfare*, p. 336.

55 Carpenter, *Competition and Collective Bargaining*, pp. 812–13.

56 *Congressional Record*, 28 March 1938, p. 1213.

57 Carpenter, *Competition and Collective Bargaining*, p. 815.

58 Ibid.

59 Walter Boles, "Some Aspects of the Fair Labor Standards Act," *Southern Economic Journal* 6 (April 1940): 498–99.

The elimination of so-called "unfair competition" and of regional wage differentials was also a factor of some importance. The lower wage structure of the South received its fair share of attention during the debates in Congress.[60]

Since businesses that pay above the minimum wage urge higher minimums on their competition, and since firms in the Northern United States tended to incur higher labor costs than their Southern counterparts, it is only logical that Northern firms would have pressed for passage of the FLSA. Paul Douglas states:

> So far as the employers were concerned, the northern textile industry was definitely in favor of the bill, and opposed to the granting of any regional differentials. It welcomed a national scale as a means of protecting themselves against southern competition with lower wages.[61]

According to Senator Walsh (Mass.), the new minimum wage was to provide protection for Northern industry:

> Industries in New England that now operate on a forty hour week ... and pay reasonable minimum wages will not continue to be subject to competition in the trade markets with goods produced by industries that can undersell New England producers due to the fact that they are working their employees longer hours and paying lower wages."[62]

A telegram sent to Representative Healey from Governor Charles F. Hurley of Massachusetts demonstrates the fact that the FLSA was favored in the North because of the protection it afforded. The telegram did not hide the fact that the law was in the interests of this particular Northern state.

> We here in Massachusetts are deeply interested in having the pending wage and hour bill adopted by Congress during this session. As a Massachusetts Congressman I am sure you realize how important it is for such Federal legislation to be adopted and for Massachusetts to have equal competition with other sections of the country, thus affording labor and industry of Massachusetts some degree of assurance that our present industries will not move out of the State.[63]

And on 6 April 1938, Rep. John F. Dockweiler (Calif.) openly admitted that he could not think of a single trade or industry in his state where the prevailing minimum wage was not

---

60   John F. Moloney, "Some Effects of the Fair Labor Standards Act Upon Southern Industry," *Southern Economic Journal* 8 (July 1942): 15.

61   Douglas, "Fair Labor Standards Act," p. 501.

62   Ibid.

63   *Congressional Record*, 3 May 1938, p. 1800.

considerably higher than the 30 cents per hour proposed in the FLSA.[64] Of course, he then went on to throw his unbending support for its passage. On 4 May 1938, Rep. Robert Allen (Penn.) introduced in the *Congressional Record* a radio address of Representative Healey from the previous day. Healey's comments again show his concern for Massachusetts:

> Sweatshops and low-wage areas have grown like mushrooms in all sections of the country … They have … undermined decent industry by ruinous competition, snatched away markets, lured factories out of high-standard areas …

> … Massachusettes, long preeminent in the manufacture of textiles, has seen its commanding position swept away by the corrosive competition of sweated industries, Between 1923 and 1933, the New England textile industry lost nearly 120,000 jobs, mostly from Massachusettes. One hundred and twenty thousand jobs were taken out of that industrial region, principally because of low wages elsewhere … [65]

We find congressmen from Indiana making similar statements:

> There are in the state of Georgia, canning factories working … women 10 hours a day for [$]4.50 a week. Can the canning factories of Indiana and Connecticut or New York continue to exist and meet such competitive labor costs? [66]

A common explanation for the passage of the ELSA—the protection of the helpless working poor—is blatantly deficient in that it completely ignores the geopolitical struggle that pervaded the issues.[67] The driving force behind the establishment of the minimum wage was Northern unions and businesses. They lobbied hard for the law and were successful.[68] To the delight of such unions as the International Ladies Garment Workers Union and the Amalgamated Clothing Workers of America, the law completely destroyed the Puerto Rican needle trades. Owners of Northern textile firms who watched the government drive their competition out of business expressed little regret at that outcome.

Henry Simons demonstrated keen perception of the entire minimum wage issue some years later when he declared:

---

64 *Congressional Record*, 6 April 1938, p. 1353.

65 *Congressional Record*, 4 May 1938, pp. 1840–41.

66 Grossman, "Fair Labor Standards Act," p. 27.

67 Boles, "Some Aspects of the Fair Labor Standards Act," p. 499.

68 S. Charles Maurice and Margaret Jane Hobson, *Minimum Wage Laws: Who Benefits, Who Loses?* (College Station, Tex.; Center for Education and Research in Free Enterprise, Texas A & M University, 1983), p. 18.

Southern workers may be intrigued by the wage expectations held out by organizers from northern unions and by the Fair Labor Standards Act. They may in a few cases get such wages, but it will be only in spite of the intentions of the northern unions and Massachusetts senators.[69]

The objections raised by Southern congressmen that the minimum wage was detrimental to the economy of the South were always conveniently pushed aside by politicians representing the North. In January 1954, Sen. John F. Kennedy published an article entitled "New England and the South: The Struggle for Industry" in the *Atlantic Monthly*. In that article Senator Kennedy made clear his belief that raising the minimum wage would help stem the migration of industry from Massachusetts to Southern states such as Mississippi:

> But the final reason for migration, with which I am particularly concerned, is the cost differential resulting from practices or conditions permitted or provided by Federal law which are unfair or substandard by any criterion. Massachusetts manufacturing industries in May of 1953 paid an average hourly wage of $1.64; but because the Federal minimum is only 75 cents an hour, many industries migrating to the rural communities of Mississippi pay workers only that less-than-subsistence wage, and those employees under "learners permits" even less. Practically all New England woolen textile mills pay a wage of at least $1.20 an hour; but ... the New England Mills must bid for government contracts against southern mills paying only $1.05 an hour.[70]

The 1955 debates over increases in the minimum wage were the sharpest North-South confrontation on this issue. With reference to Puerto Rico, President David Dubinsky of the International Ladies Garment Workers Union urged a congressional subcommittee to raise the minimum wage. The reason he gave was that the Puerto Rican brassiere industry was growing and that Northern knitting mills had begun to move to the island.[71]

In the 19 July 1955 House debate Representative Mack (Wash.) reveals why he supported an increase:

> Mr. Chairman, in the three Pacific coast states of Washington, Oregon, and California about 600,000 men are employed in forest-product industries ... The lumber, plywood, shingle, veneer, doors, and furniture which these workers produce must be sold in competition with similar products made by workers in southern states ... The southern manufacturers thereby have a competitive advantage over our west coast mills, where wages are higher ... It is not fair that western producers of lumber, plywood, furniture, and other forest products who pay an average of $1.80 an hour must compete with the southern lumber, plywood and furniture manufacturers who pay an average wage of

69   Henry Simons, *Economic Policy for a Free Society* (Chicago: University of Chicago Press, 1948), p. 135.

70   John F. Kennedy, "New England and the South: The Struggle for Industry," *The Atlantic*, January 1954, p. 33

71   Rottenberg, "Minimum Wage Laws in Puerto Rico," p. 338.

only about 86 cents an hour. This unjust differential can be remedied by requiring that southern manufacturers pay at least a minimum wage of $1 an hour.[72]

In the same House debate, Representative Nelson (Maine) summarized his feelings about the minimum wage in these words: "Today the statutory minimum wage has a far broader purpose than that ... In brief, it is a salutary and excellent device to prevent competition between states and sections of this country."[73] He also conveyed the findings of a committee appointed by the Conference of New England Governors. They found that the major explanation of New England's decline in textiles was the large wage differential between New England and the South.[74]

In 1960, Representative Lindsay (N.Y.) reminded his colleagues that he was supporting an increase in the minimum wage to protect the apparel industry in his district.[75] In 1966, Representative Resnick (N.Y.) favored increases in the minimum wage to protect farmers in the Northeast who paid workers $1.25 to $1.75 per hour from farmers in Mississippi who paid only $3.00 per day.[76]

Marshall Colberg, who views the minimum wage as a basic tool of the North to stifle Southern competition, recently tested North-South records on key votes. He looked first at the voting on the 1961 Monroney Amendment, which would have limited the coverage of the minimum wage for retail, gasoline station, laundry, and construction workers to firms established in more than one state. Colberg found that senators from Southern states voted 75 percent in favor of the amendment, while Northern senators voted 75 percent against it.[77]

Surprisingly, however, Colberg also found that Southern senators voted by a large majority in favor of a 1966 bill extending minimum wage and overtime provisions to a larger number of workers in the District of Columbia. Indeed, "even such strong opponents of the federal minimum wage as Spessard Holland of Florida, Everett Dirksen of Illinois, and Sam Ervin of North Carolina voted yea. Evidently, voting on the minimum wage is not strictly a matter of principle."[78] In what has been called the "Colberg hypothesis," Colberg determined the anomaly was only apparent: legislators from more industrialized areas—including relatively more industrialized areas in the South—will always support the minimum wage as a device to reduce business migration

---

72 *Congressional Record*, 19 July 1955, p. 10978.

73 Ibid., p. 10961.

74 Ibid. Representative Gwinn (N.Y.) had some interesting comments to his colleagues that are still relevant today. He asked (ibid., p. 10955):

Where did Congress ever get its power except to seize that power, to say to a working man in America, "You shall not work for less than 75 or 90 cents an hour." That is the way this statute reads, in effect. It is not just that the employer must not pay less than 90; the employee must not work for less than 90.

75 *Congressional Record*, 30 June 1960, p. 15212.

76 Marshall Colberg, "Minimum Wages and the Distribution of Economic Activity," in *Economics of Legal Minimum Wages*, edited by S. Rottenberg, p. 249.

77 Ibid., p. 251.

78 Ibid., p. 253.

from their districts to districts with lower wages. This hypothesis has found support in a test conducted by Jonathan Silberman and Gary Durden.[79]

V. THE PROSPECTS FOR CHANGE

Before one can hope for the abolition of the minimum wage, the influence of the well-organized, special-interest groups that receive the bulk of the benefits from it must be reduced. There is, however, little chance that such groups as Northern unions and businesses, or interest groups in general, could be barred from the political process in the near future. Other options for change would include (1) payoffs to the vested interests, (2) two-tiered minimum wages, (3) inflation, and (4) general economic education of voters and victims.

Although paying off vested interests is theoretically possible, it would not seem very promising for two reasons. First, in order to compensate Northern unions and firms for their lost rents, taxes would have to be increased. This would merely shuffle the burden of the law, shifting it from teenagers to the general taxpayer. Second, it may be politically impossible to make direct transfer payments to these groups because the visibility of such payments could put the entire rent-seeking scheme in jeopardy. Since the societal costs of the minimum wage law could no longer be hidden, the payoff scheme would have to include a high risk premium to compensate for the probability of abolition by angry taxpayers.

Two-tiered minimum wage rates have been recently proposed by President Reagan, who asked Congress for a sub-minimum wage of $2.50 per hour for teenagers for work done in the summer months.[80] In spite of evidence that such a minor reduction would result in the additional employment of 400,000–600,000 youths,[81] the sub-minimum wage is legislatively dead. In 1977, Congress also turned a deaf ear to pleas from private youth-employment centers for a lower minimum wage for younger workers.[82] The intellectual tide of opinion is moving toward favoring a two-tiered minimum wage, but it is not clear whether this movement will be translated into actual labor policy.

Inflation is sometimes considered an escape from the current minimum wage dilemma because it erodes a fixed minimum wage, eliminating its effectiveness. But this "method" poses serious problems. By using inflation to reduce minimum wage—created unemployment, greater unemployment could be created if in the process of monetary expansion relative prices are distorted in the structure of production, thus causing malinvestment.[83] That is, inflation could initiate a trade cycle, bringing with it an ensuing depression.

---

79   Jonathan Silberman and Gary C. Durden, "Determining Legislative Preferences on the Minimum Wage: An Economic Approach," *Journal of Political Economy* 84 (April 1976): 327.

80   Maurice and Hobson, *Minimum Wage Laws*, p. 18.

81   Ibid., p. 33.

82   *Congressional Record*, 6 October 1977, p. 32704.

83   See Friedrich Hayek, *Unemployment and Monetary Policy: Government as Generator of the Business Cycle* (Washington, D.C.; Cato Institute, 1979).

Educating voters about the minimum wage may be the only lasting solution to the problem. The large number of victims must be made aware of the links between the minimum wage law and their plight. But this can be very difficult when politicians use the law to their political advantage and intentionally cloud the issue with emotional rhetoric. In trying to convince Americans of the necessity of the minimum wage provision in the FLSA, President Roosevelt used tactics like the following: "Do not let any calamity-howling executive with an income of $1,000 a day ... tell you ... that a wage of $11 a week is going to have a disastrous effect on all American industry."[84] Politicians have been extremely effective in making the minimum wage popular with well-intentioned voters.[85] Economists, on the other hand, have much work to do in the slow process of giving the average voter the economic education he needs to understand—and then abolish—the minimum wage.

VI. CONCLUSION

George Stigler may have startled some economists in 1946 when he claimed that minimum wage laws create unemployment and make people who had been receiving less than the minimum poorer.[86] Fifty years of experience with the law has proven Stigler correct, leaving very few defenders in the economics profession.[87]

But economists have had little success in criticizing this very destructive law. Simon Rottenberg demonstrated the government's disregard for what most economists have to say about this issue in his investigation of the Minimum Wage Study Commission created by Congress in 1977. He noted the numerous studies presented to the commission that without exception found that the law had a negative impact on employment and intensified the poverty of low-income earners. The commission spent over $17 million to conduct the investigation and on the basis of the evidence should have eliminated the law. What was the outcome? The commission voted to *increase the minimum wage by indexing and expanding coverage.* As dissenting commissioner S. Warne Robinson commented about the investigation:

> The evidence is now in, and the findings of dozens of major economic studies show that the damage done by the minimum wage has been far more severe than even the critics of forty years ago predicted. Indeed, the evidence against the minimum wage is so overwhelming that the only way

---

84   Grossman, "Fair Labor Standards Act," p. 22.

85   William Keech, "More on the Vote Winning and Vote Losing Qualities of Minimum Wage Laws," *Public Choice* 29 (Spring 1977): 134.

86   George Stigler, "The Economics of Minimum Wage Legislation," *American Economic Review* 36 (June 1946): 358–65.

87   Although there are a few supporters left such as John K. Galbraith, many "liberal" economists such as Paul Samuelson and James Tobin have recently come out against the minimum wage. See Emerson Schmidt, *Union Power and the Public Interest* (Los Angeles: Nash, 1973).

the Commission's majority was able to recommend it be retained was to ask us not to base any decisions on the facts.[88]

It cannot be that our elected representatives in Congress are just misinformed with respect to the minimum wage law. To the contrary, the *Congressional Record* demonstrates that they fully understand the law's effects and how the utilization of those effects can ensure reelection. Economists would do well to realize that governments have little interest in the truth when its implementation would contradict self-serving government policies. Rather than attempting to bring government the "facts," economists should educate the public. This is the only solution to the malaise created when people uncritically accept such governmental edicts as the minimum wage.

---

88   Simon Rottenberg, "National Commissions: Preaching in the Garb of Analysis," *Policy Review* no. 23 (Winter 1983): 139.

Exploitation in the Jim Crow South: The Market or the Law?

By Jennifer Roback

MOST AMERICANS BELIEVE that the economic oppression of blacks in the Jim Crow South was the natural result of white racism. According to this view, southern whites were so economically dominant that—given their views on race—the regime of segregation and job discrimination that prevailed in the South was the inevitable result. Indeed, the Civil Rights Act of 1964 can be said to reflect this idea in its prohibition against discrimination by private citizens. But many scholars of the Jim Crow era, impressed by mounting evidence that state and local governments played a crucial role in shoring up the edifice of discrimination, now question this view.

Understanding the exact role of government in the creation of the segregated South is crucial to designing policies for ending segregation. The standard interpretation argues that whites were able to impose segregation on the job market without any special help from the government. If this is correct, then civil rights laws that seek to control private behavior, like those that we have today, may be the only way to prevent discriminatory outcomes. The other interpretation argues that effective discrimination could not persist without the active assistance of government. The latter thesis relies heavily on the theories of economist Gary Becker. Becker holds that in a free market employers and other economic actors would lose money if they indulged their "taste" for discrimination. Thus there is constant economic pressure to drive discrimination out of

> **[One] interpretation argues that whites were able to impose segregation on the job market without any special help from the government ... The other interpretation argues that ... discrimination [required] ... the active assistance of government.**

the market. This thesis would suggest that the government will be more effective in combating segregation if, instead of regulating private decisions, it scrutinizes carefully the racial impact of its own policies, especially those that interfere with competitive markets.

Before we decide which view is better, let us explore the economics of the southern labor market during the Jim Crow era, defined roughly as the period from *Plessy v. Ferguson* (1896) to *Brown v. Board of Education* (1954). I use a beginning date in the mid-1890s because scholars generally agree that full-scale racial segregation in every area of life did not get underway until about then. That decade saw the disenfranchisement of blacks and hence the end of black political participation in virtually every southern state. Once disenfranchisement was a fact, other forms of segregation and discrimination followed, including the labor laws discussed here.

For most of this time, the southern agricultural economy was dominated by white planters who were heavy employers of black labor. The planters wanted to collude to hold down black wages, both to increase their own profits and to solidify the dominant position of the white race. Throughout the Jim Crow period, they pleaded with one another to hold the line on black wages. "White men must stick together" was the common theme, ex-pressed in the newspapers and magazines of the time.

But as Robert Higgs shows in his book *Competition and Coercion* (1977), class interest and white solidarity were not adequate to over- come the economic incentive for individual plant-ers to offer higher wages to blacks. Despite all the admonitions, white employers competed vigorously with one another for black labor, and blacks frequently left lower-paying jobs to take higher-paying ones. The planters, however, had a weapon to combat those defections: labor laws designed to limit migration of black workers and to limit increases in their wages. These laws may best be understood as attempts to enforce an otherwise unenforceable labor-market cartel among white employers. The laws were necessary, in other words, to do what racial prejudice could not do by itself.

THE JIM CROW LAWS

Four basic types of legislation aided the enforcement of a labor-market cartel. These were (1) enticement laws and contract-enforcement laws, designed to restrict competition in the labor market to a time at the beginning of each contract year; (2) vagrancy laws, designed to pre-vent blacks from having periods of unemployment during which they could shop for higher wages; (3) emigrant agent laws, designed to restrict the activities of labor recruiters; and (4) the convict-lease system, which increased the effective punishment for blacks convicted of breaking the other laws. As Table 1 shows, most of these laws were passed in the 1890s or later.

Enticement and Contract-Enforcement Laws.

The enticement laws, which were directed primarily at white employers, made it a crime for an employer to "entice" a laborer who had a contract with another employer. Their purpose was to prevent employers from actively competing with each other for contract labor. Ten of the eleven southern states that passed such laws made enticement a criminal rather than a civil offense. The contract-enforcement laws, which were directed primarily at black farm laborers, imposed criminal sanctions for the breach of an employment contract. In The Shadow of Slavery (1972), Pete Daniel writes, "Under such laws … a laborer who signed a contract and then abandoned his job could be arrested for a criminal offense. Ultimately his choice was simple: he could either work out his contract or go to the chain gang."

The economic motivations behind the enticement and contract-enforcement laws were similar. Both sets of laws sought to limit competition for farm labor by mandating that it could only take place legally at the beginning of the contract year.

Vagrancy Laws

The second type of law used to enforce the labor-market cartel was the Vagrancy law, which essentially made it a crime to be unemployed or out of the labor force. Alabama's vagrancy law, passed in September 1903, was fairly typical. It defined a vagrant as "any person wandering or strolling about in idleness, who is able to work, and has no property to support him; or any person leading an idle, immoral, profligate life, having no property to support him …" Although vagrancy was usually considered a misdemeanor, this does not mean that the punishment was trivial: misdemeanants were often sentenced to state or county chain gangs.

Obviously, a statute that makes unemployment crime reduces the amount of searching for new and more renumerative employment; more important, it vastly increases the cost of being out of the labor force altogether. Blacks who traveled, even to visit relatives, faced the possibility of arrest. And blacks who were not working—that is, who were out of the labor force—were often round up as vagrants and put to work on local public-works projects or farms. As William Cohen has written, "So common were such practices that the Atlanta *Constitution* could quip to the police: 'Cotton is ripening. See that the 'vags' get busy'" (*Journal of Southern History*, 1976).

Emigrant-Agent Laws

The third type of statute was the emigrant-agent law, enacted to limit the activities of agents who recruited labor from one state or country for work in another. These laws regulated the white recruiters rather than the black workers and required agents to be licensed at fees of up to $5,000 for each county in which the recruiting took place. They were often passed in reaction to a wave of out migration, and many of the states raised the fees and penalties periodically in response to increased out migration.

By the time of the "great migration" of blacks to the North during World War I, we find the city of Montgomery, Alabama, passing an ordinance forbidding persons from enticing laborers to leave the city to take employment elsewhere, under penalty of a $100 fine or up to six months at hard labor, or both. The scope of the ordinance was far-reaching.

The main economic effect of the emigrant-agent laws was to make it more costly for black laborers to find out about job opportunities outside their local market area. The fact that the city of Montgomery attempted to keep its laborers from straying beyond even the city limits

Table 1

Dates of Passage of the Jim Crow Labor Laws

State	Vagrancy	Enticement	Contract Enforcement	Emigrant Agent	Convict Leasing
Virginia	1904			1924	1900–1910
North Carolina	1905	1905	1889	1891	1880–1890
South Carolina	1893	1880	1908	1891	1880–1890
Georgia	1895	1901		1876	1880–1910
Florida	1905	1865	1891	1903	1880–1920
Kentucky					1880–1890
Tennessee	1875	1875		1917	1880–1900
Alabama	1903	1866	1885	1879	1880–1915
Mississippi	1904	1890	1906	1912	1880–1890
Arkansas	1905	1875	1907		1880-1890
Louisiana	1908	1890			1880–1900
Texas	1909			1929	

Notes: Reconstruction ended in 1877. The first disenfranchisement amendment to a state constitution (South Carolina's) was adopted in 1895. The Supreme Court decided *Plessy v. Ferguson* in 1896.
   Sources: Available on request

shows how narrowly the local area might be characterized. The laws could be and were evaded, but not without cost to the agents and the laborers themselves.

The Convict-Lease System

The final prop to the labor-market cartel was the convict-lease system, a statutory practice of leasing out state or county convicts to private firms. Convict leasing was widely used in the South, especially during the 1880s. Unlike forms of convict labor in which the government maintains control over the day-to-day management of the prisoners, the lease system was worse than slavery. The slaveholder could expect to profit from a slave's future output for his entire working life and thus had an incentive to maintain the slave's health. But the lessee firm had no interest in keeping a convict alive past the end of his sentence or contract period, since the man had no "scrap" or "resale" value. The death rates on these chain gangs illustrate this difference: mortality rates were as high as 45 percent a year.

The significance of the convict-lease system was that its victims were often black misdemeanants, such as violators of the vagrancy and contract-enforcement statutes. The cost of breaking any law can be gauged by a combination of the probability of punishment and the severity of punishment. We have no direct measure of the probability of being punished for vagrancy or contract jumping, but a 45 percent chance of punishment by death certainly must have provided a powerful incentive for black laborers to stay out of the clutches of the local sheriff.

Postbellum Southern Agriculture

To see why these labor laws evolved in the way they did, we must examine the agricultural sector of the South more closely. The Civil War had brought physical and financial devastation to the southern states, destroying much of the region's material capital and wiping out family fortunes. Agriculture, the South's primary business, was and is capital-intensive and risky. Resources must be committed at the beginning of the season, but financial returns do not come until the end of the season. Emancipation increased this riskiness, putting former slave owners and others who managed farms in the position of being unable to guarantee the availability of labor during the crucial planting and harvesting seasons. For a plantation to succeed, something had to be done to ensure a steady flow of labor.

> **For a plantation to succeed [after Emancipation], something had to be done to ensure a steady flow of labor.**

Some planters simply hired laborers on a daily or weekly basis, but those who did so faced the risk that other planters would offer higher wages and lure their workers away. This was a particularly crucial problem at harvest time when the work could not be delayed, a fact that raised the value of the laborers during harvest and made planters particularly vulnerable to immediate competition. In effect, hiring workers on a short-term basis meant paying them the day-by-day value of their marginal product. Wages would be low in mid-season and relatively high during planting and harvesting.

Planters resisted this approach for a number of reasons. They believed they were being cheated when they had to pay high wages during the peak seasons. They disliked not knowing for sure whether they would have workers when they needed them. And finally, they undoubtedly were offended at the sight of their former slaves leaving jobs whenever they chose—and for higher wages to boot. A better arrangement, one that most planters seemed to prefer in the immediate postbellum period, was a year-long contract-with the laborer paid a steady wage over the life of the contract.

This system, however, had some disadvantages. A fixed-wage contract pays wages that are higher than the value of the worker's labor during some periods and lower during others. Thus, sometimes the employer will be giving implicit advances on the employees' wages and at other times the employees will be making implicit payments to the employer. For agricultural workers, the harvest is the high-productivity time when they earn less than the value of their labor; during the rest of the contract period, they are receiving implicit advances from the employer.

The most obvious flaw in the fixed-wage contract system was therefore that it gave the workers an incentive to cheat on the contract by quitting right before the harvest and then hiring out as day laborers. This reasoning served as the rationale for the contract-enforcement and enticement statutes. The assistant attorney general of Mississippi argued in 1917 that enticement laws were a necessity "in an agricultural state where long time contracts are made and monies necessarily advanced in anticipation of the fulfillment of a contract." In short, if the planter offered a fixed-wage contract, he faced the risk that the employees would breach the contract at harvest time. On the other hand, if the planter hired and paid employees on a short-term basis, he still could not guarantee that he would have enough harvest labor. Also, he could not predict the harvest wage that the competitive market would demand.

With all these problems it would have been surprising if some alternative form of contract had not emerged. In fact, as early as 1867, "a majority of planters and laborers were ready to explore alternative crop-making arrangements," according to economic historian Joseph Reid (*Journal of Economic History*, March 1973). Such alternatives—sharecropping contracts and rental contracts—became wide-spread soon after the Civil War.

Under a typical sharecropping contract, the worker, or "cropper," provided labor for the whole season in return for a share of the crop (usually a quarter to a half) when it was sold, while the landlord provided fertilizer, mules, equipment, and management skills. Some contracts specified noncultivation tasks, such as barn repair and the like, and stipulated that the cropper would receive a smaller share of the crop if he failed to perform these tasks. Sharecropping contracts still involved employer advances to the workers-which the employer, who usually marketed the entire crop, would simply deduct from the cropper's share before settling up. But the practice succeeded in reducing the employer's default risk considerably by giving the worker an incentive to stay and work out the contract. Since the worker had a stake in the crop on that particular farm, he was not likely to abandon his job, even for the promise of a high wage; and he was less likely to shirk in his effort than he would under a fixed-wage contract.

Rental contracts differed from sharecropping contracts in that they usually required the tenant to pay a fixed rent for the land he cultivated-sometimes a fixed dollar amount, sometimes a fixed quantity of the crop. The rental system placed all the risk of crop failure on the tenant and, even more than sharecrop-ping, minimized his incentive to shirk or run away. Both kinds of arrangements actually made the tenants much more vulnerable to breach of contract than they had been, because they often had to rely on the landlord's calculation of their earnings at the end of the season. In fact, most authors who discuss the period emphasize the weak position of the indebted tenants relative to the landlord.

In short, sharecropping and rental arrangements could reduce the problems the laws were meant to address and indeed were used by a significant number of employers. By 1880, 28 percent of southern farms were sharecropped and 17 percent were rented, large enough percentages to suggest that the contract-enforcement and enticement statutes were not really needed for agricultural stability.

The Impact of the Laws

If the laws were not really needed to ensure agricultural stability, they nonetheless provided southern planters with certain definite advantages. In particular, they kept workers from migrating from the low-wage southern agricultural sector to higher-wage northern and southern cities. Such migration would have tended to raise agricultural wages and decrease other wages until the wages in the various sectors were equal. The resulting system can justly be regarded as one of exploitation, since black workers were not earning the wage they would have earned had they (and their potential employers) been left free to move and change jobs as they wished.

The contract-enforcement and enticement laws reduced competition for labor directly, while the vagrancy and emigrant-agent laws reduced it indirectly by curbing mobility from one area to another.

The contract-enforcement and enticement laws reduced competition for labor directly, while the vagrancy and emigrant-agent laws reduced it indirectly by curbing mobility from one area to another. Emigrant agents functioned very much like labor arbitrageurs, bringing costly information about jobs in higher-wage areas to workers in lower-wage areas. The emigrant-agent laws made this type of arbitrage more costly and hence reduced the amount of information available to black farm laborers. This, in turn, must have increased the costs involved in moving to a new location. Note that there could be extensive mobility within a local area, so that some local markets were effectively competitive; but mobility be-tween counties or states was in many cases quite limited.

There is anecdotal evidence to support the view that blacks were restrained from leaving a county or state not only by law but by unofficial force and the threat of force. Emmett J. Scott reports numerous instances of legal and extralegal violence designed to prevent blacks from moving to northern cities, including harassment at train stations and the actual delaying of trains (Negro Migration during the War, 1920). Cohen's 1976 article gives another example:

> In September 1937 Warren County, Georgia, cotton growers sought to prevent the farmers of adjoining Glascock County from enticing away their black laborers. Desperate for hands, the men from Glascock County had offered almost to double the rate being paid for cotton pickers in Warren County. Unwilling to abide by the law of

supply and demand, Warren County planters mobilized to stop the depletion of their labor force. Sheriff G. P. Hogan de-scribed the ensuing events: "There was no trouble, although a number of [the Warren County men] carried guns and fired them into the air. They told the pickers there was plenty of cotton to pick in Warren County and asked them to stay home and pick it. They decided to stay."

There is also statistical evidence to support the view that the laws limited mobility. The first is evidence on productivity, drawn from Stephen DeCanio's excellent econometric study. The second consists of demographic evidence on the relative mobility of blacks and whites in the southern states. Both of these data sources focus on the beginning of the Jim Crow period, in an attempt to learn whether the rise of Jim Crow in the 1890s was associated with any significant change in either productivity or migration.

The Productivity Evidence.

Stephen DeCanio carried out a thorough econometric study of agricultural productivity for ten states in his book *Agriculture in the Post-Bellum South* (1974). Using decennial census data, he calculated an economic measure of factor productivity for blacks and whites in southern agriculture from 1870 to 1910. If the laws were successful in hampering black mobility, the greater relative supply of black farmers should have caused a decline in their marginal productivity relative to white farmers.

In the period from 1870 to 1890, most states had still not passed the major Jim Crow laws: only Tennessee had a vagrancy law, for example. Black labor was at least as productive as white during this period, with the single exception of Arkansas in the decade 1870-1880. During the decade 1890-1900, two more states (South Carolina and Georgia) passed vagrancy laws. And it was in these states—plus Alabama, which had passed contract enforcement in 1885—that black productivity fell below white.

The next decade saw the enactment of vagrancy laws in all seven of the other ten states, along with a number of other Jim Crow laws. This time black productivity fell below white in three of those seven states. There was one counter-trend: in Georgia, which had passed a vagrancy law in the previous decade, black productivity caught back up with white productivity.

Another way to look at DeCanio's data is this. In three of the ten states, black productivity was equal to white during the whole forty-year period. These states were Texas, Florida, and Tennessee—states on the fringe of the Old South and not, as the Deep South was, dominated by plantation culture. The other fringe state, North Carolina, had higher black productivity throughout the period. In five of the remaining six Deep South states, vagrancy laws were closely associated with lower black productivity, although the effect seemed to wear off in Georgia and began before the vagrancy law was passed in Alabama. The only Deep South state that did not show any effect, Louisiana, passed its vagrancy law very late in the period under study (as did Texas). Thus, despite some noise in the data, DeCanio's evidence is broadly consistent with the hypothesis that restrictive labor laws, particularly the vagrancy laws, succeeded in depressing black wages.

Migration Evidence.

Data on mobility within states are not readily available, but we do have data for net migration in and out of states. If the restrictive legislation was effective in reducing black mobility, black migration rates should have been cut relative both to their previous levels and to the migration rates for whites.

Table 2 displays net migration rates for each race by state and decade from 1870 to 1910. The first thing to note is that both whites and blacks were mostly migrating out of the South during this period. The exceptions were Florida, the southwestern states of Arkansas and Texas and, to a lesser extent, Louisiana. Clearly, the general westward movement of the American population took place within the South as well.

The second observation is that in the first decade under study, the net migration rates were roughly equal for the two races in almost all the states. By the next decade, however, black migration in Tennessee, Alabama, and Mississippi fell relative both to white migration and to previous black migration. In the 1890s the pattern extended to include Georgia, Kentucky, and Arkansas. These migration trends cannot be linked as strongly to state-by-state changes in legislation as can the productivity differences. But it is clear that some force was operating to reduce black migration in these six states of the central South.

The Law Versus the Market

Many influential whites in the South had an interest in keeping blacks from switching jobs easily or moving North. Individually, each specific white employer did not want to lose its workers; and collectively, white planters in general benefited from the low wages that arose from the general intimidation of the black populace. Privately, however, each employer could profit by "cheating" on the labor market cartel, by offering higher wages as inducements to the laborers. When social pressure, economic power, and custom proved insufficient to pre-vent such "cheating" and enforce discrimination against blacks, the southern elite resorted to restrictive labor laws. The evidence indicates that the laws were invoked to keep the market from bettering the condition of blacks.

> **To the extent that racial exploitation requires the backing of law, there are important implications for modern policy. One is that it is government, not private individuals, that must be restrained if disfavored minorities are to make substantial economic progress.**

Table 2
Migration Rates for Twelve States, By Race, 1870–1910
(per 1,000 whites or 1,000 blacks)

	Rates of Net Migration			
	1870-1880	1880-1890	1890-1900	1900-1910
Virginia				
White	-28	-50	-32	-35
Black	-83	-101	-115	-89
North Carolina				
White	-13	-29	-49	-52
Black	-24	-85	-82	-54
South Carolina				
White	33	-58	-32	-22
Black	38	-36	-91	-107
Georgia				
White	-39	-56	-40	-31
Black	-39	18	-18	-18
Florida				
White	79	166	52	156
Black	21	131	160	189
Kentucky				
White	-45	-83	-46	-107
Black	-65	-98	-34	-92

Source: Hope T. Eldridge and Dorothy Swaine Thomas, Population Redistribution and Economic Growth, United States, 1870-1950, vol. 8 (1954), tables A1.19 and A1.22.

Table 2
Migration Rates for Twelve States, By Race, 1870–1910
(per 1,000 whites or 1,000 blacks)

	Rates of Net Migration			
Tennessee				
White	-90	-75	-71	-101
Black	-87	-54	-34	-81
Alabama				
White	-61	-26	-61	-38
Black	-80	-11	13	-29
Mississippi				
White	-72	-135	-83	-36
Black	40	-24	-2	-39
Arkansas				
White	132	42	-118	-74
Black	193	215	-11	67
Louisiana				
White	-45	-36	19	26
Black	2	14	-24	-26
Texas				
White	347	80	59	25
Black	84	35	32	-19

Source: Hope T. Eldridge and Dorothy Swaine Thomas, Population Redistribution and Economic Growth, United States, 1870-1950, vol. 8 (1954), tables A1.19 and A1.22.

To the extent that racial exploitation requires the backing of the law, there are important implications for modern policy. One is that it is government, not private individuals, that must be restrained if disfavored minorities are to make substantial economic progress. At first glance, this may seem a strange recommendation, but we should keep in mind that a main focus of the Civil Rights Act of 1964 is the prohibitions on various discriminatory actions by government. The economic progress many blacks have made since 1964 may very well have resulted from these new curbs on government rather than from the far more visible prohibitions on discrimination by individuals.

The Jim Crow period also provides an interesting related lesson on the ability of market forces to combat discrimination. Racism was at least as prevalent in the Jim Crow period as it is now. Communities were smaller and more cohesive, making enforcement of social norms easier than today. Yet social and economic pressures by themselves were not enough to enforce a regime that called for the exploitation of black labor. This suggests that those same market forces could serve minorities well today-and that the benefits of a competitive economy go beyond those of prosperity to include social justice as well.

The Emergence of Nonperforming Loans: From the Commons of Risk

By Carrie T. Milton

TRADITIONAL MACROECONOMIC ANALYSIS OF NONPERFORMING LOANS

EXAMINING THE CURRENT phenomenon of nonperforming loans one need only consider the variables that have been in motion. At the heart of the nonperforming loans is the question of whether people involved in the interactions that generated these loans were behaving rationally, and whether the outcome that emerged could have been any different given the optimizing choices that all the actors faced. Underlying the decisions of every player in this was the assessment of risk that was being borne by the decision maker as compared to the expected benefit of engaging in a transaction. The resultant nonperforming loans are the unintended consequences of policy making intended to steer individuals toward home ownership, removal of risk from decision-makers, and rational players optimizing in a prisoners' dilemma.

The current pool of nonperforming loans that we observe is the result of the risk of loan originations being shifted from the loan originators to the commons, backed by the United States taxpayers. As the risk became increasingly shifted away from the decision-makers and left to the commons, it was more attractive and optimal to engage in transactions that produced riskier loans.

EVOLUTION OF LOW-RISK ENVIRONMENT FOR LOAN GENERATION

When savers and investors mutually engage in the trading of funds, the result is that risk is borne through the interaction. In the past, when savers deposited money in financial institutions (who act as brokers between the savers and investors), the savers faced the possibility of losing their deposits. Congress created the Federal Depository Insurance Corporation (FDIC) in the Banking Act of 1933[1] to alleviate the perceived risk of savers in order to stabilize the banking industry. Within an environment of bank failures all over the United States, the FDIC provided confidence for savers that their deposits would be safe in the event that the bank in which they deposited their money failed. It emerged as a public policy reaction to the highly unstable banking environment during the Great Depression.[2] This insurance alleviated risk faced by savers and induced more people to supply funds to investors via the banking institutions. At the time, the American Bankers Association expressed concern that the FDIC would create a system of rewarding poor banking performance.[3]

In 1938, the United States government created Fannie Mae to supply more money for mortgages. Thirty years later it became a private, government-sponsored enterprise (GSE).[4] Fannie Mae, and later its government-created competitor, Freddie Mac, purchase mortgages from banks and lenders in the primary mortgage industry, package them into securities, and then resell them to investors. This exchange produces a flow of funds from investors to the financial markets to mortgage borrowers.[5] The moneylenders assume the risk of not being repaid, but in this system the risk travels with the loan. Thus, the money moves forward to homebuyers and the risk moves backwards to the investors.

The Community Reinvestment Act of 1977 set as its purpose "to encourage [insured depository financial] institutions to help meet the credit needs of the local communities in which they are chartered [that is] consistent with the safe and sound operation of such institutions."[6] This policy required that all subsidiaries of financial institutions that were FDIC insured had to meet "the credit needs of its entire community, including low- and moderate- income

1   Christine M. Bradley, "A Historical Perspective on Deposit Insurance Coverage." *FDIC Banking Review.* Vol 13, No. 2:(2000). http://www.fdic.gov/bank/analytical/banking/2000dec/index.html (Accessed 4 December, 2008).

2   Community Business Bank. *The History of FDIC: The Federal Deposit Insurance Corporation.* 2008. http://www.cbbwi.com/fdic.htm.

3   Christine M. Bradley, "A Historical Perspective on Deposit Insurance Coverage." *FDIC Banking Review.* Vol 13, No. 2:(2000). http://www.fdic.gov/bank/analytical/banking/2000dec/index.html (Accessed 4 December, 2008).

4   Fannie Mae, *About Fannie Mae.* http://www.fanniemae.com/aboutfm/index.jhtml;jsessionid=S1BLUQYEM ZHQ3J2FECHSFGQ?p=About+Fannie+Mae.

5   Freddie Mac, *Our Mission.* http://www.freddiemac.com/corporate/company_profile/our_mission/.

6   Federal Deposit Insurance Corporation, *TITLE VIII—Community Reinvestment. Section 801 of title VIII of the Act of October 12, 1977 (Pub. L. No. 95--128; 91 Stat. 1147), effective October 12, 1977.* http://www.fdic.gov/regulations/laws/rules/6500-2515.html#6500hac801.

neighborhoods."[7] With nonspecific wording, this law forced financial institutions to make mortgages available to clients who otherwise may have posed excessive risk. [8]

Within this atmosphere, the moral sentiment that low-income, minority, and woman-headed families had a right to home ownership had the effect of pressuring Fannie Mae and Freddie Mac to purchase increasingly riskier loans. In 2000, the United States Housing and Urban Development (HUD) increased the "the required percentage of mortgage loans for low- and moderate-income families that finance companies Fannie Mae and Freddie Mac must buy annually from the current 42 percent of their total purchases to a new high of 50 percent - a 19 percent increase."[9] According to HUD, as of 2001 "HMDA data show that the number of home-purchase loans originated during the 1990s for low-income borrowers and their neighborhoods grew at substantially higher rates than did the overall market."[10]

Many of these loans were made possible through the Federal Housing Administration[11], which required smaller down payments, and which relaxed standards for buyers to access mortgage money.[12] Within the same time period that the U.S. government enacted policy measures to increase the rate of minority homeownership, financial institutions developed new and creative ways to repackage mortgages and offer them on the secondary mortgage market. Jan Kregel provides an in-depth discussion of the evolution of mortgage-backed-securities, and how they came to dominate the mortgage industry within the past twenty years. The structure of the mortgage industry itself evolved from one of a community bank originating and holding a loan for thirty years, collecting the monthly payments and applying it toward the balance of

7   Federal Deposit Insurance Corporation, *TITLE VIII—Community Reinvestment. Section 801 of title VIII of the Act of October 12, 1977 (Pub. L. No. 95--128; 91 Stat. 1147), effective October 12, 1977.* http://www.fdic.gov/regulations/laws/rules/6500-2515.html#6500hac801.

8   It is important to note that the formation of Fannie Mae and Freddie Mac, as well as the introduction of the Community Reinvestment Act of 1977 did not appear out of nowhere. These environmental factors that set the backdrop for what would occur in the future were themselves the product of relationships and exchanges between politicians and voters. The charters and laws created by members of Congress are borne out of a need to appease voters, to tangibly display to constituents that "something is being done" in order to earn future votes. These were not exogenous shocks, but rather products of a common underlying moral order that enough people believed in to create a legal order to support it.

9   United States Department of Housing and Urban Development, "Press Release," Tuesday, Oct. 31, 2000. http://www.hud.gov/library/bookshelf12/pressrel/pr00-317.html (Accessed 22 Nov. 2008).

10   United States Department of Housing and Urban Development, Office of Policy Development and Research, *First-Time Homebuyers: Trends from the American Housing Survey.* http://www.huduser.org/periodicals/ushmc /fall2001/summary-2.html.

11   Alphonso Jackson Secretary, Department Of Housing And Urban Development "Millions of Minority Owners." National Mortgage News, January 31, 2005, 4. http://mutex.gmu.edu:2233/ (accessed December 6, 2008).

12   Federal Housing Administration, *About the Federal Housing Administration.* http://portal.hud.gov/portal/page?_pageid=73,1828027&_dad=portal&_schema=PORTAL.

the loan and interest, to a completely innovative way of conducting mortgage transactions.[13] Banks evolved into loan originators, who then passed loans forward to either a GSE or other financial institution, which then pooled many mortgages together and packaged them into securities that were traded on the financial markets.

The intention of the securitization of the mortgages into pools was to create a product akin to corporate bonds where income streams would be guaranteed without investors having to assess the individual mortgage borrower's risk. The securities were in essence treated the same as corporate bonds, although the potential risk inherent in the structure of the securities was far different than that for corporate-issued bonds.[14] In order to allay investor concerns over this issue, the assets that were being developed and traded needed sufficient ratings from reputable ratings agencies. According to Kregel, "the credit ratings that were assigned were based on the design of the [over collateralization] of the securitized assets, rather than on any assessment of the credit-worthiness of the borrowers of the underlying mortgages."[15] The market-traded assets were designated as AAA, because they were insured by "a bond-insuring company that itself had been granted AAA ratings."[16]

EMERGENCE OF HOUSE PRICE APPRECIATION

Within this environment of strong encouragement to become homeowners, many renters found themselves poised to join millions of others who had realized the American dream. People "act to remove uneasiness by forming plans to secure what they anticipate will be more desired states of being."[17] The policies that steered people in the direction of home ownership, combined with increasingly available funds affected individual decision-makers, whose choices both reflected and generated the environment in which house prices continued to rise and loan originations became increasingly unconventional in order to maintain the affordability of mortgage payments.

Interest rates dropped during the period of early 2000 through mid-2003. Figure 1 shows the change in interest rates during the period of 1996 through the present, and Figure 2 and Figure 3 show the corresponding appreciation of house prices in new and existing residential housing markets during the same time. "The annual appreciation of house prices was at its

13   Jan Kregel, *Changes in the U. S. Financial System and the Subprime Crisis*. Working Paper No. 530, The Levy Economics Institute of Bard College, April 2008. http://www.levy.org/pubs/wp_530.pdf (Accessed 29 November, 2008).

14   Ibid.

15   Ibid.

16   John Bellamy Foster "The Financialization of Capital and the Crisis." *Monthly Review* 59, no. 11 (April 1, 2008): 1–19. http://mutex.gmu.edu:2233/ (accessed November 15, 2008).

17   Richard E. Wagner, *Mind, Society, and Human Action: Toward a Neo-Mengerian Program for Social-Economy*. Manuscript. Copyright, 2008.

highest when interest rates were at their lowest,"[18] but housing prices started to rise when President Clinton removed the capital gains taxes from primary residences that were sold, up to $500,000.[19] Many have targeted interest rates as the primary culprit for the rapid housing price appreciation during the early 2000s, but interest rates did not act directly on housing prices. Individual decision-makers made the choices to purchase homes during a short period of time, which created a shortage of the housing available at the price level, which drove up the housing prices. The incentives that drove them to make those decisions are the underlying reason for the housing price appreciation. While lower interest rates do serve as an incentive for purchasing a home, they are not the only incentives to consider.

On the consumer side of the interactions were new homebuyers, or entrants into the housing market. These people consisted of those who were "coming of age" at the time when they would have entered the market for home purchasing no matter what. For these consumers, buying a home had been part of the plan that they had set in motion before they entered the market, and they had generated the necessary income and stock of wealth needed for a down payment and regular mortgage payment. As the housing prices appreciated, it became necessary for them to rely on more creative mortgage structures to buy a home. Eventually market entrants who would have been able to assume a conventional home mortgage relied on alternative loan structures alongside their riskier counterparts.

Also among the market entrants were those who decided to enter at the margin, meaning that something within their immediate environment induced them to enter the market and if that something were missing, they would not have done so. The increasing values of homes signaled to them that house prices were going in a certain direction at a certain rate. Their expectations were based on the recent history of appreciating house values and the expectation that things would continue as they were. House values were expected to rise, and by waiting to enter the housing market, they would encounter much higher prices in the future. The cost of waiting to buy could be very high. These marginal market entrants added to the increasing demand for housing. Speculators also emerged as an increasingly important population of consumers. As housing prices climbed, it signaled entrepreneurs and profit-seekers that the housing market was a profitable medium for investment.

Another part of the total consumer population was the existing homeowners, who decided it was time to cash in their old properties for newer, larger, or "better" ones. Within this subgroup were those who would have been ready to change domiciles no matter what the circumstances were, and those who were induced at the margin to trade in their old home for a new one because of the newly created wealth from the appreciation of value of their own property. At some tipping point, the surging value of their own home induced them to cash in this new wealth. Some of these people recycled the money into a new mortgage, as they turned around and purchased an even bigger house. Others converted that newly created wealth into other

---

18   Robert Murphy, "Did the Fed, or Asian Saving, Cause the Housing Bubble?" Daily article, Ludwig von Mises Institute, 19 Novemeber, 2008. Email to author.

19   Ibid.

tangible assets. Still others did not directly cash in on the value of their homes, but they used the newly created wealth as equity toward loans for other consumable and durable goods.

The competition that occurred between the different consumers resulted in quickly appreciating home values. As prices rose, additional buyers were induced to enter the housing market, which caused prices to rise. "Certain expectations are of such a character that they induce the kind of behavior that will cause the expectations to be fulfilled."[20] People expected the housing prices to continue to rise, which induced them to continue spending more money on housing, which in turn caused house prices to rise. A model illustrating this effect is in Figure 3. It demonstrates the positive feedback mechanism of rising home prices inducing actions which themselves induced higher home prices. This is a reinforcing mechanism. Also in the model is the contribution of new homes being built, which acted to mollify the appreciation rate. This is a balancing mechanism, but the rate at which this happened was not sufficient to keep housing prices from appreciating at the observed rates.

The commons is "a paradigm for situations in which people so impinge on each other in pursuing their own interests that collectively they might be better off if they could be restrained, but no one gains individually by self-restraint."[21] The surging house prices, while inducing buyers to continue to enter the market and compete for the available housing, were not beneficial for the buyers. Generally, buyers try to get the maximum utility at the least cost. As housing prices continued to soar, collectively if everyone decided not to buy, then the house prices would cease rising. Individually, each homebuyer had an incentive to purchase a home as prices were rising, because they expected the price to continue rising, which would make their purchase less expensive relative to future prices. By doing this, prices continued to rise.

It became a prisoner's dilemma for the buyers. By abstaining, a buyer faced much higher prices in the future. By participating in the buying process, a buyer contributed to the increased housing prices. Prices rose depending on how many people bought houses within a certain time frame, which depended on how quickly house prices rose. "Some activity [is] self-sustaining once the measure of that activity passes a certain minimum level."[22] Figure 3 illustrates this self-sustaining process.

PERCEPTION OF RISK AND OPTIMIZING BEHAVIORS

As housing prices inflated, the amount of money needed for borrowers to purchase homes increased dramatically. Many first-time homebuyers lacked the necessary down payment for a conforming loan, and so mortgage originators offered buyers various alternatives[23] in order to

---

20   Thomas C. Schelling, *Micromotives and Macrobehavior* (New York: W.W. Norton & Co., Inc, 2006), 115.

21   Ibid, 111.

22   Ibid, 95.

23   Alt-A mortgages were those that were given to borrowers without proper income documentation; subprime mortgages included those offered at a "teaser" rate initially and that would increase to market rate consistent with the buyers' risk category in the future and also to 100% financing (Source: Gerald P. O'Driscoll, "Subprime Monetary Policy." *The Freeman* (November 2007):9.)

compete for buyers' business. Because the GSEs and various other top financial institutions purchased these alternatively structured loans, the risk that came with the new loan creations passed from the originators to the secondary mortgage market. It was optimal behavior for the loan originators to make the loans. Loan officers received commission for the mortgages while they assumed none of the risk.

Although risk was funneled to the investors, the ratings agencies allayed any concerns that investors might have had. The structure of the mortgage-backed-securities combined with the bond insurance together made the loans very low risk for investors. It was optimal for the investors to invest in the mortgage-backed-securities. In essence, the risk became the property of the commons.

The GSEs implicitly guarantee that the United States taxpayers, because of the GSEs' special status as quasi-governmental agencies, back all of the loans in their portfolios. The structure of Fannie Mae and Freddie Mac are such that were the riskier loans to fail, investors would still be able recover their losses. Also, during the 1980s several Savings and Loan institutions that provided mortgages to homeowners failed, and the federal government bailed them out.[24] This created a moral hazard that financial institutions expected that in the event that the structure of loans upon which this new system was predicated imploded, the government would come to the rescue. The people who took out loans on homes with zero money down and subprime interest rates incurred very little risk. In mortgage structures that required no money down for a home, the buyers assumed equity would be the result of the appreciating value of the home through time. As long as the buyer could sell the home for more than the purchase price, the buyer could realize real wealth in a very short period of time. Even if the house prices stopped appreciating or started to depreciate, nothing would be lost, because nothing was put into the house in the first place. At worst, the buyers were acting as if they were renters. The expected benefit of taking the mortgages far outweighed the expected cost. It was optimal for buyers to assume the mortgages.

DEPRECIATING ASSET VALUES, DELINQUENCIES, AND FORECLOSURES

As interest rates on the subprime and alternative loans reset to produce higher payments, buyers found themselves facing payments that were not part of the original decision-making calculus. Efforts to unload the properties in light of higher monthly mortgage costs transformed the housing market from one of many buyers relative to sellers to one of many sellers relative to buyers. As the market stagnated, housing prices ceased appreciating at the same rate, and in some instances the prices began to depreciate. As housing values depreciated, some owners were faced with owing more on the property than its market value.

The determination of house prices generally comes from other home sales in the neighborhood. Once one property enters foreclosure, the banks that service the loans try to recover the loan amount by selling it for the value of the loan. In many cases, initially this value was below

---

24 The Great Savings and Loan Debacle. 1994. *Eastern Economic Journal* 20, no. 2 (April 1): 229. http://mutex. gmu.edu:2233/ (accessed November 30, 2008).

the market value for the neighborhood home prices, which affected the value of all of the homes in a neighborhood. If more than one house entered foreclosure in a neighborhood, especially in a neighborhood where many of the homes were purchased with little equity as down payments, and where the owners had entered the loan terms with the expectation of future appreciating values, it caused a spiral of declining values. This caused more delinquencies, which caused more foreclosures, which further depressed the home values. This is illustrated in Figure 4. This phenomenon is aptly called contagion, because it is analogous to an illness. The eruption of foreclosures created "breakouts" of areas where foreclosures became very common, infecting entire neighborhoods.

Kelly Edmiston and Roger Zelneraitis describe how certain events contribute to the foreclosure problem of households who do have equity in their homes, such as sudden unemployment, accidents, or interest-rate changes on the loan that cause higher payments. When these occurrences coincide with low equity in the home, the optimal behavior tends to be defaulting on the loan. [25] Edmiston and Zelneraitis further describe the optimizing behavior of the borrower in the event that the balance owed on the home exceeds the market value of the home:

"One possibility for explaining default (and subsequent foreclosure) is a pure wealth-maximizing motive. The mortgagor in essence can at any time sell his property to the lender for the outstanding balance of the mortgage. He exercises this option to sell by defaulting on payments and, through foreclosure, receives value by purging his payment obligation on the mortgage. This transaction increases wealth if the home is worth less than the outstanding balance on the mortgage."[26]

A cycle of deflating home values and foreclosures erupts from this process, generated through a positive feedback loop with no balancing mechanism, as shown in Figure 4. When this spiral occurs, the cycle becomes critical. Only homes in a neighborhood where owners either choose to wait out the deflationary period and expect that eventually their home values will go back up and owners who have massive equity in their homes that will not entirely disappear from this process break the cycle.

CONCLUSION

Many events that occurred through an extensive history have led up to the current crisis that the United States faces with the nonperforming loans. Although the phenomenon exists on a macroeconomic scale, its emergence from human transactions on the microeconomic level lie at its roots. Both environmental factors and interactions among optimizing individuals created a commons of risk, where essentially no one player in the interaction carried the full burden of risk associated with their actions. Risk became a negative externality in the process, biasing peoples' calculus of benefit-to-cost ratio toward an assumption of great benefit and little risk.

---

25   Kelly D Edmiston, Roger Zalneraitis. "Rising Foreclosures in the United States: A Perfect Storm." *Economic Review - Federal Reserve Bank of Kansas City* 92, no. 4 (October 1, 2007): 115-145,4. http://mutex.gmu. edu:2233/ (accessed November 22, 2008).

26   Ibid.

This emergence of the risk as a commons to society was generated out of political, social, and innovative strategies.

The nonperforming loans that emerged as a result of human responses to an environment of low risk and high payoffs are now essentially the commons as well. Since the government has moved to "bail out" the current financial institutions from the consequences of their and others' interactions, the liabilities that coincide with the nonperforming loans have borne a cost to all American taxpayers. Moral hazard persists, and from the solutions that the government devised to correct the emergent problems of now, we can expect there to be future emergent crises as a result of optimizing behavior in an environment of no personally owned risk.

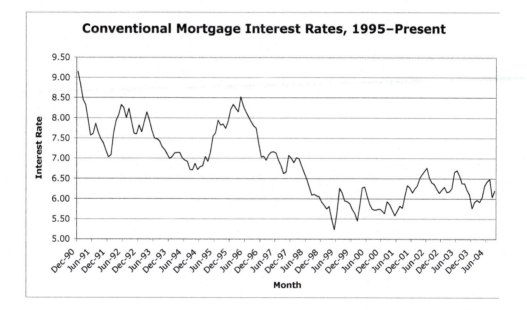

Figure 1: Conventional Mortgage Interest Rates, 1995–Present[27]

---

27   United States Federal Reserve, *Federal Reserve Statistical Release: Special Interest Rates, Historical Data.* http://www.federalreserve.gov/releases/h15/data/Monthly/H15_MORTG_NA.txt (Accessed 16 November 2008).

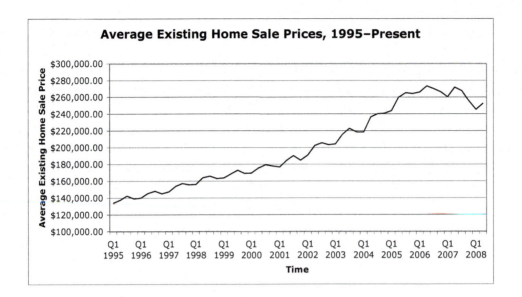

Figure 2: Average Existing Home Sales Prices, 1995–Present

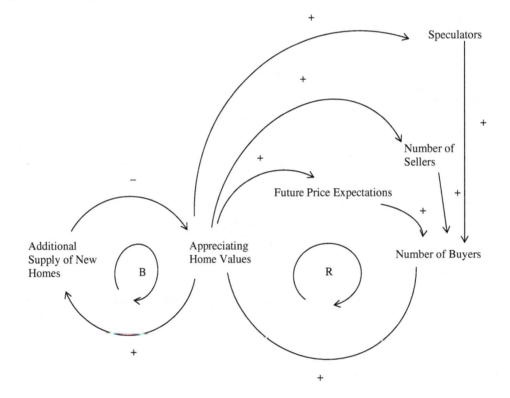

Figure 3: Model of Interaction Among Optimizing Individuals and Prices. This illustrates the positive feedback mechanisms present in driving up prices and balancing feedback mechanism of new homes being built.

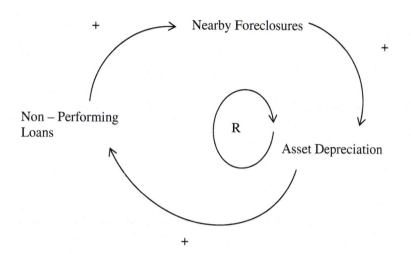

Figure 4: Model of non-performing loan cycle

BIBLIOGRAPHY

Community Business Bank. The History of FDIC: The Federal Deposit Insurance Corporation. 2008. http://www.cbbwi.com/fdic.htm

Bradley, Christine, "A Historical Perspective on Deposit Insurance Coverage." *FDIC Banking Review.* Vol 13, No. 2:(2000). http://www.fdic.gov/bank/analytical/banking/2000dec/index.html

Edmiston, Kelly D, and Zalneraitis, Roger. "Rising Foreclosures in the United States: A Perfect Storm." Economic Review - Federal Reserve Bank of Kansas City 92, no. 4 (October 1, 2007): 115-145,4. http://mutex.gmu.edu:2233/

Federal Deposit Insurance Corporation, TITLE VIII—Community Reinvestment. Section 801 of title VIII of the Act of October 12, 1977 (Pub. L. No. 95--128; 91 Stat. 1147), effective October 12, 1977. http://www.fdic.gov/regulations/laws/rules/6500-2515.html#6500hac801

Fannie Mae, About Fannie Mae. http://www.fanniemae.com/aboutfm/index.jhtml; jsessionid=S1BLUQYEMZ HQ3J2FECHSFGQ?p=About+Fannie+Mae

Federal Housing Administration, About the Federal Housing Administration. http://portal.hud.gov/portal/page?_pageid=73,1828027&_dad=portal&schema=PORTAL

Freddie Mac, Our Mission. http://www.freddiemac.com/corporate/company_   profile/our_mission/

Foster, John Bellamy "The Financialization of Capital and the Crisis." Monthly Review 59, no. 11 (April 1, 2008): 1-19. http://mutex.gmu.edu:2233/

Kregel, Jan. Changes in the U. S. Financial System and the Subprime Crisis. Working Paper No. 530, The Levy Economics Institute of Bard College, April 2008. http://www.levy.org/pubs/wp_530.pdf (Accessed 29 November, 2008).

Jackson, Alphonso. Secretary, Department Of Housing And Urban Development "Millions of Minority Owners." National Mortgage News, January 31, 2005, 4. http://mutex.gmu.edu:2233/

Murphy Robert P.. "Did the Fed or Asian Saving, Cause the Housing Bubble?" Daily Article, Ludwig von Mises Institute, 19 Novemeber, 2008.

O'Dricoll, Jr., Gerald P. "Subprime Monetary Policy." *The Freeman* (November 2007): 9.

Rosen Richard J.. The Federal Reserve Bank of Chicago. Chicago Fed Letter. "The Role of Securitization in Mortgage Lending." November 2007, no. 244 http://www.chicagofed.org/publications/fedletter/cflnovember2007_244.pdf

Schelling, Thomas C., Micromotives and Macrobehavior (New York: W.W. Norton & Co., Inc, 2006), 150.

Smith, Vernon L., Suchanek, Gerry L., Williams, Arlington. "Bubbles, Crashes, and Endogenous Expectations in Experimental Spot Asset Markets." *Econometrica (1986 – 1998)* 56, no. 5 (September 1, 1988):1119. http://mutex.gmu.edu.2233/

United States Department of Housing and Urban Development, "Press Release," Tuesday, Oct. 31, 2000. http://www.hud.gov/library/bookshelf12/pressrel/pr00-317.html

United States Department of Housing and Urban Development, Office of Policy Development and Research, First-Time Homebuyers: Trends from the American Housing Survey. http://www.huduser.org/periodicals/ushmc

United States Department of Housing and Urban Development, Compilation from : U.S. Housing Market Conditions. 1995 – Present. http://www.huduser.org/periodicals/ushmc

United States Federal Reserve, Federal Reserve Statistical Release: Special Interest Rates, Historical Data. http://www.federalreserve.gov/releases/h15/data/Monthly/H15_MORTG_NA.txt

Wagner, Richard E., Mind, Society, and Human Action: Toward a Neo-Mengerian Program for Social-Economy. Manuscript. Copyright, 2008.

Public Goods
and Public Choice

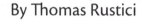

By Thomas Rustici

The man of system on the contrary, is apt to be very wise in his own conceit, and is often so enamored with the supposed beauty of his own ideal plan of government, that he cannot suffer the smallest deviation from any part of it. He goes on to establish it completely and in all its parts, without regard either to the great interests or to the strong prejudices which may oppose it: he seems to imagine that he can arrange the different members of a great society with as much ease as the hand arranges the different pieces upon a chess-board: he does not consider that the pieces upon the chess-board have no other principle of motion besides that which the hand impresses upon them; but that, in the great chess-board of human society, every single piece has a principle of motion of its own, altogether different from that which the legislature might choose to impress upon it.
Adam Smith[1]

INTRODUCTION

Government plays a pervasive role in international economic affairs. World trade, international investment and political coordination exist within a system of nations. Currently, 192 governments claim sovereignty over every continent and much of the oceans.[2] Governments range from democracies, including federal and parliamentary systems, to autocracies such as monarchies and dictatorships. This chapter explores whether economic theory can explain the existence of government and, if so, the economic principles that underlie the decisions made by the widely divergent forms of government.

---

1   Adam Smith, The Theory of Moral Sentiments (Indianapolis: Liberty Classics, 1976), pp. 380-381..
2   **World Almanac and Book of Facts** 1997, (Mahaw, New Jersey: K-III Reference Corporation), pp. 737-837.

GOVERNMENT DEFINED

Government is not poetry, it is not eloquence—it is force.
George Washington[3]

Both the private market and government coordinate exchange. Unlike the private market, which involves voluntary trades, people within a given region conduct coercive transfers through the government. While some find coercion unsettling, it is useful in certain instances. People with guns ensure serial killers, and other, outlaws, involuntarily stay in prison. Of course, "roving bandits"[4] or criminals, induce coercive exchanges. However, only the state exercises *police power,* the moral authority to use violence against anyone within the community.

The police power separates government from other institutions. Violate a religious tenet and excommunication may result. Neglect familial duty and ostracism could occur. Breach a government edict and people authorized to use deadly force shall compel you to visit a robed dignitary who may deprive you of your property, freedom or life. Only government may wield this power with the tacit approval of the community. Government is the institution with a monopoly on the use of force to secure compliance with its decision makers' resolutions.

SHARED FEATURES AMONG GOVERNMENTS

Despite the myriad forms, every government shares certain attributes. The following four features make an economic theory of government possible:

- every government contains a set of constitutional or *institutional rules* that constrain the various agents in the political market;
- every government is operated by human beings who respond to *incentives* within the context of the institutional rules;
- every government contains *politicians* and an administrative *bureaucracy* that execute the operations of state and require the support of various *special interest groups* that may include nonvoters and noncitizens; and,
- every government provides certain goods, whether financed by compulsory *taxation* or through *regulation,* and enforces its decisions using the police power.

At first glance, whether an abstract theory can predict the actions of governments ranging from the United States Congress to Saddam Hussein or the People's Republic of China seems improbable. The real world is extraordinarily complex. To reach general conclusions, a model must overlook many important aspects of the real world. As stated in Chapter 1, theory cannot

---

3   Quoted in H.L. Mencken, *Prejudices*, , 2nd. ser. (New York: Knopf, 1924), p. 221

4   Mancur Olson and Martin C. McGuire, "The Economics of Autocracy and Majority Rule: The Invisible Hand and the Use of Force," *Journal of Economic Literature* Vol. 34 (March 1996), p. 72; Robert Carniero, *A Theory of the Origin State* (Menlo Park, Ca.: Institute for Human Studies, 1977); Franz Oppenhiemer, *The State* (New York: Arno Press, 1972).

contain every characteristic of the real world; otherwise, it would be reality and not a theory. Theory is a road map. The utility of a road map consists in its abstraction that makes the complex comprehensible.[5]

ECONOMIC JUSTIFICATION FOR GOVERNMENT

Furnishing *public goods* provides one economic justification for government.[6] In the 1950s, Paul Samuelson and Francis Bator examined this rationale.[7] According to Samuelson and Bator, the free market's price system occasionally misallocates scarce resources. This blind spot in the price system occurs in the provision of public goods. When all four of the following conditions hold, economists contend that voluntary exchange fails to provide the optimal amount of a good:

- the good exhibits *nonrivalry* in consumption, meaning one person's use leaves the total quantity and quality of the good unaffected;
- the good contains a *joint-consumption* feature, meaning many may consume the good simultaneously;
- the good's consumers display *deceptive self-interest*, meaning consumers may not reveal their true preferences for the good; and,
- once produced, *free-riders* cannot be feasibly excluded from receiving the good's benefits.

These conditions imply many may consume the public good simultaneously and receive its benefits; furthermore, consumers may lie about the benefits they receive with little fear of detection. This suggests a prisoners' dilemma game[8] describes the markets for public goods. Under this scenario, consumers have an incentive to *free-ride* on the efforts of others. The consumer

---

5 Suppose a student desires to travel from New York to California. If the road map were just a photographic reproduction of reality, instead of a three-dimensional portrayal, the map would include 3,000 miles of pages depicting every tree, sidewalk, road-side building, etc. The map's usefulness comes from providing a means, or route of travel, to an end or destination. While theory must abstract from reality, theory may not arbitrarily rearrange aspects of reality at will. Theory must structurally conform with reality. For example, a map would prove useless if Interstate 70 were arbitrarily transposed from an east-west direction to a north-south direction.

6 This section assumes the public good is a final consumer good rather than an intermediate producer input. For a discussion of the problems associated with public goods as inputs and their relationship with externalties and joint production problems, see *Modern Fiscal Issues, Essays in Honor of Carl S. Shoup*, eds. Richard M. Bird and John G. Head (Toronto: University of Toronto Press, 1972), "Joint Production Externalities and Public Goods," by Itirofumi Shibata, 18–4.

7 Paul A. Samuelson, "The Pure Theory of Public Expenditure," *Review of Economics Wild Statistics* XXXVI (November 1954), pp. 387–390. Francis Bator, "Anatomy of Market Failure," *Quarterly Journal of Economics 1958*

8 Previously outlined in Chapter 12, the prisoners' dilemma game arises as a strategic incentive problem between the individual's interest and the individual's interest as a member of a group. When these interests diverge, economic theory predicts that rational agents pursue their personal interests at the expense of the group. For a

reasons (i) her trivial contributions toward producing the public good will not prevent its production and (ii) detecting her nonpayment is not easy. Since all consumers face the same incentive, very few consumers voluntarily pay their full share and not enough public good is produced. Moreover, the incentive to free ride increases as the number of public good consumers increases because the share per person declines and detecting nonpayers typically becomes more costly. Correcting the private sector's undersupply of public goods provides one economic justification for government. Government's ability to coerce payment overcomes the free riding inherent in public goods' production. Through government, consumers trade compulsory tax payments for public goods.[9]

Externalities provide another economic argument for government. Externalities are a transaction's unintended effects absorbed by others not directly involved in the exchange. Externalities may be positive or negative. Like public goods, positive externalities result in the underproduction of a good because the participants do not acquire all the benefits from the exchange. For instance, many economists view education as providing positive externalities since no one can completely capture the benefits from the student's better civic responsibility and lower propensity for crime. On the other hand, negative externalities result in the overproduction of a good since buyers and sellers do not bear all the costs of the good's production. Economists often cite pollution as an example of a negative externality.

The problem of externalities revolves around the lack of well-defined property rights, information costs and transaction costs. Given well-defined property rights and no information costs or transaction costs, the Coase Theorem[10] holds that externalities would not exist in a free market. Unfortunately, property rights are often ill-defined, transaction costs exist and information is costly to acquire, process or distribute. Yet, the Coase Theorem illuminates the causes of externalities—causes that were unclear before Coase's Nobel-winning work.

Theoretically, government's police power permits correction of externalities by enforcing property rights and regulations, as well as imposing taxes and granting subsidies designed to yield the socially optimal amount of a good. The goal is equating marginal social costs with marginal social benefits.

Pollution provides a classic example of a negative externality. All living things generate waste or pollution. Pollution becomes an issue when polluters do not incorporate pollution's adverse effects into their costs. As described in Chapter 12, this may occur from a common ownership problem that prevents charging a fee to polluters for their discharges. Pollution of the air and water does not respect political boundaries. Therefore, nonusers of the good may bear the harm caused by the pollution generated in the good's production. The graphs below illustrate several government remedies for pollution.

---

classic illustration of this problem, see Mancur Olson's, *The Logic of Collective Action*, (Cambridge: Mass.; Harvard University Press, 1965).

9 James Buchanan, *The Limits To Liberty, Between Anarchy and Leviathan* (Chicago: University of Chicago Press, 1975).

10 Ronald Coase, "The Problem of Social Cost," *The Journal of Lawand Economics* (October 1960),Vol. 3, pp. 1-44. 5.

BLOCKED EXAMPLE: NATIONAL DEFENSE

Many economists believe national defense illustrates the classic features of a public good. Imagine a situation where consumers crave security from invaders, but lack a government to levy compulsory taxes. Consumers desire defense but private producers will find supplying consumers' demand for protection unprofitable. Therefore, a suboptimal amount of national defense will be produced. The prisoners' dilemma game below further demonstrates this point.

AL

	Cooperate	Cheat
Cooperate	A, T $50, $50	A, T $100, $0
Cheat	$0, $100	$0, $0

(Row labels on left: **TOM**, with **Cooperate** and **Cheat**)

In the above game, Al and Tom face the following payoffs: (i) if both cooperate, each pays $50 and receives $100 in protection for a net gain of $50, (ii) if no one cooperates, each will pay nothing and receive no protection, and (iii) if one person cooperates and the other does not, the cooperative person pays $100 and the defector pays nothing, however, both receive $100 in protection. Given these assumptions, rational consumers free ride on the contributions by others toward national defense. Since this incentive exists for all, very few consumers voluntarily pay for their benefits and less than the optimal amount of national defense results. Everyone wants defense, but none will pay, unless everyone else contributes his share. Moreover, excluding nonpayers is neither economically nor militarily practical.

GRAPH 14-1(A)

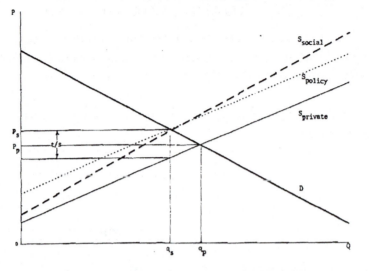

Graph 14-1(a) portrays a solution to a negative externality where the government taxes or subsidizes the polluter.[11] The polluter pays a per unit tax of *t/s* on each unit of output, or receives a per unit subsidy of *tis* on each unit of output the polluter does not produce. In Graph 14-1(a) *t/s* equals the difference between the private marginal cost of producing the good and the marginal social cost of producing another unit. The tax or subsidy shifts the supply curve from $S_{private}$ to S_{social} and reduces output from q_p to q_s, the socially optimal output.

GRAPH 14-1(B)

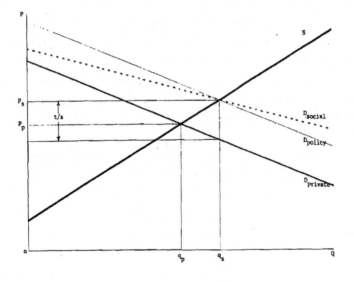

---

11   A.C. Pigou, *Economics of Welfare* (London: McMillan and Co., 1932). Yet, externalities are a two-way street -one person's loss is another's gain. The above analysis only holds when the government *actually* transfers resources between those harmed and those who benefit from the pollution. See, James Buchanan and W.C. Stubblebine, "Externality," *Economica*, (November 1962), pp. 371–84.

Graph 14-1(b) illustrates a solution to a positive externality where the government taxes or subsidizes the consumer. In the case of pollution, this would occur where the smog generates positive benefits, like spectacular sunsets, that are valued more than the smog's adverse effects. The consumer receives a per unit subsidy of *t/s* for each unit of smog-producing good consumed, or pays a per unit tax of *t/s* for every unit not consumed. In Graph 14-1 (b), *t/s* equals the difference between the private marginal benefit of the good and the marginal social benefit of consuming another unit. The tax or subsidy shifts the demand curve $D_{private}$ to D_{social} and output increases from q_p to q_s, the socially optimal output.

Depending of the scheme, taxing or subsidizing the producer or consumer results in the socially optimal output. The above graphs make several stringent assumptions. The graphs presume either one firm produces the good or all firms have identical cost structures. Also, the graphs assume government bureaucrats know each firm's cost structure in order to set the appropriate tax or subsidy. Graphs 14-1(c) relaxes the assumption that firms have identical cost structures.

GRAPH 14-1(C)

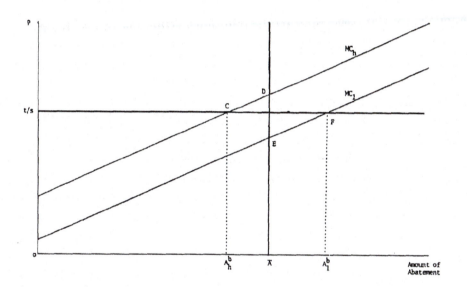

Graph 14-1(c) depicts a regulatory solution and a solution with tradable property rights to pollute. Assume two firms: a high-cost firm which must spend a substantial amount per unit of pollution abatement and a low-cost firm which can spend less. In Graph 14-1(c), MC_h is the marginal cost per unit of pollution abatement for the high-cost firm, and MC_l is the marginal costs per unit of abatement for the low-cost firm. Let A equal the average level of abatement both firms must achieve.

Suppose, an agency requires each firm to spend A on reducing pollution. While resulting in the socially optimal amount of pollution, the regulatory regime generates deadweight loss equal to the trapezoid $A_h{}^bCDA$ *plus* trapezoid $AEFA_l{}^b$ Dead-weight losses occur because the regulation prevents the low-cost producer from providing the good, instead of the high-cost producer. Establishing mandatory limits on output waste scarce resources.

Instead of dictating the amount of pollution reduction, assume the government gives each firm "bonds" which grant the holder the right to pollute A. If the government imposed a tax of *t/s*, the firms would trade bonds until each firm's marginal cost of pollution abatement equaled *tis*. While the average pollution reduction among firms remains A, the low-cost firm will engage in more pollution abatement than the high-cost firm. The socially optimal amount of pollution and production of the good occurs without any dead-weight loss.

The solution producing the optimal amount of output with the least dead-weight loss depends on the difficulties encountered in implementing the remedy. Typically, government officials possess more information about the socially optimal level of pollution than every polluter's cost structure. For stationary polluters like factories, the government solution creating the least dead-weight loss usually involves setting the aggregate level of pollution and letting the private sector decide the appropriate methods for attaining the goal.

The Traditional Explanation of Government Behavior: Public Interest Theory

Public Interest Theory represents the traditional economic view of government behavior. Public interest theory assumes agents in political markets consider society's best interest as their primary objective. The political agent's self-interest may be a secondary concern, however, the public interest remains paramount. In democratic systems, supporters of this theory believe government officials and bureaucrats faithfully reflect the popular will. Representatives of the people increase social welfare by guaranteeing sufficient public goods production and alleviating the market failures caused by externalities. In essence, government officials and bureaucrats strive to set marginal social benefit equal to marginal social cost.[12]

The public interest theory does not imply the creation and enforcement of rules and regulations by selfless individuals who simply obey the will of the people. An occasional misanthrope in the form of a petty bureaucrat or self-serving politician may commandeer the reins of power. Nevertheless, the theory assumes the cause of this problem involves inappropriate people in government rather than the inappropriate scope, scale or institutional rules of government.

The notion that government primarily serves the public interest pervades a vast array of government interventions in the private sector. For instance, many believe antitrust laws protect consumers from price gouging monopolies or minimum wage laws and other labor legislation help the working poor avoid monopsonistic exploitation by firms. Public interest theory undergirds the perception that safety regulation shields employees from potentially hazardous work conditions and consumers from unsafe products. This theory also supports the argument that regulations and taxes protect the environment from polluters and save endangered species. In essence, public interest theory presumes government actions strive to enhance social welfare.

---

12 Graphs 14-1(a) through (c) assume government officials actually attempt to equate marginal social benefit with marginal social cost.

Not So Fast: The Limits of Public Interest Analysis

The economic rationale for government depends on a market failure resulting in the misallocation of resources. The misallocation occurs from externalities or public goods. Yet, market failure only creates a *necessary condition* for government not a *sufficient condition*.[13] Nothing designed by humans is perfect and government solutions contain flaws. Thus, the free market may exhibit a second-best characteristic. In a second-best situation, a market failure clearly exists but any solution results in more dead-weight loss than that generated by the market failure.

For example, a central problem in the provision of public goods involves *demand revelation*.[14] Problems with demand revelation happen whenever exclusion of free riders becomes infeasible. By not revealing their preferences, self-interested consumers seek an escape from paying for their benefits from the public good. Government provision of the public good does not eliminate strategic free riding. Rational self-interested voters aspire to shift their tax burden onto others. Voters consuming the public good have an incentive to conceal their true preferences in the hope of free riding on other taxpayers' contributions. This shift of the tax burden misallocates resources. Whether difficulties in demand revelation produce more dead-weight loss in the private provision of public goods than in public provision remains questionable.

Moreover, government solutions contain potential defects not found in private markets. The *forced carrier* issue provides an example. Forced carrier problems stem from the government requiring taxpayers to purchase the public good despite their true preferences.[15] The same asymmetric information problem that allows free riding also prevents the government from objectively determining each taxpayer's true preference. By compelling the purchase of public goods, forced carrier problems make any improvement in social welfare problematic.

A pervasive forced carrier problem may result in the **oversupply** of a public good by the government. Over-supply may reduce net social welfare more than the underproduction by the private sector. Graph 14-2 illustrates the welfare implications from overproduction of a public good.

Suppose q_p represents the private provision of a public good and q_s signifies the socially optimal level of output. Triangle ABC represents the potential welfare improvement from the government providing the public good. Between q_p and q_s, the benefits from additional units of the public good exceed the opportunity cost of its production. However, government may set an output level at q_r which illustrates the forced carrier problem. In this case, the losses bounded by the triangle **CEF** offset the gains **ABC**. Given the lack of omniscient beings in government, achieving q. would be purely accidental.

---

13 A necessary condition holds when a potential opportunity exists for an Pareto improvement in social welfare, while a sufficient condition requires an actual possibility exists to exploit the opportunity. Harold Demsetz, "The Private Production of Public Goods," *The Journal of Law and Economics* (October 1970).

14 Joseph Kalt, "*Public Goods and the Theory of Government,*"The Cato Journal Vol. I *No.2* (Fall 1981), p. 569..

15 With national defense, for example, anarchists must contribute even though they consider national defense an economic bad.

GRAPH 14-2

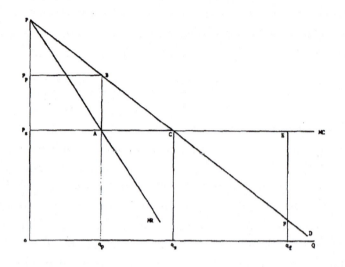

Moreover, a government-owned monopoly typically supplies public goods and may exhibit **X*inefficiency*.**[16] X-inefficiency plagues monopolistic production. Immunity from competition furnishes little incentive to operate like a competitive firm. As a result, a monopoly's marginal costs rises as its managers and administrators take the potential profits in the form of an easy life, larger offices and a plush working environment. The problem becomes more severe in government-owned firms since, unlike owners; bureaucrats do not benefit from any monetary savings resulting from improved efficiency.[17] Since government-owned firms generally employ less cost-effective technology or use a suboptimal mix of labor to capital, economic theory predicts they are less cost-effective in transforming resource into public goods and services than firms in the private sector.

Graph 14-3 incorporates the consequences of X-inefficiency. Assume the government correctly picks the q. level of public good output. Over time, X-inefficiency will shift the marginal cost curve from $MC_{private}$ to MC_{public} and total production costs for q_1 increase by rectangle P_gECP_p. These increased production costs offset the net benefit triangle ABC. Instead of a net social welfare gain of triangle ABC, a net loss of rectangle ABCE *minus* triangle ABC occurs. In this instance, the private provision of public goods manifests as much welfare loss as the government solution.

---

16 Harvey Leibenstein, "On the Basic Proposition of X-Efficiency," *American Economic* Review (May 1978),pp. 328–332.

17 This result holds true even when the government contracts with private sector suppliers to produce the public good. For an analysis of the problems and complexities involved with contracting with monopolistic suppliers, see, Oliver Williamson, "Franchise Bidding for Natural Monopolies-In General and With Respect to CATV," *Bell Journal of Economics and Management Science,* Vol. 7, No. I (Spring 1976), pp. 73–104; and Victor Goldberg, "Regulation and Administered Contracts," *Bell Journal of Economics and Management Science,* Vol. 7, No .2 (Autumn 1976), pp. 426–446.

GRAPH 14-3

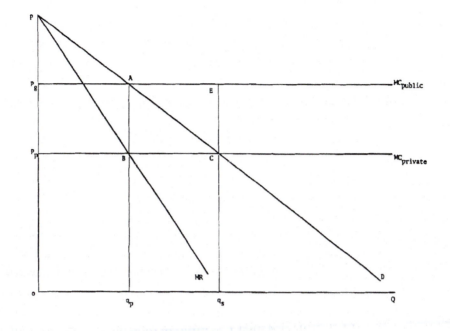

PUBLIC CHOICE: THE ECONOMICS OF POLITICS

Until now, the analysis has assumed a government run by benevolent beings with a desire to improve social welfare. Public choice employs the traditional economic assumption of rational self-interest when it explores decision making within the *political marketplace*. The motivations affecting people in the private market also influence the political market. Public choice does not assume politicians, voters, or bureaucrats primarily act to maximize social welfare.[18]

Public choice hinges on the concepts of *rational ignorance* and *transactions costs*. Rational ignorance occurs because information is costly to acquire, process or distribute. Agents in the political market acquire, process or distribute information until the expected marginal costs equal the expected marginal benefits from being better informed. Transactions costs include the cost of voting, organizing political campaigns, administering the bureaucracy, or removing agents or politicians from office by recall or impeachment. Without information and transaction costs, voters can force self-interested policy makers to improve social welfare or face removal from political office.

---

18 While the rest of this chapter outlines the American system of representative democracy, the basic principles of public choice provide a general framework for understanding other political systems including parliamentary government and dictatorship. Wayne Brough and Mwangi Kimenyi,"On the Inefficient Extraction of Rents by Dictators," *Public Choice* (1986), pp. 37–48.

CONSTITUTIONAL CONSTRAINTS ON POLITICAL MARKETS

If men were angels, no government would be necessary. If angels were to govern men,
neither external nor internal controls on government would be necessary.
James Madison[19]

Every political market exists within a set of institutional rules called a ***constitution***. Constitutions usually outline a set of powers granted to the government as well as impose important procedural constraints on political agents. A nation's constitutional rules can be drafted into a legal document or take the form of unwritten rules delineating the political market's boundaries.[20] Yet, the effectiveness of explicit or implicit constraints on the political markets may vary dramatically across countries or within a nation across time.[21] In short, constitutions are the "rules" of the game called politics.

Many political theorists believe the writers of the United States *Constitution* intentionally designed the federal government to mitigate the normal incentives found in political markets. America's political founders distrusted concentrated political power and believed Lord Acton's adage: "**power corrupts and absolute power corrupts absolutely**." Because of the founders' suspicions, the *Constitution's* rules scattered authority along horizontal and vertical dimensions.[22] The *Bill of Rights* was added to the original *Constitution* to explicitly protect individual rights from the encroachment of federal power. In short, the *Constitution's* rules assume the political marketplace exhibits the worst aspects of self-interest.

INCENTIVES MATTER

Representative democracies govern most of the industrialized countries. According to public choice, utility maximization guides political activity within democracies, just as it guides people in the private sector. Public choice models all behavior as a rationally consistent response to incentives. Political decisions conform with the incentives and rules of existing institutions. Utopian angels maximizing social welfare do not control the levers of political power.

---

19   James Madison, Federalist No. 51, in *The Federalist Papers*, pp. 86

20   For example, the United Kingdom has no official written constitution. The British courts implicitly find the constitution of the UK in the common law. See, A.V. Dicey, *The Law of the Constitution* (Indianapolis: Liberty Press, 1982)

21   For example, the formal constitution in the former Soviet Union under Joseph Stalin provided guarantees for free speech. While spelled out on paper, exercising the right to free speech during this time was impossible. For the changing and porous nature of constitutional constraints over the course of American history, see Bernard Seigan's *Economic Liberties and the Constitution* (Chicago: University of Chicago Press, 1986)

22   The horizontal dispersion of power is the concept of checks and balances among three branches of government, executive, legislative and judiciary. The vertical dispersal of power is the concept of federalism which delegates certain powers to lower levels of government.

In 1896, the Swedish economist Knut Wicksell suggested self-interest may plausibly explain the operation of political markets.[23] In 1957, Anthony Downs outlined a model of democracy based on self-interest that could make testable predictions. Kenneth Arrow and Duncan Black added important pieces to the public choice model in the 1950s. Both Arrow and Black examined decision making by a committee, for which Arrow later received the Nobel Prize.[24] In 1962, James Buchanan and Gordon Tullock published the public choice classic, *The Calculus of Consent*. The Nobel committee cited *The Calculus of Consent* when it awarded Buchanan the prize in 1986. According to Buchanan:

> *If men should cease and desist from their talk about their search for evil men or purely goodmen, and commence to look instead of institutions manned by ordinary people, wide avenues or genuine social reform might appear.*[25]

Public choice ends the split-personality theory of economic incentives. People remain people inside and outside government. Self-interested consumers, workers, and producers do not magically exchange the "horns" of greed for the "halo" of altruism when they enter government. Human motivations remain the same in both private and public sectors. Understanding the political process requires focusing on the institutional rules that guide and constrain political behavior. According to public choice, enhancing societal welfare does not require better people participate in government, instead, better results demand better rules governing political institutions.

PLAYERS IN THE POLITICAL MARKET: POLITICIANS, VOTERS AND BUREAUCRATS

Every government contains politicians responsible for creating laws and policies, various special interest groups supporting or opposing various political agents and bureaucrats who administer public policy. Public choice isolates the three key players in the political market of a representative democracy: politicians, voters, and bureaucrats. Individuals in each group primarily maximize their own utility just like their counterparts in the private sector. While civic pride exists, it plays a secondary role in public choice models. Politicians compete in elections that require them to *maximize votes*. Voters participate in elections to increase their wealth by *maximizing net benefits*. The administrative bureaucracy must *maximize budget* if it wants to survive in the political world.

---

23   Knut Wicksell, *Finanztheoretische Utersuchungen* (Jena: Gustar Fisher, 1896).

24   Kenneth Arrow, *Social Choice and Individual Values* (New York: John Wiley & Sons, Inc., 1951); and Duncan Black, *The Theory of Committees and Elections* (Cambridge: Cambridge University Press, 1958).

25   James Buchanan, *The Limits of Liberty: Between Anarchy and Leviathan* (Chicago: University of Chicago Press, 1975) p. 149.

POLITICIANS

Politicians in our model never seek office as a means of carrying out particular policies;
their only goal is to reap the rewards of holding office per se.
Anthony Downs[26]

The public interest theory of government models politicians primarily seeking elective office so they can enact legislation that increases social welfare. Public choice, on the other hand, assumes politicians chiefly pursue office for their own ends. Even purely civic-minded candidates must get elected before they can change public policy. To get elected, politicians must capture the most votes cast in the election. With the principle of majority rule, a politician's behavior follows the logic of the *median voter model.*[27] The five assumptions of the model include:

- an election were only one issue is voted upon;
- candidates from just two political parties run for office;
- parties try to maximize the total vote their candidate receives in the election;
- during the campaign, candidates can change their stand on the issue; and,
- the largest concentration of voter preferences occurs near the center of the political center; the model excludes multimodality of voter preferences.

The median voter model hypothesizes a somewhat bell-shaped distribution of voter preferences.[28] The middle of the political spectrum contains the largest number of prospective votes because very few voters embrace the radical ideologies found at either end of the distribution. While voter preferences exhibit a stable bell-curve the entire ideological spectrum may shift over time.[29]

In democracies with closed primaries,[30] the model predicts political parties nominate candidates that reflect views more consistent with the ideological tail of the voting spectrum. In a closed primary system, the party's median voter is either to the right or left of the nation's political spectrum. Graph 14-4 illustrates this point. The Democratic nominee stakes out position **D** while the Republican candidate is at **R**. After the primary, however, candidates move toward the center because all voters participate in the general election. Thus, *political convergence* becomes

---

26   Anthony Downs, *All Economic Theory of Democracy* (New York: Harper and Row, 1957), p. 28

27   For empirical evidence validating the predictions of the median voter model, see Randall Holcombe, "An Empirical Test of the Median Voter Model," Economic Inquiry Vol. XVIII NO.2 (April 1980), pp. 260–64.

28   In the elections with three or more candidates, graph 14-4 becomes multidimensional.

29   A wide range of evidence suggests that the 1980 Presidential election between Jimmy Carter and Ronald Reagan reflected a more conservative shift in the ideology of the electorate. A clear example of this shift came with the 1978 tax revolt called Proposition 13 in California.

30   In closed primaries only those members registered with the party may vote to nominate the party's candidate. In open primaries the political opposition also votes in the nominating process.

likely. Candidates converge on the ideological center by strategically changing their position to **D'** and **R'**. As election day nears, rival candidates stakeout virtually indistinguishable positions such as **D"** and **R"**. Given majority rule, the politician's optimal strategy mimics median voter preferences.

MEDIAN VOTER MODEL
GRAPH 14-4

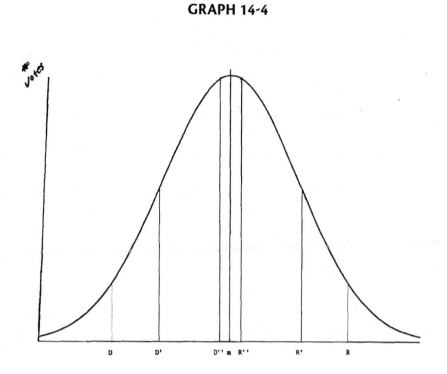

The model also predicts competitive candidates will label their opponents as an "extremist" while claiming they are more moderate. Initially, politicians provide voters with information or misinformation to distinguish themselves from opponents. Once a candidate falls behind in the pre-election polls, however, they start sounding like their political rival. A successful campaigner makes appeals to the opposition parties' members without alienating their ideological base of supporters. Candidates must quickly learn the skill of speaking in generalities and avoiding specific positions that might alienate certain groups of voters. The voters' rational ignorance permits successful candidates to claim they represent the rich, poor, and middle class as well as favoring "good jobs," a "strong national defense," or "a chicken in every pot." Candidates display a strong affinity for political symbolism such as defending the nation's flag, family values, or kissing babies because it generates positive public support with little political costs.[31]

---

31 In the 1995 Russian elections, Liberal Democratic Party candidate Vladimir Zhirinovsky promised every unmarried women a husband if he were elected!

ELECTION RULES, AGENCY PROBLEMS AND THE MEDIAN VOTER

The median voter model is a powerful tool that explains elections in a two-party democracy. The model predicts public policy accurately reflects median voter preferences. However, this implication may not always hold. Under a variety of situations, public policy can significantly deviate away from median voter preferences. *Agency problems* provide the fundamental reason for this departure.

AGENCY PROBLEMS IN THE POLITICAL MARKET

Political democracy attempts to copy the consumer sovereignty of the free market.[32] In the private sector, consumers vote their preferences with the dollars they spend. In the political market, eligible citizens legally cast one vote per election race. However, **not every vote counts**. Only the votes cast for the winning candidate count. The winner-take-all principle forms the basis of most democracies.[33] Citizens who vote for the losing candidate do not get their views expressed by the winner. For the winner, every vote after 50% + 1 has zero marginal benefit.

Another type of problem exists for voters near the median. Rational politicians may lie to voters about their views in the hopes of obtaining the votes necessary to win. Therefore, an incentive *exists* for extensive fraud in campaign advertising called *political bait and switch*. In the private sector, entrepreneurs who "bait and switch" by lying about their products can be prosecuted for fraud. Political entrepreneurs, however, make extensive use of "bait-and-switch" tactics because false campaign promises are inunune from prosecution. Politicians understand this type of legal double-standard.[34] After an election, the victorious candidate often betrays baited voters with a simple, "I've changed my mind," or "conditions have changed." Voters remain vulnerable to "baiting" because legally enforceable contracts do not exist between politicians and voters.

A dramatically reduced range of possible options also exacerbates agency problems in political markets. In the private sector, the consumer makes individualized purchase decisions. A consumer can buy one good without purchasing another. In political markets, however, elections compel voters to choose a bundle of unrelated policies. While this *bundling effect* is unimportant for the median voter model, in real-world elections, bundling creates additional rational ignorance by allowing politicians maneuvering room away from median voter preferences. The median voter might agree with Candidate Smith's position on some policies but disagree on others. It is impossible, however, to elect a person with Smith's views on taxes, spending and regulation while simultaneously electing his opponent's contradictory position on abortion, and public school prayer.

---

32 Ludwig von Mises, *Human Action: A Treatise On Economics* (Chicago: Contemporary Books, 1963),p. 271

33 Proportional representation in some European parliamentary systems alleviates this type of political market failure.

34 James Bennett and Thomas DiLorenzo, *Official Lies: How Government Misleads Us* (Alexandria, Va.: Croom Books, 1992)

A *delayed recall policy* magnifies agency problems in political markets. In the private sector, unhappy consumers may reverse market transactions through legally binding guarantees, warranties, and return policies. In political markets, voters only "repurchase" or vote after an election cycle of two, four or six years. Furthermore, reversing mistakes through impeachment or recall imposes large costs on individual voters.[35] Delayed recall and rational ignorance permits politicians to break campaign promises made to individuals near the ideological median.

Sometimes politicians purposely create agency problems by redrawing electoral boundaries because of demographic changes. Redesigning political jurisdictions can effectively deny a competitive vote. *Gerrymandering* rearranges voting districts to neutralize voters who support the opposition party. Example 14-1 illustrates gerrymandering. Suppose two political parties Red and Blue exist, and constitutional rules specify an equal number of eligible voters must reside within each district. Gerrymandering allows the Blue party to have a competitive edge in Districts 2 through 4 while being at a disadvantage only in District 1. Though an equal number of voters support each party, the Blue Party will dominate the legislature.

Example 14-1
Gerrymandering of District Voters

	Red	Blue
District 1	375	25
District 2	165	235
District 3	160	240
District 4	150	250
District 5	150	250
Total Voters	1,000	1,000

Once elected, politicians can engage in *log-rolling* by swapping votes with other politicians. Representatives log-roll to form coalitions that guarantee successful passage of legislation that benefits constituents at the expense of the national interest. For example, the Kansas Senator may pledge his vote to expand federal aid to urban cities in exchange for the New York Senator's vote to increase agricultural subsidies. Log-rolling allows politicians to impose *invisible costs* on their own district for the benefits of *highly visible* legislation. Yet, log-rolling can create a "lose-lose" situation for median voters in all jurisdictions. The combined losses for each district may vastly exceed the combined gain.[36]

---

35 Imagine the consumer dissatisfaction if defective products were only allowed to be returned after a two year delay.

36 See, Richard McKenzie and Gordon Tullock, "Rent-Seeking," *The New World Of Economics* (Homewood, Illinois: Richard Irwin, 1981), Ch. 15.

IS MAJORITY RULE SOCIALLY EFFICIENT?

If the social benefits of collective action exceed its social costs, will a majority of voters pursue such a course of action? Consider the case of a public playground for local children. Suppose there are 1000 voters who pay equal taxes. The playground costs $10,000 and each voter pays $10 in taxes to finance the project. Assume six hundred voters value the playground at $15 each, but the other 400 voters attach no value to the project. The playground will pass in a democratic election even though the total social value of $9000 is less than its $10,000 cost. Alternatively, suppose four hundred voters value the playground at $50 each, but six hundred voters attach no value to it. The playground's social worth of $20,000 far exceeds its $10,000 costs, but will fail in a democratic election.

Still, economist Donald Wittman maintains that democracy is a socially efficient market mechanism for translating voter preferences into policy.* In the first instance, the voters who value the playground less than its cost could make side-payments of $6 to 101 voters, provided they switch their vote on the issue. Thus, the playground does not get built when social costs exceed social benefits. In the second circumstance, the first 400 voters could make side-payments of $11 to 101 voters to encourage a favorable vote on the project. Thus, construction of the playground occurs when social benefits exceed social costs.

While potentially profitable exchange possibilities exist in political markets, a variety of drawbacks may prevent the efficient outcome. First, side-payments are indistinguishable from other forms of bribery prohibited by law. Second, information costs and **demand revelation** problems encourage every voter to conceal their true preferences to receive bribes. Third, the transactions costs associated with enforcing side-payments are probably prohibitive given the secretive nature of the voting booth. Finally, the time **horizon bias** of democratic majority rule may make political markets inefficient. In the private sector, investors capture the present the value of discounted future benefits from long-term investments.** In the political sector, however, the time horizon coincides with the election cycle of two, four or six years. Few politicians survive reelection when the short-run costs of their policies are highly visible, even when the future payoff exceeds the short-run costs. Politicians cannot capture future votes in the present elections. As a result, a narrowed time horizon skews outcomes.

* Donald Wittman, *The Myth of Democratic Failure: Why Political Institutions are Efficient* (Chicago: University of Chicago Press, 1995).

** The present value discount formula is $PV = \sum[R_i / (1+r)^i]$, where

PV = present discounted value

R_i = net returns from the investment in period i

r = interest rate

n = number of time periods that the investment generates net returns

Agenda control is another way politicians depart from the preferences of the median voter.[37] Suppose newly elected Senator Smith promised to build a road in his district. He introduces a bill and the legislative committee overseeing transportation affairs reviews the project. If Smith is a low-ranking member, his bill may fall to the bottom of the legislative itinerary. Although the road's benefits may exceed its costs, the project may never come up for a committee vote. The bill's position in the voting hierarchy, or project's position in the funding order, may skew the outcome away from the median voter's preferences.

VOTERS

> *Liberty is to faction what air is to fire, an aliment without which it instantly expires. But it could not be less folly to abolish liberty, which is essential to political life, because it nourishes faction, than it would be to wish the annihilation of air ...*
> **James Madison**[38]

The public interest view of government assumes that pure civic pride explains most voting behavior. According to this view, patriotic citizens principally cast their vote for the good of the country. Public choice economists do not deny the relevance of civic pride. Nevertheless, self-interested voters consider other costs and benefits of voting. Voters try to capture personal benefits through the political process by **rent-seeking**. Voters rent-seek by voting to direct social or economic benefits to themselves while shifting the cost to other citizens.

Voters are the consumers in the political marketplace. While self-interested, voters' interests may be frustrated because of rational ignorance. Suppose Citizen Smith wants to be a knowledgeable voter with respect to nuclear power. Before voting, Smith does not spend thousands of dollars acquiring a Ph.D. in nuclear physics because Smith knows his increased knowledge will have a trivial impact on the vote. A Ph.D. is too expensive for Smith given the very small probability his vote decides the outcome of the election. A **return to voting equation**[39] describes the payoff for voters.

$$R = P(CW) - CV + CP$$

where: R = Net returns from voting;

P = Probability of the voter's ballot determining the election's outcome;

CW = Net difference in benefits offered by each candidate;

CV = Costs of voting, including all opportunities foregone, and

CP = Civic pride and other psychic rewards.

---

37   Randall Holcombe, *Public Finance: Government Revenues and Expenditures in the United States Economy* (New York: West Publishing Co., 1996), pp. 185–8.

38   James Madison, *Federalist 10*, p. 17.

39   William H. Riker and Peter C. Ordershook, "A Theory of the Calculus of Voting," *American Political Science Review,* Vol. 62, No. 1 (March 1968), pp. 25–42

THE VOTING PARADOX

Nobel Laureate Kenneth Arrow demonstrated a more serious problem with translating median voter preferences into public policy. Even if the voters' political preferences remain constant, cycling of outcomes may arise. The combination of intransitive preferences and majority rule may produce a *paradox of voting*. For example, suppose **A**, **B** and **C** represent three different policies and each pair-wise vote proceeds: **A** vs. **B**, **B** vs. **C** and **C** vs. **A**. In such a case, policy makers may not reach a stable equilibrium. Example 14-2 illustrates this paradox.

Example 14-2
Cyclical Majorities

Voter		1	2	3
preference	1st	A	C	B
priority	2nd	B	A	C
	3rd	C	B	A

In the vote between A and B, voters 1 and 2 *prefer* A to B. Policy **A** wins in a democratic election. In the vote between B and C, voters I and 3 *prefer* B and policy **B** prevails in the election. However, in a contest between A and C, voters 2 and 3 *prefer* C and policy **C** triumphs! Even with stable preferences, majority rule may exhibit cycling results. With intransitive preference, constant cycling frustrates the median voter and imposes substantial transaction costs from continuous change in public policy initiatives.

Suppose Candidate Jones offers the median voter benefits exceeding those promised by candidate Thomas by $1,000. Also, assume 100,000 may vote on election day. The expected return for the median voter is one cent *minus* the cost of voting *plus* civic pride. Since a voter must forgo wages, leisure time, and other goods, voting is generally irrational unless a strong civic pride component exists. Given the negative returns to voting, economic theory has difficulty explaining why people would vote.[40] Yet, some people vote and they are often rationally ignorant, like Citizen Smith. On the other hand, many citizens correctly perceive their vote makes no difference in a large democracy. Consequently, pervasive *voter apathy* generally dominates elections.[41] Low voter turnout may not reflect a loss of civic pride; instead, the negative returns to voting make engaging in civic life very costly.

With the multitude of complex issues involved in a political campaign many voters remain rationally ignorant. For evidence for this phenomenon, ask your friends and family the

---

40   Gordon Tullock, *Toward a Mathematics of Politics* (Ann Arbor: University of Michigan Press, 1968), Chapter 7; and Downs, *An Economic Theory of Democracy,* pp. 36–50, pp. 260–276.

41   In the 1994 congressional elections only 36% of the voting age population cast votes. See, *Statistical Abstract 1996,* p. 287

following: Who is your Congressperson? Do you how your Congressperson voted on five issues and can you name the bills? Chances are most voters cannot name five issues, let alone the voting record of their elected representatives which covers hundreds or thousands of legislative bills.[42] On the other hand, there exists a subsection of well-informed voters. While the median voter may not hold intense policy preferences, voters on the tails of the ideological spectrum generally do. Voters at the tails often hold in common a few political values very intensely. In this situation, these voters might collectively join and act as *special interest groups*.

THE IMPORTANCE OF DISTRIBUTIONS

Economist Mancur Olson developed the links between the formation of special interest groups, information costs and voting behavior.[43] According to Olson, special interest legislation dominates when groups rent-seek through the political process. The return to voting equation implies individuals in special interest groups vote more often than voters within the general population. Consider the lobbying activities of the AFL-CIO. As a special interest group, the union economizes on *information costs* by reducing its members' rational ignorance with respect to political issues. For union members who vote, information and monitoring costs are prohibitive when thousands of new laws and regulations potentially affect their interests. If the AFL-CIO obtains a contribution of 10 cents from its 13.1 million members, it could amasses over one million dollars. With the money, the AFL-CIO creates a permanent group to effectively monitor and lobby politicians as well as draft rent-seeking legislation for the benefit of its members. At election time, the union informs its membership how to vote their interest.

The *distribution of benefits and costs* implies most laws are special interest legislation. For example, Candidate Jones claims every international economist should receive a $25,000 per year subsidy out of the federal budget (for the public interest, of course). If 1,000 international economists receive this subsidy, the transfer program costs $25 million dollars. Twenty-five thousand dollars becomes a powerful reason for international economists to learn about wealth transfers. Yet, this program costs an average of about 25 cents for other 100 million taxpayers. This creates little incentive for the average taxpayer to oppose this transfer of wealth. An outraged taxpayer might mail a letter to their congressional representative, but letter writing requires time, effort and a 32 cent postage stamp! For most taxpayers, it is more profitable to remain rationally ignorant. A politician proposing this transfer legislation receives almost unanimous support from international economists, but does not lose many votes from the

---

42 Michael Caprini and Scott Keeter, "Stability and Change in the U.S. Public's Knowledge of Politics," *Public Opinion Quarterly* (Winter 1991) Vol. 55, pp. 583–612. For example, 62% of respondents could not name their congressional representative in 1947 and 71 % did not know the answer in 1989. Also see, Bernard Seigan's, *Economic Liberties and the Constitution*, p. 276. According to Seigan:

"The California legislature reportedly considered more than 7,000 proposals during the 1975-76 session. Congress was expected to process as many as 6,000 items in the session beginning in 1977."

43 Mancur Olson, *The Logic of Collective Action* (Cambridge: Harvard University Press, 1971).

other taxpayers. The most effective vote maximizing strategy in political markets comes from concentrating the benefits and widely dispersing the costs.

Through *pork-barrel legislation*, successful political entrepreneurs enact legislation that brings tangible benefits to special interests within their district at the expense of voters in other jurisdictions. Pork-barrel legislation succeeds even when it creates a negative net effect for the nation as a whole. A rational politician generally puts the interests of her own constituency before the larger national interest because voters in other jurisdictions do not vote in the politician's

THE GROWTH OF POLITICAL ACTION COMMITTEES

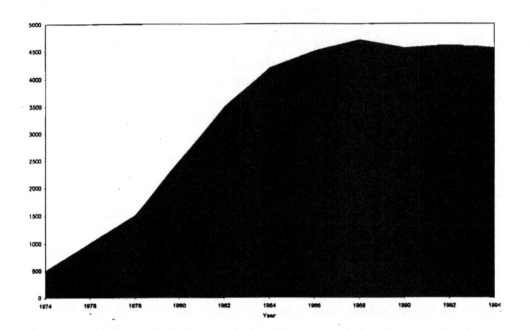

CAMPAIGN CONTRIBUTIONS BY POLITICAL ACTION COMMITTEES

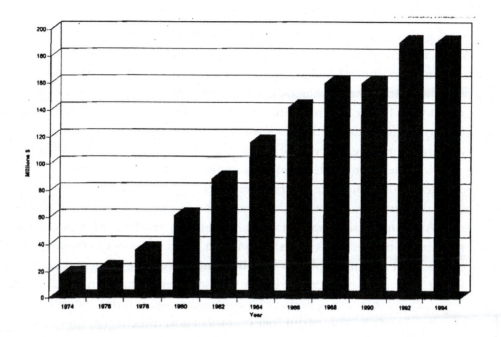

SOURCE: FEDERAL ELECTIONS COMMISSION

district. Politicians not proficient at finding "what's good for America starts with what's good for my district" find themselves quickly eliminated from the political market. Former Speaker of the House Tip O'Neil understood this incentive when he remarked that politics is always local.

Since the political market contains many self-interested voters, public choice predicts that many different special interest groups organize around the legislative process. For instance, 4,618 political action committees registered with the Federal Elections Commission in 1994.[44]It seems implausible that these interest groups act selflessly to "do good" for society.

---

44   Larry Makinson and Joshua Goldstein, *Open Secrets: The Encyclopedia of Congressional Money and Politics* (Washington, D.C., Congressional Quarterly Inc., 1996).

"Use it or lose it"

Rational government bureaucrats maximize budgets. Yet, bureaucracies lack a *residual claimant* to any monetary gains arising from efficient operation.[45] A wasteful government agency is a rational government agency. This conclusion does not denigrate the patriotism of civil servants who staff the bureaucracy. If Citizen Smith genuinely wants to "save the whales," he might work for the Environmental Protection Agency. Smith, like his private-sector counterpart, always prefers more budget to less. More whales can be saved with more funding directed toward the effort. The structure of the rules governing the agency's funding and scope of authority provides the key to understanding wasteful bureaucratic behavior.

Suppose a civic-minded employee enters government service to save money for the taxpayers. If successful, the bureaucracy's money left over at the end of the fiscal period returns to the federal Treasury. At the next fiscal appropriations, the bureaus' funding gets reduced accordingly.[46] The civic-minded bureaucrat is punished with an inevitable loss of employment for her cost-saving efforts. Government employees have little incentive to be efficient, because efficient employees do not survive the political market. A reverse incentive exists in which a larger and growing bureaucracy offers more opportunities for higher pay, prestige, power, and in-kind perquisites for administrators.[47] Successful "reinvention of government" requires a restructuring of the rules, not simply hiring efficient businesspersons to run the bureaucracy like a business.[48]

Parkinson's Law also plagues government bureaucracies. Parkinson's Law postulates the work expands to fill the time allotted for the task.[49] In a fiscal twist, bureaucracies frequently exhaust all of their budget allotted for their tasks. About 14 years ago, the United States Department of Agriculture decided the US pickle standards needed revision. The USDA took *eight* years revising pickle standards! After such an exhaustive review the only change was to "permit a bit more stem on the pickles.[50] While bureaucracies wastefully cost-maximize, taxpayers are typically rationally ignorant about any specific abuse. Some programs cost the average taxpayer only a few pennies per year, but gamer strong political support from a small group of select benefi-

---

45   Ludwig von Mises, *Bureaucracy* (Cedar Falls, Ia.: Center for Futures Education, 1983)

46   Aaron Wildavsky, *Thte Politics of the Budgetary Process* (Boston: Little Brown, 1964).

47   McKenzie and Tullock, pp. 184–87.

48   The Grace Commission established by President Reagan on June 30, 1982 enlisted the volunteer efforts of 161 of the top CEOs in America. The Grace Commission took 18 months scanning all of the explicit excess of existing government programs. They made 2,478 recommendations on cutting waste, fraud and abuse. If fully implemented the federal government would have saved 424 billion dollars from 1984–87. While meticulous in detail, very few of the Grace Commission's recommendations were ever enacted. See, J. Peter Grace, *Burning Money* (New York: Macmillan Publishing Co., 1984).

49   C.N. Parkinson, *Parkinson's Law and Other Studies in Administration* (New York: Ballantyne Books, 1957).

50   Mike McGraw and Jeff Taylor, "Failing the Grade: Betrayals and Blunders at the Department of Agriculture," *The Kansas City Star* (December 8–14, 1991) special ed., p. 1. The Pulitzer Prize winning journalists uncovering the pickle standard revision commented about the USDA, "Indeed, department programs at times seem as if they were created to generate waste!" p. 3

ciaries. Through the combination of voter rational ignorance, and special interest beneficiaries, budgetary waste aids politicians in their reelection by transferring wealth to key voting blocs.

By maintaining an extensive array of agricultural subsidies for domestic farmers, governments around the world demonstrate the symbiotic relationship between small special interest groups and politicians. As of 1991, the 12 members of the European Community appropriated approximately $135 billion dollars for farm subsidies.[51] A small subset of the population accrues substantial benefits from these programs and beneficiaries become highly vocal whenever their subsidies are threatened. For example, farmers comprise only 6% of the population of France. But, when the European Community's common agricultural policy jeopardized lucrative agricultural subsidies, over 200,000 farmers gathered in a "tractorcade protest" through the streets of Paris.[52] Farm subsidies cost individual citizens small amounts of money per year, therefore, they usually remain rationally ignorant.[53] Because farmers are a small interest group with a common goal—higher crop prices, they exert a disproportionate influence over prospective legislation.

In America, the federal bureaucracies waste taxpayer money on certain special interest groups. For example, federal bureaucracies have spent $436 for $7 dollar hammers, $511 dollars for 60 cent light bulbs, and $200 for 25 cent widgets![54] In each case, the benefits of this extravagance accrues to a small group of suppliers, as well as budget maximizing bureaucrats with excess funds near the end of the fiscal year. In the private sector, this leads to bankruptcy. Government bureaucracies, however, can not be forced into bankruptcy. As a result, public choice predicts government bureaus will be vastly more inefficient when compared to the private sector. Over 100 empirical studies suggest that privatization of public sector services results in cost reductions ranging from 20 percent to 50 percent.[55]

ARE BUREAUCRACIES MERE PUPPETS ON A STRING?

In their actions, bureaucrats are not purely passive. Bureaucrat entrepreneurs engage in strategic behavior to increase budgets or scope of authority, or to prevent budget cuts or reduction of authority. Bureaucracies compete against each other for fiscal appropriations. Yet, when politicians are rationally ignorant, an asymmetric information bias allows government bureaus to increase their budgets by exploiting the system.[56] Bureaucracies strategically behave in three ways: (i) engage in actions that bring additional votes to their Congressional overseers, (ii) punish politician perceived as threats to the agency's interests or (iii) go underground.

---

51 *Economist,* "Agricultural Trade: Head in the Muck," (October 12,1991), p. 72.

52 *Economist,* "French Fanners: The Foul Smell of Success," (October 5, 1991), p. 54.

53 Farmers do not explicitly frame agricultural subsidies as a wealth redistribution mechanism. Instead, farmers portray the policy in civic pride terms such as "saving the family farm"

54 *Burning Money,,* pp. 88–89; and, Steven Rubenstein, "It Must Be Good For Something," *San Francisco Chronicle* (April 20, 1991), C, 12:1

55 John Hilke, *Competition in Government Financial Services* (New York: Quorum Books, 1992).

56 William Niskanen, *Bureaucracy and Representative Government* (Chicago: Aldine Press, 1971).

THE SANTA CLAUS EFFECT

"The most expensive things in life are free"

Bureaucracies occasionally reward certain amenable Congresspersons around reelection time. For example, the USDA's milk price-support program allows the Commodity Credit Corporation (CCC) to accumulate surplus butter and cheese. The tax-financed CCC purchases of dairy products forces milk consumers to compete against the CCC. This makes butter and cheese unaffordable for the marginal consumers who typically have low incomes. Moreover, the CCC's surpluses of perishable dairy must be destroyed or given away.

However, as election day draws near, the CCC provides the key Congressional representatives with surplus dairy to "give away" to the poor in their district. The consequence is the **Santa Claus Effect**. The individuals receiving "free" product are rationally ignorant about the existence or consequences of price support programs. By using this strategy, important members of Congress portray themselves as generous benefactors of the poor—a political Santa Claus. Nevertheless, "free" surplus dairy exists from crowding out poor consumers the rest of the year.[57]

THE WASHINGTON MONUMENT SYNDROME

Sometimes bureaucracies try to punish budget cutters in Congress. Suppose a congressional committee tries to enhance their chances of reelection by reducing the funding for Agency X and expanding the budget for Agency Z. Agency X might propose a downsized budget that includes shutting down the most popular programs for influential Congresspersons or their constituents. This is called the *Washington Monument Syndrome*. The Department of Interior employed this strategy in 1995 when Congress slated the department's budget for reduction. The Department proposed saving money by closing either the Washington Monument, Yellowstone Park or Grand Canyon National Park during the peak of the tourist season.[58] The Washington Monument Syndrome shifts the political cost of budget cutting from the bureaucracy back to the Congress.

---

57 The USDA has utilized Santa Claus practices since its inception. According to McGraw and Taylor, p. 4:
The Agriculture Department: always has played politics. Mindful of protecting its budget, the department's first commissioner, a Pennsylvania dairyman named Isaac Newton, started lobbying Congress right away. In his first year, he distributed 306,304 packages of seeds and cereals, along with thousands of free cuttings, bulbs and plants, to congressmen and their constituents. Congress has stood by the department ever since.

58 During the 1995 federal government shutdown, the Interior Department closed Grand Canyon National Park to the 20,000 tourist who visit daily, instead of closing less popular facilities. When Arizona governor Fife Symington proposed using state employees and the National Guard to reopen the park, the Interior Department rejected the offer. See, "Effort to Reopen Grand Canyon Halted," *Los Angeles Times* (November 18, 1995), A, 20: 1

UNDERGROUND BUREAUCRACY

Occasionally, the legislature establishes constraints on the operation of the bureaucracies. For many years Congress imposed restrictions on the number of full-time federal employees that an agency may staff. By using *underground government tactics,* agencies evade this constraint. Twenty years ago, for example, the Office of Management and Budget only counted full-time employees when auditing an agency. Some bureaucracies creatively rescheduled employee job assignments during the week of the audit. Federal agencies placed thousands of employees on part-time status for the one week per year. Immediately after the audit, the employees returned to full-time status. The growing use of private-sector consultants by agencies provides another method of evading employment constraints.[59] If adverse rules constrain bureaucracies, political entrepreneurs react by moving underground or off-budget to escape the constraints.[60]

INTEREST GROUPS, INFORMATION COSTS AND REGULATION

The Public Interest Revisited

As alluded to earlier, the public interest view remains a popular explanation for government regulation. However, public choice calls this belief into question. Like other humans, regulators serve their own interests as well as the public interest. Whatever motivates producers and consumers in the private sector also motivates bureaucrats. Saints are rare. Very few regulators enhance social welfare by sacrificing their own.

A variant of the public interest theory is the *capture theory of regulation.* Capture theory, like public interest theory, assumes regulation originate to improve social welfare. As time passes, the watchdogs in the regulatory agencies become corrupted by the regulated industries and begin serving the interests of the regulated instead of protecting the people. Corporations capture the regulators by offering future employment in exchange for lenient enforcement. Empirical evidence suggests many regulatory commissioners find future employment in the industry they previously regulated.[61] According to the capture theory, regulations initially enacted to improve the public welfare eventually degenerate into furthering private interests.

Capture theory appears a more plausible version of the public interest theory of regulation; yet, serious deficiencies exist. Historians and public choice economists question the public interest origin of most regulation. Special interest rent-seeking entangles the birth of legisla-

---

59 James Bennett and Manuel Johnson, *The Political Economy of Federal Government Growth: 1959–1978* (College Station, Texas: Center for Education and Research in Free Enterprise, 1980), pp. 36–41.

60 James Bennett and Thomas DiLorenzo, *Underground Government: The Off-Budget Public Sector* (Washington, D.C.: Cato Institute, 1983)

61 Robert Fellmeth, *The Interstate Commerce Commission: The Public Interest and the ICC* (New York: Grossman, 1970); Ross Eckert, "The Life Cycle of Regulatory Commissioners," *The Journal of Law and Economics* (April 1981), pp. 113–20.

tion such as antitrust,[62] minimum wage,[63] food and drug quality standards,[64] transportation,[65] communications,[66] occupational licensing[67] and public utility regulation.[68] Also, capture theory fails to explain regulations that impose substantial costs on big business or further the interests of small businesses, labor unions, consumers or other groups which cannot offer future employment or benefits to the regulators. Moreover, capture theory cannot explain the trend toward deregulation that began with the abolition of Civil Aeronautics Board in 1978.

THE PUBLIC CHOICE THEORY OF REGULATION

The economic theory of regulation by Nobel Laureate George Stigler articulates the public choice theory of regulation.[69] Stigler suggests producers form groups that lobby the government to use its police power for the advancement of the producer's interests. By restricting entry into an industry, for example, the government allows the existing firms to earn monopoly profits. Like the capture theory, regulation often serves the interests of the regulated; however, unlike capture theory, regulation starts out only to benefiting private interests.

Since the political market produces regulation, public choice makes predictions diametrically opposed to those made by the public interest theory. For instance, instead of politicians empowering bureaucracies to supply regulation that enhances social welfare, politicians create bureaucracies to serve the politicians' interests. The demand for regulation often comes from producers in competitive markets and not from widely dispersed and rationally ignorant consumer-voters. Special-interest groups seek regulations that create a private monopolistic advantage.[70] Graph 14-5 illustrates the economics of regulations which restrict entry into an industry.

---

62   Thomas Dilorenzo, "The Origins of Antitrust: An Interest Group Perspective," in *The International Review of Law and Economics,* 1985 *No.5,* pp. 73–90.

63   Bernard Seigan, *Economic Liberties and the Constitution* (Chicago: University of Chicago Press, 1980), pp. 143-150.

64   Jack High, *Regulation: Economic Theory and History,* (Ann Arbor: University of Michigan Press, 1991).

65   Robert Spann and Edward Erickson, "The Economics Of Railroading: The Beginning Of Cartelization And Regulation," *The Bell Journal of Economics and Management Science* (1974). Also, see William Jordon, *Airline Regulation in America: Effects and Imperfections* (Baltimore: Johns Hopkins Press, 1970).

66   Ronald Coase, "The Federal Communications Commission," *The Journal of Law and Economics* (October 1959.)

67   Reubin Kessel, "Price Discrimination in Medicine," *The Journal of Law and Economics* (October 1958), pp. 20-53.

68   Greg Jarrell, "The Demand For State Regulation Of The Electric Utility Industry," *The Journal of Law and Economics* (October 1978).

69   George Stigler, "The Theory of Economic Regulation," *The Bell Journal of Economic and Management Science* (1971), pp. 1–23.

70   Sam Peltzman, "Toward a More General Theory of Regulation," *The Journal of Law and Economics* (1976), pp. 3–21.

TULLOCK RECTANGLE
GRAPH 14-5

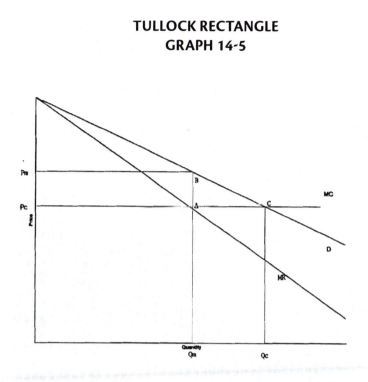

Suppose P_c and Q_c are the price and output in a perfectly competitive market. Assume producers receive government protection from competition. Over time, the market becomes monopolized and the equilibrium price changes to P_m and quantity Q_m. Triangle **ABC** equals the social dead-weight loss. Rectangle $P_m BAP_c$ represents the abnormal profits producers receive from consumers. The producers are wealthier by exactly the amount the consumers are poorer. This method of government-sanctioned transfer is called ***rent-extraction.***

The value of area $P_m BAP_c$ provides an incentive for small producers to form groups that lobby the government for entry restrictions. Public choice predicts competitors expend resources on lobbying for the restrictions up to the area of $P_m BAP_c$. This area is called the ***Tullock rectangle.*** Since lobbying does not create goods or services which consumers value, the social loss equals the entire trapezoid $P_m BCP_c$, rather than the triangle **ABC**. The social loss increases whenever consumers overcome rational ignorance and expend resources to counter-lobby against the producers. Consumer lobbying efforts that resist rent extraction are called ***rent-avoidance.***

THE IRON TRIANGLE

Politicians, special interest groups and bureaucracies comprise the iron triangle of politics. Politicians generate voter support and campaign contributions by establishing bureaucracies with broad regulatory authority. The bureaucracy then creates rules that confer concentrated benefits to special interest groups. If successful, the special interest groups reward the politicians with votes and campaign contributions, and the politicians reward the bureaucracies with increased budget, authority and freedom from oversight. In this complex exchange, politicians act as purveyors of favors and the bureaucracy becomes the broker negotiating the terms of trade with the industry. To ensure the agency's do not harm their special interest supporters, politicians oversee the bureaucracy from appropriate committees or subcommittees in Congress.

FEDERAL REGULATIONS

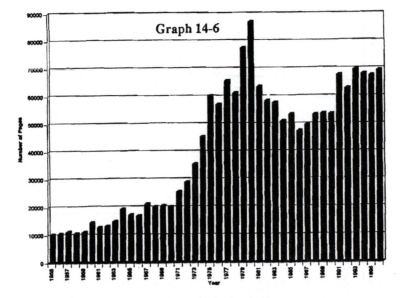

SOURCE: FEDERAL REGISTER

Occasionally, regulations impose visible harm on the Congresspersons' supporters. To correct the situation, politicians review the bureaucracy's procedures at congressional hearings and publicly blast the wasteful regulations emanating from an agency "out-of-control." This signals the agency to shape up or face reduced budgets, stricter oversight or less authority in the future. Congressional oversight mitigates the problems caused by the politicians rational ignorance concerning the actions by an agency. Also, Congressional oversight disciplines the agency to adopt a set of vote maximizing regulation.[71]

REGULATION AS IMPLICIT TAXATION

As previously suggested, government transfers resources through regulations as well as taxes and subsidies. In 1971, economist and Federal appellant judge Richard Posner argued

---

71 Barry Weingast and Mark Moran, "Bureaucratic Discretion or Congressional Control? Regulatory Policy Making by the Federal Trade Commission," *The Journal of Political Economy* Vol. 91 No.5 (1983), pp. 765–800.

regulations constitute a method of implicit taxation.[72] Suppose government raises property taxes on apartment buildings by one million dollars and uses the money to subsidize low-income renters. In the short-run, the property owners are poorer by the amount of the tax and the subsidized renters are richer by the subsidy that equals the tax revenue less the costs of administering the program. Over time, the market price of apartment buildings falls to reflect the new tax and low-income renters lose the subsidy's benefits as landlords raise rents to reflect their higher costs from the tax. Yet, the tax and subsidy program transfers wealth in the open. This diminishes rational ignorance problems by reducing the costs of acquiring information on the program's benefits and drawbacks.

Now, assume a different scenario where the government controls the rent on apartments. If the controls force rents below the market-clearing price, a shortage of rental housing results. The regulation affects landlords and renters in a similar manner as the property tax and subsidy scheme. Graph 14-7 illustrates the implicit tax effects of the rent-control regulation. The renters receive a wealth transfer just as if they obtained a direct subsidy. Area **ABCD** represents the transfer from landlords to tenets. Triangle **EBC** shows the amount of pure loss below opportunity cost of production of rental units. Unlike the tax and subsidy scheme, the burdens of regulation remains hidden from view and increase the problems of rational ignorance.

In 1992, Thomas Hopkins estimated the implicit tax of federal regulation amounted to nearly 600 billion dollars.[73] From 1987–96, federal agencies generated 615,776 pages of new regulations.[74] This does not include the new regulations promulgated by the fifty states, 3,043 counties, 19,279 municipalities, and tens of thousands of city and local governments.[75] Using regulation, politicians provide special interest supporters with benefits, while claiming they have not raised taxes. Public choice predicts politicians prefer less-visible methods of transferring wealth to favored constituents. The rational ignorance of those hurt by the wealth transfer reduces the chance they know the costs of the regulation or whom to blame.

---

72   Richard Posner, "Taxation by Regulation," *The Bell Journal of Economy and Management Science* (October 1971), pp. 22–51.

73   Thomas Hopkins, "Costs of Regulations: Filling in the Gaps," *Regulatory Information Service Center* (August 1992).

74   *Federal Register, 1987–1996.*

75   Glenn Miller, "Are There Too Many Governments in the Tenth District?" *Economic Review,* (Kansas City: Federal Reserve Bank of Kansas City) Second Quarter 1993, p. 69; Bureau of the Census, *Statistical Abstract,* 1996 (Washington, D.C., 1996), 295. Over 85,006 governmental subdivisions exist below the federal level.

REGULATION AS IMPLICIT TAXATION
GRAPH 14-7

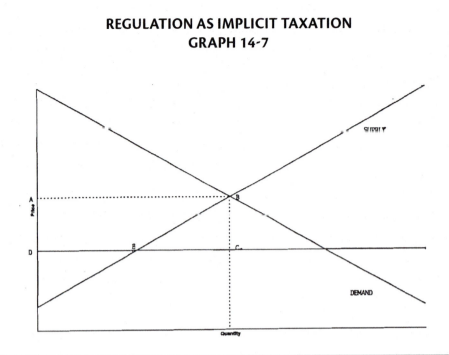

THE HIGH COST OF TRADE RESTRICTIONS

Governments impose a variety of restrictions on foreign imports such as tariffs, quotas, and voluntary export restraints. Although the costs are widely dispersed, the benefits from trade restriction generally accrue to a small subset of the population. A recent study by Gary Hufbauer and Kimberly Elliot estimated the *net* losses to the US economy from trade barriers in twenty-one industries.* In 1990, according to Hufbauer and Elliot, the trade barriers cost the U.S. economy nearly $70 billion dollars, or 1.3 percent of GDP. The various restrictions cost the average consumer approximately $280 per year.

The jobs saved from limiting foreign competition come at a very high price. In five of the twenty-one industries, the cost per job saved exceeded $500,000. The average was $170,000 per job. Charles Rowley, Richard Wagner and Willem Thorbecke, revised the Hufbauer and Elliot estimate of dead-weight loss by incorporating rent-seeking costs.** The inclusion of rent-seeking costs raises the social welfare loss to over $117 billion or roughly $287,000 per job saved. Neither study include the dead-weight loss arising from X-inefficiency. This suggests that the true costs of these trade restrictions are substantially higher.

*Gary Clyde Hufbauer and Kimberly Arm Elliot, *Measuring the Costs of Protection in the United States* (Washington, D.C.: The Institute for International Economics, 1994), p. 3.

** Charles Rowley, Richard Wagner and Willem Thorbecke, *Trade Protection in the United States* (Aldershot, UK: Edward Elgar, 1995), pp. 321–322.

Many regulations intentionally subvert constitutional constraints. A politician's survival in the political market depends on devising ingenious mechanisms that deliver benefits to their constituents at the expense of other voters. This incentive insures high-ranking committee members of Congress greater reelection probabilities. For example, Congressperson Smith's reelection depends on "bringing home the bacon" to the voters in his district. Of course, the bacon comes from the hide of voters in the other 434 Congressional districts. Incumbents representing different areas compete to directly or indirectly transfer resources to their respective constituents. The voters return those best at bringing home the bacon and replace the inept.

Occasionally, politicians propose legislation that they never intend to pass into law. Through *milker bills,* politicians induce campaign contributions from targeted groups by threatening to change the current law. Incumbents like milker bills because they can "troll for dollars" by threatening a change in the law. In the private sector, entrepreneurs not carrying out a potential threat of harm in exchange for money are usually called *extortionists.*[76]

Regulation can confer a legally transferable property right to collect abnormal profits, called monopoly rents. In 1937, for example, New York City limited the number of legal taxis to 11,787. Existing taxi companies received a medallion. Taxis without a medallion could not legally operate in the city. By issuing the medallion, the city created a property right to collect monopoly rents from taxicab patrons. Over time, new entrants purchased the medallions from the original owners. The purchase price included the discounted value of the expected future stream of monopoly rents from higher fares. Any price change in the medallion reflects a change in the capitalized value of the medallion, that is the expected stream of future earnings from driving a taxi. The current price for a New York City taxi medallion exceeds $200,000.[77]

The capitalization of monopoly rents may cause a *transitional gains trap.*[78] All but the original owner of the medallion paid up front for the right to enter the market. While benefiting from the regulation, purchasers of the medallions do not necessarily enjoy monopoly profits. The medallion's cost reduces the purchasers' rate of return by the discounted benefits from owning a medallion. This creates a perverse trap. Rationally ignorant taxicab patrons must endure high prices and poor service. However, current taxicab owners only earn a competitive return because the rate of return includes the medallion's purchase price. A continuation of the medallion program hurts consumers and potential new taxicab owners. Deregulating the taxicabs destroys the property right of the medallion purchased by the current owners. The New York City taxi market is stuck in the quicksand of the transitional gains trap. Transitional gains traps create a stable equilibrium where perpetual dead-weight losses occur.

---

76 Fred McChesney, "Rent Extraction and Rent Creation In the Economic Theory of Regulation," *Journal of Legal Studies* (January 1987). McChesney labels this practice "political blackmail," p. 104

77 "New York City Cabs: A Revolution," *The Economist* (February 3, 1996), p. 21

78 Gordon Tullock, "The Transitional Gains Trap," *Bell Journal of Economics* (Autunm 1975), pp. 671–8.

CPSIA information can be obtained
at www.ICGtesting.com
Printed in the USA
LVOW02s1954050917
547627LV00003B/183/P